Microcomputer Dictionary

Second Edition

by

Charles J. Sippl

A TANDY CORPORATION COMPANY

International Standard Book Number: 0-672-21696-5
Library of Congress Card Number: 81-50565

Edited by: *Frank N. Speights*
Illustrated by: *R. E. Lund*

Printed in the United States of America.

Preface

Electronic, communications, and industrial automation literature is filled with promises and proofs of a microcomputer revolution. For the more enthused proponents and product developers, it has turned into a craze. Statements such as ". . . more important than the invention of the transistor . . .", ". . . greater impact than the electric motor . . .", ". . . a computer in every home . . .", and "When the history of digital electronics is written, 1976 will be remembered as the year of the microcomputer explosion . . ." resound everywhere. Most of us have heard or read these claims and so far, practically no one disagrees.

However, a major problem is one of verbal communications—the need for newcomers and oldtimers alike to learn the nomenclature, the new language, the developing terms, and concepts with all the nuances, cross-meanings, and varied interpretations. Quite frenzied efforts are in progress in many markets to educate the potential users of microcomputers. Efforts are being developed in the standard ways: advertisements, product manuals, articles in periodicals, conferences, college courses, etc. Perhaps the most intense and effective methods are: (1) the concentrated, in-depth, traveling and in-house teaching classes and seminars, and (2) the efforts of microcomputer clubs and user groups and their publications. Thus, the need for a *Microcomputer Dictionary* that offers clear explanations of products, procedures, systems, techniques, and components appears quite apparent. However, the dictionary and its definitions cannot be standard, pure, or "idealized." The work must reflect the current literature—the use of the words as they are spoken and written down by the inventors, teachers, lecturers, writers, and leaders of today. Few "explanations" can be curt or brief because they must be "real"—down to earth and simplified, but also tutorial and expository. Microelectronics dictionaries cannot wait for the perfection of microscript rhetoric that appeals to purist lexicographers. The definitions and concept explanations must come from the industry, from the developers and users of these systems. The dictionary cannot be a reshuffle of words: it must be developed to establish the many facets of microcomputer operations and applications, and the newest developments—"the way it is," nothing more, nothing less. *Microcomputer Dictionary* attempts to fill this need with over 5000 entries of terms and definitions.

Current literature was the source of virtually all of the up-to-date information on microcomputer technology and its utilization. The definitions were derived from or based on product, system, and design manuals, and on scholarly reports, and conference proceedings, etc. Rapid changes in the microprocessor/microcomputer field continuously spawn several hundreds of new concept, product, and technique definitions. Thus, emphasis has been placed on how the terms are *used* in the industry by product manufacturers, system designers, and application developers. Many of the explanations are relatively long, and most "browsing" readers of this book will welcome the depth of analysis shown. Most terms are not so exotic but they still require a deeper treatment than mere "dictionary phrasing."

For most people, the new micro technology is exciting, esoteric, and complex. The microprocessor is the basic building block for hundreds of new microcomputer control systems. The digital "processor on a chip" performs the same arithmetic, logic, information, and device control that standard and minicomputers can achieve, but, at from one-tenth to one-hundredth of the cost, size, and power requirements. "Chip sets," a term that has recently evolved into popular usage, develop the microprocessor power, expand the computer memory using ROM and RAM, and, with appropriate interface and input/output devices, complete a total computer system that can be held in one hand. These micropower marvels are also known as microcontrollers, and they are being designed into "smart" computer terminals, miniature communication-switching devices, versatile production machines, and an uncountable number of consumer appliances, calculating equipment, and entertainment devices.

Microprocessor "chips" are presently selling for as little as $10.00 (in large-quantity purchases). When combined with various auxiliary circuits, a power supply, an input/output device, and a few control switches, they become a complete microcomputer system capable of performing an almost unimagined number and variety of functions. All this functional power is available to millions of people— from amateur hobbyists to atomic scientists for just a few hundred dollars. The benefits of this technological revolution are becoming tremendous. These technical advances should lead to a great new generation of products which will be more cost effective, more useful, and more reliable. Because personal computers are now cost effective and only a few hours of training are required, more and more systems are being used in homes and businesses. As a result, they are reaching users who are totally uninitiated in the use of computers.

When the first computer is installed in a business, not only are the owners and managers of the business apprehensive, but the majority of the office and administrative personnel are also suspicious and even frightened by the changes that take place. These users, especially those in the business community, need to learn exactly what the move to microelectronics is all about. As they search for answers, they are perplexed by the jargon used in the computer industry, and they discover that they must quickly educate themselves in computer language. They must study and master at least the basics because it is becoming very unbusiness-like, and even unfashionable, to ask "Exactly what is a 64K RAM?, . . . a semiconductor?, . . . a bubble memory?" Management must help these people with a calm and knowledgeable approach to explaining what is happening. Therefore, they must know something about the "mysterious" computer jargon. Filling that need for information is the purpose of this book.

An April 10, 1975 *Survey and Report,* developed by Frost and Sullivan, a major New York research firm, projected that by 1984, ". . . about 2-million minicomputers and 15-million microcomputers will be installed." The total value of the market was estimated to be $45 billion. The report further states, "A microprocessor system will sell for $100 or less, so the potential applications are mind-boggling." One manufacturing official suggests that we will soon be buying microcomputers as we would ". . . buy a toaster." The current rate of production of microcomputers suggests that the 15-million projection will be reached well before 1984. The competition is furious, and product prices continue to fall. New educational, entertainment, and industrial markets are opening for orders in the hundreds of thousands. None of us can afford to "backslide" while this onrushing progress expands. The *Microcomputer Dictionary* can be one of the basic tools that will let you stay with it.

The statements noted at the beginning of this Preface were published in 1975 just as the microcomputer was starting to be used commercially. These and other rather optimistic forecasts appear to be pragmatically true at this later date. Indeed, one school superintendent who has experience with elementary school students using microcomputers, in Apple Valley, Minnesota, stated, "It is the fourth basic skill." The head of a school that specializes in "computer literacy" in California, agreed with Donald N. Michael, the author of *"The Unprepared Society,"* who stated, "Ignorance of computers will render people as functionally illiterate as does ignorance of reading, writing, and arithmetic." A Purdue University computer specialist remarked, ". . . computer literacy will become a prime job requirement," and a University of Missouri professor stated, "By the end of this decade, we'll see some colleges and universities that will refuse to teach the basics of computers. They will expect entering students to know them." Indeed, that is not at all the problem. It has been found that children are more than anxious to know about computers and learn how to use them.

That "everything is going digital" is also well established. There are telephones, videodics, and so on, in use now. Hitachi, Ltd. in 1980 offered a voice (single chip) watch radio, and several firms have offered calculator watches. "Dick Tracy"-type wrist-computer radios have been offered to venturous capitalists and are expected to be very plentiful very soon. A half dozen companies will start selling digital records in quantity in 1981, and RCA, CBS, and others are now using "pure" digital tapes to transfer music and other information to records. Why? By digitally recording music, in a studio, engineers are permitted to use computers that are not subject to speed variations and the other drawbacks of typical tape recorders. Extraneous noise and distortion are eliminated. The records that are manufactured are of the highest quality, with little or no distortion, hiss, etc. But, it is not simply in education, entertainment, and toys that microcomputers will see their greatest use. Microcomputers are being used in automobiles (some began doing so in 1980), in office typewriters, and in a great many other devices. Xerox Corporation's "Star" system is an executive's workstation for offices. It has two full-page display screens—one a common crt, and the second, an optical character-recognition (OCR) page reader that enables executives to hold sheets of paper up to the screen and enter information into an electronic file bank (prices run about $15,000 to $17,000). The system is a touch-sensitive video display, with sophisticated text-handling/editing capability that is also an electronic messaging system (with graphics) that almost anyone can handle, with little or no training. IBM and at least two Japanese companies announced "voice-controlled" typewriters, and Sony Corporation has made a "big splash" with its very compact, easy-to-use, and low-cost word-processing system and personal computer combination. Just as voice chips are expected to be very common in cars, toys, and telephones, and are expected to be used as used as automated warning advisors in many public and factory buildings, voice input/output chips are expected to be sold in multimillion quantities as early as 1982, and are expected to move onward and upward from there.

The point of these comments is to stress the near pervasion of a "need for knowledge," not simply of computers, but of microcomputers, in particular. Microcomputers are a distinct and different technology that is based on semiconductor chips, whereas, standard or minicomputers have a fundamentally different architecture, although a great many computer programs can be run or converted to run on all types of computers. Nevertheless, most computer textbooks, computer dictionaries, and computer periodicals do not "fit" the microcomputer era, and microcomputers and their peripherals could soon overtake the other types in total sales, worldwide use, and, certainly, in pragmatic popularity.

Microcomputers have created a total revolution in communications. They will be used in telephones, display phones, tv sets, satellites, video-conferencing systems, and in every type of "distributed processing" systems. Thus, there is a great need for a dictionary that offers clear explanations of products, procedures, systems, techniques, and components. Hopefully, this book accomplishes that need.

CHARLES J. SIPPL

Acknowledgments

Deep appreciation flows to my wife and our seven children whose patience, forebearance, and encouragement were very necessary and were generously given to help maintain the persistence required to complete this volume.

Particular respect and thanks must be given to my wife, Margaret, whose valuable assistance was most significant in developing the degree of thoroughness that the work required.

My appreciation and respect also flows out to the leaders of the electronics industry who have written and produced a wealth of excellent literature, including articles, manuals, reference notes, speeches, monographs, conference reports, and research project summaries, in which these terms and definitions found their origin.

Contents

APPENDIX A

Semiconductor Chips—16-Bit Microprocessing Units—32-Bit Micro-processors—VLSI—Designer Problems—Single-Chip Devices—Peripheral Interfaces—From 8-Bit Chips to Micromainframes—CMOS Technology—Memories—EPROM Erasers—Bubble Memory Boards—Voice Synthesizer Chip—Videodiscs

APPENDIX B

Cheap Chips—Applications—Microcomputer Markets—Hand-Held Computers—Computers in Education—Computers in Business—Robotics—Viewdata and Teletext Services—Miscellaneous

How To Use This Book

In the dictionary entries, all terms of more than one word have been alphabetized as though they were one word. For example, "diskette drives" appears between "diskette" and "diskette initialization." Abbreviations are alphabetized as though they were words; for example, LCD appears between "layout" and "leader" instead of at the beginning of the L section.

For ease in locating terms, the first and last entries on each page appear as catch words at the top of the page.

Extensive cross-referencing has been used as an aid in locating terms you might look for in more than one place. For example, there are entries for both "executive program" and "program, executive."

A

A and not B gate—A specific binary logic coincidence (two-input) circuit used to complete the logic operations of A AND NOT B, i.e., result is true only if statement A is true and statement B is false.

abend—An error condition that results in the abnormal termination of a program.

abend dump—An error report provided to the programmer to aid him in interpreting the cause of an abend.

abend exit—A means that can be established by an applications program to gain control after a program has been abnormally terminated.

abend recovery program — A program that permits a system (a data base, for example) to be reloaded and restored to the point where the abend occurred.

abend, unrecoverable—A condition in which an error has caused the abnormal termination of a program, and no provisions have been included in the program to check for the reason for the termination.

aborted cycle—The interruption or removal of the initial signal or input power before the time period has been completed.

absolute address—1. An actual location in storage of a particular unit of data; an address that the control unit can interpret directly. 2. The label assigned by the engineer to a particular storage area in the computer. 3. A pattern of characters that identifies a unique storage location or device without any further modification. (Synonymous with machine address.)

absolute maximum rating—This refers to the limiting values of the operating and environmental conditions applicable to any electronic device, as defined by its published data, which are not to be exceeded under the worst conditions. It is the rating beyond which the reliability of a device can be expected to decline.

absolute-value device — A transducer that produces an output signal equal

in magnitude to the input signal but always of one polarity.

absolute-value sign—A specific horizontal line sign indicating that the absolute value of a number is to be taken, i.e., the value of the number irrespective of the sign.

absorption—Absorption is the deposition of a thin layer of gas or vapor particles onto the surface of a solid. The process is also known as chemisorption if the deposited material is bound by a chemical bond.

absorption current—Refers to the current flowing into a capacitor, following its initial charge, due to a gradual penetration of the electric stress into the dielectric. It also relates to the current that flows out of a capacitor following its initial discharge.

access, content-addressable memory—Refers to read/write RAMs having an access mechanism that retrieves the addresses of data which match an attribute presented to the inputs. The attribute to be matched is usually some code related to the meaning or content of the filed topic.

access, instantaneous — Pertaining to the ability to directly obtain data from, or place data in, a storage device or register without serial delay due to other units of data.

access time—The time between the application of a specified input pulse and the availability of valid data signals at an output. Access time varies with temperature, supply voltage, input conditions, and output loading. It can only be defined with reference to an output signal.

access time, address—The time from address valid to output valid. In a typical memory, $t_{\text{AVQV}} = 250$ ns (max).

access time, memory — Refers to the time between the application of a specified input pulse during a read cycle and the availability of valid data signals at an output.

access time, RAM—A time interval that is characteristic of a storage device, and is a measure of the time required to communicate with that device.

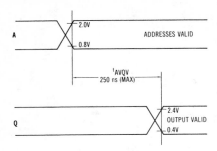

Access time, address.

ac controller, small computer—An isolated switch that can be used to control relatively heavy loads, such as home-appliance motors, lamps, ac solenoids, and heaters. One type of board incorporates the equivalent of 8 solid-state relays, where on-board jumpers determine the address of the controller card, while each bit of the data word corresponds to one of the 8 loads to be energized or not energized. Individual loads up to 12 ampere rms may be controlled with such board systems.

accumulator—The accumulator (ACC) is a 4-, 8-, 12-, 16-, or 32-bit register that functions as a holding register for arithmetic, logical, and input-output operations. Data words may be fetched from memory to the ACC or from the ACC into memory. Arithmetic and logical operations involve two operands, one held in the accumulator, the other fetched from memory. The result of an operation is retained in the accumulator. The ACC may be cleared, complemented, tested, incremented, or rotated under program control. The ACC also serves as an input-output register. Programmed data transfers pass through the accumulator.

achieved reliability—Refers to reliability that is determined on the basis of actual performance or on operations based on standards or benchmarks under equal or equivalent conditions and circumstances. Also referred to as operational reliability.

ACIA—Abbreviation for Asynchronous Communications Interface Adapter. ACIA provides the data formatting and control necessary to interface serial asynchronous data communications information to bus organized systems. The bus interface of some systems includes select, enable, read/write, interrupt, and bus interface logic to allow data transfer over an 8-bit bidirectional data bus. The parallel data of the bus system are serially transmitted and received by the asynchronous data interface, with proper formatting and error checking. The functional configuration of the ACIA is programmed via the data bus during system initialization. A programmable Control Register will typically provide variable word lengths, clock division ratios, transmit control, receive control, and interrupt control. In peripheral or modem operation, several control lines are provided. These lines allow the ACIA to interface directly with the digital modem.

ACIA interface signals (for MPU)—The signals that, in conjunction with the system valid memory address (VMA) output, permit the MPU to have complete control over the ACIA. In some systems, the ACIA interfaces to a typical MPU via an 8-bit bidirectional data bus, three chip select lines, a register select line, an interrupt request line, a read/write line, and an enable line.

ac input module, controller—An I/O rack module that converts various ac signals originating in user switches to the appropriate logic level for use within the microprocessor.

ACK—Signal for affirmative acknowledgement as used in a transmission to indicate that a previous transmission (block) has been accepted by the receiver. ACK signifies that the receiver is ready to accept the next block of transmission.

acoustic coupler—An inductive device that converts specific characters to multiple tones that can be transmitted on a communications line.

acoustic coupler, auto-answer modem—A 1200-baud acoustic coupler that is combined with a hardwired auto-answer modem to provide full-duplex asynchronous data operation over voice-grade lines. Features often include originate and answer modes, and acoustic and DAA private-line interfaces. The pair of units are generally compatible with all Bell 103-type systems and data terminals.

acoustic coupler operation—A typical coupler accepts a serial data stream from a data-processing device, modu-

Acoustic coupler (Courtesy Digi-Log Systems, Inc.).

lates it in the audio spectrum, and then produces the modulation as an audible tone. Acoustic couplers are equipped with cradles or fittings that will accept a conventional telephone handset and can couple the acoustic energy directly into the mouthpiece. At the receiving end, a similar device picks up the audible tones from the telephone earpiece and demodulates them to a serial data stream.

ac output module, controller—An I/O rack module that converts the logic levels of the microprocessor to a usable output signal in order to control a user's ac load.

ac test—A general term describing those tests that measure dynamic or switching parameters. Examples include tests that check access time, set-up time, or output delays.

active element—1. An element in its excited or being used state, i.e., a tube, transistor, or device that is on or alive rather than off, dead, or in a grounded state. 2. A file, record, or routine that is being used, contacted, or referred to. Computer components are active when they are directed or excited by the control unit.

active transducer — Any transducer in which the applied power either controls or modulates locally supplied power, which becomes the transmitted signal, as in a radio transmitter.

Ada language—Ada is a modern programming language that has been developed at the initiative of the U.S. Department of Defense, in cooperation with the United Kingdom (English), French, and German Defense Ministries and with extensive contributions from industry and universities worldwide. Ada was developed by a Honeywell-Bull team operating under the direction of Jean D. Ichbiah. The language is specifically aimed at improving software reliability, portability, and maintainability while significantly reducing system life cycle costs. Ada is designed for implementations ranging from large complex systems to embedded real-time applications and is expected to become the dominant language of the 1980s and 1990s.

Ada language structure—The Ada language gives preference to full English words and has 62 words "reserved." Specifications require very specific tasking controls, most of which are neglected by other high-level languages. In Ada, the task declaration simplifies task coordination. A task is very similar to a module, the major building block of an Ada program. For timing purposes, *delay* and *select* statements supplement interrupts. General program structure and "visibility" of program components are other focal points in Ada's design. A program consists of a nested structure (*package, module, procedure*), and names can be declared *private* or *restricted*. Thus, new names can be introduced without fear of conflict with previous names.

adapter—A connective device designed to affect operative capability between different parts of one or more systems and/or subsystems.

adapter, GPIB interface — A type of adapter that permits users to interconnect the IEEE parallel GPIB (general-purpose interface bus) with RS-232C systems. It provides 2-way transmission of data and can be used to adapt older instruments and terminals, designed to RS-232C standards, to control processing systems that use the newer GPIB parallel format.

adapter plug—Refers to a fitting designed to change the terminal arrangement of a jack, socket, or other receptacle, so that other than the original electrical connections are possible.

a/d (analog-digital) converter—Circuit used to convert information in analog form into digital form (or vice versa), e.g., in a digital voltmeter, and other devices.

ADCCP — Abbreviation for Advanced Data Communication Control Procedures.

ADC, flash or parallel type—These are the fastest and the most expensive ADCs. These high speed but limited resolution converters are used mostly for radar and video systems.

ADC, integrating—These are the slowest form of ADC, although they provide very high accuracy and low power consumption. Because it has the lowest cost and best accuracy/cost ratio, this type of converter is gaining popularity very rapidly.

ADC interfacing, systems—This is the link between the "real" world and the microprocessor. The actual measurement of a physical variable is performed by a transducer, which converts the variable—for example, a flow rate—to a voltage roughly proportional to the size of the quantity measured. However, this analog (or continuously varying) signal must be converted to a digital format by an analog-to-digital converter (ADC) before the computer can process it. This interfacing is found in systems that use computers to measure and control physical quantities or variables such as speed, temperature, and pressure.

ADC/MPS support hardware — This is the support hardware usually required to link an a/d converter to a microprocessor system (MPS). It includes level-translation buffers for handling the control-bus TTL levels, control logic to start conversion, read data and service interrupts, 3-state buffers to drive the data bus, and a data register to hold previous results while a new conversion occurs. A typical μP-to-ADC interface has such key items as input, reference and supply voltages, clock frequency, control lines, external parts, and bus-interface devices.

a/d converter, charge balancing — A conversion method that employs an operational integrator within a pulse-generating feedback loop. Current pulses are balanced against the analog input by the integrator and

counted to produce the digital output. Also called quantized feedback.

a/d converter controller—In some systems, several analog inputs are connected to an analog-digital (a/d) converter through an analog multiplexer. The controller selects an analog channel for conversion by the a/d converter. When conversion is complete, the END OF CONVERSION signal is asserted. The binary value of the converted signal is then read into the controller for processing. Errors are tested for, and out-of-circuit checks are performed on the digital representation of the analog signal.

a/d converter, counter type—A simple, inexpensive conversion method employing a counter-driven a/d converter which generates a ramp waveform that increases in value until it equals the analog input. Also called a servo-type a/d converter.

a/d converter, successive approximation—A conversion method that compares a series of binary weighted values against an analog input, in sequence, to produce an output digital word in just *n* steps, where *n* is the number of bits. The process is analogous to weighing an unknown quantity on a balance scale by using a set of fixed weights.

a/d converter, video—A low-cost modular a/d converter designed primarily for video digitization; used to convert high bandwidth video signals to a parallel digital format with 8-bit accuracy, at random or periodic word rates of dc through 11 MHz. One typical unit designed for color television digitization operates at rates through 3 times the NTSC color subcarrier frequency (10.74 MHz).

adder—A device that forms, as an output, the sum of two or more numbers presented as inputs. Often no data retention feature is included; i.e., the output signal remains only as long as the input signals are present.

adder-accumulator—In some systems, the adder is a 4-bit parallel binary adder with an internally connected carry for implementing precision arithmetic operations. The adder operates with the 4-bit accumulator to form the Arithmetic Logic Unit (ALU) section of the CPU. In addition to its arithmetic functions, the accumulator is the primary working register in the CPU and is the central data interchange point for most all data transfer operations occurring in the system. During internal data transfer, the accumulator is the interfacing data register for both RAM and ROM. For external data exchanges (Input/Output) the accumulator is the source of the output data and the receiver register for the input data.

addition time, microprocessor—Register-to-register addition time is a popular estimate of the processing speed of a computer. This specific instruction is often chosen as a selection factor because nearly every computer has a comparable add instruction. Microprocessors with more than one programmer-accessible register for data manipulation on the CPU chip can usually perform a fast register-addition in a minimum instruction execution time. Some processors, however, are organized as one-accumulator computers so that register-to-register additions are not provided. In these cases, the addition of the contents of an arbitrary storage location to the accumulator is often scored as the minimum addition time. The incrementing of a register by one is not considered a good test of addition time. Addition time should not be the only criterion used in timing estimation. (Some computer makers have been known to treat that one instruction uniquely so that the machine appears to the casual observer to be faster than it really is.)

add-on memories, LSI—On some systems, any combination of memories can be used with the LSI processor, in any mixture of types and speeds. This means that the user can configure the combination that best suits his other needs exactly, and can later change the combination to meet new needs merely by exchanging or adding the appropriate processor or memory boards. Thus, many LSI systems can "grow up" or change easily and quickly, even in the field.

address—1. A character or group of characters that identifies a register, a particular part of storage, or some other data source or destination. 2. To refer to a device or an item of data by its address.

address error exception—Address error exceptions occur when the processor attempts to access a word, or a long word operand, or an instruction at an odd address. The effect is much like an internally generated bus error, so that the bus cycle is aborted and the processor ceases whatever processing it is currently doing and begins the exception processing. After exception processing commences, the sequence is the same as that for a bus error including the information that is stacked, except that the vector number refers to the address error vector instead. Likewise, if an address error occurs during the exception processing for a bus error, address error, or reset, the processor is halted.

address field—The field that defines the source or destination of a frame; it follows the opening flag of a frame.

address format—1. The arrangement of the address parts of an instruction. The expression "plus-one" is frequently used to indicate that one of the addresses specifies the location of the next instruction to be executed. Expressions used are such as one-plus-one, two-plus-one, three-plus-one, four-plus-one. 2. The arrangement of the parts of a single address such as those required for identifying channel, module, track, etc., in a disk system.

addressing, bit set/clear mode—This mode of addressing applies to instructions that can set or clear any bit on page zero. The lower three bits in the opcode specify the bit to be set or cleared while the byte following the opcode specifies the address in page zero (on some single-chip systems).

addressing capabilities—Much of the power of microcomputers is derived from wide ranges of addressing capabilities. Addressing modes include sequential forward or backward addressing, address indexing, indirect addressing, 16-bit or 32-bit word addressing, 8-bit byte addressing, and stack addressing. Variable-length instruction formatting allows a minimum number of words to be used for each addressing mode. The result is efficient use of program storage space.

addressing capacity—The programming addressing range determines how large a program can be written without resorting to special external hardware and internal software techniques. A range that is too small means that extra hardware will be required to extend the addressing. Excessive capacity means that extraneous address bits will be carried in every instruction that refers to storage.

addressing capacity, microprocessor— 1. The addressing capacity of a microprocessor is a function of the number of address lines maintained by the processor. The number of address lines is usually determined by the number of memory locations. A typical size is 65,536 memory locations, and is referred to as 64K bytes of memory. (K stands for 1024 bits.) 2. The addressing capacity of a microcomputer often defines both the number of memory locations and the number of input/output (I/O) devices accessible, since many of the microprocessors access I/O devices directly via memory addresses.

addressing, extended — Extended addressing is used to reference any location in memory space. The EA is the contents of the two bytes following the opcode. Some extended addressing instructions are three bytes long.

addressing, indexed (16-bit offset)— This addressing mode calculates the extended address (EA) by adding the contents of the two bytes following the opcode to the index register. Thus, the entire memory space may be accessed.

addressing, inherent — The inherent mode of addressing has no extended address (EA). All the information necessary to execute an instruction is contained in the opcode. Direct operations on the accumulator and the index register are included in this mode of addressing.

addressing level—1. In zero-level addressing, the address part of an instruction is the operand (for instance, the addresses of shift instructions). 2. In first-level addressing, the address of an instruction is the location in memory where the operand may be found or where it is to be stored. 3. In second-level addressing (indirect addressing), the address part of an instruction is the place in memory where the address location of the operand may be found or is to be stored.

addressing modes — Data stored in memory must be accessed and manipulated. Data handling is specified by instructions (such as MOV, ADD, etc.) which usually indicate the func-

tion (operation code), the general-purpose register to be used when locating the source operand and/or the destination operand, and the addressing mode (which specifies how the selected register(s) are to be used). A large portion of the data handled by a computer is usually structured (in character strings, arrays, lists, etc.), and the addressing mode provides for efficient and flexible handling of structured data.

addressing modes, instruction — The addressing mode of a given instruction defines the address space it references and the method used to compute the address itself. Addressing modes are specified or implied by the instruction.

addressing modes, microprocessor — Microprocessor addressing modes include sequential, forward, or backward addressing, address indexing, indirect addressing, 16-bit or 32-bit word addressing, 8-bit byte addressing, and stack addressing. Variable length instruction formatting allows a minimum number of words to be used for each addressing mode. The result is an efficient use of program storage space.

addressing modes, relocatable code— The addressing modes determine whether or not a processor can support a relocatable object code without requiring overly sophisticated linking loaders and the like. Relative branching is essential to the relocatable code. If much of the processor's use is for table-driven software, then the ability to use indirect addressing and indexed addressing is important.

addressing, symbolic—Refers to a fundamental procedure or method of addressing that uses an address (symbolic address) chosen for convenience in programming or for the convenience of the programmer. In this method of addressing, a translation of the symbolic address into an absolute address is required before it can be used in the computer.

address, memory—Every word in memory has a unique address. A word may be defined as a set of bits comprising the largest addressable unit of information in a programmable memory. The address of a word is its location in memory.

address, memory and I/O—In some

microprocessors, the memory and I/O occupy a common address space and are accessed by the same instructions. With this type of microprocessor, the hardware decoding of the address bus determines whether the Read or Write is to a memory or I/O element. Other microprocessors have separate address spaces for memory and I/O. These microprocessors use different instructions for a memory access than for an I/O access, and they provide signals on the control bus to distinguish between memory and I/O. One advantage of this second type of approach is that the I/O address space can be made smaller to simplify device decoding. However, the I/O instructions that are available are usually not as powerful as the memory reference instructions.

address path, microprocessor — The address path is the selection path for memory and I/O data. For data processing, memory and I/O often use separate addressing or selection schemes. This suits the need for maximum memory and extensive peripherals. For logic processors, a combined addressing path for memory and I/O is the most efficient. Interconnection is simplified and the package pin limitation is not overextended.

address, single-level—An address that indicates the location where the referenced operand is to be found or stored with no reference to an index register. (Synonymous with first-level address.)

address, symbolic—Arbitrary identification of a particular word, function, or other information without regard to the location of the information.

address, track—Binary codes on magnetic tape or magnetic disk used to locate data stored in other tracks by actual code patterns (as indicated by the address), or by completing a count, or by simply noting their positions.

add time (in microseconds) — The time required to acquire from memory and execute one fixed-point add instruction using all features such as overlapped memory banks, instruction look-ahead, and parallel execution. The add is either from one full word in memory to a register, or from memory to memory, but not from register to register.

a/d interface — A "building block" subsystem offered by several manufacturers that is useful for implementation of the analog-to-digital conversion (ADC) function. These devices permit the construction of high-performance ADCs at a fraction of the cost of comparable modular units. With this subsystem, the critical analog processing is done on the monolithic chip and the less critical digital system of counters and gates is left for the system designer to implement.

Advanced Data Communications Control Procedure (ADCCP)—The American National Standards Institute's version (BSR X3.66) of Synchronous Data Link Control (SDLC) standards.

Advanced Data Link Controller (ADLC) —The ADLC converts the data that is transmitted and received in a synchronous serial form, in a bit-oriented data communication system, into parallel form, analyzes it, and stores it (for use by the MPU) so that data link management can be accomplished. Similarly, parallel data from the MPU system is serialized with the appropriate frame control information in order to conform to the bit-oriented protocol standards.

alarm systems, microprocessor—CPUs scan input-output points at preselected intervals. Data are read, processed, and checked against alarm limits. Critical deviations from normal operating conditions are detected and alarms are sent to the control/acknowledgement terminal. The CPU at the terminal formats and routes the alarm data to an operator's display panel. The operator on duty observes the detected alarm and takes the necessary steps to correct the problem.

Alarms corresponding to "crisis" situations can be detected directly by limit switches, circuit-continuity breaks, or by the manual depression of a button. Examples include floods, fire, burglary, or accidents. These conditions require immediate attention and would, therefore, be assigned as priority vector interrupts in the CPU monitor.

ALGOL—One of the international program languages designed for the concise, efficient expression of arithmetic and logical processes, and for the control of these processes. Taken from *ALGO*rithmic *L*anguage.

algorithm—A prescribed set of well-defined rules or processes for the solution of a problem in a finite number of steps; for example, a full statement of an arithmetic procedure for evaluating sin x to a stated precision. Contrast with heuristic.

algorithm, transfer — A specific algorithm design used in a demand fetching system to determine the order in which segments demanded by concurrent processes are transferred from a backing store to an internal memory.

alignment — The process of adjusting components of a system for proper interrelationship. The term is applied especially to the synchronization of components in a system.

alignment pin—Refers to any pin or device that will insure the correct mating of two components designed to be connected.

allocate—Refers to the assignment of storage in a computer to main routines and subroutines, thus fixing the absolute values of symbolic addresses.

alloy—Refers to a composition of two or more elements, of which at least one is a metal. It may be either a solid, a solution, a heterogeneous mixture, or a combination of both.

alphabetic coding—A system of abbreviation used in preparing information for input into a microcomputer. Information may then be reported in the form of letters and words as well as in numbers.

alpha flux—Alpha flux is defined as the number of alpha particles emitted from a surface over a period of time. It is measured in alpha particles per square centimeter per hour (α/cm²/hr).

alpha particles — Alpha particles are helium nucleii (consisting of two protons and two neutrons, for an atomic mass of 4) ejected from atoms during the nuclear decay of radioactive elements. Trace elements in ceramic are one source of alpha particles.

alpha-particle sensitivity — This is a problem in MOS dynamic memory arrays. The impact of an alpha particle in certain areas of a semiconductor causes the generation of close to one million electron-hole pairs. When scaling reduces the charge stored in a memory cell to about the same size, an alpha-particle hit can effectively wipe out the stored charge and cause a soft error. Depending on where the alpha particle hits the device, it can cause an error in a binary 1 or 0, or both.

alpha radiation — Alpha radiation can be found almost everywhere since it comes from naturally occurring substances. For example, typical soil samples produce 1 or 2 α/cm²/hr. (In fact, as little as one part per million of a radioactive contaminant will produce this level.)

alter switch—The alter switch, when toggled, causes the contents of the switch register to be copied into the register selected by the display switch, or into the memory location contained in the program counter, if the display switch is so set.

ALU architecture — A microprocessor can constitute an ALU (Arithmetic Logic Unit) and control portions of a general-purpose microcomputer. However, because of the different objectives of each equipment manufacturer, architectures vary widely. For example, one major system has only two 8-bit programmer-accessible data registers in the CPU, while another processor has an 8-bit accumulator and sixty-four 8-bit data registers. Generally, the ALU handles 8-bit quantities through the accumulator, and the register file is composed of three 16-bit registers. Because the accumulator and ALU are often only 8 bits wide, these three general registers can be accessed by instructions that treat them as six 8-bit registers. The choice of concept is often up to the programmer. From a hardware standpoint, the processor on many systems operates on 8-bit bytes and all I/O operations use an 8-bit data path.

ALU (Arithmetic Logic Unit)—The ALU is the heart of the microprocessor, and it is one of the essential components of the microprocessor. It is the operative base between the registers and the control block. The ALU performs various forms of addition, subtraction, and the extension of these to multiplication, division, exponentiation, etc. The logic mode relates to the operations of gating, masking, and other manipulations of the contents of registers.

ambient conditions — Ambient conditions are the conditions of the surrounding medium (pressure, noise, etc.).

ambient operating temperature — The temperature of air around an object, neglecting small localized variations.

ambient temperature, power-supply— The temperature of still air surrounding a power supply. It should be noted that the temperature of circulating air, such as in a temperature chamber with a fan, is not a correct ambient-temperature measurement since the power supply is being cooled by the circulating air. For power supplies, the following is a good practical definition: It is the temperature measured at a point ½ inch from the body of a power supply which is protected from direct air movement by a suitable enclosure.

ambiguity, controller—This is the inherent error caused by multiple bit changes at code transition positions, which is eliminated by various scanning techniques. Used in relation to encoders.

American Federation of Information Processing Societies (AFIPS) — An organization of computer related societies. Its members include: The Association for Computer Machinery; The Institute of Electrical and Electronic Engineers Computer Group; Simulation Councils, Inc.; American Society for Information Science. Its affiliates include: American Institute of Certified Public Accountants; American Statistical Association; Association for Computational Linguistics; Society for Industrial and Applied Mathematics; Society for Information Display, Association of Data Processing Services Organizations.

American National Standards Institute (ANSI) — Formerly American Standards Association (ASI) and, prior to that, United States of America Standards Institute (USASI), this organization organizes committees formed of computer users, manufacturers, etc., to develop and publish industry standards, e.g., ANSI FORTRAN, ANSI Standard Code for Periodical Identification, etc. It is a nonprofit, nongovernmental organization which serves as the national clearinghouse and coordinating body for voluntary standards in the United States.

American Standard Code for Information Interchange (ASCII) — Usually pronounced "ASKEE." A standard data-transmission code that was introduced to achieve compatibility between data devices. It consists of 7 information bits and 1 parity bit for error-checking purposes, thus allowing 128 code combinations. If the eighth bit is not used for parity, 256 code combinations are possible.

amplitude distortion—A condition that occurs in an amplifier or other device, when the output amplitude is not a linear function of the input amplitude. Amplitude distortion should be measured with the system operating under steady-state conditions and with a sinusoidal input signal. When other frequencies are present, the term "amplitude" applies to the fundamental only.

analog — In electronic computers, the term refers to a physical system in which the performance of measurements yields information concerning a class of mathematical problems.

analog amplifier—In some systems, an analog amplifier performs two functions. First, it supplies the dual-delayed sweep comparators with the proper dc levels. Second, it accepts the dc level from the vertical channel, processes this level, and provides two pieces of information for the processor through the input interface. The two pieces of information are the polarity of the dc level and whether the level is greater or lesser than some reference. If it is greater, the processor increases the reference until it is within 1 LSB of the unknown. Conversely, if it is lesser, the processor decreases the reference until it is within 1 LSB of the unknown. In both cases, it displays the reference level that is now equal to the unknown.

analog channel—A computer channel in which transmitted information can have any value between the defined limits of the channel.

analog computer — A computer which operates on the principle of creating a physical (usually electrical) analogy of a mathematical problem to be solved. Variables such as temperature or flow are represented by the magnitude of a physical phenomenon such as voltage or current. These variables are manipulated by the computer in accordance with mathematical formulas "analoged" on it.

analog gate—A logic gate, the output signal of which is a linear function of one or more input signals.

analog input card—A module that contains an instrumentation amplifier, an input multiplexer (that can select up to 16 single ended or 8 differential mode signals), a track and hold buffer, and a high-speed A/D converter. Amplifier gain and input, bipolar or monopolar, are user selectable. Low input drift permits the connection of transducers, such as thermocouples, and a short conversion time allows digitizing almost all of the entire audio spectrum.

analog output—As opposed to digital output, the amplitude is continuously proportionate to the stimulus, the proportionality being limited by the resolution of the device.

analog output card—A module that permits the generation of analog data to many devices, such as oscilloscopes, amplifiers, motor drivers, XY recorders, and other voltage controlled devices. Unlike some multichannel converters which require cumbersome software refresh, some units contain their own memory and refresh circuitry. Up to 16 channels of analog output are available, and the output range is user-adjustable, on many systems.

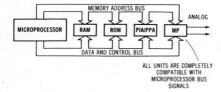

Analog output card.

analog representation—A representation having discrete values but continuously variable.

analog-to-digital-converter (ADC)—Refers to a device which produces a digital output from an input which is in the analog form of physical motion or electrical voltages.

analytic relationship—The relationship which exists between concepts and

their corresponding terms, by their definition and inherent scope of meaning.

analyzer, electronic differential—A form of analog computer using interconnected electronic integrators to solve differential equations.

ancillary equipment—A term, often interchangeable with peripheral equipment, which relates to all types of input-output, communication, and interface equipment.

AND element—One of the basic logic elements (gates or operators) which has at least two binary input signals and a single binary output signal. The answer or variable which represents the output signal is the conjunction (set theory) of the variables represented by the input signals.

AND gate—Refers to a gate circuit in an electronic computer that has more than one control (input) terminal. No output signal will be produced unless a pulse is applied to all inputs simultaneously. The AND gate truth table is:

$$0 + 0 = 0$$
$$0 + 1 = 0$$
$$1 + 0 = 0$$
$$1 + 1 = 1$$

AND operation—A basic operation in Boolean algebra which, for the two integers I and J, may be defined by the statement:

If I and J are both 1, then the result is 1. Otherwise, the result is zero.

The dot is used to indicate the AND operation. When letters are used (in general cases), the dot is sometimes omitted; thus, I and J may be represented as I●J or IJ.

AND operator—1. A logical operator that has the property that if P is a statement and Q is a statement, then P AND Q is true if both statements are true, and false if either is false or if both are false. Truth is normally expressed by the value 1, falsity by 0. The AND operator is often represented by a centered dot (P ● Q), by no sign (PQ), by an inverted "u" or logical product symbol (P ∩ Q), or by the letter "X" or multiplication symbol (P × Q). Note that the letters AND are capitalized to differentiate between the logical operator and the word "and" in common usage. 2. The logical operation that makes use of the AND operator or logical product.

annealing, laser—Annealing refers to the repair of lattice damage and dopant activation in a semiconductor following ion implantation. A pulsed laser anneals by melting the surface of the wafer to a depth significantly beyond the ion-implantation damage. As the melted area refreezes, the single-crystal structure is re-established by liquid-phase epitaxy. The implanted dopant is distributed very evenly throughout the melted area.

ANSI—Abbreviation for American National Standards Institute (formerly ASA and USASI), an organization that develops and publishes industry standards.

anticoincidence circuit—Refers to a counter circuit that produces an output pulse when either of two input circuits receives a pulse, but not when the two inputs receive pulses at the same time.

anticoincidence unit — A binary logic coincidence circuit for completing the logic operation of Exclusive-OR, i.e., the result is true when A is true and B is false or when A is false and B is true, and the result is false when A and B are both true or when A and B are both false. Same as difference gate, nonequivalence gate, distance gate, diversity gate, add-without carry gate, exjunction gate, nonequality gate, symmetric difference gate, partial sum gate, and modulo-two sum gate.

APL language — A programming language developed by Iverson. An unusually extensive set of operators and data structures are used to implement what is considered by many to be the most flexible, powerful, and concise algorithmic/procedural language in existence. Primarily used from conversational terminals, its applicability to "production" job processing is limited but its value for educational and investigative work is great.

application notes, microcomputer — Application notes are a particular form of documentation endemic to the semiconductor business; they are not common in the community of computer vendors. However, the rapid engineering changes and the problems of designing microprocessors into final systems virtually require the use of application notes for release rapidity. Some microprocessor vendors publish one circuit diagram. Others publish alternative ways of accomplishing the same objectives, complete with hardware and software considerations.

applications package—A set of computer programs and/or subroutines used to solve problems in a particular application, i.e., business, scientific, financial, etc.

applications program—A program written to accomplish a specific user task (such as payroll) as opposed to supervisory, general-purpose, or utility programs.

applications support package—Applications support packages assist users in: (1) evaluating the operation of the microcomputer family of parts in an actual application, (2) reducing the engineering time and development costs required in developing and constructing prototype systems using the microcomputer family of parts, (3) comparing the software and firmware programs of the user's system, (4) reducing the time required to evaluate and debug system hardware, software, and firmware, and (5) providing a working model of the user's system.

applications study—The detailed process of determining a system or set of procedures necessary to using a computer for definite functions or operations, and the establishing of specifications to be used as a base for the selection of equipment suitable to the specific needs.

APT (Automatically Programmed Tools)—A language for programming numerically controlled machine tools. There are many other similar languages with different names.

APT III—APT III is a system for the computer-assisted programming of numerically controlled machine tools, such as flame cutters, drafting machines, and similar equipment. It is production-oriented; that is, it was written to simplify the effort, time, and money needed to take full advantage of numerically controlled techniques in engineering and manufacturing. In addition to providing machine-tool programming capabilities that are virtually impossible by manual methods, numerical control permits: reduced lead time, greater design freedom and flexibility, lower direct costs, greater accuracy, improved production forecasting, lower tooling costs, better engineering control of the manufacturing process, and simplified introduction of changes.

AQL test—The acceptable quality level (AQL) of groups of parts and components are laboratory-tested by most manufacturers to a specified percentage value—for example, 1%. Then, if more than 1% of these parts fail, the entire lot fails to meet the acceptable quality level and is rejected.

arbitrary-function generator — A specific function generator (analog) which is not committed by its design function exclusively, so that the function that it generates can be changed at the discretion of the operator.

architecture—Any design or orderly arrangement perceived by man, i.e., the architecture of the microprocessor. Since the extant microprocessors vary considerably in design, their architecture has become a bone of contention among specialists.

argument — An independent variable; for example, when looking up a quantity in a table, the number, or any of the numbers, that identifies the location of the desired value.

arithmetic and logical operations, microprocessor—In most systems, all arithmetic and logical operations utilize the accumulator, with the second operand coming either from the general registers or the main memory. Several different addressing methods may be used for accessing the main memory including: immediate, absolute, indexed, and auto-increment modes. Instructions to manipulate the index registers make other addressing modes, such as stack addressing, easy to implement. A large complement of move instructions allows data transfers between the accumulator, the general registers, and the memory in many combinations.

arithmetic and logic unit (ALU)—The part of the CPU logic chip that actually executes the operations requested by an input command is called the Arithmetic and Logic Unit (ALU) since, in every case, some combination of arithmetic and/or logical operations is required. Another part of CPU chip logic, the Control Unit, decodes the instruction (stored in the instruction register) in order to enable the required ALU logic and, thus, implement the arithmetic and/or logical operations required by the instruction.

arithmetic logic unit data flow—Data flow in many processors centers around the arithmetic logic unit (ALU). This module generally consists of two operand/shift registers, a status register, carry control logic, and an arithmetic-logic function generator. Each of the operand inputs to this function generator is fed by a multiplexer, allowing the selection of one of four operand sources. The output from the function generator feeds the output data bus (DBO) that goes to the memory and I/O system, to the operand and status registers, and to the general register unit.

arithmetic registers—Arithmetic registers are those on which arithmetic and logic functions can be performed; the register can be a source or destination of operands for the operation. Registers that can supply but not receive operands for the ALU are not considered arithmetic registers by many evaluators.

armed interrupt — Interrupts may be armed or disarmed. An armed interrupt accepts and holds the interruption signal. A disarmed interrupt ignores the signal. An armed interrupt may be enabled or disabled. An interrupt signal for an enabled condition causes certain hardware processing to occur. A disabled interrupt is held waiting for enablement.

armed state—The state of an interrupt level wherein it can accept and remember an interrupt input signal.

ARQ (Automatic Request for Repeat) —A protocol or data-link control. This is a prescribed set of rules used to provide two major functions, establish a connection between the transmitting and receiving stations, and ensure the error-free transmission of the block(s) of one or more characters that are contained in a message. The two major classes of data-link controls are the stop-and-wait ARQ and the continuous ARQ.

array—A series of items arranged in a meaningful pattern. Also, refers to a data structure in which each element is identified by one or more unique position indicators. In mathematics, arrays are often operated upon as units by applying matrix algebra rules. In many programming applications, the term simply refers to an area assigned to store program data.

array processor — Also called coprocessor. These ultrafast processors reduce the time to do strings of iterative arithmetic (such as matrix operations, FET signal-processing operations) by several orders of magnitude. They are especially suitable for image processing, medical research, scientific computation, seismic exploration, and other applications, such as sonar, radar, speech, acoustics, communications, simulation, etc. Various 32-bit programmable floating-point array processors are available for use with 16- and 32-bit micro- and minicomputers as attachable or coworker dedicated computers.

array vectoring, FORTRAN—A unique automatic array vectoring feature of some types of FORTRAN IV. It eliminates the time-consuming multiply operations required in array subscripting. Precompiled FORMAT statements make formatted input and output conversions faster and smaller. On some systems, FORTRAN IV does an extensive local (or peephole) optimization, examining each sequence of operations output, and substituting a shorter and faster group if possible.

array, virtual—Designed to permit the random access of large data files that are too large to be contained in memory at one time. Often, one or more virtual arrays are stored on a disk and can contain string, integer, and floating-point matrices.

artificial intelligence—The development or capability of a machine that can proceed or perform functions that are normally concerned with human intelligence, such as learning, adapting, reasoning, self-correction, and automatic improvement. The research and study of methods for the development of a machine that can improve its own operations. In a more restricted sense, the study of techniques for the more effective use of digital computers by improved programming techniques.

artwork—The original oversize accurately scaled drawings and plastic overlays of the microcircuit topological layout that are used to produce the master mask plates.

ARU (audio-response unit)—A device that connects a computer system to a telephone in order to provide voice response to inquiries made.

ASCII code — 1. A contraction for "American Standard Code for Information Interchange." This standard defines the codes for a character set that is used for information interchange between equipments of different manufacturers and which is the standard for digital communications over telephone lines. 2. A code which relates 96 displayed characters (64 without lower case) and 32 nondisplayed control characters to a sequence of 7 "on" or "off" choices.

assemble—1. In digital computer programming, to put together subprograms which finally make up a complete program. 2. To perform some or all of the following functions: (A) Translation of symbolic operation codes into machine codes. (B) Allocation of storage, to the extent at least of assigning storage locations to successive instructions. (C) Computation of absolute or relocatable addresses from symbolic addresses. (D) Insertion of library routines. (E) Generation of sequences of symbolic instructions by the insertion of specific parameters into macro instructions.

assembler—1. The capability of an assembler essentially is to translate symbolically represented instructions into their binary equivalents. A well designed computer is reflected in a versatile efficient assembly language instruction set. It is a computer program which operates on symbolic input data to produce machine instructions from such data. 2. An assembler is a program that translates assembly language statements into a machine code that the processor can execute.

assembler, hardware—A hardware assembler is a program that translates a symbolic assembly language into bit patterns suitable for microcomputer control storage programming.

assembler language — A source language that includes symbolic machine language statements in which there is a one-to-one correspondence with the instruction formats and data formats of the computer.

assembler, macro—A two-pass assembler on some computers that is available with subprogram, literal, and powerful macrofacilities. The output, which can be directly processed by a debugging program, provides symbol tables for effective program checkout in terms of the source language symbols.

assembler program—The assembler is a program for a symbolic coding language. It is composed of simple but brief expressions that provide a rapid translation from symbolic to machine-language relocatable object coding for the computer. The assembly language includes a wide and sophisticated variety of operators that allow the fabrication of desired fields based on information generated at assembly time. The instruction-operation codes are assigned mnemonics which describe the hardware function of each instruction. Assembler-directive commands provide the programmer with the ability to generate data words and values based on specific conditions at assembly time.

assembler pseudo-operations — Some assemblers provide more sophisticated features. These are usually pseudo-operations, or assembler instructions, that do not assemble into microcomputer instructions directly but which control the assembly of instructions that do. The more significant and common pseudo-operations are: origin, comments, equal, etc.

assembly, conditional—Conditional assembly permits the assembler to include or delete sections of code, which may vary from system to system, such as the code required to handle optional external devices.

assembly language processor—A language processor that accepts words, statements, and phrases to produce machine instructions. It is more than an assembly program because it has compiler powers. A macro-assembler permits the segmentation of a large program so that positions may be tested separately. It also provides an extensive program analysis to aid in debugging.

assembly language program—A program that consists of a series of symbolic statements that are normally written on coding forms and later transcribed to paper or magnetic tape for input to the assembler. The assembler converts the symbolic statements into machine code.

assembly listing—Refers to a printed list made by the assembler to document an assembly operation. It generally shows, line for line, how the assembler interpreted the assembly language program.

assembly program—Refers to a computer program flexible enough to incorporate subroutines into the main program. It is a program that is able to translate a program written in symbolic language into a machine language program. Principally designed to relieve the programmer of the problem of assigning actual storage locations to instructions and data when encoding a program. It permits the use of mnemonic operational codes rather than numeric operation codes. The address scheme used may be either numeric or mnemonic.

Association for Computer Machinery (ACM)—A professional and technical society whose publications, conferences, and activities are designed to help advance the art, specifically as regards machinery and system design, language and program development, and other related activities. It is a member of the American Federation of Information Processing Societies (AFIPS).

Association of Data Processing Service Organizations (ADAPSO) — An association of U.S. and Canadian data-processing service organizations.

associative storage—A storage type in which storage locations are identified by their contents, not by their names or positions. Synonymous with content-addressed storage and parallel-search memory.

associative storage registers — Concerns various registers that are not identified by their name or position but which are known and addressed by their content; used to locate indexed items.

astable circuit—Refers to a circuit that continuously alternates between its two unstable states at a frequency determined by the circuit constants. The circuit can be synchronized by applying a repetitive input signal of slightly higher frequency.

asynchronous communications — A method of transmitting data in which the timing of character placement on connecting transmitting lines is not

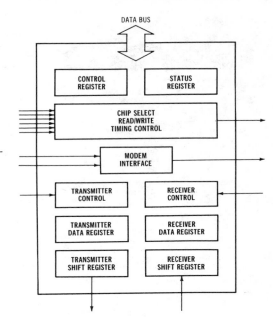

Asynchronous Communications Interface Adapter (ACIA).

critical. The transmitted characters are preceded by a start bit and followed by a stop bit, thus permitting the interval between characters to vary.

asynchronous communications interface adapter (ACIA)—A typical asynchronous communications interface adapter will provide the data formatting and control necessary to interface serial asynchronous data communications to bus organized systems. The ACIA devices include select enable, read/write, interrupt, and bus interface logic to allow data transfer over various 8-bit bidirectional data buses. The parallel data of a bus system is serially transmitted and received by the asynchronous data interface, with proper formatting and error checking. The functional configuration of an ACIA is programmed via the data bus during system initialization. Word lengths, clock division ratios, and transmit control through the Request to Send output may be programmed. For modem operation, three control lines are often provided to allow the ACIA to interface directly with the various digital modems.

asynchronous computer—1. An automatic digital computer which goes from one operation to the next controlled by signals that the previous operation has been completed. 2. A computer in which each event or the performance of each operation starts as a result of a signal that is generated or by the availability of the parts of the computer that are required by the next event or operation. 3. Having a variable time interval between successive bits, characters, or events. In data transmission, this is usually limited to a variable time interval between characters and is often known as start-stop transmission.

asynchronous machine—Refers to any machine whose speed of operation is not proportionate to the frequency of the system to which the machine is connected.

asynchronous modem controller diagnostic—A device that uses a loop-back mode along with a special connector (that cross-connects all EIA control signals) to completely test all controller functions.

asynchronous multiplexer — A typical unit will provide interfacing for up to

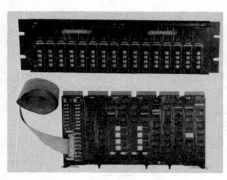

An asynchronous multiplexer (Courtesy Plessey Peripheral Systems).

16 communications devices, teleprinters, keyboard/display terminals, and data sets at programmable rates from 57 to 2400 baud. Programmable functions include parity generation and checking.

asynchronous operation—1. Relates to the timing of internal operations or switching networks and the free-running pulses that signal successive instructions. The completion of one instruction triggers the next. There is no fixed time for each specific cycle. 2. A system in which the speed (or frequency) of operation is not related to the frequency of the system to which it is connected. The performance of any operation starts as a result of a signal that indicates that the previous operation has been completed (e.g., teletypewriter signals).

ATE — Abbreviation for automatic test equipment.

attenuation—Refers to the decrease in amplitude of signal (current, voltage, or power) during its transmission from one point to the next. It may be expressed as a ratio or in decibels (by extension of the term).

attenuator—An arrangement of resistors, capacitors, etc., that introduces a known attenuation into a measuring circuit or line. A variable attenuator uses switching to vary the attenuation introduced into the circuit.

auctioneering device—A specific device designed to automatically select either the highest or the lowest input signal from among two or more input signals. This is often referred to as a high or low signal selector.

audio-cassette interface—A device that allows virtually unlimited memory storage for data or software. Operates by modulating audio frequencies in the record mode. Demodulates recorded data in the playback mode.

audio response — A form of output which gives a verbal reply to inquiries. The computer can be programmed to seek answers to inquiries that are made on a time-shared online system and, then, utilize a special audio-response unit which elicits the appropriate prerecorded response to the inquiry. Inquiries must be of a nature, however, for which the audio response has been prepared.

audio-response calculator—One type of audio-response calculator announces each entry and the results of every calculation using a solid-state synthesized voice stored on ROMs after digitizing. The CMOS circuits pronounce the ten numerals and the four algebraic functions of the calculator. They include: inverse, square root, square, and percent plus memory. The calculator's original use was for vocational education of the blind and, in its early development, an audio reinforcement of basic math concepts for sighted students.

audio-response unit (ARU)—A device that can connect a computer system to a telephone to provide voice response to inquiries made.

audio system—Relates to various types of special equipment which have capabilities of storing and processing data obtained from voice sources, either recorded or transmitted. Voice answer-back (VAB) systems are a type of audio-output system as a contrast.

autodoping—The introduction of impurities from the substrate into the epitaxial layer during the process of epitaxy.

auto loader—A program that allows program loading to be initiated automatically, remotely, or from a front panel switch. The signal operation provides loading from a teletypewriter, paper tape, cassette, magnetic tape, and/or disk.

automata theory—Relates to the development of the theory which relates the study of principles of operations and applications of automatic devices to the various behaviorist concepts and theories.

automatic calling unit (ACU)—A dialing device which permits a machine (business) to automatically dial calls over a communication network.

automatic coding—Refers to a technique by which a digital computer is programmed to perform a significant portion of the coding of a problem.

automatic dialing unit—A modem or device that is capable of automatically generating pulses representing the dialed digits of a call.

automatic interrupt — 1. Interruption caused by a program instruction as contained in some executive routine; an interruption not caused by the programmer but due to the engineering of devices. 2. An automatic program-controlled interrupt system that causes a hardware jump to a predetermined location. There are at least five types of interrupts: input/output, programmer error, machine error, supervisor call, and external. Unwanted interrupts, such as an anticipated overflow, can be masked out.

automatic loader—This is a loader program implemented in a special ROM that allows the loading of binary paper tapes or the first record or sector of a mass storage device. The program is equivalent to a bootstrap loader plus a binary loader. When an automatic loader is installed, it is seldom necessary to key in a bootstrap program to load the binary loader.

automatic loader diagnostic—This program aid reads out and verifies the contents of the automatic ROM. It verifies proper sequencing when the automatic loader switch is depressed.

automatic programming—Refers to any technique designed to simplify the writing and execution of programs in a computer. For example, an assembly program which translates from the programmer's symbolic language to the machine language, or one which integrates subroutines into the main routine.

automatic punch—A device which automatically punches a card or tape, and moves it as necessary under control of electrical or electronic signals.

automatic reset—Refers to a stepping relay that returns to its home position

either when a pulsing circuit fails to energize its driving coil within a given time or by an overload relay that restores the circuit as soon as the cause of the overload is corrected.

automatic routine—A routine that is executed independently of manual operations, but only if certain conditions occur within a program or record.

automatic sequencing — Refers to the ability of a microcomputer to perform successive operations without the necessity of additional instructions.

automatic stop—An automatic halting of a microcomputer processing operation as the result of an error.

automatic switchover — An operating system, which has a stand-by machine, that is capable of detecting when the on-line machine is faulty and which can switch to the alternate machine once this determination is made.

automatic test—A capability of some analyzers that allows the storage of a partial or complete test procedure, plus the expected results, in an auxiliary memory. Tests are then executed with minimal user intervention.

automatic test equipment (ATE) — A tester system that is capable of inspecting in a few seconds a complex printed-circuit board containing components from simple resistors and capacitors to complex LSI devices. Repairs required to correct component or workmanship problems on the assembly are printed out specifying the necessary corrections.

automatic test generation (ATG)—This is a sophisticated technique that uses a computer program to analyze a software model of complex circuit boards. It calculates a list of conditions in which the design might be failure prone, and then generates programs to test for these specific faults. The generated programs are then executed on automatic test equipment to evaluate the product's design.

automatic voltage regulator—A device or circuit which maintains a constant voltage, regardless of variations of the input voltage or load.

automation—1. The implementation of processes by automatic means. 2. The theory, art, or technique of making a process more automatic. 3. The investigation, design, development, and application of methods of rendering processes automatic, self-moving, or self-controlling. 4. The conversion of a procedure, a process, or equipment to automatic operation.

automaton—1. A machine designed to simulate the operations of living things. 2. A mechanism that is relatively self-operating. 3. A robot.

automobile computer—An algorithm-processing computer (MPU) that measures engine revolutions per minute (using reference pulse), temperatures, pressures, and other signals. In addition, some computes new parameters for air/fuel mix or injector pulse length, the spark advance or retard position, and any requisite adjustments pertinent to idle speed or cruise control. Often, new control parameters are then passed to the engine controller, which will maintain the settings while the processor executes another pass through the algorithm.

autonomous working — 1. A specific type of concurrent or simultaneous working; i.e., the carrying out of multiple instructions at the same time. 2. The initiation and execution of a part of a computer or automation system independent of a computer, or other operations being performed on other parts of the system. The independent set of operations on various data are themselves often monitored.

auxiliary equipment — Equipment not under direct control of the central processing unit. Synonymous with ancillary equipment.

auxiliary memory—A place in memory in addition to the active recording memory. It may include RAM and PROM and is used in comparing data, halting on difference, automatic testing, and other functions.

auxiliary processor — A specialized processor such as an array processor, fast fourier transform (FFT) processor, or input/output processor (IOP), generally used to increase processing speed through concurrent operation.

auxiliary routine—A routine designed to assist in the operation of the microcomputer and in debugging other routines.

auxiliary storage—A storage device in addition to the main storage of a microcomputer, e.g., magnetic tape, disk, or magnetic drum. Auxiliary storage usually holds much larger amounts of information than the main storage; however, the information is accessible less rapidly.

average transfer rate—A particular rate of data transmission through a channel, over a relatively long period of time, to thus include gaps between blocks, words, or records. Also included in this time period are regeneration time and other items not subject to program control. Starting, stopping, rewinding, searching, or other programmed control items are not included.

average transmission rate—Relates to the rate at which data is transmitted through a channel, over an extended period of time, to allow for gaps between words, blocks, records, files, or fields. Starting, stopping, rewinding, searching, or other operations subject to program control, in the case of magnetic tapes, discs, drums, are excluded. Included is regeneration time for electrostatic core or main storage, since the time period delays continuous transfer from storage and is not subject to program control.

available power—The maximum power obtainable from a given source by suitable adjustment of the load. For a source that is equivalent to a constant sinusoidal waveform, emf in series with an impedance (that is independent of amplitude), it is the mean-square value of the emf divided by four times the resistive component of the source impedance.

avalanche breakdown — Relative to a semiconductor diode, a nondestructive breakdown caused by the cumulative multiplication of carriers through field-induced impact ionization.

avalanche conduction — Refers to a form of conduction in a semiconductor in which the charged particle collisions create additional hole-electron pairs.

avalanche diode—Also called a breakdown or zener diode. A diode which switches the circuit through it rapidly whenever the applied voltage increases. This switch uses the avalanche breakdown principle, and the transit time is on the order of a trillionth of a second.

avalanche noise—Refers to a phenomenon in a semiconductor junction in which carriers in a high-voltage gradient develop sufficient energy to dislodge additional carriers through physical impact.

avalanche photodiode—A photodiode that takes advantage of the avalanche multiplication of photocurrent. It is particularly suited to low noise and/ or high speed applications.

B

back coupling—Any form of coupling which permits the transfer of energy from the output circuit of an amplifier to its input circuit.

background processing—In time-sharing and multiprogramming, the lower-priority work done by the computer when real-time, conversational, high-priority, or quick-response programs are inactive. This work can be interrupted as necessary on orders from terminals or inquiries from other units. Batch processing, such as inventory control, payroll, housekeeping, etc., is often treated as background processing.

background program—1. In multiprogramming, the program with the lowest priority. Background programs execute from batched or stacked job input. 2. Under time-sharing, a program executed in a region of main storage that is not swapped.

backlash—Property of most regenerative and oscillator circuits by which oscillation is maintained with a smaller positive feedback than is required for inception.

backplane—Connector blocks and wiring units constituting most or all of the interconnecting circuits of a system. For example, the printed-circuit modules of a personal microcomputer that make up the system are mounted by plugging into the backplane.

backplane, microcomputer—A bus-oriented backplane is typically used as the data highway between logic memory and process input/output modules. Some backplanes are configured so as to give each module (card), that is plugged into it, its own unique address.

As a result of this "card address" design, users can interchange memory and input/output modules throughout the chassis. One typical

backplane has in its chassis 3 control slots, 1 terminator slot, and 16 multipurpose addressable slots. Since only 3 of the 16 addressable slots are used in many basic systems, 13 slots are available so that users can plug in any additional memory or interfacing required.

backplane testing — New solid-state-switched systems connect to the backplane via daisy-chained "fixture cards" to minimize the interface wiring, and use the power of the computer to learn, in product nomenclature, the wiring scheme of a known-to-be-good backplane or a prototype. Wiring error rates on backplanes usually run between 0.1% and 5% depending on the type of wire-wrap equipment used. Manual wiring produces the highest error rates, between 2% and 5%. These errors are usually due to missed connections, misplaced wires, and loose solder. Semiautomatic connection errors run between 0.1% and 1%, with most errors resulting from machine malfunction, operator mistakes, and broken wires. Using completely automatic wrapping equipment, error rates seldom are above 0.2%.

back-porch effect—The prolonging of the collector current in a transistor for a brief time after the input signal (particularly if large) has decreased to zero.

back-to-back devices — Refers to two semiconductor devices connected in parallel but in opposite directions so that they can be used to control current without introducing rectification. Also referred to as an inverse-parallel connection.

back-up system—1. Systems that combine several sophisticated error detection and correction techniques to spot and correct equipment and transmission errors. 2. Systems that take over when the primary system is down for various reasons.

B address—The high-order position of the instruction code indicating the location of data to be processed.

badge reader—A device that senses data from a card or badge inserted in it. The use of machine-readable badges ensures that employees can quickly and uniquely identify themselves to a computer system without the need to use names, employee numbers, or passwords. In addition, badges are also extremely useful in identifying machines, tools, or other frequently used items, as well as the tasks to be performed. Data-capture terminals can read the most commonly used types of badges.

balanced amplifier—An amplifier having two outputs is considered to be balanced when the difference between the quiescent dc-output voltages is reduced to zero or to a specified level. Also, an amplifier having only one output is considered to be balanced when the quiescent dc-output voltage is reduced to zero or to a specified level.

balanced circuits—Those circuits that are terminated by a network whose impedance balances the impedance of the line so that the return losses are negligible.

band—1. A group of tracks on a magnetic disk or on a magnetic drum. 2. In communications, the frequency spectrum between two defined limits. 3. Also a group of specific radio channels assigned by the Federal Communications Commission to a particular type of radio service.

band-edge energy—The band of energy between two defined limits in a semiconductor. The lower limit corresponds to the lowest energy required by an electron to remain free, while the upper limit is the maximum permissible energy of a freed electron.

band-elimination filter—A filter having a single attenuation band, with neither of the cutoff frequencies being zero or infinite; for example, a filter to eliminate the 60-hertz signal picked up from ambient electrical power devices.

band ranges, channel — 1. Narrow band: Data communication capabili-ties up to 300 bps. 2. Voice band: Communications channels having effective bandwidths of about 3000 Hz. Equipment is available for data transmission at speeds up to 9600 bps. 3. Broad band: Data communication rates higher than those of voice-band channels. Higher reliability is also provided. Current facilities can provide transmission rates up to several million bps.

bandwidth, channel—In addition to the direction of transmission, a channel is characterized by its bandwidth. In general, the greater the bandwidth of the assigned channel, the higher the possible speed of transmission. This speed is usually measured in terms of the number of line-signal elements per second; this is known as the baud rate. If a signal element represents one of two binary states, the baud rate is equal to the bit rate. When more than two states are represented, as in multilevel modulation, the bit rate exceeds the baud rate.

bandwidth, mid-band gain—Bandwidth is the range of frequencies within which the gain of the amplifier is not more than 3 dB below the value of the mid-band gain. Mid-band gain is the gain at a specified frequency or the average gain over a specified frequency range.

bar code—Coding of consumer and other products by marking packages or labels with combinations of bars of varying thicknesses to represent characters and numerals. The various codes, Universal Product Code (UPC) and others, are designed to be read by optical wands or stationary in-counter readers.

bar-code optical scanner—See optical scanner, bar code.

bar-code reader—This is a device that can "read" the various product-marking codes (UPC, CODABAR, etc.) currently in use. The devices are designed either as hand-held pen-like wand scanners or as counter-installed scanners. With optional selectors, they may be equipped to scan all or specific types of codes. See bar-code optical scanner.

base number—Specifically, the radix of a number system. For example, 10 is the radix, or base number, for the decimal system. 2 is the radix for the binary system (base 2).

UPC

VERSION A

VERSION E

MSI

MODULUS 10 CHECK DIGIT
397401

MODULUS 11 CHECK DIGIT
46164105

MONARCH CODABAR

A000168 $12 8BT

Bar code.

base time—A designed and precisely controlled function of time by which some particular process or exercise is controlled or measured.

BASIC — Beginner's All-purpose Symbolic Instruction Code. A common high-level time-sharing computer programming language. It is easily learned. The language was developed by Dartmouth College.

basic control system (BCS) satellites —A computer satellite usually has an interrupt-oriented system providing fast execution of dedicated programs, without time scheduling capability.

basic linkage—A linkage which is used

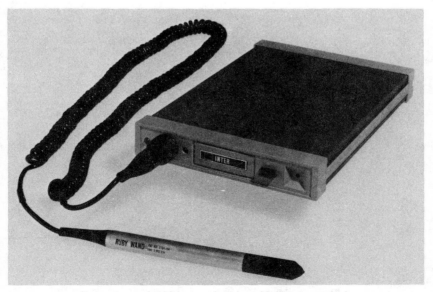

Bar-code reader (Courtesy Interface Mechanisms, Inc.).

repeatedly in one routine, program, or system and which follows the same set of rules each time. See linkage.

BASIC, multiuser—Multiuser BASIC is a fast incremental compiler developed for use as a conversation programming language. This is an interpretive system that provides interactive entry and execution of programs written in the popular BASIC language developed by Dartmouth College. It provides on-line time-shared access to the microcomputer. Several users simultaneously can develop programs, enter and retrieve data, examine files, and communicate. Multiuser BASIC supports up to nine concurrent users in some systems and provides many language extensions and features not usually included in the BASIC language. A "desk calculator" mode of operation allows immediate execution of statements without the need to write a complete program. This feature is useful for program debugging as well as for performing calculations. In addition to all the elementary and advanced features normally included in the BASIC language, some versions include extensions for string operations, matrix operations, trigonometric functions, random numbers, etc.

basic operating system (BOS)—One of many operating systems (see operating system).

basic telecommunications access method—An access method that permits read/write communications with remote devices. Abbreviated BTAM.

batch processing—1. In computer terminology, batch processing refers to a specific method of processing in which a number of similar input items are grouped for processing during the same machine run. 2. Batch-processing computer systems generally do not require immediate updating of files. In batch processing, data is gathered up to a cutoff time and is then processed. In off-line processing, data is batched (collected) via terminal-like devices for later transmission to a computer. Contrast with on-line data processing.

battery backup board—A typical battery backup board is a device designed to provide temporary power for periods ranging from 3 minutes for 128 kilobytes to 4.5 minutes for 32 kilobytes of dynamic random-access memory. It includes a watch-dog timer that sets off an external alarm when the central processing unit fails to activate the battery backup by a predetermined time. Those times are selected for intervals of between 1 and 30 seconds.

battery pack—These units generally provide backup power to support components, such as RAM, etc. The length of support time is dependent upon the amount of RAM to be kept under power; for example, 4K bytes can be supported for 8 hours and 20K bytes can be supported for 1 hour, in some systems.

baud—1. A unit of signalling speed equal to the number of discrete conditions or signal events per second. For example, one baud equals one-half dot cycle per second in Morse Code, one bit per second in a train of binary signals, and one 3-bit value per second in a train of signals, each of which can assume one of eight different states. 2. In asynchronous transmission, the unit of modulation rate corresponding to one unit interval per second, i.e., if the duration of the units interval is 20 milliseconds, the modulation rate is 50 baud.

baud rate—A type of measurement of data flow in which the number of signal elements per second is based on the duration of the shortest element. When each element carries one bit, the baud rate is numerically equal to bits per second (bps).

baud rates, selectable—This is often the baud rate that is the fastest that the communications or transmission line(s) of a terminal will allow. Standard telephone lines transmit at 1200 baud; special dedicated lines allow rates as high as 19,200 bps. Some terminals provide as many as 15 switch-selectable baud rates.

B box—A register that contains a quantity which may be used to modify addresses. (Synonymous with B-register.)

BCD (binary-coded decimal)—A type of positional value code in which each decimal digit is binary coded into 4-bit "words." The decimal number 12, for example, would become 0001 0010 in BCD. BCD is based on, and sometimes called, the 8421 code. It derives its name from the value assigned to each of four bit positions, with each set of four bits equal to one decimal.

Decimal Digit	8421 Binary
0	0000
1	0001
2	0010
3	0011
4	0100
5	0101
6	0110
7	0111
8	1000
9	1001

beam lead—A metal strip (beam) deposited directly onto the surface of the die (chip) as part of the wafer processing cycle during the fabrication. After separation of the die, the beam is left protruding from the edge of the chip and can be bonded directly to interconnecting pads without any wire connections.

beam penetration, crt—A viable alternative to raster-scan technology is beam penetration. This random-scan technology, used primarily in stroke-refresh or calligraphic systems, draws continuous lines on a crt with an electron beam. The intensity of the beam determines which of four phosphor layers is activated and, therefore, what color is displayed. Such systems achieve dot resolutions dependent on the accuracy of the DACs they employ.

Beam-penetration crt's require little memory in order to display virtually any pattern because the system stores the picture as a list of drawing tasks; it doesn't use memory space to store information about unused screen locations, as digital tv does. Because the location of every drawn point resides in memory relative to the figure drawn, beam penetration works well with light-pen systems. An example of a beam-penetration system is the stroke-refresh system. It draws clean, straight lines in one of four colors—no color mixing or shading occurs. Colors are either ON or OFF; no display point can be any more or less than one color.

bel—A nondimensional unit used for expressing ratio of power units (P_1 and P_2).

$$N = \log_{10} (P_1/P_2) \text{ bels.}$$

Ten times the size of the more frequently used decibel (q.v.). In Europe, the term neper is used instead of bel.

benchmark—In relation to microprocessors, the benchmark is a test point measuring the performance characteristics of products offered. A benchmark program is a routine or program selected to define or compare different brands of microprocessors. A flowchart in assembly language is often written out for each microprocessor, and the execution of the benchmark time, accuracy, etc., is evaluated.

benchmark problem — 1. A problem used to evaluate the performance of hardware or software, or both. 2. A problem used to evaluate the performance of several computers relative to each other, or a single computer relative to system specifications.

benchmark routine—A set of routines or problems that will help determine the performance of a given piece of equipment.

bias—1. A term that denotes an electrical, mechanical, or magnetic force or voltage applied to a relay, transistor, vacuum tube, or other electrical device to establish an electrical or mechanical operational reference level. 2. The amount by which the average of a set of values departs from a reference value. 3. In teletypewriter applications, the uniform shifting of the beginning of all marking pulses from their proper positions in relation to the beginning of the start pulse.

biconditional gate — Same as Exclusive-NOR gate.

bidirectional—Generally refers to interface ports or bus lines that can be used to transfer data in either direction, e.g., to or from the microprocessor.

bidirectional bus—A data bus in which digital information can be transferred in either direction. With reference to some microcomputers, the bidirectional data path by which data is transferred between the microprocessor chip, memory, and I/O devices.

bidirectional bus driver—Typically, a 4-bit parallel high-speed unit. It provides inverted I/O. Three-state outputs enable it to isolate and drive external bus structures. Some driver and receiver gates have three-state outputs with pnp inputs. When the drivers or receivers are tri-stated, the inputs are disabled, presenting a low current load, typically less than 40 amps, to the system bus structure.

bidirectional lines—Bus lines with bidirectional and asynchronous communications, permitting devices to send, receive, and exchange data at their own rates. The bidirectional nature of a bus allows utilization of common bus interfaces for different devices, and simplifies the interface design.

bidirectional operation—An operation in which reading, writing, and searching may be conducted in either direction, thus saving time and providing easy access to stored information.

bidirectional transistor — A particular type of transistor in which the emitter and collector can both be used interchangeably. Either electrode can be used as the input or the output.

bifurcate — 1. To divide into two branches or parts; thus, two-pronged or forked. 2. The lengthwise slotting of a flat contact in a connector to provide additional points of contact.

bifurcated contact — One which is forked or pronged. A movable contact that is divided (forked) to provide two parallel mating surfaces for a more reliable mating contact.

BiMOS—New technology that combines MOS and bipolar devices on the same chip, and promises an additional dimension of freedom to the systems designer. With near-ideal operational-amplifier parameters and digital and linear functions cohabiting

BiMOS—dual comparators (Courtesy RCA).

the same IC, these new high-density devices could be among the dominant trends in the semiconductor field for the next few years.

binary—1. A characteristic, property, or condition in which there are but two possible alternatives. 2. The binary number system using 2 as its base and using only the digits zero (0) and one (1).

binary cell—In computer technology, a binary cell is an elementary unit of storage which can be placed in either of two stable states.

binary chain—An entire series of separate binary circuits, each capable of existing in either one of two states. They are arranged so that each circuit can affect or modify the condition of adjacent circuits.

binary code—A code in which every code element is one of two distinct types of values; for example, the presence or absence of a pulse, on or off, etc.

binary-coded character—Refers to an alphabetic letter, a decimal digit, a punctuation mark, etc., as represented by a fixed number of consecutive binary digits.

binary-coded decimal (BCD)—A system of number representation; that is, an information code, in which each decimal digit is represented by a combination of four binary digits (bits), as follows:

Binary	Decimal	Binary	Decimal
0000	0	0101	5
0001	1	0110	6
0010	2	0111	7
0011	3	1000	8
0100	4	1001	9

binary-coded decimal (place value) — The 8421 system represents each decimal digit with four binary digits with the place value of each bit equal to 8, 4, 2, or 1, reading from left to right. A conversion of the decimal number 3571 into its BCD equivalent using the 8421 place value concept would be as follows:

Digit:	3	5	7	1
Binary value:	0011	0101	0111	0001
Place value:	0021	0401	0421	0001

binary counter — A flip-flop or toggle circuit that gives an output pulse for two input pulses, thus dividing by two.

binary digit—1. Often abbreviated to bit. 2. A numeral in the binary scale of notation. This digit may be either zero (0) or one (1). It is the equivalent of an on or off condition, or a yes or a no. 3. The kind of number that computers use internally. There are only two binary digits, 1 and 0, otherwise known as "on" and "off."

binary dump program—A program that provides a means for printing, displaying, or punching a binary paper-tape copy of any portion of memory. The output may be selected as either absolute or binary relocatable.

binary loader—This is used to load a binary format, such as those produced by a binary dump program, a link editor, or an assembler, into memory.

binary point — The point mid-way between integral powers of two in a particular binary number.

binary row — A method of representing binary numbers on a card, where successive bits are represented by the presence or absence of punches in a successive position—in a row as opposed to a series of columns. The binary row method is especially convenient in 40-bit-word computers, wherein the card frequently is used to store 12 binary words on each half of the card.

binary signalling—A communications mode in which information is passed by the presence and absence, or the plus and minus variations, of one parameter of the signalling medium only.

binary synchronous communications (BSC)—Binary synchronous communications (BSC), first introduced in 1966, became the industry standard for medium- and high-speed data communications. However, as new digital networks, satellite communications, and other advanced transmission techniques came on the scene, they created a need for a full duplex line protocol that was more efficient than BSC. This need is being met by newer standards, such as the high-level data link control (HDLC).

binary tape assembler—A binary tape assembler converts source program tapes to the binary tape format that is loaded into memory and produces an assembly listing that shows the converted code alongside the original assembly language mnemonic source program text. Source tape input to the assembler is via a teletypewriter or a high-speed reader. The binary tape may be punched on either a teletypewriter or a high-speed tape punch. The assembly listing is printed on the teletypewriter. Some assemblers require a minimum of 4K of RAM.

binary-to-decimal conversion—The actual process of converting a binary number to its equivalent in conventional decimal notation.

binding—The act of assigning absolute addresses to a program.

biometrics — The science of statistics when applied specifically to biological observations.

bionics—1. The application of biological techniques to the problems of design of electronic devices and systems. Bionics can also refer to the science of systems which function in a manner resembling living systems. 2. A branch of technology relating the functions, characteristics, and phenomena of living systems to the development of hardware systems.

biosensor—A mechanism for detecting and transmitting biological data from an organism in such a way that processing, display, or storage of results is permitted.

bipolar—1. Having two poles. 2. Refers to a device in which both majority and minority carriers are present. 3. In connection with integrated circuits, the term describes a specific type of construction. The general name applied to ICs that use bipolar transistors.

bipolar CPU slice—A bipolar CPU slice is a chip that provides many of the speed advantages of discrete logic and all of the processor-oriented advantages of a microprocessor. It does require a new level of system design; users must build their own instruction set (macroinstruction) by using techniques like those used to create microprogrammed CPUs.

bipolar decoders, Schottky — Devices with eight or more outputs that are used to expand systems that use input ports, output ports, and memory components with an active low chip-select input. In very large systems, the decoders can be used in sets, with each decoder driving eight or more other decoders for arbitrary memory expansions.

bipolar devices — *See* bipolar. Semiconductor devices in which there are both minority and majority carriers present. A bipolar device is a current-driven device.

bipolar fabrication—Bipolar fabrication typically requires 12 masking steps and 4 diffusion steps. Bipolar fabrication is complex because of the need for isolation rings around each device. and because of the number of alternating diffusion steps that are required to create the npnp layers.

bipolar IC, complementary—A complementary bipolar semiconductor integrated circuit is one which employs both npn and pnp bipolar transistors in the same monolithic semiconductor substrate.

bipolar LSI microprocessors—The first bipolar LSI microprocessor chips featured a machine-cycle time of less than 200 nsec. This was 10 times faster than NMOS microprocessors (which usually had $2\text{-}\mu\text{sec}$ machine cycles). The architecture was 2-bit-slice building blocks, and the instruction set was (and is) microprogrammable. At the time, these products were definitely intended for the OEM manufacturer who had the capability to tailor them in word length and implement only those instructions necessary for a particular application. Now, bipolar 4- and 8-bit-slice chips and processors are in great demand.

bipolar microprocessor slice, 4-bit — A high-speed cascadable-circuit design intended for use in CPUs, peripheral controllers, programmable microprocessors, and numerous other applications. The microinstruction flexibility will allow efficient emulation of almost any digital computing machine.

bipolar PROM—Bipolar programmable read-only memories (PROMs) include fusible links that can be opened to allow the user to configure the data pattern. Once programmed, however, the contacts cannot be restored to their initial state. Bipolar PROMs offer very fast access time and provide an economical means for changing programs "in-house." Just replace an old PROM with a newly programmed unit. Bipolar PROMs have access times in the 50 nanosecond and 90 nanosecond region.

bipolar semiconductors—Bipolar processes, as applied to memories, are less varied than the MOS process. The bipolar processes of today are more mature than MOS because many variations have been tried and abandoned. The basic processes have become known by the logic circuit built with the process (i.e., TTL— Transistor-Transistor Logic and ECL — Emitter-Coupled Logic). Actually, all common bipolar technologies are remarkably similar, being based on the formation of silicon layers with different electrical properties. The usual difference is the number and sequences of diffusion operations required to manufacture the part.

bipolar transistor — A semiconductor device that has a base of either a p-type or n-type material sandwiched between two masses of the opposite type of material (the collector and emitter). The two types of transistors (pnp or npn) have opposite applied voltage polarities.

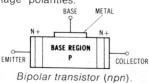

Bipolar transistor (npn).

bistable circuit—A circuit capable of assuming either one of two stable states (same as a flip-flop). Bistable states can be illustrated as follows: If the bistable component is in stable state A, an energy pulse will drive it to state B; if the bistable component is in stable state B, an energy pulse will drive it to state A. Thus, it is easy for a bistable component to represent the number 0 or 1.

bistable multivibrator—A specific circuit which has two stable states, requiring two input pulses in order to complete a cycle.

bistable relay—A relay which requires two pulses to finish one cycle composed of two conditions of operation. Frequently referred to as a locked, interlocked, or latching relay.

bistable trigger circuit—A circuit that can be triggered to adopt one of two stable states.

bit—1. Bit is an abbreviation for **binary** digit. Most commonly, a unit of information equalling one binary decision, or the designation of one of two possible and equally likely values or states. It is usually conveyed as a 1 or 0 of anything that can be used to store or convey information (such as 1 or 0, which may also mean "yes" or "no"). 2. A single character in a binary number. 3. A single pulse in a group of pulses. 4. A unit of information capacity of a storage device. The capacity in bits is the logarithm to the base two of the number of possible states of the device.

bit density—A specific number of bits of information contained within a given area, such as the number of bits "written" along an inch of magnetic tape.

bit memory organization — Each element of a memory is a binary digit (bit), capable of representing either a 1 or 0. At any instant during the execution of a program, the memory is a grid of binary 1s and 0s, with each bit representing one small piece of information.

bit parity—Bit parity schemes are the simplest approach to error correction and detection. Vertical bit-parity schemes add a ninth bit to each 8-bit byte in memory. If the number of 1s in a byte is even, its parity bit is set to 1 by supervisory hardware. The total number of 1s in every group of 9 bits thus becomes odd. Given the remoteness of two errors occurring in a single data byte, any group with an even number of 1s contains an error. This scheme only detects errors, however. It cannot correct them.

bit position — A specific location in memory, space, or time at which a binary digit occurs or is located.

bit rate—The rate at which binary digits, or the pulses representing them, pass a given point on a communications line or channel.

bit-slice architecture—With the discovery that a complete central processing unit (CPU) could be placed on a single chip, it was found that additional functions (principally, a memory) could be added to form a computer-on-a-chip. However, it was also found that certain advantages could be achieved (namely, speed) by partitioning the CPU into "slices" rather than putting it all on one chip. A typical control section is assembled with several identical 2- and 4-bit "slices" for the arithmetic and logic unit (ALU) and the registers. The slices are connected in parallel, making it possible to put together units that have several different word lengths. This approach is used to form microprocessors with word lengths ranging from 4 to 32 bits.

Bit-slice architecture allows the word length to be tailored to the accuracy and precision requirements of scientific calculations. Software architecture allows the user to develop high-speed floating-point instructions and function instructions, as required for scientific calculations. Bit-slice architecture usually employs bipolar technology because of the necessity for limiting component densities to facilitate the dissipation of heat.

bit-slice microcontrollers — A typical processor employs four 4-bit microcontroller chips. Each chip consists of a 16-register file that may be read simultaneously by two address multiplexers, A and B. Data contained in the selected registers pass through the respective latches. The B-address input is also used to select the register to be loaded with new data. When the register is loaded, the A and B latches hold output data, thereby providing edge-triggered, master/slave operation. One specific chip also contains an ALU (arithmetic logic unit) and variant multiplexers to provide data routing and shifting of results prior to their storage. An internal Q register, with its own shift multiplexers, can be used for temporary storage of results and for double-precision shift operations.

bit-slice microprocessor—The bit-slice microprocessor represents a special class of semiconductor device for computers. Most bit slices are designed for microinstruction rates between 5 and 10 MHz for high-performance applications. All contain data path circuits, such as arithmetic logic units, accumulators, and shifters, that are expandable to any word length. Each bit slice also has a microprogram control or sequencer circuit that can address the microinstruction stored in ROM or PROM, test flag bits, and execute conditional branches, while allowing the nesting of subroutines.

Although most bit slices use Schottky TTL technology, some use CMOS, ECL LSI, and I²L technology. Packaging and architecture also varies. In essence, the bit-slice approach lets users design their own microprocessor and develop a variety of specialized instruction sets.

bit stream—Generally, a binary signal without regard to groupings by character. The term is often used in connection with synchronous transmission and the devices operating in this mode.

bit string—A string of binary digits in which the position of each binary digit is considered as an independent unit.

bit stuffing, communication—One technique used to achieve data transparency is referred to as bit stuffing. To ensure that a flag character does not appear in the data field, a zero-bit is inserted wherever five one-bits appear in a row. When the receiver detects five ones followed by a zero-bit, it removes or deletes the zero-bit. If it receives six ones and a zero, it is a legal flag character that indicates end-of-message.

black box—A generic term which describes any unspecified device performing a special function where the inputs produce specific outputs.

blanked scope—This concerns the Z-axis intensity modulation of the display beam in an oscilloscope. When the beam is "blanked," the screen will not be illuminated by the electron beam.

blank transmission test — This feature allows the checking of any data field for all blank positions. As a microcomputer control, it can be used to prevent the destruction of existing records in storage, indicate when the last item from a spread card has been processed, skip calculation if a rate or factor field is blank, etc.

blast—The release of various specified areas or blocks of either main or auxiliary storage no longer needed by an operational program. This type of program will execute a blast macroinstruction that causes the control program to return the address of the area blasted to its list of storage available for use by future operational programs.

blastable read-only memory—A blastable read-only memory (ROM) provides a high-speed nondestructive memory in applications where the contents of memory do not change. Some chips operate at a cycle time of 1.5 μsec and are available in units of 1K, 2K, 4K, 8K, 16K, or more words on a single module.

blinking characters—Self-explanatory. These characters are especially useful for drawing the operator's attention to errors caught by the system, and to areas of the video screen that require attention. However, excessive use of blinking characters can be distracting to an operator, and even irritating. Generally, it is recommended that use of blinking characters be limited to items that require immediate action on the part of the operator.

block diagram—A diagram of a system, instrument, or microcomputer in which the principal parts are represented by suitably annotated geometrical figures to show both basic functions and functional relationships between the parts. Contrast with flowchart.

blocked list—A catalog of the processes that at any given time are waiting for CPU time or for completion of an I/O operation.

blocking oscillator—A tube- or transistor-tuned oscillator, which has more than sufficient positive feedback for oscillation, but in which a condition periodically supervenes to suspend normal oscillation, e.g., by integration of grid current by a capacitor. Discharge of the capacitor removes the condition and restores the initial state. The cycle is continuously repeated, producing sawtooth and pulse waveforms for up to very high frequencies.

block input processing—Blocks can be handled by the terminal, character by-character, as they arrive. However, on some systems, the terminal can delay handling a block until the entire error-free block has been transmitted (or retransmitted).

block length—A measure of the size of a block, usually specified in units such as records, words, computer words, or characters.

blocks—Records are transferred to and from tapes in the form of blocks (sometimes called physical records). A block (a physical record) may contain one or more records (logical). Records may be reduced to blocks on tape to reduce the acceleration and deceleration time.

block synchronization — Block and message synchronization is more a matter of framing or recognizing the beginning and end of a block or message than it is of an exact time dependency. It is directly dependent on the Data Link Control procedure.

block transfer function — The block transfer function is a microcoded sequence executed by the I/O processor that allows high-speed transfer between a source and a destination address as defined by a user program. Where source/destination data widths differ, the microcode automatically compensates for word alignment and bus width, making the most efficient use of the available bus bandwidth. The block transfer function supports three synchronization options: free running, source sync, and destination sync. In addition, it supports four transfer modes: port-to-port, buffer-to-port, port-to-buffer, and buffer-to-buffer.

blue-ribbon program — A handwritten and independently designed program that is written by a programmer and so checked that no mistakes or bugs are therein contained; i.e., the blue-ribbon or star program should thus run correctly the first time, excepting machine malfunctions.

bode diagram—A unique plot of log amplitude ratios and phase angle values on a log frequency base for a transfer function. This may be an element, output, or loop transfer function.

bonding pad—A metallic area on the surface of a chip for a wire connection.

bond, thermocompression—A bond in which two members are joined together through the combined application of heat and pressure.

bond, ultrasonic—A bond in which two members are joined together through the combined application of pressure and an ultrasonic oscillatory lateral motion.

Boolean algebra—A mathematical system of logic functions named after George Boole, the famous English mathematician and logician. It deals with classes, propositions, on-off circuit elements, etc. Associated by operators such as AND, OR, NOT, EXCEPT, IF . . . THEN . . . which permits computations and demonstrations as in any other mathematical system.

Boolean calculus—Basically, Boolean algebra modified to include the element of time.

Boolean equation—Expression of relations between logic functions.

booster response—An automatic controller method of operation in which there exists a continuous linear response between the rate of change of the controlled variable and the position of the final control element. Also called rate action, time response.

bootstrap—1. A technique or device designed to bring itself into a desired state by means of its own action, e.g., a machine routine whose first few instructions are sufficient to bring the rest of the routine into the computer from an input device. 2. To use a bootstrap. 3. That part of a computer program used to establish another version of the computer program.

bootstrap circuit—A single-stage amplifier in which the output load is connected between the negative end of the plate supply and the cathode. The signal voltage is applied between the grid and the cathode. The name stems from the change in voltage that changes the potential of the input source (with respect to ground) by an amount that is equal to the output signal.

bootstrap loader — A bootstrap loader is a short routine that is input when there is no loader in memory. It enables users to enter data or a program into the RAMs from a teletypewriter, paper tape, or a keyboard. Bootstrap loaders are generally available for all input devices. The principal criterion for the bootstrap loader is that it contains as few instructions as possible, in case it has to be keyed in via the computer console. For paper tape, it requires that only eight words be keyed in from the console (some systems).

bootstrap loader, automatic—An automatic bootstrap loader allows system restart from a variety of peripheral devices without manual switch toggling or key-pad operations.

bootstrap loader, cassette — A typical cassette bootstrap loader will automatically locate the top of memory and relocate itself to the top of memory, thus enabling program loading from memory location "zero." During the process of locating the top of memory, a full memory test is made every time the load button is pressed (some systems).

bootstrapping, data-link control — A data-link control procedure should be capable of bootstrapping. However, secondary stations on an unbalanced link may not be able to configure themselves for data-communications operations. Bootstrapping provides a means for the primary station to set the initial states and control modes of all such secondary stations on an unbalanced link. It is done in a transient state, however, when no other communications are permitted.

boundary—The surface in the transition region between p-type and n-type semiconductor material at which the donor and acceptor concentration are equal.

boundary register—A special register, in a multiprogrammed system, used to designate the upper and lower addresses of each user's memory block.

bps—Abbreviation for bits per second. In serial transmission, the instantaneous bit speed with which a device or channel transmits a character.

branch—1. Concerns the capability and procedure of a microprocessor program instruction designed to modify the function or program sequence. The actual modification is an immediate change in direction, meaning, or substance of intent of the programmer. 2. To depart from the normal sequence of executing instructions in a computer. Synonymous with jump. 3. A sequence of instructions that is executed as a result of a decision instruction.

branch circuit—In a wiring system, the branch circuit is the portion that extends beyond the final over-current protective device protecting the circuit.

branch, conditional — See conditional branch.

branch impedance—As it relates to a passive branch, the impedance obtained by assuming a driving force across and a corresponding response in the branch, no other branch being electrically connected to the one under consideration.

branching—When applied to computer technology, branching is a method of selecting, on the basis of the computer results, the next operation to execute while a program is in progress.

branch instructions — An instruction logic which, when executed, may cause the arithmetic logic unit (ALU) to obtain the next instruction from some location other than the next sequential location. A branch is one of two types: conditional, unconditional.

branch (network)—As a part of an electronic network, a section between two adjacent branch points. Also, a portion of a network consisting of one or more 2-terminal elements in series.

branch-on indicator—Branching takes place when appropriate indicators (switches, keys, buttons, etc.), or conditions, have been set to point to a particular group of registers; i.e., a branch may occur dependent upon whether the magnetic tape units are ready to receive a new block of data.

branch point—The junction of more than two conductors in an electric network. When applied to computers, a point in the routine where one of two or more choices is selected under control of a routine.

breadboard construction—A temporary arrangement of electronic components fastened to a board for experimental work. Usually refers to an experimental or rough construction model of a process, device, or construction.

breakpoint—1. Relates to a specific point in a program (usually indicated by a breakpoint flag) that requests interruption of the program to permit the user an opportunity to check, correct, or modify the program before continuing its execution. 2. A place in a routine specified by an instruction, instruction digit, or other condition, where the routine may be interrupted by external intervention or by a monitor routine.

breakpoint switch—A manually operated switch which controls conditional operation at breakpoints; used primarily in debugging.

B register—1. A computer register that has the capability of storing a word which can change an instruction before it is carried out by the computer. 2. Same as index word register. 3. A register used as an extension of the accumulator during multiply and divide processes.

bridge—1. In a system of measurement, the instrument in which part or all of a bridge circuit is used in measuring one or more electrical quantities. 2. In relation to a fully electronic stringed instrument, the bridge converts the mechanical vibrations produced by the strings into electrical signals.

bridge circuit—A network of circuits arranged so that, when an electromotive force is present in one branch, the response of a detecting device located in another branch may be zeroed by the adjustment of the electrical constants of other branches.

bridge limiter—A limiter is a unit intended to prevent a variable from exceeding specified limits. A diode bridge used as a limiter is called a bridge limiter.

bridging connection—Refers to a parallel connection by means of which some of the signal energy in a circuit may be withdrawn with imperceptible effect on the normal operation of the circuit.

bridging contacts—A set of electrical contacts in which the moving contact touches two or more stationary contacts simultaneously during a transfer.

broad band — A general term used to describe wide bandwidth greater than a voice-grade channel (4 kHz). Also, equipment or systems that can carry a large proportion of the electromagnetic spectrum. A broad-band communications system can accommodate all broadcast bands and many other services. Transmission that uses a bandwidth greater than a voice-grade channel (4 kHz) and, therefore, capable of higher-speed data transmission. Sometimes referred to as "wideband."

broad-band systems — Until recently, CCTV, CATV, and MATV systems were 3 distinctly separate fields. Now, many of the functions of these types of systems are being incorporated into unified systems known as broad-band communications systems. Broad-band communications systems can economically transport many video channels, plus audio, remote control, telemetry, data, and other signals over many miles of a single coaxial cable. It can also link an unlimited number of terminal locations.

broad–band coaxial-cable transmission —Though none of the basic concepts are radically new, the development of more sophisticated contention protocols and the availability of large-scale (LSI) and very large-scale (VLSI) integrated circuits has made it possible to implement wideband communications on standard coaxial cable. This makes the integration of voice, video, and data transmission feasible and it provides the framework for the integration of office automation systems. An example is the bus interface unit that is based on a microprocessor and which provides the necessary control logic for "listen-before-talk" and "listen-while-talk" protocols, enabling the effective use of the total bandwidth presently available on coaxial cable.

bubble cassette systems—These combine the nonvolatility and the storage capacity of a bubble memory with removability. Users can plug in a bubble memory as they would insert a tape cassette. One system consists of a controller card, a cassette holder, and bubble cassettes. The cassettes, which measure just 0.8 inch high $\times$ 1.8 inches wide $\times$ 2.4 inches deep, feature a write-prevention switch that protects the memory from being inadvertently erased. Cassettes are available with 64 and 256 kilobits.

The controller card accepts 8-bit parallel data. The card also features an average access time of 370 msec and can operate in the CPU or DMA mode from an external device. Up to eight bubble cassette "readers" can hang on one card, for a maximum capacity of 256 Kbytes. The TTL-compatible cassette holder, controlled by the card, has a 24-pin front-panel receptacle into which the bubble cassettes are plugged.

bubble memories — These memories are actually tiny cylinders of magnetization whose axes lie perpendicular to the plane of the single-crystal sheet that contains them. Magnetic bubbles arise when two magnetic fields are applied perpendicular to the sheet. A constant field strengthens and fattens the regions of the sheet whose magnetization lies along it. A pulsed field then breaks the strengthened regions into isolated bubbles, which are free to move within the plane of the sheet. Because the presence or absence of bubbles can represent digital information, and because other external fields can manipulate this information, magnetic bubble devices could find uses in future data-storage systems. However, the magnetic bubble memory needs various circuits to operate as a complete bubble memory system. These circuits include a controller (to provide a CPU interface and generate enable pulses to a function timing generator), coil and function drivers, and a sense amplifier (to amplify the signal of the bubble detector).

bubble memory (data)—Data is stored as magnetic "bubbles" in a very thin film of synthetic garnet. The bubbles are microns in size and move in a plane of the film when a magnetic gradient is present. Viewed under a microscope with a linear polarized light, the bubbles appear to be fluid circular areas that step from space to space following fixed loops and tracks. Bubble memories are compact, nonvolatile mass storage elements processed in a manner similar to silicon wafer fabrication. The typical device is organized as a serial-in parallel loop serial-out shift register.

bubble memory fabrication—The circuitry required to operate bubble memory, while well established, is unique. The basic material used in the fabrication of magnetic bubble devices is a slice of garnet. Tiny patterns, etched in the metal coating on the garnet, serve as avenues for bubble movement. Arrays of forty-eight 70,000-bit bubble circuit chips are fabricated on each slice of garnet.

Standard photolithography is used to make conductor and magnetic permalloy patterns on the chip. A pair of ac-driven crossed wire-wound

Bubble memory fabrication (Courtesy Bell Telephone Laboratories).

coils are slipped over the chip to provide the rotating magnetic field. The system is stabilized with a pair of permanent magnets and is protected from external magnetic influences by a sleeve of shielding material. This protection allows the device to be used around crt coils, transformers, and other equipment that produces magnetic fields.

As a device, the basic bubble memory consists of a bubble memory chip, magnetic field coils that produce the rotating magnetic field, and two permanent magnets that maintain the magnetic bubble domains and nonvolatility. However, before bubbles can be shifted through the magnetic film, they must be generated and they must correspond to input data. A microscopic one-turn metallized loop, located in a secondary layer just above the magnetic film, is used to produce the magnetic bubbles. A precisely defined current pulse passing through the loop alters the local magnetic field and generates a magnetic bubble. Once a bubble is created, it is moved along a path determined by chevron-shaped patterns of soft magnetic material deposited on the magnetic epitaxial film. Under the influence of the rotating magnetic field, these chevron-shaped patterns set up magnetic polarities that shift the magnetic bubble domains.

Scientists at Bell Laboratories, however, instead of using field-access coils to move bubbles along their loops, have succeeded in moving them with one or more perforated sheets of conductive materials. Like the permalloy patterns, these layers are situated over the magnetic garnet where the bubbles reside. The main advantage is a simplified package due to the absence of coils. But this scheme can also mean +5-V-only operation, more easily automated testing and packaging, and faster operation because there is no coil inductance to set limits to bubble speed.

bubble memory (loops)—Patterns of a permalloy metal are deposited on epitaxial film to define the path of bubble domains in the presence of a rotating magnetic field. As the field rotates, the bubble domains move under the permalloy pattern in shift register fashion. Device architecture is major loop/minor loop. Data bits are written into and read out of the major loop; data bits are transferred to minor loops for storage. Bubble control functions such as generate, transfer in, transfer out, replicate, and annihilate are executed by providing current pulses through the appropriate control elements on the chip.

bubble memory movement—In current devices, small cylindrical magnetic domains, called magnetic bubbles, are formed in single-crystal thin films of synthetic ferrites or garnets when an external magnetic field is applied perpendicularly to the surface of the film. A rotating magnetic field is used to move the bubbles, in a shift register fashion, along a path outlined by a deposited layer of metal on the surface of the magnetic filter. The presence of a magnetic bubble represents a digital 1, and the absence of a bubble represents a digital 0. Types of material and techniques used for processing magnetic bubbles are similar to those used for semiconductor memories.

bubble memory operation — Since the presence of a bubble is read as a "one" and its absence as a "zero," data is written by the selective formation of bubbles. This is accomplished by applying a weak external magnetic bias to the supporting sheet film, which in its normal state contains an equal mix of oppositely polarized magnetic regions. The external bias field shrinks regions of opposite polarity to the field into the much smaller bubbles. By lining up and moving the bubbles via a magnetic

overlay around a closed loop, a "bucket brigade" shift register is formed in a manner not unlike the scheme employed by charge-coupled devices (CCDs). An essential difference between bubbles and CCDs is that bubbles, being magnetic rather than electronic, are nonvolatile, i.e., their bit pattern is retained if power fails.

bubble shift registers—Shift registers, while they are the simplest bubble memory applications, are not the only type of memory that can be made using bubbles, nor, for that matter, is bubble technology limited to memory applications. Certain properties of magnetic bubbles, related to their interaction and their deformation or annihilation as a function of the bias field strength, hold promise for switching and logic applications.

bucket brigade device (BBD)—1. A charge-transfer device that stores charge in discrete regions in a semiconductor and transfers this charge as a packet through a series of switching devices that interconnect these regions. 2. A shift register that transfers information from stage to stage in response to timing signals.

buffer—A "device" designed to be inserted between other devices or program elements to match impedances or peripheral equipment speeds, to prevent mixed interactions, to supply additional drive or relay capability, or to simply delay the rate of information flow. Buffer types are classified as inverting or noninverting.

buffer capacitor—A type of capacitor connected across the secondary of a vibrator transformer, or between the anode and cathode of a cold-cathode rectifier tube, to suppress surging voltage which could cause damage to other circuit parts.

buffer circuit — 1. A specific isolating circuit that avoids a reaction of a driven circuit on the corresponding driving circuit. 2. A circuit inserted between other circuit elements to prevent interactions, to match impedances, to supply additional drive capability, or to delay the rate of information flow.

buffer, data communications — This type buffer enables devices (for example, addressable hard-copy printers) to operate at different speeds independently of communications line speeds.

buffering, simple—A technique for obtaining simultaneous performance of input/output operations and computing. This method involves associating a buffer with only one input or output file (or data set) for the entire duration of the activity on that file (or data set).

buffer storage—1. A synchronizing element between two different forms of storage, usually between internal and external. 2. An input device in which information is assembled from external or secondary storage and stored ready for transfer to internal storage. 3. An output device into which information is copied from internal storage and held for transfer to secondary or external storage. Computation continues while transfers between buffer storage and secondary or internal storage, or vice versa, takes place. 4. Any device which stores information temporarily during data transfers.

buffer storage locations—A set of locations used to compensate for a difference in rate of flow of data, or time of occurrence of events, when transmitting data from one device to another, and, importantly, used also to retain temporarily a copy of the data as a safeguard against faults and unintentional erasures.

bug—1. A program defect or error. Also refers to any circuit fault due to improper design or construction. 2. A mistake or malfunction.

bug patches—As bugs are uncovered in a program, patches can be inserted and documented in order to fix the mistakes. When a number of patches have been made, they should be incorporated into the source program and the program should be reassembled. This ensures a well-documented program.

building block principle—Relates to a system designed to permit the addition of other equipment units to form a larger system. Also called modularity.

bulk-channel charge-coupled device (BCCD) — A synonym for buried-channel charge-coupled device.

bulk metal technology—A multidisciplined technology, employing metallurgy, polymer chemistry, optics, photoetching, and stress analysis. These combine to form resistive elements made of metal film about 10 times thicker than conventional evaporated films. This photo-etched resistance is adjustable to provide tolerance to 0.001%. This minimizes stress and thermal effects to provide stability, and minimum inductance and capacitance for high speed response.

bulk resistor—A resistor made by providing ohmic contacts between two points of a homogeneous uniformly doped crystal of silicon material.

buried channel — A transfer channel lying beneath the surface of the semiconductor.

buried-channel charge-coupled device (BCCD) — A charge-coupled device that confines the flow of charges to a channel lying beneath the surface of the semiconductor.

buried layer — A heavily doped (N+) region directly under the N doped epitaxial collector region of transistors in a monolithic integrated circuit that is used to lower the series collector resistance.

burst—1. Refers to separation of continuous-form paper into discrete sheets. 2. In data transmission, a sequence of signals counted as one unit in accordance with some specific criterion or measure.

bus—1. As applied to computer technology, one or more conductors used as a path over which information is transmitted. 2. A circuit over which data or power is transmitted. Often one that acts as a common connection among a number of locations. (Synonymous with trunk.) 3. A path over which information is transferred, from any of several sources to any of several destinations.

bus arbitration — Bus arbitration is a technique used by master-type devices to request, be granted, and acknowledge bus mastership. In its simplest form, it consists of:
1. Asserting a bus mastership request.
2. Receiving a grant that the bus is available at the end of the current cycle.
3. Acknowledging that mastership has been assumed.

bus available (BA) signal — The bus available signal will normally be in the low state; when activated, it will go to the high state indicating that the microprocessor has stopped and the address bus is available. This will occur if the haltline is in the low state or the processor is in the WAIT state as a result of the execution of a WAIT instruction. In some systems, at such a time, all 3-state output drivers will go to their off state, and the other output devices to their normally inactive level.

bus circuits—Usually a group of circuits that provides a communication path between two or more devices, such as between a central processor, a memory, and peripherals.

bus cycles — The typical bus cycles (with respect to the processor) are: Data word transfer in: equivalent to read operation; Data word transfer in, followed by word transfer out: equivalent to Read/Modify Write; Data word transfer in, followed by byte transfer out: equivalent to Read/Modify Write; Data word transfer out: equivalent to Write operation; Data byte transfer out: equivalent to Write operation.

bus driver—Generally refers to a specially designed integrated circuit that is added to the data bus system to facilitate proper drive to the CPU when several memories are tied to the data bus line. Such circuits are required because of capacitive loading that slows down the data rate and prevents the proper time sequencing of microprocessor operation.

bus driving circuits — When information can be supplied to a bus from more than one source, special bus-driving circuits must be used to select and control the outputs from each source so that they do not interfere with each other. Basically, the bus drivers are designed to ensure electrical compatibility between each of the sources connected to the bus and to control the connections and disconnections of sources from the bus. They also multiplex the information onto the bus.

bus extender module — This module provides the capability to extend the bus for the purpose of scoping or signal tracing—not for expansion.

bus lines, microcomputer — Bus lines are the means of communication used by a microcomputer, and the bus organization is one of the most important factors determining a computer's architecture. Most microcomputers use one of two bus schemes for transferring data between the CPU, memory, and peripheral devices. One scheme provides a single bus containing lines for address, data, and control information with all data transfers occurring on this one bus. The other common scheme provides for a memory bus on which all data transfers between the CPU and memory occur, and a separate I/O bus on which all data transfers between the CPU and the peripheral devices occur.

The data bus of a computer card is a set of signal lines transmitting data to or from the CPU chip input and output pins. A typical data bus will have 60 or more signal lines transmitting data, addresses, and control information that indicates the type of operation in progress. The input and output pins of a CPU chip represent a universal interface between the CPU chip and all external devices. The single bus is a universal interface connecting all components of a microcomputer system. The dual bus system treats the CPU as a unique focal point for the microcomputer system, with separate interfaces to memory and peripheral devices.

bus master—1. A bus master is a dynamic board that takes control of the bus by asserting address and control lines. Only one bus master may control the bus at any given moment. Examples of bus masters include single-board computers and direct memory access (DMA) controllers. 2. The device controlling the current bus transactions in a system where the control of data transfers is shared between the CPU and associated peripheral devices.

bus program counter—Data and instructions enter into some chips through an 8-bit data bus. Instructions are sent to the instruction register and are decoded to control the processor. Under the processor's control, data can be shipped along many of the open paths. Input-output is done through the accumulator. Often 16-bit counting registers are incorporated on a chip, with one used for the program location counter and another as a push-down stack counter. The program counter contents are sent out on the address bus for use by memory modules to fetch the ap-

44

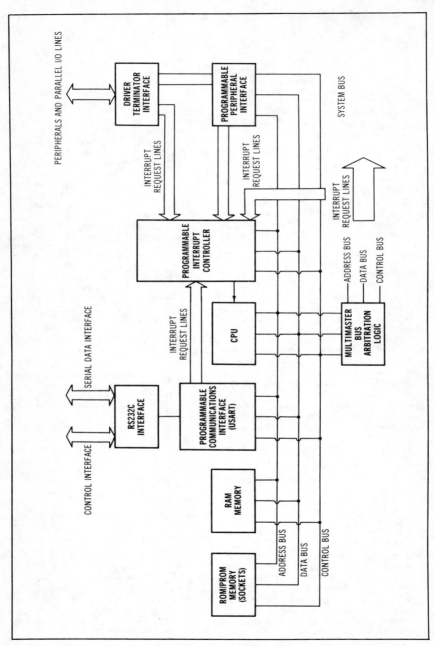

Bus lines, microcomputer.

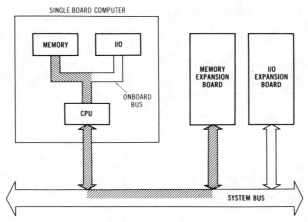

SINGLE BOARD COMPUTER

Bus master and bus slaves (Courtesy Intel Corp.).

propriate instructions; the processor increments the program counter by one after each use in many systems.

bus organized structures — Microcomputers generally employ bus organized structures for the input/output of data and control information. Often in these bus systems, information can flow in both directions and, generally, more than one "talker" and "listener" share a single interconnecting wire. The voltage levels and impedances at the bus interface are set to allow rapid transmission of information to minimize errors due to interjected noise, and to allow a number of units to share the line without excessively loading the signal that is present. These devices provide the interface necessary to mate common digital logic to the several popular bus systems that are employed in modern computers. In addition, an MPU bus transceiver overcomes another requirement of the bus structure that is associated with MPUs; i.e., the limited drive capability of the MPU necessitated by the types of device geometries used in these LSI MOS devices.

bus polling protocol—In some systems, the bus protocol allows for a vectored interrupt by the device. Hence, device polling is not required in interrupt processing routines. This results in a considerable savings in processing time when many devices requiring interrupt service are interfaced along the bus. When an interrupting device

receives an interrupt grant signal, the device passes an interrupt vector to the processor. The vector points to two addresses which contain a new processor status word and the starting address of the interrupt service routine for the particular device.

bus priority structure — Since many buses are used by processors and I/O devices, there is a priority structure to determine which device gets control of the bus. Every device on the bus that is capable of becoming a bus master is assigned a priority according to its position along the bus. When two devices that are capable of becoming a bus master request use of the bus simultaneously, the device with the higher priority position will receive control.

buses, data and address—Among the features that minimize package count and improve performance are: multiple independent data and address buses that eliminate time multiplexing and the need for external latches; three-state output buffers with high fanout that make bus drivers unnecessary except in the largest systems; and the separate output-enable logic that permits bidirectional buses to be formed simply by connecting inputs and outputs together.

bus signals—Current bus architectures carry anywhere from 50 to 150 signals, that can be grouped into four broad categories.

1. Address and data lines have signals that are used by the processor to indicate the location it wants to communicate with, and these lines are used to carry data between the processor and the other boards in the system.
2. Control, status, and interrupt lines use signals that coordinate the operation of all system components and these lines are the most critical to a bus design.
3. Power lines distribute power to the boards in the system. The number and range of voltage signals determine the kinds of peripheral devices and the memories that can be used in the system.
4. Spares are usually signal lines that are included to enable future expansion or special interboard communications.

bus slave—A bus slave is a passive element on the bus that does not assert address and control lines. Examples of bus slaves include memory or I/O expansion boards and intelligent slaves.

bus structures—Typical bus structures include the shared-bus, daisy-chain, and party-line configurations. The buses may be unidirectional, as in a daisy-chain structure, but are usually bidirectional, as in a party-line structure. Bus signals not only control how quickly information flows on the bus, but they also serve as functional controls. They can indicate which way information flows on a bidirectional bus, specify the type of information on a shared bus and, also, define which microcomputer elements control the information flow.

In a party-line structure, each device is linked directly to a single bus. In a daisy-chain configuration, the bus line is interconnected with all units in such a way that a signal passes from one unit to the next in a serial fashion. In the shared-bus approach, the microprocessor has free access to both memory and the peripheral devices. Thus, if only one device is to act as a source of information, the bus can be unidirectional. More often, however, a bidirectional bus is used so that information can pass between a number of sources and acceptors.

bus structures, serial vs. parallel—The choice between serial or parallel bus structures depends on the system application. When the system is oriented around the exchange of global variables and words, parallel techniques offer an advantage. The increased bandwidth usually associated with a parallel bus diminishes the delays in accessing and updating variables. However, due to their simplicity, bit-serial interfaces are more attractive where processors become geographically dispersed. Such systems tend to be loosely coupled when the communications become more message oriented.

bus system — Refers to a system or network of paths within the microprocessor designed to speed data flow. Several important types of buses in microcomputer systems are labeled: data bus, address bus, control bus, etc.

bus system, multiple—Microprocessor size and type dictates the bus structure that is used in a microcomputer. This is an important factor affecting performance. The common bus approach is where a single bus is used alternately for data, addresses, and control signals. However, a multiple-bus system will use at least one separate dedicated bus for data and another for addresses. Control signals may or may not have a dedicated bus.

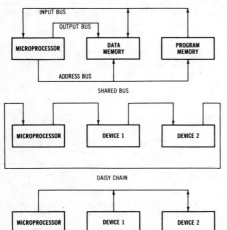

Bus structures.

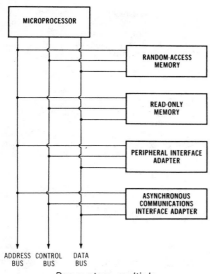

Bus system, multiple.

By using a multiple-bus system, data and addresses can be moved during the same cycle without waiting for a serial usage of a common bus.

bus transceiver — Refers to a type of high-performance low-power Schottky bus transceiver that is intended for bipolar or MOS microprocessor applications. Such devices typically consist of four D-type edge-triggered flip-flops with a built-in two-input multiplexer on each. The flip-flop outputs are connected to four open-col-lector bus drivers. Each bus driver is internally connected to one input of a differential amplifier in the receiver. The four receiver differential amplifier outputs drive four D-type latches that feature three-state outputs.

byte—A term used to indicate a specific number of consecutive bits treated as a single entity. A byte is most often considered to consist of 8 bits which, as a unit, can represent one character or two numerals.

byte addresses — Some computer words are divided into a high byte and a low byte. In some systems, word addresses are always even numbered. Byte addresses can be either even or odd numbered. Low bytes are stored at even-numbered memory locations and high bytes are stored in odd-numbered memory locations.

byte manipulation—Refers to an ability to manipulate, as individual instructions, groups of bits such as characters. A byte is considered to be 8 bits in length, in most cases, and forms either one character or two numerals.

byte multiplexer channel—Refers to a multiplexer channel which interleaves bytes of data from different sources, as contrasted with a selector channel.

byte multiplexing—Refers to a procedure in which time slots on a channel are assigned to individual slow input/output devices so that bytes from one device after another can be interlaced on the channel (to or from main memory).

C

C — A somewhat structured high-level programming language designed to optimize run time, size, and efficiency. C language was developed by Dennis Ritchie at Bell Laboratories as the systems programming language of the UNIX operating system on the PDP 11/70 minicomputer from Digital Equipment Corporation. C is not machine-dependent, so programs can be freely transferred from machine to machine with a reasonable expectation that they will run correctly without modification.

C provides a lot of features that make difficult programming jobs easier. It is designed for professional programmers and has several aspects that make it better for a wide range of applications—especially systems programming. C's declaration syntax is designed to help describe data, rather than have the data force form on a program. C supports the basic data types found in modern computers—types such as bytes, long and short integers, floating-point numbers, and pointers to all defined data types. C's data language enables the definition of data aggregates in the form of arrays and structures of any data type. Structures may even access individual bits or sequences of bits in order to allow C to interface to any existing data environment.

The major advantage of this full set of data types is that any construction that arises in system programming, including hardware control registers, can be represented in C. Furthermore, if the hardware can be addressed in memory, it can be directly manipulated from within a C program. C functions are called by value. Simple data objects passed to functions have their values passed rather than their addresses, making it impossible to accidentally overwrite the original. Since the value of a pointer may be passed, calls by reference are also provided. (*See also* C compiler.)

cable, optic—Optic cable is a generic term applied to any flexible continuous fiber or group of fibers capable of conducting light from one end of the fibers to the other with relatively low loss. An individual fiber is usually referred to as an optical fiber or optical waveguide, while a group of fibers packaged together to form a cable is called a bundle. A conductor that passes an image without distortion is usually called either a "coherent fiber optic" or an "image conduit." A coherent fiber optic cable requires that the exact relative location of every fiber must be maintained at both ends of the bundle. Glass fibers are commonly used for data communication links, while plastic fibers are used for transmission of light images or for short runs in data links.

cache—A buffer type of high-speed memory that is filled at medium speed from main memory, often with instructions and programs.

cache memory—1. A high-speed low-capacity memory similar to a scratch-pad memory except that it has a larger capacity. 2. The fastest portion of the overall memory that stores only the data that the microcomputer may need in the immediate future.

CAD—Abbreviation for computer-aided design. A CAD system is an automated design and drafting system that speeds up the design process by eliminating many tedious time-consuming tasks previously performed by hand.

CAD/CAM systems — A CAD system offers practical and up-to-date design and drafting capabilities while providing a link to numerical control and other computer-aided manufacturing (CAM) functions. The critical link between CAD and CAM systems is the effective control and flow of data among the respective systems. CAD/CAM systems can be used to help design parts and machinery, diagram complex wiring arrangements and printed-circuit boards, generate schematics, list parts, and calculate manufacturing specifications. CAD/CAM technology allows manufacturers to go from a design on a crt screen to a finished part, all with greater productivity and a better use of re-

Cache memory (Courtesy Plessey Peripheral Systems).

sources than was offered by earlier technology.

CAD N/C tapes — Numerical-control (N/C) tapes for operating drill machines, and other manufacturing machines, are end products of CAD/CAM processes. They are automatically generated by the graphics capability on some systems. Also, tapes for axial- and DIP-insertion soldering machines and pc board profiling may be generated.

cages, card frame—*See* card cage.

calculator—1. A data processor especially suitable for performing arithmetic operations that require frequent intervention by a human operator. 2. Generally and historically, a device for carrying out logic and arithmetic digital operations of any kind.

calculator, scientific programmable— Many of these units produce fast accurate answers to complex everyday scientific and engineering problems. They are ideal as a desktop scratch pad for scientific programmable calculations. Typically, they feature a 10-digit display that automatically operates in scientific notation. Results of the functions can be computed in degrees or radians at the touch of a switch. Difficult programming of functions are "inside" incorporated. Typically, a total of 15 or more scientific functions are hard-wired in, including trigonometrical, inverse trigonometrical hyperbolic, exponential, and logarithmic functions. Some units offering 64 or more steps of programming on 8 or more registers are available for formula and equation evaluation. Users can choose several decimal point positioning systems, including the floating decimal point and the exponential system.

calculator structure—New directions in computing have occurred with the emergence of calculator chips. The present-day calculator can be defined as a small highly specialized computer. The memory structure consists of both a fixed and a variable memory. The fixed portion, a read-only memory (ROM), provides a system control program called firmware — meaning nonchangeable instructions. This contrasts with general-purpose computers programmed by software, and random-logic systems that use hard-wire circuitry.

calibrated instrumentation—A procedure to ascertain, usually by comparison with a standard, the specific locations at which scale/chart graduations should be placed in order to correspond to a series of values (of the quantity) which the instrument is to measure, receive, or transmit.

calibration accuracy—Calibration accuracy is the limit of error in the finite degree to which a device can be calibrated (influenced by sensitivity, resolution, and repeatability of the device itself and the calibrating equipment). Usually it is expressed in percent of full scale.

CAM—Abbreviation for computer-aided manufacturing.

CANCL status word—This status word indicates that the remote computing system has deleted some information.

capacitance—Also referred to as capacity. The property which permits the storage of electrically separated charges when a potential difference exists between conductors.

capacitor, solid tantalum—A tantalum capacitor with a solid semiconductor electrolyte instead of a liquid electrolyte. A wire anode is used for low-capacitance values and a sintered-pellet is used for higher values. Also called a solid-electrolyte tantalum capacitor.

capacitor storage—1. A device which stores a digital bit or an analog voltage by charging a capacitor. 2. A storage device that utilizes the capacitance properties of materials to store data.

card—1. A machine-processable information storage medium of special quality paper stock, generally 7⅜ × 3¼ inches (187.3 mm × 85 mm) in size, but other standards exist for different types. 2. An internal pluggable unit used for printed-circuit wiring and components.

card-address backplane — The key to a typical system's flexibility is its unique "card-address" backplane. This printed-circuit backplane, which serves as the bus, assigns an address to each card or module. Users plug into it. The result is that users can assemble nearly any combination of memory and interfacing modules and can plug them into the standard backplane—and will still have a system that requires no hardwiring. The pro-

Card cages (Courtesy Cromemco, Inc.).

gram contained in the CPU refers to the address of each card in the package.

card cage — 1. A unit designed to permit installation of pc cards (*see* 2. Card) without the necessity of hardwiring. The card cages themselves are sturdy steel construction and usually include a retaining bar to ensure that cards cannot be shaken from their sockets. The cage backplanes include full sets of edge connectors soldered in place on the cage's bus. 2. Many suppliers offer one 12-connector card cage with a basic microprocessor. It is often prewired to hold the CPU, two memory cards, a front panel interface, and a card reader controller. An additional 6-connector card cage may be installed to allow for expansion. Generally, if still more expansion is required, the power supplies may be removed and installed remotely, thus providing space for an additional pair of 6-connector card cages (in some systems).

card code—Refers to an arbitrary code in which punched holes are assigned numeric or alphabetic values.

card column—1. A line of punch positions parallel to the Y datum line of a punch card. 2. A single line of punch positions parallel to the short edge of a 3¼- by 7⅜-inch (85 mm × 187.3 mm) punched card.

card encoder/reader — A typical unit has a write capability that allows it to encode as well as read magnetic-stripe cards, badges, and passbooks. Dual heads are independently suspended on parallelogram springs, in a gimbal mount, and this provides minimum encoder head and card wear (one system).

card extender — A passive card extender is a typical device used as a troubleshooting aid. It extends any of the card (device) "family" members to a position that is external to the card cage to permit easy access. The card extender is often equipped with labeled test-point terminals on each of the system bus lines to allow ease of measurement or the attachment of probes.

card field — The fixed columns on a punch card in which the same type of information is routinely entered.

card frames—A basic card connector and guide assembly used for most card cages. Up to 40 cards may be mounted within a standard 5¼- × 17-inch (133.4 mm × 431.8 mm) card frame. Frames can be supplied assembled with connectors, and bused power terminations with connector options. Memory busing and factory wiring of computer elements are often available as options.

card guides and edge connectors — Typically, most devices that are available are steel cadmium-plated card guides that are ABS plastic insulated and properly sized for microcomputer modules. They are typically provided in standard slot spacing of 1 inch (25.40 mm). Optional spacing of ½ inch (12.70 mm) and ¾ inch (19.05 mm) are available on special order. A 22/24 (pair/contacts) edge-type connector (with gold contacts and necessary polarizing keys) is generally provided, along with necessary mounting brackets and screws.

card modules, microprocessor—Functional modules that are generally provided on 8½ - by 11-inch (215.9 mm × 279.4 mm) printed-wiring cards by manufacturers are:

1. CPU Module — Typically, one card comprising the central processing unit, bus interface logic, and sockets for ROM and RAM.
2. Memory Modules—In some systems, they contain one memory timing and control card and up to four storage cards.
3. Interface Modules—Some cards contain both teletypewriter and card reader interface and are included in the system, as in one card devoted to the control-panel interface function.
4. Prototyping Cards—Blank cards drilled to accept 64 or 90 wire-wrap sockets that are made available. These cards facilitate development of interface circuits.

card punch—A machine which punches cards in designated locations in order to store data which can be conveyed to other machines or devices by reading or sensing the holes that were punched.

carry—A type of signal produced in an electronic computer by an arithmetic operation (on a one-digit place) of two or more numbers that is expressed in a positional notation and transferred to the next higher place for processing. Also, a signal or expression which may arise when the sum of two digits in the same digit place equals or exceeds the base of the number system being used.

carry, cascaded—*See* cascaded carry.

carry-complete signal — A signal generated by a digital parallel adder, indicating that all carries from an adding operation have been generated and propagated, and the addition operation is completed.

carry look-ahead—A circuit that, in ef-

fect, predicts the final carry from propagate and generate signals supplied by partial adders. It is used to speed up binary addition significantly by eliminating the carry propagation (or ripple) delay.

carry, partial—A technique in parallel addition wherein some or all of the carries are stored temporarily instead of being allowed to propagate immediately.

carry time — 1. The time required for transferring a carry digit to the higher column and, there, adding it. 2. The time required for transferring all the carry digits to higher columns and adding them for all digits in the number.

carry types—1. If a carry into a digit place will result in a carry out of the same digit place, and if the normal adding circuit is bypassed when generating this new carry, it is called a high-speed carry, or standing on nines carry. If the normal adding circuit is used in such a case, the carry is called a cascaded carry. If a carry resulting from the addition of carries is not allowed to propagate (e.g., when forming the partial product in one step of a multiplication process), it is called a partial carry. If it is allowed to propagate, the process is called a complete carry. If a carry generated in the most significant digit place is sent directly to the least significant place (e.g., when adding two negative numbers using nine complements), that carry is called an end around carry. Synonymous with cascaded carry, complete carry, end around carry, high-speed carry, and partial carry. 2. A signal or expression in direct subtraction, as defined in 1 above, which arises when the difference between the digits is less than zero. Such a carry is frequently called a borrow. Related to borrow. 3. The action of forwarding a carry. 4. The command directing a carry to be forwarded.

cartridge drive system — Generally, three basic methods can be used to integrate a cartridge magnetic tape drive into a host system. These are host system controlled, peripheral controlled, and common controlled (disk and cartridge). The host system can provide the cartridge tape drive control function if it can be dedicated to the back-up function instead of nor-

*Cartridge drive system, disk
(Courtesy Fujitsu Ltd.).*

mal system operation during the save and restore periods. The host system memory is used as a data buffer and time shares the CPU to provide the necessary intelligence for the cartridge tape drive. A full disk controller is assumed in this configuration. This arrangement is the lowest cost approach from a hardware viewpoint. A second, more typical, arrangement is to provide a peripheral controller that will relieve the system of direct-supervision responsibility. For this, a tape streamer is often used. The interface is an inexpensive assembly and can be efficiently implemented with a few ICs. The host system in many cases is an 8-bit processor.

cascade carry—In parallel addition, a carry process in which the addition of two numerals results in a partial sum numeral and a carry numeral which are, in turn, added together, with this process being repeated until no new carries are generated.

cascade connection—Refers to two or more similar component devices arranged in tandem, the output of one connected to the input of the following device.

cassette—A self-contained package of reel-to-reel blank or recorded film, videotape, or electronically embossable vinyl tape, for recording of sound, video, or computer input signals, which is continuous and self-

rewinding. Similar to a cartridge, but of slightly different design.

cassette diagnostic—Refers to a test for all functions of the cassette controller, and for up to four cassette drives (some systems).

catastrophic failure—A failure which is total or nearly so, such as: breakdown of the power supply, making all circuits inoperative. Any type of failure which renders the useful performance of the computer to zero.

cathode ray — Stream of negatively charged particles (electrons) emitted normally from the surface of the cathode in a rarefied gas.

cathode-ray tube—1. A vacuum tube in which a beam of electrons can be focused to a small cross-sectional area on a luminescent screen and which can be varied in position and intensity to produce a visible pattern. Abbreviated crt. 2. An electronic vacuum tube containing a screen on which information may be stored by means of a multigrid modulated beam of electrons from a thermionic emitter; storage is effected by means of charged or uncharged spots. 3. A storage tube. 4. An oscilloscope tube. 5. A picture tube.

cathode-ray tube memory — Cathode-ray tube memories use photosensitive surfaces as a target upon which an electron beam reads and writes information. These photosensitive surfaces are incorporated into a cathode-ray tube (crt), and the circuitry for addressing the photosensitive surface is used to control the electron beam of the crt.

CCD—Abbreviation for charge-coupled device. A CCD is a semiconductor that stores localized packets of charge and transfers them to adjacent locations when stimulated by externally manipulated voltages. The charge in each packet—which depends on the CCD's capacitance and its applied voltage — can represent digital information.

CCD advantages and applications— Advantages of CCDs include their high packing density and their low power dissipation. They are also fast; a CCD memory's upper operating limit will lie close to the 5- to 7-MHz range, because its peripheral and interface circuits will probably be implemented with MNOS technology, whose speed lies in that range. Primary applications of CCDs have been in image sensing and signal processing. But their basic shift register organization also suits them for applications as high-density semiconductor memory components. Foreseen as replacements for disks, drums, and other peripheral storage devices, CCDs may also ultimately find application in many mainframe requirements, as systems architecture evolves to take advantage of these fast, lower-cost, block-oriented components.

CCD architecture—CCD units basically simulate the operation of rotating drums. For example, one type of chip is organized so that it can combine both serial and random-access functions. It is arranged as 64,256-bit shift registers in which four-phase clock signals simultaneously shift the data. Each shift register can be thought of as representing a single track in a conventional drum, and each track can be thought of as being divided into 256 sectors, corresponding to the 256 CCD data storage cells in each line. The "rate of rotation" of this semiconductor drum therefore is controlled by the four-phase clock.

CCD memory—Physically the CCD is a linear array of closely spaced MOS capacitors or gates. Beneath the gates are "potential wells" at or near the surface of the silicon. The device operates by storing and transferring charge (data) between these potential wells, which are the unit storage elements or cells of a CCD memory. The wells are formed and controlled by the closely spaced MOS capacitors and by a phased voltage applied to the gates. Charge-coupling is the process of transferring the mobile electric charge within a storage element or well to an adjacent well when a periodic clock voltage is applied to the gates. Quantity of stored electric charge in this mobile packet can vary considerably, depending on capacitance of the storage element and applied voltages.

CCD operation—While similar in operation to dynamic flip-flops and while using solid-state technology, CCDs are nothing more than a series of very small capacitors, which are used to store "0s" and "1s." In a CCD, a substrate acts as the common-ground

return for a chain of very small MOS capacitors. Application of a voltage to the small insulated area of these capacitors causes a charge to build up. The capacitors have, in sequence from left to right, a zero, then a positive, and then a negative charge. These charges are applied to the capacitors by signals from three control lines connected to a single square-wave source—a Clock. The charges on the capacitors represent data when originally loaded. However, the charges will eventually leak off. To prevent this, the Clock causes the signals to be phase shifted so that the charges appear to move along the substrate from one capacitor to another.

CCDs can be considered as a series of dynamic shift registers, with the information circulating in an endless loop. In addition to physical size (they can have up to 1-million bytes of memory), CCDs offer a much faster memory operation, a shorter "fetch" cycle, and no moving parts. However, CCDs are volatile and, thus, all information in the CCD is lost when the power is removed.

CCD structure—There are two common CCD types that are referred to as surface channel and buried channel. The surface channel type is characterized by the storing and transferring of charge (data) along the surface of the substrate. The buried channel type, because of additional substrate doping, stores and transfers the charge (data) further into the bulk of the substrate. The primary differences in characteristics between the surface channel and buried channel types is that the surface channel has: (1) higher total charge carrying capability, (2) lower charge transfer efficiency at extremely high charge transfer rates, (3) simpler fabrication process. Charge transfer efficiency (number 2, above) is defined as the percentage of the total charge packet (data) which is actually shifted or transferred per shift (the efficiency is typically greater than 99.9% per shift).

CCITT—Abbreviation for Comité Consultatif International Télégraphique et Téléphonique. This is the International Telegraph and Telephone Consultative Committee, an international organization concerned with devising and proposing recommendations for international telecommunications.

C compiler—A structured general-purpose programming language for various microprocessors, the C compiler accommodates a wide variety of operating systems and numerical text-processing and data-base programs. Relatively small, compact, and easy to learn, this compiler deals effectively with characters, numbers, and addresses. Because these tasks are manipulated efficiently in combination with the arithmetic and logical operations, the C compiler is claimed to achieve higher efficiency than most high-level languages in terms of the amount of code generated. (*See also* C.)

cell—1. The storage area for one unit of information, usually one character or one word. 2. A location specified by whole or part of the address and possessed of the faculty of store. Specific terms such as column, field, location, and block are preferable when appropriate.

central distributed system — A central system usually has a Control Communication Executive (CCE) that simultaneously handles and queues all the multiple satellite transactions.

centralized data processing—Data processing performed at a single central location on data obtained from several geographical locations or managerial levels. Decentralized data processing involves processing at various managerial levels or geographical points throughout the organization.

central processing unit (CPU)—1. A unit of a microcomputer that includes the circuits controlling the interpretation and execution of instructions. Synonymous with mainframe. 2. The central processor of a computer system contains main storage, arithmetic unit, control registers, and scratchpad memory.

central processing unit operation—A central processing unit consists of a central processing unit (CPU) and a memory that has a stored sequence of instructions for the CPU. The CPU is operated by a clock circuit to alternately fetch and execute the memory instructions. The central processor performs control, input-output, arithmetic, and logical operations by executing instructions obtained from the memory sources. The instructions use a 4-, 8-, 12-, 16, or 32-bit machine word. Depending on the number of separate memory accesses required, the processor may require one, two, or three memory cycles to complete the execution of an instruction. The typical microprocessor logic section includes a parallel arithmetic-logic unit (ALU) that performs two's complement arithmetic operations, and a parallel shifter unit that performs logical and shift operations, etc.

central processor organization—A microcomputer can essentially be divided into three main sections: arithmetic and control, input/output, and memory. The arithmetic and control section carries out the directives of the program. The calculations, routing of information, and control of the other sections occur in this part of the processor. All information going in and coming out of the central processor is handled by the input/output section. It also controls the operation of all peripheral equipment. The memory section is the heart of the central processor; it provides temporary storage for data and instructions. Because of its importance, the total cycle time of the memory is often the main determining factor in the overall speed of the processor.

ceramic capacitors—Ceramic capacitors, both chip and packaged versions, have been the fastest growing segment of the capacitor industry. Prior to 1975, unpackaged ceramic chips were strictly fixed-value devices. Ceramic chips have capacitances that can be adjusted incrementally without adversely affecting device performance. A significant step in ceramic capacitors was the successful transition from a precious-metal system to a base-metal system. Manufacturers are now using a nickel alloy to make the internal electrodes and the terminations for the capacitors, permitting price reductions of 30% to 50% in many instances.

ceramic packaging — One packaging concept makes use of chips mounted in hermetically sealed, leadless, ceramic carriers. These carriers are reflow soldered, by means of a heatsink/mounting pad on their back, to a ceramic substrate. The carriers mounted to the substrate form a system module, which is simply inverted and mounted to a pc motherboard. The thermal characteristics of these modules are such that they operate in a 70°C, still-air environment. One industry standard high-performance, high-reliability ceramic package is made of three layers of Al_2O_3 ceramic and nickel-plated refractory metal. The cavity is sealed with a glazed ceramic lid, using a controlled devitrified low temperature glass sealant. Package leads are of Kovar, nickel-plated and solder-dipped, for insertion or soldering.

cerdip package — Cerdip dual-in-line packages generally have the same high-performance characteristics as the standard three-layer ceramic package, yet approach plastic in cost. It is a military-approved-type package, with excellent reliability characteristics. The cerdip concept has been around for a number of years, and some manufacturers lead the technology with this package, having eliminated the device instability and corrosion problems of earlier cerdip processes. One brand of package consists of a 96% Alumina base and the same material lid, hermetically fused onto the base with Corning 7583 solder glass (at approximately 475°C). Inert gases are sealed inside the die cavity. Generally available in: 16-, 18-, 22-, 24-, and 28-pin configurations.

cermet—A dielectric mixture used in making film resistive elements. The first half of the term is derived from ceramic, the second from metal.

chad—The tiny piece of paper removed when a hole is punched into a card or paper tape.

chadless tape — A specific type of punched paper tape in which the holes are partially prepunched. Each chad is left fastened by approximately a quarter of the circumference of the hole. Chadless punched paper tape must be sensed by mechanical fingers, as it interferes with conventional electrical or photoelectrical reading.

chain—1. Any set of records or items linked together either physically or logically in a specified sequence. 2. Pertaining to a routine in specified segments that is run through the computer in tandem, only one segment being within the computer mainframe at any one time and each segment having access to the output from previously executed segments. The order in which the segments are executed may be data dependent.

chained files—Chained files are ideal for the user desiring open-ended sequential data handling. These data files consist of a series of data blocks chained together with forward and backward pointers.

chained list—A list of items, each of which contains an identifier for the next item in a particular order, but such order does not have any particular relation to the order in which they are stored.

chaining—1 A system of storing records in which each record belongs to a list or group of records and has a linking field for tracing the chain. 2. The ability of an executing program to call another program for execution after its own execution is complete.

channel—1. That portion of a computer's storage medium which is also accessible to a given reading station. 2. A path along which signals can be sent, e.g., a data channel, an output channel. 3. The portion of a storage medium that is accessible to a given reading or writing station, e.g., a track, a band.

channel adapter—A device which permits the connection between data channels of differing equipment. The device allows data transfer at the rate of the slower channel.

channel, analog—Usually refers to a channel that will pass alternating current, but not direct current. A switched voice channel is an analog channel, while most teletypewriter circuits are digital (dc) channels. If an analog channel is said to carry digital data, it is actually carrying analog representations of the digital data in the form of various frequencies.

channel bandwidth—Besides transmission direction, a channel is characterized by bandwidth. Generally, greater bandwidth allows proportionately higher transmission rates—usually specified as the number of line-signal elements per second, or baud rate. For binary-signal elements, the baud rate equals the bit rate. When a signal element represents more than two states, as in multilevel modulation, the bit rate exceeds the baud rate.

channel capacity — 1. The maximum number of binary digits or elementary digits to other bases which can be handled in a particular channel per unit time. 2. The maximum possible information transmission rate through a channel at a specified error rate. The channel capacity may be measured in either bits per second or bauds.

channelizing—The process of subdividing wideband transmission facilities for the purpose of putting many different circuits, requiring comparatively narrow bandwidths, on a single wideband facility.

channel-select setup time, minimum— The shortest time interval between the leading edge of the channel-select input and the leading edge of the signal input that allows a full-width (or useful) signal at the output.

channel-select signal—A signal that allows the selection of a particular channel by a gating mechanism.

channel-select time—The time interval between the leading edge of the channel-select pulse and the leading edge of the output signal of the selected channel.

channel, semiconductor—A region of semiconductor material in which current flow is influenced by a transverse electrical field. Physically, a channel may be an inversion layer, a diffused layer, or bulk material. The type of channel is determined by the type of majority carriers during conduction; i.e., p-channel or n-channel.

channels, videodisc—A videodisc is a high-density information storage medium that loads as easily as a phonograph record, and the picture and sound of a program coexist on a single disk medium, assuring synchronization. Thus, two parallel sound channels can be programmed for two audience levels, for two different languages, or for a question and answer combination. Electromechanical switching between channels is also quick and easy. Microprocessor-controlled players can easily be interfaced with a mainframe computer permitting increased interactive capabilities.

channels, wideband common carrier— Wideband channels are facilities that common carriers provide for transferring data at speeds up into the 1-million baud region. The availability of these facilities depends upon what equipment the common carrier has in the subscriber's geographical area. There are many modems available for use with common-carrier facilities, many of which are supplied by the common carriers.

channel synchronizer — The channel synchronizer, often housed with the peripheral control unit in a single cabinet, provides the proper interface between the central computer and the peripheral equipment. Other control functions of the channel synchronizer include: primary interpreting of the function words; searching, by comparison of an identifier with data read from a peripheral unit; and providing the central computer with peripheral-unit status information.

channel, voice grade—A channel suitable for transmission of speech, digital or analog data, or facsimile, generally with a frequency range of about 300 Hz to 3000 Hz.

character—One of a set of elements, which may be arranged in ordered groups to express information. Each character has two forms: (1) A man-intelligible form, the graphic, which includes the decimal digits 0-9, letters A-Z, punctuation marks, and other formatting and control symbols, and (2) Its computer-intelligible form, the code, which consists of a group of binary bits.

character fill (to)—To replace all data in a storage location or group of locations with the repeated representation of a specific character, usually zeros or Xs.

character, highlighting—A blinking, reverse video, underlining, half bright, or security (nondisplay) character. Generally, it is not possible for a host computer system to cause a character to be displayed on the screen in reverse video on traditional conversational crt terminals. These built-in highlighting features have become so commonplace that they are being found increasingly on "dumb" terminals which have no other advanced capabilities.

character reader—A specialized device which can convert directly into machine language data that is represented in one of the type fonts or scripts read by human beings. Such a reader may operate optically, or if the characters are printed in magnetic ink, it may operate either magnetically or optically.

character recognition — 1. The computer process of reading, identifying, and encoding a printed character. 2. The technology of using a machine to sense and encode into a machine language characters which are written or printed so as to be read by human beings.

character sets, multiple—A capability that is found on more advanced terminals is multiple character sets, such as foreign languages, graphics, and mathematical and editing symbols. Key considerations when choosing a terminal that has multiple character set capability are: the ability to switch character sets from time to time during an application; the ability to display different character sets simultaneously, especially in adjoining screen locations; and the ability for users to modify and/or create their own character set, either through insertion of a ROM/PROM, or downline loading directly into terminal memory.

character shift-in (SI)—1. A code extension character used to terminate a sequence that has been introduced by the shift-out character, that makes effective the graphic characters of the standard character set. 2. A code extension character that can be used by itself to cause a return to the character set in effect prior to the departure caused by a shift-out character.

character string—1. A group of characters in a one-dimensional array, in an order due to the reference of relations between adjacent numbers. 2. A sequence or group of connected characters, connected by codes, key words, or other programming or associative techniques.

character/block transmission — On some systems, there are two configurations—character transmission and block transmission. Character transmission lets users operate the microcomputer just like using a teletypewriter. Block transmission provides sophisticated editing capabilities, however, such as insert/delete and full cursor control, along with such

field functions as blinking, high-intensity, and protected fields. Many models are able to generate all 128 ASCII codes. Accessible setup switches in most keyboards permit users to select functions such as line speed, parity, scroll, and reverse video. The movable keyboard is much like a modern typewriter.

charge-coupled device — Abbreviated CCD. A microelectronic circuit element whose function could not be duplicated by a practical assembly of discrete components. The device can be regarded as a stretched MOS transistor with a long string of gates (perhaps as many as 1000) between the source and the drain. In a p-channel device, a charge packet, consisting of a concentration of holes, can be held in place for a short time by applying a steady negative voltage to one of the gates. If that voltage is then dropped and, simultaneously, the next gate in line is energized, the charge packet moves to a new position under the second gate. Thus, by applying pulses to alternate gates, a sequence of charge packets can be transferred from source to drain.

charge-coupled device memory—CCD memories contain an unprecedented number of bits. This increased storage capacity is due to two separate factors. First, the memory requires a smaller area for each bit. Second, the number of contact openings or diffusions is not large, simplifying processing to the point where it should be able to produce acceptable yields on larger chips than those that can be used with conventional MOS LSI. (These predictions all assume conventional photolithographic processing, which is the factor that limits cell size.) However, even smaller CCD cells appear capable of operating without signal-to-noise ratios being reduced beyond the point of practical operation. Consequently, the exploitation of high-resolution electron-beam definition in CCD fabrication appears likely. The goal is a chip approaching 500 mils on a side and containing almost half a million bits, and an industrywide effort is being directed to this end. (See CCD definitions.)

chatter—Rapid closing and opening of contacts on a relay, which reduces its life.

check—A process of partial or complete testing of the correctness of machine operations, the existence of certain prescribed conditions within the microcomputer, or the correctness of the results produced by a program. A check of any of these conditions may be made automatically by the equipment or may be programmed.

check, arithmetic — An operation performed by the microcomputer to reveal any failure in an arithmetic operation. Can also be used to ascertain whether the capacity of a register has been exceeded after an operation.

check, automatic — Refers to various provisions constructed in hardware for verifying the accuracy of information transmitted, manipulated, or stored by any unit or device in a microcomputer. Synonymous with built-in check, built-in automatic check, hardware check.

check bit—A binary check digit, for example, a parity bit.

check digit — 1. An alarm signal that consists of a digit carried along with a machine word. It can report information about the other digits in the word. If a single error occurs, the check fails and an alarm signal is initiated. 2. Relates to one or several digits generated and carried in microcomputer processes for ascertaining error and accuracy control of data in batch processing, in real-time, or in subsequent operations; i.e., often periodically regenerated and compared with the original data.

check indicator—A device that displays or indicates a check indicator and announces an error has been made; or a checking operation that has determined that a failure has occurred.

check-indicator instruction—A specific instruction designed to direct a signal device to be turned on so as to call an operator's attention to the fact that there is some discrepancy in the instruction that is then in use.

checking, automatic — Refers to the numerous internal checks that continually monitor the accuracy of the system and guard against incipient malfunction. Typical are the parity and inadmissible-character check, the automatic readback of magnetic tape and magnetic cards as the information is being recorded, or the electronic tests that precede each use of magnetic tape or magnetic cards to ensure that the operator has not inadvertently set switches improperly.

checkpoint—A point in a microcomputer routine at which it is possible to store sufficient information so as to permit restarting the computation from that point. To establish checkpoints, processing intervals are determined, each being based upon a certain number of items, transactions, or records processed. At each processing interval or checkpoint, the stored program identifies input and output records and then records them along with the contents of important storage areas, such as counters and registers; at the same time, accuracy of processing up to that point is established.

checkpoint and restart procedures—Checkpoint and restart procedures are techniques associated with microcomputers that make it possible, in the event of an error or an interruption, to continue processing from the last checkpoint rather than from the beginning of a run. These techniques are included in applications which require many hours of processing time, since heavy machine scheduling and deadlines generally do not permit a complete rerun. Restart procedures are the means by which processing is continued after an error or interruption.

check problem—1. A test problem that can indicate an error in programming or operation of a microcomputer. When it is solved incorrectly, an error in programming or operation is indicated. 2. A problem chosen to determine whether the microcomputer or a program is operating correctly.

check register — A register used to store information temporarily so it may be checked with the result of a succeeding transfer of the information to verify that the transferred information agrees precisely.

check reset key—A push-button switch which when pushed acknowledges an error and resets the error detection mechanism indicated by the check light (some systems). This is required to restart a program after an error has been discovered in batch mode.

check, summation—A redundant check in which groups of digits are summed, usually without regard for overflow, and that sum checked against a previously computed sum to verify accuracy.

check, unused command—1. A check, usually automatic, which tests for the occurrence of a nonpermissible code expression. 2. A self-checking code or error-detecting code that uses code expressions such that one or more errors in a code expression produces a forbidden-pulse combination.

chemical deposition — Refers to the process of depositing a substance on a surface by means of the chemical reduction of a solution.

chemically deposited printed circuit— A printed circuit formed by means of a chemical reaction on the base material.

chemical etching—Chemical etching is a process in which a dielectric and copper foil are sandwiched together, and a circuit pattern is imaged on the copper foil with a material that is resistant to etching chemicals (the resist). The copper which is not intended to be part of the circuit is then removed by chemical etching.

chip—1. An unpackaged semiconductor device. A die from a silicon wafer incorporating an integrated circuit. 2. A tiny piece of semiconductor material on which microscopic electronic components are photoetched to form one or more circuits. After connection leads and a case are added to the chip, it is called an integrated circuit.

chip architecture — Functionally, a microprocessor chip includes the arithmetic logic unit (ALU), the general-purpose registers, and the control-bus structure. The architecture is to some degree dependent on the positioning of the processor and the on-chip memory on one or more chips, the number of pins each chip has, the chip size, the off-chip memory, and I/O bus structure. Speed or throughput is very dependent on architecture. Clock speed (or frequency) is not necessarily indicative of execution speed. Speed is a function of data and address widths, the number of separate paths, and the overlap in the fetch and execute cycles.

chip, beam-lead — A chip employing electrical terminations in the form of tabs that extend beyond the edge of the chip for direct bonding to a mounting substrate.

chip, bubble memory—In the simplest terms, bubble memories are sandwiches. The filling is a chip wrapped by two coils, and that filling lies between two permanent-magnet "slabs." The coils create a rotating magnetic field that moves "bubbles," or cylindrical magnetic domains, through a film on the chip. Films may consist of magnetic metals, synthetic ferrite, or garnet crystals. In addition, control functions are located in aluminum-copper elements on the magnetic film.

chip-carrier—This is an intermediate package called a leadless package or chip-carrier (which looks like a small flat-pack with the leads removed). The chip-carrier functions like a conventional package but its reduced size permits mounting on a substrate which installs on a larger package. For very complex dice, it affords a hybrid manufacturer the opportunity of extensively testing a die before further assembly, thus avoiding expensive rework. The ability to burn-in dice prior to assembly improves yields.

chip, circuit—In a microprocessor, a single device composed of transistors, diodes, and other components as interconnected by various chemical processes. It usually has been cut from a larger wafer, usually of silicon.

chip device configuration — Refers to the size and dimensional proportions of the channel, drain, and source regions of each transistor; the spacing between circuit elements and between interconnections; the thickness of oxide and metal deposits. (Most of these dimensions are incorporated into the final masks used in manufacturing.) To fully appreciate the difference between MOS processes, one must understand both the basic device characteristics and how a designer optimizes them with the choice of a particular material, process steps, and device dimensions.

chip enable $(\overline{CE})$—This is the primary device selection pin. By agreed standards, the function that substantially affects power dissipation is called CE. Any memory device that has a CE function has both an active and standby power level associated with it.

chip-enable input—A control input that, when active, permits the operation of an integrated circuit for input, internal transfer, manipulation, refreshing, and/or output of data, and, when inactive, causes the integrated circuit to be in a reduced-power standby mode.

chip-in-tape — An automated hybrid bonding technique that provides multiple simultaneous bonding of leads by means of thermal and mechanical energy transmission through a deformable, prepunched tape.

chip, IOP—Some special-purpose microprocessors are emerging with processing power tailored for specific jobs. One such example is the input/output processor, or IOP. The IOP performs the same function in a microcomputer system as an I/O channel processor performs in a mainframe computer system. As a processor, the IOP executes an input/output channel program to initialize and communicate with peripheral devices in the system. The IOP functions independently of the central system CPU, which does only data processing. In this manner, the IOP relieves the central CPU of the system I/O interface tasks and increases the data processing capability of the entire system.

chip materials—Refers to the kind of substrate to be used, its doping concentrations, the choice of silicon or aluminum for the gate electrode, etc.

chip microprocessor—Chip microprocessors have brought the state-of-the-art where complete microcomputers are available on a single chip of silicon. No larger than a ¼-inch square, they contain all the essential elements of a central processor, including the control logic, instruction decoding, and arithmetic processing circuitry. To be useful, the microprocessor chip or chips are combined with memory and I/O processor (IOP) chips to form a microcomputer "system." They usually fill no more than a single printed-circuit board and sell for less than $300.

chip reduction—This refers to the reduction of die size as technology advances permit, in order to increase overall yield, as measured in good dice per wafer. This is sometimes accomplished with software operating on the graphic data base. Chips are often designed with subsequent reduction in mind, as not all dimensions are optimally scaled down by the same amount, and more room must be left for the unscaled features (which "grow" in size relative to the other features). For example, it is desirable to leave pads the same size.

chip resistor—Used in hybrid microelectronic circuits, and available in either thick- or thin-film construction. Thick-film devices are screened onto a ceramic or glass substrate; thin-film devices are vacuum deposited. By definition, a thick-film resistor is one in which the conducting material is greater than one millionth of an inch thick, while a thin-film resistor has a conductive material that is less than one millionth of an inch thick. Resistance is obtained by scribing, sandblasting, or otherwise adjusting the resistor element to tolerance.

chip-select input—A gating input that, when inactive, prevents the input or output of data to or from an integrated circuit.

chip, semiconductor — The uncased form of a monolithic integrated circuit or circuit element.

chip size — Individual chip size has been growing steadily in spite of shrinking dimensions of individual features integrating more complex functions. For example, memories have grown from 64 bits/chip to 4096 and up. Users began buying chips with 64,000 bits in the early 1980s. Since expanded chip area and reduced feature size increase the sensitivity of pattern defects to smaller line-width control margins, product yield becomes more of a problem.

chip size limits — Die size limitations are set by the economics of "yield." Many circuits are made, the defective ones are thrown away, and the good ones are sold. Defects can arise from many sources. The photomasks used may have pin holes in dark areas, or opaque spedks in areas which should be clear. Severe defects in the basic silicon crystal can make the circuit inoperative. Dust in the photoprinting operation or other processing steps, which affects a critical spot in the circuit, will cause failures. Errors of misaligning successive photoengraving steps, or of lack of control of critical dimensions and impurity concentration, will make the circuit inoperative. The correction and elimination of these defects is a difficult task, and represents a major portion of the effort and expense of semiconductor device development and production.

chips, memory—The memory section of a microcomputer usually accounts for a major portion of the chips. Primarily, three kinds of memory are used. Random-access memory (RAM) chips are used primarily for variable data and scratchpad purposes. Read-only (ROM) chips are used to store instruction sequences. Programmable read-only memory (PROM) chips are used for quickly tailoring general-purpose microcomputers for specific applications. RAMs are expensive compared to ROMs, but the data in the ROMs must be stored at the time they are created, so there is a production delay associated with them as well as a "programming" cost. PROM chips, some of which can be erased by ultraviolet light and reprogrammed, are used in place of ROMs when small quantities are involved.

chip technology, LSI—The large-scale integration (LSI) technology used to build microprocessor chips primarily centers around metal-oxide semiconductor (MOS) devices. Chip densities on MOS devices range from 500 to 10,000, or more, transistors per chip. The chip's size typically ranges from 0.15 inch square to 0.25 inch square. The chips are mounted into dual-in-line packages (DIPs) which typically have 18, 24, or 40 pins for mounting on a printed-circuit card. P-channel MOS (PMOS) had been the predominant technology for calculator chips and most of the early 4-bit and 8-bit processors. The PMOS 8-bit microprocessors with especially good design are still sometimes competitive with the newer NMOS 8-bit chips. PMOS processors typically are offered with a family of interface chips tailored to reduce the demands on the programs to support external devices. NMOS, however, has become the preferred approach by many of the IC manufacturers.

chip technology, microprocessors — Microprocessor designers can choose from among single or multichip processors, chip sets, or pc-board assemblies, and from among a wide range of technologies. A common technology is silicon-gate p-channel MOS (NMOS) and silicon-on-sapphire MOS (SOS/MOS) to achieve manufacturers are also using n-channel MOS (NMOS) and silicon-on-sapphire MOS (SOS/MOS) to achieve speeds that are higher than those possible with PMOS. Bipolar processes are employed for the highest speeds—about 200-ns per cycle vs. 2 μs for some NMOS types. Complementary MOS (CMOS) is used for the lowest power dissipations — microwatt-range chip dissipation vs. milliwatt range for other types.

circuit, anticoincidence—Refers to a specific logic element which operates with binary digits and is designed to provide input signals according to specific rules; i.e., one digit is obtained as output only if two different input signals are received.

circuit, astable—Refers to a circuit which continuously alternates between its two unstable states. It can be synchronized by applying a repetitive input signal of slightly higher frequency.

circuit, bistable trigger—A name given to a type of circuit that is binary; i.e., it has two states, each requiring an appropriate trigger for excitation and transition from one state to the other. Also called binary pair, trigger pair, and flip-flop.

circuit, bus—Usually a group of circuits that provide a communications path between two or more devices, such as between a central processor, memory, and peripherals.

circuit, bus driver—A circuit designed to amplify a bus data or control signal sufficiently to assure a valid receipt of that signal at its destination.

circuit capacity—1. The number of communications channels that can be derived from a given circuit at the same time. 2. The information capacity, measured in bits per second, of a circuit.

circuit card — A printed-circuit board containing electronic components.

circuit fabrication, thick-film — Thick-film circuit fabrication involves the use of stable materials, precision screening and firing techniques, and balanced-bridge selective trimming of resistors. Conductors, resistors, and dielectrics are screened onto alumina substrates and fired at 800°C or higher. Other components, such as capacitors, inductors, and silicon devices are attached to the thick-film substrate by eutectic, solder, or epoxy methods. Wire bonding is accomplished with a gold wire ultrasonic ball bonder. The completed circuit is then placed in a metal or ceramic package and hermetically sealed.

circuit fabrication, thin-film—Thin-film and microwave integrated circuits use high-purity alumina substrates that have been vacuum coated with chrome-gold or tantalum-chrome-gold. Photolithographic masking and selective etching techniques are employed to delineate resistor and/or conductor patterns. Components are mounted to the substrates by eutectic bond, epoxy, or solder. Circuits are sealed in hermetic packages or in custom-machined housings for microwave integrated circuits.

circuit gettering—Gettering is an important part of most semiconductor processes. The term refers to the reduction of mobile defects and certain impurities in the crystalline structure of wafers, at their active or critical portions of the circuits built on them, by physically damaging or chemically treating the back side of the wafer. One satisfactory method is to use a pulsed laser to getter the back side of the wafer. There is no problem of contamination or doping of the front side with laser gettering. The individual pockets of damage that are created seem to resist annealing longer than the damage created by older methods. In addition, lasers cost less than ion implanters.

Gettering is more important in leakage-sensitive devices such as dynamic RAMs and CMOS circuits. As junctions get shallower (as in VLSI) and narrower, defects are more of a problem and gettering becomes a necessity.

circuit, integrated—Refers to one of several logic circuits, gates, flip-flops, etc., that are etched on single crystals, ceramics, or other semiconductor materials. Some chips with many resistors and transistors are extremely tiny, others are in effect "sandwiches" of individual chips.

circuit limiter—A circuit of nonlinear elements that restrict the electrical excursion of a variable in accordance with some specified criteria. Hard limiting is a limiting action with negligible variation in output in the range where the output is limited. Soft limiting is a limiting action with appreciable variation in output in the range where the output is limited. A bridge limiter is a bridge circuit used as a limiter circuit. In an analog computer, a feedback limiter is a limiter circuit usually employing biased diodes shunting the feedback component of an operational amplifier; an input limiter is a limiter circuit usually employing biased diodes in the amplifier input channel that operates by limiting the current entering the summing junction.

circuit, linear—A circuit whose output is an amplified version of its input or whose output is a predetermined variation of its input.

circuit, logic—One of the circuits used to perform certain logical functions. The functions are AND, OR, NOR, and Exclusive-OR, among many others. The output of these circuits is dependent on the state, or level (1 or 0), of the inputs.

circuit noise—Noise brought to a receiver electrically as opposed to acoustically from an electrical system.

circuit noise level—The circuit noise level at any point in a transmission system is the ratio of the circuit noise at that point to some arbitrary amount of a circuit noise chosen as a reference. This ratio is usually expressed in decibels above reference noise, abbreviated dBm, signifying the reading of a circuit noise meter, or in adjusted decibels.

circuit parameters—Refers to the values of the physical quantities associated with circuit elements. For example, the resistance (parameter) of a resistor (element), the amplification factor and plate resistance (parameters) of a tube (element), the inductance per unit length (parameter) of a transmission line (element).

circuit, printed—*See* printed circuit.

circuit reliability—The percentage of time a circuit meets operational standards.

circuit, single-shot—Relates to circuits or logic elements arranged to perform signal standardization in order to convert an imprecise input signal into one conforming to the requirements of a particular machine.

circuits, instruction control—The circuits that cause the microcomputer to carry out the instructions in proper sequence, and which can control by permitting only the coded conditions to continue or function.

circuits, inverting — Refers to various types of gate circuits in which the signals are inverted as they pass through, so that it is not necessary to use separate inverting circuits. Some types of circuits provide complementary outputs; that is, there are two output terminals instead of one, with the normal output appearing at one terminal and the inverted output at the other. In some dynamic circuits, transformer coupling is used, in which case the secondary windings may readily be connected to furnish either normal or inverted outputs.

circuit, sequential—Some state-storage outputs provide inputs to the logic array, thus providing the previous state information which influences the next state of the machine at $T(n + 1)$. Combinatorial logic arrays may contain AND, OR, EXOR, NAND, NOR, or NEXOR gates, ROMs, PROMs, PLAs, FPLAs, EAROMs, CAMs, or RAMs. Sequential circuits may contain any of the elements found in combinatorial logic arrays in combination with state-storage elements like flip-flops, R/W, RAMs, or CAMs. Higher-level sequential circuits have used microprocessors, microcomputers, programmable calculators, minicomputers, or even large scale computers as the logic array, storage array, state sequencer, or a combination of the three.

circuits, storage — Refers to various storage circuits that can be switched, or "triggered," into either of two stable states. One of these states can be defined as the "0" state and the other as the "1" state (zero and one). Input circuits are provided for triggering the storage circuit into either state. Because these circuits can be made to flip into one state or flop into the other, the name "flip-flop" has been applied to them. The input that triggers the flip-flop into the "1" state is frequently called the "set" input while the input that triggers it into the "0" state is called the "reset" input.

There may be more than one kind of "set" and "reset" input, providing the logical designer with considerable flexibility. One type of input is obtained by joining a "set" and a "reset" input together in such a way that a signal applied to this "T" input will trigger the flip-flop to its opposite state.

circuit, voice-grade—A circuit suitable for the transmission of speech, digital or analog data, or facsimile, and generally with a frequency range of 300–3000 Hz.

circulating storage—A device or unit that stores information in a train or pattern of pulses, where the pattern of pulses issuing at the final end are sensed, amplified, reshaped, and reinserted into the device at the beginning end.

cladding, fiberoptics—A low refractive index material that surrounds the core of the optic fiber and protects against surface contaminant scattering. In all-glass fibers, the cladding is glass. In plastic-clad silica fibers, the plastic cladding also may serve as the coating.

clamp—Refers to a circuit in which a waveform is adjusted and maintained at a definite level when recurring at various intervals.

C language—*See C.*

clear—1. An activity to place one or more storage locations into a prescribed state, usually zero or the space character. Contrast with set. 2. To return a memory to a nonprogrammed state, usually represented as "0" or OFF (empty).

cleared condition — Usually concerns destructive reading in which a flux configuration is permanently changed to some predetermined state and is also called the cleared condition. Also called a zero condition.

clock—1. The most basic source of synchronizing signals in most electronic equipment, especially computers. 2. That specific device or unit designed to time events. 3. A data communications clock which controls the timing of bits sent in a data stream, and controls the timing of the sampling of bits received in a data stream.

clocked signals — Refers to various signals within the control that are synchronized in time by a master oscillator or clock. The timing is accomplished by digital logic gating. The primary purpose of clocking (or gating) the signals is to maintain the correct time and phase relationship among the pulse signals.

clock frequency — With reference to digital computers, the master frequency of periodic pulses that are used to schedule computer operations.

clock generator—The clock generators generate clock and CPU time-phasing signals. In addition, a system clock is often provided for distribution outside of the processor for synchronization of peripheral units. Only an external crystal is required for many units.

clock generator, pulse — Refers to a specifically designed generator which generates pulses for purposes of special timing or gating, i.e., pulses which are used as inputs to gates to aid in pulse-shaping and timing.

clocking, internal — In synchronous communication, a terminal or computer is Internally Clocked when the bit-timing signal is provided from within the terminal or computer rather than from a modem.

clock, input—The terminal on a flip-flop whose condition or change of condition controls the admission of data and thereby controls the output state of the flip-flop. The clock signal performs two functions:
1. It permits data signals to enter the flip-flop.
2. After entry, it directs the flip-flop to change state accordingly.

Some J-K flip-flops permit data entry when the clock goes to "1" and then causes the flip-flop to react to the data when the clock goes to "0."

clock-pulse generator—1. An instrument or device designed to generate pulses that control the timing of the switching circuits in microprocessor operation. Clock frequency is one determination (but not the only one) of data flow or manipulation. However, clocks are a primary requisite for most microprocessors, and multiphased clocks are common in most MOS CPUs. 2. Refers to a specifically designed generator which generates pulses for the purpose of special timing or gating in a digital computer, i.e., pulses which are used as inputs to gates to aid in pulse-shaping and timing. Same as time-pulse generator.

clock rate—1. Refers to the rate at which a word or parts of characters of a word (bits) are transferred from one internal computer element to another. 2. The time rate at which pulses are emitted from the clock. The clock rate at which logical or arithmetic gating is performed with a synchronous computer. 3. The speed (frequency) at which the processor operates, as determined by the rate at which words and bits are transferred through internal logic sequences.

clock, real time—Refers to a register and the circuitry that automatically maintains time in conventional time units for use in program execution and event initiation. A typical module unit will provide programmable time bases from one microsecond to one hour. Time-base reference is from a 1-MHz crystal-controlled oscillator. On completion of a time interval, the microcomputer will receive an interrupt from the module, if enabled.

closed loop—1. A circuit in which the output is continuously fed back to its source for constant comparison. 2. The complete signal path in a control system, represented as a group of units, which is connected in such a manner that a signal started at any point follows a closed path and can be traced back to that point. 3. A group of indefinitely repeated computer instructions.

closed-loop system—Refers to a feedback control system involving one or more feedback control loops, which combines functions of controlled signals and of commands, in order to keep relationships between the two stable.

closed routine — A computer routine that is entered by basic linkage from a main routine rather than by being inserted as a block of instructions within a main routine.

closed subroutine—1. A subroutine not stored in the main path of the routine. Such a subroutine is entered by a jump operation and provision is made to return control to the main routine at the end of the operation. The instructions related to the entry and reentry function constitute a linkage. 2. A subroutine that can be stored at one place and can be linked to one or more calling routines. Contrast with open subroutine.

CML—See current-mode logic.

CML architecture—CML is a logic form similar to ECL logic. Each CML array cell consists of two pairs of common-collector npn transistors, a current source with two active emitters, plus the necessary load resistors and crossunders. This architecture permits the implementation of two 2-input NOR gates using a single array cell. A 3-input NOR gate and a 2-input NAND gate also use a single cell while a D flip-flop can be integrated using only three array cells.

Their fast toggle rate and low power consumption make these arrays useful to designers of digital systems, especially in the fields of computers, telecommunications, measurement systems, scientific instrumentation, and military or aerospace systems. Some specific applications include disk and crt controllers, keyboard scanners, ALU accumulators, high-speed modems, signal processors, and interface logic.

CML gate—A CML gate can be compared to the familiar ECL (emitter-coupled logic) gate. The elements of a simple ECL gate when connected as an inverter are a current source and a nonsaturating signal amplifier. A simple CML gate also employs a current source and a nonsaturating signal amplifier. However, the ECL amplifier is constructed as a differential pair of transistors with the base of one transistor connected to the input and the base of the other connected to a reference voltage while the amplifier in the CML gate is not a differential pair but is a single transistor and a load resistor connected in series with the current source. Finally, the operation of an ECL gate involves steering the current either through the input transistor or through the transistor connected to the reference voltage. The operation of the CML gate involves switching the current source from ON to OFF as the input goes from HIGH to LOW.

In actual operation, the CML gate is easy to use. The NOR gate is the basic building block. A NOR gate is constructed by simply paralleling transistors and using a common load resistor and a current source. Thus, 2-, 3-, and 4-input NOR gates may be implemented.

CMOS — Abbreviation for complementary metal-oxide-semiconductor. CMOS technology uses both p- and n-channel devices on the same silicon substrate. Basic CMOS construction uses n- and p-channel devices connected in series. Only one device is turned on at one time, keeping power dissipation low. Switching of devices through the active region and the charging and discharging of capacitance are the main causes of dissipation. Major advantages are (1) low power dissipation, (2) good noise immunity, (3) high fanout to other CMOS devices, (4) an allowance for very wide power-supply variations, (5) shorter propagation delay than with p-MOS devices, and (6) full temperature range capabilities. Chip size, however, is larger than p-MOS chips. CMOS technology is used in battery-operated systems, aerospace logic systems, and in portable digital communications equipment. It is also used for components in digital instruments that operate in noisy environments. See also complementary MOS (CMOS).

CMOS applications — Because CMOS offers low power and low voltage operation, it has opened new markets for IC's in battery operated systems such as watches and portable equipment. Operation over wide supply and temperature ranges with good noise margin make it a natural for automotive electronics and machine or process control. Standard logic families with increasingly competitive prices and multiple sources are pushing CMOS into areas once dominated by TTL. A fertile area for growth is memories. Memory systems make good use of the low standby power, wide operating range, and moderate speed of CMOS. Communications applications include CMOS phase-locked-loop frequency-control circuits and single-chip two-to-eight tone encoders for telecommunications terminals.

CMOS circuits—Complementary MOS refers to a family of integrated circuits whose output structure consists of an n-type MOSFET and a p-type MOSFET connected in series. The term complementary is used since the n-

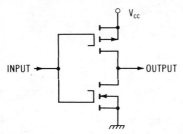

CMOS circuits (CMOS inverter).

and p-type MOSFETs are complements of each other.

CMOS contamination — Linear and CMOS ICs are subject to higher yield shrinkages than standard bipolar digital ICs. Contamination and mask registration problems are far more critical, and moisture is an important influence. Water is the vehicle that makes ions form, makes them mobile, and then puts them where they'll do the damage. Water and ions create contamination problems for the devices with the smallest geometries and the most sensitive parameters.

CMOS converters — Although bipolar technology has the advantage in speed and process versatility, CMOS has the advantage of small device structure, low-power consumption, and high packing density. Because CMOS switches are bilateral, CMOS DACs can handle multiplying functions. Both digital and analog functions can be placed together on the same chip, making CMOS a good medium for a/d and d/a converters. The CMOS parts are usually much less expensive than comparable bipolar devices.

CMOS devices—A few CMOS devices, such as bidirectional analog switches, exploit the unique features of CMOS technology; some take advantage of the smaller device size and higher potential packing density to achieve true LSI complexity, but most of the available CMOS elements today are of SSI and MSI complexity and perform logic functions that have been available in DTL or TTL for many years. Therefore, it is both helpful and practical to compare the performance of CMOS with that of the more familiar DTL/TTL. Numerous CMOS circuits are pinout identical to their TTL counterparts; others are functionally identical only. Still others are similar, but in most cases, offer added features. The CMOS family uses isoplanar technology to achieve superior electrical performance. Most of these devices are functional equivalents and pin-for-pin replacements of other circuit series; some are equivalent to TTL circuits and some are proprietary logic designs.

CMOS ion implantation — One of the most significant contributions made by ion-implant technology in recent years is in the manufacture of CMOS circuits that operate from a 1.5-V power supply. Such CMOS circuits could never have been economically made with standard diffusion techniques. CMOS circuits employ p- and n-channel enhancement-mode devices on the same chip. The p-channel devices are formed in the conventional manner on an n-type substrate. The n-channel devices are built in shallow, low-concentration, accurately doped, p-type mesas formed in the n-substrate. The threshold of the n-channel device is set primarily by the concentration of the p-dopant in the mesa. With conventional diffusion techniques, this concentration is difficult to control and the yield is low. Ion implantation is a more precise method of forming these p-mesas, and it permits accurate and reproducible n-channel threshold voltages. If an additional implant operation is used, the threshold voltages of p-channel devices can also be shifted to match those of the n-channel.

CMOS isoplanar C technology — One CMOS logic family uses isoplanar C technology for high performance. This technology combines local oxidation-isolation techniques with silicon-gate technology to achieve an approximate 35% savings in area. Operating speeds are increased due to the self-alignment of the silicon gate and reduced sidewall capacitance. Conventional CMOS circuits are fabricated on an n-type substrate transistor. The p-type substrate required for complementary n-channel MOS is obtained by diffusing a lightly doped p-region into the n-type substrate. Conventional CMOS fabrication requires more chip area and has slower circuit speeds than isoplanar C CMOS.

This is a result of the n- or p-channel stop which surrounds the p- or n-channels, respectively, in CMOS. Silicon-gate CMOS has a negligible reduction in area, though transient performance is improved.

CMOS memory evolution — The evolution of memory capability has always been governed by three principal factors: speed, power, and economics. If the user needs high speed, he pays for it in increased power dissipation and higher component cost. Much of the increased cost is package related. A ceramic or cerdip package can dissipate more heat for a given package size than plastic, but its cost is four times that of plastic. By contrast, CMOS allows a given function to be implemented such that it achieves the same performance as NMOS with regard to speed, but with greatly reduced power dissipation. For large fast memories, this can mean the difference between using a low-cost plastic package or a more expensive cerdip.

CMOS noise immunity — One of the most advertised and, also, most misunderstood CMOS features is noise immunity. The input threshold of a CMOS gate is approximately 50% of the supply voltage, and the voltage transfer curve is almost ideal. As a result, CMOS can claim very good voltage noise immunity — typically, 40% of the supply voltage, i.e., 2 V in a 5-V system and 4 V in a 10-V system. Since CMOS output impedance, output voltage, and input threshold are symmetrical with respect to the supply voltage, the LOW- and HIGH-level noise immunities are practically equal. Moreover, the inherent CMOS delays act as a noise filter; 10 ns spikes tend to disappear in a chain of CMOS gates, but are amplified in a chain of TTL gates. Because of these features, CMOS is very popular with designers of industrial control equipment that must operate in an electrically and electromagnetically "polluted" environment.

Unfortunately, these impressive noise margin specifications disregard one important fact, the output impedance of CMOS is 10 to 100 times higher than that of TTL. CMOS interconnections are, therefore, less "stiff" and much more susceptible to capacitively coupled noise. In terms of such current-injected crosstalk from high-noise voltages through small coupling capacitances, CMOS has about six times less noise margin than TTL. The nearly ideal transfer characteristic and the slow response of CMOS circuits make them insensitive to low-voltage magnetically coupled noise. The high output impedance, however, results in a poor rejection of capacitively coupled noise. CMOS appears to be the ultimate answer to power-supply costs and noise immunity. When operated with a 10-V supply, it has a worst-case noise immunity of 3 V. Even when operated at 5 V, ac and dc noise immunities are superior to those of any other logic.

CMOS-on-sapphire process — In the complementary - MOS - on - sapphire process, silicon islands are first defined photolithographically on the sapphire wafers and are then etched. The islands are exposed to radiation from an excimer laser operating at a 2490-Å wavelength with an energy density in the range of 0.5 to 1 joule per square centimeter. The islands are ion-implanted with gate oxidation; polysilicon deposition, contact, and metalization steps then follow. Although more expensive than normal CMOS, CMOS/SOS offers many performance advantages. The insulating substrate reduces device capacitances in the circuit and, thus, permits higher operating frequencies at reduced power consumption.

CMOS power — CMOS is virtually immune to noise, runs off almost any power supply, and is an extremely low-power circuit technique. In the off state, CMOS draws zero power, and even when operating at moderate speeds, an entire 100-gate logic array will typically draw less than 0.1 milliwatt. The low power of CMOS follows from its basic inverter configuration, with n- and p-channel transistors connected in parallel. When one device is on, the other is off, and the net quiescent current is simply the leakage current of the off device — less than 1 nanoampere, in modern MOS processing. But even when operating, both transistors are only partially on for only a fraction of the operating interval, so that the current drawn is still in the microampere region. At moderate speeds, in the 10-

to 11-kilohertz range, power dissipation is less than a microwatt per gate. The power dissipation does rise at higher frequencies, however, so that at TTL speeds, metal-gate CMOS structures may dissipate quite high values for each gate. Also, unlike every other logic family, CMOS circuits do not need expensive close tolerance power supplies or expensive on-card regulation. Because an inverter configuration is so insensitive to voltage variations, the circuits function off anything from 3 to 15 volts. The low power and regulation requirements allow power-supply costs to be cut significantly.

CMOS power requirements—CMOS requires only a single power supply, which may be a nonregulated battery. In general, CMOS is a very forgiving process for digital applications. While CMOS gates in the quiescent state draw negligible power, they can switch at respectable speeds which satisfy numerous applications. Moreover, the power-supply voltage can vary, and signals can get noisy, but the complementary structure of CMOS is conveniently insensitive to such variations. Circuit and system design is relatively straightforward, as there is a direct correlation between breadboard prototype and final LSI circuit performance. -

CMOS product evolution — The well-known advantages of CMOS technology are what have offset its higher manufacturing costs and increased "silicon real estate" requirements. Very low power dissipation and an ability to operate from low supply voltages led to its rapid usage in timepiece applications, where it remains as the dominant technology today. As the technology matured through the early 1970s, several general-purpose logic families evolved. Here, a wide supply-voltage range, high-noise immunity, and temperature independence made CMOS a natural choice for industrial logic design. Various families prevalent in the market have found wide acceptance in the industrial and automotive markets, and the expansion of these lines through the addition of complex medium-scale integration (MSI) and large-scale integration (LSI) functions insure their continued popularity. The mid-seventies saw a rapid growth in the consumer segment of the electronics market, with demand particularly heavy for hand-held calculators, battery-operated toys, and personal communications products. A plethora of special function CMOS LSI devices was developed for this market. A major outgrowth of these developments was the CMOS microprocessor, and with this advancement came the need for high-density CMOS-compatible memory.

CMOS propagation delay — Compared to TTL, all CMOS devices are slow and very sensitive to capacitive loading. One family uses both advanced processing (isoplanar) and improved circuit design (buffered gates) to achieve propagation delays and output rise times that are superior to any other junction-isolated CMOS design. (Silicon-on-sapphire can achieve similar performance but at a substantial cost penalty.) Isoplanar processing (CMOS) achieves lower parasitic capacitances which reduce the on-chip delay and increase the maximum toggle frequency of flip-flops, registers, and counters. Buffering all outputs, even on gates, results in lower output impedance and, thus, reduces the effect of capacitive loading. Propagation delay is affected by three parameters: capacitive loading, supply voltage, and temperature.

Propagation delay is a function of ambient temperature. The temperature dependence of CMOS is much simpler than with TTL devices, where three factors contribute—increase of beta with temperature, increase of resistor value with temperature, and decrease of junction forward-voltage drop with increasing temperature. In CMOS, essentially only the carrier mobility changes, thus increasing the impedance and, hence, the delay with temperature. For some devices, this temperature dependence is less than 0.3% per °C, or practically linear over the full temperature range. Note that the commercial temperature range is −40 to +85 °C, rather than the usual 0 to +75 °C.

CMOS technology—CMOS technology, hailed as the technology of the future because of its extremely low power requirements and packing density, had by the end of 1980 yet to fulfill that promise. The technology was still more expensive than NMOS or PMOS techniques because of the additional production steps required and because the final chip area is larger than that of comparable NMOS or PMOS designs. However, closed-loop CMOS eliminates the isolation wells around the device, thus permitting almost a doubling of density by permitting devices to be placed closer together. In addition, tighter lithography rules and better optical equipment permit circuit designers to obtain performance close to that of current NMOS while retaining the advantages of CMOS. Complementary MOS digital-logic building blocks of SSI and MSI complexity have been considered the ideal logic family. They are rapidly gaining popularity as more and more manufacturers introduce increasing numbers of parts at reasonable prices. Originally designed for aerospace applications, CMOS now finds its way into portable instruments, industrial and medical electronics, automotive applications, and computer peripherals, besides dominating the electronic watch market.

COBOL — Abbreviation for Common Business Oriented Language. 1. A data-processing language that makes use of English language statements. 2. Pertaining to a computer program which translates a COBOL language program into a machine language program.

CODASYL — Abbreviation for Conference On DAta SYstems Languages. The conference which developed the COBOL language.

code—1. A system of characters and rules for representing information. 2. Relates to transformations or representations of information in different forms according to a preassigned convention. 3. Digital codes may represent numbers, letters of the alphabet, control signals, and the like, as a group of discrete bits rather than as a continuous signal.

code, C—A code written in C, a structured high-level programming language. C can manipulate computer hardware in the same direct manner that assembly code does, making it especially useful for programming small computers. At the same time, C offers portability and productivity advantages.

codec—Codec is a short term for mi-

croelectronic coder-decoder. Codec units provide the essential translation between analog voice signals and the digital pulse-code modulation representation used in most advanced PABX equipment and short-haul telecommunications carrier gear. Codec devices are essentially a/d and d/a converters and are necessary to interface voice-telephone circuits with time-division multiplex systems.

codec designs — Multiline, or shared, codec devices can encode/decode several voice channels in a multiplexed transmission line in the allowed 125 microsecond time frame. In the same time frame, single-line codec units can encode or decode only one voice channel. However, multiline devices require a filter and a 2- to 4- wire converter on each line. Codec units and filters are being combined almost routinely on one chip. One such single-chip filter/codec unit is being produced in silicon-gate CMOS, a technology that offers density, fast logic, and low power for the chip's analog and digital circuits. As the filtering is digital, the chip is partitioned more toward digital logic than toward analog circuitry.

One type codec device contains all the elements for converting one channel of voice input to standard 8-bit pulse code modulation (PCM) and, then, back to voice. It has a companded d/a converter and a successive-approximation register that

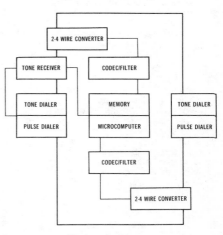

Codec designs.

makes it possible for the converter to perform the a/d encode function. Instead of two on-chip converters, a 2-chip codec shares a single d/a converter between the code and decode functions. Since the a/d conversion always takes longer, it is continuous until d/a conversion is necessary. Then an interrupt takes place, and the a/d information is stored in memory until the d/a conversion is accomplished. The use of separate chips (an encoder/filters chip and a decoder/filters chip) is said to eliminate any possibility of crosstalk between transmit and receive PCM channels.

code conversion—A process for changing the bit grouping for a character in one code into the corresponding bit grouping for a character in a second code.

code, reentrant — A code executed simultaneously by more than one software module, each of which must maintain its own data area. If one software module is interrupted while executing reentrant code, the interrupt service may execute the reentrant code, even though the first module has not been completely executed.

codes—1. A set of unambiguous rules specifying the way in which data may be represented, e.g., the set of correspondences in the Standard Code for Information Interchange. 2. In data communications, a system of rules and conventions according to which the signals representing data can be formed, transmitted, received, and processed. 3. In data processing, a method used to represent data or a computer program in a symbolic form that can be accepted by a data processor.

codes, mnemonic operation — 1. The writing of operation codes in a symbolic notation that is easier to remember than the actual operation codes of the machine. This code must be converted to actual operation codes before execution, which is done as part of any assembly, interpretive, or compiling routine. 2. An instruction code using conventional abbreviations instead of numeric codes in order to facilitate easy recognition. Examples: MLT for multiply and SUB for subtract.

code (to)—Refers to an action to originate, structure, or devise a program. "To code" most often concerns the analysis of the problem, preparation of the flowchart, designing and testing a set of developing subroutines, and the specification of the input and output commands and formats.

coding — The process of representing different characters within a computer. Also, the converting of program flowcharts into a particular computer language.

coding, BCD—Refers to a system of representing decimal equivalents with a series of four binary digits.

coding, skeletal — Sets of instructions in which some addresses and other parts remain undetermined.

coding tools—The basic tools available to simplify the designer's tasks in microcomputer design and program coding include assemblers, editors, loaders, compilers, and microprogramming. In addition, hardware or software simulators are available for program testing and error locating.

COGO (COordinate GeOmetry)—A language useful for solving coordinate geometry problems in civil engineering. Can be used as geometrically oriented urban data-management systems under ICES.

coincidence AND signal—A signal circuit with two or more input wires in which the output wire gives a signal, if and only if, all input wires receive coincident signals.

coincidence circuit — A circuit which produces a specified output pulse only when a specified number (two or more) or combination of input terminals receives pulses within a specified time interval.

collector diffusion isolation — In conventional processing, much of the silicon area is consumed by the isolation diffusion which separates transistors, resistors, and diodes from one another. This isolation technique ensures that, under all biasing conditions, there will be at least one reversed-biased diode preventing current flow either into the substrate or to other devices on the same chip. The area consumed by this diffusion is inherently large and is increased further due to mask registration tolerances and the sideways drift of the diffused dopants. While modern bipolar processes use thinner epitaxial layers and shallower diffusions, the isolation diffusion is still the limiting factor in device sizes and packing density.

COM—Abbreviation for computer output microfilm. Refers to outputting computer information onto microfilm through a COM printer.

combinational logic—Refers to various circuit arrangements designed so that the output state is determined by the present state of the input. Also referred to as sequential logic.

combined symbol matching—Abbreviated CSM, this is a dual-mode encoding system for optical character recognition. It is based on the detection of recurrent patterns (for example, alphanumeric characters) in the document being transmitted. This encoding technique has been compared to both symbol matching and facsimile operational modes. In a special test of 1000 samples with identical sets of symbols, CSM algorithms rejected all damaged characters and no mismatches were reported for this bandwidth compression technique.

COM images—Computer output microfilm imagery can be alphanumeric characters, graphical line drawings, pictures, or digital encoding marks. The output can be in black and white or full color. This makes possible the generation of graphs, Pert charts, block diagrams, and engineering drawings. Audio-visual slides can be produced from computer-created designs. Movies can be produced using 35-mm sprocketed film. Specialty recording includes additive retrieval codes and synthetic holograms. Actually, any image that can be created by a computer and shown on a display screen can be recorded on microfilm or added to noncomputer-generated information on film.

COM indexing—The means by which the information on a microfiche is retrieved. There are several indexing techniques available today. These include corner indexing, column indexing, master-file indexing, and cross-reference indexing.

command—1. For microprocessors, an electronic pulse, signal, or set of signals to start, stop, or continue some operation. It is incorrect to use command as a synonym for instruction. 2. The portion of an instruction word which specifies the operation to be performed.

command, channel—An instruction that directs a channel, control unit, or device to perform an operation or set of operations.

command file processor—This permits the user to enter any series of valid system commands as an editor-compatible file. This file may be edited as any other file. When this file is invoked, it becomes the user's own higher-level operating system program. One type of command file processor includes the ability to pass up to 10 parameters and allows the display of user messages. Therefore, a command file could: request a pair of file names, call the editor, set up one of the files as the destination file, set up the other file as the source file, load from the source file, allow the user to edit from the keyboard, copy the edit buffer to the destination file, repeat until the file has been edited end to end, exchange the file names, assemble the modified file, link the relocatable file to other files, call the debugger, load the object file, and wait for the user to debug the program. All this can be done with a single command to invoke the command file.

COM/microfiche software—Microfiche conversion can be accomplished through the use of parameter tables accessed by vendor-supplied software. Thus, an application program can be converted from paper output to microfiche output by simple parameter table values which define the format of the output report. No logic changes are required to the operational application program. Current microfiche software can be divided into six categories:
1. Conversion modules that use the parameter table to drive the COM recorder.
2. Modules that create or modify parameter tables.
3. Driver modules that interpret input file formats.
4. Utility programs.
5. Software debugging aids.
6. Hardware diagnostics.

common — An area of memory maintained for the purpose of passing data or parameters between programs.

common business-oriented language (COBOL) — A specific language by which business data-processing procedures may be precisely described in a standard form. The language is intended not only as a means for directly presenting any business program to any suitable computer, for which a compiler exists, but also as a means of communicating such procedures among individuals.

common-mode interface — A specific type of interference that appears between measuring circuit terminals and ground.

common-mode output voltage (V_{oc})— Two definitions are in common usage for this term:

1. The average of the voltage at two output terminals of a circuit.
2. The ac voltage between two output terminals (or the output terminal and ground for circuits with one output) when ac signals of identical phase and amplitude are applied to the input terminals.

common-mode range — That range of total input voltage over which specified common-mode rejection is maintained.

common-mode rejection—The ability of a device to reject the effect of voltage applied to both input terminals simultaneously.

common-mode rejection ratio—The ratio of the differential voltage amplification to the common-mode voltage amplification.

common-mode rejection voltage—The maximum sinusoidal voltage at a given frequency that can be applied *simultaneously* to both inputs with respect to output ground and still not produce an error signal in the system output. In optocouplers, the value of this voltage is very high at low frequencies and decreases with increasing frequency until it reaches a minimum. The effect is caused by the effective intercircuit capacitance of the emitter and detector chips, and the detector gain and bandwidth.

common-mode voltage — An undesirable signal picked up in a transmission line by both wires making up the circuit, to an equal degree, with respect to an arbitrary "ground."

common-mode voltage amplification— The ratio of the change in voltage at the output terminal, with respect to ground (or the change in voltage between the output terminals), to the change in the common-mode input voltage with the differential input voltage held constant.

common software — Programs or routines which usually have common and multiple applications for many systems; i.e., report generators, sort routines, and conversion programs which can be used for several routines in languages common to many computers.

Comm-Stor II — This communications storage unit is a versatile single- or dual-drive diskette system used for storage of messages received on line or prepared locally for transmission. It provides three high-speed ports with the standard RS-232 interface for direct connection with a terminal, a printer, and a data set. It is compatible with the Bell System 43 Teleprinter and DATASPEED 40/2 terminal, and it can be used in either multipoint private line or switched network applications.

communicating word processors (CWP)—These devices are special desktop-type computers that have been combined with copiers and communications capabilities. Used with or without optical fiber networks, these word processors allow desk-to-desk and intra- or inter-company communications at speeds of seconds per page. The output can be printed out by another desktop CWP. They could possibly replace the office electric typewriter.

communication control character—Refers to a specific character which designates the operation to be performed by some peripheral device. As with other characters, it is represented by a pattern of printed binary digits or holes in tapes or cards. Its execution usually causes control changes on printers; for example, back space, skip line, or rewind on tapes.

communication interface circuit — A communications interface circuit, USART is a peripheral device programmed by the CPU to operate using virtually any serial data-transmission technique currently in use. It will typically have a speed of 4 megabits per second for synchronous operation and 250 kilobits per second for asynchronous operation. USART is the abbreviation for Universal Synchronous/Asynchronous Receiver/Transmitter.

communication, real-time processing —A real-time system is a combined data-processing and communications system which involves the direct communication of transaction data between remote locations and a central computer, via communication lines, and allows the data to be processed while the transaction is actually taking place. A real-time system may be thought of as a communications-oriented data-processing system which is capable of performing batch-processing functions while concurrently processing inquiries or messages and generating responses in a time interval directly related to the operational requirements of the system.

communications control device—Data devices that can be attached directly to the system channel via a control unit that is designed to perform character assembly and transmission control. The control unit may be either the data-adapter unit or the transmission control.

communications, computer—Generally refers to the communication between computers or between computer terminals, and the use of computers to manage transmission and/or switching media.

communications, development module —The typical development module is designed to provide the user with an easy access to all circuitry, and, thus, is external to the actual microcomputer system. It connects to any microcomputer system with an RS-232C interface cable (included). The "module" is placed in the serial communications link between the system console device (crt) and the serial port of the computer system. This method of connection enables software to be transferred between the module and the system without requiring a special interface in the specific host. Software is transferred to the module using the LOAD command and taken from the module using the SEND command. These commands are provided by the host "software development package."

communications executive—Similar to the input/output executive, the communications executive provides the necessary handlers and protocol management for various communications line disciplines and terminal types.

communications monitor — Communications monitors are computer operating systems specifically designed for handling communications. Their functions essentially parallel those of a local-mode operating system except that lines, rather than devices, are the managed entities. Users must examine the special tasks demanded of communications monitors, the ways they handle these tasks, and the manner in which they interact with both higher (network) level and lower (device) level control software.

communication statements—Communication statements provide the mechanism for main program to subprogram linkage. They provide the means by which subprograms are called from and returned to memory. There are many kinds of communication statements. Some examples are the Procedure Call Statement, the Declaration Statement, and the Return Statement.

A Procedure Call Statement's typical use is to transfer control from a calling program to the called subprogram. There is no single procedure call statement. Any procedure name which has been defined as such may be coded as a valid statement. Declaration Statements describe and define the data, constants, and variables in a program or subprogram. Three sample Declaration Statements are the Constant Statement, the Scalar Statement, and the Result Statement. A Return Statement is used to transfer control from a called subprogram to a calling program.

communications systems, data — Refers to a specialized area of data processing involving terminal devices and special interfacing equipment. Data communications is an advancement over conventional teletypewriter transmission. Much data communications is carried over ordinary telephone lines, but often it requires specially conditioned leased lines where, in effect, several telephone lines are linked "side by side" to provide the required wide carrier bandwidth necessary to carry a heavy and broad flow of information traffic. This is in contrast to voice-grade communication for which narrower carrier bandwidths are assigned.

communications word—In computing, an ordered set of characters that is the normal "unit" in which information may be stored, transmitted, or operated upon within a computer.

commutator pulse—A pulse developed at a particular instant in time relative to a specific reference pulse, which may be a major or minor cycle pulse. A pulse that is often used to mark, clock, or control a particular binary digit position in a computer word.

compaction—Refers to a series of techniques used for the reduction of space, bandwidth, cost, transmission, generating time, and the storage of data. These techniques are designed to eliminate repetition, remove irrelevances, and employ special coding techniques.

companding converter — An a/d and d/a converter which employs a logarithmic transfer function to expand and then compress the analog signal range. Generally used in voice communications.

compare data—Any form of display in which a captured data record is manipulated with the data set in an auxiliary memory in such a way as to make differences conspicuous.

compatibility — The ability of various specified units to replace one another, with little or no reduction in capability.

compatibility, firmware—Compatibility among data-processing systems to facilitate the execution or conversion of existing programs, data interchange, and the implementation of compilers having equivalent execution-time semantics. Compatibility can be achieved via the basic hardware design or by (software or firmware) interpretation. Firmware, or microprogramming, has attracted attention in this context as promising hardware-like compatibility using software-like implementation techniques.

compatibility, hardware—The characteristic of computers by which one computer may accept and process data prepared by another computer without conversion or code modification.

compatibility, instruction — The characteristic of an instruction that allows it to be executed on more than one class of computer.

compatibility, microprocessor — The electrical compatibility of microprocessors with other logic circuitry is required in most applications. Most microprocessors offer some degree of TTL compatibility; however, numerous variations in input/output logic levels are common—even on one chip. An MOS-to-TTL conversion is "delicate" at best for many manufacturers.

compilation time — The time during which a source language is compiled (translated) as opposed to the time during which the program is actually being run (execution time).

compile, machine language — To prepare a machine language program from a computer program written in another programming language, by making use of the overall logic structure of the program or by generating more than one machine instruction for each symbolic statement, or both, as well as performing the function of an assembler.

compiler—An automatic computer coding system which generates and assembles a program from instructions that are written by a programmer or which are prepared by equipment manufacturers or software companies. Compilers allow programs to be written in a high-level language. High-level language programs are compact, easy to read, and much easier to write. Compilers eliminate the need to write detailed codes to control loops, to access complex data structures, or to program formulas and functions. Thus, with programming details lessened, errors are reduced.

compiler languages — High-level languages that are sometimes supplied with the computer by the computer manufacturer. These compiler-level languages include APL, ALGOL, COBOL, Pascal, C, PL/M, PL-1, BASIC, and FORTRAN. Using a compiler language, the same operation can be coded in the same way regardless of computer used; the compiler performs the binary conversion for a particular machine. The programmer will find few differences in the FORTRAN language, for example, among different computers, whereas assembly languages will vary substantially in their differences.

compilers—All higher-level languages require compilers or compiler programs to translate their commands and instructions into machine code before microcomputers can begin operations with such nonmachine language programs. Once users have written a source program in a higher level language, a special program called a Compiler converts the program to a sequence of machine instructions which becomes the binary object program. The compiler breaks out statements using format identifiers and delimiters and builds up executable binary code sequences from standard modules. Compilers are further away from machine language than assemblers are (often several machine instructions for every compiler language command statement). However, they perform many services, and, to a greater or lesser extent, take over the responsibilities of machine-code generation. The compiler takes care of much of the programmer's decision making such as: choosing register assignments, assigning memory areas to programs and subroutines, linking labels in one program with addresses in another program. If users were to program in a compiler language, the compiler will, for all practical purposes, become the computer; users could program for years and never know or care how many registers the computer has, or what the instruction set is; they need not even be aware that the compiler has a host computer.

compiler vs. interpreter—Compilers require a completely defined source code, but they produce programs that are relatively fast. Interpreters, on the other hand, need only have available the actual or condensed source code. In many applications, the combined size of an interpreter and its source code will be much smaller than the code produced by a compiler from the same language.

compiling programs — A unique, but basic, translating program designed to transform, to assemble, or to structure programs, expressed in other languages, into same or equivalent programs that are expressed in terms of the particular computer language for which a particular machine was designed. Compiling programs or compilers most often include assemblers (or programs) as well as diagnostic and generating programs within them. The computer that is using the compiling program or compiler is called the source or compiling computer, and the computer in which the program is used, or is to be used, is called the object or target computer. The occasion, or run of compilation or translation, is called the compiling phase while the use of the newly translated program is called the run. The time necessary to translate is called the compile duration.

compiling routine—A routine that enables a computer to construct a program to solve a problem.

complement—A quantity expressed to the base n, which is derived from a given quantity by a particular rule and which is frequently used to represent the negative of the given quantity.

complementary metal-oxide semiconductors—Pertains to n- and p-channel enhancement-mode devices that are fabricated on a silicon chip and connected into complementary push-pull digital circuits. This process, using n- and p-channel MOS transistors in combination, tends to reduce the slow gate-setting time of n- and p-channel MOS devices. This structure is referred to as a complementary metal-oxide semiconductor or CMOS. These circuits feature low quiescent power dissipation and potentially high speeds, but they are more complex than circuits in which only one channel type (generally p channel) is used. CMOS has some disadvantages. Even though it solves the problem of slow switching time, CMOS retains the second disadvantage of n- and p-channel MOS—the parasitic capacitance caused by a layer of silicon dioxide separating a metal conductor from a doped substrate. There also is the possibility of parasitic conduction between a p channel and a p substrate. To prevent such an undesirable side effect, isolation barriers, referred to as channel stops, or guard rings, must be provided.

complementary MOS (CMOS) — This approach combines both n- and p-channel transistors on the same chip by diffusing or implanting isolated doped substrate regions for the n-channel transistors. Since most CMOS diffused interconnections are similar to conventional p-channel circuits, CMOS has less exposure to leakage-current variation than straight n-channel circuits. However, because extra diffusion is required for the n-channel substrates as well as extra source/drain diffusion, CMOS is more expensive to manufacture than either n- or p-channel devices. Further, the special substrate region takes up considerable space, giving CMOS lower packing density than either n- or p-channel units. The major CMOS advantage is that since transistors of both polarities are available, one can design circuits with very low quiescent power. Speed and transient power (the major element of power when dynamic circuits are being operated a full repetition rate) are similar for both CMOS and n-channel circuits. *See also* CMOS.

complementary operations — In any Boolean operation, a complementary operation is the negation of the result of the first or original operation. In computing, it is represented when 0 (zero) is substituted for a 1 and 1 is substituted for a 0 in the tabulated values for the first or original operation.

complementary operator — The logic operator whose result is the NOT of a given logic operator, i.e., NOR or NAND.

complementary SCR (CSCR)—A silicon-controlled rectifier in which control current flows from anode to gate rather than from gate to cathode.

complementing — A way of producing the negative of a number by obtaining its complement.

complete carry — In parallel addition, this is a technique in which all of the carries are allowed to propagate.

complete operation — Refers to those operations which include (1) obtaining all operands from storage, (2) performing the operation, (3) returning resulting operands to storage, and (4) obtaining the next instruction.

complex bipolar—To produce memories significantly faster than standard TTL or ECL, a method called "complex bipolar" must be used. This involves an extra diffusion (to produce such things as small resistors, and low base and collector resistance

in the transistors) and two layers of aluminum interconnection (to reduce interconnection resistance). These approaches produce extremely fast memories, but at considerably higher manufacturing cost. However, for many applications that need ultimate performance, few other technologies can do the job. Since these applications are becoming more important, complex bipolar will remain a significant memory technology. Also, since speed is the prime requirement, the ECL circuit form is used. These ECL memory components can easily be made TTL compatible.

component—One of the essential functional parts of a subsystem or equipment, possibly a self-contained element, or a combination of parts, assemblies, attachments, or accessories.

component density—The volume of a circuit assembly divided by the total number of discrete circuit components utilized, usually expressed in components per cubic inch.

component error — Concerns various errors related to the operational amplifier but specifically its components, as the input and feedback impedances.

component stress—The particular factors of usage or test, such as voltage, power, temperature, frequency, etc., which tend to affect the failure rate of component parts.

composite cable — A cable in which conductors of different guages or types are combined in one sheath.

composite conductor—Refers to those conductors in which strands of different metals are used in parallel.

composite filter—Concerns the combination of a number of filter sections, or half sections, all having the same cutoff frequencies and specified impedance levels.

composite video signal—The video signal of a crt, consisting of the picture signal, the blanking pulses, and the sync pulses.

compound logical element—Computer circuitry that provides an output from many inputs.

compressed video vs. facsimile—Compressed video has a distant relationship to facsimile in that both are systems for the transmission of images over telephone circuits. Facsimile is primarily characterized by relatively slow transmission of documents and photographs with high definition. Compressed video is faster, has lower definition, and is much more flexible in its image communication format. Facsimile operates with flat copy only, while the tv camera in the compressed video system can view subjects from microscopic to macroscopic, flat or three-dimensional, near or distant, and, if required, in color. At the receiving location, pictures can be rapidly displayed on one or many standard tv screens, with sizes ranging from a 5-inch desktop monitor to a large screen projection for group viewing. Compressed video consumes no paper as does facsimile, and is free of the mechanical wear problems associated with facsimile. Applications of compressed video fall into four general categories: two-way communications, one-way communications, monitoring of remote scenes or areas, and the interconnection of tv signals to computers for image analysis.

computer-aided design (CAD)—Refers to the capability of a computer to be used for automated industrial, statistical, biological, and other types of design through the use of visual devices and graphics symbols.

computer, analog — A computer which represents variables by physical analogies. Thus, any computer which solves problems by translating physical conditions such as flow, temperature, pressure, angular position, or voltage into related mechanical or electrical equivalent circuits as an analog for the physical phenomenon being investigated. In general, it is a computer which uses an analog quantity for each variable and produces analog values as output. Thus, an analog computer measures continuously whereas a digital computer counts discretely. Related to machine data processing.

computer-assisted instruction (CAI)— Refers to microcomputer applications in which a computing system is used to assist in the instruction of students. The application usually involves a dialog between the student and a computer program which informs him of his mistakes as he makes them.

computer, asynchronous — Refers to those types of microcomputers in which the performance of each operation starts either as a result of a signal that the previous operation has been completed, or that the parts of the microcomputer required for the next operation are now available. Contrasted with computer, synchronous.

computer code—The code by which data are represented within a microcomputer system; for example, a binary-coded decimal code. Also referred to as machine language.

computer communications system — Generally considered to be a microcomputer system that handles online, real-time applications. A typical communications system would consist of the following: a teletypewriter, a visual display, or possibly, an audio answer-back device connected to an ordinary telephone line through a communication multiplexer. (That is a device which converts the keyed-in characters to electronic pulses for transmission over a telephone line or a microwave system.) An interface device in the computer center translates these pulses into binary code and delivers the character to computer storage. After receipt of the entire message, the central computer searches or stores the requested information and sends back the appropriate response. Important elements of any communications system are the modems (MODulator/DEModulator) which connect the communications multiplexer from the remote output to the interface device in the computer center. On the transmission end, the modulator converts the signals or pulses to the right codes and readies them for transmissions over a communication line. On the receiving end, a demodulator reconverts the signals for communication to the microcomputer via the computer interface device.

computer graphics—By harnessing the power of the computer to translate statistical printout into immediately meaningful graphs, charts, diagrams, maps, and renderings, computer graphics can provide overviews and visual aids that would take hours or even days to produce by hand. High-performance graphics are now easy to make, affordable, and highly versatile. Present-day graphics have revolutionized countless branches of science, industry, and education, and created whole new ones. High-quality graphics take the form of computer-display terminals. However, there are stand-alone graphic computers and plotters that draw directly onto paper or overhead projector film. There are also hard-copy units that reproduce on-screen graphics onto paper in seconds, and there are a variety of other capabilities that are built for specific needs.

computer graphics technology—Three different technologies are used in interactive computer graphics: storage tubes, random scan, and raster scan. Storage tubes are monochromatic; random-scan crt's can have limited color capabilities; raster-scan terminals can provide a full range of colors.

computer image processing—The objectives of computer-assisted image processing fall into three categories: the removal of known image degradations, a procedure known as "image restoration"; the exaggeration of obscure details, or "image enhancement"; and the location and mensuration of specific details, a process called "information extraction."

computer-independent language — A language designed for use in any microcomputer equipped with an appropriate compiler, and relatively independent of such characteristics as word size, code representations, etc.; i.e., COBOL, FORTRAN, RPG, etc., are computer-independent languages.

computerized numerical control (CNC) —A numerical control system for which a dedicated stored-program computer is used to perform some or all of the basic numerical control functions.

computer, large-scale — Large-scale computers provide, in conjunction with high-level languages and operating systems, extremely complex and powerful programmable logic in order to attack complex problems which require highly centralized computing power. Some examples are CDC 7600, CRAY L, AMDAHL 470, ILLIAC IV, and others. Some are HMS machines that operate at speeds of 100 million instructions per second.

computer network components—Three types of facilities, in addition to the host computer, are generally required to accomplish computer networking. These consist of (1) the user communication interface, (2) the communications subnetwork, and (3) facilities for the network control function.

computer-operated memory test system — Computer-operated test systems are designed to test semiconductor memories. They combine the reliability and productivity necessary for production testing with the versatility required for device characterization and evaluation. Typical units test both bipolar and MOS memories, both RAMs and ROMs. Generally, they can be configured with multiple test stations, each of which is under independent program control and which can perform both functional and dc parametric tests. Functional tests are performed at a programmable rate by a high-speed memory exerciser. The following are also under program control: the high and low levels of the address, clock, and data inputs to the memory under test, the levels against which device outputs are compared, the time at which output data is strobed, and the delay and width of the clock pulses. A precision dc measurement system provides the ability to measure voltages and currents with any combination of device terminals. These measurements can be made with the memory under test in a static condition or while it is being exercised at a programmed frequency. Some systems contain full provision for testing devices in conjunction with wafer probers, automatic handlers, and environmental chambers, without degradation of measurement performance.

computer power center (CPC)—One type of power device that has existed for only a few years is the computer power center (CPC). Instead of using rigid conduit or the "hard-wired" approach to energize the various machines in a computer room, the CPC requires only one connection to the main power source. The regulated power is then distributed to each machine or device in the computer room. Most small systems do not require such an elaborate power distribution system but for those that do, CPCs are getting more sophisticated, especially in power monitoring and crt displays. CPCs facilitate moving equipment around the computer room as well as moving an entire computer facility from one location to another. They also provide the computer with power regulation and protection from power disturbances.

computer run—1. Refers to the processing of a batch of transactions while under the control of one or more programs, and against all the files that are affected to produce the required output. 2. Performance of one routine, or several routines, automatically linked so that they form an operating unit, during which manual manipulations are not required of the computer operator.

computer, self-learning—Refers to processes by which computers modify programs according to their own memory or experience, i.e., changes of logic paths, parameter values. An example is a chess-playing computer. Also, in process-control, an analog or hybrid computer can alter its parameters by a continuous process, according to temperatures or other reports it receives.

computer stores—A fairly new form of merchandising operation that is an outgrowth of the computer explosion (revolution). These outlets can be started by either dealer discount arrangements or by a franchise arrangement. These stores are dedicated to the sale and use of computers, microcomputers, and their associated peripherals and software.

computer, synchronous — A computer in which all operations and events are controlled by equally spaced pulses from a clock. Contrasted with computer, asynchronous and clarified by frequency, clock.

computer systems—In a typical computer system, the "control section" includes the control logic and the instructions for decoding and executing the program stored in "memory." "Registers" provide the control section with temporary storage in the form of random-access memories (RAMs) and their associated functions. The arithmetic and logic unit (ALU) carries out the arithmetic and logic operations under the supervision of the control section. Input/output (I/O) ports provide access to the peripheral devices, such as the keyboard, the crt display terminal, the

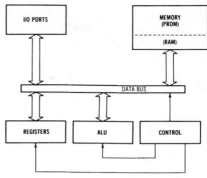

Computer systems.

information-storage "floppy disk," and the line printer.

computer systems, distributed — The arrangement of computers within an organization in such a way that the organization's computer-complex has many separate computing facilities, all working in a cooperative manner, rather than the conventional single computer at a single location. Versatility of a computer system is often increased if small computers, in geographically dispersed branches, are used for simple tasks and a powerful central computer is available for larger tasks. Frequently an organization's central files are stored at the central computing facility, with the geographically dispersed smaller computers calling on the central files when they need them. Such an arrangement lessens the load on the central computer and reduces both the volume and cost of data transmission.

computer, wired-program—The operations of such a computer are performed, or their sequence is controlled, by the placement and interconnection of wires, as on a plugboard.

computer word—Relates to that sequence of bits or characters that are treated as a unit and capable of being stored in one computer location. Synonymous with machine word.

COM recorders, on-line—On-line COM recorders are designed to eliminate the need of magnetic tape to store print data for later production of microfiche. Print data is transmitted directly over the I/O interface to the COM recorder which appears to the host system as an on-line peripheral. The microfiche conversion software may execute on the host computer, if a nonintelligent COM recorder is attached on-line. This allows application programmers to tailor microfiche output to their particular needs. The conversion software could also execute on the front-end minicomputer, if an intelligent COM recorder is used. The major benefit of this is off-loading the microfiche conversion processing from the host.

COM recorder types—There are essentially two types of COM recorders: nonintelligent and intelligent. Nonintelligent COM recorders require the use of host computer software to convert print files into COM-formatted types. These tapes contain COM control codes together with index and title pages, and can be processed off-line by the nonintelligent recorder to produce microfiche. Intelligent COM recorders have a minicomputer front-end to perform indexing and titling without the need of host computer software.

COMSAT—The Communications Satellite Corporation, known as COMSAT. It is a unique, privately owned U.S. communications carrier company operating under a mandate from the Congress of the United States. It was incorporated in early 1963 under the provisions of the Communications Satellite Act of 1962, which directed that: (1) A commercial communications satellite system be established as quickly and expeditiously as practicable, in conjunction and cooperation with other countries of the world; (2) The services of the system be made available to all countries of the world without discrimination; and (3) The benefits of the new technology be reflected in the quality and charges for such services.

concatenate — To link together; to chain; to unite in a series.

concatenated data set—Refers to various temporary data sets formed by uniting the content of several independent data sets in a specific sequence.

concurrent I/O — The concurrent I/O feature of some systems provides the capability for automatic block transfers between main memory and I/O controllers connected to the I/O interface. The concurrent mode transfer rate is a function of the firmware set used in the computer. Once started the transfers are fully automatic and proceed without program intervention. Concurrent I/O operations take priority over instruction execution and force a break in the execution of long instructions such as multiply, divide, and shifts to ensure that concurrent I/O servicing delays are not excessive. Concurrent I/O operations make use of pairs of address control words stored in dedicated main memory locations. One pair of address words is used by each controller. The control words, which contain the address of the current byte being transferred and the address of the last byte in the block, are initially set by the software program and thereafter are manipulated automatically by firmware for each byte transferred (some systems).

concurrent operating control—Operating systems provide the ability for several programs to share the computer at the same time. Concurrent operations include job processing while performing inquiry or peripheral utility operations, time sharing, and multiprogramming. For example, in the operation mode, a teleprocessing application servicing terminals can be under way concurrently with both stacked job batch processing and peripheral utility type operations.

concurrent operations—Refers to various methods in electronic data processing in which multiple instructions or the operations of different instructions are executed simultaneously. Concurrent operations refer to computers working as multiprocessors. This concept is one of the basic tenets of time-sharing, priority processing, etc.

conditional branch—An instruction that is interpreted as an unconditional transfer if a specified condition or set of conditions is satisfied. If the condition is not satisfied, the instruction causes the computer to proceed in its normal sequence of control. A conditional transfer also includes the testing of the condition.

conditional breakpoint instruction—A conditional jump instruction which, if some specified switch is set or a situation exists, will cause the computer to stop, after which either the routine may be continued as coded, or another jump may be forced.

conditional code — A term or label which is concerned with a limited group of program conditions, such as: borrow, overflow, carry, etc. These are all pertinent to the execution of instructions, and such codes are generally listed in a Condition Code Register.

conditional dump — *See* conditional branch.

conditional jump—1. An instruction to a computer which will cause the proper one of two (or more) addresses to be used in obtaining the next instruction, depending on some property of one or more numerical expressions of other conditions. Also referred to as conditional transfer of control. 2. A specific instruction which will basically depend upon the result of some arithmetical or logical operation, or upon the state of some switch or indicator, as to whether or not that instruction will cause a jump or skip to another preset instruction.

conditional stop instruction — An instruction that can cause a program to be halted if some given condition is discovered; i.e., the program may be required to stop if it finds that a console switch has been set by the operator.

conditional transfer — An instruction which, if a specified condition or set of conditions is satisfied, is interpreted as an unconditional transfer. If the condition is not satisfied, the instruction causes the computer to proceed in its normal sequence of control. A conditional transfer also includes the testing of the condition. Synonymous with conditional jump and conditional branch.

condition codes — Condition codes generally contain information on the result of the last CPU operation. The bits can be set as follows:

$Z = 1$, if the result were zero.
$N = 1$, if the result were negative.
$C = 1$, if the operation resulted in a carry from the MSB (most significant bit) or a 1 were shifted from LSB (least significant bit).
$V = 1$, if the operation resulted in an arithmetic overflow.

(The bits are set after execution of all arithmetic or logical single operand or double operand instructions.)

conditioning signal — To process the form or mode of a signal so as to make it intelligible to or compatible with a given device, including such manipulation as pulse shaping, pulse clipping, digitizing, and linearizing.

conductive elastomers — Conductive elastomeric materials are formed from a rubber that is made conductive by incorporating a metalized filler or carbon. Originally used for gasketing against electromagnetic and radio-frequency interference, recent large-scale production of digital watches has opened up a large new market for conductive elastomers as connectors for the liquid crystal readouts. As opposed to metals, the elastomers filled a need for a high-contact-density, shockproof, springy, reliable connector.

conductivity-connected charge-coupled device (C'D)—A charge-coupled device that uses doped regions between the potential wells and, hence, becomes a hybrid between a charge-coupled device and a bucket-brigade device.

conductor flat cable (d/c bus)—One standard type of cable consists of 50 wires and the desired number of connectors. This flat cable eliminates open wire problems, cross-connector shorts, and loose contacts. Each connector in the flat cable is constructed with alignment grooves to ensure proper positioning of the cable. Some manufacturers suggest a minimum space of one inch between the connectors.

confidence level—A degree of probability and/or of certainty that can be expressed as a percentage.

connectors, cable—Cable connectors can be grouped into eight general classifications according to the type cable they accommodate and their use; flat ribbon cable, flat mylar cable, flat coaxial cable, round coaxial cable, flat shielded cable, round cable, bus interconnection and termination, and miscellaneous connectors. Most of the connectors are general-purpose connectors; some, however, are specific-use connectors. These connectors are described relative to the specific use. The descriptions of some of the general-purpose connectors cite application examples. The cited examples are popular widely used applications, and are not intended to imply that a particular connector cannot be used with other equipment. A cable clamp and two eyelets are often supplied with each cable connector.

connect time—Refers to the amount of time that elapses while the user of a remote terminal is connected to a time-shared system. Connect time is usually measured by the duration between "sign-on" and "sign-off."

connect time, remote system—A measured amount of time that elapses while the user of a remote terminal is connected to a distributed system. Connect time and related costs concern transmission speed, amount of memory used, and terminal type.

console — 1. The unit of a computer where the control keys and certain special devices are located. This unit may contain the start key, stop key, power key, sense switches, etc., as well as lights which display the information located in certain registers. 2. A portion of the computer which may be used to control the machine manually, correct errors, determine the status of machine circuits, registers, and counters, determine the contents of storage, and manually revise the contents of storage.

console debugging — Some systems permit the programmer to debug at the machine console, or at a remote console, by slowly stepping the machine through each instruction and observing the contents of appropriate registers and memory locations.

console, designers — A typical front-panel designer's console provides an easy means of monitoring and controlling system operation, manually moving data to and from memory and input/output devices, setting hardware breakpoints, and executing or debugging programs.

consoles, crt — Cathode-ray tube (crt) display consoles have received much interest and attention, as a crt terminal overcomes most of the disadvantages of a typewriter console. Its display rate is very fast—thousands of characters per second. It is quiet. Its output is flexible, easily modified, and rearranged. The more sophisticated

forms of crt consoles have pictorial capabilities allowing line segments to be displayed. Pointing facilities, such as light pens, allow users to easily designate symbols or vectors of interest.

console, visual display—Consoles often contain as standard equipment, a visual display unit to enhance operator-system communications. The advantages of a visual display to the operator are obvious, and the possible display functions endless.

Constructs—Constructs is a computer-directed system that can produce detailed construction drawings by means of a computer and a plotter, but which allows humans to intervene conveniently when required. The system was designed by Meiscon Corporation, a subsidiary of Control Data Corporation, and is commercially available.

contact, bifurcated—Contacts used in printed circuits that have slotted flat springs which increase flexibility of the spring and which provide extra points of contact.

contact encoders — Contact encoders provide a means of translating the rotation of a shaft into a digital form that permits computer input in numerical control systems and for visual display.

contact float—Concerns the amount of "give," or movement, or side-play which a contact has within the insert cavity to thus allow self-alignment of mated contacts, i.e., easy insertion of the plug or other contact surface.

contacts, bump — Contacting pads which rise substantially above the surface level of the chip. The term is also applied to raised pads on the substrate which contact the flat land areas of the chip. Also called ball contacts, raised pads, pedestals.

contact sense module—In some systems refers to various devices which are designed to monitor and convert program-specified groups of field switch contacts into digital codes for input to the computer. Inputs are scanned by the computer at programmed intervals.

contact-separating force — Concerns exertion or force necessary to separate or remove pins from sockets.

contact-symbology diagram — Commonly referred to as a ladder diagram, it expresses the user-programmed logic of the controller. in relay-equivalent symbology.

content-addressable memory (CAM)— The unique characteristic of content-addressable memories as logic elements is that the location of a desired data pattern can be retrieved on command. CAMs also provide a normal read/write across method that allows programming or switching of the data base to be scanned. These features make CAMs ideal for quick data searches, correlation checks, and sorting by value or attribute. One specific application of fast CAMs is in large virtual memory systems. Another is in airline reservations systems where searches by attribute (freight number, destination, departure, credit card, etc.) comprise a very high percentage of the computing effort.

CAMs have found limited application due to low bit densities, high costs, and relatively low speeds. Most present CAM applications are either very cost insensitive or require only a few bits of content-addressable storage. CAMs are likely to remain much more expensive than R/W RAMs in the foreseeable future due to several factors. CAMs have a complex dual-accessing mechanism that consumes considerable array space which results in large die sizes. Second, a CAM bit/pin ratio is very low and cannot be increased without eliminating that one-line-per-matching-address output required for many applications. Therefore, large packages and high-pin counts are required and, again, high cost is the result.

content-addressed storage—A memory mechanism that interrogates the microcomputer memory for content rather than memory location. Normally, a microcomputer memory is accessed by address location, such as 07294, rather than by content, such as "Print Total Balance of I.M. Prince." Synonymous with associative storage.

contention—Refers to a method of line control in which the terminals request to transmit. If the channel in question is free, transmission goes ahead. If not, the terminal will have to wait until it becomes free. The queue of contention requests may be built up by the computer.

contingency interrupt — Refers to instances where a program is interrupted if any of the following events occur at the operator's console: the operator requests use of the keyboard to type in information; a character has been typed in or out; a type-in has been completed; or the operator requests a program stop. Contingency interrupts also occur if an arithmetic operation resulted in an overflow, an invalid operation code was specified, or the clock was addressed after clock power was removed.

continuous-data-stream mode — Continuous-data-stream mode refers to a mode of serial data transmission in which the word boundaries between consecutive transmissions are not defined by any type of synchronization periods. That is, the next consecutive word is transmitted immediately following the previous word. When no further data is to be transmitted, the serial data line goes to a logic high state until a new word is to be transmitted. Continuous data stream offers the advantage of a higher data rate than synchronized transmission schemes.

continuous simulation — The type of simulation which may be represented by continuous variables considered at regular intervals. The system is therefore suitable for representation by a set of differential equations. These may be further classified as linear or nonlinear. Example: missile flights, respiratory control system, etc. (Contrast with discrete simulation.)

contract programming—The hiring or contracting of a programmer/analyst or a consulting firm to custom design software and implement a system specifically for one particular business. This provides the advantages of a staff programmer/analyst without incurring the on-going overhead costs. However, the security of having a knowledgeable person on the staff to correct any problems that may arise is forfeited.

control—1. Those parts of a computer which carry out instructions in proper sequence, interpret instructions, and apply proper signals. 2. The one or more components in any mechanism that are responsible for interpreting and carrying out manually initiated directions. Sometimes, it is called manual control. 3. In some business applications, a mathematical check. 4. In programming, instructions which determine conditional jumps are often referred to as control instructions, and the time sequence for execution of instructions is called the flow of control.

control block — Refers to the circuitry that is designed to perform the control functions of the microcomputer CPU. It is designed to handle the decoding of microprogrammed instructions, to generate the internal control signals that perform the requested operations, and to carry out other basic operating functions.

control bus—One of several types of buses, the control bus generally conveys a mixture of signals designed to regulate system operations. These signals function much like "traffic" signals or commands. They may also originate in specific items of peripheral equipment, and are generally used to transfer to or receive signals from the CPU.

control card—A card containing the input data or parameters for a specific computer-program application of a general routine.

control, cascade—Refers to an automatic control system in which various control units are linked in sequence, each control unit regulating the operation of the next control unit in line.

control character — 1. A character whose occurrence in a particular context initiates, modifies, or stops a control function. A control character may be recorded for use in a subsequent action. A control character is not a graphic character, but may have a graphic representation in some circumstances. 2. A character whose occurrence starts, changes, or stops a process. 3. A character used to cause nonprinting functions, such as line feed and carriage return, to occur. 4. A character which controls an operation, such as recording, interpreting, transferring, transmitting, etc.

control circuits—Digital computer circuits that carry out instructions in proper sequence. They also interpret instructions and then apply the proper commands to the arithmetic element and other circuits in accordance with interpretation.

control, comparing—Comparing, as a control technique, permits data fields to be machine-checked against each other to prove the accuracy of machine, merging, coding, balancing, reproducing, gang punching, and record selection from magnetic drum, disk, and tape storage. In wired control-panel machines, this is accomplished with comparing magnets and, in a stored-program machine, it is accomplished with a compare instruction.

control console—The control console of an electronic data-processing system is designed to enable the operator to centrally control and monitor all processing functions. The panel is designed for efficient supervision and provides what is necessary for the operator, as well as the needs of the service engineers. However, some controls have been placed within individual components of the system. Thus, an electric typewriter provides direct communication with the processor memory and data can be entered into the memory through the typewriter keyboard. Also, the processor can transmit data to the typewriter for output through the typewriter printer.

control counter—A device that records the storage location of the instruction word, which is to be operated upon, following the instruction word in current use. The control counter may select storage location.

control data—One or more items of data which control the identification, selection, execution, or modification of another routine, record file, operation, data, value, etc.

control, dynamic — Operating a digital computer in such a manner that the computer can alter the instructions as the computation proceeds, or during the sequence in which the instructions are executed, or both.

control field—A constant location where control information is placed, usually in a sequence of similar items, in a computer.

control function—Refers to various actions that affect the recording, processing, transmission or interpretation of data, e.g., starting or stopping a process, carriage return, font change, rewind, and end of transmission. Synonymous with control operation.

control, input/output—Directs the interaction between the processing unit and the input/output devices.

control instructions—The instructions in this category are used to manipulate data within the main memory and the control memory, to prepare main-memory storage areas for the processing of data fields, and to control the sequential selection and interpretation of instructions in the stored program.

controller—1. An element or group of elements that takes data proportional to the difference between input and output of a device or system and converts this data into power that is used to restore agreement between input and output. 2. A module or specific device which operates automatically to regulate a controlled variable or system.

controller, bubble memory — A magnetic bubble memory controller is a high-level interface between the microprocessor and the bubble memory. The controller performs parallel-to-serial conversion from the microprocessor to the bubble memory, and serial-to-parallel conversion from the bubble memory to the microprocessor. The primary functions of the controller are to stop and start bubble movement, maintain page position, and raise or lower flags for such bubble memory functions as generate, swap, block replicate, and redundancy replicate. Control signals from the bubble memory controller are sent to a function timing generator—a monolithic IC that provides the precise timing signals necessary to operate the function driver, coil driver, and sense amplifier during each field cycle.

controller functions—The main function of a controller is to accept instructions from memory via the data bus, decode the instruction, and then provide the individual control signals to the CPU, memory, and I/O. These control signals are generated by combining the decoded instruction with a multiphase clock to provide a properly timed sequence of control words to the various system elements.

controller, program—The unit in a central processor that controls the execution of the computer instructions and their sequence of operations.

controlling system—Generally refers to

a feedback control system; i.e., that portion which compares functions of a directly controlled variable and a set point, and adjusts a manipulated variable as a function of the difference. It includes the reference input elements: summing point, and forward and final controlling elements, as well as feedback elements (including sensing element).

control operation—Refers to the various control actions and the interpretation of data, e.g., the starting or stopping of a process, the carriage return, a font change, rewind, and the end of transmission.

control-oriented microcomputer — Characteristics of a control-oriented microcomputer should be to efficiently process and easily connect to a multiple number of commands and status/data paths of variable widths. As control devices are characterized by different numbers of bits associated with their command signals, their status signals, and their data signals, there are no standard command, status, or data widths. A microcomputer designed with these objectives in mind would require a minimal amount of both hardware interface overhead and programming overhead in order to implement a control system. These are the design objectives that are used in the design of the microcontroller/microcomputer.

control output module — A device in some systems that stores computer commands and translates them into signals that can be used for control purposes. Some modules can generate digital outputs to control on-off devices or to pulse set-point stations. Others can generate analog outputs —voltage or current—to operate valves and other process-control devices.

control panel—1. A panel that has a systematic arrangement of terminals for use with removable wires and used to direct the operation of either a computer or peripheral equipment. On computers, it is used primarily to control input and output functions. 2. A device or component of some data-processing machines that permits the expression of instructions in a semifixed computer program by the insertion of pins, plugs, or wires into sockets or hubs in the device, in a pattern to represent instructions and, thus, make electrical interconnections which may be sensed by the data-processing machine. (Synonymous with plugboard and related to pinboard.) 3. A part of a computer console that contains manual controls.

control panel interrupt transfer — One type of control panel is implemented in software. The software implementation of the control panel need not use any part of the main memory or change the processor state. This is an important feature since the final version of the system may not have a control panel and since the system designer would probably like to use the entire capacity of the main memory for the specific system application.

control panel, transparent — A unique feature of some microprocessors is the provision for a dedicated completely independent control panel with its own memory separate from the main memory. The concept of a "transparent" control panel is an important one for microprocessors since microprocessor-based production systems normally do not have a full-fledged panel and the system designer would like to use the entire capacity of the main memory for the specific system application. A number of panel options which can greatly increase the usefulness, flexibility, and reliability of the system, such as test, maintenance, and diagnostic routines, bootstrap loaders, etc., can be incorporated just by increasing the size of the panel memory to handle more software. The panel can be considered as a portable device which can be plugged into a socket on the CPU board, whenever the panel functions are needed, and disconnected when not needed, without disturbing any part of the user program.

control program — A specific designed sequence of instructions that guides the CPU through the various operations it must perform. Most often this program is permanently stored in ROM memory where it can be accessed but not erased by the CPU during operations. Most control programs contain many routines that would otherwise have to be put into individual programs. Such routines include sequences for handling error conditions, interruptions from the console, or interruptions from a communications terminal. There are also routines for handling input and output equipment. Because these routines are prewritten, the programmer is saved a good deal of effort and the likelihood of programming errors is reduced.

control register — Also called instruction register, the control register stores the current instruction governing the operation of the computer for a cycle.

control routine — 1. Refers to primary routines which control loading and relocation of routines and which, in some cases, make use of instructions that are known to the general programmer. Effectively, control routines are part of the machine itself. (Synonymous with supervisory program.) 2. A set of coded instructions designed to process and control other sets of coded instructions. 3. A set of coded instructions used in realizing automatic coding.

control routine interrupt — A routine entered when an interrupt occurs that provides for such details as the storage of the working details of the interrupted program, an analysis of the interrupt to decide on the necessary action, and the run of control to the interrupted program.

control section — Refers to the primary sequence of instructions or data within a program that can be transferred from outside the program segment in which it is contained. The control section can be deleted or replaced with a control section from other program segments.

control sequence — Refers to the normal order of selection of instructions for execution. In some computers, one of the addresses in each instruction specifies the control sequence. In most other computers, the sequence is consecutive except where a transfer occurs.

control sequencer — The control sequencer contains a microprogram counter that points to the microinstruction to be executed. The microinstruction is fetched and is passed to the function registers in the bit-slice microprocessor. After each microinstruction is completed, another microinstruction is fetched to direct the next step the processor is to take.

control, set-point — This control is used where the power and flexibility of direct digital control is not required, or where the system is installed in a plant with existing auto/manual stations that contain stepping motors for driving the analog set points.

control statements—1. Generally, these are statements that are used to direct the flow of the program, either causing specific transfers to take place or making transfers dependent upon meeting certain specified conditions. 2. Instructions which convey control information to the processor, but which do not develop machine-language instructions, i.e., symbolic statements.

control, supervisory—1. Characters or signals that automatically actuate equipment or indicators at a remote terminal. 2. A control system that furnishes intelligence, usually to a centralized location, to be used by an operator to supervise the control of a process or operation.

control-system output module—Refers to devices in some systems that store commands and translate them into signals that can be used for control purposes. Some can generate digital outputs to control on-off devices or to pulse set-point stations. Others can generate analog outputs (voltage or current) to operate valves and other process-control devices.

control unit—1. That section of a digital computer that directs the sequence of operations, interrupts coded instructions, and sends the proper signals to other computer circuits to carry out the instructions. Also referred to as the control section. 2. An auxiliary component of a computer located behind or within the "mainframe" and other component equipment, such as tape units, printers, and optical readers, for the purpose of controlling these components.

control word—1. A word, usually the first or last of a record (or first or last word of a block), that carries indicative information for the following words, records, or blocks. 2. A word which is used to transmit processing information from the control program to the operational programs, or between operational programs. Most systems normally contain several significant fields within the record.

conventional equipment—Refers to that equipment which is generally considered to be part of the computer system but which is not specifically part of the computer itself. Various input handling devices, tape handlers, and disk units, if not built into the main frame or wired in, would be conventional equipment.

conventions—Concerns various standard and accepted procedures in programs and systems analysis, and the abbreviations, symbols, and their meanings as developed for particular systems and programs.

conversational—Refers to various programs or systems that carry on a dialog with a terminal user, alternately accepting input and then responding to the input in a real-time mode.

conversational guidance — Refers to typical user/computer communications in a conversational or dialog mode, where the user takes some action and the system responds. The system then requests a specific category of input or takes other action and the user again responds. In this alternating stimulus-response mode, the system can and should provide guidance to the user on the form and content of the user response.

conversational language — Refers to various languages that utilize a near-English character set which facilitates communication between the computer and the user. For example, BASIC is one of the more commonly used conversational languages.

conversational mode—Refers to various processes for communication between a terminal and the computer in which each entry from the terminal requires a response from the computer and vice versa.

conversion device—Refers to various devices or pieces of peripheral equipment which convert data from one form into another form or medium, but without changing the data, content, or information.

conversion equipment—Refers to the equipment that is capable of transposing or transcribing the information from one type of data-processing medium in order to render it acceptable as input to another type of processing medium.

conversion time—Time required for a complete measurement by an analog-to-digital converter. In sucessive-approximation converters, it ranges typically from 0.8 microsecond to 400 microseconds.

convert—1. Concerns the process of changing numerical information from one number base to another. 2. To transfer information from one recorded medium to another.

converter—An interface used to transform information from one form to another.

converter, code — On some systems, this device automatically converts any input code to any output code. This simplifies the data stream code-conversion problems. A typical unit can be combined in data-communications subsystems with various other line converters.

converter, data—A data-processing device designed to change one form of data into another form, i.e., microfilm, strip chart, etc., into an optical reader format, a paper-tape format, or some other type format.

converter, flash — Parallel techniques provide fast a/d converters. Sometimes called "flash" converters, these circuits use a group of parallel comparators to simultaneously sample the input signal at weighted reference voltages. All comparators that are biased below the input voltage are then turned on by it, while the others remain off. The outputs from the comparators thus provide a unique digital code corresponding to the input voltage.

converter systems—An a/d converter samples analog data at specified rates and allows the program to store the equivalent digital value for subsequent processing. Sample and hold circuitry ensures accurate conversions, even on rapidly changing signals, by holding the input voltage constant until the process is completed. The input voltage range can be program selectable for unipolar (0 V to +5 V), or bipolar (−2.5 V to + 2.5 V) operation.

core—Refers to tiny "doughnuts" of magnetizable metal that can be in either an "on" or "off" state and can represent either a binary 1 (on) or a binary 0 (off). Commonly called magnetic core and used as the basic type of main memory for older computers.

core memory — 1. A computer memory device containing magnetic cores. 2. A programmable random-access memory consisting of many ferromagnetic toroid coils strung on wires in matrix arrays. Each toroid coil acts as an electromagnet to store a binary digit. 3. A device used to store information in ferrite cores. Each may be magnetized in either polarity, which are represented by a logical "1" or "0." This type of memory is nonvolatile; that is to say, the contents of the memory are retained while power is off.

correction program—A particular routine that is designed to be used in or after a computer failure, malfunction, or program or operator error, and which, thereby, reconstitutes the routine being executed before the error or malfunction, and does it from the most recent or closest rerun point.

counter—1. A circuit designed to count input pulses. Also called an accumulator, a device capable of changing from one to the next of a sequence of distinguishable states upon receipt of each discrete input signal. 2. A device or location which can be set to an initial number and increased or decreased by an arbitrary number by stimuli applied one at a time.

counter, B-line—A specification or name for the index register, which is a special counter that can be set to any desired number from storage, changed by a certain number, and tested to see if the new number is equal to another number in storage. Index registers are useful for address modification and in problems involving repetitive calculations.

counter, control — A device within a digital computer that records the storage location of the instruction word to be operated on that follows the instruction word in current use.

counter, cycle—A special counter constructed of hardware and contained in the control unit. See also counter.

counter, cycle index—Utilized to count the number of times a given cycle of program instructions has been done. It can be examined at any selected time to determine the number of repetitions still required in a loop.

counter, program—A register that holds the identification of the instruction word to be executed next in the time sequence, following the current operation. The register is often a counter that is incremented to the address of the next sequential storage location, unless a transfer or other special instruction is specified by the program.

CPE—Abbreviation for central processing element. It can provide a complete 2-bit, 4-bit, or 8-bit wide slice through the data-processing section of a computer. CPEs may be arrayed in parallel to form a processor of any desired word length. The multiple bus structure and masking capability of the CPE enables functions to be executed in a single microcycle—functions normally requiring multiple microcycles for execution. Other unique CPE features, such as conditional clocking and the Carry "OR" function, minimize microprogram memory and increase system throughput.

CP/M operating system—CP/M is the abbreviation for Control Program for Microprocessors. It is the registered trademark of Digital Research. CP/M is divided into four subsystems—the basic input/output system (BIOS), the basic disk-operating system (BDOS), the console command processor (CCP) and the transient program area (TPA). Together, the BIOS and BDOS form the floppy-disk operating system (FDOS), which acts as the system hardware supervisor. The CCP interfaces the user's console to the FDOS and to information stored on disk. The TPA holds nonresident operating system commands and user programs for execution. (All programs are loaded and executed at 0100H.)

BIOS is a hardware-dependent module that must be written by the user to fit his hardware configuration. It contains the basic interface routines for all standard peripherals, including the floppy-disk drives and user-defined peripherals. Customized BIOS (CBIOS) includes subroutines for system initialization; simple character I/O with the console, list, punch, and read devices; and disk I/O. Entry into these routines is through a jump table located at the 'start of CBIOS. All disk-dependent parts of CBIOS are contained in a disk-parameter block that describes the characteristics of the disk system—the number of active disks, starting and ending sector numbers, sector stagger factor, checksum vector size, and number of reserved tracks.

Low-cost CP/M can be customized to run on almost any 8080- or Z80-based hardware configuration. Its file management system uses minidisks, floppy disks, or hard disks for mass storage. Programs that are created, edited, debugged, assembled, and executed on one CP/M-based configuration will run on all other configurations. Thus, CP/M acts as a standard software interface between user programs and system hardware. BASIC, COBOL, FORTRAN, Pascal, APL, and PL/1 are among the high-level language packages that run with CP/M.

CP/M vs. MP/M — CP/M stands for Control Program for Microprocessors and MP/M stands for Multiprogramming Control Program for Microprocessors. Both are compatible operating systems and trademarks of Digital Research, Pacific Grove, CA. CP/M is a general all-purpose operating system that grew up fast and became almost a "standard" for small microcomputer systems. CP/M is an example of a simple operating system that handles one terminal. MP/M differs from CP/M in that it handles up to 4 terminals—each one doing different things. MP/M is a more complex system that treats each terminal as a "task." It schedules tasks so that they do not bump into each other, take up too much time, or monopolize any resource. A program that does this is called a "task scheduler."

CPU—Abbreviation for central processing unit. The CPU is the primary functioning unit of any computer system. Its basic architecture consists of storage elements called registers, computational circuits designated as the Arithmetic-Logic Unit (ALU), the Control Block, and Input-Output ports.

The CPU is the most complex part of the microcomputer. It fetches the control instructions stored in memory and then decodes, interprets and carries them out. The CPU handles the temporary storage and retrieval of data while regulating the exchange of information with the outside world through the microcomputer's input and output ports. It includes the arithmetic and logic unit (ALU), where all operations are performed, and a certain number of registers. Moreover, it synchronizes the operation of the various components. A microprocessor built with LSI technology often contains a CPU on a single chip. Because such a chip has limited storage space, memory implementation is added in modular fashion on associated chips. Some microprocessors consist of several CPU chips with other chips for memory and I/O.

CPU chip—A CPU chip may be visualized as one universal chip which performs the functions of numerous individual chips. The CPU chip requires two sets of input signals to generate one set of output signals. The input and output signals correspond to the chip inputs and outputs. The instruction signals tell the CPU chips which individual logic chip to emulate. In order for a CPU chip's versatility to be useful, it must emulate logic equivalents to more than one chip. CPU chips will vary depending on whether the chip designer planned to sell to the chip market or the computer-card market. For the CPU chip market, chip design emphasizes easy-to-use CPU signal sequences; for the computer-card market, chip design emphasizes powerful instruction sets and fast instruction execution.

CPU computer card — Computer designs have evolved to fill a need in the marketplace and, thus, for many applications the most economical way of including computer capability in a product is via the standard expansion of a CPU chip into a computer card. For example, every microcomputer CPU chip must operate in conjunction with a memory module, and it must have CPU-to-memory interface logic. If the CPU communicates with standard peripheral devices (e.g., a teletypewriter, disk unit, or line printer), the computer card will supply the necessary interface between the CPU chip and peripheral device controller. The following list is the extra logic needed to convert a CPU chip into a computer card:
1. Communications—the ability to transmit data between the CPU chip pins and external devices.
2. Timing—a clock that generates timing signals used by the CPU chip.
3. Control logic — the means for knowing where data is to be read, and where data must be sent.

CPU elements—The principal elements of the central processing unit (CPU) control the interpretation and execution of instructions. Generally they include the ALU, timing and control, accumulator, a scratchpad memory, program counter and address stack, instruction register and decode, parallel data and I/O bus, and memory and I/O control.

CPU expander — A unit designed to permit a user to run several types of software on a single system without modifying the software. Some of the first units contained 8080, Z80, and 6800 chips on the same board, with four PIAs for control, and several multiplexers and demultiplexers.

CPU handshaking—The interaction between the CPU and various peripheral devices. For example, a printer might have some logic to designate when it is ready for a new character, or the CPU can act upon several status conditions of all the ranges of signals from I/O devices.

CPU slices—CPU slices are generally 2- or 4-bit parts of a CPU. Users must define an instruction set and the architecture that executes that instruction set. They must then develop the interface between that architecture and the memory containing the control program and the I/O system that connects into the devices. Then, a system package must be provided.

CPU time—The actual computational time necessary to process a set of instructions in the arithmetic and logic units of the computer.

crash—A breakdown, i.e., an event in which a system becomes inoperative or lost in a loop or is blocked—most often due to a hardware failure or a software malfunction. For example, in a disk system, a head crash concerns an accidental impact of the Read-Write head on the disk surface. Each peripheral has its specific type of crash.

credit-card reader—A microprocessor-based card reader for credit authorization and security applications. It can read the magnetic stripe imbedded in most major credit cards.

CRC — Abbreviation for cyclic redundancy check — an error-checking technique that uses a sophisticated mathematical algorithm. Following the transmitted control information is the data portion of the data block. It is variable in length, depending on the number of active channels and their activity rates. The block ends with a cyclic redundancy check (CRC) character, which is recalculated by the receiver to ensure that the data block was received correctly. The CRC is the 16-bit result of a polynomial calculation performed on the bits in the block, giving only a one in 10^{12} probability that a CRC will check out correctly with a block in error.

crippled leapfrog test — Refers to a standardized variation of the leapfrog test, modified so that it repeats its tests from a single set of storage locations rather than from a changing set of storage locations.

criterion—Refers to a value used for testing, comparing, or judging; e.g., in determining whether a condition is plus or minus, true or false. Also, a rule or test for making a decision, either in a computer or by humans.

criterion, cycle—*See* cycle criterion.

critical path—The longest time path in a project which has to be done as quickly as possible. Because the overall time required to complete the project cannot be less than that required along the critical path, it requires the most careful monitoring. Any delay along this path causes the project to be delayed, while minor delays along noncritical paths do not. *See* PERT network.

critical current — That current, at a specified temperature and in the absence of external magnetic fields, above which a material is normal and below which it is a super conductor.

critical path scheduling — A project planning and monitoring system used to check progress toward completion of the project by scheduling events, activities, milestones, etc.

CROM—Abbreviation for control read-only memory. A specific ROM that has been designed and microprogrammed to decode control logic. It is a major component of several types of microprocessors.

cross- and resident-assembler programs—In some systems, both cross- and resident-assembler programs are available as options to support the preparation of the user's application programs. A cross assembler may be used on a large-scale computer

system to assemble programs written in the system language. Also cross assemblers are often installed on nationwide time-share computer utilities. Another technique available for assembling application programs is the resident-assembler program, which can be loaded into the system memory and then used to assemble the user's application programs. A number of loader programs and debug programs are often available to support development of a user's application programs.

cross assembler—1. Refers to a program run on one computer for the purpose of translating instructions for a different computer. 2. Programs are usually assembled by the assembler or assembly program contained within or used by the processor on which they will be run. Many microprocessor programs, however, are assembled by other computer-type processors. A cross assembler translates a symbolic representation of the instructions and data into a form that can be loaded and executed by the microprocessor. "Cross assembler" means an assembler that is executing on a machine other than the microprocessor which generates the object code for it.

crossbar—A type of common control switching system using the crossbar or coordinate switch. Crossbar switching systems are ideally suited to data switching due to their low-noise characteristics.

cross compiling/assembling — A method in which an existing minicomputer, large computer, or time-sharing service can be used to write and debug what will become a microcomputer program. The advantage is that the designer has access to all of the conventional peripherals, and the object code he or she produces on them can, in the final stage, be loaded into the microcomputer system.

crossfire—Interference from one telegraph circuit to another telegraph circuit or into telephone circuits.

crossfoot—1. The addition of several horizontal fields of information from cards or across a document. 2. To add several horizontal fields of numeric information, usually for checking or totaling purposes. 3. The process whereby numbers in different fields of the same punch card are added or subtracted and the result punched into another field of the same card. Or, a check in which totals secured by one method in a given problem are compared with totals obtained by another method. The totals should be equal if no error has been made.

crossfooting—Crossfooting is the addition and/or subtraction of factors in a horizontal spread to prove processing accuracy. It can be used on a payroll register to prove that the final totals of net pay and deductions equal the final total earnings; this provides control on report preparation as well as calculating and card-punching operations. In posting transactions to records that are stored in a computer (e.g., accounts receivable), crossfooting is used to prove the accuracy of posting either as each transaction is posted, or collectively at the end of the run, or both.

cross hatching—Refers to the breaking-up of large conductive areas where shielding is required on a printed-circuit board.

crossover—The crossing area where a portion of the interconnect pattern passes over another conductive portion of the circuit and is separated from it by a thin dielectric layer.

cross-reference generator — A device that permits symbols (labels, variables, constants) to be correlated with their storage locations.

crossunder—A crossing of two conductive paths where one path is fabricated into the active substrate for the sole purpose of interconnection.

crowding, character—The reduction of the time or space interval on magnetic tape between characters.

crt—Abbreviation for cathode-ray tube.

crt, beam-penetration—There are two types of color crt's—monochrome and full color. Monochrome crt's rely on color phosphors, and more than one color is possible on a crt screen by layering phosphors. Different colors appear one at a time, depending on the anode potential—how far the electron beam penetrates the phosphor layers. This technique for producing color is called beam penetration.

crt function key—A key on a crt terminal that, when depressed, transmits a signal to the computer which can be equated to a prestored typewriter message of many strokes. Special consoles of various types have been developed for particular users. Examples are airline agent's sets, badge readers, and stockbroker's inquiry consoles.

crt highlighting — A display capability used for distinguishing between variable data and protected data, such as field labels or error messages. This can be done by blinking, underlining, or varying the intensity of the characters.

crt polarizing filters — Made in two bonded layers, polarizing filters are plastic or glass overlays used in front of a crt. The layer closest to the observer is a linear polarizer; the one next to the crt face is a quarter-wavelength filter. Polarizing filters cause minimal degradation of focus, resolution, and light output, but they are usually used only over small screen size crt's because of their high cost.

crt, raster-scan—In a raster-scan display, the electron beam provides only a slice of each character, one row at a time, as it scans a line. The row outputs of the ROM are latched into a parallel-input serial-output shift register, and are then shifted into the video-generation circuits in serial fashion.

crt refresh, DMA — With direct-memory access (DMA), the refresh memory is part of the computer system's memory. But this scheme has pitfalls. The microprocessor is interrupted by refreshing of the screen, and when the display controller accesses the memory to refresh the data, it forces the microprocessor to relinquish control of the address and data buses to the DMA controller. The controller transfers information from the RAM to the crt buffer memory, which is read out by the sync generator and put on the screen. While this method eliminates the interference problem of the video RAM, it is more complex and expensive to implement. In addition, when a DMA occurs, the processor must stop, thus slowing down any other CPU activities.

crt storage — 1. Often this relates to the electrostatic storage characteristics of cathode-ray tubes in which the electron beam is used to sense the data. 2. The storage of data on a dielectric surface, such as the screen of a cathode-ray tube, in the form of the presence or absence of spots bearing electrostatic charges. These spots can persist for a short time after the removal of the electrostatic charging force. 3. A storage device used as in the foregoing description.

crt terminal—A terminal containing a cathode-ray tube that is used to display programs as ladder diagrams which use instruction symbols similar to relay characters. A crt terminal can also display data lists and application reports.

Crt terminal, portable (Courtesy Digi-Log Systems, Inc.).

crt terminals, portable—One such terminal is the Digi-Log Telecomputer. It is a portable interactive terminal designed to replace or operate in conjunction with Model 33 Teletype® units. Weighing less than 10 pounds, it can be carried in a briefcase and plugged into any video monitor or network of monitors for large audience viewing. It can be acoustically coupled (an option) or hard-wired to any communications line.

cryogenic—Refers to materials whose temperatures have been reduced so as to approach absolute zero.

cryogenic element—Refers to various high-speed circuits which use the superconductivity characteristics of materials operating at or near absolute zero.

cryogenic memory—*Same as* cryogenic storage.

cryogenics—The study and use of devices utilizing properties of materials near absolute zero in temperature. At these temperatures, large current changes can be obtained from relatively small magnetic-field changes.

cryogenics, Josephson junction — A junction formed by separating, with a thin insulator, certain metals cooled to a few degrees above −273°C. Studies in Josephson junction technology indicate a potential for memory and logic devices that can perform 100 times faster while requiring one-thousandth as much power as the best currently available alternatives.

cryogenic storage — One which depends for its operation on the properties of specific materials that can become superconductive when their temperatures and the magnetic fields in which they are situated fall below certain very low temperatures. Since superconductors have zero resistance, they have the ability to maintain or store a current almost indefinitely.

cryostat—Refers to a device that uses evaporative and condensing cycles to achieve extremely low temperatures and is often used to liquefy gases.

cryotron—Refers to a device utilizing properties or metals at near absolute-zero temperature so that large current changes can be obtained by relatively small magnetic-field changes.

Curie point—1. The temperature above which ferromagnetic materials lose their magnetization (whether permanently or transiently magnetized). 2. The temperature above which ferroelectric materials lose their polarization. 3. In industry, the temperature at which the initial permeability (μ_o) of a material assumes 1/10 of its maximum value.

current instruction register — A computer register that contains the instruction currently being executed.

current-mode logic — Logic in which transistors operate in the unsaturated mode as distinguished from most other logic types which operate at the saturation region. This logic has very fast switching speeds and low logic swings. Also called ECL or MECL.

cursor—1. Refers to various position indicators frequently employed in a display (on a video terminal) to indicate a character to be corrected or a position in which data is to be entered. 2. A solid underscore which may appear under any character location on the video screen. In some systems, the cursor always appears under the location where the next character will appear.

cursor selection—Allows hardware selection of the cursor presentation—blink or nonblink, block or underline, etc.

curve conformity — Relates to curves, the closeness to which they approximate a specified functional curve (i.e., logarithmic, parabolic, cubit, etc.), and usually expressed in terms of nonconformity, i.e., the maximum deviation between an average curve and a specified functional curve. The average curve is determined after making two or more full-range traverses in opposite directions. The value of nonconformity is referred to the output unless otherwise stated. *See* linearity.

custom CMOS circuits—Custom CMOS manufacturers provide very fast development cycles, quite modest tooling charges, and low-cost chips for low and moderate volumes. Master MOS is one approach to the manufacture of custom CMOS integrated circuits. A Master CMOS circuit is a predesigned and preprocessed array, ready to be customized for each special requirement. Each chip is a matrix arrangement of CMOS elements that may be interconnected in a vast variety of patterns, forming any sort of complex or specialized logic function.

custom-design technologies — Most custom integrated circuits are designed for standard NMOS, CMOS, and PMOS. A small number are designed in bipolar and emitter-coupled logic (ECL) technologies. Because MOS processes are used to fabricate high volumes of standard parts, the processes are widely understood and steadily improved. Normally, only proven custom circuit "design rules" (the specifications for transistor lay-

out, line spacing, mask levels, etc.) are used. The purpose of custom is to achieve design, rather than processing, innovations. For this reason, even PMOS, which is now rarely used for new standard products, is still used for custom circuits because of its power-handling ability, low cost, and high yields. Most new circuits, however, are designed for NMOS, with silicon-gate CMOS rising rapidly, owing to its low-power requirements.

custom ROMs (PROM)—With custom-programmed ROMs, the manufacturer places the binary information (links or no links) into the memory as specified by the user. However, custom programming of ROMs is expensive when only small quantities are ordered. To reduce the high cost of small quantities of ROMs, manufacturers offer the field-programmable ROM or PROM. The PROM is an ordinary ROM that has all of its on-chip fuses intact. (A 256-bit PROM would have 256 of these fuses, one for each bit of memory.) The user can program information into the PROM simply by blowing open selected on-chip fuses. The fuses are blown open by passing a specific amount of current through them.

cybernetics—1. The science of systems of control and communication. The study of the automatic control system formed by the nervous system and the brain, and by electrical-mechanical communications systems, so as to understand and improve communications. 2. This diverse field encompasses (A) integration of communication, control, and systems theories, (B) development of systems engineering technology, and (C) practical applications at both the hardware and software levels. Recent and projected developments in cybernetics are taking place in at least five important areas—technological forecasting and assessment, complex systems modeling, policy analysis, pattern recognition, and artificial intelligence. Applications have moved far beyond the feedback control systems described in Norbert Wiener's book "Cybernetics," first published 25 years ago.

cycle (noun)—1. The functioning of an alternating waveform that goes from zero to its negative and positive peaks, and then back to zero. The

number of cycles each second is called the frequency or alternation. 2. A complete sequence of a waveform pattern that recurs at regular intervals. The number of cycles occurring in 1 second is the frequency of the waveform, expressed in hertz. 3. An interval of space or time in which one set of events or phenomena is completed.

cycle (verb)—1. Refers to performance of a nonarithmetic shift in which the digits dropped off at one end of a word are returned at the other end in circular fashion, cycle right and cycle left. 2. To repeat a set of operations a prescribed number of times including, when required, supplying necessary address changes by arithmetic processes or by means of a hardware device such as a b-box or cycle counter.

cycle, action—Specifically refers to the complete operation performed on data. Includes basic steps of: origination, input, manipulation, output, and storage.

cycle availability — That specific time period during which stored information can be read.

cycle counter—A mechanism or device which measures the number of times a specified cycle is repeated.

cycle criterion—The total number of times the cycle is to be repeated; the register which stores that number.

cycle error, initial—A deviation from the desired timing period when the timer has been inactive for an extended period. Crystal-controlled and pulse-counting timers do not normally suffer from initial cycle error.

cycled interrupt—The change (by sequence or specific operation cycle) of control to the next or a specific function in a predetermined manner or order.

cycle, index—1. The number of times a cycle has been executed, or the difference between the number of times a cycle is desired and the number of times it has been repeated. 2. The number of cycle iterations in digital computer programming. A cycle index register may be used to set the number of cycles desired. Then, with each cycle iteration, the register count is reduced by one until the register reaches zero and the series of cycles is complete.

cycle shift—Refers to the removal of digits of a number, or characters of a word, from one end of the number or word and their insertion, in the same sequence, at the other end.

cycle stealing, controller — On some systems, external control lines initiate a pause in microprocessor operation by suspending instruction execution within the instruction cycle. The processor clock is halted, and the memory-control lines of the microprocessor are disabled. The controller takes over and "steals" several machine cycles for data transfer. After the transfer, the pause-control lines are reset, the clock restarts, and the instruction cycle continues executing the instruction. The only negative result is that the instruction execution takes longer. However, microprocessors using dynamic memory on the processor chip restrict the number of machine cycles that may be stolen, so that no internal status is lost. Inputting or outputting a long block of data may require several separate "thefts."

cycle stealing, data channels — Data channels give the processor-controller the ability to delay the execution of a program for communication of an I/O device with main storage. For example, if an input unit requires a memory cycle to store data that it has collected, the data channel with its "cycle stealing" capability makes it possible to delay the program during execution of an instruction and store the data word without changing the logical condition of the processor-controller. After the data is stored, the program continues as though nothing had occurred. This capability should not be confused with "interrupt" which changes the contents of the instruction register. Cycle stealing by the data channels can occur at the end of any memory cycle. Maximum delay before cycle stealing can occur is one memory-cycle time.

cycle time—1. The interval between the call for, and delivery of, information from a storage unit or device. 2. A specific interval of time that recurs regularly and in the same sequence —for example, the interval required for completion of one operation in a repetitive sequence of operations or the time interval required to execute a specific group of operations which can be repeated in their entirety.

cyclic binary code—1. Positional binary notation for numbers in which any two sequential numbers whose difference is 1 are represented by expressions that are the same except in one place or column, and in that place or column differ only by one unit. 2. A type of cycle unit-distance binary code.

cyclic check—A method of error detection which checks every nth bit, $n + 1$ bit, $n + 2$ bit, etc. It is more powerful and efficient that horizontal checks, vertical checks, or combinations of both.

cyclic code—Refers to any binary code which changes by only one bit when going from one number to the number immediately following.

cyclic code polynomial—A very practical code which achieves perfect detection of single, double, and odd number of errors and very good detection of burst of error. Given an integer r, the data is multiplied by 2^r (left shifted r places) and divided by a polynomial P. The remainder is appended to the original message. Upon receipt, the total message is divided by P. If the remainder is nonzero, an error has occurred. This division is implemented in a shift register, thus providing an automatic low-cost check sum. If the data is recycled through the shift register, the process is called a cyclic sum check.

cyclic decimal code—Refers to a 4-bit binary code word in which only one digit changes state between any two sequential code words, and which translates to decimal numbers. Categorized as one of a group of unit-distance codes.

cyclic memory — Memory that constantly stores information but provides access only at multiples of a fixed time, commonly referred to as the cycle time.

cyclic redundancy check—In one system, the cyclic redundancy check (CRC) generator/checker is a 16-bit programmable device that operates on serial data streams and provides a means of detecting transmission errors. Cyclic encoding and decoding schemes for error detection are based on polynomial manipulation in modulo arithmetic. For encoding, the data stream (message polynomial) is divided by a selected polynomial. This division results in a remainder that is appended to the message as check bits. For error checking, the bit stream containing both data and check bits is divided by the same selected polynomial. If there are no detectable errors, this division results in a zero remainder. Although it is possible to choose many generating polynomials of a given degree, standards exist that specify a small number of useful polynomials.

cyclic redundancy check, character—An operations character designed as a redundant character and introduced for error detection purposes, in various modified cyclic codes.

cyclic shift — 1. A particular computer operation that produces a word whose characters are obtained by a cyclic permutation of characters of a given word. 2. A shift in which the digits dropped off at one end of a word are returned at the other end in a circular fashion, e.g., if a register holds the eight digits 23456789, the result of a cyclic shift two columns to the left would be to change the contents of the register to 45678923. Synonymous with logical shift and nonarithmetic shift.

cyclic storage access — Relates to a storage unit designed so that access to any given location is only possible at specific, equally spaced times. Concerns units such as magnetic drums, delay lines, etc.

cycling—Refers to the periodic change imposed on a controlled variable or a function by a controller.

Czochralski process — In the conventional Czochralski approach, a seed crystal is immersed in molten silicon that is heated to about 1420 °C, and is then rotated while being lifted to grow an ingot of single-crystal silicon. Normally, convection currents in the crucible agitate its surface, and the temperature near the surface varies erratically by several degrees. The convection currents also accelerate the chemical reaction between the melt and its silica crucible, causing oxygen to dissolve in the molten silicon. Ingots grown under these conditions have striations caused by the irregular growing conditions and segregation of impurities, together with defects caused by an excessive amount of oxygen.

D

daisy chain — Refers to a specific method of propagating signals along a bus. This method is a bus line that is interconnected with units in such a manner that a signal passes from one unit to the next in serial fashion. Each chip connects to its associated unit to accomplish a daisy-chaining of interrupt priorities, beginning with the chip closest to the CPU.

daisy-chain bus—A daisy-chain bus is very similar to the party-line bus, except that the connections are made in serial fashion. Each unit can modify the signal before passing it on to the next device. This approach is used mainly for signals related to interrupts or polling circuits. Whenever a device requires service, it blocks the signal. A priority is thus established, since the devices that are closest to the microprocessor usually have the first chance to request service.

daisy-chain interrupt—The daisy-chain concept is used to organize interrupt priorities. Each RAM or ROM chip—which also provides I/O ports—can accept one interrupt input. And each chip can connect to its neighbors to establish priorities. The daisy-chain technique as a system's bus structure depends on the CPU used. Pin-limited first-generation CPUs have a single bus that must be time-shared between memory addresses, instructions, input and output data, device addresses, and control signals. This time-sharing requires involved peripheral circuitry, consisting of numerous latches, multiplexers, and timing circuits. Also, output information has to be latched before it can be directed toward the appropriate output device—usually another latch. Hence, output bus structures usually have to be of the party-line type.

damped natural frequency—Related to the frequency of an oscillator following a transient input, usually a step function or pulse.

damping—Refers to characteristics built into electrical circuits and mechanical systems to prevent rapid or excessive corrections which may lead to instability or oscillatory conditions, i.e., connecting a register on the terminals of a pulse transformer to remove natural oscillations, or placing a moving element in oil or sluggish grease to prevent a mechanical overshoot of the moving parts.

damping signal—The final manner in which the output settles to its steady-state value after a change in the value of measured signal; i.e., when the time response to an abrupt stimulus is as fast as possible without overshoot, the response is said to be "critically damped." It is "underdamped" when overshoot occurs and "overdamped" when response is slower than critical.

Darlington power transistors—Darlington power transistors are actually monolithic circuits that consist of two bipolar power transistors, two resistors, and a diode fabricated by monolithic techniques on a common silicon chip and interconnected to function as a single high-gain power transistor. The dc current gain of Darlingtons typically ranges from 1000 to 20,000 at a collector current in the order of 3 to 5 amperes. Most circuit configurations are npn types. The configuration for a pnp Darlington differs only in that pnp types are used for the transistors and the polarity of the diode is reversed. Some monolithic Darlingtons operate at currents up to 10 amperes and at supply voltages that range from 40 to 120 volts. They are available in both hermetic (TO-3 or TO-66) and molded plastic (TO-220) packages. The high gain of these devices makes it possible for them to be driven directly from integrated circuits.

data—1. A general term that is used to denote any or all facts, numbers, letters, symbols, etc., that can be processed or produced by a computer. 2. In a restricted sense, data refers to numerical information as contrasted with nonnumerical information. 3. Implying source data or raw data as contrasted with information that is defined to mean the knowledge obtained by the processing of data.

data access register—In some systems, the data access register (DAR) performs memory address arithmetic for RAM resident stack applications. It contains three 4-bit registers intended for program counter, stack pointer, and operand address use. The device implements 16 instructions which allow either pre- or post-decrement/increment and register-to-register transfer in a single clock cycle. It is expandable in 4-bit increments and can operate at a 10-MHz microinstruction rate on a 16-bit word. The 3-state outputs are provided for bus-oriented applications.

data acquisition and control (DAC)—A DAC system is designed to handle a wide variety of real-time applications, process control, and high-speed data acquisition. Each system is individually tailored with modular building blocks that are integrated to meet specific system requirements. A large family of real-time process input/output (I/O) devices may be included,

such as analog input, analog output, contact sense, and contact operate, as well as data processing I/O units, such as magnetic tape, disk storage, line printer, graph plotter, card and paper tape input and output. Data are received and transmitted on either a high-speed cycle-steal basis or under program control, depending on the intrinsic data rate of the I/O device.

data acquisition, automated—An automated data acquisition system receives analog signals from a specific process, and those signals reflect a temperature, pressure, or other physical variable. Signal conditioners, such as amplifiers, filters, linearizers, or sample-hold circuits, condition the analog input and present it to an analog-to-digital converter (A/D converter) that converts the reading to a computer-compatible digital format. A computer "reads" the data, analyzes it in accordance with prewritten instructions, and sends out process control commands and/or operator information so that the process can be adjusted as may be necessary.

data, analog—A physical representation of information such that the repre-

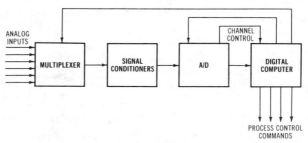

(A) Multichannel system.

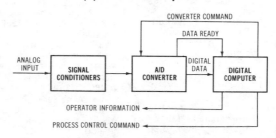

(B) Single-channel system.

Data acquisition, automated.

sentation bears an exact relationship to the original information.

data array—A representation of data in the form of signs and symbols as recorded on tape, cards, etc.

data bank—A collection of data pertaining to a given subject or application.

data base—A typical data base is a vast and continuously updated file of information, abstracts, or references on a particular subject or subjects. Online data bases are designed so that by using subject headings, key words, key phrases, or authors, users can quickly and economically search for, sort, analyze, and print out data on their terminal.

data base files — In a microcomputer-based system, all the files are probably time-series files: two-dimensional arrays with data values along one axis and time along the other. This is the simplest form of data storage and handling for a small computer. While other programs in the system can create cross-sectional displays from the data files, almost all users of these systems are interested in how certain variables are performing over time. The user gets a rapid access and high flexibility in the manipulation of time-series data at the expense of a somewhat more cumbersome access and a slower response for cross-sectional data, which is the best compromise for typical executive decision making.

data base layering—Layering is a feature of modern CAD-type data bases that provides a number of different layers for data (e.g., 256), any of which (individually or in combination) the user can extract for special kinds of output.

data base management—Refers to a software product that controls a data structure containing interrelated data stored so as to optimize accessibility, control redundancy, and provide or offer multiple views of the data to multiple applications programs. Data base management systems also implement data independence to varying degrees. Utilities, multiprogramming capabilities, and the sophistication of the data dictionary vary with different products and different vendors.

data base management system — A data base management system is a software package designed to operate interactively upon a collection of computer-stored files, or what is called a data base. Its primary operation is to count data base records that have user-specified common characteristics and retrieve those records for further processing and display. A typical system includes a high-level compiler-like language that can be used to describe the location, contents, relationships, and security level of data that are stored in the data base. It also has subroutines that are used to manipulate and extract data from the data base, such as "Query," or some other type of an English-like language that acts as an impromptu report generator. Off-line routines, or utility programs, are used to load the data base on to disk from other media and to duplicate the data base as a backup.

data base size—Increasing the size of the common data base in a one-processor system is often limited to the capabilities of the central processor. Either a larger or a second machine must be added, forcing the user to either rewrite his software or sacrifice his common data base. The common data base of some systems is expanded by simply adding additional file processors and disk drives as necessary. Thus, software revision is not necessary, and the data base of these systems can be arbitrarily large and still remain common to all users.

data base sort options—Many systems permit the user to change the order of records in a data base either logically or physically. Depending on the options specified in the command, the logic flow will often effect: (1) a Logical Sort, which does not physically rearrange the data file, but instead creates an inverted list in the form of an index or pointer file for subsequent data accessing, (2) a Sort and Select, which performs a logical sort of the file but includes only records that meet user-specified criteria, or (3) a Physical Sort and Compress, which actually rearranges the data file records, dropping those that have been logically deleted.

data block—All the data for one group of items that is entered into a microcomputer for processing, or the microcomputer output that results from processing. An example of an input data block is an itemized order form, and an example of an output data block is the check that must be sent.

data buffer register—Refers to a temporary storage register in a CPU or a peripheral device that is capable of receiving or transmitting data at different I/O rates. Data buffer registers are most often positioned between the microcomputer and slower system components, allowing data to flow at the established input-output rate of the microcomputer.

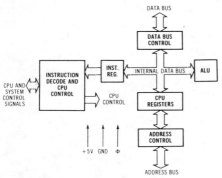

Data bus.

data bus—Most microprocessors communicate through the use of a data bus. Most buses are bidirectional, e.g., capable of transferring data to and from the CPU, memory storage, and peripheral devices. A typical bus system is composed of three signal buses. An example is a data bus that consists of 16 bidirectional data lines. The timing bus provides the basic system clocks as well as the address and data strobes which indicate when data is valid on the bus. The control bus provides a priority system for bus access, and signals to indicate whether the current transaction is a Read or Write from memory or a peripheral, plus an extended cycle signal, and a response line to indicate that a peripheral device has accepted an order sent over the system bus.

data bus enable—A typical input is a three-state control signal for the MPU data bus, and it will enable the bus drivers when in the high state. In some systems, this input often is TTL compatible; however, in normal operation, it would be driven by the Phase

2 clock. During an MPU read cycle, the data bus drivers will be disabled internally. When it is desired that another device control the data bus, such as in direct-memory access (DMA) applications, the data bus enable should be held low.

data bus, system—In many microsystems, all communication between modules in a microcomputer occurs over the System Data Bus. This bus is usually independent of the processor and handles communications between any two devices connected to the bus. In order to transfer information over the bus, a device first requests access through the Bus Priority Network of Bus Control. If no higher priority request is present, control of the bus is granted and the device then becomes the bus master for one bus cycle. During this cycle, the master may address any other bus-connected device (which becomes the slave) and may command a transfer of data to or from the slave.

data capture, direct—A technique employed in the use of cash registers, or with sales slips, whereby the customer account number, the amount of the purchase, and other information is read by an optical reading device, automatically recorded, and sent to the computer to be processed. Its use permits the generation of more timely and accurate transaction data.

data cartridge — A typical cartridge contains 300 feet of ¼-inch computer-grade magnetic tape certified error free by the tape manufacturer. The cartridge assembly consists of a high-impact plastic cover mated to a metal base. Further protection is afforded by a plastic door that closes over the tape-head opening when the cartridge is removed from the drive. The precision-drive system within the cartridge assures a constant tape tension throughout start/stop and run modes.

data cartridge, ANSI — Where data integrity is important, an ANSI-compatible cartridge (and recorder) guarantees that all tapes will be interchangeable regardless of the manufacturer—an important consideration when data interchange from recorder to recorder is necessary.

data cell—The smallest unit of data that cannot be further subdivided, such as a magnetic bit.

data chaining—Refers to the gathering (or scattering) of information within one physical record, from (or to) more than one region of memory, by means of successive I/O commands.

data channel—Refers to a bidirectional data path between the I/O devices and the main memory in a digital computer that permits one or more I/O operations to happen concurrently with computation.

data code conversion—The translation of alphanumeric data into a form acceptable to the computer. This is usually done by the computer itself during the input of the data.

data code, numeric — A digital code used to represent numerals and some special characters.

data collection — The act of bringing data from one or more points to a central point.

data communications — Generally relates to the movement of computer-encoded information by means of electrical transmission systems.

data communications buffer—Enables addressable hard-copy printers to operate at different speeds, independently of communications line speeds.

data communications control unit — The unit that scans the central terminal unit buffers for messages, and transfers them to the central processor.

data communications network—A data communications network consists of an interconnected group of computers, each of which may have human as well as data base interfaces. They can range from as simple a unit as an intelligent terminal linked to a host processor to a complete network of terminals, concentrators, remote processors, and multiple-host computers. Each processor in such a system is selected on the basis of its ability to perform the task required at its location. The individual processors may vary considerably in their speed, interfaces, languages, and other characteristics. It is only important that they be efficient in the performance of their assigned tasks.

data compaction—Refers to a specific series of techniques used for the reduction of space, bandwidth, cost, transmission, generating time, and the storage of data. These techniques are designed for the elimination of repetition, removal of irrelevancies, and employment of special coding techniques. Same as null suppression.

data complementation—Logical negation of the data at the inputs.

data compression — 1. Various techniques that save storage space by eliminating gaps, empty fields, redundancies, or unnecessary data to shorten the length of records or blocks. 2. Any display technique used to reduce the time and effort required to examine an entire data record. The simplest form converts binary words into hexadecimal words.

data concentration formatting — The formatting of data is an aspect of information concentration. ASCII formatting of raw data for remote transmission to a host is one example. The numerical data can be packed into four bits per digit (a nibble) and two digits per byte. With this type of packing, memory usage is very efficient. Systems that process hexadecimal information make extensive use of packed data formats. Typical applications for data concentration occur in line concentration for POS (point of sale) terminal devices, multiterminal key-to-tape and key-to-disk systems, and scientific data accumulators.

data design — A particular layout or format of computer storage or machine storage allocation, i.e., for input and output. Often related to flowcharts and diagrams to define procedures and practices for problem solution.

data design layout—1. A predetermined arrangement of characters, fields, lines, punctuation, page numbers, etc. 2. A defined arrangement of words, totals, characters, stubs, headings, etc., for a desired clear presentation of data or print output, such as a financial record.

data, digital—Information represented by a code consisting of a sequence of discrete elements, i.e., a zero or a one.

data element—A specific item of information appearing in a set of data, i.e., in the following sets of data, each item is a data element: the quantity of a supply item issued, a unit rate, an amount, and the balance of stock items on hand, etc.

data element dictionary (DED) — An organized listing of data elements (and their associated information) in a given system.

data error — A deviation from correctness in data, usually an error, which occurred prior to processing the data.

data field—An area located in the main memory which contains a data record.

data files—Aggregations of data sets for definite usage. The file may contain one or more different data sets. A permanent data file is one in which the data is perpetually subject to being updated, e.g., a name and address file. However, a working data file is a temporary accumulation of data sets which is destroyed after the data has been transferred to another form.

data flowchart — A flowchart showing the path of the data step by step in a problem solution or through a system.

data-flow computers—A data-flow machine is a total departure from the architecture of mathematician John von Neumann that has been the basis for all computers till now. The data-flow machine would have no single central processor. Instead, it would have a processing section with tens, hundreds, or even thousands of processor units in it, each perhaps the equivalent of a simple arithmetic and logic unit. Instead of a shared random-access memory, there would be a memory section with a large number of "instruction cells," each holding an operation code, the data operand, and a destination address. In place of data paths and storage registers, a packet-switching system, called an arbitration network, would direct the output of an instruction cell to a processor unit. VLSI technology makes these machines and processes both easier and cheaper to make. In early machines, designers used only one or two types of processing units. But with the economies of VLSI, designers can use units with 512 to 2048 processing units.

data format — Rules and procedures that describe the way data is held in a file or record, whether in character form, as binary numbers, etc.

data-formatting statements—Refers to various statements that instruct the assembly program to set up constants and reserve memory areas and to punctuate memory to indicate field boundaries.

data frames—The array of bits across the width of a magnetic or paper tape. Data frames are written on some tapes at a density of either 200 or 556 bits per inch. In paper-tape systems, one frame is equivalent to one character.

data gathering—*Same as* data collection.

data handling — 1. The production of records and reports. 2. The performance of those data-processing chores common to most users such as sorting, input/output operation, and report generation.

data-handling system—1. A system of automatic and semiautomatic devices used in the collection, transmission, reception, and storage of information in digital form. 2. A system in which data is sorted, decoded, or stored in a particular form; related to data reduction.

data hierarchy—A data structure consisting of ordered sets and subsets, of such a form that every subset of a set is of lower rank than the data of the set.

data independence—A quality of a data base environment that allows changing the logical or physical structure of a data base without changing the applications software that manipulates it. Data independence can be implemented on many levels. The physical implementation, arrangement, and proximity of the data on storage media may be changeable without altering the logical view expected by programs. Further independence is demonstrated by systems that allow the logical view of the data to be changed without requiring changes to programs that do not use that data.

data input — 1. Any data upon which one or more of the basic processing functions are to be performed, such as coding, sorting, computing, summarizing, and reporting, recording, and communication. 2. Data ready for processing and on the input channel of an input device such as an optical reader, card reader, logic element, or gate.

data input bus (DIB) — Some microcomputers feature a single bus structure with the processor, memory, and input-output channels all sharing a common data input bus (DIB). The data input bus is the mechanism whereby address information and data are transferred between the switch register (SR) and the processor, between the processor and the memory, between the memory and the input-output interface, and between the processor and the input-output interface.

data input/output register—This register is used for temporary storage of all input/output data received via or transmitted over the 8-bit bidirectional data bus during the data transfer interval of each input/output cycle. On some systems, the data input/output register is not accessible to the programmer.

data interchange code—A variation of the ASCII code, this is primarily different from ASCII in that some printing characters are replaced by nonprinting control characters, and the parity is specified to be odd. This code is now readily adaptable to computer-to-computer communications.

data in voice—A special type of transmission in which digital data displaces voice circuits in a microwave channel.

data link—An assembly of terminal installations and the interconnecting circuits that are operating according to a particular method that permits information to be exchanged between the terminal installations. The specific method of operation is defined by particular transmission codes, transmission modes, direction, and control.

data link, multipoint — For multipoint operation (often called multidrop), one station in the network is always designated as the control or primary station. The remaining stations are designated as tributary or secondary stations. The control station controls all transmissions within the multipoint data link, which is normally established over leased (nonswitched) lines. This is called a centralized multipoint operation. The control station initiates all transmissions by selecting or polling a secondary station. Any transmission over the data link is between the designated primary station and one of the secondary stations. The other stations in the network are in a passive monitoring mode. Multi-

point channels may be full-duplex or half-duplex. Frequently, only a primary station on a multipoint channel will operate full-duplex while the secondary stations are half-duplex. This is known as multi-multipoint operation.

data link protocol—Data link control protocol provides for the reliable interchange of data between data terminal equipment via a communications link. The protocol is a set of rules by which a logical data link is established, maintained, and terminated, and data transferred across a link. It includes the format by which control information is passed and the rules by which it is interpreted, in order to transfer data across the logical data link.

data link, switched network — On a switched network, the data link is disconnected after the two stations complete their transmissions. A new data link is created for each subsequent transmission by standard dialing procedures (manual or automatic). The new data link may be established with any other station in the network. Information flow is in one direction at a time (half-duplex) on the switched network.

data logger—A typical logger combines analog, digital, and clock data, and converts it to serial ASCII code for interface with any RS-232 device. Typically, 10 or more analog inputs and 32 to 64 bits of digital data can be recorded when using a printer, a cassette, or disk recorder. The RS-232 interface also permits connection to a terminal or modem.

data logging equipment — Equipment ranging from the simple devices which provide only visual readout, to systems which include a microcomputer or minicomputer and all of their available peripherals. In general, the number of inputs which can be accommodated is independent of the complexity of the equipment; all equipment can handle any number of inputs desired. This excludes the large computer-based systems, since they are principally closed-loop process-control systems, not data logging systems.

data logging transducers and applications — The transducers used with particular data logging equipment can be any or a mix of several types, depending upon the applications. Digital inputs, in the form of contact closures from limit switches, or digitized angles from shaft encoders, etc., are accepted by most data loggers along with the analog measurements. Some of the more common applications of data acquisition and logging equipment are process monitoring, environmental testing, structural testing, R & D engineering, etc. In most environmental applications, both the time scale and physical placement of equipment are different. Often 1% accuracy is adequate, and a sample per minute or hour is satisfactory, or a series of readings taken over many hours, days, or months might give the desired result. Sensing equipment is frequently on board a ship, in a balloon, on a glacier, etc. As a result, many systems provide telemetering of data from a transducer site to the central processing station. Others use self-contained data loggers equipped with battery and tape cassette which can be left on a mountain top for several months, then retrieved, and the data recovered from the tape.

data, machine readable—Being able to be sensed or read by a specific device, i.e., capable of being read by a machine.

data, master—A set of data which is altered infrequently and supplies basic data for processing operations. The data content of a master file. Examples include: names, badge numbers, or pay rate in personnel data, or stock numbers, stock descriptions, or units of measure in stock-control data.

datamation—A shortened term for automatic data processing; taken from data and automation.

data medium—The selected medium used to transport or carry (communicate) data or information. Punched cards, magnetic tapes, punched paper tapes and, lately, portable disks, are examples of the most often easily transported mediums. They are independent of the devices used in reading or interpreting such data or information.

data migration—Refers generally to the moving of data from an on-line device to an off-line or low-priority device, as

determined by the system or as requested by the user. Contrast with staging.

data path (microprocessor)—The data path is a transfer bus for input/output and data handling operations. Data path width is suggested by application where random logic suggests individual bit manipulation. Numeric operations such as calculators suggest a 4-bit width for BCD representation. Alphanumeric data handling suggests an 8-bit representation and scientific processing suggests larger byte sizes. Regardless of what byte size the application suggests, data path width is actually only limited by the speed desired in performing the operation. A 1-bit microprocessor can handle a 16-bit operation and, in the same sense, a 16-bit microprocessor can do individual bit manipulation. The real tradeoff is between speed and cost.

data processing—1. The basic generic term used for all the operations carried out on data according to precise rules or procedures. 2. A generic term for computing in general as applied to business situations and other applications. 3. Any procedure for receiving information and producing a specific result. The rearrangement and refinement of raw data into a form suitable for further use. 4. The production of records and reports. (Synonymous with data handling.)

data processor — 1. A device capable of performing operations on data, such as a digital computer, an analog computer, or a desk calculator. 2. A person who processes data. 3. A standardized term representing any and all devices that have the capability of performing the reduction, summarizing, processing, or inputting and outputting data or information; the devices include calculators, optical-type equipment, computers, and subsidiary systems.

data purification—The reduction of the number of errors as much as possible prior to using data in an automatic data processing system.

data rate—The clock rate for synchronous systems. It must not exceed the specified maximum clock rate of the analyzer.

data, raw—Data that have not been

processed. Such data may or may not be in machine-sensible form.

data reduction—Refers to the process of transforming raw data into intelligible form by smoothing, adjusting, scaling, ordering, and other statistical methods.

data registers—Special registers provided in many microcomputer CPUs for the temporary storage of data. These CPU registers also may often be used when performing simple data manipulating operations, such as incrementing or decrementing the value of a number.

data reliability—A ratio used to measure the degree to which data is error free.

data set—A collection of similar and related data records that is recorded for use by a microcomputer. A recordable medium such as a data file.

data sink—A communications term referring to a device capable of accepting data signals from a transmission device. It may also check these signals and originate error control signals. Contrast with data source.

data source—A communications term referring to a device capable of originating data signals for a transmission device. It may also accept error control signals. Contrast with data sink.

data station—A multipurpose remote-terminal device which can be used for a broad range of communications applications, as well as for off-line jobs. This device gives branch offices, warehouses, remote reporting locations throughout a plant, or any other company outposts, the power to prepare source data locally and communicate directly with a centrally located computer. The data station features a wide choice of input/output devices, including paper tape, magnetic-stripe-card equipment, a keyboard, page printers, and an optical bar-code reader that introduces new applications possibilities.

data stream—Generally all data transmitted through a channel in a single Read or Write operation.

data structures—A data structure is an organizing principle used to impose order on a collection of data or information. Strings and matrices are data structures. A *string* is a data structure that groups a number of

characters into a sequence. A *matrix* is a data structure that groups a number of characters or integers (or more complex numbers) into a rectangular array like a table.

data tablet—The data tablet is a graphical input device that enables the entry of visual images into a computer. Just as a keyboard enters alphanumeric characters (the elements of text), so a data tablet enters lines and points (the elements of images). Data tablets are now commercially available for personal computer systems. To use a data tablet, a pen-shaped stylus is moved over a flat electromagnetically sensitive board. The position of the pen over the board is monitored by a controller which relays information to a computer. Thus, it is possible to "draw" images directly into memory.

data terminal—1. A device that modulates/demodulates data between an input/output device and a data transmission link. 2. Various manual, audio, and visual devices used to put information in or receive information out of microcomputers.

data terminal equipment (DTE)—DTE equipment is comprised of devices for the data source, the data sink, or both. All types are related to the communication control function (protocol). Data terminal equipment is actually any piece of equipment at which a communications path begins or ends.

data transfer — There are generally three types of data transfer — programmed data transfers, program interrupt transfers, and direct-memory-access transfers. Programmed data transfers are the easiest and most direct methods of handling data I/O. Program interrupt transfers provide an extension of programmed I/O capabilities by allowing the peripheral device to initiate a data transfer. The data break system uses direct-memory access for applications involving the fastest data transfer rates.

data transfer controller — Signal sequences enable data transfers across the I/O bus. Actual controllers will always have their own special requirements that will cause them to depart from the various signal schemes but, in principal, the sequences should hold. Many computers have far more complex I/O signal sequences with no increase in data transfer capabilities. Users should examine carefully how complex the I/O bus signal sequences are on the computer of their choice. It is important to note the types of I/O bus lines provided and the CPU's signal generation logic.

data transfer register—The temporary storage device which eases the communication or movement of data within the computer. It is often called Memory Data Register (MDR).

data transmission—The sending of data from one part of a system to another part.

data transmission systems—A series of circuits, modems, or other devices which transfer (or translate) information from one site (or location) to another.

data under voice (DUV)—A transmission system which carries digital data on a portion of the microwave radio spectrum below the frequency used for voice transmission.

data validation—Refers to various measures it takes to verify data, i.e., the results of specific tests performed on the data, such as the forbidden code check. Such tests and checks verify the reliability of the data and, thus, its validity or degree of acceptability.

data validation operation—Some data entry systems have extensive arrays of data validation and error-checking features. Any attempt to enter incorrect data is often caught on a field-by-field basis before it gets into the computer system. On some systems, when an incorrect character is detected, the entry is disallowed, the cursor remains in the field, and an audible "beep" indicates the identified error. To continue operation, the operator merely keys in the correct character.

dc-synchronization mode—In the dc-synchronization mode, word boundaries are separated by two bit times at a high logic level. When no data is to succeed the previous transmission, the serial data line goes to a logic high state until a new word is to be transmitted. When new data is to be transmitted after an extended (greater than two bit times) idle period, the current synchronization period will be completed prior to transmission (i.e.,

idle periods are always a multiple of two bit time sync periods). Dc synchronization offers the advantage over continuous data stream in that word boundaries are defined by the synchronization period.

DCTL (direct-coupled transistor logic) —Logic employing only transistors as active circuit elements.

dead front — A connector that is designed in such a way that its contacts are recessed below the surface of its body, in order to prevent accidental short circuits, and to prevent the contacts from contacting other objects.

dead time—Any definite delay deliberately placed between two related actions, in order either to avoid an overlap that might cause confusion or to permit a particular different event, such as a control decision.

debit card system—Various terminals that are activated by magnetically encoded plastic "debit cards" such as issued by banks and loan companies. The operator simply inserts his card and then keys the applicable 4-digit security code into the terminal, followed by the amount of the transaction. The terminals are on-line to a controller which is a part of the system. The controller, in turn, communicates with a computer to ascertain account balances, and to debit or credit accounts.

debug—1. An instruction, program, or action designed in microprocessor software to search for, correct, and/or eliminate sources of errors in programming routines. There are many types of "bugs" or "glitches" that can be located by single-step testers, specifically designed programs, or operational procedures. 2. To locate and correct any errors in a computer program. 3. To detect and correct malfunctions in the computer itself.

debugged program—Refers to various programs that will perform actions in the logical sequence that is expected and will produce accurate answers to one or more test problems that have been specifically designed to execute all foreseeable paths through the program.

debuggers—Debuggers are a class of system software that is designed to help the programmer discover the causes of problems found during the run-time testing in the checkout phases of his software development. Their features include the ability to stop the executing program and inquire as to the state of the machine. The machine state includes the content of all memory locations and registers. The features of the debuggers are a function of the machine architecture and special hardware facilities. Another type of debugger is called a "simulator." The simulator is a software program that takes as input the machine code for the "target" machine and simulates the target machine's changes of state on a "host" machine while offering various debugging facilities. However, the simulator cannot duplicate the actions of the input and output, particularly when the peripheral device timing is part of the run-time and check-out.

debugging—1. The process of isolating and removing any errors or malfunctions from a computer or computer program. Also, it can refer to a process to take equipment or parts through a period during which catastrophic failures occur at a prohibitively high rate. 2. The process of determining the correctness of a computer routine, locating any errors in it, and correcting them. Also, the detection and correction of malfunctions in the computer itself.

debugging aids, reference—Refers to a specific set of routines which provides a means of utilizing the computer to assist the programmer in debugging his programs.

debugging programs—During testing, the programmer will want to examine and modify the contents of registers and memory in order to observe the results of the operation of the program and make changes in the program. Programs used for this function are called debugging programs.

debugging statements—The debugging statements are often part of the operating statements and provide a variety of methods for manipulating the program itself in an attempt to identify program errors ("bugs"). The user may: (1) insert or delete statements, (2) execute selectively, (3) print changes of values as the change occurs and transfer control as the transfer occurs, and (4) obtain a static printout of all cross-reference relationships among names and labels

with the dynamic exposure of partial or imperfect execution.

debugging, symbolic — *See* symbolic debugging.

debugging, test instruction — Most good compiler systems are designed to automatically remove various temporary tracing (debugging) instructions after the tests are made to insure accuracy and precision. Such instructions are often combined with various switch settings.

decentralized data processing — The housing and handling of data by individual subdivisions of an organization, or at each geographical location of the parts of an organization.

decibel meter — Refers to a specific meter which has a scale calibrated approximately uniformly in logarithmic steps and labeled with decibel units; used for determining the power levels in communication circuits, relative to a datum power level, now 1 mW in 600 ohms.

decimal-to-binary conversion — Refers to the process of converting a number written in base 10 into a number written in base 2.

decision—1. The computer operation of determining if a certain relationship exists between words in storage or registers, and the taking of alternative courses of action. This is effected by conditional jumps or equivalent techniques. Use of this term has given rise to the misnomer "magic brain." Actually, the process consists of making comparisons, by use of arithmetic, to determine the relationship of two terms, e.g., equal, greater than, or less than. 2. Usually by comparison, a determination that concerns the existence or nonexistence of a given condition as a result of developing an alternative action. 3. The computer operation of determining if a certain relationship exists between words in storage or registers, and the process of taking specific courses of action.

decision box — A rectangle or other symbol on a flowchart that is used to mark a choice or branching in a sequence of programming.

decision circuit — A circuit that performs a logical operation on one or more binary digits of input information (representing "yes" or "no"), and expresses the result in its output.

decision gates—A logic circuit having two or more inputs and one output. The output depends upon the combination of logic signals at the input.

decision integrator—1. A digital integrator changed in such a way that when used in incremental computers, it has an output increment that is maximum negative, zero, or maximum positive dependent upon the same input values. It is used when negative feedback is necessary, as in various types of adders. 2. A specific servomechanism that is used to develop a rotational speed of a shaft which is proportional to its input current.

decision level—A predetermined signal amplitude that serves as a standard for determining the value of a signal pulse. If the signal amplitude is above the decision level at the time of sampling, a binary 1 is indicated. A binary 0 is indicated if the signal amplitude is below the decision level at sampling time. Ideally, a signal pulse is measured at its time center.

decision table—A tabulation or array of possible courses of action, selections, or alternatives that can be possible and, thus, considered in the analysis of various problems, i.e., a graphic aid to problem description, flow, and potential results, much as the purpose of a flowchart.

declarative operation—1. Generally, a coding sequence consisting of a symbolic label, a declarative operation code, and an operand. It involves writing symbolic labels and operation codes for data and constants. 2. The process or procedures that provide the object program with various input, output, work ideas, and other constants that may be desired or required.

decoder—1. Refers to a specific device which determines the meaning of a set of signals and initiates a computer operation based thereon. 2. A matrix of switching elements which selects one or more output channels according to the combination of input signals present.

decrement—1. To decrease the value of a number. 2. The quantity by which a variable is decreased. 3. In some computers, a specific part of an instruction word. 4. A programming device or instruction designed to de-

crease the contents of a storage location.

dedicated — Generally refers to machines, programs, or procedures that are designed or set apart for special or continued use. For example, a dedicated microprocessor can be one that has been designed or specifically programmed for a single or special group of applications, such as computerized games, appliances, traffic lights, calculators, etc. ROMs, as control devices, are usually the means of developing dedicated microprocessors. 2. Synonymous with leased or private lines, or with machines, and usually referring to communications equipment. 3. Reserved or committed to a specific use or application.

dedicated channel—A specific channel that has been reserved or committed or set aside for a very specific use or application.

dedicated circuit—Refers to a communications circuit or channel that has been reserved or committed or allocated for a specific user or use, i.e., for emergency, ultra high-level priorities, or for very distinct purposes.

dedicated control application—A dedicated control application is one in which a piece of hardware performs a limited task repeatedly on demand. When power is applied, it does a job. There is little or no need to process volumes of data. Every job is unique and a canned program is not necessary. The job is precisely defined. It either has a requirement or very low cost for a high-volume market or it must be easy to design and change because of its one-of-a-kind nature.

dedicated leased line, private—A service offered by the common carriers in which a customer may lease, for his exclusive use, a circuit between two or more geographic points.

dedicated line characteristics—1. Data set may be telephone company type or from some other vendor. 2. Service terminal is charged for on a monthly rental basis plus a one-time installation charge. 3. The transmission speed may require additional monthly line conditioning charges for each termination or drop point on the line including the computer location. 4. Mileage is charged for on a monthly rental basis with no installation charge.

dedicated machine control—A microcomputer dedicated to production machinery control. The main benefit is increased operational flexibility, since the entire system becomes programmable. With microcomputer control systems, it is practical to build multifunction machines, since diverse tasks can be performed under the command of the controller. An economic advantage is possible if one such machine can be used where several were previously necessary. Plus, programming may allow complex equipment to be modified for new production requirements, rather than have them fall into obsolescence. Examples are: (1) Automatic armature coil-winding machines controlled by the microcomputer. The number of turns, turn counts, and turn positions are fully programmable. Plus, on-line testing for parts control can be easily implemented. (2) A bottling machine controlled by a microcomputer that provides instructions for the loading of bottles of different sizes and also gives the command to initiate each step in the loading process A related characteristic of a machine with a dedicated microcomputer is the ability to be manually or automatically tuned for optimum operation under a given set of conditions. An example is an automatic surface grinder whose stepping motors are tuned to give maximum performance by programming the stepping rate versus the load.

dedicated microprocessor techniques —In data processing, multiple overlapping tasks requiring interrupt are assigned to the data processor to maintain its productivity. In random-logic designs, where microprocessors are dedicated to limited tasks, the productivity requirement relaxes. Instead of the logic processor waiting for an external interruption, it is put to work analyzing the external situation, continuously scanning and testing for inputs. The logic processor has complete command of the operation, and knows when to accept or ignore inputs. This simple, but effective, technique eliminates the need for expensive and complex interrupt structures.

dedicated processor, array—Array processors are computers dedicated by their design to performing repetitive arithmetical calculations on large arrays of data with high precision, wide dynamic range, and high throughput. Usually, most input/output operations and file management chores are left to the host computer, in order to free the peripheral array processor to concentrate on its calculations. As they become more popular, however, a semantic distinction must be made between array processors and other specialized processors with similar sounding names. An array processor consists of a single computer that operates on one piece of data at a time (see vector processor).

deferred addressing—An indirect addressing mode in which the directly addressed location contains the address of the operand, rather than the operand itself.

degauss—A procedure to demagnetize a magnetic tape. A degausser is a coil that is momentarily energized by an alternating current and which disarranges the impulses on a magnetic tape when the coil is placed close to the magnetic tape.

delay circuit—A specific circuit that can delay the passage of a pulse or signal from one part of a circuit to another.

delay line—1. A device capable of retarding a pulse of energy between the input and output, based on the properties of materials, circuit parameters, or mechanical devices. Examples of delay lines are material media such as mercury, in which sonic patterns may be propagated in time, lumped-constant electrical lines, coaxial cables, transmission lines, and recirculating magnetic-drum loops. 2. A line or network designed to introduce a desired delay in the transmission of a signal, usually without appreciable distortion.

delay line, acoustic — Refers to a specific delay line that bases its operation on the time of propagation of sound waves.

delimiter—Refers to a computer character that limits a string of characters and, therefore, cannot be a member of the string.

delimiter, data—Generally, a flag character marks the ends or bounds of a series or a string of bits or characters, and, thus, it is not a part or member of such a string unless it is the first or last member. Most frequently, certain special patterns of data are proposed and used by each computer center as a convention or rule of that center and are used as markers, end-of-message signals, etc.

delta clock—A clock whose primary use is in timing subroutine operations. If a momentary fault throws the computer into a closed programming loop, or if a fault occurring during the execution of an instruction halts the computer, the delta clock restarts the computer by means of an interrupt, thus providing automatic fault recovery. The interrupt can be programmed to notify the operator that a closed loop has occurred. If completing an operation takes longer than desired, this clock is also used to interrupt the computer and thereby allow program attention to be diverted to items of more immediate importance.

demodulator—1. Refers to various devices which receive tones from a transmission circuit and convert them to electrical pulses, or bits, which may be accepted by a machine. 2. A device which detects the modulating signals, removes the carrier signal, and reconstitutes the intelligence.

descriptor—Refers to a specific computer word used specifically to define characteristics of a program element. For example, descriptors are used for describing a data record, a segment of a program, or an input/output operation.

desk check—A procedure of analyzing or inspecting a written program or specific instructions for errors in logic or syntax without the requirement or use of computing or peripheral equipment.

desktop computer systems—A typical desktop computer is a complete highly integrated system, generally ready to use as it comes out of the crate. Desktop computers are often heavily I/O oriented. Thus, most contain a typewriter-like keyboard, a block of user-programmable keys, cartridge drives for program and data storage, and a crt display that is all in one enclosure. Often a hard-copy unit, such as a thermal printer, is also built in. It often doubles as a plotter. The typical system has up to 64

Desktop computer systems
(Courtesy Hewlett-Packard Co.).

Kbytes of Read/Write RAM memory and a ROM-based operating system that includes an editor, a language interpreter, and an I/O scheduler. The microprocessors selected for I/O intensive applications are often byte-oriented and highly parallel in organization, e.g., the data and address lines will be separate rather than multiplexed. The major trend in high-performance desktop computers is toward increased throughput, with simplicity of design and low cost.

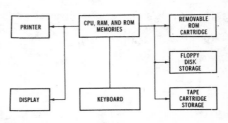

Desktop computer systems
configuration.

development time — A part, portion, or section of operating time during which new routines or hardware are tested and debugged.

device character control — A control character which is used to control various devices associated with computing or telecommunications systems, i.e., particularly the switching to on or off of the devices.

device independence — Refers to the ability to request I/O operations without regard for the characteristics of specific types of input/output devices.

device priority — Each device has an I/O priority, in some systems, based on its distance from the processor. When two or more devices request interrupt service, the device electrically closest to the microcomputer will receive the interrupt grant (acknowledge).

device selection check—1. A check that verifies the choice of devices, such as registers, in the execution of an instruction. 2. A check (usually automatic) to verify that the correct register (I/O device, etc.) was selected in the performance of a program instruction.

device status word (DSW)—A computer word containing bits whose condition indicates the status of devices.

diagnosis, breakpoint conditions — A variety of breakpoint conditions can be specified to stop a program: memory read, memory write, I/O read, and I/O write. These conditions may be further qualified by prototype logic operations, combined with such functions as stack operations or instruction fetch. For example, some users will monitor a device such as flip-flop A in a prototype, and specify a breakpoint halt when A is set and a specific stack address is being accessed. This enables the development team to make sure the flip-flop is set at the proper point in a control, data-processing, or interrupt-handling routine.

diagnosis, single-step mode — In the single-step mode, one instruction is executed, and a "snapshot" is taken of system states, including memory address, data, and status, which are translated into readable images that can be displayed on the system console. Following instructions are then executed upon operator command. In multiple single-step operation, the system appears to run continuously. It single-steps automatically, pausing only long enough between instruction cycles to display or log the data that has been collected. This mode is particularly useful when an engineer or programmer wants to look at system behavior throughout an operating sequence. He can note operations that appear to be troublesome, as well as retrieve the images from bulk memory for detailed off-line analysis.

diagnostic—Refers to the detection, discovery, and further isolation of a malfunction and/or mistake.

diagnostic function test — A program used to test overall system reliability.

diagnostic program — A user-inserted test program that is used to help isolate hardware malfunctions in the programmable controller and the application equipment.

diagnostic routines—1. A routine designed to locate a malfunction in the computer or a mistake in coding, or both. 2. Routines used for diagnosing programming mistakes are most often service routines, whereas, routines used for diagnosing mistakes in data are usually specific to a particular application.

diagnostic test—The running of a machine program or routine for the purpose of discovering a failure or a potential failure of a machine element, and to determine its location or its potential location.

diagnostic test routine—A test program used to detect and identify hardware malfunctions in the computer and its associated I/O equipment.

diagnostic trace routine—A particular type of diagnostic program designed to perform checks on other programs or to demonstrate such operations. The output of a trace program may include instructions of the program that is being checked and the intermediate results of those instructions arranged in the order in which the instructions were executed.

diagram, set-up—A graphic representation showing how a computing system has been prepared and the arrangements that have been made for operation.

die—Sometimes called a chip. A single piece of semiconductor material that has been cut from a slice (semiconductor wafer) by scribing and breaking. It can contain one or more circuits but is packaged as a unit. Plural is dice.

die bond—1. A process in which chips are attached to a substrate (hold, epoxy, wax, etc.). 2. The joint between a die and the substrate.

dielectric guide — Possible transmission path of very-high-frequency electromagnetic energy functionally realized in a dielectric channel, the dielectric constant of which differs from its surroundings.

dielectric heating — Radio-frequency heating in which energy is released in a nonconducting medium through dielectric hysteresis.

dielectric hysteresis — Phenomenon in which the polarization of a dielectric depends not only on the applied electric field, but also on its previous variation. This leads to power loss with alternating electric fields.

dielectric isolation, IC—In certain IC diffusion applications, the parasitic junction capacitances or leakage currents associated with the junction isolation methods may not be acceptable. In such cases, a superior electrical isolation is obtained by insulating each pocket with a dielectric layer. Normally, thermally grown SiO_2 is used as the dielectric material. In forming the dielectrically isolated pockets on the wafer surface, a number of alternate fabrication techniques can be utilized.

differential amplifier—Refers to a circuit that will produce an output signal derived from the difference between two input signals.

differential analyzer—Refers to various analog computers using interconnected integrators to solve differential equations.

differential, electronic — An input or output type of circuit that only amplifies or responds to the difference of two signals, and does **not** respond to the signal with respect to ground or a supply voltage.

differential, switching—The difference between the operate and release points of a switch, caused by hysteresis. It can be in units of amps, volts, inches, gauss, etc.

differential transducer—A type of device that can simultaneously measure two separate stimuli and provide an output proportionate to the difference between them.

differentiating amplifier — A specific type of amplifier whose output current is proportional to the derivative

with respect to time, related to the input current, as used in analog computers.

diffused-alloy transistor — A transistor constructed by combining the diffusion and alloy techniques. First, the semiconductor wafer is exposed to gaseous dissemination to produce the nonuniform base region. Alloy junctions are then formed comparable to a conventional alloy transistor.

diffused-base transistor—Also referred to as a graded-base transistor. This type of transistor is made by combining diffusion and alloy techniques. A nonuniform base region and the collector-to-base junction are formed by gaseous dissemination into a semiconductor wafer which constitutes the collector region. The emitter-to-base junction is then formed by a conventional alloy process on the base side of the diffused wafer.

diffusion capacitance — The rate of change of injected charge with the applied voltage in a semiconductor diode.

diffusion constant—The ratio of diffusion current density to the gradient of charge carrier concentration in a semiconductor.

diffusion, floating — A doped region without ohmic connection to which charge packets are transferred in and out by overlapping or adjacent transfer gates. A floating diffusion can be used as the sense node for the charge signal in detection or regeneration circuits.

diffusion, mesa—Refers to a technique used to manufacture semiconductors having diffused pn junctions. A single base region is diffused over the entire wafer, and an acid is then used to etch a mesa configuration for the transistor elements.

diffusion of solids—In semiconductors, the migration of atoms into pure elements to form a surface alloy for providing minority carriers.

diffusion, planar—A technique used to manufacture semiconductors having diffused pn junctions. All the junctions emerge at the top surface of the wafer.

diffusion, semiconductor — A process used in the production of semiconductors that introduces minute amounts of impurities into a substrate material, such as silicon or germanium, and permits the impurity to spread into the substrate. The process is very dependent on temperature and time.

digital/analog converter (DAC)—Converts digital signals into a continuous electrical signal suitable for input to an analog computer.

digital bar-code wand — A digital barcode wand is a hand-held scanner designed to read all common barcode formats (with the narrowest bars having a nominal width of 0.3 mm or 0.012 inch). The wand contains an optical sensor (with a visible light source), a photo IC detector, and precision aspheric optics. Internal signal-conditioning circuitry converts the optical information into a logic-level pulse-width representation of the bars and spaces. A push-to-read switch is used to activate the electronics.

digital cassette—A typical digital cassette holds at least 282 feet of 0.15-inch tape. Differences between digital and most audio cassettes include an ANSI locating notch, reusable write-enable tabs, pullout-proof leaders, and holes at the beginning and end of the tape. The recording qualities of the two types also differ. A flat belt provides built-in direct drive and tensioning for the recording tape. Internal guides align the tape.

digital circuit—Refers to circuits which operate in the manner of a switch, that is, it is either "on" or "off." More correctly, they should be called binary circuits.

digital clock—Clocks that have output signals in a digital representation. They allocate time to each program as set by priorities. Used in computing systems with developed time-sharing procedures.

digital computer — A computer which processes information represented by combinations of discrete or discontinuous data as compared with an analog computer for continuous data. More specifically, it is a device for performing sequences of arithmetic and logical operations, not only on data but on its own program. Still more specifically, a stored-program digital computer that is capable of performing sequences of internally stored instructions, as opposed to calculators on which the sequence of instructions is impressed manually. Related to data processor.

digital converter—A modem or device which completes the process of putting information into digital form.

digital multiplier—Refers to a specific device that generates a digital product from the representation of two digital numbers, by additions of the multiplicand in accordance with the value of the digits in the multiplier. It is necessary only to shift the multiplicand and add it to the product if the multiplier digit is a 1, and just shift the multiplicand without adding, if the multiplier digit is a 0, for each successive digit of the multiplier.

digital output—A type of output signal that represents the size of a stimulus or input signal in the form of a series of discrete quantities which are coded to represent digits in a system of numerical notation. This particular type of output is to be distinguished from one which provides a continuous signal as opposed to a discrete output signal.

digital output module, isolated—A typical module provides a data output interface and electrical isolation (1500 volt) between the microcomputer and user-defined processes or peripheral devices. Provides outputs up to 50 volts on contact closure.

digital subset—A collection of data in a prescribed format described by the control information to which an operating system has access. It constitutes the principal unit of data storage and retrieval within the system.

digital-to-analog converter (DAC) — A particular type of computing device that changes digital quantities into a physical motion or a voltage. For example, a number output changed into a specific number of turns of a potentiometer.

digital voltmeter—A type of indicator which provides a digital readout of a measured voltage as opposed to a pointer (scale) indicator.

digitization—Refers to the conversion of an analog signal to a digital signal, with steps between specified levels. Also quantization.

digitize—A process that is used to convert an analog measurement of a specific physical variable into a num-

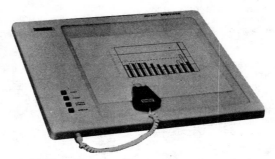

Digitizer (Courtesy Houston Instruments, Inc.).

ber expressed in digits in a system of notation.

digitizer — Refers to a specific device which converts an analog measurement into digital form.

diode matrix — A hardware pattern in which diode leads may be inserted to change solid-state control logic.

diode, Schottky high-power — The Schottky high-power diode is a special rectifier favored for its fast switching speed and is popular in switching power supplies. Having only half the forward voltage drop of ordinary pn diodes, Schottkys boost power conversion efficiency, dissipating only half the power for the same amount of forward current. Power Schottkys are available in the current range of 25 A to 75 A.

diode-transistor-logic (DTL) — Logic employing diodes with transistors used only as inverting amplifiers.

DIP—Abbreviation for dual-in-line package. A most popular IC packaging in the mid-1970s was the plastic dual-in-line case. Plastic was used for economic reasons and the dual-in-line package (DIP) configuration for manufacturing efficiency. IC chips were enclosed in the dual-in-line packages which take their names from the double parallel rows of leads that connect them to the circuit board. DIPs are sometimes also called "bugs."

dipole modulation—Refers to the representation of binary digits on a magnetic-surface medium such as disks, tapes, drums, cards, etc., but in which a specified part of each cell is magnetically saturated in one of two opposing senses, depending upon the value of the digit represented. The

remainder of the cell is magnetized in a predetermined sense and remains fixed.

direct access—Refers to a basic type of storage medium which allows information to be accessed by positioning the medium or accessing mechanism directly to the information required, thus permitting direct addressing of data locations.

direct-access unit—A memory device which allows a particular address to be accessed in a manner independent of the location of that address; thus, the items stored in the memory can be addressed or accessed in the same amount of time for each location. Access by a program is not dependent upon the previously accessed position.

direct addressing—A basic addressing procedure or mode designed to reach any point in main storage directly instead of by the usual indirect manner. Direct addressing is usually restricted considerably in most microprocessors.

direct-coupled flip-flop — A flip-flop composed of electronic circuits in which the active elements are coupled with resistors.

direct-coupled transistor logic — Abbreviated DCTL. Logic employing only transistors as active circuit elements.

direct-current balancer—Refers to the coupling and connecting of two or more similar direct-current machines so that the conductors connected to the junction points of the machines are maintained at constant potentials.

direct instruction—A standard instruction which contains an operand for the operation specified by the instruction.

directive commands, assembler—Assembler directive commands provide the programmer with the ability to generate data words and values based on specific conditions at assembly time. The instruction operation codes are assigned mnemonics which describe the hardware function of each instruction.

directive statements — Directive statements define program structure. There are four directive statements: Program Statement, Procedure Statement, End Statement, and Origin Statement.

directly controlled system—Refers to various modules, processes, or machines directly guided or restrained by the final controlling element, i.e., designed to achieve a prescribed value of the directly controlled variable.

direct-memory access (DMA) — 1. Direct-memory access, sometimes called data break, is the preferred form of data transfer for use with high-speed storage devices such as magnetic disk or tape units. The DMA mechanism transfers data directly between memory and peripheral devices. The CPU is involved only in setting up the transfer; the transfers take place with no processor intervention on a "cycle stealing" basis. The DMA transfer rate is limited only by the bandwidth of the memory and the data transfer characteristics of the device. The device generates a DMA request when it is ready to transfer data. 2. High-speed data transfer operation in which an I/O channel transfers information directly to or from the memory. Also called "data break."

direct-memory access transfer—A direct-memory access (DMA) device sets up a high-speed data path to link memory with peripheral electronics. The DMA circuit when working in conjunction with the interface may not require overhead electronics to keep track of memory addresses, bytes transferred, and handshaking signals. The data transfer is initiated by the CPU under program control. Once started, the DMA transfer will continue without CPU intervention. The CPU can sense the enable line of the DMA to determine the comple-

tion of a transfer. The entire DMA transfer will take place without halting the central processor (in some systems).

directory—A file containing information concerning the other files on a mass-storage device, such as a diskette; also termed a catalog.

direct page register — The direct page register serves to enhance the direct addressing mode. The content of this register appears at the higher address outputs during direct addressing instruction execution. This allows the direct mode to be used at any place in memory, under program control. To ensure compatibility, all bits of this register are cleared during processor reset.

direct reference address—A virtual address that is not modified by indirect addressing, but may be modified by indexing.

disabled—1. Refers to a state of the central processing unit that prevents the occurrence of certain types of interruptions. Synonymous with masked. 2. In communications, pertaining to a state in which a transmission control unit cannot accept incoming calls on a line.

disarmed state—Concerns that state of an interrupt level that cannot accept an interrupt input signal.

disassembly—Retranslation of machine language into mnemonics during debugging.

disaster dump — A dump or printout which occurs as a result of a nonrecoverable program error.

discrete circuits—Refers to the many various electronic circuits built of separate, individually manufactured, tested, and assembled diodes, resistors, transistors, capacitors, and other specific electronic components.

discrete data—A representation for a variable which may assume any of several distinct states; i.e., sex, race. Usually coded. Conventional usage in computing excludes measures of a quantal nature (i.e., number of children in a family). (Contrast with continuous data.)

discrete wired circuits—A compromise approach exists between printed-circuit and wire-wrapped boards called discrete wired circuits. In discrete wiring, an automatic tool lays down

Disk controller board (Courtesy Ampex Corp.).

a conductor pattern of insulated wires from point to point. The wired board is then sealed in an epoxy layer to freeze the wires in position.

discrimination—Refers to the skipping of various instructions as developed by a predetermined set of conditions as programmed. If a conditional jump is not used, the next instructions would follow in the normal proper sequence.

disk accessing—Refers to the process of or methods used in transferring data to and from a disk file. Disk units and access routines vary widely in their sophistication: access can be accomplished either by using physical addresses (actual disk locations) or various levels of symbolic or keyed-record addressing procedures. Some disk drives can locate a desired record by using addressing logic contained within the unit itself to find a keyed record, thus leaving more productive time available to the central processing unit while the record is being sought.

disk controller board — The controller board accepts software commands from the program in execution, decodes them, and manages the disk drive in such a way as to produce the required operation. When a controller simply accepts orders, such as "access specified track and sector," it is then called a "dumb" controller. Whenever a controller is equipped with its own sophisticated software

capabilities, such as a file management system, it is termed an "intelligent" controller, in the same way that a dumb display is opposed to an intelligent display. An "intelligent device" is one that can decode complex commands that it receives, both on input and on output.

disk crash—This refers to a disk Read/Write head making destructive contact with the surface of a rotating disk. Loosely refers to any disk unit failure that results in a system malfunction.

disk drives — Typical disk drives are highly reliable, random-access, moving-head memory devices, compactly designed for use as peripheral units in large, small, and, now, microcomputer systems. Typically, a photoelectric positioning system, working in conjunction with a velocity transducer and a voice-coil-driven actuator, provides fast and accurate head positioning over a wide temperature range. Cartridge interchangeability is becoming standard.

A typical disk drive provides 10-million bytes of storage. Some reliable drives have an average access time of 53 milliseconds, and a data transfer rate of 6.3 million bits per second.

diskette—Generally refers to a thin flexible platter (floppy disk) that is coated with a magnetic material. It is used as the storage medium in a floppy-disk unit.

Disk drives, Winchester (Courtesy Priam Corp.).

Diskette drives (Courtesy PerSci, Inc.).

diskette drives—See disk drives.

diskette initialization — Each diskette must be initialized before it can be used for data storage. The initialization operation consists of prerecording sector information on the diskette. During this operation, each track is written on in one continuous operation from index to index. The leading edge of an index pulse is always used as the starting point for the initialize operation.

disk file—1. Refers to various disk units consisting of a drive, channel, and the fixed or removable disks. 2. An associated set of records of the same format, identified by a unique label.

disk, hard sector—Generally refers to magnetic disk systems that are divided into sectors around the disk. These sectors may be marked either by the hardware, called the hard sector, or the software (the soft sector).

Hard sectoring is older, consisting of actual holes in the diskette.

disk index holes — Both soft-sectored and hard-sectored disks have index holes—indicators to the drive that the disk is rotating. Sector holes in hard-sectored disks (there are 32 in an 8″ diskette) are used as indicators to the drive controller that data is to be read or written.

disk index/sector signal — This status signal is generated whenever a hole is sensed in the disk. In a soft-sectored disk, this will be an index hole; in a hard-sectored disk, it will be a sectored hole.

disk interfacing — Disk interfacing is quite simple in principle. The disk drive is equipped with the minimum electronics needed to manage the few control signals it generates. These control signals allow an external controller board to sense the mechanical and electronic status of the drive and provide the required orders needed to position the head over the required track and sector. Because the formatting of the disk itself is well rationalized, in the case of IBM-compatible diskettes, it has been implemented in single-chip disk controllers. A number of additional facilities are desirable in order to provide an easy interface with the user program. Ideally the user software should be able to specify any file name and have all functions taken care of automatically. This is performed by an intelligent disk controller. The set of commands usually available in a disk-operating system varies widely with the manufacturer. However, recently, CP/M (trademark of Digital Research) has become a virtual standard in the hobbyist and small business systems world and is likely to be widely used in the future as it makes disk-based program files compatible.

disk operating system, CP/M—In the early 1980s, CP/M was the leading industry defacto standard operating system for small machines. It was one of the original hardware-independent "bus" systems for those users who were working with the broad array of languages, word processing, and applications software that was available from scores of suppliers. CP/M 2.2 was the 1980 version of the efficient reliable system.

disk operating system (DOS) — Many such programs are data communications-oriented disk-based operating systems. They feature both multiterminal and multitasking capabilities and allow full control of both hardware and software operations through the system console, or any batch input device.

disk operating system, MP/M—MP/M is a popular small computer disk operating system that provides multiterminal access with multiprogramming at each terminal. It is compatible with its predecessor CP/M and, thus, can run many programming languages, applications packages, and development software developed for various systems. It offers such advanced capabilities as run editors, translators, word processors, and background print spoolers. Users can write their own system processes for operation under MP/M.

disk pack—Refers to various removable direct-access storage devices containing magnetic disks on which data is stored. Disk packs are mounted on disk storage drives.

disk storage—A computer memory device capable of storing information magnetically on a disc similar in appearance to a phonograph record.

disks, Winchester — "Micro-Winchesters" are disks less than 8 inches in diameter, both rigid and flexible, which rotate at speeds that are approximately ten times faster than floppies and which use "flying" (air bearing) recording heads. "Mini-Winchesters" are 5¼-inch diameter hard disks, whose access speed advantage over floppies will facilitate the appearance of virtual memory, data base management, and multitasking on microcomputer systems.

disorderly close-down—A system stoppage due to an equipment error wherein it is impossible to do an orderly close-down. Special precautions are necessary to prevent the loss of messages and duplication in record updating.

dispersion, fiber optics—Two types of dispersion—modal and chromatic—occur in optical fibers. Modal dispersion is the spreading of light as it takes different paths (travels in different modes) along the fiber. Because different modal paths have different lengths, some of the light arrives late at the receiver, causing pulse spreading. Chromatic dispersion depends on the wavelength or "color" of the light. Light travels along a fiber at a speed that depends on its color and on the characteristics of the fiber. Therefore, if the light source is not truly monochromatic (of just a single wavelength), the various color components of the light will travel at different speeds and arrive at the detector at different times. Again, the result is spreading of the received light pulse, with a resulting limitation on the useful bandwidth.

displacement transducer—A device capable of converting mechanical energy into electrical energy, usually by moving a rod or an armature. Output voltage is determined by the amount the rod or armature is actually moved.

display adapter—The display adapter unit controls the transmission of data, unit control information, and unit status information, and the sequencing and synchronizing of the various units in the system. In addition, digital data received from computer storage is formatted for deflection commands for the crt devices.

display controller — A typical device displays data in the form of a 1024 by 1024 dot array. Under program control, a bright dot may be produced at any point in the array. A series of these dots may then be programmed to produce a graphical output. Basically, a controller fetches data to be displayed from storage, converts the data into dot matrix patterns representing characters, and then, converts the dot patterns into electrical signals to create a video display.

display cursor—A cursor is a moveable mark that locates a character on the screen. By pressing cursor control keys, the operator can move the cursor from line to line and from character to character in the display. A cursor can be used to direct-display editing functions such as "delete character." Thus, if the cursor is moved to underline a certain displayed character, and the "delete character" key in then pressed, that character will be removed. Some terminals use a blinking cursor to call the operator's attention to its position.

display editing functions—These programmed functions permit the removal of characters, words, or larger pieces of text, the insertion of new text, and the movement of text from one position to another. Such functions are essential to word processing operations, but they are also very useful features for any display work station. Operators always make mistakes, and editing allows these mistakes to be easily corrected.

display, electrochromeric — Electrochromic displays, or ECD displays, are low-voltage, low-current devices that chemically transform themselves from a transparent to an opaque state when tickled by an external electrical field. Even after this electrical field is turned off, the devices maintain their opacity; only when subjected to a field with an opposite polarity do they return to their initial state. Thus, electrochromism can find uses both in displays and in information storage devices. The devices can operate in either a transmissive or a reflective mode, against any color background. They do not require polarizers, and are claimed to have distinctly superior appearance, contrast, and legibility in dimly lit ambients. In addition, they are legible over wide viewing angles and are compatible with IC technology.

display, highlighting—A method used to distinguish or emphasize data on a crt display. This is done by reversing the field, blinking, underlining, changing color, changing light intensity, or some combination of the above. A typical keyboard terminal should have at least three different methods for emphasizing or highlighting information on the display.

display modes — Refers to various modes such as vector, increment, character point, etc., which indicate the manner in which points are displayed on a screen.

display module—An optical device that stores a computer output and translates this output into literal, numerical, or graphic signals which are distributed to a program-determined group of lights, annunciators, and numerical indicators for use in operator consoles and remote stations.

display register—The display register consists of up to twelve (or more) indicators that display the contents of the register selected by the display switch.

display resolution—Essentially, resolution is the extent to which an observer can discriminate between closely spaced dots or lines. Parameters used to specify resolution are spot size, trace width, or lines per unit length. Since these vary with crt beam current and display brightness, the beam current or brightness at which the parameter was measured should be stated in the specifications.

display scrolling—This feature allows text to be moved up or down, so as to show material that does not fit on the display screen. When the scrolling key is pressed, the entire displayed text moves up or down. The first line in the direction of motion disappears and a new line appears at the opposite edge of the screen. An alternate approach is to display the text in "pages." Then, when the page advance key is pressed, the currently displayed text is succeeded by a new full screen of text.

display services, refresh graphics — Generally, the refresh-graphics display serves not only as an output device but as an input device as well. The display can provide the designer or draftsman with a precise visible record of the location and content of all drawing data stored in the computer. With a touch of a light pen, any piece of content and location data can be instantly created or modified and the results viewed at once. Some user-oriented systems permit an intimate dialogue between man and machine. The machine takes over the tedious, routine, error-prone work of drawing, moving, editing, and scaling.

display storage, direct-view — Direct-view storage display methods need no refreshing. This is an important memory-saving feature. In a direct-view storage-tube display, graphics information is stored in the phosphor of the crt screen. The technique of

Display storage, direct-view (Courtesy Digital Equipment Corp.).

scanning works like that of vector scanning, with the beam of crt describing geometric end points and connecting them. In addition, it has high-resolution capability and low flicker content. The drawbacks are that color capability is limited, and erasure is not selective. If a part of the display has to be erased, the entire display must be erased. Brightness levels are relatively low, as well.

display window manager—Some subsystems use a type of display window manager to manipulate screen information. The window manager partitions the screen into separate areas or windows. Windows may be moved around the screen, enlarged or contracted in two dimensions, scrolled and clipped under direct user control. Windows can overlap each other, and can be as large as the entire screen or as small as a postage stamp. Menus and "light buttons" are also supported by the window manager. The process mechanism uses the window manager to allow direct user control of multiple concurrent processes when used with special software.

disruptive discharge — A sudden and large increase in current through insulation that is due to the complete failure of the insulation when exposed to an intense electrostatic stress.

distortion—1. A disruption of a waveform of an original signal which can result in unfaithful signal reproduction. Distortion is classified as nonlinear, frequency, or phase, depending on how the waveform has been affected. 2. Distortion caused by transients which, as a result of the modulation, are present in the transmission channel and depend on its transmission qualities. 3. The unwanted change in waveform that occurs between two points in a transmission system.

distortion, asymmetrical—Refers to that type of distortion affecting a two-condition (or binary) modulation (or restitution) in which all the significant intervals corresponding to one of the two significant conditions have longer or shorter durations than the corresponding theoretical durations of the excitation. If this particular requirement is not met, distortion is present.

distortion delay—1. The distortion that results when the phase angle of the transfer impedance is not linear with frequency within the desired range, thus making the time of transmission or delay vary with frequency in that range. Also called "phase distortion." 2. A characteristic distortion of a communication channel that causes some of the frequency envelope to be delayed.

distortion, frequency—A type of distortion in which certain frequencies are lost or discriminated against.

distributed systems—Refers to various arrangements of computers within an organization in which the organization's computer complex has many separate computing facilities all working in a cooperative manner, rather than the conventional single computer at a single location. Versatility of a computer system is often increased if small computers in geographically dispersed branches are used for simple tasks and a powerful central computer is available for larger tasks. Frequently, an organization's central files are stored at the central computing facility, with the geographically dispersed smaller computers calling on the central files when they need them. Such an arrangement lessens the load on the central computer and reduces both the volume and cost of data transmission.

DMA—Abbreviation for direct-memory access. A procedure or method designed to gain direct access to main storage in order to achieve data transfer without involving the CPU. This means that the CPU must be periodically disabled while DMA is in progress. The manner and modes of achieving this differ considerably in the many microprocessor models that have DMA capability.

DMA channel — A direct-memory access channel capability permits faster data transfer speeds. The basic approach is to bypass the registers and provide direct access to the memory bus. Another significant feature included in some of these is a vectored interrupt capability. Typically, the number of separate interrupt lines accommodated is four or more. These newer designs have been referred to as the second generation in microprocessors. Second-generation design features include separate address and data bus lines, multiple address modes (e.g., direct, indirect, relative, and indexed), more instructions, more versatile register stack operation, vectored interrupts, direct-memory access, and standard RAM and ROM. The result of these improvements is an operation that is 10 times faster for typical instruction times, over first generation micros.

DMA control—Various types of controls depend on the speed of the processor. Higher throughput results can be obtained from the use of a direct-memory access (DMA) bus. In this arrangement, a peripheral device communicates directly with memory without disturbing the CPU. Interfacing is more complex because request and acknowledge signals must be exchanged between the device and an autonomous bus controller. When a single bus is used, data and addresses must be time-multiplexed, and latches must be provided to hold the address stable while the memory or a peripheral are accessed.

DMA controller — The direct-memory access (DMA) controller is an example of an interface chip that is purely a controller; it does not handle data directly. The data transfer is con-

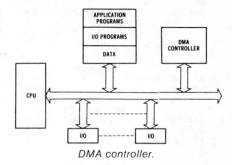

DMA controller.

trolled by the DMA controller, a dedicated high-speed logic circuit that can operate faster than the microprocessor. For DMA data transfer, the DMA controller must take over the microprocessor memory. A typical DMA controller contains a set of programmable registers that specify a starting memory address, the number of bytes to be transferred, and the direction of transfer, i.e., to or from memory. Once initialized, the DMA controller sits idly by until an associated peripheral device has some data to be transferred. Basically, the DMA controller operates as a slave to the CPU. Registers in the controller are down-loaded by the CPU, and when the controller has finished its job, it signals the CPU via an interrupt or control flag.

DMA cycle stealing—Cycle stealing is a condition where the microprocessor allows the direct-memory access controller to take control of the system bus while it (the microprocessor) is doing internal work. The microprocessor is not using the bus anyway, so the direct-memory access controller steals that clock cycle (or cycles).

DMA data transfers—In order to effect DMA data transfers, a device controller has buffers to hold the current memory address (to or from which data are to be transferred) and the word count. After transferring the data address to the in-bus data lines, the device controller logic must increment the memory address and decrement the word count.

DMA interleaved processing—On some systems, DMA is an interleaved process, with CPU operations and DMA transfers running simultaneously. The CPU and DMA devices contend for the memory bus in a similar manner, with the CPU having a lower priority (which is optimum for its memory-access requirements) so DMA devices can gain command of the memory bus.

DMA transfer cycle—Generally, all DMA transfers occur in one memory cycle. The signal sequence that initiates and controls the DMA transfer occurs in parallel with the preceding memory cycle.

DNC—Abbreviation for direct numerical control.

document—1. Relates to a form, voucher, or other written evidence that pertains to various types of transactions. A medium that contains a representation of stored information, such as printed paper, punched cards, etc. 2. To instruct, as by citation of references, or to substantiate, as by listing authorities. 3. Any representation of information that is readable by human beings, usually used in connection with information of interest to the originator of a data processing activity, rather than to the operators of the computer. More commonly applied to input information rather than output information.

documentation — Refers to the orderly presentation, organization, and communication of recorded specialized knowledge, in order to maintain a complete record of reasons for changes in variables. Documentation is necessary, not so much to give maximum utility, as to give an unquestionable historical reference record. Such documents usually contain: (1) The name of the responsible individual who ordered or is directing the program, (2) A brief outline of the system, with some notes relating to the benefits to be obtained, and (3) A type of "handbook" that is developed for use by those who will use the system and programs. It explains such things as paper flow, the coding required, and the output file instructions. Other items explained are equipment utilization change-over procedures, systems test data, program descriptions, etc.

donor—Refers to those elements which enter or are introduced (in small quantities) as impurities into semiconductor materials. They have a negative valence greater than the valence of the pure semiconductor.

donor ion—An atom in a doped semiconductor crystal which gives up an electron.

dopant—1. An impurity added to a semiconductor to increase its ability to conduct electricity. 2. Chemical elements that are introduced into the lattice structure as impurities to form desired properties; for example, phosphorus and boron used to create n and p regions in a silicon chip.

dope additive—Specific impurity added to an ultrapure semiconductor in order to give required electrical properties, e.g., indium to germanium.

doped junction — A semiconductor junction created by adding an impurity to the melt during crystal growth.

doping—1. Increasing the level of impurities in semiconductors in order to make n- or p-type semiconductor devices. 2. The process of adding alien elements to a semiconductor crystal in order to supply it with charge carriers—electrons or holes.

DOS—Abbreviation for disk operating system.

DOS booting — After initially applying power to some systems, the DOS must be "booted." Booting is the process of loading only those segments of the DOS that will enable the system to function. For example, one such portion, called the monitor, decodes the various commands and then transfers control to the appropriate software segment to carry out the command. After the command is executed, control returns to the monitor.

double bus fault—This problem happens when two bus errors occur in a row. When a bus error exception occurs, the processor will attempt to stack several words containing information about the state of the machine. If a bus error exception occurs during the stacking operation (before the execution of the next instruction), there will have been two bus errors in a row, or what is commonly referred to as a double bus fault. When a double bus fault occurs, the processor will halt.

double-doped transistor — A particular type of transistor created by growing a crystal and then adding p- and n-type impurities to the melt while the crystal is being grown.

double precision — Data requiring two computer words to contain it. Often called Double Length.

double-precision arithmetic—1. Using two computer words to represent a number, usually to obtain greater accuracy than a single word of computer storage is capable of providing. 2. Arithmetic used when more accuracy is necessary than a single word of computer storage will provide.

down-loading—Direct transfer of code from the host system into the target system or into a PROM programmer.

down time—The period during which a computer is malfunctioning or not operating correctly because of mechanical or electronic failure, as opposed to available time, idle time, or stand-by time, during which the computer is functional.

DPMA Certificate—A certificate given by the Data Processing Management Association which indicates that a person has a certain level of competence in the field of data processing. The certificate is obtained by passing an examination that is offered yearly throughout the United States and Canada.

drift—Refers to a change in the output of a circuit, i.e., an amplifier, which takes place slowly. Usually caused by voltage fluctuations or changes in environmental conditions. Circuits can be designed to include correction for drift and are used in analog computers to eliminate the errors which would otherwise occur.

drift-corrected amplifier — Refers to various high-gain amplifiers that have been separately equipped with a means for reducing drift and thus preventing drift error.

driver — Refers to various small programs which control external devices or execute other programs.

driver modules—Various major output signals from the standard computer, that are used in programmed and data-break information transfers and are power amplified by bus driver modules in order to allow them to drive a very heavy circuit load.

driver software — The final processing of data signals by peripherals is accomplished by software routines called drivers. Drivers cause the processor unit to produce, manipulate,

and present the appropriate signals, in the appropriate format, at the appropriate times, in order to cause the peripheral device to perform its required functions. Although this process is explicit, it is often not evaluated or considered in the selection process. Driver software is a small but critical part of the overall systems software complement. The driver software must be properly integrated between the operating system, the processing unit, the peripheral controller, and the actual applications programming process of the system.

drop dead halt—Concerns a type of halt which may be deliberately programmed or which may be the result of a logical error in programming, but from which there is no recovery.

drop in—Refers to the reading of a spurious signal whose amplitude is greater than a predetermined percentage of the nominal signal.

drop out — 1. In data transmission, a momentary loss in signal, usually due to the effect of noise or system malfunction. 2. A failure to read a bit from magnetic storage.

dry contact—Refers to a part of a circuit containing only contact points and resistive components.

dry reed contact—Refers to various encapsulated switches consisting of two metal wires which act as the contact points for a relay.

dry running—Relates to the examination of the logic and coding of a program from a flowchart and the written instructions, and the recording of the results of each step of the operation before running the program on the computer.

DTE — Abbreviation for data terminal equipment. Usually refers to devices that connect to data communication equipment (DCE) and which act as sources or sinks for data crossing the boundary. A DTE can be a computer, a telecommunication device, etc. Often, the distinction as to whether a device is a DCE or DTE device is made on the basis of ownership.

DTL (diode-transistor-logic) — Logic employing diodes, with transistors used only as inverting amplifiers.

dual clocking—Input organized as two words, each with its own clock input. User may select positive- or negative-going edges for each clock—a necessary capability when the analyzer is used with a microprocessor that multiplexes data and address information on the same bus.

dual-in-line package—Abbreviated DIP. The most popular IC packaging in use in the mid-1970s was the plastic dual-in-line case. Plastic was used for economic reasons and the dual-in-line package (DIP) configuration was used for manufacturing efficiency.

dual-processor system — Dual-processor systems, supported by standard system software, help guard against system failures. In these, two systems are usually interconnected. One acts as a message concentrator while the second runs on a "standby" status. If the on-line system fails, the backup system takes over the workload automatically, with virtually no data lost.

dual slope converter — An integrating a/d converter in which the unknown signal is converted to a proportional time interval which is then measured digitally.

dual systems — Special configurations which use two computers to receive identical inputs and execute the same routines, with the results of such parallel processing subject to comparison. Exceptionally high-reliability requirements are usually involved.

dumb terminal—A dumb terminal consists of a keyboard and a screen for basic I/O, an interface to a communications line, and very little else. Once data are entered at the keyboard, the terminal is limited to displaying and transmitting codes to the computer, which are then interpreted by the host for subsequent transmission and display. Any intelligence involved is in the device interfacing with the terminal.

dummy address — Generally refers to artificial address, instruction, or record of information inserted solely to fulfill prescribed conditions, such as to achieve a fixed word length or block length, but without itself affecting machine operations except to permit the machine to perform desired operations.

dummy argument — A prototype card field in a macro-definition that is variable and is to be replaced with a parameter (quantity or symbol) when the macro-operation is used. It is also called a dummy definition.

dummy instruction—Refers to an artificial instruction or address inserted in a list of instructions solely to fulfill prescribed conditions (such as word or block length) without affecting the operation.

dummy load—1. Refers to devices such as a resistor, in which the output power can be absorbed. A dummy load is used for simulating conditions of operation for test purposes. 2. To effect the finding, and transfer to storage of a program or set of programs without any actual execution in order to determine that all relevant specifications and components exist in the proper forms in the library.

dump — 1. Frequently referred to as power dump, meaning to withdraw all power from a computer, either accidentally or intentionally. 2. To transfer all or part of the contents of one section of computer memory to another section. 3. A small program that outputs the contents of memory onto hard copy, which may be printed listings, tape, or punched cards.

dump and restart—Concerns specific software routines used for making program dumps at specified times, and for restarting programs at one of these points, in the event of program failure.

dump, binary—Refers to a dump or printout of the contents of a memory unit (in binary form) onto some external medium, such as paper tape or printout forms.

dump, change — Concerns a printout or output recording of the contents of all storage locations in which a change has been made — since the previous change dump.

dumping — A technique designed to provide a periodic "write out" of a complete program and its data (i.e., the contents of the working storage area) to a backup storage or memory unit. A dumping program usually incorporates restart procedures that enable the program to be resumed at the last dump point, in the event of an interruption due to a machine failure or some other job interruption.

dump point — Refers to a designated point in a program at which it is desirable to "write" the program and its data to a backup storage, as a protection against machine failure. Dump points may be selected to effect dumping either at specific time intervals or at predetermined events in the running of the program.

duplex — In communications, a simultaneous two-way and independent transmission in both directions (sometimes referred to as "full duplex"). Contrast with half-duplex.

dynamic cell—Refers to a memory cell that stores data as charge (or absence of charge) on a capacitor. A typical cell isolates the capacitor from the data line (bit line) with a transistor switch. Thus, when no Read or Write operation is desired, there is essentially no power required to maintain data. However, normal leakage requires that the charge be periodically restored by a process called refresh. Characteristics of a dynamic cell are very low data retention power, fewer transistors per bit (a one-transistor cell is common), and, usually, less area and lower cost per bit than for static cells.

dynamic circuits—Dynamic circuits use the absence or presence of charge on a capacitor to store information, typically with three or four transistors per cell. Fewer transistors give higher packing density and lower cost. Since the capacitor that stores the charge has a leakage current, the stored information degrades slowly and, therefore, must be refreshed (normally by simply addressing the memory periodically so that every address is covered eventually).

dynamic dump — A dump that is performed periodically during the execution of a program.

dynamic memory—1. A type of semiconductor memory in which the presence or absence of a capacitive charge represents the state of a binary storage element. This charge must be periodically refreshed; this is accomplished by the application of an external control signal(s).

dynamic memory elements—Types of semiconductor memory elements that are not able to retain data more than a few thousandths of a second unless "refreshed" by activity on their address lines.

dynamic memory, Read/Write — A read/write memory in which the cells require the repetitive application of control signals in order to retain stored data. Such repetitive application of the control signals is normally called a refresh operation. The control signals may be generated inside or outside the integrated circuit.

dynamic RAM—A device in which data are stored capacitively, and which must be recharged (refreshed) periodically (every 2 msec or so), or it will be lost.

dynamic relocation program — The moving of a partially executed program to a different location in main memory without detrimentally affecting its ability to finish its normal processing.

dynamic response — The specific behavior of the output of a device as a function of the input, both with respect to time.

dynamic storage—1. Refers to stored computer data which remain in motion on a sensing device. For example, an acoustic delay line or magnetic drum, as opposed to static storage. 2. The storage of data on a device or in a manner that permits the data to move or vary with time. Thus, the data are not always available.

dynamic storage, permanent — A distinct type or form of dynamic storage. Examples are a magnetic disk or drum, in which the maintenance of the data stored does not depend on a flow of energy.

dynamic subroutine—As it relates to computer programming, a subroutine which involves parameters (such as placement of a decimal point) from which a properly coded subroutine can be derived. The computer adjusts itself or generates the subroutine according to its particular parametric values chosen.

E

EAM — Abbreviation for electrical accounting machine.

EAROM — Abbreviation for electrically alterable read-only memory. A specialized random-access read/write memory with a special, slow Write cycle and a much faster Read cycle; programmed by writing into the array and generally used as a ROM. Contents can be erased en masse. These nonvolatile memory devices are programmed much like ordinary RAMs. They have no fusible links and do not require UV irradiation. (*See* electrically alterable ROM.)

EBCDIC Code — An acronym for Extended Binary-Coded Decimal Interchange Code. A standard code consisting of a character set that uses 8-bit coded characters; used for information representation and interchange among data processing systems, communications systems, and associated equipment.

echo—Refers to that portion of a transmitted signal that has been reflected or otherwise returned with such sufficient magnitude and delay as to be received as interference.

echo check — Refers to various error control techniques wherein the receiving terminal or computer returns the original message to the sender to verify that the message was received correctly.

ECL microprocessor — A typical ECL microprocessor set contains five chips: a 4-bit slice, a control register function, a timing function, a slice memory interface, and a slice lookahead. The various chips can be used as building blocks to construct a microprocessor with capabilities larger than four bits. ECL provides significant advances in speed, roughly six times that of standard TTL. This extra speed is essential in fast systems.

edgeboard connector — The printed-circuit or edgeboard connector is a reliable, inexpensive, and simple method for interconnecting pc boards and for connecting pc boards to other devices. Selection of the edgeboard connector is based primarily on the contact density required. Contact density is defined as the pin-to-pin and row-to-row spacing of the contacts on the termination end of the connector.

edit commands—In some systems, edit commands are implemented as single-, double-, or triple-letter mnemonics followed by optional command parameters. All commands are

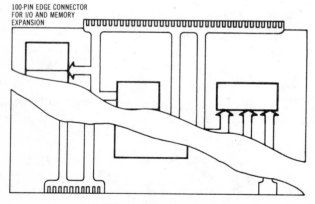

100-PIN EDGE CONNECTOR FOR I/O AND MEMORY EXPANSION

Edgeboard connector.

electric polarization—The dipole moment per unit volume of a dielectric.

electric transducer—A type of device activated by electric waves from one system, that supplies power, also in the form of electric waves, to a second system.

electrochromeric displays (ECDs) — Electrochromic displays are low-voltage, low-current devices that chemically transform themselves from a transparent to an opaque state when tickled by an external electric field. Even after this field is turned off, the devices maintain their opacity; they return to their initial state only when subjected to a field with the opposite polarity. Thus, electrochromism can find uses both in displays and in information storage devices. The devices can operate in either a transmissive or a reflective mode, against any color background. They do not require polarizers, and are claimed to have distinctly superior appearance, contrast, and legibility in dimly lit ambients. In addition, they are legible over wide viewing angles and are compatible with IC technology.

electrodeposition — The deposition electrolytically of a substance on an electrode, as in electroplating or electroforming.

electrodynamics—Science dealing with the interaction of currents, or forces between currents, or the forces on currents in independent magnetic fields.

electroencephalograph—Instrument for the study of voltage waves associated with the brain. It effectively comprises a sensitive detector (voltage or current), a dc amplifier of very good stability, and an electronic recording system.

electrofluor — A transparent material that has the property of storing electrical energy and releasing it as visible (fluorescent) light.

electrokinetics — Science of electric charges in motion, without reference to the accompanying magnetic field.

electrolysis — The chemical change, generally decomposition, effected by a flow of current through a solution of the chemical, or in its molten state, based on ionization.

electromechanics — That branch of electrical engineering concerned with

machines producing or operated by electric currents.

electrometallurgy—The branch of science concerned with the application of electrochemistry to the extraction or treatment of metals.

electron beam — A narrow stream of electrons moving in the same direction under the influence of an electric or magnetic field.

electron-beam fabrication — E-beam equipment dramatically cuts turnaround time for new designs and could prove cost effective for producing low-volume custom chips. Because not every level of wafer processing is critical, manufacturers could use the E-beam process just on the few critical levels and stay with the more relaxed and less expensive photolithographic techniques for the remainder of the wafer-processing task. Electron-beam fabrication eliminates at least two processing steps and their attendant defects, an important factor, because in the final analysis, yield, not the number of wafers per hour, is the most important production parameter. E-beam fabrication is also a shallow-processing technique, so wafers can be fabricated at lower temperatures and, thus, have a better chance of surviving the production process in working order.

electron-beam lithography—This is a complex and expensive lithography process in which the radiation-sensitive film or resist is placed in the vacuum chamber of a scanning-beam electron microscope and is exposed by an electron beam under digital computer control. After exposure, the film is removed from the vacuum chamber for conventional development and other production processes. Processing by electron beam lithography uses a nonthermal beam to expose a thin polymeric film which, after development, becomes a high-resolution contact mask. Subsequent steps transform the original resist device structures without edge definition loss.

electron camera—Generic term for a device that converts an optical image into a corresponding electric current directly by electronic means, without the intervention of mechanical scanning.

electronic data processing (EDP) — 1.

Any machine or group of machines which has the capability to automatically enter, receive, classify, sort, compute, and/or record alphabetical or numerical accounting or statistical data (or all three) without the intermediate use of tabulating cards. 2. Data processing by way of electronic equipment, such as an internally stored program, electronic digital computer, or an automatic data processing machine.

Electronic Funds Transfer System — 1. Abbreviated EFTS, this refers to various electronic communications systems which transfer financial information from one point to another. Although EFTS encompasses many diverse electronic automation projects, it is most frequently used to describe three types of systems: Automated Clearing Houses, Automated Tellers, and Point-of-Sale Systems. 2. A type of national banking or money settlement and clearing function.

Electronic Industries Association (EIA) —A trade association of the electronics industry which formulates technical standards, disseminates marketing data, and maintains contact with government agencies in matters relating to the electronics industry.

electronic mail—The sending or receiving of point-to-point or multipoint messages via a consumer-oriented communication system based on telephone lines and/or radio transmission.

electronic mail network—A communications system that electronically links together individuals and information via radio transmissions and/or telephone lines. Some network service companies cater to all types of data and facsimile terminals. Thus, these networks can accept electronic mail from, or transmit to, practically any device, including word processors, data phones, Telex machines, or various types of computers. This service is achieved through a computerized digital-input store-and-forward system that makes all terminals compatible with practically any other terminal.

electronic neuron network simulation —Refers to the study and duplication of neuron cells and networks in order to build multiple-purpose systems using analogous electronic components. Computers have been programmed to act as neuron system simulators, and this type of research holds much potential for the future.

electronic packaging—The coating or surrounding of an electronic assembly with dielectric compound.

electronic pen (stylus) — Refers to a pen-like device that is commonly used in conjunction with a crt (cathode-ray tube) for inputting or changing information under program control. The electronic stylus is often called a light pen, and works by signalling the computer with an electronic pulse. The computer acts on these signals and can change the configuration plotted across the tube

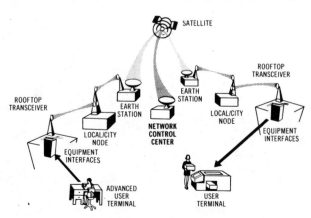

Electronic mail network.

face or perform other operations using the imputted data according to previously programmed instructions.

electronics—1. Branch of science that deals with the study and application of electron devices, e.g., electron tubes, transistors, magnetic amplifiers, etc. 2. The field of science and engineering concerned with the behavior of electrons in devices and the utilization of such devices.

electronic switch — A circuit element that, electronically, causes a start and stop action or a switching action, usually at high speeds.

electron jet—Narrow stream of electrons, similar to an electron beam, but not necessarily focused.

electron lens — A composite arrangement of magnetic coils and charged electrodes that is used to focus or divert electron beams in the manner of an optical lens.

electron mass—A result of the relativity theory, that mass can be ascribed to kinetic energy, is that the effective mass (m) of the electron should vary with its velocity according to the experimentally confirmed expression:

$$m = \frac{m_0}{\sqrt{1 - \left(\frac{v}{c}\right)^2}}$$

where, m_0 is the mass for small velocities, c is the velocity of light, and v that of the electron.

electron octet—The (up to) eight valency electrons in an outer shell of an atom or molecule. Characterized by great stability, in so far as the complete shell around an atom makes it chemically inert, and around a molecule (by sharing) makes a stable chemical compound.

electronogen—Photosensitive molecule which may emit an electron when illuminated.

electron optics—Control of free electrons by curved electric and magnetic fields, leading to focusing and formation of images.

electron pair — Two valence electrons shared by adjacent nuclei, thus forming a nonpolar bond.

electron paramagnetic resonance — Resonance arising from conduction electrons in metals and semiconductors.

electron trap—An acceptor impurity in a semiconductor.

electro-optical effect—Interaction between a strong electrical field and the refracting properties of a dielectric.

electroscope—Indicator and measurer of small electric charges, usually two gold leaves which diverge because of repulsion of like charges; with one gold leaf and a rigid brass plate, indication is more precise.

electrostatic adhesion—The adhesion between two substances, or surfaces, due to electrostatic attraction between opposite charges.

electrostatic bonding—Valence linkage between atoms arising from the transfer of one or more electrons from the outer shell of one atom to the outer shell of another, with the transfer leading to a more near completion of the outer shells of both atoms, producing ions on dissociation.

electrostatics—That section of the science of electricity which deals with the phenomena of electric charges substantially at rest.

electrostatic screen — 1. Conducting shield surrounding instruments or other apparatus to prevent their being influenced by external electric fields. 2. A grounded conducting plate interposed between two circuits to prevent any unwanted capacitance coupling between them.

electrostatic separator—An apparatus in which materials having different permittivities are deflected by different amounts when falling between charged electrodes and, therefore, fall into different receptacles.

electrostatic shield — A metal mesh used to screen one device from the electric field of another.

electrostatic storage—1. The storage of data on a dielectric surface, such as the screen of a cathode-ray tube, in the form of the presence or absence of spots bearing electrostatic charges that can persist for a short time after the electrostatic charging force is removed. 2. A storage device so used.

electrostatic units — Units for electric and magnetic measurements in which the permittivity of a vacuum is taken as unity.

electrostatic voltmeter—One depending for its action upon the attraction or repulsion between charged bodies; usual unit of calibration is the kilovolt.

electrostatic wattmeter — One which utilizes electrostatic forces to measure ac power at high voltages.

electrostriction—The change in the dimensions of a dielectric that accompanies the application of an electric field.

emission — The release of electrons from parent atoms on the absorption of energy in excess of the normal average. This can arise from (1) thermal (thermionic) agitation, as in X-ray tubes, cathode-ray tubes; (2) secondary emission of electrons, which are ejected by impact of higher energy primary electrons; (3) photoelectric release on absorption of quanta above a certain energy level; and (4) field emission by actual stripping from parent atoms by a high electric field.

emittance — The power per unit area radiated by a source of energy.

emitter character—An electromechanical device which emits a timed pulse or group of pulses to form a character in some code.

emitter-coupled circuits (ECL)—These circuits do not saturate, obviating either Schottky clamps or gold doping. However, to realize ECL's speed potential, one or two extra diffusions are needed in manufacturing. The net result: ECL memories are faster than TTL but more expensive. Certainly, for applications requiring small memories to be mixed with ECL logic, there will always be a requirement for ECL memories. Also, since ECL memories are faster than CMOS and N-channel, they will be used in applications that need extra speed. Since this is not true with TTL, ECL should eventually become a more important memory form than TTL.

emitter-coupled logic (ECL)—A bipolar digital integrated-circuit family that uses a more complex design than transistor-transistor logic (TTL) to speed up IC operations. ECL is costly, power hungry, and difficult to use, but it could become important in the next generation of large computers because it is four times faster than TTL.

emitters, fiber optic — Fiber-optic signal transmission would be impossible without emitters (which generate light in response to electrical signals) and detectors (which transform the light signals back into electrical signals at the receiving end of the link). Two types of solid-state emitters find use in fiber-optic systems. These are the light-emitting diode (LED) and the laser diode. Strictly speaking, the laser diode is a special subclass of LEDs but is classified separately, because, like its nonsolid-state cousins, it employs internal amplification to stimulate light emission with a "lasing" action. Conventional LEDs merely generate light directly by biasing a semiconductor junction. There is a continuing search for higher-powered emitters and more sensitive detectors—which could combine to make possible longer signal transmission paths without using repeaters.

emulate—A procedure designed to imitate one system with another so that the imitating system accepts the same data, executes the same programs, and achieves the same results as the imitated system. Contrast with simulate.

emulation — Refers to various techniques using software or microprogramming in which one computer is made to behave exactly like another computer; i.e., the emulating system executes programs in the native machine-language code of the emulated system. Emulation is generally used to minimize the impact of conversion from one computer system to another, and is used to continue the use of production programs—as opposed to "simulation" which is used to study the operational characteristics of another (possibly theoretical) system.

emulator—1. Refers to various devices or computer programs that emulate. 2. The combination of programming techniques and special machine features that permits a given computing system to execute programs written for another system. Usually provides full capability for developing and debugging a user's application hardware and software. *See also* integrated emulator.

emulator generation — Refers to the process of assembling and link-editing an emulator program into an operating system during system generation.

Emulator, in-circuit (Courtesy Intel Corp.).

emulator, in-circuit—In-circuit emulation provides more than just a sophisticated debug environment. Integrated hardware/software development can be a reality. During a development cycle, there occurs some moment when hardware and software must be joined. The later this occurs on a project, the greater are the chances for problems and the greater the difficulty in correcting these problems. In-circuit emulation lets the software designer run his programs on the actual prototype hardware at the earliest possible time. In addition, the hardware designer gets the benefit of running the actual system software on his prototype for hardware debugging. Microcomputer product design can become easier, faster, and cheaper. Diagnostic programs developed at the early stages of a project may be used to debug the prototype hardware during all stages of prototype development. The hardware will no longer provide any "surprises" to the software designer due to misunderstandings or poorly documented specifications. Thus,: systems integration can be accomplished in a more efficient manner. For manufacturers, this means that the product will be on the market sooner, capturing a larger market share and minimizing the effects of price erosion. In-circuit emulation permits faster product introduction.

emulator, stand-alone — Refers to an emulator whose execution is not controlled by a control program; it does not share system resources with other programs and excludes all other jobs from the computing system while it is being executed. (An example is the ZSCAN 8000 from Zilog Corporation which operates stand-alone or with

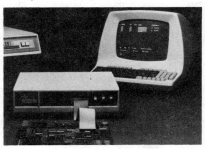

Emulator, stand-alone (Courtesy Zilog Corp.).

a host computer to provide Z8000 emulation.)

emulator vs. simulator — In a basic sense, emulation means the modification of a computer system to execute programs that are written for another system. This modification may consist of the addition of software, microprograms, or hardware. Historically, an emulator has been used as support during the transitional period of converting or upgrading one data processing system to another. Whereas, an emulator uses added microprograms or hardware, a simulator uses only the software of the host machine to simulate instructions of the machine to be realized.

emulsion-laser storage—Refers to a digital data storage medium which uses a controlled laser beam to expose very small areas on a photosensitive surface.

encoder—A network or system in which only one input is excited at a time and each input produces a combination of output signals.

encoder interface, microprocessor—A

keyboard encoder can interface with a microprocessor in either a scanned or interrupt-driven mode. In a scanned system, the microprocessor periodically monitors the encoder to determine whether any switches have been pressed. If it detects a switch depression, the microprocessor collects and processes the key data. In an interrupt-driven system, a key depression interrupts the microprocessor program flow and causes an interrupt service routine to process the key data.

end-of-data marker—Refers to a character or code that designates that the end of all data held on a specific storage unit has been reached. Not to be confused with end-of-file marker.

end-of-file (EOF)—Refers to the termination or point of completion of a quantity of data. End-of-file marks are used to indicate this point.

end-of-message (EOM) — Refers to a specific character or sequence of characters that indicates the termination of a message or record.

end-of-run routine—A specific routine provided by the programmer to deal with various housekeeping operations before a run is ended; i.e., rewinding tapes, printing control totals, etc.

end-of-tape routine — A specific program, either provided by a housekeeping package or written by the user, that supplies the special processing required when the last record on a reel of magnetic tape has been reached.

end-of-transmission (EOT)—Refers to a unique character or group of characters used to denote the end of a data transmission to or from a remote terminal.

energy band—In a solid, the energy levels of individual atoms interact to form bands of permitted levels with gaps between. Normally, there is a valence band with a full complement of electrons and a conduction band which is empty. When these overlap, metallic conduction is possible. In semiconductors, there is a small gap and intrinsic conduction occurs only when some electrons acquire the energy necessary to surmount this gap and enter the conduction band. In insulators, the gap is huge and, normally, cannot be surmounted.

engineering graphics — Graphics can be considered the primary language of engineering as analysis often requires a graphic representation in the form of circuits, free bodies, block diagrams, and flowcharts. The design process frequently utilizes working drawings, plot plans, and other pictorial representations in formal presentations. Graphic displays facilitate data manipulation, arithmetic calculations, simulation, and the building and testing of models. Thus, besides serving as a tool for computer-aided design, computer graphics can also be applied to the solution of problems in finite element analysis, structural loading, fluid flow, heat transfer, and other complex engineering problems. They maximize communication between user and machine by permitting interaction through pictures rather than words.

engineering improvement time — That particular time set for installing, acceptance testing, or approving equipment which is added; i.e., that time spent for modification of an existing system to improve reliability without adding to the facilities is supplementary maintenance time, while engineering improvement time is a part of the scheduled engineering time along with the scheduled maintenance time and it includes all the tests needed to ensure all the improvements necessary for satisfactory operation.

engineering time — The total machine "down time" necessary for routine testing and for machine servicing measures. This includes all test time needed following breakdown and the subsequent repair or preventive servicing. Synonymous with servicing time.

enquiry character (ENQ) — Refers to data communications. It is a special control character designed to elicit a response from some remote station, usually for station identification or for the description of the station equipment and status.

entry block—Refers to a block of main-memory storage assigned on receipt of each entry into a system and which is associated with that entry throughout its life in the system.

entry instruction—Generally refers to the first instruction to be executed in a subroutine.

entry point—1. Refers to various specific locations in a program segment which other segments can reference. 2. The point or points at which a program can be activated by an operator or an operating system.

epitaxial film—A type of film with a single-layer semiconductor material that has been deposited onto a single-crystal substrate.

epitaxial growth—Epitaxial growth is a process in which the single crystal structure of a semiconductor is extended by careful control of process variables. Expitaxial growth, or deposition, is carried out in a special furnace called a "reactor" where silicon wafers having a clear and chemically polished surface are heated up to temperatures comparable to those encountered in the diffusion step (i.e., 1000 to 1200 °C). During the epitaxial growth, vapors containing silicon are passed over the heated substrate. Normally, hydrogen is used as the carrier gas, with either silicon tetrachloride ($SiCl_4$) or silane (SiH_4) as the source of silicon. During the epitaxial growth process, the source compound is chemically reduced resulting in free silicon atoms, some of which are deposited on the single-crystal substrate. Under proper deposition conditions, the interatomic forces of the single-crystal silicon lattice constrain the deposited silicon atoms to follow the original crystal structure. Thus, structurally, the deposited epitaxial layer forms a continuation of the original crystal structure.

epitaxial-growth mesa transistor — A particular type of transistor made by overlaying a thin mesa crystal over another mesa crystal.

epitaxial growth process—Refers to the process of growing semiconductor material by depositing it in a vaporized form on a semiconductor seed crystal. The deposited layer continues the single-crystal structure seed.

epitaxy — Epitaxy, derived from the Greek word meaning "arranged upon," is a growth technique wherein the single-crystal structure of a silicon substrate can be extended by vapor-phase deposition of additional atomic layers of silicon. By controlling the deposition rates and by introducing controlled amounts of im-

purities into the carrier gases utilized during the epitaxial growth process, the thickness and the resistivity type of the deposited layer can be accurately controlled. Thermal growth or deposition of a dielectric layer, such as SiO_2, on top of the silicon wafer provides a convenient means of electrically passivating the silicon surface and forming a protective mask against contamination of the surface by undesired impurities.

epitaxy, solid-state — Annealing ion-implantation damage by use of continuous-wave laser heating involves a process known as solid-state epitaxy. This technique has the advantage that it does not redistribute the implanted dopant atoms. Laser annealing eliminates the potato-chip effect of furnace annealing since it only heats the top of the water. This factor (wafer flatness) is vital to accurate lithography at levels near and below 1 μm. In addition, laser annealing achieves a greater degree of dopant activation than furnace annealing.

EPROM—*See* electrically programmable read-only memory.

equivalence — A logic operator having the property that if P is a statement, Q is a statement, R is a statement, . . . , then the equivalence of P, Q, R, . . . , is true if and only if all statements are true or all statements are false.

equivalence element — A unique logic element which has two binary input signals and only one binary output signal. The variance or variable of the output symbol signal is the equivalence of the variables represented by the input signals, i.e., a two-input element whose output signal is 1 when its input signals are alike.

equivalence operation — Refers to a Boolean operation on two operands (P and Q), with the result (R) being as follows:

Operands		Result
P	Q	R
1	1	1
1	0	0
0	1	0
0	0	1

erasable and programmable read-only memory (EPROM)—A field-programmable read-only memory that can have the data content of each memory cell altered more than once. An

Erasable and programmable read-only memory (EPROM) (Courtesy Intel Corp.).

EPROM is bulk erased by exposure to a high-intensity ultraviolet light. Sometimes referred to as a reprogrammable read-only memory.

erasable storage—1. A storage device whose data can be altered during the course of a computation. 2. An area of storage that is used for temporary storage. 3. A storage medium that can be erased and reused repeatedly, e.g., magnetic-drum storage, magnetic-tape storage, magnetic-disk storage, etc.

error—1. Refers to any incorrect step, process, or result in a microcomputer or data-processing system. The term also refers to machine malfunctions or "machine errors," and to human mistakes or "human errors." 2. Any discrepancy between a computed, observed, recorded, or measured quantity and the true, specified, or theoretically correct value or condition. Contrast with mistake.

error ambiguity — Considered a gross error, usually transient, occurring in the reading of digits or numbers and imprecise synchronism which causes changes in different digit positions, such as in analog-to-digital conversion.

error burst—Concerns a sudden outbreak of errors in a short amount of time compared to the period of errors immediately before and after the occurrence.

error, coincidence—Refers to the specific difference as related to time for switching different integrators to the compute mode or the hold mode.

error condition — Concerns the state that results from an attempt in a computer program to execute instructions that are invalid or that operate on invalid data.

error, conscious—An error that was instantly recognized as such by an operator, but which was such that his reflex actions were unable to prevent the error.

error control—Refers to various provisions or arrangements made to detect the presence of errors. In some systems, refinements are added in order to correct the detected errors, either by operations on the received data or by retransmission from the source.

error correction, automatic—Refers to various techniques, usually requiring the use of special codes and/or automatic retransmission, which detect and correct errors occurring in transmission. The degree of correction depends upon the coding and equipment configuration.

error correction code—A digit or digits, carried along with a moved computer word or record, which may be used to partially reconstruct the moved record in case of partial loss.

error correction (transmission)—Refers to blocks of data containing transmission errors that can be retransmitted correctly. Such retransmission is immediate and fully automatic.

error detecting code—1. Refers to a system of coding characters entered in a computer so that any single error produces a forbidden or impossible code combination. 2. A code in which each expression conforms to specific rules of construction, so that if certain errors occur in an expression, the resulting expression will not conform to the rules of construction and, thus, the presence of the errors is detected. Synonymous with self-checking code.

error detecting system—A system employing an error detecting code and so arranged that any signal detected as being in error is (1) either deleted from the data delivered to the data sink (in some cases, with an indication that such deletion has taken place), or (2) delivered to the data sink (together with an indication that it has been detected as being in error).

error detection, automatic — Refers to various programs which are embedded in a more complicated system. They are usually designed to detect the system's errors, print them out with the cause and, if so designed, take steps to correct them.

error detection routine—A routine used to detect whether or not an error has occurred, usually without any special provision to find or indicate its location.

error diagnostics—Using diagnostics, some compilers will continue to the end of the program. Thus, complete error diagnostics may be obtained in one compilation. The errors are listed on the same device as the source-language listing.

error dump, program — The dumping onto tape, etc., of information and core storage by a priority program so that the cause of an equipment or program error interrupt may be assessed by the analysts.

error messages, assembler—The ability of assemblers to detect and point to a variety of errors in source statements is a valuable feature on many systems. These errors are often syntactic—they deal with misuse of the actual language. Assemblers normally cannot catch logic errors in the program, errors of intent, or other subtle problems. A statement that contains an error is often printed in the list file with a code letter—a flag—beside it. Or, the entire error message may be printed.

Some common errors that can be detected include duplicate address labels, undefined label, and unrecognized instruction mnemonic (due perhaps to the misspelling of an operation code). Other detectable errors include undefined operand field names, wrong number of operands, and an invalid number in the number system chosen. In addition, an assembler could be made to detect the error of an address referred to the same ROM page, as in a short JUMP when a long JUMP is required. Not all errors of syntax are flagged in current microprocessor assemblers. For example, when the labeled address for a JUMP or CALL instruction is not the start of an executable instruction, the error is not generally detected.

error signal—1. A signal whose magnitude and sign are used to correct the alignment between the controlling and the controlled elements of an automatic control device. 2. Relating to closed loops, that specific signal resulting from subtracting a particular return signal from its corresponding input signal.

etched printed circuit—Refers to a specific type of printed circuit, formed by chemically or electrolytically (or both) removing the unwanted portion of a layer of material that is bonded to the base.

eutectic bond—Method of die attachment (or bonding) of two metal surfaces using heat and pressure.

Exclusive-NOR gate—A two input (binary) logic circuit designed to perform the logic operation of Exclusive-NOR, i.e., if A and B are input statements, the result is true or 1 when both A and B are true or when both A and B are false. The result is false when A and B are different.

Exclusive-OR — 1. A logical operator having the property that if P is a statement and Q is a statement, then the OR of P and Q is true if, and only if, at least one is true; it is false if all are false. The statement P or Q is often shown as P + Q or P U Q.

Exclusive-OR operator—A logical operator which has the property that if P and Q are two statements, then the statement P*Q (where the * is the Exclusive-OR operator) is true if either P or Q, but not both, are true, according to the following table. The numeral 1 signifies a binary digit or truth.

P	Q	P*Q	(even)
0	0	0	(odd)
1	0	1	(odd)
1	1	0	(even)

Primarily used in compare operations.

EXEC—1. An abbreviation for Executive Statement. 2. An abbreviation for the Executive system.

execute statement—A basic job control command which identifies a load module to be accessed and executed, plus the specification of job steps.

execution cycle—Refers to a portion of a machine cycle during which the actual execution of the instruction takes place. Some operations (e.g., divide, multiply) may need a large number of these operation cycles to complete the operation, and the normal instruction/operation alternation will be held up during this time. Also called operation cycle.

execution time—1. Relates to the specific time required to carry out an instruction, procedure, or cycle. The time is often expressed in clock cycles. Because the clock frequency is known, the actual time can be calculated accurately, although clock frequencies can be varied. 2. The portion of an instruction cycle during which the actual work is performed or the operation executed, i.e., the time required to decode and perform an instruction.

Executive—In systems where the write-edit-assemble-execute sequence is in any way predictable, users can have the computer schedule, load, and execute each system software module. The program that provides this service is called the Executive. The Executive (also called the Supervisor or Monitor) is a program (or set of programs) that coordinates the controls for the running of other programs on the computer. As such, the Executive is the key element that converts a collection of system software programs into an operating system. Portions of the Executive are normally resident in the computer memory at all times. The general duties of the Executive generally are: job scheduling, storage allocation, and monitoring the device control. The object programs rely on the Executive and the Library Utilities for all I/O and mathematical functions.

executive control — Primary control of the executive system is by control information that is fed to the system by one or more input devices. These devices may be either on-line or at various remote sites. This control information is similar in nature to present control-card operations, but it allows additional flexibility and standardization.

executive control statement—The basic format of an executive control statement is quite simple, and is amenable to a large number of input devices. Statements are not restricted to card image format, and they may be of variable lengths. Each statement consists of a heading character for recognition purposes, followed by a command (which categorizes the statement), followed by a variable number of expressions. The end of a statement is signified by the end of a card, a carriage return, or an equivalent signal, depending on the type of input device.

executive cycle—Refers to a specific period of time during which a machine instruction is interpreted and the indicated operation is performed on the specified operand.

executive diagnostics — A part of the executive system is an integrated system of diagnostic routines designed to provide the programmer with information of maximum utility and convenience in checking out programs. The programmer can be highly selective about what is to be printed, and may receive diagnostic listings with source-code symbolics collated with the contents of both registers and central store. Both dynamic (snapshot) and post-mortem (PMD) dumps of registers and central store are often provided.

executive dumping—The facility to obtain printable dumps of the contents of areas of film or main memory, in case unexpected errors cause premature termination of supposedly debugged programs. The dumps are recorded on tape or disks for later printing on a high-speed printer.

executive instruction—Similar to a supervisory instruction, this instruction is designed and used to control the operation or execution of other routines or programs.

executive language—1. A set of control commands capable of performing all of the desirable or mandatory functions required in a modern executive system. The command language is open-ended and easily expanded, so that features and functions may be added as the need arises. 2. *See* Executive.

executive program — 1. An executive program usually controls the loaders, and an editor, an assembler, a specific compiler, a debug monitor, an input/output subsystem with device drivers, and a utilities library of mathematical routines. Once the executive program has been loaded into memory, all further operations are executed using various types of commands to the executive, editor, and debug programs. 2. *Same* as executive routine.

executive routine—A routine designed to control the loading, relocation, execution, and possibly the scheduling of other routines. An executive routine is part of the basic operating system and, effectively, may be considered as part of the computer itself. Such a routine maintains ultimate control of the computer at all times and control always returns to the executive routine when any controlled routine finishes its functions or when an unexpected stop or trap occurs. Synonymous with supervisory routine and routine, monitor.

executive system control—Usually the primary control of the executive system is developed from the control information fed to the system by one or more input devices. These devices may be either on-line or at various remote sites.

exit—The means of halting a repeated computer cycle of operation in a program.

exjunction—A reasonable element applied to two operands that will create a result depending on the bit patterns of the operands.

expander, CPU—These units are designed to permit a user to run several types of software on a single system without modifying the software. Thus, expanders have become popular with home computer enthusiasts and industrial users alike, as building blocks and flexible performers. Some of the first units contained 8080, Z-80, and 6800 chips on the same

board, with four PIAs for control, and with several multiplexers and demultiplexers.

explicit address—Refers to an address reference that is specified as two absolute expressions. One expression supplies the value of a displacement. Both values are assembled into the object code of a machine instruction.

extended addressing — 1. Concerns a specific type of addressing mode designed as an operation that can reach practically any place in memory. 2. With extended addressing, the contents of the two bytes immediately following the opcode fully specify the 16-bit effective address that is used by the instruction. The address generated by an extended instruction defines an absolute address and is not position independent (some systems).

extended arithmetic element — Refers to a fundamental central processor logic-circuit element which provides hardware-implemented multiply, divide, and normalize functions.

extender card—On many development systems, "extender card" provisions provide a probe access to card-module test points, and thus become excellent time savers.

external clocking—A time base oscillator supplied by the data set for regulating the bit rate of transmission. Also called data set clocking.

external delay — Computer down time (lost time) attributable to circumstances that are not the fault of the computer system, and which are beyond the reasonable control of the system operator or maintenance engineer. Examples of external delay are a power failure to the building and transmission difficulties or faults.

external interrupts—External interrupts are caused by console switching, by the timer going to zero, or by either an external device requiring attention (such as a signal from a communications device).

external labels—Labels are normally defined in the same program in which they are used as operands. However, it is possible to define a symbol in one program; use it in a program assembled independently of the first program, and then execute both programs together. A label is termed an ENTRY point in the program in which it is defined; it is an EXT (external) label in the program in which it is used as an operand.

external observation—External observation is the use of software and hardware outside a system to observe the system's behavior. Tools for external observation include hardware monitors, hybrid monitoring systems consisting of hardware and software, and software or firmware monitors that are associated with the operating system that supports the system of software being observed. Such a monitoring system is set up to watch for telltale signs of system malfunctions, such as performance degradation and unexpected or invalid sequences of events or states.

external priority interrupts—The external interrupt system of some MPUs operates through an I/O interface in the computer mainframe. Interrupts can originate from device controllers or from an optional priority-interrupt interface board connected to the byte I/O bus. The priority-interrupt interface board provides control of 8 external interrupt signals. The I/O interface contains a single external interrupt-request line common to all I/O controllers on the byte I/O bus and a priority line that is carried sequentially through all controllers on the bus. Each I/O controller receives priority from the preceding controller in the priority chain and passes it along to the next controller in line, if it is not ready to request an interrupt. When a controller receives a priority and is ready to request an interrupt, it stops the progression of the priority signal and activates the interrupt-request signal. After receiving acknowledgement of the interrupt request, the interrupting controller places an address byte on the I/O bus that the processor uses to transfer program control to the proper interrupt servicing routine.

external registers—Refers to those registers which can be referenced by the program and which are located in control store as specific addresses. These are the location (registers) that the programmer references when he desires that some sort of computational function be carried out.

external storage—1. Storage facilities separate from a computer itself but holding information in a form acceptable to the computer, such as magnetic tapes, disks, bubble cassettes, etc. 2. A facility or device, not an integral part of a computer, on which data usable by a computer are stored, such as off-line magnetic tape units, or optical-disc devices. Synonymous with external memory.

external symbol—Refers to a specific symbol whose value is of interest to a number of program modules—not only the program module in which it is defined but also as a symbol contained in a program module dictionary.

extracode—Specifically, a sequence of machine code instructions stored within the operating system, and sometimes in read-only memory, that is used to simulate hardware functions. Extracodes may be used to provide floating-point operations, for example, on a machine that does not have floating-point hardware.

extract—1. A procedure to replace the contents of specific columns of a quantity (as indicated by some other quantity called an extractor) with the contents of the corresponding column of a third quantity. 2. To remove from a set of items of information all those items that meet some arbitrary criterion.

extract instruction—A specific instruction that requests the formation of a new expression from selected parts of given expressions.

extrinsic properties—The properties of a semiconductor, modified by impurities or imperfection within the crystal.

extrinsic semiconductor — A semiconductor whose electrical properties depend on its impurities.

F

facsimile — 1. Refers to a process by which pictures are electronically scanned and the information converted into signal waves. These signals then produce a likeness of the subject copy at a remote operating point. 2. A system for the transmission of images. The image is scanned at the transmitter, reconstructed at the receiving station, and duplicated on some form of paper. Abbreviated FAX.

facsimile, computer compression — A process where letters, memos, drawings, and other forms of correspondence are processed by a scanning unit. The information is digitized and entered into the computer portion of the system, where it is compressed; that is, large areas of white space (such as the space between lines) are condensed. This compression allows a high throughput of the system. Data transmission speed of a system can be up to 448 kilobits per second.

facsimile, multicopy — When multiple copies of a document are required at a receiving location, only one copy is transmitted. At the receiving end, the system then creates the number of copies specified by the sender. An outgoing document can be addressed to several recipients, with the receiving unit automatically addressing each copy to the appropriate individual. For example, if the originator designates 10 recipients, the address sheet at the sending end will contain the names and locations of all of the recipients. At each receiving location, each copy is addressed only to a specific individual and the names of the other recipients are not shown (some systems).

facsimile transmission—Refers to the transmission of signal waves that are produced by a facsimile machine.

fail soft—Refers to a method of system implementation designed to prevent the irretrievable loss of facilities or data in the event of a temporary outage of some portion of the system.

fail-soft system — A computer system which will continue to run (with deteriorated performance) despite failure in parts of the system.

failure logging—An automatic procedure whereby the maintenance section of the monitor, acting on machine-check interrupts (immediately following error detection), records the system state. This log is an aid to the customer engineer in diagnosing intermittent errors (some systems).

failure, mean-time-to (MTTF)—The average time a system or a component of the system works without faulting.

failure prediction — Refers to various techniques which attempt to determine the failure schedule of specific parts or equipments so that they may be discarded and replaced before failure occurs.

fallback—Refers to a specific condition in processing where special computer or manual functions must be employed as either complete or partial substitutes for malfunctioning systems. Such procedures can be used anywhere between complete system availability and total system failure.

fallback procedure—Refers to various procedures to circumvent all equipment faults. The fallback may give degraded service and may include switching to an alternate computer, or to different output devices, and so on.

fallback recovery—The restoration of a system to full operation from a fallback mode of operation after the cause of the fallback has been removed.

fan-in—Refers to the number of inputs available to a specific logic stage or function.

fan-out—Concerns the number of circuits that can be supplied with input signals from an output terminal of a circuit or unit. The changes of digital circuits depend basically on the number of devices that can drive or be driven by one circuit of a specific type. The number of elements that one output can drive is related to the power available from the output and the amount of power required for each input.

faraday—A unit equal to the number of coulombs (96,500) required for an electronic reaction involving one electrochemical equivalent.

Faraday cage—Grounded wire screen (e.g., a number of parallel wires joined at one end that are grounded) completely surrounding a piece of equipment in order to shield it from external electric fields and designed so that there can be no electric field within. Also called a Faraday shield.

Faraday's laws of electrolysis—1. The amount of chemical change produced by a current is proportional to the quantity of electricity passed. 2. The amounts of different substances liberated or deposited by a given quantity of electricity are proportional to the chemical equivalent weights of those substances.

Faraday's law of induction—The emf induced in any circuit is proportional to the rate of change of the number of magnetic lines of force linked with the circuit (a principle used in every motor).

fault—Refers to various physical conditions that cause a device, a component, or an element to fail to perform in a required manner, for example, a short circuit, a broken wire, or an intermittent connection.

fault current—The maximum electrical current that will flow in a short-circuited system prior to the actuation of any current-limiting device. It is far in excess of normal current flow. It is limited only by the electrical system generating capacity and the cable impedance.

fault-location program—Concerns various programs used for identification or information regarding faulty equipment. They are designed and used to identify the location or type of fault and are often part of a diagnostic routine.

feasibility study — 1. Usually the initial procedures and criteria for determination of suitability, capability, and compatibility of computer systems to various firms or organizations. A preliminary systems analysis of potential costs savings and new higher level of operations and decision-making problem-solving capacity as a result

of computer procurement. 2. A study in which a projection of how a proposed system might operate in a particular organization is made to provide the basis for a decision to change the existing system.

feedback, analog—Normally, feedback in circuits is obtained by means of a resistor from output to input. An important property of some types of amplifiers is that if a suitable capacitor is used in the feedback path instead of a resistor, the output will be the integral of the input. Conversely, the input will be the derivative of the output. Hence, the operations of the calculus can be performed, giving the machine great computational power.

feedback control — A type of system control obtained when a portion of the output signal is operated upon and fed back to the input in order to obtain a desired effect.

feedback control loop—A closed transmission path which includes an active transducer and consists of a forward path, a feedback path, and one or more mixing points arranged to maintain a prescribed relationship between the loop input and output signals.

feedback control signal—That portion of the output signal which is returned to the input in order to achieve a desired effect, such as fast response.

feeding, cyclic — A system used by character readers, in which each individual input document is issued to the document transport at a predetermined and constant rate.

ferric oxide (Fe_2O_3)—1. A red iron-oxide coating used for magnetic-recording tapes. 2. The magnetic constituent of practically all present-day tapes, in the form of a dispersion of fine particles within the coating.

ferrite — A chemical compound that consists of iron oxide and other metallic oxides that are often combined with a ceramic material to form storage devices. Ferrite has characteristics of high magnetic-flux properties.

ferrite core—1. A core made from iron and other oxides that is usually shaped like a doughnut. It is used in circuits and magnetic memories and can be magnetized and demagnetized very easily. 2. Concerns various types of magnetic materials, but usually toroidal in shape, which are pulsed or polarized by electric currents carried in a wire or wires wound around it. These devices are capable of assuming and remaining at one of two conditions of magnetization, thus providing storage, gating, or switching functions.

ferrite core memory, magnetic — The physical construction of memory in which cores are placed in the same number of columns and rows on a flat surface.

ferrites—Chemical compounds of iron oxide and other metallic oxides combined with a ceramic material. They have ferromagnetic properties, but are poor conductors of electricity.

ferroelectric—Pertaining to a phenomenon exhibited by certain materials in which the material is polarized in one direction or the other, or reversed in direction by the application of a positive- or negative-electric field of magnitude greater than a certain amount. The material retains the electric polarization unless it is disturbed. The polarization can be sensed by the fact that a change in the field induces an electromotive force that can cause a current.

ferroelectric materials—These are dielectric materials (usually ceramics) with a domain structure, which exhibit spontaneous electric polarization. Analogous to ferromagnetic materials (see ferromagnetism). They have relative permittivities of up to 10^5, and show dielectric hysteresis. Rochelle salt was the first to be discovered. Others include barium titanate and potassium dihydrogen phosphate.

ferromagnetic—1. The ability of certain materials such as iron, nickel, and cobalt to be highly magnetized. 2. A property of substances that can cause an electric force of current with a change in polarity.

ferromagnetic material — A particular material having a specific permeability greater than unity, the amount depending on the magnetizing force. A ferromagnetic material usually has relatively high values of specific permeability and it exhibits hysteresis.

ferromagnetics — The science which deals with the magnetic polarization properties of materials.

ferromagnetism — 1. Refers to a high degree of magnetism in ferrites and similar compounds. The magnetic moments of neighboring ions tend not to align parallel with each other. The moments are of different magnitudes, and the resultant magnetization can be large. 2. Phenomenon in which there is a marked increase in magnetization in an independently established magnetic field. Some magnetism is retained in some ferromagnetic substances but can be removed by demagnetization. Certain elements (iron, nickel, cobalt) and alloys with other elements (titanium, aluminum) exhibit relative permeabilities much in excess of unity, up to 10^6 (ferromagnetic materials). Some have marked hysteresis, leading to permanent magnets, storage devices for computers, magnetic amplifiers, etc.

ferrous oxide spots—Refers to a specific medium by which information is represented on magnetic tape. Specific ferrous oxide spots represent information in binary form that is interpreted by the magnetic-tape drive and then stored in computer memory for processing.

fetch—1. That portion of a computer cycle during which the location of the next instruction is determined, the instruction is taken from memory, and modified, if necessary, and then entered into the control register. 2. To obtain a quantity of data from a place of storage. 3. To bring a program phase into main storage from the memory image library for immediate execution. 4. The routine that retrieves requested phases and loads them into main storage. *See* system loader. 5. The name of a macro instruction (fetch) used to transfer control to the system loader.

fetch cycle—The portion of an operational sequence in which an instruction or directive is obtained from the location in memory identified by the contents of the program counter.

fetching, demand — A memory multiplexing design in which segments are kept on a backing storage and only placed in an internal storage when computations refer to them.

fetch instruction—Refers to a basic instruction or procedure to locate and return instructions that are entered in the instruction register. Generally, the next, or some later step in the program, will cause the microprocessor to execute that segment of the program related to the fetched instructions.

fetch phase—Refers generally to an alternate part of the cycle of the computer's operation wherein the instruction is brought from memory into the program register.

fetch phase, microprogram—Some microprograms provide a "fetch" phase to form an address, to access the machine instruction from the system memory (external to the CPU) and store it in the CPU instruction register. Also, the microprogram has an "interpret" or "execute" phase to carry out the operations specified by the instruction. Microprogramming techniques can be extended to other programmable storage means besides conventional memories and to systems that include a number of programmable control sections operating in parallel or in a hierarchy.

fetch (program)—A routine to obtain a requested phase, load it into main storage at the locations assigned by the linkage editor, and transfer control to the phase entry point.

fiber loss—Fiber loss, or the decrease in the intensity of a light pulse as it travels through an optic fiber, increases with fiber length. Loss can result from the scattering of light that is produced by fiber composition or density fluctuations, which occur on a small scale compared to the wavelength. Called Rayleigh scattering, this scattering, or loss, is inversely proportional to the fourth power of the wavelength. Light can also scatter due to geometrical imperfections that are large compared to the wavelength, i.e., scattering (independent of wavelength). In addition, material impurities can absorb light.

fiber optic acceptance angle—The angle of acceptance is the maximum angle within which light may be coupled from a source or emitter. It is measured relative to the axis of the fiber.

fiber optic bandwidth—See fiber optic bit rate and fiber optic capacity.

fiber optic bit rate — The ultimate bit rate (or bandwidth) of a fiber, like loss, proves critical to the economics of the lightwave system, for the more information carried per fiber, the fewer fibers are needed. A recently developed time domain technique serves to measure the information-carrying capacity of fibers. In this technique, a narrow pulse of optical power, generated by the optical signal generator, excites a fiber and detector in tandem. The output voltage is measured by scanning the sampling gate of a wide-band sampling oscilloscope. The combined frequency responses of the fiber and the detector distort the output. Calculations take this into account to extract the response of the fiber from the output pulses.

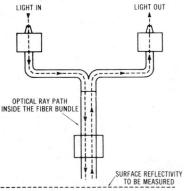

Fiber optics cable, bifuricated and randomized.

fiber optic cable, bifuricated and randomized—In a bifuricated and randomized fiber optic cable bundle, one end of the cable bundle is split in two. The other end of the cable bundle is a single end where the fibers from the two split ends are randomly mixed together. A typical cable bundle is comprised of 125 μm-cladding-diameter single fibers. The diameter of the single-end part of the bundle is 1.5 mm while each of the split-end bundles are 1 mm in diameter. Typically, each split end is terminated with a fiber optic connector, and the single end is terminated with a metal ferrule. One of the fiber optic connectors attaches to a light source and the other attaches to a light receiver.

fiber optic capacity — See fiber optic dispersion.

fiber optic cathode-ray tubes — In a fiber optic cathode-ray tube, the normal faceplate is replaced with a plate composed of millions of microscopic optical fibers running from the inter-

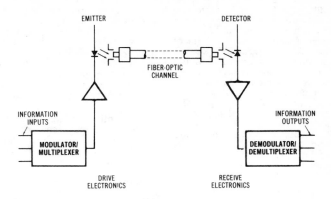

Fiber optics communications.

ior surface to the exterior surface of the plate in a tight coherent bundle. The phosphor is deposited directly on the ends of the fibers inside the tube. Thus, an image generated at the phosphor plane is transferred from the phosphor on the inner surface, through the fibers, and appears on the outer surface. The fibers run only the thickness of the cathode-ray tube (crt) face. Use of a fiber optic faceplate permits the coupling of an image, generated at the crt's phosphor plane, to be recorded on film that is in contact with the outside plane of the faceplate, with little or no spreading. With conventional tubes, coupling to film is normally accomplished by placing a lens between the crt face and the film, thus imaging the information generated at the phosphor plane onto the film. Fiber optic coupling not only eliminates the space required for an optical path, making the system much more conpact, but provides a light-transfer efficiency on the order of 30 times that of a common lens.

fiber optic communications—Fiber optic communications avoids all of the electromagnetic interference to which wire systems are susceptible because of the dielectric nature of optical fibers. Data is converted into modified infrared light, transmitted, then reconverted into electronic signals.

fiber optic components—The fiber has a core of a light-transmitting material with a high index of refraction, surrounded by a cladding or optical insulating material with a lower index of refraction. Light enters the fiber at an infinite number of angles, but only those rays entering the fiber at an angle less than the critical acceptance angle are transmitted. Light is propagated within the core of a multimode fiber at specific angles of internal reflection. When a propagating ray strikes the core-cladding interface, it is reflected and zigzags down the core.

fiber optic dimensional parameters— Unlike electrical conductors, optical fiber "conductors" must match dimensionally and align precisely at connections. Optical power transmitted through the core of a fiber distributes throughout the fiber's cross-sectional area and any mismatch in core cross-sections can result in a loss of optical power. Also, the connecting scheme makes use of the outer fiber diameter in alignment; to ensure the proper alignment of fiber cores, the outside (cladding) diameters must match, as must the positions of the cores in the fibers.

The critical dimensional parameters are: the core and cladding diameters (determined indirectly by optical means), core eccentricity (a measure of the displacement of the center of the core relative to the cladding center), and ellipticity (the degree of distortion from circularity of the core).

fiber optic dispersion—The capacity, or bandwidth, of a fiber optic system is the maximum rate at which the pulses comprising the signals can be sent and received without error. A form of distortion called dispersion sets a practical limit to the speed at which pulses can be transmitted without error. Dispersion means that a pulse is spread out in time and part of it arrives at the wrong time—too late to be correctly interpreted at the receiving end. Because the pulse is blurred, the decoders at the receiving end of the link may see an erroneous bit of data after the intended bit—and this binary "one" instead of a "zero" constitutes an error.

fiber optic distortion—*See* fiber optic dispersion.

fiber optics — A fiber is a transparent material system that conducts or "guides" light. This guiding phenomenon is a result of a dissimilar set of material refractive indices. That is, an optically dense core material (high refractive index n_1) is usually surrounded by a less optically dense cladding material (lower refractive index n_2). The magnitude of the resulting optical density difference between the core and cladding determines the maximum angle at which guiding occurs (numerical aperture). Only rays which are at the maximum angle or less are "accepted" and guided along the fiber, while all other rays escape from the side of the fiber and are "radiated." A very simple fiber structure would consist of a simple strand of glass ($n_1 = 1.5$) surrounded by air ($n_2 = 1.0$).

Because optical fibers are nonmetallic, fiber optic systems provide safe, noise-free communications circuits. Fibers are not susceptible to electromagnetic interference, and they provide isolation from ground-potential rise. Fiber optic systems are also not affected by heavy rain and lightning, which can cause outages in conventional cable and radio systems.

fiber optics cladding—A covering for the core of an optical fiber that provides optical insulation and protection. Generally fused to the fiber, it has a relatively low index of refraction.

fiber optic signal transmission — Though signals can be transmitted through a fiber either digitally (by pulsing the light) or in analog form (by varying the brightness of the light), the trend is towards digital transmission—even when the original source is an analog signal such as that from a telephone. Users look at fiber performance in terms of what happens to digital pulses — though similar types of losses and distortion occur with analog light transmission.

fiber optics, "lightpipe" — *See* "lightpipe" fiber optics.

fiber optics, step index—*See* step index fibers.

fiber optic transmission system — Abbreviated FOTS. A transmission system utilizing small-diameter glass fibers through which light is transmitted. Information is transferred by modulating the transmitted light. These modulated signals are detected by light-sensitive semiconductor devices.

Fick's law—The rate of molecular diffusion is proportional to the negative of the concentration gradient. This law holds for mass and energy transfer and also for neutron diffusion.

field — 1. In computers, area obtained by a vertical division of a punched card. 2. A set of scanning lines that, when interlaced with other such sets,

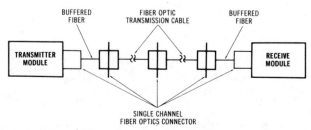

Fiber optic transmission system.

constructs the complete tv picture. 3. The interaction of bodies or particles is explained in terms of fields, viz., electric, magnetic, gravitational, and acoustic fields.

field, computer — 1. A group of computer characters that can be treated as a single unit of information. 2. In a series of punch cards, a column or columns regularly used for a standard item of information. 3. Source statements are made up of a number of code fields, usually four, that are acceptable by the assembler or assembly program. The four fields might connote: Label, Operand, Comment, and Operator. 4. Fields are also applicable to data storage procedures. For example, two 8-bit words might contain two 4-bit fields, eight 1-bit fields, etc.

field density—The number of lines of force normally passing through a unit area of an electric or magnetic field.

field discharge—The passage of electricity through a gas as a result of ionization of the gas; it takes the form of a brush discharge, an arc, or a spark.

field-effect transistor—A transistor having a circuit application similar to that of a vacuum tube. The main conduction path is through a bar of n-type silicon, with control through depeletion layers on each side of the n-type bar.

field marker — A symbol used to indicate the beginning or the end of some set of data, i.e., group, file, record, block; in this case, a particular field.

field protected—A display field in which the user cannot enter, modify, or erase data from the keyboard.

field strength — 1. Frequently referred to as field intensity. The value of the vector at a point in the region occupied by a vector field. Also the amount of magnetic flux produced at a particular point by an electromagnetic or permanent magnet. 2. Vector representing the quotient of a force and the charge (or pole) in an electric (or magnetic) field, with the direction of the force; also called field intensity. 3. In radio, electromagnetic wave in volt/meter, i.e., that which induces an emf of 1 volt in an antenna of 1 meter effective height. Usually measured with a frame or loop antenna.

FIFO — A first-in/first-out memory as compared to a conventional random-access memory (RAM). For applications where it is desirable to read out information in the same order that it was written in, a FIFO memory greatly simplifies system operation. As with any memory system, Read access time is an important FIFO parameter. An excessive Read time directly delays the response of a system to a FIFO input. In some communication systems, the rate at which information can be entered into or Read from a FIFO memory is also important. This is especially true when different data rates are required between the input and output of the FIFO memory. Another important feature used to measure the performance of a FIFO memory is the ease with which data can be entered into the memory.

FIFO memory—First-in/first-out memories are commonly used to store information in digital processing systems. However, these memories can also be designed to interface subsystems operating asynchronously or at different data rates. Ideally, FIFO Read and Write operations should be completely independent of each other and of the system timing. This is especially true with asynchronous operation where the data inputs and Write clock must always be ready to accept data. Any time the Read cycle interferes with the ability to Write in information, the memory cannot accept asynchronous data without additional buffer circuitry.

Data to be written in the memory is automatically stored in the next available location and a Read operation advances the outputs to the next unread memory word. Once the Read is advanced, the previous word normally cannot be used again. The big advantage of a FIFO memory is the absence of external memory addressing. It is automatically controlled within the memory, requiring only data inputs, Read outputs, and the associated clock lines.

FIFO queue—A first-in/first-out queue in which the most recent arrival is placed at the end of the waiting list and the item waiting the longest receives service first. Same as push-up list, push-up storage.

file-control block —A data structure in

main memory that is used for keeping track of files in use.

file, data—The aggregation of data sets for definite usage. The file may contain one or more different data sets. A permanent data file is one in which the data is perpetually subject to being updated; e.g., a name and address file. A working data file is a temporary accumulation of data sets that are destroyed after the data has been transferred to another form.

file gap—An interval of space or time used to indicate or signal the end of a file.

file management system — The part of a disk operating system that controls the organization and allocation of disk files, which may consist of one or more sectors.

file manager—A file manager often is an on-line executive program that provides the ability to create, delete, and retrieve programs by name from a bulk storage device. The file manager can be designed to provide program storage for systems as small as 4K words where a full operating system cannot be used. File manager supports disks, magnetic tapes, cassettes, etc.

file manipulator—The manipulator is a collection of statistical programs. The common features of a manipulator include software for smoothing data, forecasting, setting confidence limits, lagging and leading data, calculating averages, means, and other statistical data, and performing trend analysis. These programs should be chosen or designed to meet the user's requirements. The manipulator is entered from the data base program or from the display program. A menu often enables the user to select the type of statistical operation desired; the system then prompts the user to enter the names of the data files. Results can be stored temporarily in work files or permanently as data files.

file protection — A device or method which prevents accidental erasure of operative data on magnetic tape reels.

film resistor — A type of fixed resistor having a resistance element made of a thin layer of conductive material on an insulated form. An overlaying insulating coating that is a sort of mechanical protection is placed over this layer.

filter, digital—A filtering process performed on a digitized signal by a general- or special-purpose computer. Although digital filtering is far more flexible than analog filtering, it is also generally slower and more expensive and, hence, largely limited to experimental applications when relatively few frequencies are being filtered.

firmware—1. A term usually related to microprogramming and those specific software instructions that have been more or less permanently burned into a ROM control block. 2. An extension to a computer's basic command (instruction) repertoire to create microprograms for a user-oriented instruction set. This extension to the basic instruction set is done in read-only memory and not in software. The read-only memory converts the extended instructions to the basic instructions of the computer. 3. Firmware is a machine component of a computer system, similar to a computer circuit component or a terminal component, or a disk component. This software machine component can be in two forms—in source form (the source program) or in machine form (the object program). Firmware generally is limited to moving data through the data paths and functional units already present; it is able to process effectively only the instruction formats, data types, and arithmetic modes that are defined for the hardware. Attempting to use firmware for new formats, types, and modes is inherently awkward and might result in poor performance.

firmware, ROM — Refers generally to nonerasable permanently programmed memory that is usually used to store monitors and I/O drivers. These monitors and drivers are needed whenever the computer is used. Programs stored in ROM are called "firmware."

first-generation microcomputers—First-generation microcomputers use n- or p-channel MOS technology. A first-generation microcomputer is most accurately visualized as a powerful set of discrete logic that can be sequenced in innumerable ways by a stored program. One suitably programmed memory chip plus one CPU chip can replace approximately one thousand gates' worth of discrete logic, and changing logic is as simple as changing the program. To a logic designer, a first-generation CPU chip is a very attractive device; it has a very simple interaction with external devices and, therefore, is easy to understand and use.

first-in/first-out memory — 1. *See* FIFO memory. 2. In computing systems, FIFO memory is used for stack registers where register outputs are sequentially read in the same order that data was entered. A FIFO memory also simplifies many information-handling operations such as high-speed compiling and code conversions. Equally important to internal use in a system is the performance of a FIFO memory as an interface element between two subsystems. It is possible that the two subsystems will not share a common clock and the FIFO memory must operate asynchronously. In this case, data input is controlled by the device supplying information and the Read function is controlled by the system using the information. Also, the two systems can be operating at different data rates where several words are stored prior to being read. For example, a lower speed peripheral system may load data at a slow rate to be read by a CPU in a high-speed burst.

fixed-cycle operation — 1. A type of computer operation where a fixed amount of time is allowed for a specific operation. 2. A synchronous or clock-type arrangement within a computer in which events occur as a function of measured time.

fixed instruction/microprogramming— *See* microprogramming/fixed instruction.

fixed-length file records — Enumerable elements, each of which has the same number of words, characters, bits, fields, etc.

fixed-length record — A record whose number of characters is fixed. The restriction may be deliberate to simplify and speed processing or it may be caused by the characteristics of the equipment used.

fixed-point arithmetic—1. A method of calculation in which operations take place in an invariant manner, and in which the computer does not consider the location of the radix point.

This is illustrated by desk calculators or slide rules, with which the operator must keep track of the decimal point. Similar to many automatic computers, in which the location of the radix point is the programmer's responsibility. 2. A type of arithmetic in which the operands and results of all arithmetic operations must be properly scaled so as to have a magnitude between certain fixed values.

fixed-program computer—A computer in which the instructions are permanently stored or wired in, performed automatically, and are not subject to change either by the computer or the programmer, except by rewiring or changing the storage input. Related to computer, wired-program.

fixed word length—Having the property that a machine word always contains the same number of characters or digits.

flag—1. An indicator, usually a single binary bit, whose state is used to inform a later section of a program that a condition, identified with the flag and designated by the state of the flag, had occurred. A flag can be both software- and hardware-implemented. 2. Refers to a bit (or bits) used to store one bit of information. A flag has two stable states and is the software analogy of a flip-flop.

flag bit—Refers to a specific information bit that indicates a type or form of demarcation that has been reached. This may be carry, overflow, etc. Generally, the flag bit refers to special conditions, such as various types of interrupts.

flash-type a/d converter—An ultra fast conversion technique employing 2^n-1 comparators to quantize an analog input to n bits. Also known as parallel or simultaneous method.

flip-flop — 1. A type of circuit capable of storing 1 bit of information. It has two stable states and usually two input terminals (or signals) corresponding to each of the two states. The circuit remains in either state until the corresponding signal is applied. Also, a similar bistable device with an input which allows it to act as a single-stage binary counter. Flip-flops may be grouped together to form storage registers, counters, shift registers, or a number of other functional components. 2. A bistable device; a device capable of assuming two stable states; a bistable device which may assume a given stable state depending upon the pulse history of one or more input points and which has one or more output points. The device is capable of storing a bit of information, controlling gates, etc.; a toggle.

flip-flop, ac-coupled — Refers to a type of flip-flop made up of electronic circuits in which the active elements, either tubes or transistors, are coupled with capacitors.

flip-flop, capacitance-coupled — Same as flip-flop, ac-coupled.

flip-flop circuit — An electronic circuit having two stable states, one input line, and one output line.

flip-flop, "D"—D stands for delay. A flip-flop whose output is a function of the input which appeared one pulse earlier; for example, if a "1" appeared at the input, the output after the next clock pulse will be a "1."

flip-flop, dc—The connection by a device which passes the steady state characteristics of a signal and which largely eliminates the transient or oscillating characteristics of the signal.

flip-flop equipment — Refers to electronic or electromechanical devices that cause automatic alternation between two possible circuit paths. The same term is often applied to any mechanical operation which is analogous to the principles of the flip-flop.

flip-flop, level-enable—A specific flip-flop, set by the level-enable signal, that partially controls the ability of an interrupt level to advance from the waiting state to the active state.

flip-flop, "R-S" — A flip-flop consisting of two cross-coupled NAND gates having two inputs designated R and S. A "1" on the S input and "0" on the R input will reset (clear) the flip-flop to the "0" state, and "1" on the R input and "0" on the S input will set it to "1." It is assumed that "0's" will never appear simultaneously at both inputs. If both inputs have "1's," it will stay as it was. A "1" is considered nonactivating. A similar circuit can be formed using NOR gates.

flip-flop, "R-S-T"—A flip-flop having three inputs, R, S, and T. This unit works the same as the R and S flip-flop except that the T input is used to cause the flip-flop to change states.

flip-flops, general-purpose—Two types of general-purpose flip-flops are available in some series, both of which have built-in protection against the ambiguous state characteristic of NAND gate flip-flops. They are the D type flip-flops and J-K type flip-flops. The D type flip-flop is a true leading-edge (positive-going voltage) triggered flip-flop and the D input is locked out until the clock input returns to low. The operation of the J-K type flip-flops and J-K type flip-flops. mation present at the J and K inputs just prior to and during the clock pulse to the master flip-flop when the threshold is passed on the leading edge (positive-going voltage) of the clock pulse. The information stored in the master flip-flop is transferred to the slave flip-flop, and consequentially to the outputs, when the threshold is passed on the trailing edge (negative-going voltage) of the clock pulse.

flip-flop, sign — The specific flip-flop used to store the algebraic sign of numbers.

flip-flop storage — A bistable storage device which stores binary data as states of flip-flop elements.

flip-flop string—An important computer property is that the state of one flip-flop can be transferred to another by means of special triggering circuits. That is, a number stored in one strip of flip-flops can be transferred to another string. In this way, numbers can be transferred from place to place in a computer. This function is so important that the flip-flop circuits generally include a pair of triggering circuits for this purpose.

flip-flop, "T"—A flip-flop having only one input. A pulse appearing on the input will cause the flip-flop to change states. Used in ripple counters.

floating-point arithmetic — Arithmetic used in a computer where the computer keeps track of the decimal point (contrasted with fixed-point arithmetic).

floating-point arithmetic hardware—A processor circuitry feature that is usually found on larger computers or on scientific computers which is capable of directly performing operations on floating-point numbers without the use of subroutines.

floating-point calculation—A computer

calculation that takes into consideration the varying location of the decimal point (if base 10 is being used) or the binary point (if base 2 is used). The sign and coefficient of each number are separately specified.

floating-point representation — A specific number representation system in which each number, as represented by a pair of numerals, equals one of those numerals times a power of an implicit fixed positive integer base where the power is equal to the implicit base raised to the exponent represented by the other numeral. Contrast with variable-point representation.

Common Notation	Scientific Notation	Floating-Point Representation
0.0001234	0.1234×10^{-3}	.1234E — 03

floating symbolic address — A label chosen to identify a particular word, function, or other information in a routine, independent of the location of the information within the routine.

floppy-disk reference point — The standard diskette is designed for use with a format in which the sector information is prerecorded. In this case, a single hole on the diskette serves as a reference point. The detection of this hole is accomplished by a transducer which is made up of a phototransistor/LED combination. The transducer produces an index pulse once per revolution of the diskette. A diskette that has equally spaced fixed sector holes on the same radius as the index hole is referred to as being hard sectored.

floppy-disk sectors — On a floppy disk, each track is divided into a given number of sectors. Some manufacturers depend on timing holes in the floppy disk to locate where the sectors begin and end, while others use a single hole and electronically time where the sectors start. Still others drop the head on the proper track and read off prerecorded sector identification marks from the disk itself. **Hard Sectored** means that the sectors are timed from several holes in the disk; **Soft Sectored** means that a single sector hole is timed and counted from there. **Preformatted** means that the sector identification is prerecorded on the disk before purchase.

floppy-disk systems — A typical floppy disk provides random-access program/data storage. Hard-sector formatted, each disk will hold over 300,000 data bytes. Because many floppy controllers have all of their intelligence in microcode, some microcontrollers offer features not practical in designs implemented with hard-wired logic. The host-computer driver need only issue a small sequence of commands to Write or Read data from the disk.

floppy-disk tracks — Tracks of a disk are parallel to each other, just as cassette tracks are. Because the head is moveable, it can slide from track to track. Each track, then, forms a ring around the center hole. However, each manufacturer of disk drives has his own patented way to position the head over the proper track with the necessary accuracy so that the recording will be in the same place when played back on another drive.

flowchart — 1. A programmer's tool for determining a sequence of operations (as charted) using sets of symbols, directional marks, and other representations to indicate stepped procedures of computer operation. Flowcharts also enable the designer to conceptualize the procedure necessary and to visualize each step and item on a program. A completed flowchart is often a necessity to the achievement of accurate final code. 2. A graphical representation for the definition, analysis, or solution of a problem, in which symbols are used to represent operations, data, flow, equipment, etc. Contrast with block diagram. 3. A flowchart represents the path of data through a problem solution. It defines the major phases of the processing as well as the various data media used.

flowcharting — Refers to a method for representing a succession of events in symbolic form. The events may represent a variety of activities but, in general, a specific flowchart will record the interconnection between events of the same type. In data processing, flowcharts may be divided into systems flowcharts and program flowcharts.

flowchart, logical — A detailed solution of the work order in terms of the logic, or built-in operations and characteristics, of a specific machine. Concise symbolic notation is used to represent the information and describe the input, output, arithmetic, and logical operations involved. The chart indicates types of operations by use of a standard set of block symbols. A coding process normally follows the logical flowchart.

flowcharts, functional vs. detail — A functional flowchart defines the functional operations sequentially, but it does not contain sufficient detail to allow program writing or coding. Detailed charts overcome this limitation. They are derived from the functional flowcharts, the established command codes, and the manner in which each command code works within the system. The detailed flowcharts tell, step by step, every operation that must be performed. For the instruction writing, or coding, the programmers need only know how to program the microprocessor. Any engineer trained in assembly language for any computer fulfills this requirement.

flow diagram—1. A chart containing all the logical steps in a particular computer program; also referred to as a flowchart. A program is coded by writing down the successive steps which will cause the computer to perform the necessary logical operation for solving the problem, as presented by the flowchart. 2. Relates to a specific graphic representation of the major steps of work in process. The illustrative symbols may represent documents, machines, or actions taken during the process. The area of concentration is on where or who does what, rather than how it is to be done.

foreground — 1. In multiprogramming, refers to the environment in which high-priority programs are executed. 2. Under time-sharing option (TSO), the environment in which programs are swapped in and out of main storage to allow CPU time to be shared among terminal users. All command processor programs execute in the foreground. Contrast with background. 3. A high-priority program, process, or system part which utilizes the computer CPU immediately, or when and where and as needed, but which still allows less critical or subsidiary programs to be worked on as background tasks during the time when the high-priority programs are not being worked. This is the basis of multiprogramming or foreground/background processing.

foreground/background modes — Pertaining to a system in which programs are executed in two modes, foreground and background. Foreground programs are executed interactively under user control. Users maintain complete control over editing, execution, inputs, outputs, and other program functions. While monitoring the system programs, the microcomputer is said to be in foreground mode. All foreground mode operations are initiated by interrupts. Programs in the background are executed on the basis of time available to the computer system. The microcomputer is often idle 80% of the time, so operators will use it during its idle time for operations wholly unrelated to regular work. All required execution data is set up prior to submitting the job for execution. Users refer to these secondary programs as operating in the background mode. When a job is submitted to the background, user control is usually limited to checking program status (running, waiting, printing, etc.) or aborting the job.

foreground/background processing — Automatic execution of lower priority (background) programs when higher priority (foreground) programs are not using the system and vice versa. Background program processing is temporarily suspended to service interrupt requests from I/O devices that require foreground processing.

format—A predetermined arrangement of characters, fields, lines, punctuation, page numbers, etc.

format control—Format control permits the microcomputer to write protected data on the screen. The operator can fill in the blank (unprotected) areas but cannot change the protected data.

format conversion language—Refers to language that transforms the data between its internal and external formats and structures. Thus, a programmer must know three distinct languages to get the program down on paper: (1) an algorithmic data-manipulation and statement-sequencing language, (2) a "format conversion" language specifying the structure of the external data, and the mapping between the external organization, and the representation of data and its internal organization and representation, and (3) a language for specifying the internal structure of the data elements to be manipulated by the algorithm.

format mode — A feature of some crt terminals is a "format mode" capability. This is a dual intensity display that distinguishes between foreground and background data, and a "blinking field" that is used to highlight important data. A tab key is provided that will move the cursor from one variable field to the next.

format, packed—A binary-coded decimal format in which two decimal digits are represented within a single byte of storage, accomplished by eliminating the zone bits.

format storage, local — A system in which frequently used formats are stored at a terminal controller instead of being repeatedly sent down the communications line.

format, symbolic-coding—In writing instructions using the assembly language, the programmer is primarily concerned with three fields: a label field, an operation field, and an operand field. It is possible to relate the symbolic coding to its associated flowchart, if desired, by appending comments to each instruction line or program segment.

formatter—The formatter, when used in conjunction with a floppy disk drive, provides all the control and timing necessary to form a data storage/retrieval system suitable for use in data processing applications. In addition to Read and Write commands, formatter commands are provided for data search, Read-after-Write data checking, and Write initialize operations. The formatter also performs automatic checks on data, sector addressing, and various programming and hardware error conditions.

formatting—1. Planning the order of information to or output from a computer or crt, usually to assist or ease the human receiver's interpretation of the information. 2. Preparation of various types of magnetic media to accept data structures. Floppy disks, for example, require before use that formatting regarding track and sector information be set for the controller. After it is formatted, the disk can be used for normal I/O and retrieval operations.

format, variable—A changing description of classification for the information content in a particular area.

FORTH compiler — FORTH uses a unique organization, known as threaded code. The basic unit in FORTH, called a word, is either an assembly language routine or a sequence of FORTH words in structured reverse Polish notation (RPN). When a word is defined, it is compiled into a sequence of addresses of words. It can then be executed by an interpreter perhaps 50 bytes long, which jumps from word to word, stacking all continuations at each level of definition down to executable code and returning when the stack is empty. Commands can be entered from a terminal keyboard and interpreted, each word being looked up in the dictionary of definitions when it is to be executed.

FORTH language — FORTH is a programming language system which can be implemented readily on microcomputers, and which offers high-level means of expressing solutions to a wide range of problems. A major feature of FORTH is that user-defined operators (procedures, functions, or commands) can be used just as though they were primitives. This makes the language truly extensible. Extensions may be added at the user-program level or at the FORTH-interpreter level.

FORTH language, structured programming — Unlike other high-level languages that insulate the user from the machine, FORTH allows easy movement between higher-level, machine-transportable programming and assembly modules for input/output control or time-critical routines. It exploits what is called indirect-threaded coding, which means that statements are built from a dictionary of definitions coming both in the operating system and from the programmer. Moreover, it permits structured programming, which is to say, the programmer transfers control down a hierarchy from the most general to the most specific routines. FORTH is extensible; the user can fabricate his or her own operations, data types, etc., and these definitions are treated exactly like FORTH's own. Thus, they are immediately available when the system comes up, with no need for access to a software library or subroutine.

FORTRAN—1. *FOR*mula *TRAN*slator. A compiler language developed by the IBM Corporation; originally conceived for use on scientific problems but now widely adapted for most commercial problems as well. **2.** Pertaining to a computer program that translates a FORTRAN-language program into a machine-language program.

FORTRAN, commercial — Some systems combine FORTRAN IV with elements of BASIC and COBOL for business and computational applications.

FORTRAN compiler system—The FORTRAN compiler system consists of two basic elements: a source language (FORTRAN IV), whose structure closely resembles the language of mathematics, and a compiler that translates the statements and formulas written in the source language into a machine-language program.

FORTRAN-80, microcomputer — One type initial compiler is a fully implemented ANSI standard FORTRAN with the exception of the double precision and complex data types. It allows three data types: logical (one byte), integer (two byte) and real (four-byte floating point). Logical variables under FORTRAN-80 can represent, and store, both logical values (ones and zeros) and integer quantities from −128 to +127. This allows programmers to minimize data storage, and take advantage of fast logical arithmetic operations—with integers within that range. It is a one-pass compiler that reads source code, concurrently translates it into relocatable object code, that may be placed in ROM, and prints an optional code listing. (12 Kbytes memory required.)

FORTRAN IV—FORTRAN IV is a language that is problem oriented. The programmer may think in terms of the problem, rather than thinking in terms of the computer which is used to solve the problem. Initially designed for scientific applications, it has proved quite convenient for many commercial and industrial applications.

FORTRAN IV cross assembler—A typical program or group of programs designed to convert microcomputer assembly language to microprocessor machine code. Assembly language is fully symbolic, and symbolic cross-referencing is provided together with diagnostics of programming errors. Special assembler features are typically provided to enable efficient use of unique architectural features of specific microprocessors.

FORTRAN IV logical capabilities—FORTRAN IV logical capabilities include: type-declaration statements, logical operators, logical expressions, relational operators, logical assignment statements, and the logical IF statement.

FORTRAN IV simulator—Programs designed to functionally simulate execution of various host computer programs. Simulators are interpretive and provide bit-for-bit duplication of microprocessor instruction execution timing, register contents, etc. The system usually provides direct user control over execution conditions, RAM/register contents, interrupts, I/O data, etc.

FORTRAN language — Programs are written directly as algebraic expressions and arithmetic statements. Various symbols are used to signify equality, addition, subtraction, exponentiation, etc. Additional statements are provided to permit control over how the algebraic expressions and arithmetic statements are to be processed. These include transfer, decision, indexing, and input/output statements.

FORTRAN-77 cross compiler—This is a typical FORTRAN cross compiler that conforms to the ANSI X3.9-1978 standard at the defined subset level, with added features for use in microprocessor environments. The cross compiler translates FORTRAN programs into a sequence of microprocessor assembler statements. These may then be assembled using the cross assembler, linked with other FORTRAN or assembly language routines, and down-loaded for execution, or written into PROM. Included with these compilers is a library of intrinsic functions and run-time support routines which operate on the microprocessor to perform required run-time support functions.

forward scan — An editing operation which makes an output word conform to the control word by comparing positions from right to left and adding punctuation, such as decimals and dollar signs.

four address—1. A method of specifying the location of operands and instructions in which the storage location of the two operands and the storage location of the results of the operation are cited, and the storage location of the next instruction to be executed is cited. 2. Having the property that each complete instruction specifies the operation and addresses of four registers.

Fourier analysis—The determination of the harmonic components of a complex waveform either mathematically or by a wave analyzer device.

Fourier principle — Principle which shows that all repeating waveforms can be resolved into sine-wave components, consisting of a fundamental and a series of harmonics at multiples of this frequency. It can be extended to prove that nonrepeating waveforms occupy a continuous frequency.

Fourier series—A mathematical analysis that permits any complex waveform to be resolved into a fundamental plus a finite number of terms involving its harmonics.

fox message—A standard message that is used for testing teletypewriter circuits and machines because it includes all the alphanumerics on a teletypewriter as well as most of the function characters, such as space, figures shift, letters shift, etc. The message is: The quick brown fox jumped over a lazy dog's back 1234567890 _____ sending. (The sending station's identification is inserted in the blank space which precedes the word "sending.")

FPLA—Abbreviation for Field Programmable Logic Array. A programmable logic array device in which the internal connections of the AND and OR gates can be programmed by passing high current through fusible links.

FPLA editing — A critical feature of FPLAs, absent in bipolar PROMs, is their editing capability. A number of modifications can be incorporated in a program already stored in the FPLA. Specifically in some FPLAs, product terms can be added or deleted from any output function, input variables can be deleted from any output function, and input variables

can be deleted from any product terms. Also, outputs programmed active-high can be reprogrammed to active-low. This offers a good degree of flexibility, comparable to the versatility afforded by erasable MOS PROMs.

FPLA vs. PROM—The structure and use of Field Programmable Logic Arrays can be understood if one compares them more to memory than to logic. An FPLA is basically a PROM with one very important difference—its versatility makes it a great deal more useful. To grasp the similarities, one must examine PROMs. Industry jargon refers to PROMs as 1K, 2K, 4K, etc. These usually imply standard organizations such as 256×4, 256×8, 512×8, respectively. The larger value in each pair of numbers refers to the number of words in a PROM, and the second value represents the number of bits in each word. The product of both numbers (approximately 1K, 2K, and 4K) gives the total number of storage bits contained in the PROM. This aspect of PROMs carries over to FPLAs, meaning that FPLAs will be described as 48×8, for a total **working** storage density of 384 bits. The key word here is "working," for, although an FPLA appears to be a relatively small PROM, its usefulness is vastly magnified because of the difference in input structure.

frame—1. The array of bits across the width of magnetic or paper tape. In paper-tape systems, one frame is equivalent to one character. 2. A structure which allows a receiver to uniquely identify an information channel.

frame, main—The central processor of the computer system. It contains the main storage, arithmetic unit, and special register groups. (Synonymous with CPU and central processing unit.)

frequency, clock—Refers to a designed type of master frequency of periodic pulses which schedule the operation of the computer.

frequency division multiplexing — A multiplex system in which the available transmission frequency range is divided into narrow bands, each used for a separate channel. Channels are derived by allocating or "splitting up" a wider bandwidth into several narrower bandwidths. Abbreviated fdm.

frequency-shift-coded data — Frequency-shift coding, or FSC, is a term used for a data transmission code in which each bit period begins with a transition. A space (0) has no transition during the bit period; however, a mark (1) has one transition during the bit period. FSC formatting provides the advantage that it is self-clocking and, therefore, precludes the necessity of transmitting a clock signal to the receiving end to define the point in time in which data are valid. Some transmitters and receivers incorporate FSC data to provide a data rate of one megabit per second.

frequency-shift keying — Abbreviated FSK. A form of frequency modulation in which the carrier frequency is raised or lowered to represent binary 1 or binary 0. For example, if a frequency of 1700 Hz is shifted plus or minus 500 Hz, a frequency of 1200 Hz represents a 0, and a frequency of 2200 Hz represents a binary 1. Generally, FSK techniques are suitable for low-speed devices such as teleprinters and allow operation at speeds as high as 1800 bps.

front-end processor — Refers to minor microprocessors that are used to interface communication terminals to a "host" data processing system (an information processor). A front-end processor supports the host machine by alleviating the need for data communications software in the main computer. *See also* minicomputer, front-end.

FSK—*See* frequency-shift keying.

full adder (parallel) — A parallel full adder can be developed from as many three-input adders as there are digits in the input words. The carry output of each operation is connected to one input of the three-digit adder corresponding to the next significant digit position (some systems).

full duplex—Refers to a duplex operation that is a simultaneous communication in both directions between two points.

fully static memory—Both the periphery and array are designed with static cells. No external control signals are required to operate the memory. The access time equals the cycle time because no refresh or precharge is required. Fully static memories, the least sensitive to power supply noise, are the easiest to use because they require no controls — although controls may be used. The disadvantages of fully static operation are high power dissipation and relatively high cost per bit. In a newer system where adequate control edges are usually available, any of the other approaches will yield better cost and performance ratios.

functional interleaving—The process of having I/O and computing operations proceed independently of one another but interleaved in their sharing of the memory.

functional test system — A functional test system tests an entire circuit assembly *as a whole* with respect to the functions it is designed to perform. The circuits on the board are powered

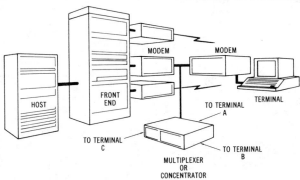

Front-end processor.

up and input signals applied, matching as closely as possible the inputs that would be encountered in actual operation. Outputs are measured and performance is compared with design specifications. Values of the various parameters at internal circuit nodes are not measured during a functional test. Connections between the test apparatus and the circuit under test are generally via a card-edge connector. A different program controls the test routine for each different circuit configuration.

function digit — A coded instruction used in a microcomputer for setting a branch order to link subroutines into the main program.

function element—The smallest building block in a microcomputer or data-processing system that can be represented by logical operators in an appropriate system of symbolic logic. Typical logical elements that can be represented as operators in a suitable symbolic logic are the AND gate and the OR gate.

function generator—Refers to a computing element designed with an output of a specified nonlinear function of its input or inputs. Normal usage excludes multipliers and resolvers.

function generator, analog—Refers to a specific network of biased diodes designed to produce a nonlinear relationship between the input and output voltages of the network. Nonlinear functions can also be generated by means of potentiometers with specially built resistance elements. Other classes of function generators use electromechanical devices which consist of motor-driven pointers that follow arbitrary curves prepared in the form of graphs. A servo motor causes the pointer to move back and forth across the curve in accordance with the value of the independent variable (the "X" coordinate).

function generator, arbitrary — Refers to a specific function generator (analog) that is not committed by its design function exclusively, so that the function that it generates can be changed at the discretion of the operator.

function generator, curve follower — A function generator that operates by automatically following a curve drawn or constructed on a surface.

function generator, diode — A device with the capability of generating an arbitrarily designed or specified fixed function (or family) by using an amplifier whose input or feedback impedance consists of networks of resistors and diodes with connections to bias supplies. See function generator.

function key — 1. A specific key on a keyboard (for example, CR, LF, LTRS, FIGS, etc.) which, when operated, causes a receiving device to perform a certain mechanical function so that a message will be received in proper form. 2. A special key or set of keys which allows functions to be specified as characteristic of given applications environment. 3. Keys on keyboards of input/output or specialized terminals which are used to query the system or have it perform certain operations. For example, on a remote-inquiry terminal used in a stock quotation system, a three letter combination identifies any stock, and earnings, sales, dividends, volume, etc., can be displayed, by punching the right function key.

function keys, (crt)—Fixed and variable function keys have been added to various crt consoles. A function key, when depressed, transmits a signal to the microcomputer that can be equated to a prestored typewriter message of many strokes. Function keys, by thus saving user actions, provide convenience and ease of operation and increased response rate of the user. Special consoles of various types have been developed for a particular user. Examples are: airline agent's sets, badge readers, stockbroker's inquiry consoles, and many others.

function keys, programmable — By changing the keyboard handling routines, the user can change the function of any key or symbol that will be displayed on the screen. This conveniently allows for any arrangement of functions for operator ease. For specific text editing applications such a feature is invaluable. Keys may be coded to perform such functions as block definition, block movement, margin definitions, tabbing, column formatting, character deletes, word deletes, search and replace, temporary data storage, file appendix, document merging, pagination, printing, and various methods of hyphenation and justification.

function mode — A communication mode that is the means by which the central computer establishes the initial communication path with a peripheral subsystem. During this mode of transmission, the central computer sends one or more function words to a peripheral subsystem. These function words direct the units to perform the desired operation (some computers).

functions library (elementary)—A typical offering of many manufacturers is a set of subroutines to perform the most common mathematical functions using floating-point number format. Some are: square root, exponentiation, hyperbolic tangent, arc tangent, sine, cosine, natural logarithm, common logarithm, Base 2 logarithm, etc.

function table—1. Refers to two or more sets of data so arranged that an entry in one set selects one or more entries in the remaining sets; for example, a tabulation of the values of a function for a set of values of the variable, a dictionary. 2. A device constructed of hardware, or a subroutine, which can either decode multiple inputs into a single output or encode a single input into multiple outputs.

G

gamma ferric oxide — The magnetic constituent of practically all present-day tapes, in the form of a dispersion of fine acicular particles within the coating.

gap—1. The portion of a magnetic circuit which does not contain ferromagnetic material, such as an air space. Also, the space between any two electrodes in a spark gap. 2. An interval of space or time used as an automatic sentinel to indicate the end of a word, record, or file of data on a tape, e.g., a word gap at the end of a word, a record, or item gap at the end of a group of words, or a file gap at the end of a group of records or items. 3. The absence of information for a specified length of time or space on a recording medium, as contrasted with marks and sentinels which are the presence of specific information to achieve a similar purpose. Marks are used primarily internally in variable word length machines. Sentinels achieve similar purposes either internally or externally. However, sentinels are programmed rather than inherent in the hardware. Related to file gap and terminating symbol. 4. The space between the reading or recording head and the recording medium, such as tape, drum, or disk. Related to gap, head.

gap, block — The space on magnetic tape separating two blocks of data or information.

gap digits — Digits are sometimes included in a machine word for various technical reasons. Such digits are not used to represent data or instructions.

gap, file — Refers to various short lengths of tape designed or left blank which contain no recorded information. It is used to separate files or blocks of data on tapes and other recorded media.

gap, head — 1. The space between the reading or recording head and the recording medium, such as the tape, drum, or disk. 2. The space or gap intentionally inserted into the magnetic circuit of the head in order to force or direct the recording flux into the recording medium.

gap, interblock—The space on magnetic tape separating two blocks of data or information.

gap, interrecord—A blank space between records or blocks of data on a storage medium; e.g., a gap on a magnetic tape that allows for acceleration of the tape to the proper speed required for the Read/Write operation, and for deceleration to a stop before the next operation. Also known as *interblock gap*.

gap, interword — The time period and space permitted between words on a tape, disk, drum, etc. Usually, such space allows for controlling specific or individual words for switching.

gap length—The dimension of the gap of a reading and recording head measured from one pole face to the other. In longitudinal recording, the gap length can be defined as the dimension of the gap in the direction of tape travel.

gap, record—1. An interval of space or time associated with a record to indicate or signal the end of the record. 2. The space between records on a tape, usually produced by tape acceleration or deceleration during the writing stage of processing.

garbage—A slang computer term for unwanted and meaningless information carried in memory or storage. Also referred to as hash.

gas discharge displays—Gas discharge displays are devices that use the glow produced by ionized neon gas to form alphanumeric characters. For computer applications, these characters are usually in the form of a 5-by-7 or 7-by-9 dot matrix. There are two kinds of gas discharge or plasma displays—dc and ac. Dc displays are the most widely available. In dc plasma panels, a glass plate with an array of holes is sandwiched between top-wire anodes (above the glass) and cathode strips and bottom-wire anodes (below the glass). The holes from cells for the neon gas become visible when the proper voltages are applied.

gate—1. A circuit having one output and several inputs, the output remaining unenergized until certain input conditions have been met. When used in conjunction with computers, a gate is also called a logic circuit. A gate can also be a signal to trigger the passage of other signals through a circuit. 2. An electrode in a field-effect transistor. 3. A device having one output channel and one or more input channels, such that the output channel state is completely determined by the input channel states, except during switching transients. 4. A combinational logic element having at least one input channel.

gateable clock—Refers to a specific device which has a start-up time equal to ½ a bit time, and whose frequency equals the baud rate of the line being sampled.

gate, AND—A signal circuit with two or more input wires in which the output wire gives a signal if, and only if, all input wires receive coincident signals. Synonymous with AND circuit.

gate array chip — This is a geometric pattern of basic gates contained in one chip. Most gate arrays are also called uncommitted or semicustom logic. With this approach, it is possible to interconnect the gates during manufacture to form a complex function that may be used as a standard production device.

gate, B OR NOT A—A binary (two-input) logic coincidence circuit for completing the logic operation of B OR NOT A (the reverse of A OR NOT B); i.e., the result is false only when A is true and B is false.

gate circuit—An electronic circuit with one or more inputs and one output, with the property that a pulse goes out on the output line if, and only if, some specified combination of pulses occurs on the input lines. Gate circuits provide much of the hardware by means of which logical operations are built into a computer.

gate, coincidence — A specific circuit designed with the capability to produce an output that is dependent upon a specified type of (or has the coincident nature of) input; e.g., an AND gate has an output pulse when there are pulses in time coincidence at all inputs and an OR gate has an output when any one or any combination of input pulses occur in time coincidence. Any gate may contain a number of inhibits in which there is no output under any condition of input, if there is a time coincidence of an inhibit or except signal.

gate, conditional implication—A binary (two-input) logic coincidence circuit for completing the logic operation of A OR NOT B; i.e., the result is false only if A is false and B is true.

gate equivalent circuit — A basic unit-of-measure used to define relative digital circuit complexity. The number of gate equivalent circuits is that number of individual logic gates that would have to be interconnected to perform the same digital circuit function.

gate, NAND—A logical operator having the property that if P is a statement and Q is a statement, then, the NAND of P, Q, and R is true if at least one statement is false, and false, if all statements are true.

gate, negation—A device with capability of reversing a signal, condition, state, or an event into its alternate or opposite condition.

gates (decision elements) — A circuit having two or more inputs and one output. The output depends upon the combination of logic signals at the input.

gate, Sheffer stroke—Same as gate, NAND.

gate, time—A time gate is a transducer that gives output only during chosen time intervals.

gating circuit—Refers to a circuit which operates as a selective switch, allowing conduction only during selected time intervals or when the signal magnitude is within certain specified limits.

gauss—The cgs unit of magnetic induction or flux density. 1 gauss $=$ 1 maxwell/sq. cm.

Gaussian distribution—Widely encountered spread of values about a nominal mean in systems where statistically large numbers of readings are obtained. Characterized by equal probabilities of values with equal positive and negative deviations from the mean. Also called normal distribution.

Gaussian noise — 1. Noise where the particular voltage distribution is specified in terms of probabilities related to a "normal" curve. 2. Unwanted electrical disturbances described by a probability density function that follows a normal law of statistics.

Gaussian response — Response for a transient impulse, e.g., of an amplifier, which, when differentiated, matches the Gaussian distribution (normal) curve.

general-purpose computer — A computer designed to solve a large variety of problems, e.g., a stored-program computer which may be adapted to any of a very large class of applications.

general-purpose interface—A general-purpose interface (GPI) includes all the necessary command, status, and data registers, as well as the handshake and interrupt-control circuitry, that is necessary and required in order to easily link various peripheral devices to a variety of computers.

general register—A register used for operations such as binary addition, subtraction, multiplication, and division. General registers are used primarily to compute and modify addresses in a program. They have also found increasing utilization as replacements for special registers, such as accumulators, particularly in microprogrammable processors.

generated address—A number or symbol that is generated by instructions in a program and is thus used as an address part.

generating routine—A form of compiling routine, capable of handling less fully defined situations.

generator program — A program that permits a computer to write other programs automatically.

generator, pulse — A specifically designed generator which generates pulses for purposes of special timing or gating in a digital computer; i.e., pulses which are used as inputs to gates to aid in pulse-shaping and timing. Same as time-pulse generator.

generic card sets—Generic capability means that users can program PROM families from one manufacturer by simply using one personality card set and different socket adapters to match the pin configurations on the different devices. Programmers from manufacturers that do not offer this benefit require that the user purchase several different card sets. The additional expense is significant, since each card set generally costs between $360 and $450. The immediate cost saving advantages to users in a programmer having generic card sets can be readily seen. Another important benefit is the design flexibility that generic capability offers. It allows a user to use additional PROMs in the same family for just the cost of a socket adapter.

germanium — A brittle light-gray metal with certain chemical properties similar to those of silicon, carbon, and tin that is used in the manufacture of transistors and semiconductor diodes.

GIGO (Garbage In-Garbage Out) — A specially coined term used to describe the data inserted into and taken out of a computer system—that is, if the input data is bad (garbage in) then the output data will also be bad (garbage out).

Gilbert—The cgs unit of magnetomotive force. The magnetomotive force required to produce one maxwell of magnetic flux in a magnetic circuit with one unit of reluctance.

glitch — An unwanted false electronic pulse. 2. Any of a variety of problems that can plague both hardware and software in digital designs.

global—Refers to that part of an assembler program that includes the body of any macro definition called from a source module and the open code portion of the source module. Contrast with local.

global variable — Refers to a variable whose name is accessible by a main program and all its subroutines.

global variable symbol—Refers to assembler programming, in which a variable symbol is used to communicate values between macro definitions and between a macro definition and open code. Contrast with local variable symbol.

gold contacts—Type of contact used in low-energy or dry-circuit switching applications because they resist the formation of surface films. Gold does have some drawbacks, however. Over and above the obvious problem of price, it is very soft and, therefore, tends to stick or cold weld. It's also not the best solution for switching levels above 0.5 A. Combining **palladium** with it, however, minimizes the cold-welding problem while maintaining favorable dry-circuit switching characteristics.

gold doping — A process sometimes used in the manufacture of integrated circuits in which gold is diffused into the semiconductor material, resulting in higher operating speeds.

gold substitute—To reduce gold consumption in the manufacturing of integrated circuits, Bell Labs and Western Electric have developed a new manufacturing process in which some of the gold is replaced by less costly metals such as copper. The new process, called TPCNA (because it involves the metals titanium, palladium, copper, nickel, and gold), uses only one-quarter as much gold as the process it replaces.

grandfather cycle—The period during which magnetic tape records are retained before reusing so that records can be reconstructed in the event of loss of information stored on a magnetic tape.

graphical-data operations — Manipulations that a system can perform on points, lines, symbols, angles, and other graphical representations. These operations include delete, insert, replace, move, rotate, expand, contact, and extrapolate.

graphic color combinations — Color combinations are important, as are backgrounds. If greater attention is needed, a higher contrast is superior. Red-on-a-black-background is harder to notice than on a white background; yellow on a white background is an even worse contrast. If yellow appears on a green background, the "vibration" (optical illusion) distracts and produces eye fatigue.

graphic display — A communications terminal (linked to a computer) that displays data in shapes and drawings on a television-like screen, usually a crt (cathode-ray tube).

graphic display systems—Two general types of graphic display systems exist —storage tubes and directed-beam refresh. Refresh display consists of stroke writing and raster scanning. Stroke writing writes on the crt like an artist using a pen while raster scanning, as is well known, does it by scanning the entire crt, with the beam brightening when desired. Raster scanning uses more memory, since each coordinate point must reference memory. This disadvantage is offset, however, by an ability to handle color graphics and selective image-erasing capability.

graphic panel—Master control panel in automation and remote control systems, which shows the relation and functioning of the different parts of the control equipment by means of colored block diagrams.

graphics applications — The areas of graphics, image processing, and pattern recognition are all particularly appropriate for interactive man-machine applications. Graphics is generally considered to be the synthesis, manipulation, and analysis of essen-

*Graphics applications
(Courtesy Ramtek Corp.).*

tially planar line abstractions. This applies particularly to drawings of block diagrams, alphamerics, outlines, maps, isometrics, perspectives, lines, topology of closed spaces, recognition of geometric shapes, description of graphical objects, concatenation, segmentation of parts, and so on.

graphics, color beam — Color is produced by the beam penetration method through variations in the velocity of the electrons. The phosphor on the face of the screen is applied in several layers of different materials. The color is determined by the distance the electron beam can penetrate into the phosphor. The number of colors is limited; variations in intensity and shading are not feasible.

graphics crt display—There are three basic forms of graphics crt displays: raster scan, directed-beam refresh, and direct-view storage tubes. The raster scan version is used in commercial television. It operates by varying the intensity of a beam that periodically scans left to right along a fixed number of scan lines from the top to the bottom of the screen. In directed-beam displays, the beam moves from point to point on the screen to produce the desired image, rather than scanning periodically. The image is maintained by being completely redrawn at the periodic refresh rate. Direct-view storage devices use the same method as directed-beam displays to draw an image. Since the image is stored in the phosphor of the screen, periodic refresh is not necessary. This type features a "write through" capability, which writes a

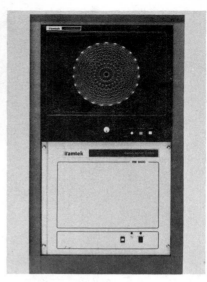

*Graphics crt display
(Courtesy Ramtek Corp.).*

beam-refreshed image of lesser intensity over the permanent image on the screen. Full color is only available on the raster and scan display devices.

graphics light pen—The light pen enables the user to interactively pick, move, and draw objects directly on the crt. This graphics tool features highly accurate picking and fast tracking, accomplished with a predictive firmware algorithm that enables the cursor to move at the same speed that the user moves the pen. The light pen is often human-engineered so that it can be switched from right to left to accommodate both left- and right-handed operators.

graphics microprocessor — On some systems, the master control of system initialization, interface handling, local data editing, and refresh control, as well as indirect addressing and multiple subroutine methods are provided by the graphics microprocessor. Arithmetic, I/O and logic functions, display refresh, and control programs are in RAM. Typically, the basic memory has 32K bytes of memory. Control of self-test diagnostics, communications between the terminal and host computer, data entry devices, and display instruction file are often in PROM. Generally, the display is managed by a specialized microprocessor that retrieves instructions from the display file located in RAM, interprets the display instructions, and sends display and control information to the appropriate character and vector generators to produce the graphic image. Hardware function generators save memory, space, and increase throughput speed. Standard facilities can include a vector position generator and a character position generator.

graphics plotting—Most graphics systems require crt terminals plus either plotters or printers or both. Interactive applications, which require many changes, must have crt's because they enable the easy modification of designs and drawings. Plotters and printers, on the other hand, can most economically accommodate static readouts of drawings stored in data banks, or plot the results of processes. In output-only applications, a plotter or printer may be all that is necessary. Plotters operate as a team with crt's when a design or simulation problem is developed on the crt and the result is to be recorded.

graphics, raster scan — Raster scan is the display method used in home tv sets. Colors are bright and may as-`sume an almost infinite variety of shades and hues. The shadow-mask color technology used in raster scan displays was developed for home color tv at great expense over a number of years. Crt color graphics thus reap the benefit of this research. Most computer crt graphics use tubes of higher quality than those used in home tv, but they employ similar techniques.

graphics, small computer — For managers and business owners who previously had to digest voluminous reports, new low-cost graph and chart presentations summarize corporate conditions more clearly, reveal trends, and generally permit managers to use information more quickly, effectively, and accurately. Today's manager can sit at a terminal and design, modify, and produce graphics quickly and easily by entering new data or by requesting rearrangements.

graphics software—Often software from the turnkey vendors includes both systems and application capabilities. Standard microcomputer operating systems are sometimes rewritten by the vendors to more efficiently support graphics, and, thus, a variety of graphic utilities for data creation, editing, output, and data base management are always included. Most of the manufacturers provide sophisticated data base management systems

	1970	1971	1972	1973	1974	1975
COMMODITIES	113.5	117.4	120.9	129.9	145.5	158.4
SERVICES	121.6	128.4	133.3	139.1	152.0	166.6
ALL ITEMS	116.3	121.3	125.3	133.1	127.7	161.2
EXCHANGE RATE	90.0	95.0	89.1	83.3	87.0	80.1

STATISTICAL DATA (ABOVE) IS EASILY TRANSFORMED INTO A BAR CHART (BELOW) BY TELL-A GRAF, A COMPUTER SOFTWARE PROGRAM DEVELOPED BY INTEGRATED SOFTWARE SYSTEMS CORP., SAN DIEGO, CA.

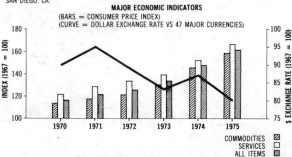

Graphics, small computer (Courtesy Integrated Software Systems Corp.).

for handling graphic and nongraphic attribute data, write the graphic display drivers in host assembler code, and provide a high-level capacity (usually FORTRAN, but sometimes in a vendor-generated graphic problem-oriented language) for the user to develop applications programs and interface them with the vendor's data base management capabilities.

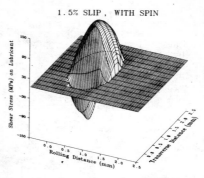

1.5% SLIP, WITH SPIN

Graphics, three-dimensional (Courtesy Integrated Software Systems Corp.).

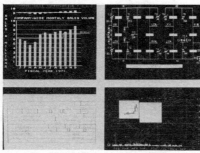

Graphics software packages (Courtesy Data Disc., Inc.).

graphics software packages — Many software packages offer plotting capability for various printer/plotters. Often written in FORTRAN, the packages are designed to run under micro- and minicomputer operating systems to provide graphic hardcopy. Some packages consist of FORTRAN and assembly language source code, and a batch job stream to compile and assemble the source and build libraries. They include callable subroutines that are compatible with basic pen plotter routines and commercial software packages. Enhancements include programmed grid overlay, area shading, graphs, bar graphs, and solid- or dashed-curved line generation.

graphics, three-dimensional — Many display systems are capable of using sophisticated graphics software in order to produce three-dimensional effects. These effects and plots are used in designing new manufacturing processes.

graphic terminals, crt—Graphic terminals are primarily of two types, crt displays and electromechanical plotters. Crt terminals for graphic applications require the ability to draw lines and move spots on the surface of the crt, as well as printing alpha-

numeric characters. Since most graphic applications require a two-way interaction between the user and the computer, some form of graphic input, such as a light pen, a RAND tablet, or a cursor is required. Most graphic applications also require an alphanumeric keyboard for manual input.

gray code—1. A positional binary number notation in which any two numbers whose difference is one are represented by expressions that are the same except in one place or column and differ by only one unit in that column or place. 2. A binary code in which sequential numbers are represented by expressions which are the same except in one place and in that place differ by one unit.

gray cyclic code—A specific positional code for numbers which have the

Graphic terminals, crt (Courtesy Intercolor Systems Corp.).

property that when some or all of them of a given length are arranged in sequence, the signal distance between consecutive numbers is one. The Gray code is a cyclic binary unit-distance code.

gray levels, image—Typical black and white photographs are called continuous-tone images because the shades of gray blend continuously both in intensity (level) and spatiality (area). However, the quantized picture is not continuous, but is composed of a number of discrete elements with each having a discrete gray level assigned to it. System resolution may therefore be defined as the ability to reproduce images with a visual quality that is comparable to the continuous-tone originals. This requires a sufficient number of picture elements to give the appearance of spatial continuity, and a sufficient number of gray levels to give the appearance of continuous depth and contrast.

grid—1. Often refers to a thin wire mesh between cathode and plate in a triode tube. 2. In optical character recognition, two mutually orthogonal sets of parallel lines used for specifying or measuring character images.

grid-spaced contacts—Refers to various types of electrical contacts, usually surfaces, spring types, or pins, arranged in parallel or equally spaced rows and columns, on any type connector or edges of printed-circuit boards.

grouped records—Refers to the result of the combining of two or more records into one block of information on tape to decrease the wasted time due to tape acceleration and deceleration and to conserve tape space. This is also called blocking of records.

group mark—A mark that identifies the beginning or end of a set of data, which could include words, blocks, or other items.

guard bit—1. Refers to a special bit contained in each word or specific groups of words of memory designed to indicate to computer hardware units or software programs whether or not the content of that memory location may or may not be altered by a program. 2. A bit designed to indicate whether a main or disk memory word or group of words is to be filed or protected.

guard digit—Refers to a specific low-order hexadecimal zero appended to each operand fraction in a single-word floating-point arithmetic addition or subtraction operation.

guarding — The technique of isolation that enables each component in a circuit to be tested independently during an in-circuit testing procedure.

gunn effect—The production of high-field intensity domains in a semiconductor diode (usually by dipole charges formed across a depletion layer, although other processes, such as charge accumulation, can produce similar effects). These domains can form the basis of negative-resistance microwave semiconductor oscillators.

H

half-add — A computer instruction that performs bit-by-bit half additions (i.e., logical Exclusive-OR without carry) on its operands. *See* half-adder.

half-adder—Refers to a circuit with two input and two output channels for binary signals (0, 1).

half-shift register — Another name for certain types of flip-flops when used in a shift register. It takes two of these to make one stage in a shift register.

halfword—Refers to a contiguous sequence of bits or characters which comprises half a computer word and is capable of being addressed as a unit.

Hall constant—The constant of proportionality R in the relationship:

$$EH = R \times J \times H$$

where,

EH is the transverse electric field (Hall field),
J is the current density,
H is the magnetic field strength.

(The sign of the majority carrier can be inferred from the sign of the Hall constant.)

Hall effect—The development of a voltage between the edges of a current-carrying metal strip when it is placed in a magnetic field perpendicular to the faces of the strip.

Hall-effect generator—A magnetic sensor using the Hall effect to give an output voltage proportional to magnetic field strength.

Hall-effect keyswitches—These devices move a magnet on a plunger assembly to or from an integrated-circuit Hall transducer chip, which produces isolated outputs that reduce encoding-logic complexity. Neither an oscillator nor an amplifier is required, but the chip does draw dc current in both operating and standby modes. Hall-effect keyswitches are extremely reliable, and are good for 100-million operations or better.

Hall-effect sensors—Hall-effect sensors make and break electrical circuits. They are thought of as being magnetically operated super-switches, because they allow users to do things that cannot be done with electromechanical switches. Sensor life is measured in billions of operations.

Hall-effect switch—Hall-effect switches can furnish two definite states, as well as magnetic isolation and sensing. For a Hall-effect switch, the Hall voltage is fed into a Schmitt-trigger circuit. The voltage level at which the output of the circuit changes state defines the basic function of the switch (bipolar or unipolar). The hysteresis built into the trigger circuit provides a stable, bounce-free operation between the device's on and off states. An active low output is provided through an open-collector transistor that can sink up to 20 mA. The open-collector output adds versatility to the device by allowing direct interface to many types of circuits. Hall-effect switches have little susceptibility to environmental (pressure and temperature) change, operate with small magnetic fields, offer solid-state reliability, and are more compact, more sensitive and less expensive than reed-relay switches.

Hall generator—A thin wafer of semiconductor material used for measuring ac power and magnetic field strength. Its output voltage is proportional to the current passing through it times the magnetic field perpendicular to it.

Hall mobility—The mobility (mean drift velocity in unit field) of current carriers in a semiconductor as calculated from the product of the Hall coefficient and the conductivity.

Hall sensor—A device made of compounds such as indium arsenide, indium antimonide, or silicon that produces a useful Hall potential. Its output is proportional to magnetic induction through the semiconductor. Sensors can be grouped into two broad categories—those used with an external magnet, and those with an integral magnet.

halt—A condition which occurs when the sequence of operations in a program stops. This can be done to a HALT instruction being met or due to some unexpected halt or interrupt. The program can normally continue after a halt unless it is a drop-dead halt.

HALT condition—This causes the processor to leave the RUN mode. The program counter (PC) points to the next instruction to be executed. In some systems, the processor goes into the HALT mode. The contents of the PC are displayed on the console terminal and the console mode of operation is enabled.

halt, drop-dead—Refers to a machine halt from which there is no recovery. Such a halt may be deliberately programmed. A drop-dead halt may occur through a logical error in programming. Examples in which a drop-dead halt could occur are a division by zero and a transfer to a nonexistent instruction word.

halted processing state — The halted processing state is an indication of catastrophic hardware failure. For example, if during the exception processing of a bus error another bus error occurs, the processor assumes that the system is unusable and halts. Only an external reset can restart a halted processor. Note that a processor in the *stopped* state is not in the halted state, nor vice versa.

halt indicator—The halt indicator is illuminated whenever the processor is in the HALT mode.

HALT mode — On most systems, only highly specific commands are executed by the processor when the system is in the HALT mode. When in this mode, the processor responds to commands and information that is entered via the console terminal, and all processor response is controlled via the processor's microcode.

HALT mode (bus)—On some systems, the HALT bus signal can be asserted low to place the processor in the HALT mode. While in the HALT mode, the RUN indicator is extinguished (on some systems), the interrupts external to the processor module are ignored, and the processor executes the special console microcode. Although the user can assert this line by a separate switch or a custom module, on some systems, it is most often asserted by the HALT/ENABLE switch or by some other user designated interface module signal.

halt, nonprogrammed—Refers to an inadvertent machine stoppage, not due to the results of a programmed instruction, such as an automatic interrupt, manual intervention, machine malfunction, power failure, or other cause.

halt, programmed — A machine stoppage or interruption of machine operations caused deliberately by a program instruction. The halt is automatic with this instruction in the program.

Hamming code—1. An error-correcting code system that was named after the inventor, R. W. Hamming of Bell Telephone Laboratories. A Hamming code contains four information bits and three check bits. 2. A data code which is capable of being corrected automatically.

hand-held computer—Today's technology and advanced design techniques bring science fiction to life with a computer that can be carried in your pocket. As powerful as yesterday's room-sized computers, they provide a vast range of information and computing services in a fully portable format. While the hand-held computer can be interfaced to hookup to a home tv set, a cassette tape recorder, or a miniprinter, their resident language and battery operation permit these small computers to be used alone as a stopwatch, a calculator, a memo recorder, or an electronic reference library. They also permit translating of foreign words and phrases and the playing of hand-held games.

handprint data-entry terminal — Refers to a peripheral device which is a local or remote terminal that can capture handwritten data at the time of writing. It recognizes ordinary handprinting, and translates alpha, numeric, and special characters directly into machine readable form. The system comprises a writing station with an integral 40-character line display. Anyone can write, using an ordinary ballpoint pen or pencil, onto documents designed to suit their applications. Data are captured as they are written. Character recognition takes place within the system and all that is transmitted to the microcomputer is the ASCII character plus its position on the document.

handshake I/O control — Provision for handshake I/O control allows convenient interfacing with peripherals of varying response time. Control flags and jump condition inputs are useful to reduce hardware decoding and software overhead. If multiple devices are to be connected over the same I/O lines, three-state or open-collector TTL logic is often required to drive the bus. The microprocessor I/O circuitry should directly interface with these signals for most systems.

handshaking — 1. A descriptive term often used interchangeably with buffering or interfacing, implying a direct connection or matching of specific units or programs. Some computer terminal programs are called "handshaking" if they greet and assist the new terminal operator to interface with or use the procedures or programs of the system. Other handshaking terms relate to direct package-to-package connections as regards to circuits, programs, or procedures. 2. Exchange of predeter-

Hand-held computer (Courtesy Quasar Co.).

mined signals when a connection is established between two data set devices.

handshaking, hardware—Refers to interaction between the central processor and the peripheral devices. The devices report their status during data transfers so that the processor knows when an operation is completed and more data can be transferred.

hang-up—1. A condition in which the central processor of a computer is attempting to perform an illegal or forbidden operation or in which it is continually repeating the same routine. 2. An unplanned computer stop or delay in problem solution, e.g., caused by the inability to escape from a loop. 3. A nonprogrammed stop in a routine. It is usually an unforeseen or unwanted halt in a machine pass. It is most often caused by improper coding of a machine instruction or by the attempted use of a nonexistent or improper operation code.

hang-up prevention—Refers to computer logic that must be designed or modified so that no sequence of valid or invalid instructions can cause the computer to come to a halt or go into a nonterminating uninterruptible state. Examples of this latter case are infinitely nested executions or nonterminating indirect addressing.

hard copy — 1. Typewritten or printed characters on paper, produced by a computer at the same time that the information is copied or converted into machine language that is not easily read by a human. 2. A printed copy of machine output that is in a visually readable form, e.g., printed reports, listings, documents, summaries, etc.

hard copy, camera — An economical way to make permanent records of oscilloscope traces, closed-circuit television screens, the alphanumeric and graphic data from computer output terminals, and the information on crt screens (both repetitive and transient). One type system uses a Polaroid CU-5 hard-copy camera for this purpose.

hard-copy interface — This generally concerns a wide variety of hard-copy devices that can be accommodated via either an optional RS-232C serial interface or a printer-compatible parallel interface. Commands to print data can be initiated either locally from the terminal keyboard or remotely from a computer.

hard-copy output—The output option on some systems allows the system to be connected to a printer or paper-tape punch to produce hexadecimal listings or paper tapes of the contents of the memory modules. This option provides easy and automatic update of the input and prepares permanent records of user-modified programs. The output paper tape is properly formatted for input back into the system.

hard-disk controller — Most units use a hard-disk controller that receives commands from the host processor and then performs disk transfers independent of the processor. Data transfers are to and from a dual-port memory buffer. The dual-port architecture and stand-alone disk controller mean that virtually no processor overhead is required for disk transfers and that all segments of disk transfers are fully interruptible. Thus, disk operation does not degrade terminal interrupt response time in multiuser systems.

hardware — Refers to the metallic or "hard" components of a microcomputer system in contrast to the "soft" or programming components. The components of circuits may be active, passive, or both.

hardware assembler (microprocessor) —1. Often consists of PROMs that plug into simulation boards, enabling the prototype to assemble its own programs. 2. A program that translates a symbolic assembly language into bit patterns suitable for a microcomputer control storage programming.

hardware interrupt facility—A hardware interrupt facility permits input-output operations to be scheduled under interrupt control. The interrupt facility may be selectively enabled or disabled under program control. When the interrupt facility is enabled, a device generates a processor interrupt each time it is ready to receive or transmit data. Use of the interrupt facility enables input-output operations to be performed simultaneously with computing.

hardware/software—The following list gives the hardware equivalents to software programming tools (Courtesy Pro-Log Corporation).

Program	Hardware
Flowchart	Block diagram
Mnemonic coding	Schematic symbols
Hexadecimal coding	Wire list or assembly-print coding
Program assembly form	Schematic and assembly print
Instruction	Component
Subroutine	Module or subsystem
PROM	Breadboard or prototype
PROM programmer	Wirewrap gun or soldering iron
Clip-on tester	Digital voltmeter

hard-wired — A fixed wired program or control system that is built in by the manufacturer and is not subject to change by programming.

hard-wire logic—Refers to logic designs for control or problem solutions that require interconnection of numerous integrated circuits that are formed or wired for specific purposes and are relatively unalterable. A hard-wired diode matrix is hard-wired logic whereas a RAM, ROM, or CPU can be reprogrammed with little difficulty to change the purpose of operation. Hard-wired interconnections are usually completed by soldering and are, thus, hard-wired in contrast to software solutions that are achieved by programmed microcomputer components.

hartley—1. Computer unit of information, equal to 3.32 bits, and conveyed by one decadal code element. 2. A unit of information content, equal to one decadal decision, or the designation of one of ten possible and equally likely values or states.

Hartley principle — General statement that the amount of information which can be transmitted through a channel is the product of frequency bandwidth and time during which it is open, whether time division is used or not.

hash, electronic—Electrical interfering noise arising from vibrators or commutators.

hash total — A sum formed for error-checking purposes by adding fields that are not normally related by unit of measure; i.e., a total of invoice serial numbers.

header—The initial portion of a message containing any information, control codes, and so on that are not part of the text (e.g., routing, destination addressee, and time of origination).

header label — Refers to a designed block of data at the start of a magnetic tape file which contains descriptive information to identify the file; e.g., file name, reel number, file generation number, retention period, and the data when the data was written to tape.

head gap — 1. The space between the reading or recording head and the recording medium, such as tape, drum, or disk. 2. The space or gap intentionally inserted into the magnetic circuit of the head in order to force or direct the recording flux into the recording medium.

heading — A sequence of characters, usually placed at the beginning of a message, that represents message routing and destination information and that is machine readable.

head-to-tape contact — The degree to which the surface of the magnetic coating approaches the surface of the record or relay heads during normal operation of a recorder. Good head-to-tape contact minimizes separation loss and is essential in obtaining high resolution.

hermaphroditic connector — Refers to those connectors whose mating parts are identical at their mating face, i.e., those which have no female or male members but still can maintain correct polarity, sealing, and mechanical and electrical couplings.

hertz—1. A unit of frequency equal to one cycle per second. 2. A hertzian wave is the wave used in radio communication; it is produced by an alternating current at the sending station and received by the antenna of the receiving set. 3. A generalized expression referring to all radio waves or oscillations of electricity in a conductor producing electromagnetic radiation. Named after Heinrich Hertz (1857-1894), a German physicist.

Hertzian waves — Electromagnetic waves from 10^4 to 10^{44} Hz which have been found useful for communicating information through space.

heuristic — Pertaining to exploratory methods of problem solving in which solutions are discovered by evaluation of the progress made toward the final result. Contrast with algorithm.

heuristic routine—A routine by which the computer attacks a problem not by a direct algorithmic procedure, but by a trial and error approach frequently involving the act of learning.

hexadecimal—Refers to whole numbers in positional notation with 16 as the base. Hexadecimal coding uses numerals 0 through 16, with the first ten digits represented by 0 through 9, and the last six digits represented by A,B,C,D,E, and F.

hexadecimal 8-bit words — The 8-bit word can represent numbers from 0 to FF_{16} (i.e., from 0 to 255_{10}).

hexadecimal notation, 4-bit system — The basic 4-bit structure of the CPU makes it convenient to use hexadecimal notation in order to express, with a single character, one of sixteen possible combinations. The single hexadecimal character notation 0–9 and A–F is used to refer to the: 16 basic instructions, 16 I/O and RAM instructions, accumulator instructions, 16 index registers, 16 pages of program memory capacity, 16 RAM register chip capacity, 16 characters in a RAM register, 16 output ports, and 16 input ports. A double hexadecimal character notation is applied to the 8-bit instruction word address for program memory where the decimal addresses are 00 through FF in hexadecimal coding.

hexadecimal numbering system — The numbering system that has a base of 16 (as contrasted with the decimal system that has a base of 10).

hierarchical file system—The utilization of a three-level hierarchical file system using symbolic file, record, and item names eliminates the requirement for a separate and complicated data base definition language. Simple English-type commands like ''update,'' ''write,'' ''get,'' ''put,'' ''add,'' ''delete,'' ''copy,'' ''lock,'' and ''unlock,'' are used to set up and access the system (available on some intelligent disk systems).

hierarchy, memory—Refers to a set of memories with differing sizes and speeds and usually having different cost-performance ratios (i.e., expensive/fast to less expensive/slower). Faster access sections contain a main computer memory hierarchy, which might consist of a very high-speed small semiconductor memory, a medium-speed cache memory, and a large slow-speed bubble memory.

high-level compiler — High-level languages allow the programmer to express operations in a less direct form that is closer to the normal human language representation of the procedures that the computer is to perform. Arithmetic operations are expressed in the form of equations, results are tested through the use of relational expressions, etc. Programs written in high-level languages must also be translated into object code by programs called compilers. Once the program has been assembled or compiled, it must be loaded into the microcomputer memory so that it can be tested. This function is performed by still another program called a loader.

high-level language — 1. Such languages are usually problem-oriented or procedure-oriented programming languages as distinguished from machine-oriented and/or mnemonic languages. Machine languages are the final target languages, after compiling, while high-level languages are source languages for many programmers and users. Examples of high-level languages are: COBOL, BASIC, C. FORTRAN, Pascal, etc. 2. A language in which each instruction or statement corresponds to several machine code instructions. High-level languages allow users to write in a notation with which they are familiar rather than in a language oriented to the machine code of a computer. Contrasted with low-level language.

high, logical — Digital logic elements must operate with two distinct states. The two states are variously called true and false, high and low, on and off, or 1 and 0. In computers, they are represented by two different voltage levels. The level which is more positive (or less negative) than the other is called the high level; the other is the low level. If the true (1) level is the most positive voltage, such logic is referred to as positive true or positive logic.

high-order digit—A digit that occupies a more significant or highly weighted position in a numerical or positional notation system.

high-mode testing, bias—The destructive read off or use caused by overloading or underloading the computer components, causing failure of substandard units to thereby minimize nonschedule down time.

high order—Pertaining to the weight or significance assigned to the digits of a number, e.g., in the number 123456, the highest order digit is one, the lowest order digit is six. One may refer to the three high order bits of a binary word, as another example.

high-pass (low-pass) filters — Filters which freely pass signals of all frequencies above (or below) a reference value, known as the cut-off frequency.

high-speed bus — A set of wires or "path" which is used to transfer numbers (electrical pulses) that represent data and instructions to various registers and counters. However, on-off and similar transfer lines or control signals are not considered as digital transfer buses.

high-speed printer — A printer which operates at a speed more compatible with the speed of computation and data processing so that it may operate on-line. At the present time, a printer operating at a speed of 300 lines per minute, 100 characters per line is considered a high-speed device.

HMOS—This refers to a newly developed n-channel, depletion load, silicon-gate technology. Use of the HMOS process gives microprocessor devices 4-micrometer scaled-down metal-oxide-semiconductor transistors and on-chip biasing that makes the microprocessor operate faster and more reliably. With this high-performance MOS technique, typical on-chip gate propagation delays of 2 nanoseconds are as short as those obtained from costly Schottky transistor-transistor logic. This results in extremely fast internal clocking rates. The HMOS process also produces denser circuitry. The entire 16-bit data and microprogrammed control structure of the typical microprocessor uses 29,000 transistors integrated onto a die about 225 mils square. Many less complex peripheral chips, that use large-scale integration, are larger. The smallness of its die means that the high-performance device will decline in cost as production experience with it grows.

HMOS devices—As a driving force behind high-performance digital technology, Intel Corporation (Santa Clara, CA) has developed several advanced processes in NMOS technology. One of these processes, called HMOS, relies heavily on device scaling, ion implantation, fine-line lithography, and very thin oxide depositions. The combining of all of these factors has made possible such devices as a 4096-bit static RAM with an access time of less than 50 nanoseconds, and microprocessors capable of operating at clock frequencies of 11 MHz. In the early 1980s, HMOS was used to upgrade the performance of Intel Corporation's previously introduced microprocessors and microcomputers by redoing the masks for the popular devices using 3-μm design rules. In addition, the clock frequency was raised to 11 MHz from the previously available high of 6 MHz.

HMOS, low voltage—This is an evolving process which provides the best speed/density relationship of all the n-channel processes. Device scaling is common with 2- to 3-micron channel lengths most frequent. Both custom and standard MOS/LSI products are now taking advantage of the benefits available from this state-of-the-art process.

HMOS processing advances—Processing advances like HMOS and HMOS II have made possible greater density, speed, power dissipation, and low-cost advances in MOS memories. HMOS, which was introduced about 1978, allowed the selective scaling down of electrical and physical parameters for a higher-performance, smaller-size chip. This was taken a step further with HMOS II, which halved access times in 1K-bit and 4K-bit dynamic MOS RAMs.

Many of these processing advances have been achieved with direct wafer-stepping photolithographic equipment, replacing the older contact printing, for higher-density 64K-bit dynamic MOS RAMs. Positive instead of negative photoresists, dry instead of wet chemical etching, and the fabrication of masks with electron beams have made it easier to meet the tighter line-dimension requirements needed for higher-density 64K-bit dynamic MOS RAMs.

HMOS II — HMOS II couples the older

HMOS techniques with advanced scaling techniques, which permits further reductions in cell size. Even though HMOS II is usually considered as a high-density technology, its inventor, Intel Corporation, puts it to work in a GPIB (general-purpose interface bus) transceiver to provide the high drive currents required by the IEEE-488 bus standard. A 5-volt-only part, the device features nine on-board drivers and receivers that meet bus line termination and hysteresis specifications, plus power-up and power-down protection to keep power transitions off the bus. The device's high flexibility derives partly from four programable modes, which reconfigure its internal circuitry to permit its functioning in both talker/listener and talker/listener/controller environments.

hobbyist computer—A hobby computer is principally a group of circuit boards that contains a CPU, memory, interfaces, and, possibly, terminals with graphics and/or voice I/O. These are all stuffed with other electronic components, and are sometimes set in "card edges" that are encased in a sheet metal or plastic box.

hold button (analog)—The hold button causes the solution to be temporarily suspended, permitting the user to study the various quantities. The integrating capacitors are disconnected during holds so that they will neither charge nor discharge.

hold instruction—A computer instruction which causes data called from storage to be also retained in storage after it is called out and transferred to its new location.

hold time—1. The interval during which a signal is retained at a specified input terminal after an active transition occurs at another specified input terminal. 2. Hold time is the actual time between two events and may be insufficient to accomplish the intended result. A minimum value is specified that is the shortest interval for which correct operation of the logic element is guaranteed. 3. The hold time may have a negative value; in which case, the minimum limit defines the longest interval (between the release of data and the active transition) for which correct operation of the logic element is guaranteed.

hole—1. As related to punched cards, the removal of paper to affect a contact and detecting a binary digit. 2. As related to transistor theory, a vacancy in a crystal lattice caused by

Hobbyist computer (Courtesy Rockwell International).

the absence of an electron. In an ordered structure of covalent bonds, thermal agitation will break the bond, causing the electron to move away from its atom leaving the hole behind. The electron may fill another hole left by another electron in the same or in an adjacent atom. The hole is considered to have a positive charge equal to that of an electron. The movement of holes and electrons constitutes current flow, and upon the application of an electric field, the flow becomes ordered rather than random, as it is under thermal agitation. 3. A freely moving positive charge in a doped semiconductor crystal.

hole current — Hole current refers to conduction in a semiconductor where electrons move into holes, creating new holes. The holes appear to move toward the negative terminal, giving the equivalent of positive charges flowing to the terminal.

hole density—The density of the holes in a semiconductor in a band otherwise full.

hole injection—Holes can be emitted in an n-type semiconductor by applying a metallic point to its surface.

hole injector — A metallic point device for injecting holes into an n-type semiconductor.

hole mobility—The ability of a hole to travel easily through a semiconductor.

hole trap—An impurity in a semiconductor which can release electrons in the conduction or valence bands and so trap a hole.

Hollerith code — The Hollerith code is used almost exclusively for punched-card applications. It is a 12-level, alphanumeric punched-card code invented by Dr. Herman Hollerith in 1889, in which the top three positions in a column are called "zone" punches (12, 11, and 0, from the top downward), and are combined with the remaining punch rows (1 through 9) to represent alphabetic, numeric, and special characters. For example, A is a combination of a Y (12) and a 1 punch; an L is a combination of an X (11) and a 3 punch, etc.

holofiche memory—An individual holofiche memory contains millions of bits of data. It can be used for such personalized data storage as medical history, credit record, and security

clearance. When tied to a crt display, the system visually retrieves instantly. It can operate as a ROM/floppy-disk replacement, as on-line mass storage, or as archival data storage.

hologram—Refers to a major type of optical "imaging" that is accomplished without the use of lenses. It is now a practical reality with the advent of the laser. The laser beam is split into two portions, one part directly illuminating a photographic film (or plate) while the other illuminates the scene. The two portions produce an optical interference pattern on the film which, when illuminated by a laser beam, will produce two images of the original scene. One of these is virtual but the other is real and may be viewed without a lens.

holographic-based system—A system that utilizes laser and holographic technology in a microform setting.

holographic recorder—A system designed to acquire and record electronic digital data in high-density holographic form on photographic film. A reader retrieves the holographic data and reconverts it to the original electronic form according to the presentation that accompanies the programmed instructions.

home safety/security system—By monitoring smoke and motion detectors, a microcomputer can alert homeowners to fires or to intruders by sounding alarms or by turning on lights. In the future, the system will be able to automatically dial the police or fire departments and will deliver a prerecorded message. The security func-

Home safety/security system (Courtesy GBC Closed Circuit TV Corp.).

tion can also control the doors of the home. Traditional door locks and keys will be replaced by an electronic keypad. When the proper access code is entered on the keypad, the door opens automatically. A voice capability can also be added to the system. The microcomputer will greet members of the family by name as they enter the home (provided they entered the proper access code on the keypad). It can also announce the correct time on the hour, if desired, and can be programmed to provide verbal warnings in the event of fire or intrusion.

homostasis—The dynamic condition of a system wherein the input and output are balanced precisely, thus presenting an appearance of no change; hence, a steady state.

host computer—1. The primary or controlling computer in a multiple computer operation. 2. A computer used to prepare programs for use on another computer or on another data-processing system; for example, a computer used to compile, link edit, or test programs to be used on another system.

housekeeping operations—1. Pertaining to a computer routine, those operations that contribute directly to the proper operation of the computer but not to the solution of the problem, such as setting up constants and variables for use in the program. 2. A general term for the operation that must usually be performed for a machine run before actual processing begins. Examples of housekeeping operations are: establishing controlling marks, setting up auxiliary storage units, reading in the first record for processing, initializing, set-up verification operations, and file identification.

housekeeping routine — The initial instructions in a program that are executed only one time, i.e., clear storage.

hunting — Refers to a continuous attempt on the part of an automatically controlled system to seek a desired equilibrium condition. The system usually contains a standard, a method of determining deviation from this standard, and a method of influencing the system, such as the difference between the standard and the state.

hybrid circuit—1. An electronic circuit utilizing two or more types of components which perform similar functions (e.g., tubes and transistors), but which have different modes of operation. 2. Circuits fabricated by interconnecting smaller circuits or different technologies mounted on a single substrate.

hybrid computer — Various specially designed computers with both digital and analog characteristics, combining the advantages of analog and digital computers when working as a system. Hybrid computers are being used extensively in simulation process-control systems where it is necessary to have a close representation with the physical world. The hybrid system provides the good precision that can be attained with analog computers and the greater control that is possible with digital computers, plus the ability to accept input data in either form.

hybrid integrated circuit—1. Refers to an arrangement consisting of one or more integrated circuits combined with one or more discrete component parts. Also refers to a combination of more than one type of integrated circuit into one integrated component. 2. A class of integrated circuits wherein the substrate is a passive material such as ceramic and the active chips are attached to its surface.

hybrid interface—Relates to a channel for connecting a digital computer to an analog computer.

hybrid microcircuit—A circuit produced by the combination of several different components in a single package. Hybrids form a middle ground between boards or modules using packaged components and monolithic ICs which may not offer sufficient performance. Hybrids are commonly formed from a combination of chip or packaged active devices and thin- or thick-film passive devices.

hybrid system checkout—These programs implement checkout of system hardware, analog wiring, and the digital program. Normal maintenance checks are performed in conjunction with a standard wired analog patch board. Digital utility programs and analog static check programs are also provided.

hybrid systems—1. Refers to the result of a number of efforts by manufacturers and designers to utilize the best properties of both digital and analog computers by building hybrid systems. In the hybrid system, a digital computer is used for control purposes and provides the program, while analog components are used to obtain the continuous solutions. 2. A combination of an on-site minicomputer for immediate response processing and an off-site large-scale computer for processing of large blocks of data.

hysteresis—1. A term referring to the amount the magnetization of a ferrous substance lags the magnetizing force because of molecular friction. Also, the difference between the response of a unit or system to an increasing and a decreasing signal.

hysteresis distortion—The distortion of waveforms in circuits which contain magnetic components. It is due to the hysteresis of the magnetic cores.

hysteresis, switching — The principle associated with sensors, which is that the operate point is not at the same level as the release point. In solid-state sensors, it is accomplished with negative-resistance devices. In mechanical switches, it results from the storing of potential energy before the transition occurs.

I

IC—The abbreviation for both integrated circuit and instruction counter.

IC doping—By adding a minute amount of phosphorus or boron to pure silicon, an n-type or p-type semiconductor material can be produced. Controlled amounts of dopant impurities are introduced into preselected parts of the silicon surface through diffusion windows in the oxide layer. This process is called *doping* and it enables a semiconductor to conduct current. Solid-state diffusion of these dopants into silicon at high temperatures results in the formulation of a pn junction within the single crystal silicon. Since the diffusion of impurities proceeds sideways as well as downward from the diffusion windows at the surface, the resulting junction edge is not exposed to air on the surface, but is protected by the surface oxide layer.

IC electrical contact — An electrical contact to semiconductor regions can be formed by depositing thin metal films of high electrical conductivity, such as aluminum, over the diffusion windows cut in the oxide layer. These conductive films can then be etched into desired interconnection patterns on the surface of the silicon wafer, thus completing the monolithic circuit structure.

IC electrical isolation—The two principal means of isolating the individual devices in an IC are junction isolation and dielectric isolation. The necessity of providing such electrical isolation is apparent, but the steps required to obtain the isolation can affect the IC design appreciably. In particular, the packing density of standard bipolar integrated circuits is limited by the electrical isolation requirement. *See also* IC isolation techniques.

IC etching—The photomasking step of a photo lithography process is followed by an etching step during which the parts of the SiO_2 layer that are not protected by the exposed resist mask are etched away, thus forming the diffusion or contact windows on the oxide. In this process, a buffered hydrofluoric acid solution is used as the etchant. Following the etching step, the photoresist is washed away by a special cleaning solution, and the silicon wafer is ready for the next diffusion step. A similar photomasking step is also used in forming the metal interconnection patterns.

IC isolation techniques—Generally, all the integrated-circuit components are fabricated simultaneously and on the same silicon substrate. It is thus necessary to employ some means of electrical isolation between them. This is achieved by fabricating the monolithic devices within electrically isolated regions of the substrate, known as isolation "tubs" or "pockets." The electrical separation between each isolation pocket and the rest of the circuit is generally achieved by reverse-biased junctions (junction isolation) or by dielectric barrier layers (dielectric isolation).

IC manufacturing process yields — IC manufacture begins with a sequence of alternating optical and chemical steps carried out on a thin wafer of silicon. The optical operation transfers circuit patterns from a set of masks to the wafer, and the chemical (or physical/chemical) processes create appropriate conducting, semiconducting, and insulating paths in the silicon locations specified by the masks. The masks typically contain patterns for tens or hundreds of identical circuit components, or chips (the actual number depends on wafer and chip dimensions). When the manufacturer finishes the processing steps on a batch of wafers, he tests the individual chips and marks the bad ones. The ratio of good chips to total chips on the wafer is called the *wafer yield,* and is a most important parameter.

Next, the manufacturer separates the chips, discarding the bad ones. He mounts each good chip on a package "header," and bonds it in place. Then he attaches the chip terminals to the package leads, and inspects the result. The ratio of good circuits to total circuits at this point is the *packaging yield.* The last steps in the manufacturing process call for the mounted chips to be capped and marked, and to undergo a final test, which cycles the finished product through a sophisticated test appropriate to its complexity. The ratio of good units to total units at this point is the *final test yield.*

IC photomasking—The wafer surface to be masked is initially coated with a photosensitive coating known as "photoresist" or "resist." The resist-coated wafer surface is then brought into intimate contact with the masking plate and exposed under an ultraviolet light. The portions of the photosensitive resist not covered by opaque portions of the mask polymerize and harden as a result of this exposure.

Then, the unexposed parts of the resist can be washed away, leaving a "photoresist mask" on the wafer surface. As a consequence of the masking step, the pattern to be etched through the oxide is transferred to the wafer surface in the form of a hardened, etch-resistant, photoresist pattern.

IC surface passivation, planar process —Passivation of the silicon surface by an inert dielectric layer is one of the basic features of the planar process. In almost all cases, surface passivation is provided by a thermally grown layer of silicon dioxide (SiO_2). This passivating layer performs three fundamental functions:

1. It serves as a diffusion mask and allows selective diffusions into silicon through the windows etched into the oxide.
2. It protects the junctions from exposure to the moisture and other contaminants in the atmosphere.
3. It serves as an insulator on the device surface on which the metal interconnections can be formed.

IC tri-metal processing—The tri-metal process requires initial production steps similar to those developed for standard ICs. After conventional diffusion, epitaxial, and photolithographic steps have created the ICs on a silicon wafer, a layer of silicon nitride is used to seal the junctions of the chips. A standard masking operation then opens contact windows, and platinum sputtered over the wafer is sintered into these windows to form platinum silicide contacts. At this point, sequential sputtering of a titanium and a platinum layer provides contact adherence and a diffusion barrier, respectively. After a standard photoresist technique defines chip interconnections, a 2-micron gold layer electroplated to the platinum interconnect runs provides conduction paths. Finally, as in a standard IC, a chemically vapor-deposited layer of phosphorous-silicate glass provides passivation and mechanical protection.

identifier word — Refers to a specific identifier word, i.e., a full-length computer word which is associated with a search or a search-read function. In a search or search-read function, the identifier word is stored in a special register in the channel synchronizer and compared with each word read by the peripheral unit (some systems).

identity element—A logical element operating with binary signals that supply one output signal from two input signals. The output signal will be 1 when, and only when, the two input signals are the same; i.e., both inputs are 1 or both 0.

identity gate—A specific n-input gate which yields an output signal of a particular kind when all of the n-input signals are alike. Same as identity unit.

identity unit — An n-input device that yields a specified output signal only when all n-input signals are alike.

idle time—1. The period between the end of one programmed computer run and the commencement of a subsequent programmed run. 2. The time normally used to assemble cards, paper, tape reels, and control panels required for the next computer operation. 3. The time between operations when no work is scheduled.

IEEE—Abbreviation of Institute of Electrical and Electronics Engineers.

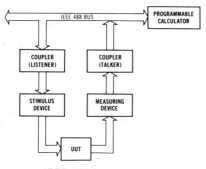

IEEE-488 bus controller.

IEEE-488 bus controller—Devices connected to the bus may be talkers, listeners, talkers/listeners, or controllers. The controller dictates the role of each of the other devices by setting up the proper communication paths and outputting commands to the other components. Addresses are set into each device when the system is assembled. Each device recognizes its own address and responds to a poll, accepts data, or outputs data de-

pending upon its function in the system. The address switch is mounted where it can be easily changed or inspected. Each device performs the following 488 bus functions depending upon its role in the system: handshake, single-address talk or listen, service request, parallel poll, device clear, and device trigger.

IEEE-488 bus coupler functions—The IEEE-488 bus interface couplers let each system engineer add 488 bus compatibility to his existing instruments. Configurations of the coupler are available for connecting measuring devices to the 488 bus (called talkers), controlling stimulus or output devices from the 488 bus (called listeners), and connecting and controlling devices in a bidirectional manner (called talker/listener). Using the coupler, the systems engineer can put his existing instruments together to form an automated instrumentation system at a minimum cost.

ignore—1. A typewriter character indicating that no action whatsoever be taken, i.e., in teletypewriter code, a character code consisting of holes punched in every hole position (paper tape) is an ignore character, this convention makes possible the erasing of any previously punched character. 2. An instruction requiring nonperformance of what normally might be executed, i.e., not to be executed. This instruction should not be confused with a No Op or do nothing instruction, since these generally refer to an instruction outside themselves.

illegal character—Refers to a character or combination of bits that is not accepted as a valid representation by the machine design or by a specific routine. Illegal characters are commonly detected and used as an indication of a machine malfunction.

illegal code—A code character or symbol that appears to be the proper element but really is not a true member of the defined alphabet or specific language. If forbidden patterns, characters, or symbols present themselves, they are judged to be mistakes or the results of malfunctions.

illegal instruction — An illegal instruction is the term used to refer to any parts of the word bit patterns that are not the bit pattern of the first word of a legal instruction. During instruction execution, if such an instruction is fetched, an illegal instruction exception occurs.

illegal operation — The process which results when a computer either cannot perform the instruction part or will perform with invalid and undesired results. The limitation is often due to built-in computer constraints.

image enhancing, spatial filtering — Spatial filtering, one method of image enhancement, creates a box around one pixel (picture element) of an image and then computes the average optical density. This local average is subtracted from the optical density of the pixel and the resulting value added back to the original. Repeating this process over the entire image yields an enhancement. Box size is important—this procedure suppresses any detail larger than 55% of the box. Edge enhancement uses the derivative of the image. The gradient, i.e., the sum of the partial derivatives of the optical density with respect to each direction, is calculated by subtracting each pixel from its immediate neighbors. The result can be multiplied by a constant and added to the original. To find the "true edge" of an object, maximum gradient analysis makes use of the second derivative of the image.

image processing fundamentals — The concept of image processing stems from the utilization of computer techniques as a means of manipulating an image into a form which is more meaningful to the user. The processing may be either analysis or enhancement. It may be as simple as a nonlinear brightness amplification or as complex as sophisticated spatial frequency modification. As a rule, image processing is the analysis and enhancement of two dimensional data; it is the manipulation of imagery to present to the viewer, or a subsequent machine, additional information or insight into some factor concerning the original unprocessed image. The original data may be in such familiar forms as medical X-rays, weather satellite pictures, smudged fingerprints, television or motion picture programming, computer-aided design models, reconnaissance photographs, earth resources satellite data, etc.

image processor graphics — Graphics overlay data are often stored in the solid-state refresh memory. These data are retrieved from storage and presented to the display simultaneously with the retrieval and display of the image data. The graphics overlay is a matrix of one bit per pixel (picture element) data with the same spatial resolution as the image data. The overlay can be used for identification and marking purposes such as alphanumeric notations, outlines, vectors, grid lines, political boundaries, etc. The graphics overlays are independent of each other, if there are more than one, and they are independent of the image data as well. They can be placed nondestructively over the image being displayed. There is additional logic to permit display of the overlay if there is a conflict between the image brightness and the graphics (some systems).

image processor, moveable target — A special feature of some image processors is a moveable target. Operating independently of either the image or the graphics presentation, the target consists of a unique pattern of pixels. This pattern is such that it is visible in any combination of image and graphics data that is being displayed. The target location is changed by an external device like a trackball or data tablet. Its position is available as X-Y coordinate data through the standard computer interface (some systems).

image, pseudo color—The arbitrary assignment of the color combinations of hue, saturation, and luminescence to the image brightness information defines a *pseudo color* presentation. Pseudo coloring, by providing a greatly improved image contrast, is often used for positive feature identification.

image restoration—This technique subdivides an image into smaller zones, each theoretically containing a feature and background. Using statistical techniques, one can assign a "best" value for the optical density of the feature, and another value for the optical density of the background. Reassignment of each pixel's optical density to either feature or background results in a less noisy and sharper image.

image sensors—Image sensors, known also as charge-coupled devices (CCDs), are nickel-sized silicon chips containing over 120,000 electronic elements. When an image is focused on the CCD, the sensor's electronic elements transform the picture into individual electric charge packets. These packets then are read out very rapidly by charge transfer techniques. The resulting information then can be processed and displayed as a tv picture. In the CCD, half the electronic elements form the imaging array and the other half are for storage and read-out. Charge-coupled devices are being developed as part of some broadly based efforts aimed at developing all solid-state tv systems, and of applying CCD technology to a wide range of other applications such as space exploration, closed-circuit television, military programs, surveillance systems, and telephone systems used to transmit tv pictures. Image sensors operate as follows:

Light photons falling on the sensors generate packets of electrons in potential wells, which are then electronically transferred and shifted out of the device by external clocking. A line of video information representing the object pattern is thus obtained for processing in various ways, depending on the particular applications.

Early in CCD development, it was apparent that this technology could be used to store digital information in very high densities. Design efforts soon produced a 9216-bit digital CCD memory to fill the cost/performance gap between MOS memories and the much slower rotating magnetic memories. The inherent capability of charge-coupled devices to manipulate information in the form of charge packets makes CCD technology ideal for analog-signal processing, i.e., delay, filtering, signal correlation, enhancement of signal-to-noise ratio, etc.

image sensor, solid-state—Some types of solid-state image sensors are specially fabricated and designed into-grated circuits. A single monolithic chip of silicon may contain thousands of photosensitive devices. These special ICs are mounted in normal IC packages, except that the top is made of a transparent material. The photosensitive elements are scanned as an image strikes the IC. This produces an electronic analog video signal. These ICs are usually either *linear* or *area* arrays—that is, the photosensitive elements are either in a straight line (linear) or in a 2-dimensional array (area).

image table — An area in pc memory dedicated to I/O data. Ones and zeroes ("1" and "0") represent ON and OFF conditions, respectively. During every I/O scan, each input controls a bit in the input-image table; each output is controlled by a bit in the output-image table.

immediate addressing — 1. A specific mode of addressing in which the operand contains the value to be operated on, and no address reference is required. 2. A particular system of specifying the locations of operands and instructions in the same storage location, i.e., at the same address. An address part contains the value of an operand rather than its address.

immediate instructions—Some systems provide a full complement of immediate instructions. The address portion of the instruction can contain the 8-bit operand itself, rather than an address. Only half as much memory is needed since both instruction and operand are contained in a single word. Immediate instructions include: Add, Subtract, Load, and Compare.

imperative statement—1. Action statements of a symbolic program that are converted into actual machine language. 2. A statement consisting of a verb and its operand(s); also, a series of such statements. A statement expresses a complete unit of procedure.

implication—A logic operation with the property of "IF . . . THEN." For instance, if "A" is a statement and "B" is another statement, then, "A" inclusion "B" is false if "A" is true and "B" is false.

implication gate—Same as gate, B OR NOT A, and gate, conditional implication.

implication gate, conditional—A binary (two-input) logic coincidence circuit for completing the logic operation of A OR NOT B; i.e., the result is false only if A is false and B is true.

implication operation, conditional—Relates to a Boolean operation where the result for the values of the operands P and Q is given by the table:

Operands		Results
P	Q	R
0	0	1
1	0	0
0	1	1
1	1	1

implicit address, assembler — In assembler programming, an address reference that is specified as one absolute or relocatable expression. An implicit address must be converted into its explicit base-displacement form before it can be assembled into the object code of a machine instruction.

impulse — 1. A pulse that begins and ends within so short a time that it may be regarded mathematically as infinitesimal. However, the change in the medium is usually of a finite amount. 2. A change in the intensity or level of some medium, usually over a relatively short period of time; e.g., a shift in electrical potential of a point for a short period of time compared to the time period. 3. A change in the intensity or level of some medium over a relatively short period of time.

impulse noise — A type of interference on communication channels characterized by high amplitude and short duration. This type of interference may be caused by lightning, electrical sparking action common in power tools, or by the make-break action of switching devices, etc. Sometimes called impulsive noise.

impurity—An atom foreign to the crystal in which it exists. Material added to a semiconductor crystal to produce excess electrons (a donor impurity) or excess holes (an acceptor impurity).

impurity level—The energy level existing in a substance because of impurity atoms.

in-circuit testing — In-circuit testing electrically isolates each *component* on a board, tests it for its own characteristics, and ignores its function in the overall circuit. All circuit-board components are tested one by one. Connections between the in-circuit test system and the board are via a vacuum-actuated, multiple-pin, "bed of nails" fixture, with each distinct circuit-board type having its own unique fixture. The tester is used to test for shorted and open circuits on bare boards, for correct values of analog components (using a guarding technique), and for correct functions of individual ICs (using a pulsing technique). Because the test fixture connects to every device, the in-circuit test system is more effective than the functional type, which connects to the edge of the pc board. The major drawback of the card-edge tester is the complex software required to isolate faults (some systems).

in-circuit testing, learning mode — Some in-circuit testers practically write their own test programs while examining a small sample of "known good" boards. In the learning mode, a system first starts testing the "known good" boards to fairly tight tolerances. Then, as it encounters values that fall outside these limits, the system opens up the tolerances to accommodate the new as well as the previous values. The ideal limits will, of course, be just outside the range of actual values measured on the sample of good boards, and the system will automatically settle in on these tolerances. After about a dozen boards have been examined, the test system will have a very good idea of what constitutes a "good board." The system, in other words, will have been programmed.

inclusion—Same as implication.

increment—1. To increase, especially in quantity or value. 2. A software operation most often associated with stacks and stack pointers. Bytes of information are stored in the stack register at the addresses contained in the stack pointer. The stack pointer is decremented after each byte of information is entered into the stack; it is incremented after each byte is removed from the stack. Increment also refers to various addressable registers.

incremental—Often refers to an arrangement of 2 bits phased 90 degrees (electrical) apart, from which direction of rotation can be sensed. Repeated sequentially and summed algebraically in an external counter.

incremental compaction—A procedure for data compaction using only the initial value, and all subsequent changes in storage for transmission. A saving in time and space is achieved when only the changes at specific intervals are transmitted or processed.

incremental data—Often refers to specific data which represents only the change from that data that just preceded it; hence, in incremental positioning, each move is referenced to the prior one.

incremental induction — Refers to one half the algebraic difference between the maximum and minimum magnetic induction at a point, in a material that has been subjected simultaneously to a polarizing and a varying magnetizing force.

index — A number that represents the relative position of an entity in either a record or a file.

indexed addressing — 1. Refers to a procedure where data for an instruction is pointed to by the contents of an "index register," plus an offset value. The offset value is in the byte immediately following the instruction code. 2. In indexed addressing, the address contained in the second byte of the instruction is added to the index register's lowest 8 bits in the MPU. The carry is then added to the higher order 8 bits of the index register. This result is then used to address memory. The modified address is held in a temporary address register so there is no change to the index register. These are often two-byte instructions (some systems). 3. Indexed addressing is similar to relative addressing but a temporary address register so there a datum address, the address part of the instruction is added to the contents of the index register by the microprocessor.

indexed addressing, single-chip system—Indexed addressing enables the programmer to address any location in memory through the use of the pointer register and the displacement. When indexed addressing is specified in an instruction, the contents of the designated pointer register are added to the displacement to form the effective address. The contents of the pointer register are not modified by indexed addressing (some systems).

indexed files—The indexed structure is ideal for applications involving a heavy volume of random access. This structure consists of a series of pointers to data blocks scattered throughout the disk. It has the open-ended characteristics of chained files with the access speed of contiguous files.

indexing — A computer technique of addressing modification that is often implemented by means of index registers.

index of refraction—This is defined as the ratio of the velocity of light in a given medium to the velocity of light in a vacuum.

index register—1. A basic register, the index register contains the addresses of information subject to modification by the control block, without affecting the instruction in memory. The IR information is available for loading onto the stack pointer when needed. 2. A register designed to modify the operand address in an instruction or base address by addition or subtraction, thus yielding a new effective address.

index value—The preset value of a controlled quantity at which an automatic control is required to aim; also the desired value.

index word register — A register that contains a quantity which may be used to modify addresses under direction of the control section of the computer. (Sometimes known as b-box.)

indicator chart—Refers to a table or schematic used by a programmer during the logical design and coding of a program in order to record items about the use of indicators in the program. A portion of program documentation.

indirect addressing — 1. Refers to the procedure of addressing a memory location that contains the address of data rather than the data itself. 2. A form of computer cross-referencing, in which one memory location indicates where the correct address of the main fact can be found. 3. Any level of addressing other than the first level of direct addressing. The translation of symbolic instructions into machine-language instructions.

indirect address, microprocessor—Indirect addresses allow a named location to contain, instead of data, the address of data. Thus, the instruction refers to a word or words that, in turn, refer to the datum. This is particularly important in generalized software. In some systems, one of the bits of the address that has been fetched indirectly may further specify an indirection.

induced environment — The vibrations, shocks, pressures, accelerations, temperatures, and other conditions imposed on a system due to the operation or handling of the system.

induced failure—A failure caused basically by a condition or phenomenon external to the item that fails.

inequivalence—1. The Boolean operator which gives a truth table quantity the value of true if only one of the two variables it connects is true. 2. A logical operator that has the property that if P is a statement and Q is a statement, then P Exclusive-OR Q is true if, and only if, either but not both statements are true, and false if, and only if, both are true or both are false. P Exclusive-OR Q is often represented by PQ.

infix notation — Refers to the natural form of writing mathematical expressions with operators appearing in between the symbols upon which they operate, such as CROSS + PROFIT, etc.

information bits—The fundamental unit of measurement for information is the "bit." One bit of information is one answer to one question, expressed in binary (yes or no) form. Basic information theory, derived from logical principles, provides that all information, no matter how complex, can be represented by some collection of bits. Physicists generally agree that bits can travel at least at the speed of light, and that the minimum mass or energy required of a bit can be made indefinitely small if the space and time required to contain it can be made indefinitely large. The limiting product of the energy and time requirements of a bit is closely related to the very small Plank's constant of the quantum theory, 6.626×10^{-27} erg-seconds. Despite rapid advances in electronics technology in recent years, the theoretical limits have not been even remotely approached.

information, input/output—The microcomputer is called upon to process three types of information — data, status, and control—and it may do so in one of three ways. It may retain complete control of the information transfer, as in polled I/O. It may allow the I/O device to initiate a transfer, but the CPU retains control thereafter, as when interrupts are used. Or

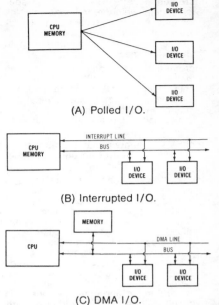

(A) Polled I/O.

(B) Interrupted I/O.

(C) DMA I/O.

Information, input/output (Courtesy Intel Corp.).

it may relinquish control completely to the input/output devices, as in direct memory access. Data generally is bidirectional, flowing to the microcomputer from the I/O devices in the system and flowing from it to them. The nature of the data—whether it's alphanumeric (ASCII) or variable-length binary — strongly influences the microcomputer's optimum word length.

information retrieval—1. A method for cataloging vast amounts of data, all related to one field of interest, so that any part or all of this data can be called out at any time that it is needed, with accuracy and speed. 2. A branch of computer science relating to the techniques for storing and searching large or specific quantities of information.

infrared-emitting diode — A semiconductor device in which radiative recombination of injected minority carriers produce infrared radiant flux when current flows as a result of applied voltage.

inherited error — A computer error which has incorrect initial values, especially that error accumulated from prior steps in a step-by-step integration.

inhibiting input—A computer gate input which can prevent any output which might otherwise occur.

inhibition gate—A gate circuit used as a switch and placed in parallel with the circuit it is controlling.

inhibit pulse — A computer drive impulse which tends to prevent certain drive impulses from reversing the flux of a magnetic cell.

initializing — The preliminary steps in arranging those instructions and data in a computer memory that are not to be repeated.

initial program loading — An initiation process which brings a program or operating system into a computer with the data records which participate in the process. Such a routine is established in memory making it possible to load and execute any other desired program.

initialize — 1. Refers to a program or hardware circuit which will return a program, a system, or a hardware device to an original state. 2. To set an instruction, counter, switch, or address to a specified starting condition at a specified time in a program.

injection laser—A solid-state semiconductor device consisting of at least one pn junction capable of emitting coherent or stimulated radiation under specified conditions. The device will incorporate a resonant optical cavity.

injection laser diode—A semiconductor device in which lasing takes place within the pn junction. Light is emitted from the diode edge.

in-line processing—1. A method of processing in which individual input transactions are completely processed and all pertinent records are updated without previously having been grouped or batched. 2. The processing of data in a random order not subject to preliminary editing or sorting.

in-line subroutine — A subroutine inserted directly into the linear operational sequence. Such a subroutine must be recopied at each point that it is needed in a routine.

input—1. An adjective referring to a device or collective set of devices used for bringing data into another device. 2. A channel for impressing a state on a device or logic element. 3. Pertaining to a device, process, or channel involved in an input process, or to the data or states involved in an input process. In the English language, the adjective "input" may be used in place of "input data," "input signal," "input terminal," etc., when such usage is clear in a given context. 4. Pertaining to a device, process, or channel involved in the insertion of data or states, or to the data or states involved. 5. One, or a sequence of, input states.

input area—The internal storage area in a computer into which data from external storage is transferred.

input block—A section of a computer's internal storage reserved for receiving and processing input data.

input buffer register—A device that receives data from input devices (tape, disk, etc.) and, then, transfers it to internal computer storage.

input converter module, analog—The device that converts analog input signals from the process instrumentation into a digit code for transmission to the computer (some systems).

input device—The mechanical unit designed to bring data to be processed into a computer, e.g., a card reader, a tape reader, or a keyboard unit.

input editing — Refers to various types of input that may be edited to convert to a more convenient format for processing and storage than that which is used for entry into the system; also, to check the inputted data for proper format, completeness, or accuracy. Often, input must be formatted in the most convenient form for preparation by humans and, then, it must be reformatted for computer use.

input equipment — 1. The equipment used for transferring data and instructions into an automatic data processing system. 2. The equipment by which an operator transcribes original data and instructions to a medium that may be used in an automatic data processing system.

input impedance — Refers to the specific impedance measured at the input terminals, such as a typewriter terminal, crt, transmission line or gate, or an amplifier, all under no-load conditions.

input mode—During this mode of transmission, data is transferred into the central computer.

input module—A general name for an input device or collective set of devices used to bring data into another device, or a channel or process device used for transferring data from an external storage to an internal storage.

input/output bus—An input/output bus provides scores of parallel lines for data, command, device address, status, and control information. This eliminates the timing problems created when data and address lines are time-shared. It makes interfacing easier, faster, and less expensive. Memory and input/output interfaces connect directly to the main bus. Each operates at its own pace. Under direct-memory access (DMA), this means that transfers can be made directly between external devices and memory without affecting the central processor, if desired (some systems).

input/output channel—Refers to a specific channel which allows independent communication between the memory exchange and the input/output exchange. It controls any peripheral device and performs all validity checking on information transfers.

input/output channels, automatic—Automatic I/O channels transfer data between memory and external interfaces in blocks of any size without disturbing the processor's working registers. Word or byte count and current address for each channel can be held in memory and each transfer automatically updates them until the count is complete. This use of memory for control registers lowers the cost of interfacing. Multiple channels can operate concurrently, with hardware priority control of each channel. Transfers can be full 16-bit words or 8-bit bytes with automatic packing/unpacking (some systems).

input/output channel bus control — Some central processor communication paths consist of a high-speed data bus, a high-speed input/output bus for computer peripheral equipment, and a low-speed bus buffer channel for slower process equipment. The transfer of data between external devices and their associated assembly registers proceeds under the control of the external device. Input/output channels may transfer data simultaneously in multichannel operation. The access to main memory from the in/out channel is made available as needed, subject to channel priority. This is often provided by channel priority logic which selects the channel of highest priority requesting transfer, that is, the lowest numbered channel requesting transfer of data.

input/output control program—Refers to the control of input and output operations by the supervisory (computer) program.

input/output device controllers — Input/output controllers consist of the necessary logic circuitry required to interconnect one or more peripheral devices with the input/output interface. An input/output controller is normally identified with a single device; however, certain types of controllers may accommodate multiple devices of the same physical type.

input/output devices—Computer hardware capable of entering data into a computer. Abbreviated I/O.

input/output equipment — Pertains to those specific units of the total computing system that are designed to accept data and to output the results of the computing and processing in a form that is readable either by humans or to other processing units.

input/output executive — A modular system of peripheral I/O device management and support, input/output executives can free the user from the need to write critical time-dependent I/O service routines for standard peripherals. It also provides a well-defined protocol and support for user-written special-purpose device handlers.

input/output interface—A typical input/output interface incorporates two or more input/output channels, a processor input/output (PIO) channel, and a direct-memory access (DMA) channel. The PIO channel interfaces with the processor via the data input bus and provides simplex character-oriented data transfer capability. The DMA channel interfaces directly with the memory, via the data input bus, and provides high-speed record-oriented data transfer capability, at rates of up to 500,000 or more words per second.

input/output operation—The input/output section acts as an autonomous processor which runs independently of the instruction-execution cycle, scanning the input channels for the presence of input or output word transfer requests and transferring data between the channels and central storage, controlled by the input/output access-control location associated with the channels.

input/output port—A typical input/output port consists of an 8-bit latch with tri-state output buffers along with control and device selection logic. Also included is a service request flip-flop for the generation and control of interrupts to the microprocessor. The device is multimode in nature. It can be used to implement latches, gated buffers, or multiplexers. Thus, all of the principal peripheral and input/output functions of a microcomputer system can be implemented with this device. Some units require only 0.25 μA input current, permitting direct connection to MOS data and address lines of the CPU.

input/output processor (IOP)—The IOP assumes all device controller overhead, performs both programmed and DMA transfers, and can recover from "soft" I/O errors without CPU intervention. Therefore, these activities may be performed while the CPU is attending to other tasks. To the CPU, I/O devices appear to transmit and receive whole blocks of data. Thus, the IOP makes both byte- and word-level transfers that are invisible to the CPU.

input/output request words — Control words for input/output requests that are stored in the Message Reference Block until the I/O is completed.

input/output, simultaneous—Generally refers to the microcomputers that can handle other operations concurrently with input and output operations. Most often this is accomplished using buffers that hold input/output data and information as it arrives (and on a temporary basis), while other operations are executed by the CPU. Thus, the computer need not wait for data from the very slow I/O units and may instead take it from the faster part of the buffer in massive quantities instead of as it arrives from slower units or terminals.

input/output switching—Refers to the connecting of various input/output devices to more than one channel and using channel switching to optimize processing.

input/output table — A plotting device used to generate or to record one variable as a function of another variable.

input/output trunks — The basic systems are equipped with many input/output trunks, each of which can be connected to a peripheral control. A control which handles both reading and writing (e.g., a magnetic tape control) connects to a pair of trunks. Data are transferred between main memory and a trunk (and thus, a peripheral device) via the Read/Write channel specified in the instruction that initiates the transfer. Additional peripheral devices can be connected to the system simply by adding several more input/output trunks to the basic configuration. The number of peripheral devices in a system depends only on the number of input/output trunks available.

input program—A routine which directs or controls the reading of programs and data into a computer system. Such a routine may be internally stored, wired, or part of a "bootstrap" operation, and may perform housekeeping or system control operations according to specific rules.

input reference—The specific reference designed and used to compare the measured variable that results in a deviation or error signal. Also referred to as set point or desired value.

input register—In a computer, the register of internal storage that is able to accept information from outside the computer at one speed and supply the information to the computer calculating unit at another, usually much greater, speed.

input signal — The control-loop signal when it enters a data block.

input storage—1. Refers to devices that hold each bundle of facts while they await their turn to be processed. This allows successive bundles to be compared either to make sure they are in the right order or for other control purposes. 2. Any information that enters a computer for the purpose of being processed or to aid in processing. It is then held until signaled for use by the control program.

input stream—Concerns the sequence of job control statements and data submitted to an operating system on an input unit that is especially activated for this purpose by the operator.

input translator—Refers to a section of some computer programs that convert the incoming programmer's instructions into operators and operands understood by the computer. This scan or search also checks the input items for desired properties and, in many cases, outputs appropriate error messages if the desired properties of the input do not conform to the proper syntax.

input work queue—Concerns a waiting line of summary information of job control statements maintained by the job scheduler, from which it selects the jobs and job steps to be processed.

inquiry—Refers to a technique whereby the interrogation of the contents of a computer's storage may be initiated at a local or remote point by use of a keyboard, touch-tone pad, or other device.

inscribing—In optical character recognition, the preparation of source documents for automatic reading, and which includes both handwritten and printed characters.

inserted subroutine — 1. A separately coded sequence of instructions that is inserted in another instruction sequence directly in low order of the line. 2. A directly inserted subroutine to the main line program that is inserted specifically where it is required. 3. A subroutine that must be relocated and inserted into the main routine at each place it is used.

insert with automatic justify — Text is automatically justified on completion of all insertions or, optionally, at any insertion.

instruction — 1. A coded program step that tells the computer what to do for a single operation in a program. 2. A set of characters, together with one or more addresses (or no address), that defines an operation and which, as a unit, causes the computer to operate accordingly on the indicated quantities. 3. A set of identifying characters

designed to cause a computer to perform certain operations. A machine instruction to specific functions.

instruction, absolute — A particular computer instruction which specifies completely a specific computer operation and is capable of causing the execution of that operation.

instruction address register—The register which contains the address of the instruction that is to be executed next.

instructional constant—A constant written in the form of an instruction but not intended to be executed as an instruction. One form of dummy instruction.

instruction, arithmetical — Specifies an arithmetic operation upon data, e.g., addition or multiplication. Arithmetical instructions form a subset of the machine instruction set and are to be considered separately from logical instructions.

instruction, blank — *See* instruction dummy.

instruction, breakpoint—1. An instruction which will cause a computer to stop or to transfer control in some standard fashion to a supervisory routine which can monitor the progress of the interrupted program. 2. An instruction which, if some specified switch is set, will cause the computer to stop or take other special action.

instruction characters—Refers to characters, when used as code elements, that can initiate, modify, or stop a control operation. Characters may be used, for example, to control the carriage return, etc.

instruction code—The list of symbols, names and definitions of the instructions that are intelligible to a given computer or computing system.

instruction codes, mnemonic — *See* codes, mnemonic operation.

instruction complement—A built-in feature designed to provide a number of instructions for each programmer instruction.

instruction counter—Refers to a multiple-bit register that keeps track of the address of the current instruction and is used as the input to the memory-address register (MAR).

instruction decoder — The part of the CPU that interprets the program instructions in binary into the necessary control signals for the ALU, registers, and control bus.

instruction diagnostic — A device that completely tests all CPU instructions in all modes including operation under interrupt.

instruction digit, unallowable—A character or combination of bits which is not accepted as a valid representation by the machine design or by a specific routine. Instruction digits unallowable are commonly detected and used as an indication of machine malfunction.

instruction, discrimination—A more acceptable term for conditional jump instruction or branch instruction. Also called decision instruction. *See* branch.

instruction, do-nothing — *See* instruction, dummy.

instruction, dummy—1. An artificial instruction or address inserted in a list to serve a purpose other than execution as an instruction. (Related to constant instruction.) 2. A specifically designed artificial instruction to serve a purpose other than its meaningful or purposeful execution; i.e., it is not data. Such an instruction is usually inserted in the sequence for a purpose, but if it is executed no disturbance to the run will occur. It is frequently a no-operation, a do-nothing, or a waste instruction.

instruction, executive—Similar to a supervisory instruction, this instruction is designed and used to control the operation or execution of other routines or programs.

instruction format—1. The allocation of bits or characters of a machine instruction to specific functions. 2. Instructions are coded in a two-address, variable-length format. However, one or perhaps both addresses may often be omitted, thereby saving memory space and speeding up instruction execution. 3. The allocation of instructions according to some particular machine or installation conventions or rules. 4. An allocation of characters of various instructions differentiating between the component parts of the instructions, such as address part, operation part, etc.

instruction, four address — Refers to a machine instruction usually consisting of the addresses of two operands, the address for storing the result, the

address of the next instruction, the command to be executed, and miscellaneous indices.

instruction, hold—A computer instruction which causes data called from storage to be also retained in storage after it is called out and transferred to its new location.

instruction, jump—A computer instruction causing a jump in the sequence of instructions. *See* branch.

instruction, logic—An instruction causing the execution of an operation defined by symbolic logic statements or operators, such as AND, OR, etc., and to be distinguished from arithmetic instructions, such as add, multiply, and divide.

instruction, look up—An instruction designed to allow reference to systematically arranged and stored data.

instruction, macro — 1. An instruction consisting of a sequence of microinstructions that are inserted into the object routine for performing a specific operation. 2. The more powerful instructions that combine several operations in one instruction.

instruction, micro — A small, single, short, add-shift, or delete type of command.

instruction, microprocessor—A typical instruction can be from one to three bytes long, depending on the addressing mode used with the instruction. The first byte always contains the operation code, which designates the kind of operation the MPU will perform. In single-byte instructions, no memory address is required because the operation is performed on one of the internal MPU registers. In multiple-byte instructions, the second and third byte can be the operand, or a memory address for the operand.

instruction, mnemonic — *See* codes, mnemonic operation.

instruction modification—Refers to an alternation in the operation code portion of an instruction or command such that if the routine containing the instruction or command is repeated, the computer will perform a different operation.

instruction, no-op — 1. An instruction that specifically instructs the computer to do nothing but process the next instruction in sequence. 2. A blank instruction. 3. A skip instruction.

instruction, n-plus-one address — Refers to a multiple address instruction in which one address specifies the location of the next instruction of the normal sequence to be executed.

instruction path, microprocessor—The instruction path is a transfer bus for retrieving instructions from the program memory. Instruction word width is determined by the size of the instruction set which affects processing power.

instruction register — The instruction register is a 4-, 8-, 12-, 16-, or 32-bit register that is used to hold the instruction currently being executed by the processor. An instruction register offers storage for the binary code of the operation to be performed. Usually this instruction represents the contents of the address just designated by the program counter. However, the contents of the instruction register or the program counter may be changed by the computations. This, of course, represents one of the key ideas of a stored-program computer—instructions, as well as data, can be operated upon and subsequent operations will be determined by the results.

instruction repertoire—The set of operations that can be represented in a given operation code.

instructions — Instructions are the means by which a computer performs data manipulations and arithmetic operations. Memory is passive; users can write into it, and can read back what they wrote, and that is all. Therefore, a computer will need a more flexible storage area in which data manipulation will take place. Most will call this storage area an Accumulator or a Working Register. It is built from flip-flops, or from logic that allows each bit to be set to 0 or 1 based on the status of other accumulator bits, or based on the results of any other logical sequence. The electronic logic that determines whether a bit is to be set to a 1 or a 0 is collected into a part of the computer called the Central Processing Unit.

instruction set—Instruction sets consist of an operator part, one or more address parts, and some special indicators, usually, and they serve to define the operations and operands for the computer. It is the total structured group of characters to be transferred to the computer as operations are executed. One typical large instruction set has 128 instructions including:
- the floating point group
- the memory reference group
- the register reference group
- the I/O group
- the extended arithmetic group
- the indexed group
- the data communications group.

instruction sets, microprocessor—From a programmer's point of view, microprocessor instructions break down conveniently into the following:
- Data movement.
- Data manipulation.
- Decision and control.
- Input/output.

Data can be moved about between a variety of internal sources and destinations. The most complex locations are those in memory—usually a RAM or RAM bank—since a variety of addressing modes can be used to specify location. The effective address of a memory location that is to be read or written can be given immediately by bits in the instruction being executed. In current microprocessors, the immediate data may be 4, 8, 12, 16, or even 32 bits long. Immediate data may be interpreted as a location (or displacement) in a previously selected page (or location) or memory.

instructions, general—Microcomputers retrieve instructions sequentially from their memories and execute them. Microcomputer instructions also move data about within CPU registers, perform arithmetic operations, test the results of these operations and branch to alter the flow of instruction execution, and transfer data to and from peripheral devices. These instructions are encoded in the binary numbering system or one of its common "shorthand" forms (octal or hexadecimal). In this form, instructions are said to be in machine language or object code. Instruction codes, data, and the names of data may be written in mnemonic form using combinations of letters and numbers. Programs written in this form are said to be written in assembly language and they must be translated by programs called assemblers into machine language in order to be executed by the microcomputer. Assembly language is easier for humans to use, read, and understand than machine language. Assemblers also permit programmers to annotate their programs with comments to explain and document the purpose and operation of the instructions.

instructions, input/output — Computer instructions which operate input/output devices like optical readers, printers, and terminals.

instructions, microprogrammable — Generally all instructions which do not reference main memory (do not contain a memory address) can be microprogrammed, allowing the programmer to specify several shift, skip, or input/output transfer commands to be performed within one instruction.

instructions, monitored — As shown in the input/output instruction repertoire, instructions calling for input, output, or function transfers may be executed either with or without monitor. When executed with monitor, an internal interrupt will be generated upon completion of the transfer. When an instruction is executed without a monitor, the interrupt is inhibited.

instructions, privileged — Protection against one problem subprogram misusing the I/O devices of another problem subprogram is provided by restricting all I/O commands to the supervisor state. A subprogram requests I/O action by issuing a supervisor call instruction. The supervisory subprogram can then analyze this request and take the appropriate action.

instruction, supervisory—This instruction is designed and used to control the operation or execution of other routines or programs.

instruction time—1. The portion of an instruction cycle when the control unit is analyzing the instruction and setting up to perform the indicated operation. 2. The portion of an instruction cycle when the actual work is performed or operation executed, i.e., the time required to decode and perform an instruction.

instruction, waste — *Same as* instruction, dummy.

instruction word—1. Refers to a specific grouping of letters or digits handled by the computer as a distinct unit in order to signify the provision of definitions of the operations to be performed or the description of further data. 2. A part of a word or all of a

word which is executed by the computer as an instruction.

instruction, zero-address—An instruction specifying an operation in which the location of the operands is defined by the computer code, so that no address need be given explicitly.

instrumentation—The application of devices for the measuring, recording, and/or controlling of physical properties and movements.

instrumentation calibration — A procedure to ascertain, usually by comparison with a standard, the locations at which scale/chart graduations should be placed to correspond to a series of values of the quantity which the instrument is to measure, receive, or transmit.

integer — A complete entity; a whole (not fractional or mixed) number.

integer programming—A class of optimization problems in which the values of all of the variables are restricted to be integers. Normally, the optimization problem without this integer restriction is a linear program; additional adjectives indicate variations— for example, integer quadratic programming.

integers—The natural or whole numbers; concepts intimately connected with the process of counting or enumeration. Because integers can be written down in endless series, they are used to indicate order or sequence, i.e., the ordinal aspect of integers. The cardinal aspect of integers concerns how many things are observed or noted and provides a basis of measurement.

integer, single-precision—A fixed-point number that occupies one word of main storage. The value varies depending on the word length of the computer.

integer variables (FORTRAN)—An integer variable consists of a series of not more than six alphameric characters (except special characters), of which the first is I, J, K, L, M, or N (some systems).

integral—In numeric notation, the integral or integer is contained in the places to the left of the assumed point. The decimal 2345.67 has four integral places.

integral action limiter—A specific program or unit which limits the value of the output signal due to integral action to a predetermined value.

integral boundary—Refers to a location in main storage at which a fixed-length field, such as a half-word or a double-word, must be positioned. The address of an integral boundary is a multiple of the length of the field, in bytes.

integral control action—A specifically designed control action in which the output is proportional to the time integral of the input, i.e., the rate of change of output is proportional to the input.

integral control programming — Programming integral control requires dealing with both control system and software design problems. It is possible that the integral will saturate—reach the maximum 16-bit value. It must not be allowed to "wrap-around," which is catastrophic to the control system. ("Wrap-around" is the term for overflowing during signed arithmetic.) This is prevented by using a signed addition subroutine that checks for overflow and limits the result to the maximum values.

integral control, servo system—Integral control is used to trim small offset errors. Any error will eventually integrate to a value large enough to cause a control action. This assures that the machine will move to a new commanded position and not just to a nearby, but different, position. Integral control is computed as the product of the integral control gain and the time integral of control error (the integration is approximated by summation). The time integral is usually stored as a 16-bit double-precision number. Control error, limited to eight bits, is added to the integral at the sampling frequency (some systems).

integrated circuit—1. Abbreviated IC. 2. A microcircuit consisting of interconnected elements, inseparably associated and formed, in situ, on or within a single substrate to form an electronic circuit function. Multiple substrates and/or a combination of film circuit elements and semiconductor circuit elements are often included. 3. Also called a functional device. An interconnect array of conventional components fabricated on and in a single crystal of semiconductor material by etching, doping, diffusion,

Integrated circuit.

etc., and capable of performing a complete circuit function. 4. A microminiaturized circuit developed by using microphotography and mounted inside a special package. The package in which it is mounted typically has pins along its sides that allow the package to be plugged into a socket or soldered to a printed-circuit card. In its most general state, an IC is an interconnected array of active and passive elements integrated with a single semiconductor substrate, or deposited on the substrate, and capable of performing at least one electronic circuit function.

integrated-circuit diode-matrix memory—An integrated circuit containing a matrix of diodes which may be individually open-circuited to represent a program.

integrated component — A number of electrical elements comprising a single structure which cannot be divided without destroying its stated electronic functions.

integrated data processing—1. Refers to an information processing system which is organized, directed, and carried out according to a systems approach. 2. Complete machine control of a sphere of interest.

integrated emulator—Refers to a specific emulator program whose execution is controlled by an operating system in a multiprogramming environment. Contrast with stand-alone emulator.

integrated injection logic (I²L)—I²L is characterized by some observers as the bipolar LSI of the future. Its primary advantages are increased density, good speed-power product, versatility, and low cost. The technology is capable of squeezing 1000 to 3000 gates, or more than 10,000 bits of memory, on a single chip. It has a speed-power product as low as 1 picojoule, compared to 100 pj with TTL logic. It can handle digital and analog functions on a single chip and is made with a five-mask process without the need for current-source and load resistors.

integrated monolithic circuit — Refers to various circuits, gates, and flip-flops that are etched on single crystals, ceramics, or other semiconductor materials, and designed to use geometric etching and conductive-ink deposition techniques all within a hermetically sealed chip. Some chips with many resistors and transistors are extremely tiny, while others are in effect ''sandwiches'' of individual chips.

integration, large-scale — Abbreviated LSI. The accumulation of a large number of circuits (say 1000 or more) on a single chip of semiconductor. Characteristic of many CPU circuits and memories.

integrator — 1. Any device which integrates a signal over a period of time. 2. Unit in a computer which performs the mathematical operation of integration, usually with reference to time. 3. A resistor-condensor circuit at the input to the vertical oscillator. 2. A device whose output is proportional to the integral of the input variable with respect to time.

integrator [computing unit]—1. Refers to a device which has two input variables (x and y) and one output variable (z), with the value of z being proportional to the integral of y with respect to x. 2. One with one input and one output variable, the value of the output variable being proportional to the integral of the input with respect to elapsed time.

integrator, incremental—A digital integrator modified so that the output signal is maximum negative, zero, or maximum positive when the value of the input is negative, zero, or positive.

integrator, storage—In an analog computer, an integrator used to store a voltage in the hold condition for future use, while the rest of the computer assumes another computer control state.

integrator, summing—An analog computer amplifier which forms the time integral of the weighted sum of the input voltages or currents as an output.

intelligence—The developed capability of a device to perform functions that are normally associated with human intelligence, such as reasoning, learning, and self-improvement. (Related to machine learning.)

intelligence, artificial — The study of computer and related techniques to supplement the intellectual capabilities of man. As man has invented and used tools to increase his physical powers, he now is beginning to use artificial intelligence to increase his mental powers. In a more restricted sense, the study of techniques for more effective use of digital computers by improved programming techniques.

intelligent communications terminals—Intelligent terminals can be adapted to communicate with one host computer after another, simply by changing the protocol of the terminal rather than adapting the host for a terminal. Protocol refers to the vast sequence of messages and responses required between a terminal and a host computer, or between a terminal and a peripheral, such as an on-line printer. Most typical intelligent terminal configurations make use of either an RS-232C type of interface or a current-loop interface. RS-422/423 is a long distance differential driver-type of communication interface that allows the user to have crt terminals located some 4000 feet away from the host computer (without using a modem). Using LSI (large-scale integration) an intelligent terminal's communications interface can now be programmable for three types of operations: asynchronous, synchronous, or isochronous. Similarly, word length, parity, and baud rate are all under program control.

intelligent terminals, special-purpose— Refers to various terminals that contain some logic and are usually polled by the computer, or, conversely, the computer polls some intermediate device, such as magnetic tape or disk. Intelligent terminals are capable of data processing with storage and a stored program that is available to the user. If the computer goes down, the terminal can continue to operate in a limited mode for a certain period of time. Applications include department stores, supermarkets, hotel systems, coffee shops, bars, banks, etc.

intelligent terminals vs. host computer —The intelligent terminal has flexible design for simplified user interface including custom keyboards, modularity to meet a variety of user requirements, including control of other terminals and buffering capability to simplify the communications interface and the impact on host computer software. In other words, more and more of the communications functions can be done inside the terminal rather than at the host computer site. Microprocessors are also being used in all functional areas of terminal design, including print mechanisms, carriage control, interface control, and maintenance testing. Potentially, the more intelligence that is placed in a rote device, the less that is required in the host computer.

intensity of magnetization — Vector of the magnetic moment of an element of a substance divided by the volume of that element.

interactive debugging system—An interactive debugging system allows users to trace the execution of the program on a statement-by-statement basis. Generally, program debugging requires a knowledge of three languages: absolute binary machine language, the symbolic assembler language for the machine (and the conventions of that language that apply to the program's executive environment), and the syntax and semantics of the debugging language and the debug control system. An interactive debugging program often generates full screen hexadecimal memory dump displays instantaneously. Commands include display, store, execute, change memory, dump memory, find data in memory, set, reset, and display breakpoints (on many systems).

interactive simulator — The interactive simulator precisely duplicates the MPU functions and calculates the timing of the specific microcomputer family. The user has total interactive control over the simulator to execute, alter, and re-execute his application.

interactive time-sharing—Time-sharing apportions computer resources among many simultaneous users, giving each a seemingly dedicated system to apply to the task at hand. Interactive time-sharing maximizes the use of the computer as a working tool by integrating user input and machine output in a dynamic give-and-take process.

interblock gap — The space on magnetic tape separating two blocks of data or information.

interface—1. Refers to instruments, devices, or a concept of a common boundary or the matching of adjacent components, circuits, equipment, or system elements. An interface enables devices to yield and/or acquire information from one device or program to another. Although the terms adapter, handshake, and buffer have similar meaning, interface is more distinctly a connection to complete an operation. 2. A common boundary; for example, a physical connection between two systems or two devices. 3. A common boundary between automatic data-processing systems or parts of a single system. In communications and data systems, it may involve code, format, speed, or other changes as required.

interface adapter (device adapter)—A unit that provides a mechanical and electrical interconnection between a tester and a device under test. It may include special stimulus, measurement, load, and switching circuitry that is unique to a device or family of devices, but which is not provided in the tester.

interface adapter, EIA—The EIA communications interface adapter makes it possible to use equipment that provides a 20-mA dc signal-line (current-loop) interface with equipment that requires EIA Standard RS-232 electrical interfacing. Designed as a convenient means of adapting teletypewriter-compatible equipment to standard communications facilities, the communications interface adapter not only permits interface crt's, printers, plotters, etc., to be used as remote computer terminals, but also offers a low-cost approach to providing remote access to a computer via its current-loop (tty) port. Solid-state circuitry is used to convert the 2-way EIA-compatible voltage interface to separate electrically isolated dc-current Send and Receive signal lines that allow the interface adapter to be used in 2-wire half-duplex, 3-wire neutral, or 4-wire full-duplex circuits. Loop current may be supplied externally or obtained from internal Send and Receive loop "battery" power supplies in the communications interface adapter.

interface, analog — Analog interfaces allow the personal microcomputer to monitor and control the nondigital world. These circuits are the key elements in environmental sensors, dc motor controls, and other interfaces to linear peripheral devices.

interface adapter, general-purpose — Abbreviated GPIA. A typical GPIA interfaces between the IEEE-488 standard instrument bus and the MPU. With it, many instruments may be interconnected and thus remotely and automatically controlled or programmed. Data may be taken from, sent to, or transferred between instruments. The typical device will automatically handle all handshake protocol needed on the instrument bus.

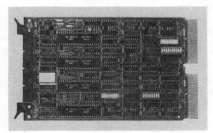

Interface card (Courtesy Plessey Peripheral Systems).

interface card — Data communication interface cards permit microcomputer users to transmit data using a wide variety of communication facilities. A typical serial line-interface board (card) will handle up to four serial

lines. Most communications interfaces conform to EIA specification RS-232C and CCITT specification V.24.

interface, CCITT — The world recommendation for interface requirements between data processing terminal equipment and data communication equipment. The CCITT recommendation resembles very closely the American EIA Standard RS-232-B or C. This standard is considered mandatory in Europe and on the other continents.

interface circuit — A circuit that links one type of device with another. Its function is to produce the required current and voltage levels for the next stage of circuitry from the previous stage.

interface circuitry—The most complex interface requirements can be solved by using a small number of integrated circuits (ICs). Entire interfaces to video terminals, graphics displays, data communications channels, and floppy disks can be designed on a single board (and recently on a single silicon chip). The availability of single-chip interfaces will simplify the task of the integrators of a system. However, all interfaces, whether they are implemented on a single chip or on multiple chips, incorporate 3 basic elements: bus interface logic, a data channel, and a control channel.

interface, communication (USART)—A synchronous/asynchronous transmitter/receiver (USART) chip is designed for data communications in microcomputer systems. The USART is used as a peripheral device and it is programmed by the CPU to operate using virtually any serial data transmission technique presently in use. The unit accepts data characters from the CPU in parallel format and then converts them into a continuous serial data stream for transmission. Simultaneously it can receive serial data streams and convert them into parallel data characters for the CPU. The unit will signal the CPU whenever it can accept a new character for transmission or whenever it has received a character for the CPU. The CPU can read the complete status of the unit at any time.

interface, current-loop—A current-loop interface option converts the EIA RS-

232-C levels of a standard communications line interface to a tty-compatible 20-mA neutral current loop. The interface consists of separate transmit and receive circuits that are electrically isolated from each other and from signal and chassis ground. The receiver and transmitter may be used separately in a 4-wire full-duplex system or externally connected in series to form a 2-wire half-duplex system.

interface, DMA—This interface has the ability to gain mastership of the bus in order to transfer data between itself and some other peripheral.

interface, EIA—Refers to a standard set of signal characteristics (time duration, voltage, and current) specified by the Electronic Industries Association for use in communications terminals. Also includes a standard plug/socket connector arrangement.

interface, general-purpose — General-purpose interfaces are contained on individual plug-in I/O cards. In addition to the appropriate data registers, many interfaces have independent flag and control logic allowing two-way communication between the computer and one, or more, external devices. Most interfaces operate under either program or direct memory access control.

interface, graphics — Multiple-chip graphics interface boards are designed to display either color or black and white images. A typical two-board interface uses direct memory access to display the contents of a display memory. Each pixel of the display is mapped from one bit of display memory.

interface, interrupt—This interface generally has the ability to gain mastership of the bus in order to give the central processor the address of a subroutine that the processor will use to service the peripheral.

interface, I/O — The type of interface and the I/O responsiveness of the microcomputer are factors in the organization of I/O activity. One method is to assign a specific class of interface to each processor. For example, one processor can do all decimal interface operations; another can handle high-speed I/O. In this way, the designer can choose the most suitable processor for each category.

interface, Kansas City Standard — Named for the meeting place of the symposium at which it found acceptance, the Kansas City Standard describes a modern technique for reading and writing digital data on audio cassette recorders, and could influence developments in the hobby computer market. Low-speed fsk modems use different pairs of frequencies for originating and answering calls and, thus, do not talk to themselves. Recording and replaying data from tape requires a modem that uses only a single pair of mark/space frequencies because the recorded data consists of these keyed frequencies. Using harmonically related frequencies permits deriving the clock frequency from the data and accommodates the wide speed variations of inexpensive cassette recorders. The standard provides both speed and software independence.

interface latch chip—On some systems that use latches for interfacing, the interface latch chip can be used as a bidirectional input/output port, a dedicated input port, or as a dedicated output port. A control signal (dynamic for bidirectional mode and static for dedicated modes) is supplied by the user, in many cases. Separate control lines enable the I/O ports; thus,

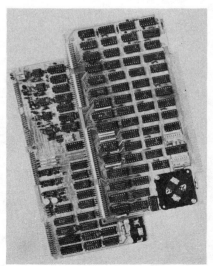

Interface, graphics (Courtesy Cromemco, Inc.).

the latch may be a high-impedance device, i.e., it does not load the system bus unless an enable signal is present.

interface (MIL STD 188B) — The standard method of interface established by the Department of Defense. It is presently mandatory for use by the departments and agencies of the Department of Defense for the installation of all new equipment. This standard provides the interface requirements for connection between data communication security devices, data processing equipment, or other special military terminal devices.

interface, slave—This interface usually has no provision in its control logic to become master. It will only transfer data onto and off the bus by command of a master device.

interfacing, bus—Physically, a bus is an etched board with rows of module connectors soldered to the board. The pin assignment can be the same on all connectors. One of the most popular buses consists of 96 signals which feed to 96 pins on the connectors. The user is generally only concerned with those signals that control data transfers, address memory, or contain the data to be transferred. However, additional signals, such as timing, are readily available on the bus to accommodate various tailor-made requirements in the event that the user should design and build his own interface module. A typical bus structure employs bidirectional data and control lines plus a few unidirectional control signals. Each bus line is a matched and terminated transmission line that must be received and driven with devices designed for that specific application.

interfacing, I/O port—Perhaps the easiest interfacing task is when a user has a microcomputer that provides I/O ports for use. Many hobby and professional microcomputers provide unused I/O ports for the user to allocate as desired. In some computers, such as those based on the S-100 bus, additional I/O ports can be accommodated merely by purchasing or building an additional I/O card. In those machines, it is easy to add on up to 256 additional ports, of which most people will only need a handful. Inputs of a D/A converter can be connected directly to the output port of

the microcomputer. This simple connection would be used by those people who have an assembled machine, instead of a microprocessor. In that case, the I/O circuitry is already provided. It also assumes that the I/O ports are *latched*. That means that the output port will retain the last valid data fed to it by the microprocessor IC, and will hold it until updated data is provided. This is the scheme used by almost all hobbyist and professional microprocessor-based computers.

interlace — In a computer, to assign successive storage location numbers to physically separated storage locations on magnetic media, reducing access time.

interleaving—1. In a computer, to insert segments of one program into another program so that the two programs can, in effect, be executed simultaneously; e.g., a technique used in multiprogramming. 2. A process of splitting the memory into two sections with two paths to the central processor to speed processing. Main memory access takes longer than logic or arithmetic operations but a second word can be read during the half-cycle when the previously read word is being written back into the memory. 3. The process of having I/O and computing operations proceed independently of one another but interleaved in their sharing of the memory.

interlock — To arrange the control of machines or devices so that their operation is interdependent in order to assure their proper coordination.

interlock (communications)—Any protective feature which helps to prevent interference to normal transmission or processing of data by other operations, such as sending from the keyboard while an automatic transmission is in progress, or to prevent sending more than one character at a time from the keyboard.

interlock time, print—The required time for the printer to accept data from the print storage area and to complete the printing.

intermediate cycle — An unconditional branch instruction that may address itself, i.e., a branch command is called, executed, and a cycle is set up, which may be used for stopping a machine.

intermediate memory storage — An electronic scratchpad for holding working figures temporarily until they are needed, and for releasing final figures to the output.

internal arithmetic—The computations performed by the arithmetic unit of a computer.

internal interrupt—Refers to a special control signal which diverts the attention of the computer to consider an extraordinary event or set of circumstances; i.e., it causes program control to be transferred to a special subordinate which corresponds to the stimulus. Many levels of control can be exercised by the numerous forms of interrupts provided. The interrupts from external sources serve primarily to synchronize the computer program with the readiness of peripheral devices, including other computers, to transmit or receive data. Internal interrupts serve primarily to synchronize the computer program with termination of input-output transfer and to signal the occurrence of an error.

internally stored program — The computer program (set of instructions) that is stored in computer internal memory as contrasted with those stored on cards, magnetic tape, etc.

internal memory—1. Also referred to as internal storage. The total memory or storage that is automatically accessible to a computer. It is an integral part of the computer and is directly controlled by it. 2. Any one of the internal parts of an automatic data-processing machine capable of retaining data.

internal sort—The sequencing of two or more records within the central computer memory; the first phase of a multipass sort program.

international temperature scale — A practical scale of temperature which is defined to conform as closely as possible with the thermodynamic Centigrade scale. Various fixed points were defined initially using the gas thermometer, and intermediate temperatures are measured with a stated form of thermometer according to the temperature range involved. The majority of temperature measurements on this scale are now made with platinum resistance thermometers.

interpolation—1. The process of finding a value between two known values on a chart or graph. 2. General procedure for determining values of a function between known or observed values, e.g., entries in a table of logarithms. There are various procedures, depending on the assumption of a curve (line or parabola) which fit localized values, imitated electrically in some controls for machine tools.

interpret — 1. To print on a punched card the graphic symbols of the information punched in that card. 2. To translate nonmachine language into machine language. 3. To decode. 4. The translation of coded characters into standard letters, numbers, and symbols.

interpreter — 1. A program that operates directly on a source program in memory. The interpreter translates the instructions of the source program, one by one, and executes them immediately. It is not common practice to use interpreters to translate and execute source programs, since they are slow, but they have several advantages on specific problems. 2. An executive routine that, as the computation progresses, translates a stored program expressed in some machine-like pseudo-code into machine code and performs the indicated operations (by means of subroutines) as they are translated. An interpreter is essentially a closed subroutine that operates successively on an indefinitely long sequence of program parameters, the pseudo-instructions, and operands. It may usually be entered as a closed subroutine and left by a pseudo-code exit instruction.

interpreter code—An interim, arbitrarily designed code, which must be translated to computer coding in order to function as designed—usually for diagnostic or checking purposes.

interpreter operation — An executive routine that, as the computation progresses, translates a stored program expressed in some machine-like pseudo-code into machine code and performs the indicated operations, by means of subroutines, as they are translated.

interpreter (program) — An essentially closed subroutine (executive) which translates a stored pseudo-code program into machine code and performs the desired and specified operations. Such an interpreter program usually consists of sequences of pseudo-instructions and operands (program parameters) which are introduced as a closed subroutine and exited by a specific pseudo-code instruction.

interpret program—1. A computer program that translates and executes each source language statement before translating and executing the next one. 2. A device that prints on a punched card the data already punched in the card. 3. To translate nonmachine language into machine language. 4. To decode.

interpretive code — A routine that decodes and immediately executes instructions written as pseudo-codes. This is contrasted with a compiler which decodes the pseudo-codes into a machine-language routine to be executed at a later time. The essential characteristic of an interpretive routine is that a particular pseudo-code operation must be decoded each time it is executed.

interpretive routine — 1. A computer routine designed to transfer each pseudo-code and, using function digits, to set a branch order that links the appropriate subroutine into the main program. 2. A routine that carries out problem solution by process of: (A) decoding instructions written in a pseudo-code, and selecting and executing an appropriate subroutine to carry out the functions called for by the pseudo-code, and (B) proceeding to the next pseudo-instruction. It should be noted that an interpretive routine carries out its functions as it decodes the pseudo-code, as contrasted with a compiler, which prepares a machine-language routine that will be executed later.

interpretive translation program — A specialized program which relates and handles the execution of a program by translating each instruction of the source language into a sequence of computer instructions and allows these to be executed before translating the next instruction, i.e., the translation of an instruction is performed each time the instruction is to be obeyed. If the interpretative program allows for programs written for one type of a computer to be run on a different type, it is often called a simulator program.

interrecord gap—1. Also referred to as interblock space. The space between records on magnetic tape caused by starting and stopping the tape motion. This gap is used to signal that the end of a record has been reached. 2. An interval of space or time, deliberately left between recording portions of data or records. Such spacing is used to prevent errors through loss of data or overwriting, and permits tape stop-start operations.

interrupt—1. A break in the normal flow of a system or routine such that the flow can be resumed from that point at a later time. An interrupt is usually caused by a signal from an external source. 2. An interrupt is a special control signal that diverts the attention of the computer from the main program, because of a particular event or set of circumstances, to a specific address which is directly related to the type of interrupt that has occurred. 3. To stop current control sequence, i.e., to jump when affected by signals from on-line peripheral equipment or to skip as triggered by results of programming test techniques. 4. An interrupt relates to the suspension of normal operations or programming routines of microprocessors and is most often designed to handle sudden requests for service or change. As peripheral devices interface with CPUs, various interrupts occur on frequent bases. Multiple interrupt requests require the processor to delay or prevent further interrupts, to break into a procedure, to modify operations, etc., and after completion of the interrupt task, to resume the operation from the point of interrupt.

interrupt, active state—The state of an interrupt level that is the result of the central processor starting to process an interrupt condition.

interrupt capabilities — Many applications require asynchronous, or unpredictable, events control and an interrupt capability. Throughput increases, since the processor can perform useful work concurrent with I/O (input/output) operations. The major characteristics of this capability include interrupt latency (time to recognize the interrupt and branch to the service routine), response (time to identify the interrupted device and begin execution of the device service code) and software overhead (to get to the service routine and return to the main program). Single line, multilevel, and vectored interrupts offer various speed/hardware tradeoffs. Cascaded interrupt capability (interrupting an interrupt) is essential if slow and fast devices are to be mixed in a system. Interrupt enable flags are used to mask or unmask individual levels.

interrupt, class — Class interrupts are used primarily to report on internal checking by the CPU. Machine check interrupts occur when the hardware malfunctions, e.g., a parity or I/O sequence problem. Program check interrupts occur when an improper instruction is attempting to execute; for example, when an invalid storage address, protection exception, or an invalid instruction is detected. Other class interrupts are power/thermal warning, supervisor call, soft exception trap, and trace and console interrupt.

interrupt, controller—Interrupts can be generated by the controller for various conditions, including the detection of an error condition or the sensing of a special character that requires immediate action. Typical conditions that may generate interrupts are receipt of end-of-message or end-of-block (EOM or EOB) characters, either on receiving or transmitting. The availability of an interrupt feature relieves the computer of the need for time-consuming scanning to sense these special conditions. Some controllers send interrupts to the processor after the receipt of each character from the line; other — the message-oriented controllers — only send interrupts at the end of the message or end of transmission.

interrupt controller ICs — Many microprocessors have only one or two interrupt input lines—not enough for many applications. For this reason, microprocessor-chip families generally include interrupt controller ICs that enable a microcomputer to handle more interrupt lines. These controllers accept as many as eight interrupt sources, each of which is vectored to a separate address specified by the programmer. Moreover, they can be cascaded together to handle virtually any number of interrupts.

interrupt count-pulse — An interrupt level that is triggered by pulses from a clock source. Each pulse of the clock source causes an instruction in a (clock) count pulse interrupt location to be executed, thus modifying the contents of a particular location (byte, halfword, or word) in memory. Each count pulse interrupt level is associated with a count zero interrupt level.

interrupt device — External interrupts are caused by an external device requiring attention (such as a signal from a communications device), console switching, by the timer going to zero, and by other procedures.

interrupt enable and interrupt disable —These are instructions that set or reset an interrupt-control flip-flop. They allow the disabling of the interrupt request, whenever necessary. In microprocessors not having this feature, one way to achieve the same result is to use the external enable to gate the interrupt signals. The hardware, in turn, can be controlled by a conventional output.

interrupt, error—Special interrupts are provided in response to certain error conditions within the central computer. These may come as a result of a programming fault (e.g., illegal instruction, arithmetic overflow), a store fault (parity error), or an executive system violation (attempt to leave the locked-in area or violation of guard mode). These faults have special interrupt locations in central store and are used by the executive system to take remedial or terminating action when they are encountered.

interrupt indicator, I/O—Input/output interrupt instructions are used to determine both the input/output unit originating an interrupt and the cause of the interrupt by testing the indicators associated with each input/output channel. When the cause of the interrupt has been determined and corrective action, if required, has been taken, the indicators may be reset and the interrupted program resumed. These instructions also provide the facility for setting, resetting, and testing the inhibit input/output interrupt indicator.

interrupt, internal—A feature of peripheral equipment using an external device that causes equipment to stop in the normal course of the program and perform some designated subroutine.

interrupt mask bit — A specific bit designed to prevent the CPU from responding to further interrupt requests until cleared by execution of programmed instructions. It may also be manipulated by specific mask bit instructions.

interrupt mask (interrupt enable)—This usually refers to a mechanism that allows the program to specify whether or not an interrupt request will be accepted.

interrupt, microcomputer—If an application involves asynchronous or unpredictable events, an interrupt capability on the processor is essential. Most units claim some form of interrupt capability, but only the newer units can handle several levels of prioritized interrupt. Most of the processors can handle single-line, multi-level, and vectored interrupts, and all their registers are automatically saved in the stack when an interrupt comes along. After the interrupt is serviced, the register contents are automatically restored.

interrupt module — In some systems, a specific device that acts as the monitor for a number of priority-designated field contacts and immediately notifies the computer when any of these external priority requests have been generated. This assures servicing of urgent interrupt requests on the basis of programmer-assigned priorities when requests occur simultaneously.

interrupt, parity (memory)—Each time control is given to the monitor, the memory parity trap is armed and the interrupt location is patched with an instruction. When a memory parity occurs, the computer halts at the location at which the parity occurred, with the console memory parity indicator light on (some systems).

interrupt, polled — With polled interrupts, the processor does not generate the interrupt acknowledge signal; rather, a programmed interrupt service routine interrogates the possible sources of the interrupt. The routine determines which sources originated the interrupts and establishes the priority of multiple requests.

interrupt priorities—Interrupt requests are frequently assigned priorities. Whenever two interrupts occur simultaneously, the one with the higher priority is considered first. Furthermore,

a higher-priority interrupt can interrupt the service routine of a lower-priority interrupt. Most microprocessors do not have built-in priorities, and these must be handled either with software or external hardware.

interrupt, processor—In many systems, processor interrupts are automatic procedures designed to alert the system to conditions arising that may affect the sequence of instructions being executed.

interrupt program, I/O — An efficient method of I/O handling that interrupts the processor whenever a peripheral device signals that it is ready for information transfer. The processor first stores the necessary information that will cause it to return to the present operating mode, then jumps to the routine appropriate for exercising the requested transfer. Upon completion of the I/O transfer, the processor restores either the previously running task or some other task, depending on priorities and available resources.

interrupt requests, jumper-selectable— Jumper-selectable interrupt requests can be automatically generated by the programmable peripheral interface when a byte of information is ready to be transferred to the CPU (i.e., input buffer is full), or when a byte of information has been transferred to a peripheral device (i.e., output buffer is empty). 2. Jumper-selectable interrupt requests can be automatically generated by the USART when a character is ready to be transferred to the CPU (i.e., receive channel buffer is full), or a character is ready to be transmitted (i.e., transmit channel data buffer is empty). 3. A jumper-selectable request can also be generated by each of the programmable timers.

interrupt response time—The elapsed time between interrupt and the start of the interrupt-handling subroutine is called the "response time." The difference between the total time elapsed and the actual execution time is referred to as the "overhead." Both times should be kept as short as possible.

interrupt, return from (microprocessors)—On return from an interrupt, the CPU must be returned to the state it was in before the interrupt occurred. This is often done by a specific instruction, Return from Interrupt (RTI). This brings the contents of the registers (especially the Program Counter) back from the stack, so that return to the main program can be accomplished. With a microprocessor, control lines other than the interrupt lines may be used as specific-purpose interrupts (in most systems they are).

interrupts, development systems — A bus generally communicates interrupt requests from one module to another in development systems. Interrupts, which may be generated by front-panel switches or by sources, such as external request lines connected to general-purpose I/O or DMA modules, are processed by the system's CPU. The user needs only to define the system responses to interrupts and assign priorities to ensure that contentions for interrupt service are handled unambiguously.

interrupt servicing, microcomputer — Some applications require that a peripheral device be serviced as soon as possible after some external condition has occurred. In some cases, especially when the microcomputer is not very busy, this can be done by program control. But, most frequently, it is necessary to establish some sort of interrupt structure that allows asynchronous external events to change the processing sequence. When interrupt facilities are not available, the only way to find out whether a device requires servicing is to interrogate it periodically by inputting a status bit and testing it. When the need for service is identified, the program branches to a special subroutine—at the end of which, the program returns to its regular operation.

interrupts, external—External interrupts originate with device controllers or interrupt modules on an I/O bus. An interrupt module provides the control of many external interrupt signals. Device controllers may generate interrupts to signify individual data transfers, end of operation, or error conditions. External interrupt systems may contain a single interrupt line, a priority line, and a select line. A device may initiate an interrupt request only if priority has been received from higher level interrupts on the priority chain. Devices not requiring interrupt

service will propagate priority to the next device in line.

Various events can lead to a program interrupt. Each interrupt is to a unique fixed memory address that is associated with the event that caused it. Addresses are reserved for these interrupts. Each external device has an interrupt address that is equal to its external device address. An external device may have more than one interrupt event and each event may have its own interrupt address. Some interrupts may occur only at the end of program instructions. It is important to the programmer that each type of interrupt results in transfer of control to a different memory address. This makes it unnecessary for the program to scan interrupt events to see what has happened. A subroutine for each interrupt event may be in the memory.

interrupt signal feedback—Refers to a steady signal indicating that an interrupt signal has advanced its associated interrupt level to the waiting or active state. The signal is dropped when the interrupt level is reset to the disarmed or the armed state.

interword gap—The time period and space permitted between words on a tape, disk, etc. Usually, such space allows for controlling specific or individuals words, for switching.

involuntary interrupt—Refers to an interrupt which is not caused by an object program but which affects the running of such a program. For example, the termination of a peripheral transfer will cause the operating system to stop the object program momentarily while the interrupt is serviced. Such an interrupt is involuntary.

I/O buffer—Permits data word transfer to and from memory to proceed without main program attention. May be programmed so that when I/O transfer is complete, the microcomputer generates an internal interrupt.

I/O bus lines—Parallel lines and control logic are referred to collectively as the I/O bus. They transfer information between microprocessor and I/O devices. The bus contains three types of lines: data, device address, and command. **Data lines** consist either of one bidirectional set or two unidirectional sets. In the latter case, one set is used exclusively for inputting of data to the CPU and the other for outputting of data. In most cases, the width of the bus—number of lines—equals the word length of the microprocessor. **Device address lines**

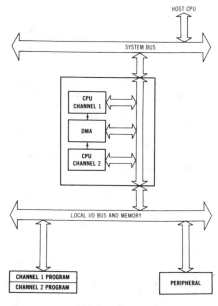

I/O bus lines.

are used to identify I/O devices. The theoretical maximum number of available address lines changes significantly from one microprocessor to another. **Command lines** allow a peripheral to indicate to the CPU that it has finished its previous operation and is ready for another transfer end.

I/O bus structures—I/O bus structures employ several schemes. Generally, the bus structures take three different forms: radial, party line, or daisy chain. A **radial system** is one of the simplest, but it limits the number of I/O units. A radial-bus system connects each I/O device to the microprocessor through a dedicated set of lines. It does not allow the connection of more than one I/O unit. A **party-line system** reduces the number of lines needed for a distributed system. The latter system also comes in a **daisy-chain** version, which connects devices serially.

I/O categories, microprocessor—Users can usually classify I/O lines into three broad categories: programmed, interrupt, and DMA. **Programmed I/O** covers most low-speed hardware, including human interaction devices (keyboards and programmer panels), which the operating software occasionally scans. **Interrupt I/O** requires a special microprocessor bus and services intermediate-speed devices. If an I/O function needs service, it interrupts the processor through the bus, redirects the processor, and processes the available data. Usually, this is a more efficient way to handle events, at least from a software point of view. Finally, a system needs **DMA I/O** when it must transfer data very quickly; for instance, when a peripheral must communicate directly with memory. Microprocessor software usually initiates a data transfer under program control and reports the finished condition under interrupt control. DMA takes control of the data and address buses and controls the actual transfer of data to or from memory.

I/O device control, executive—The executive program will often control operation of I/O devices using the I/O subsystem and device drivers that are part of the utility routines.

I/O hardware control—Hardware control of information transfer is used on many newer CPUs designed to accommodate it. The method requires a significant amount of additional hardware, since the I/O device must initiate and control the data transfer directly into or from microcomputer memory. Often the software support is limited to the initiation, termination, and recovery aspects of the transfer. These aspects are often performed automatically without microprocessor intervention. The hardware-control approach is also known as direct-memory access or data break. It can be used to transfer blocks of characters directly between a peripheral device—such as tape, cassette, or floppy disk—and the main microprocessor memory.

I/O (input/output)—Refers to devices, programs, or procedures for accepting or outputting information. As regards microprocessors specifically, package pins are tied directly to the internal bus network to enable I/O to interface the microprocessor with the associated equipment or programs.

I/O interface operation—An I/O interface provides the facility for transferring bytes over a party line I/O bus under microprogram control in some systems. Standard firmware provides both programmed I/O and concurrent I/O transfer capability, along with a priority interrupt system. Data transfers through the I/O interface are basically two-phase operations. During the first phase, a control byte is placed on the byte I/O bus before the actual transfer of data. The control byte contains a device address specifying the address of one of the I/O controllers connected to the bus, and a device order code signifying the type of operation to be performed during the transfer (data transfer, status/function transfer, etc.). In some systems, all controllers on the bus examine the device number, but only the controller with a matching address accepts the control byte and logically connects itself to the bus for the subsequent data byte transfer. During the second phase of the byte I/O operation, a single byte is transferred to or from the I/O controller. After each byte transfer, the controller disconnects itself from the bus.

I/O lines/ports—Microprocessor input/output (I/O) ranges from complex floppy-disk control peripheral chips to simple 8-bit (I/O) latches. The input and output facilities are the devices by which the CPU communicates with the external environment. If the microprocessor has an 8-bit internal structure, the I/O bus and each respective I/O port will also be organized for 8 bits. A port is a collection of individual I/O lines—their number is equal to the length of the basic microprocessor word. If a port is bidirectional, it can accept input or output, depending on the nature of the I/O command. Unidirectional structures are predetermined and can only accept one type of command. I/O ports that are "quasi" bidirectional allow input and output lines to be mixed on one port. This is convenient when the number of inputs and outputs are not even multiples of the basic word size.

ion implantation (I^2)—Refers to a process that can be used with all variations. It allows accurate control of do-

pants or impurities introduced into the silicon—in essence, a costlier, most controllable alternative to thermal diffusion. The process can selectively change the threshold voltage of MOS transistors to produce devices with no overlap capacitance. Although it has not yet demonstrated significant advantage in memories, I^2 is a potentially valuable processing tool, and may eventually be used to varying degree in all complex integrated circuits.

I/O port requirements (microprocessor) — To effectively distribute the processing load in a system, the intelligent I/O ports must have three characteristics: (1) The ability to request interrupt service from the independent monitoring of external control lines. (2) The ability to initiate DMA transfers from the independent monitoring of external control lines and the ability to signify completion of a DMA block transfer. (3) The ability to monitor data transfers for error conditions.

IOP selector—This is a particular input/output processing unit that performs bidirectional data transfer between main memory and high-speed peripheral devices. Up to 32 devices can be attached to a selector IOP, but the high data-transfer rates allow only one device to operate at a given time (some computers).

I/O scan—The time required for the pc processor to monitor all inputs and control all outputs. The "I/O scan" repeats continuously.

I/O section, microprocessor—The I/O section consists of the necessary buffering and control interfaces for connecting the system to I/O devices such as teletypes, terminals, and other types of peripheral devices. The I/O area needs very careful consideration during the process of selecting a microprocessor system. I/O inherently creates a bottleneck in small systems for applications that require heavy I/O activity. The user must analyze his intended applications carefully to assure a satisfactory ratio between processing and I/O, and to avoid having to build costly external I/O interfaces.

I/O spooling — Programs requiring a significant amount of communication with "slow" peripheral devices may have their data routed at high-speed transfer rates to the disk for later re-routing to the intended devices. This is called output spooling. The result is that tasks are completed faster, thus freeing main memory so other tasks may be executed. It also allows automatic storage of data on the disk if the intended device is nonoperational. In addition to output spooling, input spooling is available. This permits jobs and data entered through "slow" devices to be routed to the disk. When the spooled jobs are to be executed or when the spooled data is required, the executive program loads them from the disk into main memory.

I/O status/command words—A status word describes what the I/O device is doing. Each status-word bit indicates a particular condition, such as message data are ready for transmission, device is busy, device is unavailable, or transmission errors. However, in contrast, a command word controls the actual operation of the device. Each command-word bit has its own function, such as stopping the motor, incrementing a feed, or changing the transmission rate.

IPL — Abbreviation for initial program loader. An initial program load or a program that reads the supervisor into main storage and then transfers control to the supervisor.

ISAM files—Indexed sequential access method (ISAM) file management allows application software to file and retrieve records by alphanumeric name or "key." One classic use of ISAM is in a "mail list" application, where names and addresses are entered for retrieval and, typically, the family or company names are the "key" elements. Without ISAM capability, the burden of finding a given name in the file falls upon the end user or application software. A given name is entered, and the program searches the length of the file in pursuit of a match. Or, the user or program is burdened with determining that a given name is the nth entry in the file and so retrieves it. With ISAM files, the desired record is retrieved by "key" so that one simply enters the desired name (or key) and the O/S reads it directly from the file, "knowing" its exact location at all times. Application software is greatly simplified, and access to records is normally significantly faster.

ISL — Abbreviation for integrated Schottky logic. A newly emerging bipolar technology invented by Philips Gloeilampenfrabrieken of the Netherlands, and applied by its subsidiary, Signetics, in several proprietary products. These circuits combine the speed of Schottky technology with the high density and low power of I²L. ISL is not as dense as I²L, but it is about nine times denser than standard low-power Schottky circuits. The typical 0.88-pJ speed-power product is the lowest in the bipolar family and rivals that of complementary MOS (CMOS).

ISO (International Organization for Standardization)—ISO is the specialized international agency for standardization, at present comprising the national standards bodies of 86 countries. Only one organization in each participating country can be a member: the United States member body is ANSI. Participating members contribute to the work of the technical committees and have the power to vote for or against the approval of developed standards. Observer members can attend meetings but cannot vote. In addition, organizations such as CCITT participate as liaison members.

isolated I/O module — A module that has each input or output electrically isolated from every other input or output on that module. That is to say, each input or output has a separate return wire.

isolation, dielectric—The electrical isolation of one or more elements of a monolithic semiconductor integrated circuit by surrounding the element(s) with an insulating barrier such as semiconductor oxide.

isolation, junction—The electrical isolation of one or more elements of a monolithic semiconductor integrated circuit by surrounding the element(s) with a region of that conductivity type which forms a junction and, then, reverse biasing that junction.

isotropic, magnetic—A material having the same magnetic characteristics along any axis or orientation. Might be considered as the antonym of anisotropic.

I²L—A new kind of bipolar LSI, integrated injection logic (I²L) chips may contain as many as 3000 gates operating at less than 10-nanosecond speeds, and dissipating just 1 nanowatt of power per gate. Internal logic can be totally separated from the interface resulting in optimum density, correct logic interface; thus, ease of use for the system logic designs. These chips are appearing in electronic wristwatches and as single-chip controllers for industrial, automobiles, and computer systems. Some scientists feel that I²L, because of its tremendous speed-power ratios (100 times smaller than other bipolar logic), will have as much influence on the way logic is built as TTL had in the 1960s.

I²L logic devices—Integrated injection logic (I²L) is a bipolar technology spin-off. I²L combines the best of micro worlds — bipolar circuit speeds, MOS circuit densities, and one-hundredth of the power consumption of TTL circuitry. I²L devices are expected to be able to meet the stringent military specifications on vibration, acceleration, and moisture.

I²L microprocessors—One of the first LSI digital circuits built with nonisolated I²L logic was a microprocessor chip slice designated SBP 0400, which stands for "semiconductor bipolar processor, 400 series." It is a 40-pin 4-bit microprogrammable binary processor element containing more than 1450 gates—one of the most complex standard product bipolar logic chips built. Containing all the functions required for 4-bit parallel processing (except for sequencing controls), the features of the SBP 0400 could only be duplicated by using 30 to 40 small- and medium-scale TTL integrated circuits. The chip contains:

- A 16-function symmetrical arithmetic logic unit (an ALU that has full-carry look-ahead logic).
- An 8-word general-register file that includes a program counter and an incrementor.
- Two 4-bit working registers that can handle both single- and double-length operations.
- Scaled-shifting multiplexers enabling the chip to handle a wide variety of interface conditions.
- A factory programmable logic array (PLA) instead of the usual fixed-size control ROM. (This is perhaps the most innovative feature.) The 512 standard operations programmed into this on-chip logic array provide a greater degree of instruction capability than is achievable by any other standard bipolar or MOS LSI processor.

J

jack—1. A socket to which the wires of a circuit are connected at one end, and into which a plug is inserted at the other end. 2. A connecting device to which a wire or wires of a circuit may be attached and which is arranged for the insertion of a plug.

jack, data—User modems can now be connected directly to the telephone network instead of through the Data Access Arrangement (DAA) that formerly was rented from the phone companies. Various modems are equipped with a cable and keyed data jack that mates with the telephone jack. Bell Company, or other suppliers, install the data jack in walls or modem cabinets. Some types of Bell Company data jacks are programmable; a resistor inside the data jack determines the modem transmit level. Mechanically, the data jack provides a standard Bell Company 8-pin miniature connector with a keyway design.

jack panel—An assembly composed of a number of jacks mounted on a board or panel. *See* control panel.

JCL—Abbreviation for Job Control Language (IBM). A system which interprets instructions that are given to it by the user and then processes them in order to tell the central processor what to do with the user's program. Used on batch and time-sharing systems.

jitter—1. Short-time instability of a signal. The instability may be in either amplitude or phase, or both. The term is applied especially to signals reproduced on the screen of a cathoderay tube. The term "tracking jitters" is used to describe minor variations in the pointing of an automatic-tracking radar. 2. The maximum peak-to-peak value of the timing variations in synchronous data expressed as a percentage of the ideal bit period. 3. Refers to various shifts in the time or phase position of individual pulses, causing difficulty in synchronization and/or detection. Also called peak distortion.

J-K flip-flop—A flip-flop having two inputs designated J and K. At the application of a clock pulse, a "1" on the "J" input and a "0" on the "K" input will set the flip-flop to the "1" state. A "1" on the "K" input and a "0" on the "J" input will reset it to the "0" state. Placing "1s" simultaneously on both inputs will cause it to change state regardless of the previous state. Inputs of $J = 0$ and $K = 0$ will prevent any change.

job—Usually refers to an externally specified unit of work for the computing system from the standpoint of installation accounting and/or operating system control. A job consists of one or more job steps.

job control language—Specifies an environment in which a job is to be run, and the optional output desired.

job control program—A program that is called into storage to prepare each job or step to be run. Some of its functions are to assign I/O devices to certain symbolic names and set switches for program use.

job control, stacked — Under sequential-stacked job control, the jobs are performed in the sequence in which they are received by the system.

job entry subsystem, remote—A typical remote job entry (RJE) subsystem is an integrated subsystem that provides remote terminal emulation to other computer systems. On some systems, RJE consists of a communications handler, an appropriate protocol interpreter for each terminal emulation, and a remote job spooler for queueing RJE terminals. Most RJE terminals require operator interaction. The RJE subsystem performs most of the operator actions, yet it allows the user at a terminal to transfer normal status requests to the remote site and receive responses at the user's terminal.

job input stream — The input, usually consisting of tapes or diskettes, that is often the first part of an operating system. The stream contains the beginning of job indicators, directions, programs, etc.

job library—A concatenation of user-identified partitioned data sets used as the primary source of load modules for a given job.

job-oriented terminal — 1. A terminal especially designed to receive source data in an environment associated with the job to be performed, and capable of transmission to and from the system of which it is a part. 2. A terminal designed for a particular application.

job processing — The reading of job control statements and data from an input stream, the initiating of job steps defined in the statements, and the writing of system output messages.

job processing control — Job processing control program is generally part of the control section which starts job operations, assigns input/output units, and performs functions needed to proceed from one job to another.

job processing, master file—The master file contains the programs necessary for job processing. The programs in the master file are sectioned into four categories: (1) input/output drivers, (2) system programs, (3) utility routines, and (4) library subroutines.

job schedule—A control program that is used to examine the input work queue and is used to select the next job to be processed.

job statement control—Individual statements used to direct an operating system in its functions, as contrasted to information needed to process a job, but not intended directly for the operating system itself.

job step—A job step consists of the external specifications for work that is to be done as a task or set of tasks. It is also used to denote the set of all tasks which have their origin in a job step specification. A job stream consists of a set of computer jobs or job steps in an input queue awaiting initiation and processing.

job stream—*See* job step.

joint denial gate — Refers to a gate whose output is true when, and only when, all inputs are false. Same as NOR gate.

Josephson devices — Josephson devices are digital LSI circuits which operate as superconductors under very low temperatures. Heavily researched at IBM, the circuits are said to surpass silicon and gallium arsenide types in both circuit speed and system performance. These circuits are based on cryogenic operation at

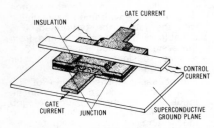

Josephson device, two-junction.

near absolute zero temperature (−273 °C). The Josephson technology was developed in 1962 by Brian Josephson, a British physicist, who predicted that if two superconductors could be separated by a sufficiently thin insulating layer, the insulator would act like a superconductor itself. The theory was verified by experiment. It was also found that the presence of a magnetic field in the insulator destroys the superconductivity. When this happens, current flow is accomplished by electron tunneling, and is accompanied by a voltage drop. The presence or absence of this voltage drop indicates the presence of a logical 1 or 0.

Josephson device, two-junction — This type of device construction allows the device to have low capacitance for high speed, but a high inductance for control sensitivity.

Josephson effect — In the most general state, it is the tunneling of electron pairs through a thin insulating barrier between two superconducting materials.

Josephson-junction memory cell — The prototype Josephson-junction memory cell contains two data junctions and a third sensing function. Write current, I_w, temporarily changes the magnitude of the current flowing in the loop and allows the sensing device to determine the current's original magnitude and direction—clockwise signifies a "one" and counterclockwise, a "zero."

Josephson junctions — A Josephson junction consists of two thin-film strips separated by a 30-Angstrom oxide barrier. Impressing a voltage across the barrier causes electrons to tunnel through it. If the junction is maintained above some critical temperature (T_c), the relationship between current and voltage is linear. If the junction is supercooled, however, electrons can tunnel even at zero voltage, and the current-voltage relationship becomes nonlinear. By sending control current (I_c) through a thin-film strip near the junction but isolated from it, users can vary the magnetic flux (ϕ) linking the junction and, thereby, vary the amount of current that flows at zero voltage.

The theory of Josephson junctions centers primarily on basic physical properties:

1. Certain materials, known as superconductors (for example, tin, lead, and niobium), when cooled to a temperature a few degrees above absolute zero (−273 °C), lose all resistance to the flow of electric current. If current is made to flow in a loop or ring of such material, it will flow continuously.

2. Magnetic flux cannot penetrate an "ideal" superconductor because shielding supercurrents are set up to oppose external magnetic fields. Consequently, magnetic flux can be trapped in superconducting rings, where it threads through a hole in the ring and is linked with persistent circulating currents in the ring.

3. If two superconducting materials form a junction with a very thin oxide layer (about 40 Å thick) sandwiched in between, the oxide, normally an insulating barrier, allows a current to flow by a tunneling mechanism. Although still in its infancy, Josephson junction technology has now reached the level where the capability for total digital computer technology—that is, for constructing all digital logic and

all necessary memories, both large and small—is within reach.

joule—Unit of work, energy, and heat in the MKS system, equal to work done when a force of 1 newton advances its point of application 1 m. One joule $= 10^7$ erg $= 0.2390$ calorie.

joule effect — 1. Production of heat solely arising from current flow in a conductor. 2. Slight increase in the length of an iron core when longitudinally magnetized. *See also* magnetostriction.

joystick—The stick or lever that can be tilted in various directions to control or indicate direction of movement of cursors, game activities, and other movement or measurement. A typical joystick's position is converted into X and Y coordinate signals that move the cursor to the indicated spot. Because the range of motion of most joysticks is small, precise positioning with them may be more difficult than with a trackball.

jump—The Jump instruction or operation, like the Branch instruction, is designed to control the transfer of operations from one point to another point in a control or applications program. Jumps differ from Branches by avoiding the use of the Relative Addressing mode (in most microprocessors). The jump is a departure from the normal one-step incrementing of the program counter. By forcing a new value or address into the program counter, the next instruction can be fetched from an arbitrary location, either farther ahead or behind. A program jump can be used to go from the main program to a subroutine, from a subroutine back to the main program, or from the end of a short routine back to the beginning of the same routine to form a loop. *Also see* branch.

jump, conditional — *See* conditional branch and conditional jump.

jump instruction—A computer instruction causing a jump in the sequence of instructions. *See* branch.

jump instruction, conditional—*Same as* conditional branch.

jump instruction, conditional transfer— *See* conditional branch.

jump operation—The computer departs from the regular sequence of instruction executions and jumps to another routine or program, or even to some preceding or forward instructions to alter control, repeat a process or loop, etc.

jump routine — A routine designed to have the microcomputer depart from the regular sequence of instruction executions and jump to another routine or program, or even to some preceding or forward instructions to alter control, repeat a process or loop, etc.

jump to subroutine instructions—Some systems offer special jump instructions that jump to subroutines and return via addresses stored in the E register. This method of return via a hardware register decreases subroutine and interrupt overhead. Using a register also permits subroutines to be executed in ROM.

jump, unconditional — *See* unconditional branch.

junction—1. A connection between two or more conductors, or two or more sections of a transmission line. 2. A contact between two dissimilar metals or materials. 3. The contact interface surface or immediate area between n-type and p-type semiconductor materials. Transistor action takes place at the junction of these differently doped materials.

junction circuit—One directly connecting two exchanges situated at a distance apart, but less than that specified for a trunk circuit.

junction diode—1. A two-terminal device containing a single crystal of semiconducting material which ranges from p-type at one terminal to n-type at the other. It conducts current more easily in one direction than the other and is a basic element of the junction transistor. When fabricated in a specific geometrical form, it can be used as a solar cell. 2. One formed by the junction of n- and p-type semiconductors, which exhibits rectifying properties as a result of the potential barrier built up across the junction by the diffusion of electrons from the n-type material to the p-type. Applied voltages, in the sense that they neutralize this potential barrier, produce much larger currents than those that accentuate it.

junction summing—Refers to computing amplifiers or operational amplifiers and to various input impedances that are connected each from a separate input terminal of a unit to a common point which is called a summing junction. This summing junction is connected to the feedback impedance.

junk—A slang expression that refers to a garbled or otherwise unintelligible sequence of signals or other data, especially as received from a communications channel, i.e., hash or garbage.

justification—The act of adjusting, arranging, or shifting digits to the left or to the right to fit a prescribed pattern.

justified margin—Arrangement of data or type printed on pages in such a manner that the left or right end characters of each horizontal line lie in the same column.

justified, right-hand—When a quantity in storage or in a register has no zeroes in the low-order (right-hand) positions, it is considered right-hand justified.

justify — 1. To adjust exactly, as by spacing; to align a set of characters horizontally (or vertically) to right or left margins. To develop an exact format or spacing in words, fields, items, or data as designed by context of exact specifications. 2. To move a data item so that a particular part of the item assumes a particular position relative to some reference point in a storage medium; for instance, to adjust the print on a printed page so that the left, right, or both margins are aligned; also to shift the item in a register to position specifically the most or least significant digit.

justify, right—To format a right margin for the type on a printed page. More difficult and expensive than left justification.

juxtaposition—The positioning or placing of items adjacent to each other or side by side.

K

K—1. Symbol for cathode or dielectric constant. 2. Abbreviation for Kelvin or kilo. 3. A symbol which is equivalent to the numeral 1024. For example, 8K would be equivalent to 8192.

Kansas City Standard—Early standardization has been of great benefit to personal computing. A meeting of manufacturers and technical editors in Kansas City produced the so-called "Kansas City Standard" for computer data encoding on standard audio cassettes using standard cassette recorders. The computer interface required is simple and inexpensive. By using audio cassettes, a hobbyist can easily store long programs, such as a BASIC interpreter, and load them into his computer in less than 30 seconds.

Karnaugh map—Usually a chart or an arrangement in tabular form which facilitates combination and elimination of duplicate logical functions by listing similar logical expressions.

kernel—The lowest level of an operating system; creates and destroys software processes used to implement abstract processes. The kernel is the root of an operating system's supervisory section. One software process can request that this kernel create another process. The kernel also serves to allocate resources to individual processes. Software processes can exist as unrelated units, in which case, they are generally created as needed and subsequently destroyed. In a kernel mode of operation, the operating system and programs have complete control and execute all instructions.

key — 1. A group of characters usually forming a field, utilized in the identification or location of an item. 2. A marked lever, manually operated, for copying a character, e.g., a typewriter paper-tape perforator, a card-punch manual keyboard, digitizer, or manual-word generator. 3. That part of a word, record, file, etc., by which it is identified or controlled. 4. The field by which a file of records is sorted into order, e.g., the key for a file of employee records by a number, department, or letter.

key, actual—A data item, in the COBOL language, which can be used for a machine address and which will express the location of a record in a storage medium.

keyboard—A device for the encoding of data by key depression, which causes the generation of the selected code element

keyboard and display control—Refers to various systems that provide up to 64-key (and more) strobing, key debounce, 2-key rollover protection, multiple key buffering, and character display buffers with automatic segment/digit strobing.

keyboard, ANSI — The American National Standards Institute keyboard is a typewriter-standard unit that offers a choice of upper-case characters only or upper-case and lower-case combined. By contrast, the Data Communications (ASR-33) keyboard offers only upper-case and some punched-tape control functions.

keyboard, ASCII — A full 128-character ASCII keyboard includes 96 upper- and lower-case letters, the numbers, and a symbol printing set, plus 32 control characters.

keyboard, ASR—ASR is the abbreviation for automatic send-receive. This keyboard is modeled after the standardized teletypewriter unit, a 33-key communications-compatible alphanumeric device. The control characters are used for special functions such as moving the cursor or shifting the keyboard into a mode for defining or calling symbols.

keyboard classes — Keyboards fall into two basic types — alphanumeric and numeric. Alphanumeric keyboards are used for word processing, text processing, data processing, and teleprocessing. Numeric-only keyboards are used on accounting machines and calculators.

keyboard, companion — An auxiliary keyboard device that is usually located remotely from the main unit.

keyboard components layout — Most available keyboards incorporate single-contact switches followed by an encoder, in order to eliminate the effect of noise and switch bounce and to convert the key closures into ASCII code. There are two types of key arrangements—typewriter and data entry. The latter, a calculator-style alphabetic arrangement and numeric keypad, provides greater speed and lower error rates for nontypists. For users who touch-type long text messages, the typing keyboard layout proves superior. In either system, the keytops should be dished inward to home the typist's fingers.

keyboard computer—A computer, the input of which employs a keyboard (possibly an electric typewriter).

keyboard contact bounce — The momentary (and decreasing) rebounds occurring between two contact surfaces suddenly thrust together, before they attain firm closure. As a switch rating, bounce is stated as a time interval required for reaching firm closure after the initial closure.

keyboard control keys — On most crt terminals, control keys move and control the cursor, switch the terminal from one application to another, switch the communication disciplines, and cause the performance of other functions.

keyboard, detachable — Crt terminals are available in two basic configurations. They can be supplied either with an integral or with a detachable keyboard. The detachable keyboard allows the operator to position the keyboard for maximum ease of operation and allows the video display to be built into a console if desired. The free-standing crt (not built into the console) allows the unit to be added to an existing system with as little difficulty as adding a typewriter. Furthermore, it offers the advantage of easy maintenance by permitting the rapid replacement with a spare unit.

keyboard, display console — 1. Some keyboard consoles make possible interpretive operations. Often a particular job is assigned by the computer program and the keys for that job are identified by removable illuminated overlays. 2. An operator control panel for those processors where the display is used in place of the typewriter control console.

keyboard editing display station—Keyboard displays are valuable tools for on-line program debugging and/or editing. Programs are displayed on the keyboard/display station with mnemonic and location in a format identical to the programmer's coding sheet, a "page" of coding at a time.

The editing features of the keyboard/display station are used to make corrections to the program. The programmer may "thumb through the pages" of his program stored in memory just as he can thumb through his coding sheets. In a data-acquisition system, the keyboard/display station may also be used for a "quick-look" display of test data or results as the test progresses. The ability to address locations on the keyboard/display station screen by the computer permits the output of only the changing information by the computer at a very rapid per character rate, rather than requiring a complete "page" of information for each change. This light demand on computer time permits a continuous presentation of important test parameters as they change (some systems).

keyboard encoder—A typical encoder identifies each key and mode with a simple binary number. The ideal keyboard encoder would be a single chip with programmable operational parameters. Requirements for four critical functions are involved in the design approach to a keyboard encoder: keyboard scanning, key debouncing, key encoding, and indication of key data availability. The rate at which a keyboard encoder scans keys determines to a large extent the size of the keyboard (number of keys) to which the encoder can be linked. Two basic scanning operations may be performed simultaneously to increase scanning speed to a more useful rate. This involves scanning the keyboard and scanning (or debouncing) a particular key at the same time.

keyboard features—Keyboards are the part of the terminal that interfaces with the operator. They should be designed in a manner that makes the operator as comfortable and efficient as possible. The most important design features are: layout, N-key rollover, edit keys, function keys, numeric pad, and control keys. Many suppliers offer terminal function keys that make it possible to strike one or two keys to call out strings of characters and formats, send a unique distinct code to the computer which may represent any amount of data, or which can conveniently activate the terminal peripherals.

keyboard, hardware encoded—A hard-

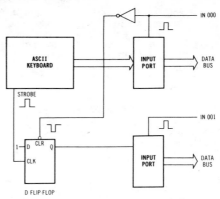

Keyboard, hardware encoded

ware encoded keyboard, regardless of the type of keys (metallic contact, Hall effect, capacitive), produces a unique code for each key (ASCII, EBCDIC, binary, or BCD). The encoder section of the keyboard also produces some sort of strobe pulse, or logic-level change, to indicate that a key is pressed. However, the encoding logic will not only produce a unique key code, but will also transmit the code as an asynchronous serial character.

keyboard overlays—1. Some keyboard consoles make possible interpretive operations. Often a particular job is assigned by the computer program and the keys for that job are identified by removable illuminated overlays. 2. An operator control panel for those microprocessors where the display is used in place of the typewriter control console.

keyboard send/receive set—Abbreviated KSR. A combination transmitter and receiver with transmission capability from keyboard only.

keyboard, touch-sensitive membrane—Available in both custom and standard designs, the monopanel keyboards offer many options previously unavailable in the keyboard industry. Utilizing touch-sensitive membrane technology, the boards are designed for a long trouble-free life. Lack of any mechanical-linkage wearout problems further enhances keyboard reliability. The layer construction of the boards incorporates a tough membrane with a conductive rear surface. Contact closure is effected when the membrane is moved approximately 0.005 inch. A 2- to 4-oz. touch sensitivity is required for switch operation.

keyed sequential access method (KSAM)—A file structure and a group of library routines which together allow users to directly read records from a file, based on content of key fields, or in sequential order, based on the ordering of key field contents.

key, index—As regards indexing, a field within an entry that is used to locate the entry. For example, surnames are the key field for the entries of a telephone directory.

keypad—A small keyboard or section of a keyboard containing a smaller number of keys, generally those used on simple calculators. These 10-, 12-, or 16-key units are often either the simplest input devices to microcomputers or they function as an extension of ASCII keyboards to permit a more extensive computational capability.

keypad, numeric — On some systems, this is used in the alternate-keypad mode. Numeral, decimal point, and enter keys transmit unique escape sequences, distinguishing them from alphanumeric keys.

key, symbolic — In COBOL, contrast with actual key.

keyword—1. Refers to various significant or informative words in a title, abstract, body, or part of the text that generally are utilized to describe a document. A keyword or set of keywords may describe the contents of a document, label the document, and/or assist in identifying and retrieving the document. 2. Refers to the word in a high-level language statement line that defines the primary type of operation to be performed.

keyword-in-context (KWIC)—An index that lists available computer programs in alphabetical order with entries for each keyword in the title. There is an index entry for each significant keyword in the title. Certain words are not accepted as indexing words but will be printed as part of the title. A KWIC index is prepared by highlighting each keyword of the title in the context of words on either side of it and aligning the keywords of all titles alphabetically in a vertical column.

keywords—The most informative words in a title or document which describe the content of that document; the significant words.

kilo—A prefix meaning one thousand. Its abbreviation is K; e.g., 8K means 8000. In computer use, it also refers to the "power of two" closest to a number; e.g., a 4K-word memory is actually 4096 words.

kit, breadboard—In general, a collection of parts and sockets (and full instructions) designed for insertion into a breadboard. These usually come with an assortment of sockets for custom circuitry. A number of circuit kits are available which allow the user to add special functions to the modular microcomputer system. Such kits are available for interfacing to ASCII keyboards, to 8-bit parallel TTL input/output sources, to the ASR-33 teletypewriter, and to other makes of printers.

Kipp relay — A widely used alternative name for a monostable multivibrator, i.e., a circuit that has one stable, or quasi-stable state, and one unstable state, and which undergoes a complete cycle of change in response to a single triggering excitation.

Kirchhoff's law—The law which states that: (1) The current flowing to a given point in a circuit is equal to the current flowing away from that point, (2) The algebraic sum of the voltage drops in any closed path in a circuit is equal to the algebraic sum of the electromotive forces in that path, and (3) At a given temperature, the emissive power of a body is the same as its radiation-absorbing power for all surfaces.

KSR—*See* keyboard send/receive set.

KWIC — A permuted title index based upon use of keywords or phrases extrinsically or automatically identified. (*See also* keyword-in-context.)

L

label—1. A set of symbols used to identify or describe an item, record, message, or file. Occasionally it may be the same as the address in storage. 2. A code name that classifies or identifies a name, term, phrase, or document. 3. Various labels are concerned with, or correspond to, numerical values or memory locations in tapes, disks, etc. The specific absolute address is not necessary, in most cases, because the intent of the label is a general destination. Labels are a requisite for jump and branch instructions as regards to software.

ladder diagram—An industry standard for representing control logic relay systems.

language—A defined set of characters that are used to form symbols, words, etc., and the rules for combining these characters into meaningful communications, e.g., FORTRAN, C, COBOL, ALGOL, English, French, etc.

language, absolute—*Same as* machine language.

language assembler, microprocessor—A microprocessor language assembler is often a paper-tape (or disk) oriented system that is used to assemble a source code on a microcomputer and convert it into a binary output that is then loaded and executed on the CPU module. Input to the assembler is usually prepared with the aid of an assembler program; source text can, however, be generated off-line on a time-sharing terminal.

language, assembly — Instructions include machine operation codes and symbolic addressing. Assembly languages are used to avoid coding directly into machine code; mnemonics are used for both the command instructions and the operands, and it is usually not necessary to label the address for every instruction. The output may be absolute or relocatable. The assembly language can feature page-free programming, fixed and floating-point pseudo-operations, and the ability to reserve storage with a COM statement. Assembly programs generate in a one-to-one fashion a set of machine-coded instructions, as contrasted to a compiler, or macro language, wherein one compiler instruction can generate many machine instructions.

language, direct-execution—One type of architecture is a microcomputer that directly executes high-level languages. Directly executing means without a separate compilation step. Instead, a circuit built into the microcomputer interprets each high-level statement directly. Such microcomputers are called direct-execution computers and are distinguished from others in that they neither compile nor assemble a program into object code. The high-level program is the only program. This architecture is extremely useful from two points of view. From the software viewpoint, high-level programs can be debugged without the compile/assemble process, thus speeding the programming activity. From the hardware viewpoint, the design is optimized for the high-level language and executes it quickly.

language features — The features of most languages accepted by a compiler or interpreter are intended to enable the programmer to express: (1) The Data Objects or Structures, their descriptions, their attributes, their groupings, their memory allocations, and a myriad of other characteristics (these correspond to nouns, adjectives, and descriptive phrases in natural language), (2) The Operations or Commands that act upon the data structures (these correspond to verbs and adverbs), and (3) Control Structures that specify the flow of control or sequencing of operations (these correspond to building of statements, conditional phrases, paragraphing, sectioning, and forming of chapters, etc.).

language interpreter — A general term for any processor, assembler, or other routine that accepts statements in one language and produces equivalent statements in another language.

language list, assembly—Refers to a listing that contains the symbolic instructions equivalent to the binary-code output of the compiler. This assembly-output listing is useful as a debugging aid. By including certain pseudo-operation codes in in-line assembly language, the assembly-language output can be assembled by the assembler (if output is obtained on either disks, paper tape, or magnetic tape). This will allow modification of programs at the assembly-language level.

language rules — Most language rules are basically designed to: (1) Prevent the programmer from making nonsensical or disallowed statements of computer operations, and (2) Allow a "shorthand" method for commonly made code sequences. Additionally, translators themselves have control options that invoke or specify various services that contribute to the programmer's efforts — like object code listings and data maps.

languages, hardware-based — Various manufacturers are setting their own language trends and are developing hardware-based languages. This is an expanding market that is making special-purpose language chips practical. In addition, applications programs can be put in ROMs, which makes them hard to pirate or tamper with. Many manufacturers are following that route and producing "applications boxes," similar in concept to the calculator plug-in modules made by Texas Instruments Incorporated. These applications boxes or plug-in modules are multiprogram "solid-state software" devices that are used in calculators, games, etc.

language, source — The original symbolic language in which a program is prepared for processing by a computer. It is translated into object language by an assembler or compiler.

language transition — In the hierarchy of programming, languages can be represented as a sphere. In the center is the machine code, and each layer that is farther away from the center is closer to human language.

language translator—1. A program that converts a language to equivalent statements in another computer lan-

(A) Calculator module.

(B) Back view of calculator.

Languages, hardware-based (Courtesy Texas Instruments Inc.).

guage, usually for a different computer. 2. A routine that aids in the performance of natural language translations, such as French to English. 3. Any assembler or compiling program that brings forth the same or equivalent output from human-readable statements.

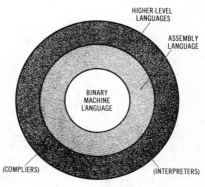

Language transition.

large-scale integration (LSI) — 1. The accumulation and design of a large number of circuits on a single chip of a semiconductor. Characteristic of many CPU circuits and memories introduced since 1970. 2. A concept whereby a complete major subsystem or system function is fabricated as a single microcircuit. In this context, a major subsystem or system, whether digital or linear, is considered to be one that contains 100 or more equivalent gates, or circuitry of similar complexity.

laser—1. An acronym for Light Amplification by Stimulation of Emission of Radiation. Sometimes called an optical maser. An amplifier and generator of coherent energy in the optical, or light, region of the spectrum. 2. A device which transmits an extremely narrow and coherent beam of electromagnetic energy in the visible light spectrum. 3. The laser is an intense light source. Light from a laser is all the same frequency, unlike the output of an incandescent bulb. Laser light is referred to as *coherent,* and has a high energy density. It can travel great distances without diverging from a tight beam.

laser-annealed solar cells—A processing breakthrough that may eventually have a significant impact on the energy crisis is laser annealing of semiconductor junctions. Recent research indicates that it is a key to extremely efficient photovoltaic conversion. Solar cells made with laser-annealed ion-implanted silicon have been found to exhibit efficiencies almost 50% greater than those of thermal-annealed cells. And, unoptimized laser-annealed cells are only slightly less efficient than those made with the most sophisticated (and, therefore, the most expensive) diffusion techniques.

laser annealing—Annealing is the process of removing the ''damage'' caused to the crystal lattice by the implanted ions. In thermal annealing, the implanted sample is heated to several hundred degrees for 30 minutes or longer and allowed to cool slowly. Laser annealing is accomplished simply by illuminating the implanted sample through laser radiation of the correct wavelength, energy level, and pulse duration. The energy is heavily absorbed in a surface layer

that is a few hundred to a few thousand Angstroms thick, causing very high local temperatures (even melting), which creates the annealing effect but, unlike thermal annealing, does not affect the rest of the substrate. Another advantage is that laser annealing does not need any special ovens or even controlled environments. It can be done in air because the surface cools so rapidly that undesirable impurities are not trapped. And, laser annealing is much faster than the thermal method.

laser creation—The basic requirements for the creation of a laser are quite simple: a material that can absorb and release energy, an energy source for exciting this material, and a container to hold and control the lasing action, such as a glass tube or a solid crystal. In the actual lasing process, the laser material is placed inside the container, and then stimulated by means of an energy source into the emission of light waves. The laser beam is created by channelling the energy of these light waves into a particular and controlled direction. The result is a highly concentrated brilliant beam of tremendous power.

laser diodes—Gallium-aluminum-arsenide double-heterojunction laser diodes are characterized by a very low threshold current and may be operated in either the cw or high duty-cycle mode at room temperature. Their wavelength peak emission of 820 nanometers is well matched with the spectral characteristics of most commercially available glass fibers as well as with silicon photodiodes. The laser diode may be operated directly from a commercial power supply. However, before such operation is effected, the power supply should be thoroughly checked for transients. Exposure of the diode to even very brief transient current spikes can cause irreversible device failure. Safe operating considerations require that the device be protected by connecting a resistor (5 to 10 ohms) in series with the laser diode. Laser diodes are ideal for very high data-rate system applications requiring a very small coherent light source, such as fiber optic communications and holographic memories.

laser-emulsion storage—Refers to various types of digital data storage media which use a controlled laser beam to expose very small areas on a photosensitive surface, thereby producing desired information patterns.

laser, helium-neon—The versatile low-power helium-neon laser is about the size of an ordinary flashlight, just as simple to operate, and has a working life of many thousands of hours. Basically an electron tube filled with a combination of helium and neon gas, the helium-neon laser produces a very intense narrow beam of coherent red light that retains its diameter over long distances. This beam can be manipulated, controlled, and detected quite easily. By expanding or focusing the beam with simple optical elements, the desired spot size can be achieved at almost any distance.

laser noise — Generally, sources of noise can contribute to fluctuations in the output of a laser. Some noise sources include the microphonic types of noise caused by vibrations due to coolant flow or acoustic pickup, as well as noise due to discharge fluctuations, competition between modes of oscillation, or air currents within the laser cavity. Before selecting a laser, users should check laser noise against that required by their system in an environment as close to the operating one as possible.

laser systems, chip processing — In ion-implantation processes, a wafer is subjected to high temperatures, yet the dopant still migrates into the wafer relatively slowly and might not go where required. However, use of a laser can actually turn the wafer's silicon surface molten. While the surface is in this temporary state, the dopant migrates seven orders of magnitude faster than through solid silicon. This capability to selectively enhance dopant migration could give rise to a technique to anneal-out the damage produced by ion implantation. During the wafer-probe stage, it would be possible to "fix" bad dies that would otherwise be discarded. Ultimately, the use of lasers could prove an even more dramatic development for microlithography than the introduction of either E-beam or X-ray production systems. It is possible to eliminate all ion implantation, masking, and etching by using only a laser to drive dopants into a wafer. Whether

such dopants should be solid, liquid, or gaseous has not yet been determined. If current programs prove fruitful, the result could be a totally dry, precisely controlled, semiconductor-fabrication process that uses 75% fewer steps than now used.

laser trimming — Laser trimming depends on several different technologies besides those required to initially fabricate the circuit. Trimming is primarily concerned with layout, geometry, the mechanism and physics for material removal, and the measurement means for terminating the trim process. Resistor layout and geometry are determined before the wafer is fabricated. The laser and its operation establish the mechanisms and physics of material removal as well as trim termination procedures.

latching—Arrangement whereby a circuit is held in position, e.g., in readout equipment, until previous operating circuits are ready to change this circuit. Also called locking.

latching logic—Refers to a signal modification that causes an output to energize and remain energized (maintained output). Latched output may be immediate or delayed.

latency—1. The time required by a digital computer to deliver information from its memory. 2. In a serial-storage system, the access time minus the word time. 3. The time spent waiting for the desired location to appear under the reader, or disk heads, or at the end of an acoustic coupler.

latency time—1. Refers to the time lag between completion of instruction staticizing and the initiation of the movement of data from its storage location. 2. The rotational delay time from a disk file.

lattice dynamics — Mechanics of the properties of the thermal vibrations of crystal lattices.

lattice filter—One or more lattice networks acting as a wave filter.

lattice network — 1. A network composed of four branches connected in a series to form a mesh. Two nonadjacent junction points serve as input terminals, and the remaining two as output terminals. 2. One formed by two pairs of identical arms on opposite sides of a square, the input terminals being across one diagonal and the output terminals across the other;

also called bridge network, lattice section.

lattice spacing (or parameter)—Length of the edge of a unit cell in a crystal.

lattice vibration—Vibration of atoms or molecules in a crystal due to thermal energy.

layout — Refers to the overall plan or design such as schematics, flowcharts, diagrams, format for card columns or fields, outline of the procedure, makeup of a book or document, etc.

LCD — Abbreviation for Liquid-Crystal Display. A liquid-crystal display consists of a thin sandwich, or cell, of two glass plates with sealed edges, containing nematic liquid-crystal material. Transparent electrodes are deposited on the inner surfaces of the glass plate in the shape or shapes of the segments and areas that form the display. When voltage is applied to the front and back electrodes, the molecular orientation of the liquid-crystal material between them is altered, modifying the amount of light that can pass through it.

leader—1. An unused or blank length of tape at the beginning of a reel of tape preceding the start of the recorded data. 2. Some records which precede a group of detail records give information about the group not present in the detail records, e.g., beginning of batch 10.

leader record—A specific record containing the description of information contained in a classification or group of records, which follow this initial document.

leapfrog test—Refers to a unique program designed to discover computer malfunction, characterized by the property that it performs a series of arithmetical or logical operations on one group of storage locations, transfers itself to another group of storage locations, checks the correctness of the transfer, and, then, begins the series of operations again. Eventually, all storage positions will have been occupied and the test will be repeated.

learning, computer — That process by which computers modify programs according to their own memory or experience, i.e., changes of logic paths, parameter values. An example is the chess-playing computer. In process-

control, an analog computer can alter its parameters by a continuous process according to temperatures or other gauge reports it receives. Examples are adaptive autopilots for aircraft, which explore different alternatives.

learning, machine—The capability of a device to improve its performance based on its past performance.

leased lines—Refers to a communications line reserved for the exclusive use of a leasing customer without interexchange switching arrangements. Also called a private line. Leased or private lines are dedicated to the user. Their advantage is that the terminal or computer is always physically connected to the line. Very short response times are met with this service. This service is billed on a 24-hour-a-day, 7-day-a-week basis, or as based on number and destination of "packets" on these type systems.

left justify—To format a left margin for the type on a printed page. Typewriters produce left justified copy.

length, block—The total number of records, words, or characters contained in one block.

length, field—The physical extent of a field. On a punch card, it refers to the number of columns. On a tape, it refers to bit positions.

length, interrecord gap—The length of the unused recording area between records written by the unit.

length, record—The number of characters necessary to contain all the information in a record.

length, register—The number of digits, characters, or bits that a register can store.

length, string—The number of records in a string.

level—1. The magnitude of a quantity in relation to an arbitrary reference value. Level normally is stated in the same units as the quantity being measured (e.g., dB—as in blanking level, transmission level, etc.). 2. Refers to the power relationship between different circuits, or different parts of the same circuit. The level at some particular point is the gain or loss of power, expressed in decibels (dB) between that point and some arbitrary reference point. The level at the reference point is zero. 3. In describing codes or characters, it is synonymous with bit, element, or channel (for example, the "levels" or rows of recorded information on paper tape). 4. A COBOL term indicating the status of one data item relative to another; indicates whether one item includes subsequent ones or whether, as reflected in the numbering scheme which must follow certain rules, data items are independent of each other. 5. The number of bits in each character of an information coding system. 6. The number of discrete signal elements that can be transmitted in a given modulation scheme.

level-enable signal—Refers to a signal generated by the CPU for the purpose of changing the state of the level-enable flip-flop from 0 to 1.

leveling zone — An analogous process to zone refining, carried out during processing of semiconductors in order to distribute impurities evenly through sample.

librarian — A program that creates, maintains, and makes available the collection of programs, routines, and data that make up an operating system. Librarian functions may include system generation and system editing.

library—Refers to a collection of standard and proven routines and subroutines by which problems and parts of problems may be solved, usually stored in relative or symbolic coding. (A library may be subdivided into various volumes, such as floating-decimal, double-precision, or complex, according to the type of arithmetic employed by the subroutines.)

library, basic software—A comprehensive library of utility software is available for many microcomputers. A typical library includes: loading and debugging programs, text editor, resident assembler, floating-point package, cross assembler, PROM programming software, tape conversion program, and a multiply/divide package.

library file editor—Some systems use a library file editor that lets users combine compiler or assembler output to form binary libraries. The result is a set of central updatable program libraries that eliminate program duplication.

library, macro—An assemblage of prepared and specialized but unparticu-larized programs, which are located in mass storage and which may be selectively found by an assembler that reads them, particularizes them by replacing general parameters with specific parameters, and incorporates them into programs.

library, object program — See library program.

library program—An assemblage or organized set of computer programs, routines, or common or specifically designed software, i.e., catalog of program titles, abstracts, etc., reels of magnetic tapes or cabinets of disks, tape containing various programs or routines, source or object programs classified for intelligence or retrieval, etc.

library routine — 1. An ordered set or collection of standard and proven routines and subroutines, usually stored in relative or symbolic coding, by which problems and parts of problems may be solved. (A library may be subdivided into various volumes, such as floating-decimal, double-precision, or complex, according to the type of arithmetic employed by the subroutines.) 2. A checked-out routine which may be incorporated into a larger routine and is maintained in a library as an aid to programmers. 3. A routine for building and maintaining a library of special programs and subroutines. It is capable of inserting, deleting, changing, or replacing routines in the library. With this routine, the library may be altered at will to conform to individual customer requirements.

library subroutine — A set of standard and proven subroutines which is kept on file for use at any time.

library tapes—Library tapes will have tape labels, skip records, and CMs (control marks) exactly as outlined for data tapes. However, the programs themselves must be stored on magnetic tape according to a particular format. Library tapes may contain two types of intermixed formats—standard format (running programs as set up by the librarian), and debugging format (this includes check data as well as the programs to be checked). Various CMs are used in this intermixing of formats.

library tracks—Tracks used to store reference data, such as titles, key words, document numbers, etc., on tapes, disks, or mass storage devices.

library, user — A basic library of general-purpose software is furnished by manufacturers to perform common jobs; to this, the user can add his own often-used programs and routines. Programs in the library can be conveniently assembled into an object program by the use of macroinstructions.

LIFO — 1. Refers to push-down stack procedures and is the acronym for last in/first out, a buffer procedure. 2. A queue discipline wherein the newest entry in a queue or file is the first to be removed.

LIFO stack — A data-storage structure in which new items are added to the top of the existing stack in a LIFO (last in/first out) fashion. Often used for subroutine linkages. A register contains the address of the current top-of-stack.

light gun—*See* light pen.

light, logic—*See* logic light.

light pen—A high-speed photosensitive device that can cause the computer to change or modify the display on the cathode-ray tube. As the pertinent display information is selected by the operator, the pen signals the computer by generating a pulse. Acting upon this signal, the computer then instructs other points to be plotted across the tube face in accordance with the pen movements, or it can exercise specific options previously programmed without the need for separate input devices. 2. A hand-held light-sensing device that detects the crt beam when pointed toward a portion of the screen. Routines are provided to allow the user to point the light pen at objects or instructions on the screen for identification or control purposes. In addition, a facility may be provided for light-pen tracking, which allows the user to point at a tracking object displayed on the screen and move it rapidly anywhere across the screen. 3. A hand-held reader for bar-code labels and tags.

light pen attention — An interruption generated by a light pen when it senses light on the screen of a crt display device.

light pen attributes—1. When the pen-like device is pointed at information displayed on the screen, it detects light from the cathode-ray tube (crt) when a beam passes within its field of view. The pen's response is transmitted to the computer which, in turn, relates the computer action to the section of the image being displayed. In this way, the operation can delete or add text, maintain tighter control over the program, and choose alternative courses of action. 2. An optional device, when used in conjunction with the incremental display, can greatly extend its usefulness. It is a high-speed, photosensitive device with which the operator can cause the computer to change or modify the display on the cathode-ray tube. As the pertinent display information is selected by the operator, the pen signals the computer by generating a pulse. Acting upon this signal, the computer can then instruct other points to be plotted across the tube face in accordance with the pen movement.

light pen operation—A light pen is a special kind of pointer used with cathode-ray tube (crt) displays. Using the light pen, an operator can select, draw, or modify pictures on the crt by means similar to using a conventional pen to draw on paper. The power of the light pen lies in the intimate relationship between the operator, the display, and the supporting computer. Operations that would be awkward on paper (erase, scale a figure, replicate, etc.) are done swiftly with the computer to perform the necessary calculations. The light pen is an effective and popular means of interfacing the human to the display-computer combination. Available light pen systems include two parts: the physical hardware, which turns out to be relatively simple, and the supporting software system, which can be arbitrarily complex. A sophisticated light pen system is pleasing to the human in the sense that the response time to execute commands is "acceptable" and that the operator need not be particularly aware of, or knowledgeable about, the intricacies of the programs. When this is done, the operator can concentrate on his task and use the light pen as a flexible extension of his finger. Using a low-cost graphics computer system that is suitable for laboratory and real-time (immediate response) applications, an operator

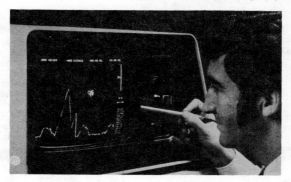

Light pen operation (Courtesy Digital Equipment Corp.).

can test real-life activities, such as guiding a "lunar module" across jagged mountain peaks in a simulated moon flight.

light pen systems—A light pen system consists of two parts: hardware and software. The hardware is easily described. The physical light pen is a cylindrical object the size of a fountain pen. One end is linked by an umbilical cord to nearby electronics; the other end contains an exposed light-detecting device such as a photodiode or phototransistor. A lens may be placed before the light sensor to collect and focus light on the active area of the sensor. The pen is held loosely in the hand and aimed at the crt screen. The function of the pen is to detect the presence of light within its field of view and to generate a narrow electrical pulse that can be fed to the computer as an interrupt signal.

The purpose of this signal can be seen by considering the software. A display file exists in the computer memory which represents a graphical entity. This file is read sequentially by the computer and the output is fed to the graphics console where each record is interpreted as a drawing command and suitable deflection signals are fed to the crt. The picture is sketched on the tube face as rapidly as possible and is made visible by the action of the electron beam on the phosphor coating of the tube. The transient light response of the phosphor requires that the display file be scanned cyclically and at a rate sufficient to prevent objectionable flicker.

At any given instant of time, the computer is pointing to a single record in the display file and the graphics console is concurrently sketching the corresponding picture element.

"lightpipe" fiber optics—A typical fiber optic data transmission system converts electrical pulses to light pulses that are then conducted by an optical fiber (sometimes called a "lightpipe") and received by a detector which reconverts the light into electrical data. This simple trio of components comprises a *link*. A link can be considered as a "black-box" from which the output data is a replica of the input data.

One approach used to detect signals from fibers is to include a short piece of fiber in the detector package. One end of this integral lightpipe is placed close to the detecting surface; the other end is accessible at the outside of the package. This method has the following advantages:

1. The detector can be hermetically sealed inside the package.
2. Coupling losses between the lightpipe and the detector surface are minimized.
3. This system is compatible with most fibers.
4. The lightpipe is sufficiently large that coupling losses between it and the fiber are small.
5. This system effectively makes the accessible end of the lightpipe the detecting surface, thus all characteristics can be referred to this surface.

light sensitive—Said of thin surfaces of which the electrical resistance, emission of electrons, or generation of a current depends on the incidence of light.

light sensors — The simplest type of light sensor, the cadmium sulfide photocell, undergoes a change in its electrical characteristics when subjected to light. With a response time longer than that of other types of light sensors, it has color sensitivities that suit it to high-sensitivity applications. The solid-state photodiode provides a much faster response than the photocell, although it is somewhat less sensitive to light. A compromise between these two devices, the phototransistor provides a greater sensitivity to light than the photodiode, and it can detect very fast pulses of light.

light, storage—The light on a control console panel which indicates that a parity check error has occurred on a character as it was read into storage.

light, tape—A light usually found on the control console which indicates an error during the read or write cycle.

limited integrator—Refers to a specific arrangement or setup which involves an integrator that has characteristics such that the inputs cease to be integrated when the output tends to exceed specified limits. In a hard-limited integrator, the output does not exceed the limits, while in a soft-limited integrator, with limited precision, the output may exceed the limit.

limiter — Any transducer in which the output, above a threshold or critical value of the input, does not vary, e.g., a shunt-polarized diode between resistors. Particularly applies to the circuit in a frequency-modulation receiver in which all traces of amplitude modulation in the signal have to be removed before final demodulation. A bridge limiter is a bridge circuit used as a limiter circuit. In an analog computer, a feedback limiter is a limiter circuit usually employing biased diodes that shunt the feedback component of an operational amplifier; and an input limiter is a limiter circuit usually employing biased diodes in the amplifier input channel that operates by limiting the current entering the summing junction.

linear—Having an output that varies in direct proportion to the input.

linearity—1. The relationship between two quantities when a change in a second quantity is directly proportionate to a change in the first quantity. 2. Deviation from a straight-line response to an input signal. 3. A constant ratio of cause and effect (as in a straight line representation).

linear magnetostriction — Under stated conditions, the relative change of length of a ferromagnetic object in the direction of magnetization when the magnetization of the object is increased from zero to a specified value.

linear program — Refers to an algorithmic program used to develop a class of problems satisfied by a set of solutions, the requirements being to select the least costly (or the most profitable) solution belonging to the set.

linear resistor — One which "obeys" Ohm's law, i.e., under certain conditions, the current is always proportional to voltage. Also called ohmic resistor.

line bias — Refers to the effect of the electrical characteristics of a transmission line on the length of teletypewriter signals.

line code—A single instruction written usually on one line, in a code for a specific computer to solve a problem. This instruction is usually stored as a whole in the program register of the computer while it is executed, and it may contain one or more addresses of registers or storage locations in the computer where numbers or machine words are to be obtained or sent, and one or more operations to be executed.

line conditioning—This refers to adjusting the properties of the communications line to prevent the signals from getting too far out of shape. Conditioning a line involves physically attaching electrical components to it, so it cannot be done on the switched network unless those components are built into the modem. For Bell System leased voice-grade lines, C1, C2, C4, D1, and D2 conditioning is offered. Bell's Long Lines Division recently began offering B1 and B2 conditioning as well, both of which are usually employed only for short-haul transmissions. In any case, if conditioning is required, line costs go up; to avoid this, many modems incorporate "equalization" circuitry that effectively accomplishes the same purpose by tuning the modems to the existing lines.

line control block—An area of main storage containing control data for operations on a line. The line control block can be divided into several groups of fields, and most of these groups can be identified as generalized control blocks.

line discipline—Relates to distinct procedures which act to adjust the operating parameters of transmission systems to achieve correct or desired line control values; includes considerations of contention, polling, queuing priority, etc.

line equalization—*See* line conditioning.

line printer — A type of high-speed printer capable of producing an entire line at one time. All characters of the alphabet are contained around the rim of a continuously rotated disc, and there are as many discs as there are characters in the line. A computer momentarily stops the discs at the right characters for each line, and stamps an impression in a fraction of a second. Generally, high-speed line printers will provide a printed output at the rate of 1000 alphanumeric lines per minute or more. The control of skipping is accomplished by either program control or by means of a punched-tape control loop on the printer. An automatic-interrupt feature for optimum time-sharing is a part of the printer, allowing processing time to be shared between print cycles.

line printer controller—A low-cost line printer controller can be completely software compatible and transparent to host computer. The controller is often a single printed-circuit board that fits into one quad slot in the computer chassis. Boards come with ribbon cables and with mating connectors furnished for connection to the line printer. There are many controller/printer packages available. A typical line printer controller gives users a total line printer capability with no change in system software. The user plugs in the module and connects his line printer through the ca-

ble furnished. Many controllers are completely compatible with host computer diagnostics, driver, and operating systems.

link — 1. A type of transmitter-receiver system connecting two locations. 2. In computer technology, the part of a subprogram that connects it with the main program. 3. In automatic switching, a path between two units of switching apparatus within a central office. 4. In some systems, a link is a 1-bit flip-flop that serves as a high order extension of the accumulator (ACC). It is used as a carry flip-flop for two's complement arithmetic.

linkage — 1. Specific instructions that are related to the entry and re-entry of closed subroutines. 2. The instructions that connect one program to another, providing continuity of execution between the programs.

link bit — Refers to a specific 1-bit diagnostic register that contains an indicator for overflow from the accumulator and, usually, from other registers It can be tested under program control.

link editor — Most minicomputer language compilers and an increasing number of microcomputer compilers support modular software development. Each code module is written and complied separately. The final program consists of several modules linked together by a special utility program (called a linker, linking loader, or link editor). Although this procedure is intended to enable designers to divide the functions of their final products into smaller more easily manageable projects, it also provides a key performance tool to the real-time software designer.

linked list—A list formed by tying together (with pointers) several items such as directory entries.

linker—*See* link editor.

link indicator — Some link indicators display the content of the 1-bit link register.

linking loader—1. The bootstrap loader can be used to load a linking loader into main memory. The linking loader is a relocatable loader—it completes memory address calculations that were partially processed by the relocatable assembler, allowing users to load and execute a program anywhere in core. 2. With the typical linking loader, any number of programs may be loaded with one command, relocatable modules may be loaded in user specified locations, and external references between modules are automatically resolved. The loader performs library searches for system subroutines and generates a load map of memory that shows locations of main program and subroutines. A cross-reference facility prints out an alphabetic listing of all program variable names along with line numbers and where they are referenced and defined (on some systems). 3. *See also* linking editor.

liquid crystal display — Producing an image, digital or otherwise, requires a conductive surface in the shape of the desired image on the front glass plate. When the liquid in the display is not electrically excited, its long cigar-shaped molecules are parallel to one another in a position perpendicular to the plates. The liquid appears transparent. When an electric current is applied, current flowing from the conductive image through the liquid crystal to the common ground backplate causes the liquid to change from clear to a frosted appearance in the current-carrying areas. Ion activity of the molecules leads to turbulence causing the liquid to scatter incident light. Depending on the type of nematic liquid used, either a dynamic scattering or field-effect display results. The images almost always are in the form of seven segments formed on the front glass with transparent oxide and with each segment having its own electrical lead. Energizing the proper segments produces the desired numerals. Lead-ins connect the segments to the external contacts on the sandwich (display).

liquid photoresists—Liquid photoresists are photosensitive materials used for etching patterns through masks on semiconductor surfaces and thin films. Both negative and positive resists are available. In a negative-resist application, ultraviolet light is shone through a photomask onto a resist-covered surface. The resist film beneath the clear areas of the photomask undergoes a physical and chemical change that renders it insoluble in· the developing solution. In a positive-resist system, the iden-

tical action produces areas that are soluble in a developing solution. At the present time, more than 85% of resist applications use the negative type.

LISP—LISP is an interpretive language developed for manipulation of symbolic strings and recursive data. LISP in an acronym for *list* processing. While the language has been developed to aid in the handling of symbolic lists, it can be and has been used successfully in the manipulation of mathematical and arithmetic logic. LISP and the techniques incorporated into it are the tools that have become popular in the development of higher-level languages. LISP lends itself quite readily as a language in which languages including itself may be written. The LISP expressions are evaluated within an interpretative routine and return the value of the expression. This interpreter accepts the first argument as the function to be applied, while the second argument is the value or list values to which the function is to be applied and the interpreted value returned.

listing, assembly — Refers to a printed list which is the by-product of an assembly procedure. It lists in logical instruction sequence all details of a routine showing the coded and symbolic notation next to the actual notation established by the assembly procedure. This listing is highly useful in the debugging of a routine.

list processing—Refers to a method of processing data in the form of lists. Usually, chained lists are used so that the logical order of items can be changed without altering their physical locations.

list processing languages — Refers to specific languages developed for symbol manipulation and used primarily as research tools rather than for production programming (i.e., LISP). Most have proved valuable in construction of compilers and in simulation of human problem solving. Other uses have been generalization and verification of mathematical proofs, pattern recognition, information retrieval, algebraic manipulation, heuristic programming, and exploration of new programming languages.

list processing structures—A programming technique in which list structures are used to organize memory. In list processing, computer memory is organized into several lists, or structures of data items. Each list has a symbolic name, a header or starting record, and some number of entries. The header contains (among other things) the address of the first data entry in that list. Each data entry contains one or more related data items and the address of the next entry in this list. The last entry cannot contain a successor address, so it may have either an end-of-list signal or the address of the header record. The header is in a known location and serves to give the list processor a fixed starting location when searching or operating on that list. Initially, all memory is organized into an empty-space list. The lists are created in space removed from this master list, and may be destroyed by returning memory addresses to the empty-space list.

list, pushdown — Generally refers to a list of items that is maintained in a stack and operates in a LIFO (last in/first out) order. Each item is effectively pushed down by the addition of a new item.

list structure — A specific set of data items combined because each element contains the address of the successor item or element, i.e., a predecessor item or element. Such lists grow in size according to the limits of fixed storage capacity, and it is relatively simple to insert or delete data items anywhere in a list structure.

literal—1. A symbol which names itself and which is not the name of something else. 2. A symbol or quantity in a source program that is itself data rather than a reference to data. 3. A character, or group of characters, used in a COBOL program to represent the value literally expressed. Thus, the literal 7 represents the value 7, whereas, seven is a name that could be used to represent the value 7.

literal operands — Refers to operands, most often in a source language instruction, that specify precisely the value of a constant rather than an address in which the constant is stored. This method enables the coding to be written more concisely than

if the constant had been allocated a data name.

load—1. The power consumed by a machine or circuit in performing its function. 2. A resistor or other impedance which can replace some circuit element. 3. To fill the inner storage of a computer with information obtained from auxiliary or external storage. 4. The process of reading the beginning of a program into virtual storage and making necessary adjustments and/or modifications to the program so that it may have control transferred to it for the purpose of execution. 5. To take information from auxiliary or external storage and place it into core storage.

load and go—A computer operation and compiling technique in which pseudo-language is converted directly to machine language and the program is then run without the creation of an output machine language.

load and store, central processing unit — The central processing unit, on some systems, contains the electronic logic to perform operations such as:

> LOAD — Load the contents of a memory byte and store it in the 8-bit accumulator. Memory is read bit by bit, and as each bit of the memory byte is read, the next sequential accumulator bit will be set or reset to reproduce the status of the memory bit just read.
> STORE—Store the contents of the 8-bit accumulator in a memory byte. This will be the reverse of the load process.

A computer will perform a variety of other operations.

load control—A procedure designed to prevent thrashing by measuring the utilization of processors and backing storage, and (if necessary) preempting processes to reduce the computational load.

loader—A program that operates as or on input devices to transfer information from off-line memory to on-line memory. There are a number of capabilities that a loader must have in order to be effective and useful:

> 1. It must load a string of bytes into memory, storing words into designated memory addresses.
> 2. It must check that each byte was correctly transmitted by the in-

put device. (Usually it makes a parity check.)

3. It must insure that each word is a valid instruction, part of an instruction, or data. This is done by checking special format codes that were imbedded into the byte string when it was recorded.

4. It must check that the right number of bytes were read. Usually, this number is recorded along with the program (e.g., as the first two bytes).

5. It must convert relocatable addresses to absolute memory addressed, depending on where in memory the program is being loaded.

6. It must satisfy external references. For example, if program A references a label in program B, then the loader must provide program A with the actual memory address of the program B label.

loader, initial program—The procedure that causes the initial part of an operating system or other program to be loaded in order that the program can then proceed under its own control. Contrast with bootstrap. Abbreviated IPL.

loader routine—A routine generated automatically according to a programmer's specification and included in an object program to perform, respectively, program-loading operations and a printout of memory content upon request.

loaders and linkage editors (microprocessors)—Loaders and linkage editors perform a number of services for the programmer. Generally they take machine code or object code as input, along with possible programmer commands, and produce the desired "memory image." Their characteristics are influenced by the available translators and the machine architecture. Relocating loaders are needed with assemblers that can generate relocatable object code. Linkage editors are needed when the assembly language allows for reference across object modules. If separately assembled (or compiled) subroutines are allowed, subroutine linkages must be accomplished. Loaders can be considered a form of translator.

loader types—A number of microcom-

puter loaders are available to complete various coding processes. Many types can be stored in ROMs. Assembled programs are often loaded into read-only memory. They can also be loaded into RAMs, in which case, a bootstrap type is often used. A relocating loader automatically adjusts program addresses and loads the resulting instructions. Some loaders have linking capability that lets users employ routines with undefined labels. These types supply the missing cross-references between separate routines.

loading (bootstrap)—1. Refers to a particular routine placed in storage for the purpose of reading into storage another program, routine, or various data. 2 A single subprogram that loads a complete object program.

local memory — A high-speed RAM memory used to store sequential data patterns that cannot be generated by a hardware pattern generator. Local memory often includes the capability to process data stores in RAM as if they were instructions, thereby modifying data in the buffer.

location counter—1. The control section of a microcomputer that contains a register with the address of the instruction currently being executed. 2. The control section register that contains the address of the instruction currently being executed. 3. A register in which the address of the current instruction is recorded. Synonymous with instruction counter and program address counter.

lockout—A portion of the buffer cycle in which the logic or arithmetic unit must cease operation or neither will be able to communicate with the memory unit.

lockout module—An electronic circuit that prevents keying of more than one keyboard output signal at a time. When two or more keys are depressed simultaneously, it either accepts only the first signal registered or prevents entry of all signals and transmits an error signal to warn the operator.

log—1. Refers to the process of recording everything pertinent to a machine run, including identification of the machine run, recording the alternation switch settings, identification of input and output tapes, copy of manual key-ins, identification of all stops, and a record of the action taken on all stops. 2. A collection of messages that provides a history of message traffic. 3. To print and record one or more values. The values might be the instantaneous values of input variables or of averaged or calculated values.

logger—1. Arrangement of thermionic valves for obtaining an output indication that is proportional to the logarithm of the input amplitude or intensity. Required in modulation and noise meters. 2. Colloquialism for recorder or printout device in control system. 3. A type of instrument which automatically scans conditions such as pressure, temperature, and humidity, and records (logs) the findings on a chart. 4. A device which automatically records physical processes and events, usually with respect to time.

logic—1. As regards microprocessors, logic is a mathematical treatment of formal logic using a set of symbols to represent quantities and relationships that can be translated into switching circuits or gates. Such gates are logical functions, such as AND, OR, NOT, etc. Each such gate is a switching circuit that has two states, open or closed. They make possible the application of binary numbers for solving problems. The basic logic functions electronically performed from gate circuits are the foundation of the often complex computing capability. 2. The science dealing with the criteria or formal principles of reasoning and thought. 3. The systematic scheme which defines the interactions of signals in the design of an automatic data processing system. 4. The basic principles and application of truth tables and the interconnection between logical elements required for arithmetic computation in an automatic data processing system. Related to logic, symbolic.

logical circuit—1. A group or set of logic elements interconnected or integrated to carry out the design of the processing task as part of the total computer logic design. 2. One of many types of switching circuits such as AND gates, OR gates, NAND gates, etc., that can perform various logic operations or represent logic functions.

logical decision—One that is made on data in accordance with criteria previously inserted into an electronic computer by a program.

logical diagram—A diagram representing the logical elements and their interconnections, but not necessarily their construction or the engineering details of an overall logic design.

logical element—1. The smallest building block in a computer or data processing system that operators can still represent in an appropriate system of symbolic logic. Typical logic elements are the AND gate and the "flip-flop." 2. Refers to that circuitry which provides an output resulting from the input of two variables.

logical file—1. A data set that is composed of one or more logical open records. 2. A data file that has been described to the disk or tape operating systems through the use of a file-definition macro instruction. Note that a data file is described to the operating system through a different defining method. Operating system publications refer to a data file that is described in this different manner as a data set.

logical flowchart—Relates to the particular detailed solution of the work-order or arrangement in terms of the logic or built-in operations and characteristics of a specific machine. Concise symbolic notation is used to represent the information and describe the input, output, arithmetic, and logical operations involved. The chart indicates types of operations by using a standard set of block symbols. A coding process normally follows the logical flowchart.

logical operations—1. The operations in which logical quantities, such as yes-no decisions, quantities expressed as zeros and ones, etc., make comparisons, decisions, and extractions. 2. Operations in which logical (yes-or-no) quantities form the elements being operated on (e.g., comparison, extraction). A usual requirement is that the value appearing in a given column of the result shall not depend on the values appearing in more than one given column of each of the arguments.

logical relation—Relates to assembler programming. A logical term in which two expressions are separated by a relational operator.

logical shift—A shift in which the sign is treated as another data position.

logical sum—1. A result, similar to an arithmetic sum, obtained in the process of ordinary addition, except that the rules are such that a result of 1 is obtained when either one or both input variables are a 1, and an output of 0 is obtained when the input variables are both 0. The logical sum is the name given the result produced by the inclusive-OR operator. 2. The result of an (inclusive-OR) operation.

logical symbol—A symbol used to represent a logical element on a graph.

logic analysis — The delineation or determination of the specific steps required to produce the desired output or intelligence information from the given or ascertained input data. The logic studies are completed for many computer processes, programs, or runs.

logic analyzer clock rate—A logic analyzer's clock rate, which determines the highest unit-under-test speed the analyzer can handle, has a different meaning for logic-state analyzers from that for logic-timing analyzers. In state analysis, clock rate is the maximum permissible pulse-repetition rate of the unit under test. In timing analysis, the clock rate is the rate at which samples of the input waveform are taken. The clock rate determines how narrow a glitch the timing analyzer can capture and display.

logic analyzer multiline analysis—Logic analyzers examine the activity on each line of a data bus. Some units have a capability in which the display for each line can be shifted to make timing measurements easier.

logic analyzers—1. A logic analyzer is a multichannel instrument that captures, records, and displays logic signals of operating digital systems. There are two basic types: data-domain (or logic-state) and time-domain analyzers. A data-domain instrument displays a block of data on a crt in binary form (ones and zeros) with either a hexadecimal or octal readout. Some instruments also provide a logic map (dot matrix signature) for the circuit under test. A time-domain analyzer displays the captured data as quasi-waveform (square-wave) pulse trains. Instruments with waveform recording capability display true signal waveforms for troubleshooting analog problems. 2. Logic analyzers generally fall into three categories: state analyzers, timing analyzers, and trigger generators. State analyzers display digital data, in the form of 1s and 0s on a cathode-ray tube or via light-emitting diodes, in a word-versus-event format. This concentration on word sequences makes state analyzers useful in examining the functional behavior of binary systems. They are especially useful in the design of microprocessor-controlled digital products for examining the flow of command and data words on multiline buses. 3. Logic analyzers are most useful in the first steps of troubleshooting—locating the problem. By examining the sequence of events leading up to a failure, an engineer can usually identify the most likely sources of the problem . . . the "where." More detailed testing to pinpoint the exact cause of the failure — the "why" — usually requires a more detailed analysis of such parameters as timing relationships and logic voltage levels. This often concerns just a few signal lines, and can be carried out by logic-timing analyzers or oscilloscopes. In deciding which logic analyzer is most appropriate for a given testing problem, the important features to look for include the number of channels that can be viewed simultaneously and the ease of connecting to these input channels, the maximum logic speed that the analyzer can handle, and the independence of the analyzer from other instruments.

logic card—Refers to a group of electrical components and wiring circuitry mounted on a board that allows easy withdrawal and replacement from a socket in the equipment. Each such card is related to a basic machine function and, on discovery of a bug in that function, the card can be replaced.

logic circuit—Refers to various types of switching circuits, such as AND, OR, and NAND gates, that can perform various logic operations or can represent logic functions. The prime function of any logic circuit is to provide a logic output to one or more loads in response to logic input. The ideal logic-coupling network should provide high isolation between the input and output, and should introduce as little signal delay as possible. Power dissipation should also be kept low, and the higher the level of integration, the more reliable and efficient the logic becomes.

logic clips—Logic clips fasten directly on integrated circuits and read the states of all pins simultaneously. This means that users can see the state of each pin by glancing at the individual LED associated with that pin. Thus, users are provided with HIGH and LOW state indications for an entire IC at once. Using a logic clip, the relationship of inputs to outputs becomes very clear. Users step a counter or shift register through a complete cycle and verify the outputs, resets, clears, and other signals. (A hand-held pulser is a valuable stimulus tool for this type of testing.) The clip quickly shows if a device is following its truth table, or if a logic fault exists. Logic clips are easy to use; there are no controls to set, adjustments to make, or external signal connections to hook up.

logic comparators — A way to track down failed devices is with a logic comparator. These instruments detect functional failures by comparing the in-circuit IC with a tested good device. Logic comparators operate on the simple principle that a known-good IC can act as a standard against which to measure the in-circuit performance of ICs that are suspected to be faulty. This means that users can check dozens of ICs quickly—an IC at a time — to detect and "map" functional failures on a faulty circuit board. The comparator performs this function by comparing the output responses of a reference IC against an in-circuit test IC and displaying subsequent errors in performance — pin by pin. Comparators connect the test and reference IC inputs in parallel, so the reference IC is exercised by the same signals as the test IC. Any differences in the outputs are detected and displayed, usually by a LED lamp corresponding to the failed pin. Thus, an IC output pin that does not correctly follow its inputs will produce an error indication, even when the error is a short-term (200 ns) dynamic fault. This also means that the inputs do not have to be correct to verify the operation of an IC, allowing use of the comparator in circuits such as digital feedback loops, where troubleshooting is very difficult at best. Perhaps the comparator's most useful function, though, is to increase the user's confidence that a fault has been tracked down to the IC that caused a problem.

logic design—The analytical detail of the working relations between the parts of a system in terms of symbolic logic and without primary regard for its hardware implementation.

logic diagram engineering—A specific logic diagram that has been referenced or addended with detailed information relating to circuitry, chassis layout, terminal identification, etc., and showing gates, circuits, etc., used in the logic as well as the types and ratings of the circuit elements. An engineer's usual approach begins with a set of functional specifications, which he translates into a block diagram and then reduces to the level of individual gates. The completed design is assembled on a breadboard, built into a prototype, and then, with a series of tests and redesigns, reduced to a form that can be manufactured in volume and sold at a profit. Meanwhile, it may be undergoing simulation on a computer as part of the design refinement.

logic, diode-transistor — Abbreviated DTL. The earliest form of integrated circuit, combining a diode and a transistor in a monolithic structure.

logic element — 1. A set of circuitry which provides an output resulting from an input of two variables. 2. A device that performs a logic function.

logic, emitter-coupled — Abbreviated ECL. A logic circuit in which the circuit generates its own clock pulse, independently of the clock pulse, for logically preceding or following circuits. This allows different circuits to work at their own speeds and not be dependent on a clock pulse which must run at the speed of the slowest circuit.

logic family—Group of digital integrated circuits sharing a basic circuit design with standardized input-output characteristics.

logic flowchart—Relates to procedures and details of the necessary steps for solution of work and their order or arrangements in terms of the logic, or built-in, operations and characteristics (of a specific machine). Concise symbolic notation is used to represent the information and describe the input, output, arithmetic, and logical operations involved. The chart indicates types of operations by use of a standard set of block symbols. A coding process normally follows the logical flowchart.

logic, formal—Concerns a branch of logic that deals with the study of the structure and forms of a valid argument without regard to content.

logic gates — An electrical component capable of performing a logical operation is called a logic gate. A gate may have multiple input signals but only one output signal: 1 (true) or 0 (false).

logic instruction — An instruction that executes an operation that is defined in symbolic logic, such as AND, OR, NOR, and NAND.

logic-level converter — Also called a logic-level translator. A circuit used to convert logic voltage levels of one family to the corresponding logic levels of another family, such as from ECL to TTL.

logic levels—1. Nominal voltages which represent binary conditions in a logic circuit. 2. The voltage magnitudes associated with signal pulses representing ones and zeroes ("1" and "0") in binary computation.

logic light — The control console light that indicates that an error has occurred in an operation.

logic operations—1. Refers to various logical or Boolean operations on n-state variables which yield a single n-state variable. 2. The operations of logical shifting, masking, and other nonarithmetic operations of a computer.

logic operator — Refers to the many switching operators or gates such as AND, OR, NAND, etc.

logic probe—A logic-testing tool easily shared in the lab and one that can also handle field-service requirements. Logic probes are designed to simplify logic testing by giving the user a direct readout of logic levels without the set-up and calibration time needed by logic analyzers and oscilloscopes. Logic probes use one or more lamps to indicate whether a point in a digital signal path is at a logic 1, a logic 0, or is toggling between these levels. Some units, for example, use three lamps—red for 1, white for 0, and blue for toggling. The relative brightness of the red and white lamps gives some indication of the signal's duty cycle, and all-lamps-off indicates the absence of logic signals (an open lead, perhaps). Other units use a single lamp—on for 1, off for 0, and blinking at a 10-Hz rate for toggling. A constant half-brightness indication means no signal is present.

logic pulsers — Logic pulsers briefly drive circuit nodes to the logic state opposite their present states. Pulse widths are usually tenths of a microsecond—short enough to prevent destroying the logic under test. Since logic pulsers cannot drive a point tied directly to the power-supply voltage or grounded to the opposite state, placing a pulser and a probe on one point and finding no change in state on application of a pulse can uncover those short-circuit conditions and eliminate many gate faults from suspicion.

logic shift—1. A type of shift in which all bits or characters are treated the same, i.e., no special consideration is made for the sign position as in an arithmetic shift. 2. A shift that affects all positions.

logic symbols — 1. A symbol used to represent a logic element graphically. 2. A symbol used to represent a logic operator.

logic, transistor-transistor — Abbreviated TTL. An integrated circuit in which two transistors are combined in one monolithic structure. These circuits are generally faster, easier to construct, and hence cheaper than DTL circuits.

long instruction format—An instruction which occupies more than one standard instruction position of length (e.g., a two-word instruction); the second word may be used for address modification or as an operand.

longitudinal current—A current which flows in the same direction in both wires of a parallel pair, the earth being its return pattern.

longitudinal magnetization — In magnetic recording, magnetization of the recording medium in a direction essentially parallel to the line of travel.

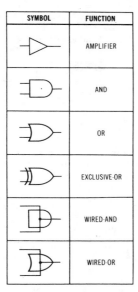

SYMBOL	FUNCTION
	AMPLIFIER
	AND
	OR
	EXCLUSIVE-OR
	WIRED-AND
	WIRED-OR

Logic symbols.

look ahead—Basically, this is a feature of the CPU that permits the machine to mask an interrupt request until the following instruction has been completed. This is also a feature of adder circuits and ALUs that permits these devices to "look ahead" to anticipate that all "carries" generated are available for addition.

look-up, binary — Relates to various techniques designed for finding a particular item in an ordered (sequence) set of items. This is accomplished by repeatedly dividing in half the portion of the ordered set containing the sought-for item until only the sought-for item remains. Binary searching is several times more efficient than sequential searching, even when the number of items is relatively small.

look-up, table—Refers to a procedure for obtaining the function value corresponding to an argument from a table of function values.

loop—1. Basically a self-contained series of instructions in which the last instruction can modify and repeat itself until a terminal condition is reached. The productive instructions in the loop generally manipulate the operands, while bookkeeping instructions modify the productive instructions and keep count of the number of repetitions. A loop may contain any number of conditions for termination. The equivalent of a loop can be achieved by the technique of straight-line coding, whereby, the repetition of productive and bookkeeping operations is accomplished by explicitly writing the instructions for each repetition. (Synonymous with Cycle [verb] 2.) 2. A communications circuit between two private subscribers or between a subscriber and the local switching center.

loopback test—Refers to a type of test in which signals are looped from a test center through a data set or loopback switch and back to the test center for measurement.

loop checking—Refers to a procedure for checking the accuracy of transmission of data in which the received data are returned to the sending end for comparison with the original data, which are stored there for this purpose.

loop, closed—1. Concerns a signal path in a control system that is represented as a group of units connected in such a manner that a signal started at any point follows a closed path and can be traced back to that point. 2. A control arrangement where data from the process or device being controlled is fed to the computer to affect the control operation; i.e., the computer can perform all control functions without intervention of an operator.

loop code—Refers to the repetition of a sequence of instructions by using a program loop. Loop coding requires more execution time than would straight line coding but will result in a savings of storage space.

loop computing functions — Those instructions of a loop which actually perform the primary function of the loop, as distinguished from loop initialization, modification, and testing, which are housekeeping operations.

loop counter — Relates to assembler programming in which a counter is used to prevent excessive looping during conditional assembly processing.

loop error—An error related to departure of the loop output signal from the desired value. If used as the loop actuating signal, it is known as the loop error signal.

loop feedback signal—Concerns that part of the loop output signal that is fed back to the input to produce the loop actuating signal.

loop, hysteresis—Concerns a graphical representation centered around the origin of rectangular coordinates, depicting the two values of magnetic induction for each value of magnetizing force — one when the magnetizing force is increasing, and one when the magnetizing force is decreasing.

looping—Refers to the repeating or recursive nature of many types of programs and instructions, often performed at delayed speeds until a final value is determined. Many looped repetitions in microprocessors are burned into ROM and are then jumped to when required. Looping occurs when the CPU is in a wait condition, or as a result of programming errors and machine malfunctions.

loop operation — Refers to a loop that has an associated set of instructions which restores modified instructions or data to their original or initial values at each entry to the loop, or to a loop that has a sequence of instructions which may be obeyed repetitively.

loop program—Refers to a specific series of instructions that are repeated until a terminal condition is reached.

loop system—A closed system in which the microcomputer controls an external program or process without human intervention. An example of a closed-loop process-control system would be a microcomputer connected directly to instrumentation through a digital-to-analog converter in order to complete the feedback loop. The computer could then take control directly of the process by setting controllers, activating switches, opening valves, etc.

loop testing—Refers to those instructions of a loop which determine when the loop function has been completed.

low-level language — 1. A language close to the machine code of a computer, whose instructions usually bear a one-to-one relationship with machine code. 2. One in which each instruction has a single corresponding machine code equivalent.

low order—That which pertains to the weight or significance assigned to the digits farthest to the right within a number; e.g., in the number 123456, the low-order digit is six. One may refer to the three low-order bits of a binary word as another example.

low-order digit—A digit that holds the low weighted position in a numeral in a positional notation system.

LSI—Large-scale integration refers to a component density of more than 100 per chip.

LSI microprocessor—An LSI microprocessor is essentially a complete system on one chip, or at most a few chips. Sometimes called a microcomputer, the system normally consists of a CPU, a RAM, an I/O, and a ROM. The ROM is predesigned and can be customized by programming.

In examining the semantics of microprocessing, it should be pointed out that the CPU was introduced first. Most people call the combination of CPU with a ROM and a RAM a microprocessor. Some LSI microprocessor systems are complete sets with no interfacing circuitry needed, and they contain a variety of LSI I/O circuits. Therefore, some industry people now call a completed system a microcomputer—a set of system-designed LSI circuits that have been programmed in the ROM to perform unique functions. All microcomputers contain a small memory that is often satisfactory for manual input, such as a keyboard.

LSI package, quad-in-line —An unconventional dual in-line package called QUIL that has two rows of staggered pins on each side with half the spacing of the conventional single-row-per-side arrangement. The new package is about half the size of the more conventional 48-pin packages —1.250 by 0.52 inches as compared with 2.5 by 0.7 inch. The package allows for much shorter internal interconnections. The larger package's longer interconnections were found to reduce circuit speed. The special QUIL lead frame has 24 leads on a side, exactly half the spacing of conventional DIP pins. The denser QUIL leads are bent into two staggered rows. The ceramic-alumna-oxide package can dissipate 1.3 watts over a temperature range extending from 0 °C to 75 °C. Motorola Semiconductor Products Inc. is the manufacturer and plans to apply this package to in-house MOS and bipolar LSI devices. There is also a lot of outside interest in the new small package. Work is in progress to make a slightly larger 64-pin version and also higher-temperature versions using beryllium oxide as the ceramic case. (*See* QUIP).

LSI technologies — The various LSI technologies are conceptually similar.

Most use the electrical properties of silicon dioxide and doped crystalline silicon. Pure crystalline silicon has a valence of 4, and a regular covalent lattice structure. Crystalline silicon can be turned into a conductor by adding a source of surplus electrons, or by introducing electron deficiencies (holes) into the crystal lattice structure. Surplus electrons can be generated by "doping" the silicon with traces of a valence 5 impurity such as phosphorus.

M

machine-check interruption—Machine-check interruptions are caused by the machine-checking circuits detecting a machine error. A system is then often automatically switched to a diagnostic procedure.

machine-code instruction — 1. Those symbols that state a basic computer operation to be performed. 2. A combination of bits specifying an absolute machine-language operator, or the symbolic representation of the machine-language operator. 3. That part of an instruction that designates the operation of arithmetic, logic, or transfer to be performed.

machine-control electronics — Computers became powerful tools as controllers. When computerized numerical control began, it was economical to use hard-wired controllers for each task. Since the prices of general-purpose computers have dropped drastically, they have become more feasible to use. One major benefit of the general-purpose computer is in the controlling of an NC-system that permits new features to be easily implemented by changing the software. General-purpose computer applications have two general areas: (1) Direct Numerical Control (DNC)—where a large computer works as a controller for more than five machines, and (2) Computer Numerical Control (CNC)—where a microcomputer controls one or two machines. Among DNC and CNC, CNC is preferred since it's very flexible. Large com-

puters are expensive to own and if the computer is down all the machines it controls will be down. On the other hand, microcomputers are less expensive and, if the microcomputer is down, only the one or two machines that are connected to that computer will be affected.

machine cycle—The shortest complete process or action that is repeated in order. The minimum length of time in which the foregoing can be performed.

machine equation—That which an analog computer is actually programmed to solve, if not identical with the equation governing the original problem.

machine instructions, mnemonic — In some systems, each machine instruction is identified by a symbolic instruction mnemonic. The assembler recognizes each mnemonic and generates a binary machine instruction which corresponds to the symbolic instruction. In some instruction descriptions, optional statement parameters are enclosed in square brackets ([]). Instruction statements often contain a label preceding the instruction mnemonic, and comment strings are preceded by a slash (/).

machine language—The final language all computers must use is binary. All other programming languages must be compiled or translated ultimately into binary code before entering the processor. Binary language is machine language.

machine-language programming—Machine-language programming involves programming instructions in assembly language and, then, assembling by hand into the machine code that is then entered into the control ROM. This process is slow and cumbersome and requires the cooperation of the process engineer(s) and programmers experienced in assembly-language programming. Assembly language is the procedure used to improve upon the method of writing programs in binary machine code. Users write a computer program that will accept coded instructions that are more meaningful to them. Assembler programs will translate symbolic instructions into the binary machine code that the computer can execute. Users want to be able to address data locations and instructions by symbolic names instead of by the absolute memory addresses. Assembler programs count memory locations and label those locations that users must reference as operands in instructions. Programs can be revised without alerting addresses every time an instruction is added or deleted. The only advantage of machine language programming is that the machine's resources can be efficiently utilized.

machine logic design—Refers to built-in methods of problem approach and function execution—the way a system is designed to do its operations, what those operations are, and the type and form of data it can use internally.

machine-oriented language—1. A language designed for interpretation and use by a machine without translation. 2. A system for expressing information which is intelligible to a specific machine, e.g., a microcomputer or class of computers. Such a language may include instructions which define and direct machine operations, and information to be recorded by or acted upon by these machine operations. 3. The set of instructions expressed in symbolic operation codes with absolute addresses, relative addresses, or symbolic addresses.

machine programming, cross-assembler—An improvement over machine-language programming is the use of a cross-assembler running on a larger computer (possibly on a time-sharing system). This is mainly a programming aid, since it relieves the programmer of the tedious task of assembling the machine code. It also provides an accurate hard copy of the programs and associated documentation. However, the computer running the cross-assembler is generally not local to the process controller, and so, the programmer must make field patches between trips to his assembly computer.

machine readable—Relates to the capability of being able to be sensed or read by a specific device; i.e., tapes, cards, cassettes, disks, etc., are capable of being machine readable.

machine units—In electric analog computing, a machine unit is the voltage used to represent one unit of the simulated variable.

machine word—1. A unit of information that consists of a standard number of characters which a computer regularly handles in a register. 2. A unit of information of a standard number of characters which a machine regularly handles in each transfer, i.e., a machine may regularly handle numbers or instructions in units of 4, 8, 12, 16, 32 binary digits. Each unit is then the "machine word."

macroassembler — A macroassembler simplifies coding when similar sections of code are used repeatedly but variations preclude the use of conventional subroutine techniques. With a macroassembler, a single instruction yields the necessary expansion without undue complexity. The macroassembler converts sequences of logical operations directly into machine code. The macroassembler generally resides in RAM, and is written in assembly language for efficiency.

macroassembler, resident — The resident macroassembler enables users to efficiently translate assembly-language programs into the appropriate machine-language instructions. The full macro capability eliminates the need to rewrite similar sections of code repeatedly and simplifies the user's program documentation. The conditional assembly feature of the macroassembler permits users to include or delete optional code segments which may vary from system to system.

macroassembler time-sharing—Various macro processors can be accessed via time-sharing computer systems to create specified sequences of microprocessor statements. They can include conditional assembly features and variable parameter capabilities.

macroassembly program — Refers to various language processors that accept words, statements, and phrases to produce machine instructions. The macroassembler permits segmentation of a large program so that portions may be tested separately. It also provides extensive program analysis to aid in debugging.

macrocode — A coding system which assembles groups of computer instructions into single code words and which, therefore, requires interpretation or translation so that a microcomputer can follow them. Macros are a form of text replacement that provides an automatic code-generation capability completely under the user's control. This permits a user to define repetitive tasks just once, and when he wishes to include a task in his coding, it is only necessary to write one line of code.

macrocoding—Refers to procedures for providing segments of coding, that are used frequently throughout a program, and which can be defined at the beginning and used and referenced by a mnemonic code with parameters. This increases coding efficiency and readability of the program.

macrocommand—Refers to those programs that are formed by strings of standard, but related, commands. Such strings are usually brought into operation by means of a single macrocommand or instruction. Any group of frequently used commands or routines can be combined into a single macrocommand — and the many individual instructions thus become one. With macros, a user can gradually build up a library of frequently used instruction sequences tailored to his application. Such a library will not only enable an experienced user to significantly reduce his program development time, but it can also enable other users who are not software experts to produce efficient machine-language code.

macrodefinition—Refers to the specification of a macrooperation. This includes specifying the name of the macrooperation and the prototype cards, which indicate the fields that

are to be fixed, and the fields that are to be variable (substitutable arguments).

macrodefinition library—A macrodefinition stored in a program library; for example, the various manufacturer-supplied supervisor and data management macrodefinitions.

macrofacility—A macrofacility is often a deluxe feature in assemblers. It is very useful when similar sections of an assembler itself are written in FORTRAN. With minor modifications, the program can be run on any computer that compiles FORTRAN programs. Thus the designer prepares source programs and assembles them on some other computer to obtain an object tape for the microcomputer. The FORTRAN-written assemblers are often made available to users through various national time-sharing computer-service companies.

macroflowchart—Refers to tables and charts utilized in designing the logic of a specific routine in which the various segments and subroutines of a program are represented by blocks.

macrogenerating program—Refers to particular types of generating programs that are designed and developed to construct the group of instructions in an object language appropriate to a particular macroinstruction in the basic source language.

macrogeneration—Refers to those operations in which a macroassembler produces a sequence of assembler language statements by processing a macrodefinition that is called by a macroinstruction. Macrogeneration takes place at preassembly time.

macroinstruction — 1. An instruction consisting of a sequence of microinstructions that are inserted into the object routine for performing a specific operation. 2. The more powerful instructions which combine several operations in one instruction. 3. Instructions that are the same as line subroutines, except that the main program executes these instructions as it comes to them rather than branching out of the main stream and then returning, as it does with subroutines. 4. A symbolic language statement for a macroassembly programming system. A statement can correspond to several computer instructions.

macroinstruction, debug—One of several types of macroinstructions which generate a debugging program testing capability within a particular program.

macroinstruction, declarative—Utilized as a portion of an assembly language to instruct the compiler or assembly program to perform some action or take note of some condition. When used, it does not result in any subsequent action by the object program.

macroinstruction design — Many efficient designs result from considering three steps together to ensure that the mocroinstruction set formats are compatible with the microcomputer family members, and that operation-code formats result in the simplest microprogram flow. The macroinstruction set may be register or stack oriented, and may be original or a copy of another machine. In general, lower cost and higher performance will result when an original macroinstruction set is developed to use the microcomputer family features most effectively. In most cases, three special-purpose registers and a few of the general-purpose registers must be reserved for microprogram "bookkeeping" operations. As a result, when realizing macroinstruction sets that use a large number of registers, an external register file will have to be added. If more than eight bits of operation code are used in a macroinstruction, the interpretation of the macroinstruction becomes more complex. In some cases, additional logic may have to be added to a basic hardware design.

macroinstruction, inner — A macroinstruction that is nested inside a macrodefinition.

macroprogramming—Refers to procedures for writing machine procedure statements in terms of macroinstructions.

macros, debug—Refers to aids built into a program by the applications programmer, in addition to those supplied by the supervisory program. Debugging macros are a type of unit testing.

magnadur — A ceramic-type material, comprised of sintered oxides of iron and barium, used for making permanent magnets. It is also a good electrical insulator, its eddy-current loss in an ac field being very small.

magnesium (Mg) — At. no. 12, at. wt. 24.312, sp. gr. 1.74, m.p. 651°C, b.p. 1120°C. A light metallic element, often alloyed with aluminum, and used in constructing electronic components.

magnet—A body which has the property of attracting iron and when freely supported in isolation from other bodies will tend to set in a north-south direction. Occurs naturally in "stones" containing magnetite and once known as a lodestone. Nowadays, permanent magnets are made artificially from hardened steel that has been magnetized by a strong magnetic flux.

magnetic—Relates to all phenomena essentially depending on magnetism, especially to the enhanced magnetic effects associated with ferromagnetism.

magnetic bubble chip simulator—This is a process that allows research scientists to test new designs before building the actual hardware. Magnetic bubbles are small regions of magnetism that exist in certain types of magnetic materials. They are used for information storage and can be relocated within the material by applying magnetic fields. This technology permits greater storage capacity potential than conventional magnetic recording methods. The design system consists of three parts: a large host processor, a display terminal, and a designer. These parts are then linked together by several computer programs. Use of these magnetic bubble chips helps produce a theoretical base for design, predicts specifications, aids in selecting design directions, and thus reduces the number of hardware iterations.

magnetic bubble memory — Magnetic bubbles are small cylindrical domains formed either in single-crystal thin films of synthetic ferrites or garnets, or in thin amorphous magnetic-metal films, when a stationary external magnetic-bias field is applied perpendicularly to the plane of the films. These domains are mobile in the presence of a magnetic-field gradient, and their direction of movement can be controlled by special structures deposited on top of the film and by a moving magnetic field. As the bias field increases in strength toward its optimum value, randomly distributed serpentine domains in the film layer shrink until they form the cylindrical domains, or bubbles. Once the bubbles are formed, they can be moved along a path defined by a deposited layer of metal on the surface of the magnetic film. The presence of a bubble corresponds to a ONE and the absence to a ZERO.

magnetic circuit — 1. Complete path, perhaps divided, for magnetic flux, excited by a permanent magnet or an electromagnet. The range of reluctance is not so great as resistance in conductors and insulators, so that leakage of the magnetic flux into adjacent nonmagnetic material, especially air, is significant. 2. A closed path of magnetic flux. The path has the same direction as the magnetic induction at every point.

magnetic core—1. A magnetic material which, once placed into one of two magnetic states, will remain in that state. Thus, it can provide storage, gating, or switching. 2. A piece of magnetic material used for functions such as switching or storing. 3. A configuration of magnetic material that is, or is intended to be, placed in a spatial relationship to current-carrying conductors and whose magnetic properties are essential to its use. It may be used to concentrate an induced magnetic field as in a transformer induction coil, or armature, to retain a magnetic polarization for the purpose of storing data, or for its nonlinear properties as in a logic element. It may be made of such materials as iron, iron oxide, or ferrite, and in such shapes as wires, tapes, toroids, rods, or thin film. 4. Commonly, the memory unit contained as an integral part of the older type central processing unit in a computer.

magnetic-core storage—A type of computer storage which employs a core of magnetic material surrounded by a coil of wire. The core can be magnetized to represent either a binary 1 or 0.

magnetic disk—Refers to a storage device or system that consists of magnetically coated disks, on the surface of which information is stored in the form of magnetic spots arranged in a manner to represent binary data. These data are arranged in circular tracks around the disks and are accessible to reading and writing heads located on an arm that can be moved

mechanically to the desired disk and then to the desired track.

magnetic drum—Refers to a standard-type storage device consisting of a rotating cylindrical drum surfaced with a magnetic coating. Data are stored as small magnetized spots arranged in closed tracks around the drum. A magnetic reading and writing head is associated with each track so that the desired track can be selected by electrical switching. Data from a given track are read or written sequentially as the drum rotates.

magnetic ferrites—Those having magnetic properties and, at the same time, possessing good electrical insulating properties by reason of their ceramic structure.

magnetic field—Modification of space, so that forces appear on magnetic poles or magnets. Associated with electric currents and the motions of electrons in atoms.

magnetic-field intensity — The magnitude of the field-strength vector in a medium (i.e., the magnetic strain produced by neighboring magnetic elements or current-carrying conductors). The MKSA unit is the ampere-turn/meter, and the CGS unit is the oersted. Also called magnetic-field strength, magnetic intensity, magnetizing force.

magnetic-field interference—Refers to specific types or forms of interference induced in the circuits of a device due to the presence of a magnetic field. It often appears as common-mode or normal-mode interference in the measuring circuits.

magnetic flip-flop—A bistable amplifier using one or more magnetic amplifiers. The two stable output levels are determined by appropriate changes in the control voltage or current.

magnetic flux—The surface integral of the product of the permeability of the medium and the magnetic-field intensity normal to the surface. The magnetic flux is conceived, for theoretical purposes, as starting from a positive fictitious north pole and ending on a fictitious south pole, without loss. When associated with electric currents, a complete circuit (the magnetic circuit) is envisaged, the quantity of magnetic flux being sustained by a magnetomotive force (co-existent with ampere-turns linked with the said circuit). Permanent magnetism is explained similarly in terms of molecular mmf's (associated with orbiting electrons) acting in the medium. Measured in lines (or megalines) or maxwells.

magnetic hysteresis — Nondefinitive value of magnetic induction in a ferromagnetic medium for a given magnetic-field intensity, depending upon past magnetic history of sample.

magnetic oxides — The iron oxides which are ferromagnetic and which, suitably fabricated from the powder form, provide efficient permanent magnets.

magnetic recording medium—A wire, tape, cylinder, disc, or other magnetizable material which retains the magnetic variations imparted to it during magnetic recording.

magnetic shift register—One in which the pattern of settings of a row of magnetic cores is shifted one step along the row by each fresh pulse.

magnetic strip—A strip of magnetizable ink on the back of a ledger card containing coded information for data. This information may or may not appear printed on the face of the ledger card.

magnetic tape—Flexible plastic tape, on one side of which is a uniform coating of dispersed magnetic material, in which signals are registered for subsequent reproduction. Used for registering television images, sound, or computer data.

magnetic-tape reader—One which has a multiple head which transforms the pattern of registered signal into pulse signals in a computer.

magnetic-tape storage—Refers to various storage devices in which data are stored in the form of magnetic spots on metal or coated-plastic tape. Binary data are stored as small magnetized spots arranged in column form across the width of the tape. A read-write head is usually associated with each row of magnetized spots so that one column can be read or written at a time as the tape traverses the head.

magnetic wire — A wire made of, or coated with, a magnetic material and used for magnetic recording.

magnetoelectric—The property of certain materials, i.e., chromium oxide, for becoming magnetized when placed in an electric field. Conversely, they are electrically polarized when placed in a magnetic field. Such materials may be used for measuring pulse electric or magnetic fields.

magnetostriction — Phenomenon of elastic deformation of certain ferromagnetic materials, e.g., nickel, on the application of a magnetizing force.

magnetostriction transducer—Any device employing the property of magnetostriction to convert electrical to mechanical oscillations, e.g., by using a rod clamped at the center and passing ac through a coil wound around the rod.

mail box — A ''Mail Box'' is often referred to as a set of locations in a common RAM storage area, an area reserved for data addressed to specific peripheral devices as well as to other microprocessors in the immediate environment. Such an arrangement enables the coordinator CPU and the supplementary microprocessors to transfer data among themselves in an orderly fashion with minimal hardware.

mainframe—Refers to the basic or main part of the computer, i.e., the arithmetic or logic unit. The central processing unit.

main routine—Coded directions which form the basis of a program in setting an electronic microcomputer to perform a required operation on data, independently supplied.

main storage — 1. Usually the fastest storage device of a computer and the one from which instructions are executed. 2. Program addressable storage from which instructions and data can be loaded directly into registers from which the instructions can be executed or the data can be operated upon.

maintenance-control signals—A panel of indicator lights and switches on which are displayed a particular sequence of routines, and from which repairmen can determine changes to execute.

major control data — Refers to various priority items of data, one or more of which are used to select, execute, identify, or modify another routine, record, file, operation, or data value.

major cycle—1. That part of a memory device that can provide serial access to storage positions. The time interval between successive appearances of a given storage position. 2. The maximum access time of a recirculating storage element. The time for one rotation, i.e., of a magnetic drum or of pulses in an acoustic delay line. A whole number of minor cycles.

major state—Generally refers to the control state of a computer. Major control states (in some systems) include fetch, defer, execute, etc.

major-state generator—Refers to one or more major control states that are entered to determine and execute an instruction. During any one instruction, a state lasts for one computer cycle. The major-state generator determines the machine state during each cycle as a function of the current instruction, the current state, and the condition of the break-request signal supplied to an input bus by peripheral equipment.

major-state logic generator—Relates to the logic circuits in the central processor which establish the major state for each computer cycle.

management information system (MIS) — 1. Refers to various management activities performed with the aid of automatic data processing. 2. An information system designed to aid in the performance of management functions.

manganese (Mn) — Grey-pink, hard, brittle, metallic element, at. wt. 54.9380, sp. gr. 7.20, m.p. 1260°C. Alloyed with other nonferromagnetic elements of copper and aluminum, it forms a ferromagnetic material. The element is used in some primary batteries.

manganin—A copper-base alloy, containing 12% manganese and 4% nickel, that is used for making resistor wires because of its low temperature coefficient and low contact potential.

manual input—Entry of data into a computer or system by direct manual manipulation of a device.

manual-input generator—A device that accepts manually input data and holds the contents which can be sensed by a computer, controller, and other devices, i.e., used to insert a word manually into computer storage for hold until it is read during the execution of a program.

manual operation—Processing of data in a system by direct manual techniques.

manual-storage switch—A specific type of storage, most often in the form of arrays of switches, including toggle switches, which are manually set for the entering of data. Data are entered by manually placing such switches in positions that represent data, control data flows, or instructions.

map—1. Refers to activities necessary to transform information from one form to another. 2. A listing provided by a compiler to enable a programmer to relate his data names to the main addresses within the program. 3. To establish a correspondence between the elements of one set and the elements of another set.

map, memory—*See* memory map.

map, memory list — *See* memory map list.

mapping—1. A transformation from one set to another set. 2. A correspondence. 3. In contrast to virtual memory which lets addressable program space exceed real memory, mapping lets real memory exceed addressable program space. Software and hardware for systems with either mapping or virtual memory usually make these benefits transparent to the user by letting him write and run location-independent code. Operating systems may also provide dynamic allocation of memory.

mapping, data base — A description of the way in which different record types (files) of a data base are associated with one another.

mapping mode—The mode of computer operation in which virtual addresses above 15 are transformed through the memory map so that they become references to actual main memory locations (some computers).

marginal checking—A means of testing circuits for incipient or intermittent failures by varying the voltages applied to the circuits.

marginal testing — Refers to various forms of tests, usually as part of preventive maintenance or a fault-finding or correcting operation, to test against safety margins for faults.

marginal voltage check — Refers to a means of testing the control unit by reducing the power-supply voltage on the logic modules. The theory is that, if there is a marginal module, it will fail at the reduced voltage.

mark — A term which originated with telegraph to indicate a closed key condition. Present usage implies the presence of current or carrier on a circuit or the idle condition of a teletypewriter. It also indicates the binary digit "1" in computer language.

marker—Refers to various types of symbols used to indicate the beginning or the end of some set of data, i.e., the end of a record, block, field, file, etc.

mark, file — An identification mark for the last record in a file, or one of the several labels to indicate end-of-file. File marks may be followed by trailer label, file mark, and reel mark.

marking bias — Bias distortion that lengthens the marking impulses by advancing the space-to-mark transition.

marking code, Codabar—Many types of portable data-entry terminals using an optical wand scanner are designed to read a modified Plessey bar code, the Universal Product Code (UPC), the Codabar code, and others. The Codabar code by Monarch Marking System is used mainly in discount and variety stores where point-of-sale (POS) terminals are already installed. However, it is also a marking method for libraries, medical institutions, industrial control, photographic processes, and other industries largely new to POS marketing efforts.

mark reader—A device capable of reading pencil marks on documents up to a size of 13 inches × 8 inches. The marks can be positioned anywhere on the document. The reader's sensing cells are switched on by special clock track marks. The procedure uses a standard No. 2 pencil, a card, and a mark-sense card reader to enter data into a microcomputer quickly and easily. Users program the card by marking it with the pencil. They feed the card into the reader slot and the reader automatically turns on. The card is fed through, and the data are instantly entered into memory.

mark, record—A special character used in some computers either to limit the number of characters in a data transfer, or to separate blocked or grouped records on tape.

mark, record-storage—A special character that appears only in the record-storage unit of the card reader to limit the length of the record that is read into storage.

mark-space multiplier—A specific analog multiplier in which one input variable is represented as a current or a voltage, and is used to control the mark-to-space ratio of a repetitive rectangular wave and whose amplitude is made proportional to the other variable, which is also represented by a voltage or a current.

mark-to-space ratio — Specifically related to the ratio of the duration of the positive and negative cycles of a square wave. A space is a negative cycle, a mark is a positive cycle.

mask—1. Usually a device made of a thin sheet of metal which contains an open pattern used to shield selected portions of a base during a deposition process. 2. A machine word that specifies which parts of another machine word are to be operated on. 3. This is sometimes a pattern, "printed" on glass, that is used to define areas of the chip on the silicon wafer. Masks are used for diffusion, oxidation, and metallization steps in chip manufacture.

maskable interrupt (INTR)—Some systems provide a single interrupt-request input (INTR) which can be masked internally by software with the resetting of the interrupt-enable Flag status bit. The interrupt-request signal is level triggered. It is internally synchronized during each clock cycle on the high-going edge of CLK. To be responded to, INTR must be present (High) during the clock period preceding the end of the current instruction or the end of a whole move for a block-type instruction. During the interrupt-response sequence, further interrupts are disabled.

mask bit—Used with a special pattern of bits that are used to extract selected bits from a string.

masking—A technique for sensing specific binary conditions and ignoring others. Typically accomplished by placing zeros in bit positions of no interest, and ones in bit positions to be sensed.

maskmaking — A procedure that converts the composite drawing made up of all device layers into individual masks, each of which defines one layer of the LSI device. Made of photographic emulsion, chrome, or iron oxide on glass, the masks contain final-size images of the areas to be etched on the surface of the silicon in the wafer fabrication process. Wafer fabrication defines the sequence of chemical processing steps which, when applied to a silicon wafer with appropriate masking, produces an array of LSI devices. Mask prices are determined by plate size, the material used to make the mask (chromium, iron oxide, or emulsion), line width requested, and defect level of the mask, as well as the type of mask ordered and whether it is produced on an E-beam system or a standard optical unit.

maskmaking process, early — Prior to the early 1970s, the maskmaking process started with a handdrawn 200x or 500x layout for each layer of the device. From this layout, the mask shop manually created a piece of artwork at the same scale as the layout. The artwork medium consisted of a Mylar sheet with a red film coating (Rubylith). Cutting and stripping the coating away from the Mylar left the desired pattern. The artwork was then reduced to 10x size on an emulsion plate by means of a large reduction camera. The 10x emulsion plate, called a "reticle," was then placed in a step-and-repeat machine which reduced the size to 1x and created an array of identical patterns on a third emulsion plate, used as the master. A chrome submaster was contact printed from this master. The submaster was then used to contact print the emulsion or chrome working masks for wafer fabrication. However, increasing die size and complexity eventually made hand cutting of artwork unfeasible.

mask-programmed read-only memory —A read-only memory in which the data content of each cell is determined during manufacture by the use of a mask, with the data content thereafter being unalterable.

Massey formula—One giving the probability of secondary electron emission when an excited atom approaches the surface of a metal.

mass storage—Peripheral devices into which large amounts of data can be deposited and recovered. Sometimes referred to as "secondary" storage to differentiate from memory.

mass storage device—Refers to various storage units with a large capacity, such as magnetic disk, tape cassette, data cells, etc.

mass storage dump/verify program — Refers to a program that allows the user to dump a specified area of memory to a mass storage device, such as a disk, magnetic tape, or cassette. In an autoloadable format, the accuracy of the dumped program is automatically verified.

master — 1. A file of data considered permanent or semipermanent, i.e., an arrangement or ordering of a series of records. 2. A single record from such a file.

master card — A card containing fixed or indicative information for a group of cards. It is usually the first card of that group.

master chip — The semicustom design approach is based on the use of a number of standardized IC chips with fixed component locations. These standardized IC chips, called Master Chips, contain a large number of *undedicated* active and passive components (i.e., transistors, resistors, logic gates, etc.). These integrated components can be interconnected in thousands of different ways, with a *customizing* interconnection pattern. Thus, each different metal interconnection pattern creates a new custom IC. The customization with a special interconnection pattern is what converts the prefabricated Master Chip to a completed custom chip. This method is called *semicustom,* rather than *full custom,* since only the last layer of tooling is changed to customize an IC chip, and the rest of the layers are standard. As a result, the development phase is very short, far less expensive, and risk free, compared to conventional full- or dedicated-custom ICs. Similarly, if a design change or iteration is necessary, it can be readily accommodated, within a matter of weeks, by simply generating a new or modified interconnection pattern.

master clock—1. Oscillator component which generates all the digital impulses required in an electronic computer. 2. The primary source of timing signals used to control the timing of pulses.

master clock frequency—The number of pulses per second produced by the master clock.

master control program — Refers to a computer program designed to control the operation of the system. It is designed to reduce the amount of intervention required of the human operator. The master control program provides the following functions: schedules programs to be processed, initiates segments of programs, controls all input/output operations to insure efficient utilization of each system component, allocates memory dynamically, issues instructions to the human operator and verifies that his actions were correct, and performs corrective action on errors in a program or system malfunction.

master control routine—1. In a program consisting of a series of subroutines, a routine that controls the linking of the other subroutines and which may call the various segments of the program into memory as required. 2. A program which controls the operation of a hardware system.

master data—A set of data which is altered infrequently and which supplies basic data for processing operations. The data content of a master file. Examples include: names, badge numbers, or pay rates in personnel data; or stock number, stock descriptions, or units of measure in stock-control data.

master file—1. A file of relatively more permanent information, which is usually updated periodically. 2. A main reference file of information.

master file inventory — Permanently stored inventory information retained for future use.

master program file—A tape on which all the programs for a system of runs are recorded.

master program file update—Programs from the old master file are deleted, corrected, or left unchanged, and new programs are added from the transaction tape. A new program master file is produced.

master/slave accumulator — The master/slave accumulator provides for fast, iterative computer operations needed in high-performing systems. These may include repeated add with accumulated sum, multiply, divide, and multiple-shift operations. A multiplexer circuit feeds the accumulator from one of three possible sources—the results of the shift network, the input bus, or the output bus. A fourth condition inhibits the accumulator clock so that stored data are retained. The accumulator is the only section of some 4-bit slices that requires clock operation. This is done to eliminate possible race conditions when the circuit is connected within a system.

master/slave computer — *See* master/slave system.

master/slave multiprogramming — A system designed to guarantee that one program cannot damage or access another program sharing the same memory.

master/slave system—A special system or computer configuration for business or scientific use (as production automation) in which one computer, usually of substantial size or capability, rules with complete control over all input/output devices, and schedules and transmits tasks to a slave computer. The latter computer often has a great capacity, and it performs computations as directed and controlled by the master unit. Availability of peripheral switches contributes to the utility of the master/slave configuration. If the slave fails, only some CPU power is lost; if the master fails, devices can be switched, and the former slave can be reloaded as the master.

master synchronizer—Refers to a primary source of timing signals. Often a ring counter synchronized by a crystal-controlled oscillator.

master tape—Refers to a specific tape, most often magnetic, which contains the program or master data file with most or all of the routines and programs for various main runs, and is considered a fundamental part of the operating system.

master terminal — In some networks, any terminal in the network can be the master, but only one terminal is master at any one time. As master, the terminal can communicate with all other terminals in the network.

master unit—Refers to various units that handle a variety of jobs being executed simultaneously and which have the capability of regrouping several units together to thus control independently a complete automatic data processing system or job.

matching—1. The coupling of two circuits or parts together so that the impedance of either circuit is equal to the impedance between its terminals. 2. The matching technique is generally used to verify coding. Individual codes are machine-compared against a group of master codes to select any that are invalid.

matching impedance—The impedance value that must be connected to the terminals of a signal-voltage source for matching.

mathematical check — A check which uses mathematical identities of other properties, occasionally with some degree of discrepancy being acceptable, e.g., checking multiplication by verifying that $A*B = B*A$. Synonymous with arithmetic check.

math chips—As microcomputers enter increasingly sophisticated computational systems, they're bringing along a new kind of processor to help them out. Called math chips, these dedicated processors unburden the central microcomputer by quickly performing such functions as arithmetic, logarithmic, trigonometric, fast Fourier transform, and floating point calculations. Math chips generally compete in areas where performing math functions in software is too tedious and too slow.

Math chips dedicated to numeric processing eliminate most of the lengthy software needed by microprocessors for this function. They can also contribute substantial improvements in system speed and precision. A typical numeric data processor performs a wide variety of arithmetic operations roughly a hundred times faster than floating point software in a CPU, and at a speed and precision comparable to minicomputers and mainframes with floating point boards. In a variety of scientific, industrial, and military applications, they can apply the usual advantages of large-scale integration in order to lower

cost, reduce size, and increase speed.

Some typical math processor chips contain a 16-bit arithmetic logic unit, a microprogrammed algorithm controller, an 8-by-16 operand stack, a 10-level working register stack, command and control registers, and a control ROM. All transfers, including operand, results, status, and command information, take place over an 8-bit bidirectional data bus. Operands are pushed onto an internal stack, and commands are issued for performing the required operations on the data in the stack. Following the operation, data results are also located in the stack.

mathematical control mode—Refers to specific types of control actions such as proportional, integral, or derivative.

mathematical subroutines — Subroutines including sine, cosine, square root, exponent, log, etc.

matrix—1. A coding network or system in a computer. When signals representing a certain code are applied to the inputs, the output signals are in a different code. A matrix is also a computer network in which a combination of inputs produces a single output, or a computer network or system in which only one input is excited at a time and it produces a combination of outputs. 2. An array of quantities in a prescribed form, in mathematics, usually capable of being subject to a mathematical operation by means of an operator or another matrix according to prescribed rules. 3. An array of coupled circuit elements, e.g., diodes, wires, magnetic cores, and relays, which are capable of performing a specific function, such as the conversion from one numerical system to another. The elements are usually arranged in rows and columns. Thus, a matrix is a particular type of encoder or decoder. 4. A data structure that groups a number of characters or integers (or more complex numbers) into a rectangular array like a table.

matrix, dot—A dot-matrix display uses individual character displays arrayed in any length. Each unit contains dots arranged in rows and columns, which can be selected in the proper pattern to display a letter, number, or other symbol when energized. Display assemblies can be obtained with power supply, programming and decoding electronics, and scanning circuitry that causes the message to traverse the display from left to right for displaying continuous messages.

Matrix printer (Courtesy Rank Numbering Machines, Inc.).

matrix printer—Based on the information obtained from the carriage sensors and the incoming data, the CPU decides where and how to print every character in a line, whether forward on reverse, in red or black, elongated or not. Since every printed character is built up in a dot-matrix format, the received data must first be converted from a digital format to its corresponding dot-matrix format. The dot-matrix format for each character is stored in the character-generator PROM. With the print head moving across the page under direct control of the CPU, a character is removed from the line buffer, converted to its dot-matrix format and transferred to the print head at the precise moment necessary for printing. The resulting matrix format is used to energize the appropriate print needles to form the dot-matrix character.

matrix printing—1. The marking of intersections of a matrix of dots so that a recognizable pattern is displayed and registered on a cathode-ray tube. 2. The printing of alphanumerical characters by means of the appropriate selection of pins contained in a rectangular array on the printing head.

matrix switch—Refers to an array of circuit elements designed specifically to perform a particular function as interconnected, i.e., the elements are usually transistors, diodes, and relay gates completing logic functions for encoding, transliteration of characters, decoding number system transformation, word. translation, etc. Most often, input is taken along one dimension while output is taken along another.

matrix table—A specific set of quantities in a rectangular array according to exacting mathematical rules and designs.

maximum clock frequency (f_{max})—The highest rate at which the clock input of a bistable circuit can be driven through its required sequence, while maintaining stable transitions of logic level at the output, with input conditions established that should cause changes of output logic level, in accordance with the specification.

maximum frequency operation — The maximum repetition or clock rate at which modules will perform reliably in continuous operation, under worst-case conditions, without special trigger pulse (clock) requirements.

maxwell — The CGS unit of magnetic flux, the MKS unit being the weber. One maxwell $= 10^{-8}$ weber.

Maxwell's circulating current—A mesh or cyclic current inserted in closed loops in a complex network for analytical purposes.

Maxwell's equations — Fundamental equations, developed by J. C. Maxwell, for expressing radiation mathematically, and describing the condition at any point under the influence of varying electric and magnetic fields.

Maxwell's law—A moveable portion of a circuit will always travel in the direction that gives maximum flux linkages through the circuit.

Maxwell relationship—That relationship between the refractive index (n) and the dielectric constant (k) of a medium. For a nonferromagnetic, $k = n\pm$.

m-derived network (or filter)—Electric wave-filter element which is derived from a normal (constant k) element by transformation, the aim being to obtain more desirable impedance characteristics than is possible in the prototype.

mean-time-between-failure (MTBF) — The special limit of the ratio of the operating time of equipment to the number of observed failures as the number of failures approaches infinity.

mean-time-to-failure (MTF)—The concept of mean-time-to-failure (MTF), in engineering circles, expresses the duration of continuous operation which may be expected of a system or component before an interruption is caused by failure. It is defined as the sum of the lengths of each service period, from start until interruption, divided by the number of such periods; in practice, it is calculated by dividing the total "service time" by the number of interruptions.

measurand—Refers to a specific physical quantity, condition, or property which is to be measured, often referred to as a measured variable. Some commonly measured variables are: pressure, rate of flow, thickness, temperature, speed, etc.

measurement error—Refers to a total anticipated error due to (1) sampling inadequacy or variability, (2) sample preparation variability, or (3) instability or lack of precision in read-out or transducer systems.

mechanical dictionary — Refers to a type of language-translating machine which will provide a word-for-word substitution from one language to another. In automatic-searching systems, the automatic dictionary is the component that substitutes codes for words or phrases during the encoding operation.

mechanical differential—A mechanical device in analog computers which provides an output mechanical rotation equal to the sum or difference of two input rotations.

mechanical interface — Mechanical mounting and interconnections between system elements.

medium-scale integration (MSI)—The accumulation of several circuits (usually less than 100) on a single chip of semiconductor. Widely used in third-generation systems, contrast with discrete components and large-scale integration (LSI).

medium, storage — The material on which data are recorded and which may be paper tape, cards, magnetic tape, strips, or devices such as magnetic cartridges, disks, etc.

membrane keyboards — Since mono-

panel keyboards have no mechanical linkages, this refers to a layer construction that incorporates a tough membrane with a conductive rear surface that effects a contact closure when moved approximately 0.005 inch.

membrane switch—The typical membrane switch is clear enough to read through. It is as easy as touching a picture, graph, word, or letter, and it activates the desired response. For analog or X-Y matrix panels, membrane switches utilize highly linear films, thus solving critical resistivity requirements. The transparent conductors do not interfere with the display. Image and readability are actually enhanced. Some other features of a membrane switch are: it can be designed to many specifications (size, resistivity, light transmission) in order to control any graphic pattern, it can be formed to the contour of many crt screens or control panels, it can be sealed for cleaning and weatherproof versatility, and it can be backlighted for many uses.

memories, associative—With associative-memory capability, high-speed memory searches within computers are based on content or subject matter rather than being limited to locating data through specified addresses.

memory — 1. One of the three basic components of a CPU, memory stores information for future use. Storage and memory are interchangeable expressions. Memories accept and hold binary numbers or images. 2. In order to be effective, a computer must be capable of storing the data it is to operate on as well as the program that dictates which operations are to be performed. Not only must the memory unit of a computer store large amounts of information, the memory must be designed to allow rapid access to any particular portion of that information. Speed, size, and cost are the critical criteria in any storage unit. Various types are: disk, drum, semiconductor, magnetic core, charge-coupled devices, bubble domain, etc. 3. A device into which information can be copied, which will hold this information, and from which the information can be obtained at a later time. (Interchangeable with storage.)

memory-address counter—Memory-address registers may be the regular

working registers, or specially designated ones, such as the program
counter. A key register in any computer, this counter points to the next
location in memory for an instruction-
fetch operation. In addition, it is common to have an independently controlled register that points to a read/
write memory location. Instructions to
load and store the program counter
are extremely important, since they
permit modification of the instruction
sequence. A special advantage results when the counter can be loaded
or modified by a value in the accumulator or other working register. This
simplifies the control of a program's
sequence through computed or external data.

memory addressing—Memory addressing can be inefficient when used with
microcomputers. One memory-ad-
dressing limitation problem encountered with microcomputers, and not
with minicomputers, is "out-of-page"
reference errors. A microcomputer
often has "paged" memory, i.e., the
memory is divided up, for addressing,
into blocks or "pages," and some of
the microinstruction formats can only
reference memory locations within
the same page as the instruction. This
technique of addressing is used to
limit the number of bits required to
specify an operand's address. However, when an attempt is made to
reference, within one of these short
instructions, a location outside the
current page of memory, an "out-of-
page" reference error occurs. This
restriction can be avoided by using
indirect addressing or using full-ad-
dress instructions.

memory addressing modes—Methods
of specifying the memory location of
an operand. Common addressing
modes are: direct, immediate, relative,
indexed, and indirect. These modes
are important factors in program efficiency.

memory address register — A register
containing the address of the selected
word in memory.

memory address, virtual—Often interpreted as addressing (1) a particular
character relative to the beginning of
a page, (2) a particular page relative
to the initial point of that segment,
and (3) a particular large memory
segment or book. Thus, programs can
be addressed into noncontiguous

areas of memory in relatively small
blocks.

memory and device control—In some
systems, the memory and device control unit provides external control signals to communicate with peripheral
devices, switch register, memory,
and/or control panel memory. During
I/O instructions, this unit also modifies the PLA outputs depending on
the states of the four device control
lines.

memory, associative — 1. Associative
memory is an extension of search
memory. It operates on the same
search-by-content principle but contains additional logic at each cell,
performing word-parallel logical,
arithmetic, and input and output operations, generally in bit-serial fashion. Among the logical functions typically offered by associative memory
is a parallel-write operation. It simultaneously modifies selected bit positions at all cells in the associative
memory or throughout a selected
subset of the cells. The bit positions
to be modified are determined by the
contents of the mask register; the
cells to be modified are selected by
the settings of the match flip-flops.
The changes to bit positions are set
in a compare register and are the
same for all selected cells. 2. Data
storage based on the data actually
stored in the memory, not the location of the data. This leads to its alternate name, content-addressable
memory (CAM). Associative memory
is a method of organization and memory design that permits the access of
all information that matches certain
"tag" bits of the address.

memory, backing — Considered to be
the same as auxiliary storage, i.e.,
those units whose capacity is relatively larger than working (scratchpad
or internal) storage but of longer access time, and in which transfer capability is usually in blocks between
storage units.

memory, bootstrap — The bootstrap
memory is a time-saving device built
into the main computer. It is programmed to fit the specialized needs
of various computer users. The program and words in the bootstrap
memory cannot be altered by the
computer but can be manually
changed when necessary. The purpose of the bootstrap memory is to

provide for the automatic reading of new programs into the computer with protection against erasing its vital instructions (some systems).

memory, bubble—Magnetic domain, or "bubble," memories may be thought of as patterns of vertically oriented bar magnets moving on tracks within a thin horizontal film or platelet. The polarity of the bar magnets (actually tiny cylindrical magnetic fields) is always perpendicular to the film plane and opposite to their surrounding region. In the most simplified model of bubble memory, the presence of a bubble is detected when its reverse magnetic field is sensed during its passage under a permanently magnetized material that changes resistance with a change in polarity. The bubbles are unaffected by their passage under the sensor.

memory buffer register—Refers to a register in which a word is stored as it comes from memory (reading) or just prior to its entering memory (writing).

memory bus—The CPU communicates with memory and I/O devices over a memory bus. In different computers, this bus has various names, including I/O bus, data bus, or one of a host of proprietary names. The memory bus actually consists of three buses: one for memory addresses, another for data to the CPU, and the third for CPU data to the memory. Typically, these three time-share a single bus. The memory-address register—which defines the address for data transfer—drives the address bus.

memory, cache—Refers to units with limited capacity but very fast semiconductor memory which can be used in combination with lower cost, but slower, large-capacity memory, giving effect to a larger and faster memory. Look-ahead procedures are required in the progress of the programs to affect locating and depositing the right information into the fast memory when it is required.

memory capacity — This refers to the number of elementary pieces of data that can be contained in a storage device. Frequently defined in terms of characters in a particular code or words of a fixed size that can be so contained.

memory, CCD—Charge-coupled memory devices (CCDs) are low-cost alternatives for bulk storage applications, filling a void between magnetic memories and semiconductor RAMs. CCDs are volatile semiconductor storage devices. They are the beneficiaries of fabrication techniques developed for MOS RAMs and are manufactured on the same production facilities. CCDs are faster than bubble memories; their 250-kHz cycle time is roughly one-fourth that of bubbles. CCDs, like RAMs, are read/write devices, and do not need the peripheral circuitry at the chip level that bubble memories need to make them read and write.

memory cell—The smallest subdivision of a memory into which a unit of data has been or can be entered, in which it is or can be stored, and from which it can be retrieved.

memory chip, bubble—Contained in a small module, bubble memory is an electronic chip that stores digital information by changing the magnetic polarity of tiny areas in the chip called bubbles. The bubbles are actually cylindrical magnetic islands polarized in a direction opposite from that of a film in which the bubbles function. The memory has no moving parts. Because it works magnetically, it retains information even when the power is turned off. Bubble memory has advantages over electromechanical mass memory devices, such as paper tape, cassettes, or floppy disks; it offers solid-state reliability, higher access speeds, smaller size, and less weight and power consumption.

memory, content-addressable — A memory that is addressable by its contents rather than by location. Often used in segmented systems to store recently used segment base addresses. Enables faster interrogation to retrieve a particular data element.

memory controller — Any computer, from micro to super mainframe, can be thought of as a memory controller. The computer simply moves and combines data in the memory it controls. Thus, computers can be used as universal digital interfaces, if the equipment being interfaced looks like a computer memory.

memory, core—A storage device composed of ferromagnetic cores, or an apertured ferrite plate, through which select lines and sense windings are threaded.

memory cycle—1. A computer operation consisting of reading from and writing into memory. 2. The time required to complete this process.

memory, cycle stealing—Many applications require the fastest possible transfer of large amounts of data between the microcomputer memory and peripheral devices. System efficiency can be increased by avoidance of time-consuming programmed word transfers in which the microprocessor supervises each operation. Increased efficiency can be achieved by addition of a direct-memory access (DMA) facility. It allows an I/O device interface to "steal" a memory cycle from the program and transfer a word of data directly from or to a memory address specified in a special address register. With an automatic increment of the address register after each word transfer, successive words of data can be transferred into successive memory locations.

memory data register—A memory data register is a 4-, 8-, 12-, 16-, or 32-bit register that holds the last data word read from, or written into, the memory location addressed by the contents of the memory-address register.

memory diagnostic—Refers to a routine that checks all memory locations for proper functioning using a set of worst-case pattern tests. By relocating quality control diagnostics into various positions in memory, the memory diagnostic is able to test all of memory.

memory dump—1. Generally refers to a listing of the contents of a storage device, or selected parts of it. (A) Dynamic: A dump of certain sections of memory under program control as a main routine is being executed. (B) Differential: A dump of only those words or characters of memory which have been changed during the execution of a routine, determined by a diagnostic routine which re-reads the original contents from auxiliary storage and compares them with the present contents. 2. A process of writing the contents of memory consecutively in such a form that it can be examined for computer or program errors. 3. Routine generated automatically according to a programmer's specification and included in an object program to perform both program-loading operations and a printout of memory contents upon request.

memory, dynamic—Refers to a characteristic of storing data on a device or in such a manner that permits the data to move or vary with time, and thus, the data are always available instantly for recovery; i.e., acoustic delay line, magnetic drum, or circulating or recirculating of information in a medium.

memory, dynamic relocation — Refers to a process that frees computer users from keeping track of exactly where information is located in the system memory. Another important attribute is its ability to keep programs flowing in and out of memory in a highly effective manner.

memory error—An error is a situation in which the data read out of a memory location are different from the data originally stored in that location. The term "error" is normally not applicable to circuits that do not contain memory elements. It can be applied, however, to complex logic arrays that contain memory elements, such as flip-flops or small arrays of RAM. Errors can be classified into three categories: hard error, medium error, and soft error.

memory expansion modules—Memory expansion modules are often small printed-circuit boards that attach to main boards using sockets and nylon bolts. Use of expansion modules is advantageous from a price/performance point of view as the price of a memory expansion module is significantly less than that of an equivalent separate memory expansion board with its own system bus interface and support circuitry. Memory expansion modules also offer higher performance since it is not necessary to use the system bus for memory transactions. All transactions take place using the on-board bus with no additional wait states or bus contention (on many systems).

memory expansion motherboard — A typical memory expansion motherboard is a card that attaches to either a standard motherboard or to a mini-type motherboard. It typically pro-

Memory expansion modules (Courtesy Intel Corp.).

vides space for 5 or more memory cards.

memory, external—A facility or device, not an integral part of a computer, in which data usable by a computer are stored. Examples are off-line magnetic-tape units and other magnetic devices. (Contrasted with storage, internal.)

memory fill—Refers to the placing of patterns of characters in the memory registers not in use in a particular problem to stop the computer if the program, through error, seeks instructions taken from forbidden registers.

memory hierarchy—A set of memories with differing sizes and speeds, and usually having different cost-performance ratios. A hierarchy might consist of a very-high-speed small semiconductor memory, a medium-speed disk memory, and a large slow-speed tape memory.

memory, interlaced — A memory with sequentially addressed locations occupying physically separated positions in the storage media.

memory interleaving—Interleaving, like cache, takes advantage of the fact that most computer programs tend to reference sequential addresses. In interleaving, sequential addresses are placed on sequential memory boards (some systems can interleave 2, 4, or 8 memory modules at a time) so that the CPU can fetch a word, manipulate it, and then fetch the next word with-

out having to wait for completion of one board's memory cycle.

memory, internal — 1. The storage of data on the primary devices that are integral parts of a computer. 2. The storage facilities forming an integral physical part of the computer and directly controlled by the computer. In such facilities, all data are automatically accessible to the computer, e.g., main memory and magnetic disk or tape on-line (contrasted with external storage). 3. All memory or storage which is automatically accessible to the computer without human intervention.

memory, laser—Typical of what may be operational in the near future is a device being developed and field tested by Holofile and the TRW Defense and Space Systems Division. The unit uses a combination of laser technology and holography to store, in digital form, the equivalent of the central Los Angeles telephone book on a single 4- × 6-inch microfiche. Access to this kind of massive memory could make other kinds of storage obsolete. Data stored in this fashion can, of course, be retrieved for computer processing. By the same token, they cannot be erased, as can data that are stored on more conventional magnetic media.

memory latency time—Refers to a measurement of the time required for the memory's control hardware to physically move the memory media, containing the desired data, to a position where it can be electrically read. Alternately, the reading device may be moved to the desired data. Latency is associated with serial memories and certain random-access memories.

memory, magnetic—Any portion of the memory that uses the magnetic properties of a material to store information.

memory, magnetic core — Formerly, cores were commonly used for memory. A core is composed of tiny ferromagnetic rings (shaped like doughnuts), each a few hundredths of an inch in diameter. Besides being extremely small, magnetic core has traditionally been less expensive than solid-state components, yet it can be magnetized in a few billionths of a second. If cores are strung on wire (like beads) and a large enough electrical current is sent through the wire, the cores are magnetized. The direction of the current determines the magnetic state or polarity of the core. If the direction of current is reversed, the polarity is changed. The cores, however, retain their polarity even after the electrical current is removed. Thus, magnetic core memory is nonvolatile.

memory, main—Usually the CPU or fastest storage device of a computer and the one from which instructions are executed. (Contrasted with auxiliary storage.)

memory map—A special type of listing of addresses, or symbolic representations of addresses, which define the boundaries of the memory-address space occupied by a program or a series of programs. Often memory maps can be produced by a high-level language such as APL, FORTRAN, etc. In addition, under operation of some computer memory management options, a dynamic memory map is maintained to guide automatic allocation of memory space to overlay programs.

memory map list—In some systems, a memory map is provided at compile time on an optional basis. The memory map is a listing of all variable names, array names, and constants used by the program, with their relative address assignments. The listing often includes all subroutines called and the last location that is called.

memory-mapped graphics — In memory-mapped graphics, each character cell is subdivided so that each scan line of the cell may be independently addressed. The crt memory block then typically provides 8 bits of direct video data, rather than 8 bits of data defining a character cell code to the character generator. The crt memory block serves double duty: crt memory storage and symbol or character generator. All the user has to do is convert this parallel video data to serial video data.

memory-mapped I/O—An alternative to separate I/O instructions is to use memory data-transfer instructions to communicate with the I/O devices. Users can assign a block of unused memory addresses to serve as device addresses. This approach, called memory-mapped I/O, is commonly used in many microcomputer systems. Although this approach shrinks the available memory-address area, it can reduce both program-storage requirements and program-execution times. The memory instructions would be Load Data (input message data or status word), and Store Data (output message data or command word).

memory-mapped I/O bus — Memory-mapped I/O organization by its very nature requires that the same bus be used for memory and I/O operations. Isolated I/O, on the other hand, may use separate buses for memory and I/O, as is the case with many minicomputers. Nevertheless, current microprocessors often use the same bus for memory and I/O, even if they have an isolated I/O instruction set. That is, the same data bus is used for memory and I/O operations, and I/O port numbers are transmitted on the memory-address bus.

memory mapping — An optional mode of microcomputer operation wherein the eight high-order bits of any virtual address greater than 15 are replaced by an alternative value, thus providing for dynamic relocatability of programs (some microcomputers).

memory map, system — In some systems for extended flexibility, four maps are included: (1) system map, (2) user map, (3) dual channel port controller Map 1, and (4) dual channel port controller Map 2.

When the system map is enabled, the program operates in privileged mode, with complete control over all maps. It is then able to alter the contents of any map, exchange data between maps, or enable another map. However, when the user map is enabled, the program operates in nonprivileged mode; only those pages of memory that the system has assigned are available. When additional memory is required, the system is responsible for altering the page addresses contained in the user's map. This assures a single source of control, regardless of the number of users or programs.

When the maps are enabled, the program can make rapid data transfers into any contiguous block of memory, or it can "scatter load" the data into noncontiguous, nonsequential pages of memory. The time penalty of setting up a transfer to each separate block is eliminated, which is especially advantageous in time critical programs. Some processors continue to operate during high-speed data transfers. The advantage of this operation becomes obvious during relatively long operations, such as floating point instructions—entire blocks of memory can be transferred while other instructions are executing.

memory map, user — When the user map is enabled, the program operates in nonprivileged mode; only those pages of memory that the system has assigned are available. When additional memory is required, the system is responsible for altering the page addresses contained in the user's map. This assures a single source of control, regardless of the number of users or programs. *See also* memory map, system.

memory, metal-oxide semiconductor— A memory using a semiconductor circuit; generally used as a high-speed buffer memory or a read-only memory.

memory, microcomputer—Some typical microcomputer main memories have a capacity of 4096, or more, 4-, 8-, 12-, or 16-bit words with a Read/Write cycle time of 1.5 microseconds (or faster). The memory is often nonvolatile; if power is removed, data stored in memory is not lost. The processor and input-output interface communicate with the memory by way of the data input bus. Typically, various hardware registers are used to hold memory address information and data received via the bus, such as the memory address register and the memory data register.

memory module — 1. A magnetic or semiconductor module providing storage locations for 4K, 8K, 12K, 16K, or more words. 2. A microprocessor module consisting of memory storage and capable of storing a finite number of words (e.g., 4096 words in a 4K memory module). Storage capacity is usually rounded off and abbreviated with K representing each 1024 words.

memory, nonvolatile — A storage medium which retains information when power is removed from the system.

memory organization, cache—An integral cache memory is a standard feature of some computers. The cache often is a high-speed solid-state memory with a 2K- to 64K-byte capacity. The cache acts in many ways like a buffer between the CPU registers and main memory. Whenever a request is made to fetch data from memory, the circuitry checks to see if the data are already in cache. If it is, the data are fetched from cache, and no main-memory read is required. If data are not in cache, byte segments are transferred in parallel from main memory for execution. When a request is made to write data into main memory, they are written both into the cache and main memory. This assures that the main memory always has the most up-to-date data.

memory page—A section of memory, typically 256 words. This arises from the fact an 8-bit computer handles memory addresses in 8-bit bytes. One byte can address 256 locations, so most 8-bit microprocessors use a total of 2 bytes to give one 16-bit word capable of addressing 65,536 (2^{16}) locations. The upper 8 bits are referred to as the page number. Thus, the address in octal page form 012 125 is location 125 (octal) on page 012 (octal).

memory parity—Refers to a procedure that generates and checks parity on each memory transfer and provides an interrupt if an error is detected. It is usually available on special order from some manufacturers.

memory, permanent—Storage of information which remains intact when the power is turned off. Synonymous with nonvolatile memory.

memory print—*See* memory dump.

memory printout—A listing of the contents of a storage device, or selected parts of it. (Synonymous with memory dump and core dump.)

memory protect — Memory protect is available for use in many processors. It protects the integrity of operating systems against accidental modifications. Memory protect sets up a fence which divides memory space into two segments, separating the operating system from user programs. If any part of a user program seeks to modify system space, the system interrupts and takes control. This is a necessity for many real-time environments and other highly interactive systems.

memory protection option—Users can reserve a portion of memory to hold unalterable program code. With the Memory Protect option, the CPU will inhibit any attempt to write into protected memory and flag as an error any instruction that attempts to do so. Large computers protect a substantial area of memory and store all vital system software in this protected area.

memory, RAM—Random-access memory (RAM) chips are temporary data-storage devices for use in computers. There are two types—static and dynamic. A static RAM cell stores a data bit in a flip-flop circuit that usually consists of from four to six transistors. A dynamic RAM cell uses a single transistor and capacitor to store a data bit. Both types can lose their data content upon removal of operating power. Moreover, the charge stored in the capacitor of a dynamic RAM cell decays in a matter of milliseconds and must be refreshed periodically (usually about every 2 ms) to avoid loss of data. Control logic provides charge refresh each time the cell is accessed for a Read or Write cycle. At the same time, all other cells in the same row are also refreshed.

memory, read-only (ROM) — Refers to memory that cannot be altered in normal use of the computer. Usually a relatively small memory that contains often-used instructions, such as microprograms or system software.

memory register—1. A so-called high-speed bus, distributor, or exchange register. In some computers, a register used in all data and instruction transfers between memory, the arithmetic unit, and the control register. 2. A register in computer storage rather than other units of the computer; same as storage register. 3. A register which is involved in all transfers of data and instructions in either direction between memory and the arithmetic and control registers. It may be addressed in some machines. Also called distributor, exchange register, high-speed bus, arithmetic register, and auxiliary register. 4. A register in which the contents can be added to or subtracted from. The contents are available until the register is cleared.

memory scan option — Memory scan provides a rapid search of any portion of memory for any word or byte value. Any block of contiguous memory locations can be scanned in a single instruction to see if it contains the desired value.

memory, scratchpad—1. A high-speed memory device used to store the location of an interrupted program and to retrieve the latter after the interrupting program has been completed. 2. Refers to the small central high-priority immediate-access memory area of the CPU, with a significantly faster access time than the larger main store. This is normally used by the hardware and/or operating system for storing microcodes, most frequently used operands, and groups of object program instructions or registers.

memory, semiconductor—1. Semiconductor flip-flop circuits can provide large-scale storage units. Although semiconductors are very fast, most require the continuous application of power to retain the data stored in them. They were originally used primarily for microcomputer storage registers and computational logic units (such as the arithmetic logic unit). 2. A memory whose storage medium is a semiconductor circuit and most often used for high-speed buffer memories and for read-only memories, but which are now becoming primary storage devices for most computers. Large-scale integration (LSI) semiconductor memories now almost totally supersede core memories for most purposes. Charged-coupled devices (CCDs) and magnetic bubbles, that represent bits as regions of charge or as magnetism that can be moved electrically on a fixed substrate, are an important recent contribution to memory technology. 3. Generally, semiconductor memory components are constructed using one of three basic technologies: (1) bipolar, (2) n-channel MOS, or (3) Complementary MOS. Early designers favored p-channel MOS, since that technology had already been developed for other componentry by the time it was realized that semiconductors could offer an economically feasible alternative to cores. There are many significant variations within each of the three technologies. To most experts, it appears that over the long term, CMOS will be the dominant process used for semiconductor memory and processing components.

memory, serial — Refers to a type of memory whose information media is continuous. Data are identified in their content or form. Data may be obtained only by performing a serial search through the contents of the memory.

memory, static—Refers to a memory device that contains no mechanical moving parts or one that contains fixed information.

memory storage, intermediate — An electronic scratchpad for holding coding temporarily until it is needed, and for releasing final figures to the output device.

memory structural units—The memory can be thought of as a large array of storage points, each of which is called a "bit." (Bit is an acronym for BInary digiT). A bit is the smallest unit of information a memory is capable of retaining. A group of bits form a single "byte." A byte is considered as the smallest complete unit of information that can be transmitted to or from the microprocessor at a given time. Bytes are made up of a varying number of bits, the exact number of which depends on the specific hardware requirements of the individual system. Generally, a byte has 8 bits. A group of 16 bits on many machines make up a 16-bit instruction, or a "word." This "word" can also be thought of as being made up of two 8-bit bytes. Because of its function in the memory, one word may also be thought of as a memory location—when a word is being used, an actual physical location in the memory

is being accessed. In various types of documentation, it is conventional to show bits with the most significant bit (MSB) at the left and the least (LSB) at the right.

memory types—Memory is divided into four main areas: (1) mainframe memory, (2) high-speed buffer memory, (3) microprocessor memory, and (4) bulk storage memory. Mainframe memories include mini- to megamemories. The buffer memory follows the mainframe memory in the hierarchy. It is rapidly growing and changing dramatically. Most microcomputers (larger than 1-chip systems) require an external memory, a microprocessor memory, sometimes in substantial size. Such systems usually need static memories, such as ROM, PROM, and EPROM. Some bulk storage memories replace the rotating mechanical storage types. These include magnetic bubble memories (not really semiconductors) and charge-coupled devices (CCDs).

memory, virtual—A technique that permits the user to treat secondary (disk) storage as an extension of main memory, thus giving the virtual appearance of a larger main memory. A type of memory with the capability of using a type of algorithm of the paging or segmenting type. In this manner, a larger memory is simulated than actually exists. Virtual memory has been used primarily on large multiprogrammed computers in order to have a larger number of active programs in main memory. In some cases, however, the minicomputer being used will be dedicated to a single program rather than being multiprogrammed. With this consideration, the virtual memory system allows a user to run large programs without having to go to the expense of buying more than a minimal amount of main memory for the machine.

memory, virtual (pointer)—Virtual memory systems are designed for storage efficiency. Some computers are structured so that parts of programs and data may be scattered through main memory and auxiliary storage. Various pointers or sets of pointers automatically keep track of the location of these program portions. The user of computers so designed may be unaware of this scattering procedure and most often operates computing procedures as though he were using normal memory.

memory, volatile—A storage medium in which information is destroyed when power is removed from the system.

menu — Generally, these are operator instructions, prompts, and messages that are displayed whenever special conditions exist or operator decisions are required, such as when selecting operating parameters.

mercury—(Hg). Metallic element, at. no. 80, at. wt. 200.59, sp. gr. 13.6, m.p. —39°C, b.p. 357°C. Used in thyratrons, arc rectifiers, switches, etc.

mesh — 1. A complete electrical path (including capacitors) in the component branches of a complex network. 2. A set of branches forming a closed path in a network—provides that if any branch is omitted, the remaining branches do not form a closed path. Sometimes called a loop.

mesh current—1. The current assumed to exist over all cross sections of a closed path in a network. It may be the total current in a branch included in the path, or a partial current which, when combined with the others, forms the total current. 2. The current assumed to exist throughout the whole section of a mesh.

mesh network—A network formed from a number of impedances in series.

meson field—That which is considered to be concerned with the interchange of proton and neutron in a nucleus, the mesons transferring energy.

message concentrator — A message concentrator stores and sends messages from low-speed remote terminals to a host processor. The messages are sent either in periodic high-speed bursts or are stored until the concentrator's line is polled. Because it efficiently handles line use, the concentrator is a key to minimizing network costs. A message concentrator is one of the sensible ways to add line-handling capability to a network.

message control flags—Refers to the specific type control flags that indicate whether the information being transmitted is data or a control-only message and whether it is the first, intermediate, or last block of a message.

message queueing — There are four general types of queues which each terminal can have: input, output, switch, and priority. The difference between the output and switch queues is that the output queue is used to store output that has been generated as a result of input from the same terminal, while the switched queue is used to store unsolicited messages generated from another terminal. Terminals may be protected or unprotected (some systems).

metal, base—Refers to the metal substrate on which one or more coatings of other materials or metals are deposited, such as in printed circuits or connections for logic elements.

metal ceramic—An alloy of a ceramic and a metal which retains its useful properties at very high temperatures. Also called cermet.

metal-film resistor—An electronic component in which the resistive element is an extremely thin layer of metal alloy, vacuum-deposited on a substrate.

metalization—The network of conductive material formed on the surface of a silicon chip or substrate to interconnect microcircuit elements.

metalization, multilayer—A metalization pattern in which the conductive network of a silicon chip is fabricated in more than one plane, and separated, except at desired contact points, by thin dielectric films.

metallic bond—Bond in which the valence electrons of the constituent atoms are free to move in the periodic lattice.

metallic conduction — That which describes the movement of electrons which are freely moved by an electric field within a body of metal.

metallic-film resistor—One formed by coating a high-temperature insulator, such as mica, ceramic, Pyrex glass, or quartz, with a metallic film.

metal-oxide resistor — A type of film resistor in which the resistance material deposited on the substrate is tin oxide, which provides good stability.

metal-oxide semiconductor — Abbreviated MOS. A technology that employs field-effect transistors that have a metal or conductive electrode which is insulated from the semiconductor material by an oxide layer of the substrate material. Whereas, a bipolar device allows current to flow in only one direction, an MOS device will permit bidirectional current flow.

metal-oxide semiconductor memory— A memory using a semiconductor circuit; generally used in high-speed buffer memory and read-only memory.

mica — A naturally occurring mineral which may be sheared into very thin sheets. In the very clear form, it is an extremely good insulator even at very high temperatures and is used in the best capacitors. It is also employed to insulate electrodes.

MICR code—Refers to the special magnetic-ink character-recognition code that consists of a set of 10 numeric symbols and four special symbols. It is standardized as Font E-13B and was developed for the American Bankers Association. The characters are visually readable through the use of magnetic sensing heads in various types of magnetic-ink recognition equipment.

microampere (μA)—Equate to 10^{-6} ampere.

microcircuit — 1. Miniaturized circuitry components common to the so-called third generation of computer equipment. Microcircuits frequently reduce cost, increase reliability, and operate faster than tubes and many transistors. 2. A specialized electronic circuit composed of elements which are fabricated and interconnected to make them inseparable and miniaturized.

microcircuit, hybrid — A microcircuit consisting of elements that are a combination of the film-circuit type and the semiconductor-circuit type, or a combination of one or both of these types with discrete parts.

microcircuit isolation — The electrical insulation of circuit elements from the electrically conducting silicon wafer. The two main techniques are oxide isolation and diode isolation.

microcircuit, module—An assembly of microcircuits, or an assembly of microcircuits and discrete parts, designed to perform one or more electronic circuit functions. It is constructed such that, for the purposes of specification, testing, commerce, and maintenance, it is considered to be indivisible.

microcircuit, multichip—A microcircuit consisting of elements formed on or within two or more semiconductor chips, which are separately attached to a substrate.

microcode—1. A list of small program steps. Combinations of these steps, performed automatically in a prescribed sequence, form a macrooperation like multiply, divide, and square root. 2. A set of control functions performed by the instruction decoding and execution logic of a computer system. The microcode defines the instruction set (repertoire) of a specific computer. It often is not accessible to programmers if the system is a large one and designed for nonuse by the owners and users, e.g., proprietary to the manufacturer. Some microcomputers are modified by microcode use by hobbyists and designers.

microcode, horizontal — Refers to a code that increases the number of simultaneous functions by adding control fields to each microinstruction, thus widening the control word. *Vertical code* reduces microinstruction width by decreasing the number of simultaneously performed functions, thus reducing execution speed.

microcode instruction set—Perhaps the most significant feature for general-purpose high-level language and operating-system optimization is the instruction set. The decision to microcode extended instructions into various types of ROMs rather than to use conventional software subroutines also is related to distributed parallel-logic theory. The tradeoff is one of increased chip cost (in ROMs) versus time-consuming software routines, and the answer is to optimize software performance by putting commonly used subroutines into various micro-coded types of ROMs.

microcoding—A system of coding that uses suboperations not ordinarily accessible in programming.

microcommand — Refers to various commands specifying elementary machine operations to be performed within a basic machine cycle.

microcomputer—A general term referring to a complete tiny computing system, consisting of hardware and software, that usually sells for less than $500 and whose main processing blocks are made of semiconductor integrated circuits. In function and structure, it is somewhat similar to a minicomputer, with the main difference being price, size, speed of execution, and computing power. The hardware of a microcomputer consists of a microprocessing unit (MPU), which is usually assembled on a pc board with memory and auxiliary circuits. Some microcomputer systems also require ROM storage for programs and data, clock circuits, input/output interfaces, selector registers, and control circuits. Power supplies, control console, and cabinet are separate. The advantages of small size, low weight and power, and high reliability are added to the ability to easily modify and enhance microcomputer-system functions through software changes. In addition, the reduction in parts count has cut inspection costs for incoming parts and has resulted in reduced material costs for the chassis, interconnects, and power supplies. Microcomputers fill the needs for low-cost applications, such as electronic games, small intersection traffic-control signals, simple industrial systems, appliances, vending machines, and for more complex control functions, such as editing typewriters and measurement systems. Many 16- and 32-bit systems can substitute for mainframe computers.

microcomputer addressing modes — Operands needed to execute an instruction are designated by addresses, such as register addresses, memory addresses, or I/O addresses. The addressing mode of a given instruction defines the address space it references and also defines the method used to compute the address itself.

microcomputer analyzers—The typical microcomputer analyzer, or logic analyzer, is a diagnostic hardware/software test set which provides both real-time emulation for testing hardware and a means of integrating the hardware with the software. It provides for single-step and full-speed operation capability in addition to display presentation. Some test units can be fitted with plug-in units which can provide the universal capability for testing different types of systems. The microsystem analyzer offers the capability of testing the microcomputer system under the conditions of the required mechanical, thermal, and electrical environment. It also allows for the testing of systems by "board-swapping" techniques. For field service, these same test units are used in smaller, portable, battery-powered versions that perform functional testing procedures similar to production testing but with field service flexibility and versatility. These units usually have provision for RS-232 port capability for remote on-line diagnostic testing.

microcomputer architecture—The typical microcomputer board is a complete single-board computer with its own self-contained memory, plus serial and parallel I/O ports. It features the use of a Z80, an 8080, a 6502, or any of the other CPU devices that have become standard components in the microcomputer industry.

microcomputer architecture, single-chip 8-bit—*See* microcomputer, 8-bit vs. 16-bit.

microcomputer buses — A bus is an

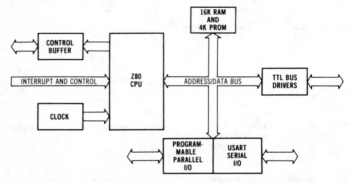

Microcomputer architecture (Courtesy Zilog Corp.).

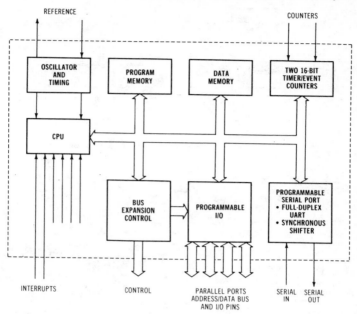

REFERENCE

COUNTERS

| OSCILLATOR AND TIMING | PROGRAM MEMORY | DATA MEMORY | TWO 16-BIT TIMER/EVENT COUNTERS |

CPU

| BUS EXPANSION CONTROL | PROGRAMMABLE I/O | PROGRAMMABLE SERIAL PORT • FULL-DUPLEX UART • SYNCHRONOUS SHIFTER |

INTERRUPTS   CONTROL   PARALLEL PORTS ADDRESS/DATA BUS AND I/O PINS   SERIAL IN   SERIAL OUT

Microcomputer architecture, single-chip 8-bit.

electrical connection that serves as a communication path between the components of a system. Some microcomputer systems use at least three types of buses: local, intersystem, and intrasystem. The local bus connects the microprocessor and support chips, while the intersystem bus provides communication between the complete system and the outside— the peripheral devices or other systems. Between the local and intersystem devices is the intrasystem bus, often called simply the "system bus," which provides the communication link between the boards that comprise the microcomputer system. This is where the memory address lines, shared data lines, and control signals transform a collection of pc cards into a working system. The system bus is usually part of the backplane, pre-wired to regularly spaced connectors, with each pin on every connector assigned a specific signal. Each system board has a corresponding connector and is linked into the system by plugging it into a backplane connector.

microcomputer bus system — Devel-oped as a simple, straightforward link between processor and peripheral elements of the system, the typical bus is comprised of numerous bidirectional signal lines, along which addresses, data, and control signals are sent. Some signals contain time-multiplexed information. Communication between devices on the bus is asynchronous. A master/slave relationship exists between two devices on the bus throughout any transaction between them (some systems). At any time, one device (the "bus master") controls the bus; this master device initiates the bus transaction. Data may be transferred either to or from the master device. Arbitration between devices (i.e., which one becomes bus master at a given time) is decided by the processor.

microcomputer card — Also called circuit board. A plug-in unit designed to accommodate printed-circuit wiring and components. The typical card is made up of a base used to mount an electrical circuit and the circuit. The base is usually a laminated or resinous-type material of an insulating

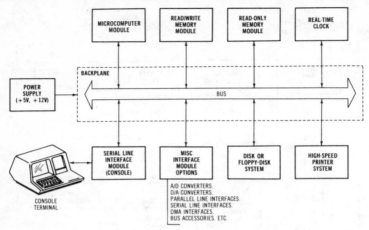

Microcomputer bus system.

type. Typically mounted on a "motherboard" in a card cage.

microcomputer cards versus a CPU chip—Often the addition of a little logic has converted a hard-to-use CPU chip into an easy-to-use computer card. The process of converting a CPU chip into a computer card illustrates some key factors which a user must evaluate before deciding which to buy. The vital ingredient is to provide an interface between the CPU chip pins and the data buses that connect to external memory and peripheral devices. If the CPU chip is to be used in a computer-like application, that is all the logic the computer card requires, since standard memory control logic and I/O device control logic will complete the interface.

microcomputer classification — Microcomputers are often classified by the number of bits that can be handled by their CPU. Performance is judged on a basis of utility of the instruction set, the number of bits that need to be stored in the program to carry out the task they are assigned, and the speed with which they execute typical programs. Though speed is an important consideration in many applications, there are some possibilities for speed-price tradeoffs due to manufacturers' capabilities involving large-scale integrated circuits. The most popular microprocessors today are not necessarily the most ad-

Microcomputer card (Courtesy Zilog Corp.).

vanced or the most efficient. Thus, a broader applications-oriented scheme has involved into five classes: (1) low-end units for simple control applications and the replacement of electromechanical devices, (2) intermediate units to replace hard-wired logic in more complex industrial controllers, communications, and other equipment, (3) high-end units with minicomputer-like structures for use in such applications as data processing and real-time control, (4) bit-slice units for very high performance applications, and (5) micromainframes.

microcomputer, communications—Four data input/output (I/O) paths typically will be required in order for a microcomputer to communicate: (1) CPU to memory, (2) memory to CPU, (3) CPU to peripheral devices, and (4) peripheral devices to CPU. It is also logical to differentiate between memory and peripheral devices during I/O operations. Memory I/O is very fast and occurs during the instruction fetch phase of every instruction's execution; also, memory is addressable to a very elementary (byte or word) level. However, peripheral device I/O is too slow to constitute an integral part of instruction execution and must be treated as an accessory to CPU operations. Typical operational examples are: (1) Front-End Processing—interfacing to a host computer, (2) Remote Data Concentration—multiplexing from many low-speed to one or more high-speed lines, (3) Message Switching—store, analyze, check, process, then transmit, (4) Terminal Control—performing control of hardware, and (5) Network Processing and Control—support of local data bases, network hardware, and protocols.

microcomputer-controlled terminal — The typical use of a microcontroller in a terminal network application is one designed to provide intelligence, system programmability, and buffer memory. The devices also control data networks, at rates up to 9600 baud, using asynchronous/synchronous adapters. A typical 8- or 16-bit microprocessor provides communications protocol control, code conversion/editing, local data processing, or custom-programming functions for one or more terminals. Also included are network-communications line adapters plus optional peripheral interfaces.

microcomputer control panel—A programmer's control panel is supplied with some systems to provide access to the CPU registers and to the memory. It generally includes an array of data switches, data and address indicators, and function switches. Using the programmer's panel, an operator can address, load, and examine memory and CPU registers, and control the operation of the microcomputer. It provides features useful in program debugging and system operations. The control-panel logic module contains the interfacing circuits needed for the control panel.

microcomputer CPU — In general aspects, the CPU consists of the following: the program counter (PC), instruction register (IR), instruction execution logic, a memory-address register (MAR), a general-purpose register file (GPR), and an arithmetic and logic unit (ALU). The CPU logic allows bus operation and an ALU operation to be executed simultaneously, or two ALU operations can be executed simultaneously. The two ALU operations can be executed at the same time, providing they do not interfere with one another (for example, by trying to load and unload the ALU adder in one operation). However, a number of ambiguities must be resolved by Control Unit logic. These relate to the No Operation, Conditional Operations, and Instruction Status statements. Instruction Status is indicated by various pins to provide external logic, with information on source of data expected by other pins

Microcomputer-controlled terminal (Courtesy Computer Devices, Inc.).

or destination of data appearing at other pins.

microcomputer development kit — In essence, these are do-it-yourself kits for use with the microprocessor prototyping systems to allow users to design, debug, and modify microprograms readily — eliminating complicated software simulation or emulation. Errors in the microprograms can be detected and corrected before masks are made. Such user-defined microprograms permit the user to increase effective processor speed, shrink system memory requirements, and protect proprietary machine programs from duplication. They also permit implementation of high-level languages directly for more efficiency, development of microdiagnostics for improved fault isolation, and emulation of larger computers with similar architecture. Many systems operate in parallel with the standard instruction set and a complete package of system software. A typical kit contains a cross assembler, a simulator, and a PROM programmer. It converts a specific computer into a microcomputer development system.

microcomputer development system — Microcomputer development systems are designed to simplify product design cycles. They provide a test bed for interfaces and related hardware, as well as a full program-preparation facility with resident on-line hardware and software debugging aids. Peripheral interfaces often include tty, high-speed paper-tape equipment, and serial line printers with magnetic-tape cassettes. Various card-level modules of the systems range from microcomputers and memory and I/O modules to general-purpose arrays. These systems, often purchased by large users of microprocessors for program development and debugging, are specially designed tools to employ software devices, such as exercisers, emulators, etc., to eliminate manual I/O and the need for the user to be fluent in hexadecimal. They often include terminals, tapes, cassettes, floppy disks, etc.

microcomputer disk operating systems (DOS) — A typical disk operating system is a complete batch processing system optimized to reduce the time and cost of program development. It provides all of the file management and utility functions required for generating, debugging, storing, and modifying programs. Using DOS, programs can be developed either for stand-alone applications or for operation under real-time executives. When running under DOS, user programs can take advantage of the DOS executive services and I/O control systems (IOCS) functions. DOS generally includes a complete device independent logical unit oriented to IOCS with dynamic physical unit assignments. Support is provided for peripheral devices, including disks, tapes, cassettes, paper tapes, printers, and terminals. File-handling facilities provide for creation and maintenance of named symbolic and binary files in random access or sequential modes, blocked or unblocked.

microcomputer, 8-bit vs. 16-bit — There is no doubt about the clear superiority of a 16-bit microcomputer over an 8-bit microcomputer for general-purpose data processing. Most 16-bit microcomputers are far more powerful in that they can process data faster and more efficiently. Data moves through the computer 16 bits at a time rather than 8 bits at a time, and, therefore, many types of arithmetic, logic, and data transfer operations take place at a higher speed. This is not only an advantage but also a must for many applications. Typically, 16-bit microcomputers have a more powerful instruction set that allows them to perform a wider variety of operations than their 8-bit cousins. This further speeds up and simplifies internal operations. While an 8-bit microcomputer can often be programmed to perform the same functions as a 16-bit computer, the 16-bit machine will typically do it faster, with fewer instructions, and using less memory. "Computing power" is the primary reason for purchasing a 16-bit microcomputer instead of an 8-bit microcomputer.

microcomputer execution cycle — The steps required for a microcomputer to execute an instruction are: (1) the instruction, in a binary code, is fetched from its memory storage location, and held in the microcomputer's instruction register, (2) the microcomputer decodes the instruction code, and (3) the microcomputer executes the operations requested by the decoded instruction.

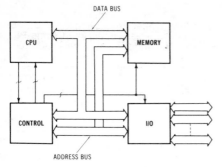

DATA BUS

ADDRESS BUS

Microcomputer functions.

microcomputer functions — All microcomputers (in fact, all practical digital computers) consist of four basic functions — central processing unit (CPU), control, memory, and input/output (I/O). Connecting the various functions are the address and data buses, plus various control lines. While all microcomputers have essentially the same general architecture (i.e., perform the same four functions), there are a number of differences in the way the various functions are implemented. The most obvious differences occur between MOS and bipolar technologies. In the MOS approach, for example, the most common implementation places the CPU and control function both on one chip. This chip —which was the original "microprocessor" — inputs instructions and data, performs the operation required by the instruction, and outputs the resulting data. It also provides the addressing function to locate the instructions in memory, and to Read or Write data in memory and/or I/O. Because the decoding circuitry for the instructions (the main portion of the control section) is hardwired on the chip, the same instruction (set of "1s" and "0s") will always cause the same operation (add, subtract, compare, etc.) to be performed, and therefore, the instruction set is said to be "fixed." This is one of the major distinctions between MOS and bipolar microprocessors.

microcomputer instruments—The typical analytical scientific instrument uses microcomputers to control the collection, conversion, and recording of data. For example, a microcomputer can control scanning in spectrographic devices like spectrometers and Fourier interferometers, automatically adjust sensors and transducers for out-of-limit conditions, compensate collected data for automatic gain adjustments, average collected data, transform data using processes like the fast Fourier transform, convert data to engineering units and provide formatted printouts. Several commercially available instruments offer these features.

microcomputer I/O architecture — The I/O architecture of a microcomputer generally breaks down into the following areas: transfer techniques, instruction formats, buses, bus structures, interrupt schemes, and memory-access techniques. Most microprocessors allow for three types of I/O transfer techniques: programmed transfer, interrupt-program control, and hardware control. In the first two cases, found in most simple applications, the microprocessor controls the transfer. In the third case, system hardware controls the transfer.

microcomputer master/slave operation —The master/slave design lends itself well to systems where there is a high degree of information transfer and I/O. Data-collection networks, instruments with intelligent plug-ins, POS terminal networks, and certain process-control systems are only a few applications that exhibit the high information transfer and high I/O activity level. In these applications, the slave microcomputers pass the I/O to and from the master. There, the data are concentrated and/or processed, and sometimes forwarded for external communication. Information can be transferred from microcomputer to microcomputer, either directly via a common bus or radially with a dedicated bus. The information flow is usually directly between elements, rather than through the common-memory scheme that is associated more closely with a master/master system. When a slave requests the attention of the master, the master— at some point based on a priority— grants the request. It then sets up the information route from the slave to the master or from the requesting slave to another destination slave. The number of slave microcomputers per system is a function of the I/O capacity of the system and the distribution to maintain an efficient information throughput. Other considerations, such as the degree of physical integration desired and the packaging cost of the microcomputer are also relevant.

microcomputer, micromainframe — In early 1981, four semiconductor manufacturers announced that they had developed 32-bit microcomputers which had the power of, in effect, putting a major mainframe computer on a chip or a chip set. Intel Corporation's iAPX-432, in three chips (with some containing 200,000 MOS devices, or almost one-half million total), offers operating system functions such as process scheduling, process dispatching, and the like. It supports modular programming, variable length data structures, and, in essence, performs with a power equal to a majority of the mainframe computer systems. Hewlett-Packard Components, Bell Labs (of AT&T), and National Semiconductor Corporation also offered similar systems (as did Fujitsu Ltd., sometime later), and Motorola Semiconductor Products Inc. is expected to follow quickly with their 32-bit chip system.

microcomputer performance criteria— Performance is what comes from "computing power." It is hard to define and is a very subtle term, but it is important. Power is wrapped up in, and influenced by, these things:

1. Number of instructions — the more instructions, the greater the power.
2. Number of registers—the more, the better.
3. Amount of addressable memory —again, the more, the better.
4. Computing speed — that is, the faster, the better. This is usually a function of semiconductor technology.
5. Software — the availability of good software is essential.

Basically, the microcomputer that can perform a specific function the fastest, with the fewest instructions, and can address a lot of memory, is the best.

microcomputer, single-board — A typical single-board microcomputer is designed to operate as a complete computer with its own self-contained memory, plus serial and parallel I/O ports. It might feature the use of a CPU (central processing unit), a CTC (counter timer circuit), and some PIO (parallel input-output) devices.

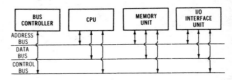

Microcomputer, 16-bit.

microcomputer, 16-bit—A 16-bit microcomputer is designed to perform in a system environment of connected units. The system consists of a central processing unit (the 16-bit microcomputer), memory units, I/O units (peripheral controllers), and a bus controller. These units communicate over a system bus consisting of a 16-bit-wide address bus, a 16-bit-wide bidirectional data bus, and a control bus. The control bus is a collection of signals that include the memory and I/O interface controls and the interrupt request lines.

microcomputer S-100 bus—The S-100 bus is a 100-wire bus used in many personal microcomputers. Because they all have the same pattern of four interconnections, the plug-in board from one microcomputer will work (usually) when plugged into another S-100 machine. The S means "standard."

microcomputer word processing—Microcomputer applications include word processing, an office equipment application, i.e., controlling one or more typewriters that are used to edit text stored on cassettes or floppy disks.

microcontroller—1. A microprogrammed machine, a microprocessor, or a microcomputer used in a control operation; that is, to direct or make changes in a process or operation. 2. Any device or instrument that controls a process with high resolution, usually over a narrow region.

microcontroller applications —- There are generally three classes of control applications: Device Control, in which a single machine tool or computer peripheral is sequenced through its different operations; Data Control, in which data from one or more sources must be moved to one or more destinations or where multiple low-speed data paths are concentrated into a higher-speed data path; and Process Control, in which discrete inputs from measured process variables are used in a closed loop environment.

microcontroller characteristics—A typical microcontroller is a general-purpose microcomputer. Several types use bipolar LSI technology. They are designed to provide an effective and practical cost/performance solution to a wide range of problems. Microcontrollers can provide significant advantages over the present methods of implementing digital system design for control. A control system should be able to respond to external variables by altering the program sequence and generating data for the outside world. A microcontroller becomes a tool for the designer to use in implementing a programmable logic design. A capability exists in the system to store and execute control sequences. The principal elements of a microcontroller system are the processor, the interface vector, and the working storage. Some interfaces use a uniform method of input/output connection that accepts variable field length sizes; thus, additional expensive custom circuitry for I/O is not required. The working storage can provide 256 or more bytes and may be viewed as an extension of the data registers in the processor. The programmed microcontroller often becomes the controlling subsystem in the overall specified system.

microcontroller external input signals—Typically, external input signals direct the operation of microcontroller systems. In some systems, the internal crystal-controlled clock sets the operating rate of the system. The reset signal establishes the initial state. User inputs via a special Interface Vector, in combination with the stored program, control the execution sequence of program steps and the consequent value of user output signals available at the Interface Vector. User input/output control signals (Byte Input Control and Byte Output Control) establish the instant at which the external user signals are input to or output from the microcontroller system (some systems).

microcontroller functional components—A typical microcontroller is a complete microcomputer system consisting of:
* A central processing unit called the Interpreter.
* Read-only program storage.
* Optional Read/Write data storage called Working Storage with a variable field access to 1 to 8 bits.
* A complete bit-addressable input/output system called the Interface Vector.

microcontroller, general-purpose — There are numerous ways to construct a good general-purpose microprogrammed controller. Many systems consist of register files that store immediate results and communicate with the outside world, an arithmetic unit for processing information, a ROM (Read-only memory) control store, and circuits which control the access to the ROM. A controller must be able to interconnect economically to many input and output points. In design examples, connections are made to the outside world using a register structure. To meet the criteria established, these registers must be both numerous and economical.

microcontroller I/O system—A typical microcontroller I/O system is treated as a set of internal registers. Therefore, data from external devices may be processed (tested, shifted, added to, etc.) without first moving them to internal storage. In fact, the entire concept is to treat data at the I/O interface no differently than internal data. This concept extends to the software which allows variables at the input/output system to be named and treated in the same way as data in storage.

microcontroller simulator — A microcontroller simulator is a programming and design test instrument. It provides the designer with a microcontroller with which he can interconnect and run his system in real-time. The operator's options include: (1) modification of the program and data, (2) specification of breakpoints, (3) starting, stopping, or single-stepping the program, and (4) instruction insertion.

microcontroller, single-chip—One type

that is designed for dedicated computing and control applications is a stand-alone 40-pin device that requires few or no support circuits. It contains its own register file, mask-programmable control ROM, output PLA, internal oscillator, and power reset circuitry. It is directly TTL compatible. An editor, assembler, and simulator are also available.

microcontroller working registers—The working registers can generally both supply data to the arithmetic unit and receive data from it. Therefore, these registers can be used to store intermediate results and also buffer data. Working registers have input and output connections to the outside world. They can be used to accept data from an external source and drive an external device. Working registers can be implemented from RAMs (random-access memories) and are, therefore, very inexpensive. Output registers can be loaded from the arithmetic unit. They can be used for presenting data to the outside world. For example, they can be employed to drive indicators, a computer data bus, or to supply data to a magnetic tape or disk. This type of register can be implemented inexpensively because of the limited number of interconnection paths to the register.

microcontroller working storage — A typical working storage provides 256 bytes of temporary storage. It may be viewed as an extension of the data registers in the processor. The processor may address a variable length field in working storage. Intermediate storage for program data or input/output data buffering are typical uses for the working storage.

microcontrol microprogramming — There are generally two sections of microcontrol. One set of outputs is used to control the data paths. It is labeled data-path control. The other set of outputs is used in the determination of the next address and it is fed into a logic network where it is combined with status information from the data paths and is then used to select the next address. The information in the data-path control section of the ROM will, for example, gate data from the various registers into the arithmetic unit, select the function that the unit will perform on the data, and gate the result into the

appropriate register. It is highly desirable to have the ROM Read cycle as small a fraction as is possible of the basic machine cycle. This gives the system the maximum amount of time to select the next microinstruction.

microcycle — Often, manufacturers use a basic cycle time or period, sometimes called a microcycle, to specify the instruction execution speed. This may be the inverse of the clock frequency or a multiple (possibly two or three times) of the clock frequency. Each instruction is then defined as requiring several microcycles for execution. As a result, a three-microcycle instruction may actually require 3, 6, or 9 clock cycles. Longer instructions, such as multiply and divide, can require tens or even hundreds of microcycles.

microdiagnostics—Troubleshooting requirements often difficult. A microdiagnostic will detect a problem in a few seconds, but locating the failing component in less than a few minutes is difficult. A test device is often controlled by the microprocessor Control Store, a ROM. The ROM can be replaced with a high-speed RAM (Writable Control Store), and a set of microdiagnostics can be written to exercise the processor and detect faults. To make the test a complete one, a memory subsystem can be used in conjunction with the software diagnostics to check the processor with memory. I/O simulators are designed to test the I/O control and logic and are often available. However, testing at CPU speed is a more difficult requirement to meet because the Control Store is located some distance away electrically. This problem can be solved, however, by using terminated twisted-pair wires and by selecting RAMs for the Writable Control Store that will operate at faster than average speeds.

microelectronic devices — Devices made up of transistors, resistors, capacitors, and similar components, and fabricated along with their interconnections on a single substrate in a single series of operations. The primary material of microelectronic circuits is usually silicon.

microelectronics — 1. Technique of solid-state circuits in which units of semiconductors are formed into several components. 2. That area of electronic technology associated with or applied to the construction of electronics systems from extremely small electronic parts or elements.

microfabrication — The smaller that most solid-state device elements are, the faster they operate, the less power they will require, and the less they will cost. A new advance in electron-beam lithography permits the design of circuits with features smaller than ever before. Features as small as 350 angstroms wide, or 1/300th of the size of a human brain cell, can be placed on conventional silicon chips. The features are visible on the scanning electron microscope screen. The new technique can be used to fabricate high-speed microelectronic devices for use in chip and telecommunications systems.

microfiche—A unit film record containing images in a two-axis coordinate system. Microfiche images are recorded by rows or by columns. Microfiche are normally 105mm × 148mm, but may be almost any length due to special application requirements. Standard microfiche reduction ratios are 24X, 42X, and 48X. Microfiche are sometimes referred to as fiche.

microfiche, laser-beam retrieval — A system, developed by the Central Intelligence Agency (CIA), speeds up the process of finding data on microfiche. Using an optical reference of interference patterns created by key words and phrases, the system "looks at" microfiche files with a laser beam. Whenever a key word is detected, the system automatically triggers a hard-copy duplication of the relevant page. The CIA developed this system to extract information on individuals and events from records of all sorts that were maintained on microfilm or fiche—newspapers, typewritten pages, or TWX messages.

microfiche viewer—An engineering data reader that enables operators to view data stored on aperture cards, microfiche, fiche jackets, or a combination of all three.

microfilm—A fine-grain high-resolution film containing an image that is greatly reduced in size as compared to its original paper form. The recording of micro-images onto microfilm utilizes numerous techniques and film types. Film widths of 16 mm, 35 mm, 82.5 mm, and 105 mm are used in COM with 16 mm and 105 mm film widths being the most common.

microfilm cartridge—Refers to a container, enclosing roll microfilm, that is designed to be inserted into readers or other retrieval devices.

microfilm, computer output (COM)—1. Normal printed output of a computer reduced to one of several available microforms by a special output device that takes the place of the line printer. The COM device allows high-quality output at speeds of 5000 or more lines per minute. 2. A microfilm printer that will take output directly from the computer, thus substituting for a line printer or tape output. *See also* COM.

microfilm image—The legend contained in a microfilm frame. The reproduction on microfilm of the words, numbers, and other information on a document.

microfilm procedures, CIM—The basic purpose of CIM (Computer Input, Microfilm) is to place information that is on microfilm into a computer in order to manipulate the data. Updating can be done by combining with new data, deleting, or rearranging the old data. Automatic interpretation of information is also possible. This is particularly useful with medical recordings, photographs, and electrical measurements. When combined with OCR software capabilities, CIM can provide the highest quality automatic reading process. The medium (microfilm) is easier to handle than paper. It is also possible to have higher accuracy when working with transmitted light rather than reflected light.

Microfiche viewer (Courtesy AM International, Inc.).

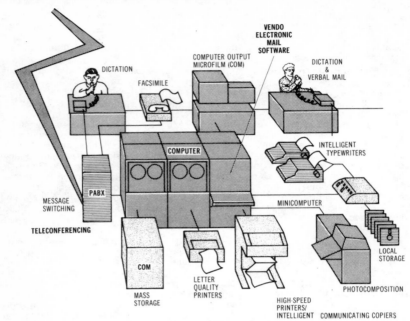

Microfilm, computer output (COM).

microform — Any reduced film image. This includes all versions of roll film and microfiche.

microinstruction — 1. A small single short type of command (add, shift, or delete). 2. A bit pattern that is stored in a microprogram memory word and which specifies the operation of the individual LSI computing elements and related subunits, such as main memory and input/output interfaces.

micromainframe — Bell Labs' 32-bit digital microprocessor (introduced early in 1981) contains 100,000 transistors and is claimed to have "three-quarters" of the processing power of current medium-sized mainframe computers. Intel Corporation offered its 32-bit 3-chip iAPX-432 system, in sample kits, early in 1981. It was acknowledged to be a more than adequate substitute for many mainframe computers. The Hewlett-Packard Components' 32-bit microcomputer system (on 6 chips) appears to be a most powerful and densely constructed microcomputer. (*See* micromainframe construction, VLSI.)

micromainframe construction, VLSI — Hewlett-Packard Components has produced a 32-bit VLSI central processor chip that contains 450,000 transistors in an area that is only ¼-inch square. It operates at a frequency of 18 MHz. The interconnect lines are on a 2.5-micron scale grid that is 1/10,000 of an inch in size. The metal conductors are only 1.5 microns wide and are spaced by 1 micron. To show them, in a slide, requires such magnification that if the entire chip were to be shown at that magnification, it would require 300,000 separate photographs. Eight masking steps, involving depositions of phosphorus and boron, using E beams, nitride and oxide growth, and dry etching (using inert zenon gas) were needed to make this complex chip. The memory alone (occupying less than one-half of the chip's area) contains a storage capacity of 9000 "words," each of which consist of 38 bits. This represents a 342-kilobit ROM (Read-only memory), or a memory so large that it can store enough code to permit the microprocessor chip to accept program instructions written in a high-level language.

microminiaturization — 1. Production and use of circuit components of very small dimensions, involving vacuum-deposited films, e.g., Nichrome on ceramic rods for resistors, oxide layers for capacitor dielectrics, etc. 2. The process of reducing the size of parts, photographs, or printed materials for economical convenient storage or packing. Microminiaturized circuits are usually etched, evaporated, or electronically deposited metals, inks, or other materials used to form extremely tiny monolithic chips, blocks, or other integrations. *See* large-scale integration (LSI).

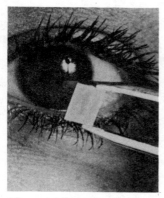

Microminiaturization (Courtesy NCR Corp.).

micromodule—Refers to an especially tiny electronic device with standardized dimensions (usually fabricated using semiconductor techniques) that is capable of performing one or more functions in a circuit.

micron — 1. Unit for electromagnetic wavelengths, one-millionth of a meter. Also used for measurement of dust, condensation, and suspensions. Abbreviated μ. 2. A unit of length equal to one-thousandth of a millimeter, i.e., one-millionth of a meter or 39-millionths of an inch.

microprocessing systems — A typical multiprocessing subgroup defines the symmetrical and the asymmetrical systems. In a symmetrical system, every processor is performing the identical task as every other proces-

sor. The only difference is in the use of different data variables. In an asymmetrical system, each processor has a different task. These tasks are related and generally dependent on data from other processors in the network.

microprocessing unit — Abbreviated MPU. The main constituent of the hardware of the microcomputer. It consists of the microprocessor, the main memory (composed of Read/Write and Read-only memory), the input/output interface devices, and the clock circuit, in addition to buffer, driver circuits, and passive circuit elements. The MPU does not contain power supplies, cabinet, or control console, and is normally understood to be an assembled printed-circuit board. The level of sophistication of the MPU is that of the named microcomputer.

Microprocessor (Courtesy Zilog, Inc.).

microprocessor — The semiconductor central processing unit (CPU) and one of the principal components of the microcomputer. The elements of the microprocessor are frequently contained on a single chip or within the same package, but are sometimes distributed over several separate chips. In a microcomputer with a fixed instruction set, the microprocessor consists of the arithmetic logic unit and the control logic unit. In a microcomputer with a microprogrammed instruction set, it contains an additional control-memory unit.

microprocessor analyzer—1. A digital diagnostic instrument for testing and debugging of MPU hardware and software. 2. An instrument for designing, troubleshooting, and testing both program and hardware in systems using microprocessors. These instruments often eliminate the need for control panels, diagnostic routines, or other data-processing tools for testing microprocessor-based systems. Used in conjunction with a standard oscilloscope, analyzers can test both program and hardware either together or individually. The analyzers display all data related to a selected instruction cycle and generate a scope sync pulse. Some types interface to the system under test through use of a DIP connector that clips onto the microprocessor.

microprocessor applications—Because of its unique system partitioning, microprocessor device sets can be applied across a wide range of applications. In automotive applications, the microprocessor operates on such inputs as engine rpm, vacuum, pressures, and temperatures, and generates ignition dwell and timing angles. The CPU performs the necessary computations with look-up tables and/or by solving engine equations directly. Such systems use RAMs, and all memory addressing is done with 12 or more address lines. In a home, a single microprocessor could assure efficient use of several heavy appliances, such as air conditioners, ovens, dishwashers, and washing machines.

microprocessor architecture — Architectural features include general-purpose registers, stacks, interface structure, choice of memories, etc.

Microprocessor architecture.

General-purpose registers are used for addressing, indexing, status, and as multiple accumulators. They simplify programming and conserve main memory by eliminating memory buffering of data. Multiple accumulators are especially important for ROM programs that have no writable memory.

microprocessor architecture, bit-slice —The basic architecture of a multiple bit-slice processor can be split into three major blocks: the bit slices, the controller, and the control store. However, for a full system, many other circuits are required. The items that are necessary for it to work include: memories, buffers, interface circuits, and clocks. The ALU (arithmetic-logic unit) and the MAR (memory-address register) are usually combined into a single circuit referred to as a bit slice.

microprocessor cache memory—A typical cache memory consists of a cluster of bipolar units arranged in four blocks of four words each. Each memory board contains one cache. When addressing memory, the CPU checks cache and main memory. If the word is in cache, the data are transferred. An error check doesn't require extra CPU time. Error-detection/correction memories use 5 bits more than noncorrecting units. The extra bits are for a computation made by both memory and CPU when they exchange data.

microprocessor cards—Typical microprocessor cards are often flexible, low-cost, self-contained 8-bit parallel processors and controllers. They are designed for computer-oriented equipment such as data terminals, test systems, communications equipment, machine tool controllers, process control systems, and peripheral device controllers. A typical microprocessor is packaged on an 8½ - by 11-inch printed-wiring card. A 144-pin edge terminal connects the circuits to interfacing units (one system). With them, the system designer can have a proven, totally debugged, processor that he may customize to his immediate application by programming rather than by hard-wiring. This technique can save considerable cost, both in terms of money and development time. This is in contrast to costly inhouse-developed processors or controllers that use hard-wired or permanent logic.

microprocessor chip — An integrated circuit that contains all the essential elements of a central processor, including the control logic, instruction decoding, and arithmetic-processing circuitry. To be useful, the microprocessor chip or chips are combined with memory and I/O integrated-circuit chips to form a microcomputer. Microprocessors are viable alternatives to hard-wired circuits for many control-oriented functions. Standing alone, a microprocessor chip can do nothing. It functions only in the context of a microcomputer system, in which appropriate integrated-circuit chips are incorporated to complement the basic function of the microprocessor—to serve as a central processing unit (CPU) in which logic and arithmetic operations and data transfers between registers, memory, and the outside world are performed. One specific microcomputer system with 4K of solid-state memory and a control panel is built around the Intel 8080 microprocessor chip. Except for a power supply, it is completely operational. The system is bus structured and has all important inputs and outputs connected to a solderless breadboarding socket, permitting interfacing with scores of devices.

microprocessor chip characteristics— A typical microprocessor chip has the following general characteristics: (1) 8-bit organization, (2) 2-μs instruction cycle time, (3) over 70 microprocessor instructions, (4) 64 general-purpose registers in the CPU, (5) binary and decimal arithmetic and logic functions, (6) up to 65,536 bytes of ROM and RAM in any combination, (7) internal-programmable real-time clocks, (8) internal power-on and reset logic, (9) multilevel interrupt handling, and (10) clock and timing circuits. For example, the typical microprocessor chip set is tied together via an 8-bit bidirectional data bus, timing, and control lines. These data, timing, and control lines connect to buses that interface to the memory and to I/O interface units.

microprocessor chip, ROM—A typical microprocessor ROM gives the user the ability to: (1) load user programs or data into memory from either the keyboard or tape, (2) execute user programs, (3) list user programs or data within specified memory locations on the terminal or tape, (4) print the data contents within the internal CPU registers, and (5) change the data in specified memory locations or the CPU registers.

microprocessor classifications—There are at least four major classifications of microcomputer systems: calculators, controllers, data processors, and general-purpose computers. Controllers and calculators are the most likely candidates for single-chip CPUs. Data processors and general-purpose computers require more flexibility and are better served by a multichip system. Most microprocessors claim to be microprogrammable since they make use of ROM to store an intermediate-level program or a higher-level program.

microprocessor compiler — A program that translates the source program into machine language. These compilers, which can be run on a medium- or large-scale computer, are available from several time-sharing services.

microprocessor controller—Some microprocessor controllers were designed to eliminate the tape reader as part of the PROM programmer system. The controller, which is built around a microprocessor, plugs into the terminal through an umbilical cord in place of the terminal microprocessor. The controller consists of a switch/light panel, similar to that used on a minicomputer, as well as the circuitry for the light drivers, switch debouncers, and certain special features. The controller provides readout of memory address and bus status, allows single stepping of program execution and substitution of memory data with data from the switches, and has hardware breakpoint capabilities. In effect, the controller is to the microprocessor what the operator's panel is to a minicomputer.

microprocessor cross-assembler — If the software that converts the programmer's listing into object code resides in a computer other than the selected microprocessor, it is called a cross-assembler. On the other hand, if conversion software resides in a computer using the selected microprocessor, it is called an assembler. Both forms produce identical outputs.

microprocessor, custom — A microprocessor can be a single chip, a self-contained component, or an un-assembled collection of processor-related components, consisting of memories, peripheral and I/O (input/output) chips, a CPU (central processor unit) chip, clocks, and interface chips. The "custom" composition varies depending on the manufacturer, the application, and the user. Software is generally not provided in component form except in the case of high-level language interpreters, which have appeared in ROM or PROM.

microprocessor debugging program — A debugging program usually resides in the microprocessor memory and is used during application program development to assist in error correcting (debugging). It permits debugging via the keyboard. The program can be a formatted tape-cassette tape or a paper tape that is punched in binary code, directly transferable into the memory of the MPS.

microprocessor, high-end — High-end microprocessors are characterized by the use of more memory, Interrupt, and DMA (direct-memory access). Such performance can be obtained by using faster microprocessors, including microprocessors with large word widths and other improved facilities. More data and control can be incorporated in the 16-bit word. Two data bytes can be stored and retrieved from a single memory location. In applications such as process control, where the natural data word is greater than 8 bits, the advantage of the large word size is more significant. Many high-end microprocessors require a combined program and data memory of between 8K and 1M words; DMA and Interrupt capabilities are a must, either directly on the CPU chip or via peripheral chips.

microprocessor instructions — Microprocessor instructions are often divided into three general classifications: (1) memory reference, so called because they operate on specific memory locations, (2) operating instructions that function without needing a memory reference, and (3) I/O instructions for transferring data between the microprocessor and peripheral devices.

microprocessor "intelligence"— In an MPU-based design, "intelligence" refers to the control program, a sequence of instructions that guides the MPU through the various operations it must perform. During system development, users have a predefined instruction set to prepare a satisfactory control program. The program, usually called "software" at this point, is then stored in memory that can be accessed by the MPU during operation, thus becoming the system's intelligence. Once in ROM memory, the program is usually called "firmware."

microprocessor I/O—Microprocessors, the central processing units in microcomputers, have I/O characteristics similar to minicomputers. They are restricted, however, by physical chip size (package pins limitation), and word length (resolution), which varies from 4 to 32 bits. The capability to interface I/O devices has evolved from the relatively primitive units to high-capacity units with advanced features included in many new units. A typical unit, for example, contains a separate bus that is 16 bits wide with a 3-state driving capability that is separated from its bidirectional 8-bit data bus. These lines can address as many as 256 I/O devices. The unit can also handle multiple interrupt requests from peripherals and can initiate DMA transfers.

microprocessor language assembler— A microprocessor language assembler is often a powerful floppy-disk-oriented system that is used to assemble a source code on a minicomputer and then convert it into a binary output. This output is then loaded and executed on the CPU module. Input is usually prepared with the aid of a special program, but source text can, however, be generated off-line on a teletypewriter or other type terminal.

microprocessor language editor — An editor can be provided in the form of a floppy disk which is loaded into memory by means of a special program, using either the low- or high-speed terminal system. The editor facilitates both program entry and program correction. Source text is entered either directly from the keyboard or via the low-speed (teletypewriter) terminal or high-speed (floppy disk) terminal. Once in memory, the program text can be freely changed, deleted, or reformatted. Some microprocessor language editors are com-

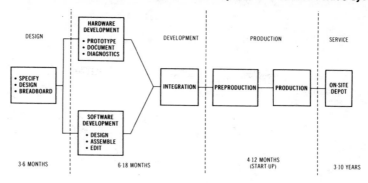

Microprocessor life cycles.

puter-based editor-oriented to paper tape usages, are interactive, and offer an extensive set of commands which can be entered from the teletypewriter terminal or similar keyboard terminal. They are used primarily as an on-line tool for the creation and modification of source program tapes.

microprocessor life cycles—Microprocessor-based products have short design cycles that typically reach the production stage within two years. Once on the market, these products can have a useful life of up to ten years. Consequently, field-service equipment must be able to accommodate several generations of products operating in the field during the the same time period.

microprocessor, low-end — A low-end microprocessor application typically has some kind of man/machine interface such as a keyboard, a series of switches, displays, an indicator, etc. Processor speeds for a low-end application are not critical. Instruction cycle times between 2 μs and 10 μs are generally acceptable. The man/machine interface also places a requirement for BCD capability on the system, since it is more convenient to handle numerical data in BCD form than in binary, where human entry and display are concerned. A low-end application will have a program memory size greater than 1K words, but less than 4K. Other characteristics of a low-end microprocessor are lots of I/O and bit manipulation, and instruction mixes that contain a large quantity of conditional branches and

jumps. Word size can be either 4 or 8 bits.

microprocessor master/master operation—In a master/master system, communication between elements is less frequent and is more formatted or refined than in a master/slave system. Communication between elements is predetermined by each master. Each master is more inclined to perform a higher degree of dedicated activity associated with a particular system entity. A master processor contacts the other processor or processors with which it needs to communicate. This communication can be direct or via a common memory. Access to the communication bus is on a priority basis, arbitrated by a common logic tree usually located within the common memory or at some central location. Master/master systems are becoming more popular than master/slave. They can be used in multi-instrument test systems where a separate processor controls each instrument but passes results to a central processor for final summarization.

microprocessor master/slave systems —Processor organization or configuration depends to some extent on factors such as: number of I/O ports and their location, type of I/O ports and activity rate, type of processing required, and microcomputer cost-performance characteristics. Two basic organizations used are master/master and master/slave. Either organization (or any other) can perform the four basic system functions. The master/slave arrangement imposes a rigid hierarchy on subsystem components. All slave processors communicate to a single master, which acts as either a concentrator or information switcher assigned to control the subsystems communication activity. An instrument with several "plug-ins," all of which require the attention of the instrument mainframe, is a specific example. The mainframe is the master and the plug-ins are the slaves.

microprocessor memory interface—For applications requiring more memory than the RAM located on the CPU, several memory interface circuits can be included in the microprocessor. Each device can generate more address lines and the signals necessary to interface with up to 65K or more bytes of RAM, PROM, or ROM memory, Other devices may be used in conjunction with standard static semiconductor memory devices.

microprocessor monitor — A system monitor gives users complete control over the operation of the system. All necessary functions for program loading and execution are provided while additional commands implement extensive debugging facilities. These facilities include the capabilty to examine and modify memory or CPU register contents, set program breakpoints, and initiate program execution at any given address. Users can dynamically reassign system peripherals via monitor commands through calls to the system monitor's I/O subroutines (some systems).

microprocessor read-only memory programmer—This unit is a computer-based program which, in conjunction with a processor and a PROM hardware programming option, allows the user to load, verify, and modify programs in a PROM chip. Data can be entered by means of binary paper tapes produced directly from a teletypewriter terminal keyboard.

microprocessor semantics — Originally the word microprocessor was used to define MOS-LSI circuit sets organized like a computer — CPU, RAM, ROM, and I/O circuits. "Micro-" was applied for various reasons: the MOS-LSI systems were smaller, slower, and less powerful than a "mini," and they were programmed through microinstructions. Early practices, in applying microprocessors, found semiconductor firms selling sets of CPUs, ROMs,

and RAMs, with equipment manufacturers supplying the TTL circuitry. Microprocessor means the subsystem of combined CPU, ROMs, and RAMs to many persons. The microprocessor system phrase is beginning to be used to indicate a programmed microprocessor (CPU-ROM-RAM) with integrated MOS-LSI I/O circuits. A "microprocessor unit" is an alternate term for microprocessor system. Some firms have begun to use microcomputer as another equivalent term for either microprocessor or microprocessor system—i.e., CPU, RAMs, I/Os, and microprogrammed ROMs. However, it is best to reserve the term, microcomputer, for a full microprocessor system: CPU, RAMs, I/Os, and microprogrammed ROMs.

microprocessor "slices"—An important variation to the fixed-word length of 4-bit and 8-bit microprocessor designs is the building block design using either 2-bit or 4-bit "slices" that can be used to build up 8-, 12-, 16-, 24-, and 32-bit wide architectures. The longer word length for both addressing and instructions provides a higher throughput and easier programming while the shorter 4-bit word length uses less hardware and smaller memories. There are many examples of this modular approach where 4-bit slices can be used to build up the registers, arithmetic logic unit (ALU), and I/O data lines to 32-bit widths. Software support and I/O interfaces for these models are not usually practical for wide general use.

Microprocessors, 16-bit (Courtesy Zilog Corp.).

microprocessors, 16-bit — See microprocessor, high-end.

microprocessor system organization— Although a specific system may be configured in a variety of ways from the available modules, the central processor module and the memory module are basic to almost any configuration. The central processing unit (CPU) provides registers for data storage; the arithmetic and logic unit (ALU) is used to process the stored data, and the microprogrammed control section is used to control the operation of the CPU. An input/output section interfaces the registers with the system data bus so data may be transferred between the registers and memory, or peripheral devices. In some systems, the Registers, ALU, and the Input/Output units are controlled by a microprogrammed control section. The operation of the data bus is controlled by the bus control section of the CPU module. Bus operation generally is asynchronous with respect to ALU and register operations, so data may be transferred between memory and a peripheral (or a second processor) independent of ALU operation. The bus control section provides for bus timing and resolves the priority of devices requesting bus access.

microprogram—1. This generally refers to computer instructions which do not reference the main memory. Microprogramming is a technique to design subroutines by programming the very minute computer operations. As regards microprocessors, microprograms can implement a higher language program by storing microinstructions in ROM. 2. A program of analytic instructions which the programmer intends to construct from the basic subcommands of a digital computer. 3. A sequence of pseudo-commands that will be translated by hardware into machine subcommands. 4. A means of building various analytic instructions as needed from the subcommand structure of a computer. 5. A plan for obtaining maximum utilization of the abilities of a digital computer by efficient use of the subcommands of the machine. 6. A type of program that directly controls the operation of each functional element in a microprocessor. 7. A program of microcode, using basic subcommands. 8. The operations making up a single step are called microopera-

tions. A collection of microoperations executed in one basic machine cycle is a microinstruction. A sequence of microinstructions is a microprogram.

microprogram assembly language — Computer-dependent machine language using mnemonics for the basic instruction set. In a microprogrammed computer, each assembly language instruction is implemented by a microprogram.

microprogram, bit-slice — A sequence of microinstructions for a microprogrammed processor (e.g., designed from bit-slice components). A regular control structure in ROM replaces random-logic control elements to control the operation of the ALU. A machine (or macro) instruction is composed of many microinstructions.

microprogram control — A ROM and counter form the basis for execution control logic. To select and generate a timing sequence, users set the counter to the start value and increment it for each step. The ROM decodes each counter value to activate appropriate ROM-output lines. This technique is called microprogram control, since the contents of the ROM control the sequence of operations.

microprogram control functions — The functions of the control portion of a microprogram-controlled central processing unit are very similar to the functions of a central processing unit. The terms "micro" and "macro" are used to distinguish the operations of the control unit from those realized by a central processor. The central processor, under the direction of microinstructions read from its control memory, fetches macroinstructions from main memory. Each macroinstruction is then executed as a series of microinstructions. The main memory contains a macroprogram, while the central processor is defined by the microprogram contained in the control memory. Thus, within a microprogrammed machine, there are at least two levels of control and two levels of programming to be considered. The designer of the central processor is usually concerned with the definition of the macroinstruction set and its realization as a microprogram. The final user of the central processing unit seldom needs to be aware that the CPU was using microprogramming. A description of the macroinstruction set is usually sufficient for his purpose.

microprogram debugging — After the user has checked out as much of the system as possible with diagnostic programs, he is ready to begin debugging his microcode. The diagnostic checkout will tend to increase user confidence that the problems he encounters are, in fact, errors in the microprogramming and not hardware system problems. Microprograms are definitely easier to debug if they have been written in assembly language. For this purpose, the user can either write his own assembler or make use of an assembly program which permits him to generate an assembler to fill his need.

microprogram development—Once the macroinstruction set has been chosen, and the hardware design established, the designer must proceed to write the microprograms for the system. To simplify the writing of these microprograms, a standardized microassembly language can be used in which symbolic representations of the various control functions are used. Programs written in the microassembly language have two main parts—a declaration part, in which various aspects of the control word, etc., are defined and a specification part, in which the contents of each word are symbolically declared. Provision is made for comment statements throughout the program so that the programmer may explain the functions being performed.

The main body of the program, the specification part, defines the sequences of states to be executed, and the operations which take place for each state. Each statement of the specification part of the program defines the action (and location) of one microinstruction, i.e., one or more words of control memory. The statement will declare, either directly or by default, the contents of each control field for the specified microinstruction. Furthermore, the statement will include assignment information designating the address in control memory where the statement is located.

microprogram emulation — Microprogrammed devices are sequential logic circuits using ROM which, within constraints of time, can be used to simulate the performance of any sequential logic network. The simulation process is often referred to as an emulation. The ability of the device to emulate effectively is determined to a great degree by the address selection or sequencing portion of the unit. From the numerous alternatives presented, some reasonable variation must be selected which meets the objectives of the designer. In microprogrammed devices with short microinstruction words, this usually involves combining a program counter technique with a global branch instruction format. In larger systems, the truncated addressing schemes are more frequently used.

microprogram fields—Parts of a microinstruction that specify one microoperation. Each of several fields may be independent of any other.

microprogram instruction set — The repertoire of machine-dependent instructions available to the assembly-language programmer.

microprogrammable computer — A computer in which part of the control store is set aside for the user, and the user is able to put microprograms in and access them.

microprogrammable instruction — All instructions which do not reference main memory (do not contain a memory address) can be microprogrammed, allowing the programmer to specify several shift, skip, or input/output transfer commands to be performed within one instruction.

microprogram machine instructions — The binary-coded bit patterns that actually control the operations of the computer through the control processor. Programs written in symbolic languages like FORTRAN are translated into machine instructions by compilers, assemblers, or interpreters.

microprogram mapping — A group of addresses stored in computer hardware that is used to access specific program and data storage space in main memory. In a computer with microprogrammed architecture, a machine instruction is not just associated with a path through the hardwired control logic, but with a microprogram. Instead of the hard-wired control logic used in the earliest computer designs, there is a control store that holds the microprogram. When a machine-language instruction is executed, it is mapped to the corresponding microprogram, which is then executed, as if the user had a computer within a computer.

microprogrammed processor — The term "microprogrammed" refers to any computer whose instruction set is not fixed but which can be tailored to individual needs by the programming of ROMs or other memory devices. Consequently, whether the computer is a mini, midi, maxi—or a microprocessor—theoretically, it can be microprogrammed. The central processor can exploit the flexibility of microprogramming to the fullest possible extent.

microprogrammed subroutines — Subroutines are programs designed to be used by other routines to accomplish a particular purpose. These routines can be called into action from numerous points within the main body of the program. In microprogramming, subroutines are also used. This is because many microprograms contain similar or identical sections of code. For example, many memory reference instructions in a computer system all use the same logical sequence in generating the address for an instruction and, therefore, this sequence could be a subroutine called from within a body of code which executes the addressing algorithm.

microprogram microassembler—A program that translates microprograms in symbolic form (similar to assembly language) into bit patterns that are then loaded into the control store.

microprogram microcode — Another name for the microinstructions that make up a microprogram, either in source-language or in object-code form.

microprogramming—Refers to the technique of using a certain special set of computer instructions that consists only of basic elemental operations which the programmer may combine into higher-level instructions as he chooses, and can then program using the higher-level instructions only. One advantage offered by microprogramming is that the computer instruction set can be modified to fit any application. Also, microprogramming is much less expensive than hard-wiring a control unit. However, microprogram-

ming is very expensive when compared to writing computer programs.

microprogramming, bit-slice microprocessor—The changing of the way the ALU (arithmetic-logic unit) reacts to instructions by altering the microprogram held in the control store. When several bit-slices and a controller are connected together with a control store, a complete processor is built.

microprogramming, diagonal—A control-processor implementation technique that combines horizontal and vertical microprogramming by encoding the contents of control store. It yields high performance with simple machine-language format instructions.

microprogramming, horizontal—A control-processor implementation technique in which many micro-operators are used in each microinstruction to provide intrinsic high-speed control almost at the gate level of the computer's operation. The technique is usually associated with very wide word widths.

microprogramming simulation—Emulation is a chief function of a microprogram that can imitate the basic instruction set of the machine being emulated. Word lengths, arithmetic, and logic details, as well as other functions of another machine, are simulated. Each fundamental instruction or operation of the imitated machine is made up of a sequence of microcoded steps allowing registers to be loaded, data to be moved, etc. Quite often the microcoded sequences which make up each basic machine operation are hard-wired into a control store. Such control stores, in many new machines, are either being made from read-only memory (ROM), which may be easily removed for substitution, or from semiconductor reloadable control store (RCS). Microprogramming offers user programmers the opportunities to tailor their own machines to their own jobs; i.e., powerful instructions can be developed that would require only a single line of program code to complete a number of complex but repetitive jobs.

microprogramming techniques—There are very few techniques that have been widely publicized for writing efficient microprograms or for developing efficient microcode. A few of the more frequently used techniques often discussed, that are finding application in microprogramming, are: indexing, subroutines, and parameterization.

Many arithmetic operations are made up of a sequence of repetitive operations. For example, a "multiply" is made up of a sequence of adds and shifts. This sequence will be executed over and over again until the operation is completed. Index registers have been used in computers to count the number of times one goes through a sequence of instructions. The same technique is applicable to microprogramming.

When macro or machine instructions are implemented in a control store in place of hard-wired logic, flexibility increases. Users can augment, modify, or completely replace the instruction set simply by adding or replacing ROMs in the control store. So microprogrammed computers are easier and less expensive to design, and a large number of computer designers now use the microprogramming technique.

microprogramming, vertical—A control-processor implementation technique in which fewer micro-operators are employed in each microinstruction to simplify user microprogramming, at the expense of performance.

microprogramming/fixed instruction— Some microprocessors come with fixed instruction sets, around which software must be developed for an application. Other units offer options for microprogramming; this is the ability to alter or totally change the original instruction set. In essence, the microprocessor's internal microinstructions are programmed by the user to obtain a macroinstruction set that is tailored to the application. One of the advantages of microprogramming is increased speed, since microinstructions are executed considerably faster than macroinstructions. Also, the technique allows a more detailed level of control that can be used to reduce hardware; the program controls more functions.

microprogram parameterization — Parameterization is a technique of storing parameters which characterize the state of program. This is sometimes accomplished by storing these in program status words. Information in

these words can be tested and actions can be initiated based on these parameters. In microprogrammed controls, similar techniques can be used. Parameters which characterize the state of the control portion of the system can be set and tested by the control processor in the same way that overflow, carry, less than, and other indicators can be tested in some of today's computers.

microprogram principles — The basic principle is to segment the microprogrammed control into two parts—one for operating the gates which control the data paths, and the other for selecting the next step in the control sequence. All microprogrammed devices are organized in a similar fashion. The essence of designing a good microprogrammed system is the selection of the proper strategies for data paths and logic function control as well as the implementation of the control sequence section.

microprogram, single-chip system—In some systems, the operation of the microprocessor consists of repeatedly accessing or fetching instructions from the program stored in external memory and, then, executing the operations specified by the instructions. These two steps are carried out under the control of an internal microprogram. (Some systems are not user-microprogrammable.) The microprogram is similar to a state table that specifies the series of states of system-control signals necessary to carry out each instruction.

microwave—1. Refers to all electromagnetic waves in the radio-frequency spectrum above 890 megahertz. 2. Line-of-sight, point-to-point transmission of signals at high frequency. Many CATV systems receive television signals from a distant antenna location with the antenna and the system connected by microwave relay. 3. Related to data communications, systems in which ultra-high-frequency waveforms are used to transmit voice or data messages.

microwave integrated circuits (MICs)— MICs are appearing throughout the vhf, uhf, and microwave field, reducing circuit size, improving performance, and cutting costs in amplifiers, oscillators, passive components, and entire systems. MIC technology is hybrid—not monolithic—it is likely to remain so for some time. The circuits require far larger substrates than digital circuits, since they use transmission lines, and the substrate materials are not suitable for "growing" transistors. In any case, the quantities of MICs needed for the foreseeable future fall far short of the numbers that make monolithic-circuit production efficient. Practically all MICs are built with microstrip transmission lines. The lines are fabricated on a substrate — most commonly, high-alumina ceramic or sapphire, but also on ferrites, quartz, beryllia and "soft" plastics or fiberglass compositions. Transistors and diodes used in the circuits may be in packages or naked-chip form, and resistors and capacitors can be either chips or deposited.

micro-Winchester disk — Winchester-disk technology provides another "dimension" with the introduction of a 5¼-inch (13.3 cm) disk drive. With a 6.38-Mbyte (unformatted) capacity aimed at small-system storage requirements, the typical micro-Winchester provides all the reliability advantages of a Winchester-type drive in a package the size of a minifloppy drive. As with 8- and 14-inch Winchester drives (20.3 and 35.56 cm, respectively), two disk platters are sealed in an airtight enclosure with an integral air filter that continuously cleans the air within the drive. The read/write heads are loaded with approximately 20 grams of loading force, another offshoot of other Winchester designs. The heads touch the disk surface only when the disk is at rest at the beginning and end of operation. In addition, a special lubricant in the disk oxide prevents damage to the disk. The micro-Winchester is the same size as the industry-standard minifloppy, 5¾ × 3¼ × 8 inches (14.6 × 8.26 × 20.32 cm).

micro-Winchester drive—The drive mechanics of these systems divide roughly into stepper and spindle-motor assemblies, a head assembly with up to four Winchester heads, and a disk assembly often with the two platters. The disk platters have an outer diameter of 130 mm (5.12 inches) and an inside diameter of 40 mm (1.58 inches). All the drive electronics are contained on one or two pc boards. The stepper motor generally uses a steel band to position the heads over 153 tracks. This stepping action allows a track-to-track access time of 3 msec with 15-msec settling time on the last step. Access time, including settling, is on average just 170 msec. The spindle is driven by a dc brushless motor that spins the disk at 3600 rpm.

MICR scan—The sensing of characters, marks, or codes printed in magnetic ink. The technique was developed by American Bankers' Association and is used on bank checks. The character size, shape, and ink are standardized by the USA Standards Institute.

migration — Refers to movement of atoms within a metal or among metals in contact, i.e., the problem, for example, of movement of atoms during the plating of one metal over another (such as on printed-circuit boards) and which often prevents one metal from performing its purpose of protective coating.

migration, data — The moving of data from an on-line device to an off-line or low-priority device, as determined by the system or as requested by the user.

migration technology, avalanche induced (AIM)—The AIM element is a minimum size, open base, npn transistor. The emitter is contacted by an aluminum "column" line and the collector is common with the collectors of other elements and the "row" driver collector. A conventional gold doped TTL process is used to fabricate the AIM element and all other transistors, diodes, and resistors on the chip. The programming technique is to force a high current through the element from emitter to collector. This forces the emitter-base junction beyond normal avalanche and into a second breakdown mode. In the second breakdown mode, the current constricts to a narrow high-temperature filament. Aluminum then migrates down the filament to the emitter-base junction and causes a short circuit of that junction. The drop in power dissipation, as soon as the emitter-base short circuit is achieved, causes a decrease in temperature. Since temperature is a driving force in the programming action, further advance of migrating aluminum is inhibited after programming is achieved. The action is thus self-limiting. The AIM programming technique assures superior reliability since the element junction where the programming action occurs is inherently hermetic.

mil—A unit of length equal to 10^{-3} inch $(2.54 \times 10^{-5}$ meters), used in measurements of small thicknesses, i.e., thin sheets.

milestone—A task or event that cannot be considered completed until all tasks that feed into it are completed.

Miller-Pierce oscillator—A crystal-stabilized oscillator in which the quartz crystal is connected between the grid and cathode of a triode tube, a parallel resonant circuit being in series with the anode.

miniassembler program — A typical miniassembler program is designed to simplify machine-level programming on various microprocessor systems. The program allows the operator to type mnemonic program symbols directly in assembler language on the terminal, while the program generates the correct object code, placing it in the proper memory location, and printing it out simultaneously on the terminal. Relative branches are calculated from the absolute address which is entered following branch instructions.

miniaturization—Refers to specific reduction of size for the purpose of increasing the packing density of magnetic and electromechanical parts and components of circuits, either single or integrated. Miniaturization or microminiaturization reduces power requirements, delay of signal propagation, and the distance signals must travel, as well as the space necessary for packing.

minicomputer — Generally, a minicomputer is a mainframe that sells for less than $25,000. Usually it is a parallel binary system using an 8-, 12-, 16-, 18-, 24-, or 36-bit word length that incorporates semiconductor or magnetic core memory, offering from 4K words to 64K words of storage and a cycle time of 0.2 to 8 microseconds or less. These units are characterized by higher performance than microcomputers or programmable calculators. They have richer instruction sets, higher prices, and a proliferation of high-level languages, operating systems, and networking methodologies. Most minicomputers, presently being sold, have operating systems that

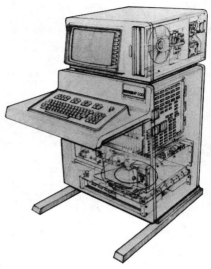

Minicomputer.

can simultaneously process real-time, time-shared, and batch jobs, manage software and hardware protection on concurrent paths, and do disk spooling on input and printed output. Multiprogram systems can also "heuristically" allocate memory, CPU time, I/O, and other system resources according to processing demands, besides having all of the standard features. Minicomputers are used nearly everywhere large computers were used in the past but at much lower cost.

minicomputer concentrator — When used as a remote concentrator, a minicomputer functions as a storage buffer with input/output capabilities. Thus, the concentrator may alter the signalling speed of a message in addition to regulating the flow of messages over the lines. The processing speed of the concentrator is sufficiently rapid that it can accept messages simultaneously from several slow-speed terminals, thus reducing terminal delays caused by waiting for an available circuit to the host processor. Like the front-end processor, a concentrator can be programmed to perform such functions as character-to-message assembly and disassembly, communications line control, message buffering, code conversion, error detection, and automatic answering.

minicomputer, front-end—The growing need for machines to communicate with other machines has prompted the development of the communications, or front-end, processor. These front-end processors alleviate the requirements for data communications software support in the main computer. Thus, the central, or host, computer is freed to do other work that uses its resources more efficiently. Minicomputers used as front-end processors have the capacity to improve the host processor's efficiency; however, problems can arise if an incorrect minicomputer system is selected. *See* front-end processor.

minidiskette—A storage medium similar to, but smaller than, the standard flexible disk. Available in hard- or soft-sectored formats, it shares the same oxide formulation, technology, and technique of manufacture. The protective jacket is 5.25 inches (13.3 cm) square.

minimal latency coding — Refers to a procedure or method for programming for those computers in which the waiting time for a word depends on its location, i.e., locations for instructions and data are so chosen that access time is reduced or minimized.

minimum access code — A system of coding which minimizes the effect of delays for transfer of data or instructions between storage and other machine components.

minor cycle—The time interval between the appearance of corresponding parts of successive words in the storage device which provides serial access to storage positions.

minority carrier — The minor or nondominant charge carrier in a semiconductor.

MIS — 1. Abbreviation for metal-insulator-silicon. A technology of silicon dioxide layers formed on a single crystal silicon substrate and, then, etched to form an electrode pattern. It is doped with phosphorous to create the desired conductivity. 2. Abbreviation for management-information system. A communications process in which data are recorded and processed for operational purposes. The problems are isolated for higher-level decision-making, and information is fed back to top management to reflect the progress or lack of progress made in achieving major objectives. An MIS gives the executive the capability of controlling the operation of a firm on a real-time basis.

MIS display program—The display program, which enables the computer to "talk" to the user graphically, is the heart of many systems. Displays include a wide selection of bar graphs, line graphs, scatter graphs, and specialized displays, such as 3-D perspective bar graphs and line graphs, 3-D pie charts and combinations. In an interactive system for executives, speed is of the utmost importance, so the computer performs data scaling and color selection automatically. However, a manual override menu can "hide" behind each graph, enabling the user to change scaling, colors, and format, and add remarks. These changes can be made a permanent part of the data file, so that each time it is graphed, the same new format will appear.

MKS system — A metric system that uses a series of multipliers, all powers of ten, which, together with Greek and Latin terminology, indicate the actual size of its units. A kilogram, for example, is 10^3 or 1000 grams. The MKS (meter-kilogram-second) system is used in preference to the CGS (centimeter-gram-second) version of the metric system, due to recommendations from the IEEE and many other engineering groups and organizations.

mnemonic — Refers to a technique to assist a programmer's memory. Mnemonics is the art of improving the efficiency of the memory in computer storage.

mnemonic address—Refers to an address code of abbreviations that has some easily remembered relationship to the name of the destination; i.e., NY for New York, JFK for New York's International Airport.

mnemonic code—Often referred to as "memory codes," these are designed to assist programmers in remembering instructions corresponding to a given operation; for example, MPY for multiply. Source statements can be written in this symbolic language and then translated into machine language.

mnemonic operation code—An operation code in which the names of operations are abbreviated and expressed mnemonically to facilitate remembering the operations they represent. A mnemonic code normally needs to be converted to an actual operation code by an assembler before execution by the computer. Examples of mnemonic codes are ADD for addition, CLR for clear storage, and SQR for square root.

mobility—A description of the drift of ions (including electrons and holes in semiconductors) under applied electric fields. This is additional to thermal agitation. Measured in $cm^2\ sec^{-1}$ $volt^{-1}$, it is related to conductivity and Hall effect. The term mobility (designated μ) refers to the intrinsic current-carrying properties of N- and P-doped silicon. In N-doped silicon, the majority current carriers are free electrons, whereas, in P-doped silicon, current is carried by means of holes. The mobility of electrons is approximately 2.5 times that of holes and, therefore, N-type transistors are faster than P-type.

mode—1. Refers to various methods of operation, e.g., the binary mode, the interpretive mode, the alphameric mode, etc. 2. The most frequent value in the statistical sense.

mode, burst—The movement of a continuous bit stream between devices until an interruption or completion of the stream occurs.

mode, byte—Refers to the movement of one byte at a time between devices, separated by an interrupt, and release of channel control. Used in multiplexing, the byte mode permits the handling of data from several low-speed devices simultaneously.

mode, conversation—Refers to a real-time communication activity between one or more remote terminals and a time-sharing computer, in which each entry from a terminal elicits an immediate response from the computer. The remote terminal thus can control, interrogate, or modify a task within the computer.

model—1. Refers in mathematical terms to a process, device, or concept. 2. A general model is a schematic pictorial representation of a system being studied.

model, mathematical—Often refers to computer characterization of a process, object, or concept, in terms of mathematics, which enables the relatively simple manipulation of variables to be accomplished in order to determine how the process, object, or concept would behave in different situations.

modem—Refers to a MODulation/DEModulation chip, or device, that enables computers and terminals to communicate over telephone circuits. A modulator/demodulator connects the communications multiplexer from the remote outlet to the interface device in the computer center. On the transmission end, the modulator converts the signals or pulses to the right codes and readies them for transmission over a communication line. On the receiving end, a demodulator reconverts the signals to direct current for communication to the computer via the computer interface device.

Modem, acoustic (Courtesy Atari, Inc.).

modem, acoustic — Various types of modulator-demodulator devices convert electrical signals to telephone tones and back again. The conversion occurs through acoustic coupling (placing speakers near the phone) or by direct coupling to the line (which provides superior frequency response). Most modems use the RS-232C interface standard.

modem audio loopback control — Test function used in conjunction with the remote modem which loops the received audio signal back to the remote site.

modem check control — Puts the modem in a loopback and terminates the audio line; may be used for modem testing or terminal testing.

modem connect-line control — Connects the telephone dial line to the modem; an indicator flashes when a ring signal is detected and illuminates when the modem is connected to the dial line.

modem data-clamp control—Forces the modem to send a known data pattern and can be used with Modem Check control to perform self-test functions.

modem digital loopback control — A test function used in conjunction with the remote modem that causes the received demodulated data to be remodulated and sent back to the remote site.

modem receive-only control—Disables the transmitter and is used in conjunction with Data Clamp control for half-duplex line diagnostic tests.

modem synchronization — Basically, some form of synchronization must be established for any useful communications to occur. Modems customarily establish synchronization at the bit level when a specified bit pattern is transmitted to a receiver that is appropriately conditioned. The interface hardware then establishes character synchronization as part of the same sequence. However, there may be no explicit indication from hardware if bit synchronization is subsequently lost. It is, therefore, advisable to resynchronize whenever an error is detected because it is not known whether or not there is still character synchronization.

modem tester—One type of tester is a small portable self-contained device that simulates data-communications control functions, evaluates system performance, and isolates equipment failures. It is intended for testing of either asynchronous or synchronous modems in simplex, half-duplex, or full-duplex mode. It determines the overall condition of a data channel consisting of a telephone line with a modem at each end. This type of tester transmits a 511-bit pseudo-random test pattern and measures the bit-error rate of the received signal.

modification loop—Refers to those instructions to or of a loop which alter instruction addresses or data.

modular—Refers to the standardization of computer-system components to allow for combinations and large variety of compatible units.

modular connector—Refers to various electrical connectors with sections that are used like "building blocks" or modules.

modular converters — Modular converters are an epoxy-encapsulated variety of converter that offers, for example, a complete data acquisition system in modular form. These units, low-profile packages smaller than a human hand, are multiple-channel systems that contain a-d converters, sample-and-hold circuits, multiplexers, and, sometimes, programmable logic.

modulation code — A code used to cause variations in a signal in accordance with a predetermined scheme, normally used to alter or modulate a carrier wave to transmit data.

modulation, differential — A type of modulation in which the choice of the significant condition for any signal element is dependent on the choice of the previous signal element.

modulation, dipole—Refers to the representation of binary digits on a magnetic surface medium such as disks, tapes, drums, cards, etc., but in which a specified part of each cell is magnetically saturated in one of two opposing senses, depending upon the value of the digit represented. The remainder of the cell is magnetized in a predetermined sense and remains fixed.

modulation, four-phase — Refers to a digital type of modulation designed for the carrier to shift between four distinct phases, the four possible phases serve to encode two bits.

modulation, frequency—1. Refers to a basic procedure for varying the frequency of a carrier of fixed amplitude above and below the normal carrier frequency, in accordance with the amplitude variations of an applied signal voltage. 2. Specifically, the rate in hertz or bits per second for a sine-wave carrier to be modulated by an intelligence-bearing signal.

modulation, frequency-shift (FSM) — Refers to a technique or form of frequency modulation in which the carrier frequency is shifted between a mark frequency and a space frequency in response to the impressed intelligence signal (frequency-shift keying).

modulation meter — A specific meter

placed in shunt with a communication channel, to give an indication that interprets, in a stated way, the instant-to-instant power level in varying modulation currents.

modulation parameters — There are three parameters of the carrier signal that can be modulated: amplitude, frequency, and phase. In amplitude modulation, users vary the amplitude of the carrier signal in line with the data being sent. In the simplest case, the carrier signal can simply be switched on and off to represent the zero (0) and one (1) bits. With frequency modulation, the frequency of the carrier signal is varied with the data, having one value for a one (1) and another for a zero (0). This two-valued form of frequency modulation is commonly called frequency-shift keying, or FSK, and is the most popular technique for lower-speed modems.

To transmit binary data by phase modulation, the zero (0) and one (1) bits are represented by carrier signals 180° out of phase with each other. With phase modulation, users can also transmit bit pairs, or "dibits," by using a succession of 90° phase shifts to represent the bit pairs 00, 01, 10, and 11. Similarly, by using successive 45° phase shifts, data can be transmitted in bit trios.

modulator/demodulator (MODEM) — Refers to the basic device that converts data from a form which is compatible with data-processing equipment (parallel) to a form that is compatible with transmission facilities (serial-by-bit), and vice versa.

module—1. Refers to a device or program unit that is discrete and identifiable with respect to compiling, combining with other units, and loading, e.g., the input to, or output from, an assembler, compiler, linkage editor, or executive routine. 2. A packaged functional hardware unit designed for use with other components. 3. An interchangeable "plug-in" item, containing electronic components, which may be combined with other interchangeable items to form a complete unit.

module boards—Blank module boards provide a convenient method of breadboarding (mounting) experimental or prototype circuits, and they provide a low-cost method of produc-

ing limited runs of production modules with special circuitry. They are generally compatible with the standard module mounting blocks. Some are glass-epoxy blank module boards that have etched and gold-plated contact fingers and have handles attached. The attached handles are usually stamped with their identification number (part number). Handles are often on copper-clad boards and are attached with reusable nylon hardware. Blank module boards are often available in three basic forms: plain, perforated, and copper-clad.

module boards, copper-clad—Copper-clad blank module boards provide a method of producing limited runs of modules with special circuitry and components. A complete selection of copper-clad blank boards is widely available. Some may be user-etched on both sides, while others may be user-etched on one side only. Many sizes are available that have etched and gold-plated contact fingers.

module boards, perforated—Perforated blank module boards provide nearly the same advantage as plain blank module boards except they are pre-drilled with 0.052-inch (0.132-cm) diameter holes spaced 0.1 inch (0.254 cm) center-to-center horizontally and vertically. This eliminates the need for user drilling and only slightly reduces the choices of component placement. Many have etched and gold-plated contact fingers.

module boards, plain — Plain blank module boards provide flexibility in the placement of components since they are not perforated (predrilled), and they permit easy changes to the circuitry since etching is not required. Component connections are made via hook-up wire. Plain blank boards are, therefore, ideal for experimental or prototype modules because they permit easy changes to the circuitry and nearly unlimited component placement, and yet they provide stability and security for the circuits and components.

module boards, special-purpose—Special-purpose blank module boards provide pre-etched mounting facilities for user-defined, supplied, and installed components. These special-purpose module boards are low-cost and ideal for prototype and limited-production runs of circuitry unique to each user. They are generally compatible with the standard module mounting blocks. Some glass-epoxy module boards have etched and gold-plated contact fingers and have handles attached, The attached handles are stamped with their identification number (part number).

module extender boards—Module extender boards are usually used to extend system modules for test and/or maintenance. Module extender boards permit access to the system module circuits and components without breaking the electrical connections between the system module and the backplane or mounting panel wiring. Extended length module extender boards should be used when the system comprises extended length system modules.

modulo check—One which anticipates a remainder when a processed number is divided by a number which is also carried with data through the process.

modulo-N—Refers to a ring of integers derived from the set of all integers according to the following rule: Let N be an integer greater than 1, and A and B be two other integers; if N is a factor of A — B, then A is said to be congruent to a B modulo-N.

modulo-N check — 1. A check that makes use of a check number that is equal to the remainder of the desired number when divided by N, e.g., in a modulo check, the check number will be 0, 1, 2, or 3, and remainder of A when divided by 4 must equal the reported check number B, otherwise an equipment malfunction has occurred. 2. A method of verification by congruences, e.g., casting out nines. Related to number, self checking.

modulo-N residue—The remainder from a division of a number by another number, i.e., the residue for 58 modulo-8 is 2, since 58 divided by 8 is 7 with a remainder of 2.

modulo, two sum—Same as nonequivalence, exclusive-OR operation, intersection, and collation.

molar conductance — The electrical conductance between electrodes 1 cm apart in an electrolyte having 1 mol of solute in 1 litre of solution.

mol(e)—Amount of any defined chemical substance which weighs its mo-

lecular weight in grams. Also gram-molecule. Symbol mol.

molecular beam — Directed stream of un-ionized molecules issuing from a source and depending only on their thermal energy.

molecular bond — Bond in which the linkage pair of electrons are provided by one of the bonding atoms; cf. atomic bond.

molecular distillation—An isotope separation in which molecules are evaporated at very low pressures from a surface and are condensed before they encounter collisions.

molecular volume — That occupied by one mole of a substance in gaseous form at standard temperature and pressure (approximately 22.414 litres).

molecular weight — The sum of the atomic weights of the constituent atoms of a molecule.

molecule—Smallest part of an element or compound which (nominally) exhibits all the properties of that specific compound or element.

mole-electronics—Technique of growing solid-state crystals so as to form transistors, diodes, resistors in one mass for microminiaturization. Also called molectronics.

molybdenum (Mo) — Metallic element, at. no. 42, at. wt. 95.94, m.p. 2625°C, b.p. 4800°C, resistivity 4.77 microhm-cm². Its physical properties resemble those of iron. Used in the form of wire for filament heaters in vacuum tubes, for electrodes of mercury-vapor lamps, and for winding electric resistance furnaces. It seals well to Pyrex glass and spot-welds to iron and steel. It is a prominent fission product from nuclear reactors as [95]Mo.

monadic Boolean operator—A Boolean operator having only one operand; for example, NOT.

monitor—1. Ionization chamber or other radiation detector arranged to give a continuous indication of intensity of radiation, e.g., in radiation laboratories, industrial operations, or X-ray exposure. 2. Unit in large computers that prepares the machine instructions from the source program, using built-in compiler(s) for one or more program languages. It feeds these into the processing and output units in sequence, once compiling is completed. It also controls time-sharing procedures. 3. To control the operation of several unrelated routines and machine runs so that the computer and computer time are used advantageously. 4. To test, check, or sequence, i.e., supervise the operation of a computer; a master schedule. 5. A black-and-white or color crt (cathode-ray tube) display consisting of rows and columns of elements. Alphanumeric characters are formed in dot-matrix elements. Multiple elements can often be combined to form larger symbols. 6. A device that observes and verifies the operations of a data processing system and indicates any significant departure from the norm. 7. Software or hardware that observes, supervises, controls, or verifies the operations of a system.

monitor, firmware—Refers to programming built into the computer executive or control program (monitor) to make its operation simpler, faster, and more versatile. Firmware is usually supplied by the manufacturers, stored in PROM memory units, with very basic functions for system control.

monitoring—A monitor checks for error conditions that can occur when a program is being executed (e.g., numerical overflow, infinite loops, or an attempt to access a protected area of main memory). The monitor attempts to provide error recovery and diagnostics.

monitoring controller — A controller used in an application where the process is continually checked in order to alert the operator to possible application malfunctions.

monitor, microcomputer — A typical basic monitor system includes a CPU board (with a console board), a keyboard with fully decoded digits, a breadboard (for assembling custom circuitry), and a PROM/RAM board (with a minimum 256 bytes of RAM), and a PROM containing a versatile monitor program. Fully assembled and tested, these systems are available as a monitor system.

monitor, microprocessor—The system resides in PROMs in the mainframe. It provides an operating system enabling program development to be carried out with a wide range of peripherals. Debugging is fast because users can do real-time breakpointing, and can examine and modify all mem-

ory and CPU status information. Linkage points are available that permit user access to monitor routines.

monitor programs—Refers to the part of an operating system that contains routines and is needed for continuous system operation.

monitor system—Refers to a major programming system which is in control of all systems functions (a subprogram of a control program). The monitor simulates the operator at processor speed. It maintains continuity between jobs and maintains status of I/O devices, while providing automatic accounting of jobs. A logical outgrowth of advanced programming systems, it is the only practical way to operate real-time systems and the only efficient method for priority applications.

monitor, time-sharing — The monitor system is a collection of programs remaining permanently in memory to provide overall coordination and control of the total operating system. It performs several functions. First, it permits several users' programs to be loaded into main memory simultaneously. The monitor makes use of the time-sharing hardware to prevent one user's program from interfering with another user's program. Each program is run for a certain length of time; then the monitor switches control to another program in a rotating sequence.

monitor unit—A device which is supervisory and which is capable of verifying the operation of another device or group in data-processing systems, production-automation systems, message-routing systems, etc. When significant departure from the normal procedures, measurements or guides (criteria) occur, the state of the system is observed, measured, and operators are alerted or various departures corrected.

monochromator—Device for converting heterogeneous beam of radiation electromagnetic or particulate) to homogeneous beam by absorption or refraction of unwanted components.

monocrystalline—Material made up of a single continuous crystal.

monolithic—Pertains to the single silicon substrate in which an integrated circuit is constructed. *See* integrated circuit.

monolithic chip — If a circuit can be built as a monolithic chip, it will usually be cheaper and theoretically more reliable than with competing methods of fabrication. The cost will be lower because monolithic fabrication is less labor intensive than other approaches, such as hybrid assembly—in which various unpackaged active and passive chips are bonded to a ceramic substrate, and then interconnected by metal films or manually attached wires. Reliability of monolithics is usually superior to that of hybrids because there are fewer parts and interconnections—and failure of any single device or connection means a failure of the complete assembly.

monolithic compandor — One type of LSI chip geared for analog telephone applications is the monolithic compandor. The analog equivalent of the codec (coder-decoder), it expands and compresses voice signals to improve the S/N ratio.

monolithic integrated circuit—1. Refers to various electronic circuits designed to be constructed on a single tiny chip of crystalline semiconductor material, usually silicon. The chip is contained in a plastic or ceramic package, often a dual-in-line (DIP) package. Electrical connections are made by having extremely fine wire welded to metal pads on the chip and to the package leads. 2. In this type of circuit, both active and passive elements are simultaneously formed in a single small wafer of silicon by the diffusion planar technique. Then, metallic stripes are evaporated on to the oxidized surface of the silicon to interconnect the elements.

monolithic storage—Refers to storage made up of monolithic integrated circuits.

monostable circuit—Refers to a basic circuit which has one stable or quasi-stable state and one unstable state and which undergoes a complete cycle of change in response to a single triggering excitation.

monostable multivibrator—Refers to a circuit which holds information for a fixed time, as determined by the nature of the circuit elements.

monostable trigger circuit — A circuit that has only one stable state.

monotonicity — A characteristic of a/d converters, whereby the output is a continuously increasing function of the input. In other words, the slope of the transfer function is never negative.

MOS — Abbreviation for metal-oxide semiconductor. This refers to the three layers used in forming the gate structure of a field-effect transistor (FET).

mosaic—1. Photoelectric surface made up of a large number of infinitesimal granules of photoemissive material deposited on an insulating support. Used as emitting electrode in some forms of electron cameras, e.g., iconoscope. Mosaics of piezoelectric crystal elements are employed in ultrasonic cameras. 2. The reconstruction of the track of a nuclear particle through a stack of photographic emulsions.

MOS character generator—A metal-oxide semiconductor (MOS) IC character generator generates voltage patterns needed to form numbers, letters, and symbols on visual displays, such as light-emitting diode (LED) arrays.

MOS circuits — Circuits that are based on metal-oxide-semiconductor technology, which offers very low power dissipation and, hence, makes possible circuits that can jam transistors close together before a critical heat problem arises. Most monolithic memories, calculators, and electronic watches use this technology.

MOS design considerations—In the design and manufacture of an MOS integrated circuit, there always are several main objectives of performance, cost, manufacturing feasibility, etc. Such objectives must be arranged in a priority and optimized. This approach is equally true for an MOS manufacturer who is planning a standard product, as for an end user considering the design of a custom circuit. Some of the essential objectives that must be considered are: speed, power, logic type, application, power supply, clock signals, interface, packaging, and cost.

MOS integrated injection logic (I²L) — Injection logic is being hailed as a new logic generation because of its extremely simple and compact LSI gate structure. Laid out on silicon, the gate needs no current-source resistors and occupies only 1 to 2 mil², or the space of one transistor. It is capable of logic speeds down to 5 nanoseconds, at power dissipations of nanowatts per gate, and so achieves speed-power products of 0.1 picojoule. Moreover, because it can be built into high-gain linear as well as digital structures, it has applications throughout the spectrum of semiconductor products.

MOS memory—Refers to a memory using a semiconductor circuit. Generally used in high-speed buffer memory and Read-only memory.

MOS, PMOS, NMOS, CMOS—These are four of the basic metal-oxide semiconductor manufacturing technologies. They are capable of high densities. The terminology used to describe power-FET devices encompasses a profusion of names to describe the architectures and processes to make power-FETs. Some of the names and acronyms are V-groove MOS (VMOS), vertical DMOS (VDMOS), lateral DMOS (LDMOS), planar double-diffused metal-oxide semiconductor (DMOS), and vertical V-groove MOS (VVMOS). However, acronyms such as TMOS, ZMOS, etc., seem to be manufacturer-generated names used for product naming.

MOS transistor capacitance—A major concern in MOS transistor design is capacitance. Capacitance usually is considered in several parts. First, the gate electrode and the surface of the silicon substrate form a parallel plate capacitor, with the silicon oxide serving as the dielectric. Second, both the source and drain region junctions with the substrate constitute a capacitor, with the depletion region acting as the dielectric. Third, there is capacitance between the gate electrode and both the source and the drain. This latter capacitance is particularly important in all transistors in which the gate electrode overlaps the source and drain regions and it does so in all except those manufactured by the self-aligning gate processors. This overlap is necessary in manufacture to allow for mask tolerances: the gate electrode-metal deposit must always reach all the way from the source to the drain and the only way to assure this is to allow a positive (overlap) mask tolerance.

MOS transistor capacitance, power consumption — Capacitance affects the speed of a transistor and also its power consumption. The more capacitance loading a transistor presents to an input signal, the more time is required to turn the transistor on. Power consumption considerations become particularly important at high operating frequencies. In addition to having undesirable effects on circuit performance, the intrinsic capacitances can also be used beneficially in MOS circuit design. In dynamic MOS circuits, capacitance is very often used for temporary storage of charge representing a logic level.

MOS transistor enhancement mode — In the enhancement mode, as the gate voltage is raised, it enhances the flow of current in the N channel between the source and drain. It is equally possible, however, to make a P-channel enhancement-mode transistor by diffusing two P regions in an N-type substrate and, then, increasing the gate voltage in a negative direction, to accumulate positive charge at the surface and, thus, create a P channel between the source and drain.

most significant digit (MSD) — Refers to the leftmost nonzero digit, or the one which contributes the largest quantity to the value of a numeral.

motherboard — A circuit board onto which various processor boards are plugged.

Mott scattering formula—Gives the differential cross-section for the scattering of identical particles arising from a coulomb interaction.

moving-domain memories (MOD)—One current MOD has 35,000 bits per substrate. Other working MODs have a density four times that. Moving-domain memories are attractive for a number of reasons: (1) they're nonvolatile, like core memories, but much smaller, (2) they operate reasonably fast, (3) they need no external magnetic bias to form and hold the domains, as do bubble memories, and (4) they can be batch-fabricated using conventional microcircuit techniques.

moving-head disk system—A disk unit in which a Read/Write head is capable of moving across the surface of the disk to access any one of a number of circular tracks of data.

MP/M operating system—MP/M stands for Multiprogramming Control Program for Microprocessors. MP/M is an operating system that provides multi-terminal access with multiprogramming at each terminal. It is CP/M compatible (CP/M stands for Control Program for Microprocessors), so users can run the many programming languages, applications packages, and development software that were developed for CP/M on their MP/M systems. It offers advanced capabilities with run editors, translators, word processors, and background print spoolers working simultaneously. The real-time facilities of an MP/M system either monitor an assembly line and schedule programs automatically, or else, control a network of micros. Users can write their own system processes for operation under MP/M.

MPS—1. Abbreviation for microprocessor system or microprocessor series. 2. Abbreviation for meters per second.

MPS software tools — MPS software tools are software packages available to the user to aid in developing MPS application programs. The packages often consist of basic programs and the programs can be provided in floppy-disk form. User's Handbooks fully describe the operation of the following programs and their interaction with the MPS: (1) Microprocessor Host Loader — loads binary-coded tapes, (2) Microprocessor Language Editor—modifies or generates source text from teletypewriter commands by reading and writing paper tapes, (3) Microprocessor Language Assembler—assembles source text into binary format by reading and writing disks and listing them, at user's option, (4) Master Tape Duplicator/Verifier — copies paper tapes and verifies their contents, (5) Microprocessor ROM Programmer — copies and modifies paper tape and PROMs, and (6) Microprocessor Debugging Program — aids in debugging of binary programs. Runs on MPS.

MPU—Abbreviation for microprocessor unit. The microprocessing unit (MPU) performs the central control function of a microcomputer, and its architecture determines the eventual applications for which the system is best suited. Some MPUs are especially oriented toward the process control and data communications fields; others are designed for alarm functions,

games, calculators, or other purposes. Guiding characteristics for superior systems are maximum power, versatility, system throughput (operating speed), and design ease.

MPU control — Whether a microcomputer consists of a totally integrated single chip, or is composed of a number of interactive LSI chips, the microprocessing unit (MPU) is the central control system that determines the eventual application for which the system is best suited. Its architecture contains the complex routines that permit the system to respond correctly to each of the different "instructions" associated with a particular system. It controls the flow of signals into and out of the computer, routing each to its proper destination in the required sequence to perform an end function.

MPU support chips — A typical set of support chips provides all the necessary I/O and other functional help. The chips include the intelligent peripheral controller, the combination parallel-interface and timer circuit, the direct-memory-access controller, the memory-management unit, the dual-port RAM, and the serial DMA interface.

multiaccess — Refers to large systems that permit several people or groups to transact with the computer through the operator's console or many on-line terminals. Access points are generally connected to the central processor by data transmission lines from remote terminals, which can be typewriters, visual display units, crt's, or satellite processors. Multiaccess multiprogramming systems have been installed by many universities, laboratories, businesses, and research groups. Most operate in a conversational mode with fast response times and are controlled by operating systems.

multiaddress—A type of instruction that specifies the addresses of two or more items which may be the addresses of locations of inputs or outputs of the calculating unit, or the addresses of locations of instructions for the control unit. The term multiaddress is also used in characterizing computers, e.g., two-, three-, or four-address machines.

multiaddress instruction—*See* multiaddress.

multibus multiprocessor—A multibus architecture in a multiprocessor system allows each processor to work asynchronously. Therefore, a fast microprocessor operates at its own speed regardless of the speed of the slowest microprocessor. This technique tolerates duty-cycle and phase-shift variations, and offers hardware modularity. When new system functions are desired, additional microprocessors can be integrated without impacting existing task partitioning (some systems).

multibus system architecture—Refers to a type of system bus architecture that isolates the I/O bus from the main high-speed CPU bus. Conceptually, its basic function is analogous to the peripheral itself, isolating the CPU from the I/O processing tasks. By establishing a secondary bus that is controlled by an auxiliary processor, the entire I/O structure can function separately but as a related entity to the main CPU. The speed of the I/O bus can be limited to 4 MHz–5 MHz, thus simplifying system layout and construction. The only element of this I/O bus structure that is required to operate at the speed of the main CPU bus is the I/O processor. The I/O processor manages all operations of the I/O bus and assumes the "master" role to all peripherals. It assumes the "slave" role to the main CPU and, in essence, functions as a high-speed peripheral to the main CPU.

multichannel—Refers to systems which divide the frequency spectrum of a signal into a number of bands which are separately transmitted, with subsequent recombination.

multichip integrated circuit — An electronic circuit comprising two or more semiconductor wafers which contain single elements (or simple circuits). These are interconnected to produce a more complex circuit and are encapsulated within a single pack.

multicomputer system functions—The main function of multicomputer systems is to separate or partition the various tasks in order to achieve improved system throughput. Examples, in larger systems, include that of separating "number crunching," done in the main CPU, from "I/O processing" that is performed in various I/O processors. In multimicrocomputer systems, the primary motivation is to separate tasks that are mostly independent, i.e., ones that require relatively little intercommunication. This partitioning enables the various microcomputers to be far more responsive to their dedicated tasks. In fact, each microcomputer may be controlling a process requiring, for example, rapid responses to interrupts. It would be difficult, perhaps impossible, for a single microprocessor to respond rapidly to a large number of interrupts; however, several microprocessors could handle them easily.

multifile sorting — The automatic sequencing of more than one file, based upon separate parameters for each file, without operator intervention.

multilayer board — A high-density printed-wiring board that consists of

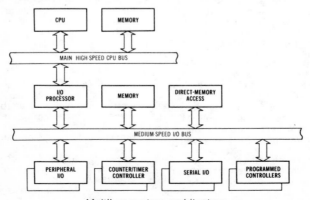

Multibus system architecture.

alternating conductive pattern layers and insulating layers bonded together. Interlayer connections are included as required by means of plated through holes.

multipass sort — A sort program designed to sort more data than can be contained within the internal memory of a central computer. Intermediate storage, such as disk, tape, or drum, is required.

multiphase charge-coupled device—A charge-coupled device in which the directionality of the charge-packet flow is determined by the sequence of the three, four, or more clock phases.

multiphase program—Refers to various programs in absolute form that require more than one fetch or load operation to complete execution.

multiple access—Reference to a system from which output or input can be received or dispatched from more than one location.

multiple address—*See* multiaddress.

multiple-address code — Refers to an instruction code in which an instruction word can specify more than one address to be used during the operation. In a typical instruction of a four-address code, the addresses specify the location of two operands, the location at which the results are to be stored, and the location of the next instruction in the sequence. In a typical three-address code, the fourth address specifying the location of the next instructions is dispensed with, the instructions are taken from storage in a preassigned order. In a typical two-address code, the addresses may specify the locations of the operands. The results may be placed at one of the addresses or the destination of the results may be specified by another instruction.

multiple-address instruction—1. An instruction consisting of an operation code and two or more addresses. Usually specified as a two-address, three-address, or four-address instruction. 2. A type of instruction that specifies the addresses of two or more items which may be addresses of locations of inputs or outputs of the calculating unit, or the addresses or locations of instructions for the control unit. 3. Relates to an instruction that

has more than one address part. 4. *Same as* multiaddress.

multiple-bus architecture — The multiple-bus architecture greatly minimizes the number of components required to build high-performance systems. A complete functional system can be implemented without external multiplexers or ancillary logic. The use of bipolar computing elements means that byte swapping, and other special functions, may be implemented directly with no external logic required.

multiple computer system — Generally regarded as a system which consists of one or more central processing units, input/output devices, and other peripheral hardware that is related and interconnected, and capable of simultaneous operation. A multiple computer system is often referred to simply as a computer.

multiple devices—Multiple devices are devices that encompass two or more transistor chips in a single package. Included in this definition are the Darlington transistors which consist of two interconnected devices functioning as a single-stage amplifier.

multiple-in-line package — Abbreviated MIP, the multiple-in-line package, developed by Bell Labs, is actually a system that allows chip carriers to be used on pc boards that have been laid out for DIPs. The MIP is a plastic chip carrier soldered to a copper-clad epoxy-glass adapter.

multiple monitor systems—As terminal systems can drive up to ten separate video monitors, the monitors can be placed at various locations for ease of visibility and large audience viewing of the data on the crt screen of the monitor. Typical applications are classroom instruction, airport reservations, process control, and message transmission.

multiple precision notation—Refers to use of two or more computer words to represent a single numeric quantity or numeral, i.e., with twice as many or more digits as are normally carried in a fixed-length word.

multiple-process operating system — Multiple-process capability gives the user the ability to have more than one context established at a time. This allows rapid switching from editor to compiler to debugger, for instance, without normal "start up" delays.

Multiple processes permit background I/O spooling, network access by other systems, etc., without disturbing the user. This type of operating system also often supports virtual memory systems which can manage very large programs with ease.

multiple programming—Refers to programming of computers by allowing two or more arithmetical or logical operations to be executed simultaneously.

multiplex — 1. Use of one channel for several messages by time-division multiplex or frequency division. 2. A frequency-modulated stereo radio system. 3. In communications applications, the concurrent transmission of more than one information stream on a single channel. 4. The process of transferring data from several storage devices operating at relatively low transfer rates to one storage device operating at a high transfer rate, in such a manner that the high-speed device is not obliged to "wait" for the low-speed units.

multiplex data terminal—Refers to specific devices that modulate and/or demodulate data between two or more input/output devices and a data transmission link.

multiplexed bus—A type of bus structure that time-multiplexes control, address, and data information. Several independent control lines support the multiplexed bus and signal external circuits (with respect to the microprocessor CPU) with the particular type of information and its stability on the bus. This bus structure provides a suitable means of circuit interconnection with inherent minimal requirements for support circuits, primarily because each peripheral circuit (memory or I/O) requires the connection of the data transfer path. All peripheral ICs essentially receive the full address and control information for free. Device selection (enabling a specific memory location or I/O register) can thus take place within the memory or I/O peripheral or integrated circuit.

multiplexed operation—Refers to various simultaneous operations which share the use of a common unit of a system in such a way that they can be considered independent operations.

multiplex drivers and receivers — The multiplex driver and receiver circuits in a CPU provide direct interfacing with the system address and instruction data bus. The bus is time multiplexed and uses a precharge technique to achieve an unusually high system fan out. Systems with a circuit complexity up to 30 or more chips can be mechanized without the need for external drivers.

multiplexer—1. A device that takes low-speed inputs from a number of terminals and combines them into one high-speed data stream for simultaneous transmission on a single channel. At the other end of the link, a demultiplexer reconverts the high-speed data stream into a series of low-speed inputs to the host computer. The channel is split into time slots (time-division multiplexing) or frequency bands (frequency-division multiplexing). 2. A multiplexer in its simplest form consists of a manual rotary switch with single- or multiple-bank operation. From this, the stepping switch was developed for sequential switching and the crossbar switch was developed for random access. However, their mechanical complexity, slow speed, and incompatibility with electronic controls limited their applications. The introduction of solid-state switches and reed relays gave the optimum combination. The reed relays offered hermetically sealed contacts, low capacitance, low crosstalk, a switching time of less than 1 millisecond, low contact resistance, and a flexibility of design for multiple-point switching of analog signals. The solid-state switches use gated DTL or TTL circuits for the switching of logic functions in the true-or-false state where no absolute value is critical. (Some systems.)

multiplexer and bus interface—A typical data line multiplexer transfers the bus address, word count, data, or the contents of the user-designed command and status register to the bus. The multiplexer is generally controlled by the two least-significant bits of the device address, which are decoded to select the appropriate information for transfer. Information can be strobed to the bus drivers when the device address is detected. Outputs of bus receivers are sometimes accessible at wire-wrap posts for connection to the user's interface logic.

multiplexer channel—1. The communications multiplexer channel is a data processing and communications "co-ordinator." Systems equipped with communications multiplexer channels can manage the myriad data-transfer problems inherent in complex configurations. 2. A channel designed to operate with a number of I/O devices simultaneously. Several I/O devices can transfer records at the same time by interleaving items of data.

multiplexer, data-line—*See* multiplexer and bus interface.

multiplexer, frequency-division — In a frequency-division multiplex (FDM) system, the voice-grade link is divided into several subchannels at different frequencies, such that each subchannel may be used as though it were a separate line. Contrast with multiplexer, time-division.

multiplexer, intelligent—In recent times, TDM (time-division multiplexer) suppliers have added intelligence and storage to their devices to duplicate many of the concentrator functions, at less cost and without the need for tampering with host software. Like concentrators, these intelligent multiplexers assign the high-speed link to active terminals only. They commonly use full-duplex protocols for in-. creased throughput and a cyclic redundancy check that provides error protection, even with asynchronous terminals. Some intelligent multiplexers also increase throughput by data compression. One technique substitutes short code words for frequently used characters within a code set and longer words for less frequently used characters.

multiplexer polling—Refers to a technique of polling, which is possible when multiplexers are used, to allow each remote multiplexer to poll the terminals connected to it. This is more efficient than polling from the central computer because each multiplexer is operating in parallel, and there are fewer control messages involving the computer itself. An alternative technique known as "hub-polling" is used on some multipoint circuits.

multiplexer, time-division — Time-division multiplexing (TDM) involves assigning discrete time slots to each terminal, during which information can be sent without interference from the other terminals. Only one signal occupies a channel at any instant, in contrast to FDM, where all the signals are on the channel at the same time, each occupying a different frequency band. *See also* multiplexer, frequency-division.

multiplexing — Refers to a process of transmitting more than one signal at a time over a single link, route, or channel in a communications system.

multiplexing, byte—Refers to a process in which time slots on a channel are delegated to individual slow input/output devices so that bytes from one after another can be interlaced on the channel to or from main memory.

multiplication shift—A shift which results in multiplication of the number by a positive or negative integral power of the radix, with special treatment to the sign digit. With floating-point numbers, only the fixed-point is treated.

multiplication table—A specific area of storage that holds the groups of numbers to be used during the tabular scanning of the multiplication operation.

multiplication time—The time required to perform a multiplication. For a binary number, it will be equal to the total of all the addition times and all the shift time involved in the multiplication.

multiplier, analog — The analog device that develops the analog product from two or more analog input signals; i.e., the output variable is proportional to the product of the input variables.

multiplier, digital—Refers to a specific device which generates a digital product from the representation of two digital numbers, by additions of the multiplicand in accordance with the value of the digits in the multiplier. It is necessary only to shift the multiplicand and add it to the product if the multiplier digit is a one, and just shift the multiplicand without adding, if the multiplier digit is a zero, for each successive digit of the multiplier.

multiplier, function — A device causing the generation of a continuously varying analog representation of a product of two continuously varying analog input signals, as particular independent variables, i.e., time or distance change.

multiplier, mark-space—A specific analog multiplier in which one input variable, which is represented as a current or a voltage, is used to control the mark-to-space ratio of a repetitive rectangular wave and whose amplitude is made proportional to the other variable, which is also represented by a voltage or a current.

multiplier-quotient register — Refers to a specific register in which the multiplier for multiplication is placed and in which the quotient for division is developed.

multiplier, voltage—Refers to a circuit for obtaining a high dc potential from a low-voltage ac supply, effective only when load current is small; i.e., for anode supply to crt. A ladder of half-wave rectifiers charges successive capacitors, connected in series, on alternate half-cycles.

multiply/divide package—A multiply/divide package is a collection of subroutines that perform single- and double-precision multiplication and division of signed and unsigned binary numbers. Since these are normally assembled with the user's program, the multiply/divide package is supplied only in the form of a source-program tape with an assembly listing of the specific microcomputer.

multipoint circuit — A circuit interconnecting several stations that must communicate on a time-shared basis.

multipole moments—These are magnetic and electric and are measures of the charge, current, and magnet (via intrinsic spin) distributions in a given state. These static multipole moments determine the interaction of the system with weak external fields. There are also transition multipole moments which determine radiative transitions between two states.

multiprecision arithmetic — A form of arithmetic similar to double-precision arithmetic except that two or more words may be used to represent each number.

multiprocessing — 1. The utilization of several computers to logically or functionally divide jobs or processes, and to execute various programs or segments asynchronously and simultaneously. 2. Two or more processors in a system configuration; one processor to control the system, with the others subordinate to it. All processors have direct access to all memory; each can perform computations and request input/output on individual programs stored in system main memory. Devices request memory access and wait until memory is available. They start immediately upon receipt of a memory access, and need not wait for the next clock cycle. 3. Processing several programs or program segments concurrently on a time-shared basis. Each processor is only active on one program at any one time, while operations such as input/output may be performed in parallel on several programs. The processor is directed to switch back and forth among programs under the control of the master-control program.

multiprocessing, mass-data — Two or more processors, each with direct access to banks of common memory, continuously process a conventional work load, and provide answers to special projects, such as product analysis, market research, site analysis, and operations research. The total system is under executive control of one processor. This results in the most efficient use of the expensive central processor and is the basis for time-sharing of single processors among multiple users, each processor having access to the mass data memories of each other's system. Handling scientific, engineering, and business data with equal ease, such a system tied into a coast-to-coast communications network can give a consolidated data-processing operation.

multiprocessing, microcomputer — A form of distributed processing is the multiprocessor type of organization. In the architecture, multiple independent microcomputers are interconnected to provide increased computing power. While this structure provides a more powerful overall processing system than the single CPU/intelligent-controller organization, the multiprocessor system is several times more expensive because each CPU requires its own support chips, and large amounts of software must be written, and the interaction of processors in the system can make the control software very complex.

multiprocessing operation—A type of

operation in which two (or more) central processors perform as one system. This configuration enables the system to perform overlapped simultaneous processing to a greater extent than does a single computing system. Multiprocessing configurations may consist of a host computer and a front-end processor, or both may be host computers. In either case, both are processing (either on segments of the same job or on entirely different jobs) simultaneously.

multiprocessing organizations — There are two generic multiprocessing organizations: loosely coupled and tightly coupled. Loosely coupled multiprocessing connects two or more individual systems by means of a communication link. Each system is capable of independent processing, but supports the link to allow at least file-system access, and perhaps task interchange for a form of load balancing. File-system access provides not only a file transfer mechanism among systems, but more generally allows a task on one system to open a file on another system. File I/O is transparent to the task so that records going to or from a file on another system are passed across the link instead of requiring direct file I/O on the task's CPU and peripherals. System software should support links of various types and speeds so that the one most appropriate for a particular operating environment can be selected.

A tightly coupled multiprocessor organization has a single shared memory and a single copy of the operating system and supporting software.

multiprocessing system—A system that is organized to contain two or more interconnected computers, which perform functionally or geographically specialized processing tasks.

multiprocessor—A computer with multiple arithmetic and logic units for simultaneous use and capability.

multiprocessor interleaving—Relates to various techniques or special processes of addressing adjacent storage modules in an even/odd fashion. It significantly reduces storage-access conflicts in a multiprocessor system and, thereby, increases overall system performance. With interleaving, the modules are divided into even and odd locations (although the address-

ing structure within the modules themselves remains unchanged). Thus, in a fully expanded 8-module system, modules 0, 2, 4, and 6 are referenced for even addresses, while modules 1, 3, 5, and 7 are referenced for odd.

multiprogramming — 1. Refers to procedures for handling numerous routines or programs, seemingly simultaneously, by overlapping or interleaving their execution; that is, by permitting more than one program to time-share machine components. 2. Multiprogramming is a process by which several related or unrelated programs or portions of programs are performed concurrently, provided that enough processing, storage, and input/output facilities are available. While one program is awaiting an occurrence, such as the completion of an input/output operation or the end of a time interval, control of the processing unit is directed to another program in accordance with a pre-established order of priority. The competition among several programs for the processing, storage, input/output, and programming facilities of the system helps to ensure that as much of the system as possible is kept busy performing useful work for as much of the time as possible. As a result, the total throughput of the system—that is, the total volume of work performed by the system during a given interval of time —is significantly increased.

multiprogramming executive — Refers to a microsystem building block that provides the operating environment of concurrent execution of more than one program. It contains such services as priority scheduler, memory allocation, and memory deallocation.

multiprogramming interrupts — Some computers are equipped with a set of control signals which are referred to as interrupts. Whenever certain conditions exist, a control signal will direct the central computer to execute the word (instruction) at a specified address in central store. Each interrupt is activated by unique conditions and directs the computer to a correspondingly unique address in central store. The occurrence of an interrupt terminates guard mode, program lockin, and central-store address assignments. (Some systems.)

multiprogramming, master-slave — Refers to a system designed to guarantee that one program cannot damage or access another program that is sharing memory. The unique operating technique used in changing from slave to master mode makes multiprogramming not only practical, but also foolproof.

multiprogramming, priority — Priority multiprogramming is oriented toward concurrent operation of several types of applications. Assignment of priority levels is at the discretion of the user. For example, one priority level can be reserved for a program that must provide rapid responses to realtime devices, such as communications control. Another can be reserved for the peripheral control package to accomplish several media conversions—disk to tape, tape to printer, etc. The third priority level could then be used to run either a production or a monitor job.

multitasking—Refers to procedures in which several separate but interrelated tasks operate under a single program identity; differs from multiprogramming in that common routines and data space as well as disk files may be used. May or may not involve multiprocessing.

multithread operation—A device used on a program which can have more than one logical path through it executed simultaneously.

multivibrator—Refers to a type of relaxation oscillator used for the generation of nonsinusoidal waves in which the output of each active device is coupled back to the input of the other to sustain oscillations.

multiwire pc board—The multiwire process involves a customized pattern of insulated wires laid down on an adhesive-coated substrate. While successful, multiwire's availability has been confined to photocircuits and a few licensees. Multiwire competes with multilayer boards in two areas—packaging density and as an interconnection method for high-speed bipolar logic. One multiwire board with an etched ground and powerplane and with signal layers on each side is the equal of a six-layer multilayer board (MLB). By adding other signal layers, equivalents of a 12-layer MLB can be had.

MUMPS—A text-oriented language with built-in data base facilities and string and pattern matching. Used in hospitals and other large organizations for unified accounting. The basic orientation of MUMPS is procedural, much like FORTRAN or COBOL. However, because of the interactive nature of the system, programs are written and fully debugged in a fraction of the time required by other high-level languages. Its capabilities are primarily directed toward the processing of variable-length string and array data. In addition, algebraic, Boolean, and assembly-like bit-manipulation operations are available.

muting—Refers to the suppression of an output of electronic equipment unless there is an adequate signal/noise ratio.

N

name, file — Alphanumeric characters assigned to identify a related set of records which constitute a particular file.

name, program—The brief reference in a program to another program or portion of another program.

name, section — The distinct qualifying term available for a paragraph name.

name, set—An identifier.

name, variable—An alphanumeric name selected by a programmer to represent a specific program variable. Rules for naming variables vary between compilers (FORTRAN, BASIC) and computing equipment.

NAND — A logical operator having the property that if P is a statement, and Q is a statement, then, the NAND of P, Q, and R is true if at least one statement is false, false if all statements are true. (An AND invert; a negated AND.)

NAND operations—The grouping of an AND gate followed by an inverter is called a NOT AND or NAND gate. If all the inputs have a value of 1, the output is 0, and if any of the inputs have a value of 0, the output will be 1. (Note that this is just the opposite of an AND gate.)

NAND element—*Same as* gate, NAND.

NAND gate—*See* gate, NAND.

NAND operation—*Same as* gate, NAND.

NAND operator—*Same as* gate, NAND.

nanocircuit—This is an integrated microelectronic circuit in which each component is fabricated on a separate chip or substrate so that independent optimization of performance is possible.

nanosecond — A measurement equivalent to one billionth of a second (10^{-9} second). Abbreviated nsec, ns.

nanosecond circuit — Refers to computer logic circuits, or other electronic circuits, which have gradient pulse rise or fall times measured in billionths of a second or less.

narrow band—Refers to a communication line similar to the common voice-grade line but which operates on a lower frequency. Communications lines are an essential element of computer communication systems. The selection of a communication service to provide a specific bandwidth depends on the volume and speed requirements of the system.

natural binary—A number system to the base (radix) 2, in which the ones (1s) and zeroes (0s) have a weighted value in accordance with their **relative position** in the binary word. "Carries" may affect many digits.

natural frequency—The free-oscillation frequency of a system.

natural-function generator—Relates to either an analog device or a specific program based on some physical law, such as one used with a digital computer to solve a particular differential equation.

native language—A communication language or coding between machine units or modules that is peculiar to or usable only for a particular class or brand of equipment.

natural language — A language whose rules reflect and describe current usage rather than prescribed usage.

n-channel charge-coupled device — A charge-coupled device fabricated so that the charges stored in the potential wells are electrons.

n-channel MOS (NMOS) — A type of metal-oxide silicon field-effect transistor using electrons to conduct current in the semiconductor channel. The channel has a predominantly negative charge.

n-channel performance—Refers to n-channel MOS devices that have several inherent performance advantages over p-channel and bipolar circuits. Since the majority carriers are electrons rather than holes, mobility is increased by a factor of two, giving a theoretical speed-improvement factor of two over p-channel MOS. In addition, the threshold voltages obtained are lower than for p-channel and allow circuits to be designed to operate over a lower supply range. This reduces the effects of parasitics and allows approximately 15% tighter packing densities if lower voltages are used. When compared with bipolar devices, n-channel offers significantly lower power consumption for equivalent speed. Bipolar devices, however, offer the highest possible speed if power and cost are secondary.

n-channel silicon JFET—This family of n-channel junction FETs are designed and characterized for vhf and uhf applications requiring high-gain and low-noise figures. The forward transconductance is relatively flat out to 1000 MHz. Applications for these devices in military, commercial, and consumer communications equipment include low-noise high-gain rf amplifiers, low-noise mixers with conversion gain, and low-noise ultrastable rf oscillators.

n-channel silicon planar epitaxial JFET —Features of this device are: exceptionally high figure of merit, radiation immunity, extremely low noise and capacitance, high input impedance, zero offset, and a high-reliability silicon epitaxial planar construction.

NC language processor—Refers to numerical control in which a computer program is developed to serve as a translating system for a parts programmer.

NC (numeric control) system—Refers to a system which uses prerecorded intelligence prepared from numerical data to control a machine or process. The NC system consists of all elements of the control system and of the machine being controlled that are, in fact, a part of the servomechanism.

negation gate—Refers to a device with capability of reversing a signal, condition, state, or an event into its alternate or opposite.

negative conductance (in semiconductors)—The use of "hot" electrons in some form of a two-terminal negative conductance, forming the basis of both avalanche transit-time devices and those devices relating to the Gunn effect. In the former, e.g., using silicon, the negative conductance arises from a phase shift (greater than 90° and preferably near to 180°) between current and voltage. In the Gunn devices, it arises within the GaAs crystal in a strong electric field with the local current density decreasing whenever the local electric field exceeds a certain threshold. Other materials showing the Gunn effect are InP, InAs, CdTe, ZnSe, etc.

negative conductor — This refers to a type of conductor connected to the negative terminal of a voltage source. Such a conductor is often used as an auxiliary return circuit in a system of electric traction.

negative crystal — Birefringent material for which the velocity of the extraordinary ray is greater than that of the ordinary ray.

negative electricity—Phenomenon in a body when it gives rise to effects associated with an excess of electrons.

negative feedback — 1. A process by which part of the output signal of an amplifying circuit is fed back to the input circuit. The signal is fed back 180° out-of-phase with the input signal, decreasing the amplification and the distortion. Also called degeneration, inverse feedback, or stabilized feedback. 2. A technique whereby the effective output of a control system is used to proportionally suppress the output of the system; i.e., a "set point" may be maintained by adjusting the feedback of a driven system to trigger at a given level, or a system can be made to oscillate by inserting a time delay in a relatively strongly weighted negative feedback loop and

a weaker but faster-acting positive feedback loop.

negative impedance—A condition existing when there is no inductance or capacitance in the circuit. This is a characteristic of certain electrical devices or circuits—instead of increasing, the voltage decreases when the current is increased and vice versa. Also called negative resistance.

negative impedance converter—Active network for which a positive impedance connected across one pair of terminals produces a negative impedance across the other pair.

negative ion—Refers to an atom with more electrons than normal. Thus, it has a negative charge.

negative resistance—A resistance exhibiting the opposite characteristic from normal. For example, when the voltage is increased across a circuit, the current will decrease instead of increase.

negative-true logic—A logic system in which the voltage representing a logical 1 has a lower or more negative value than that representing a logical 0. Most parallel I/O buses use negative-true logic due to the nature of commonly available logic circuits.

negatron—A four-electrode thermionic tube for obtaining negative resistance, comprising an anode and grid on one side of a cathode, and an anode on the other.

nesistor—Transistor depending on a bipolar field effect.

nest—1. Refers to an activity to embed a subroutine or block of data into a larger routine or block of data. 2. To evaluate an nth degree of polynomial by a particular algorithm which uses (n-1) multiply operations and (n-1) add operations in succession.

nesting—1. Concerns subroutines that are generally enclosed within each other. Those in the inner ring are not necessarily part of the outer ring or loop. Nesting is an important programming technique. 2. The inclusion of a routine or block of data (within a computer) inside a larger routine or block of data.

nesting level—Refers to assembler programming in which the level at which a term or subexpression appears in an expression, or the level at which a macro definition containing an inner macro instruction is processed by an assembler.

nesting loop—Refers to nesting loops that usually contain a loop of instructions which then also contain inner loops, nesting subroutines, outer loops, and rules and procedures relating to in and out procedures for each type.

net loss—The algebraic sum of the gains and losses between two terminals of a circuit, equal to the difference in the levels at these points.

network—1. A combination of elements. 2. An interconnected system of transmission lines that provides multiple transmissions between loads and sources of generation. 3. A series of points connected by communications channels. 4. A switched telephone network is a network of telephone lines normally used for dialed telephone calls. 5. A private network is a network of communications channels confined to the use of one customer.

network, analog—Refers to a circuit or circuits which represent(s) physical variables in such a manner as to permit the expression and solution of mathematical relationships between the variables or permits the solution directly by electric or electronic means.

network analysis—1. Process of calculating theoretically the transfer constant of a network. 2. The process of obtaining electrical properties of a network from its configuration, parameters, and driving forces.

network analyzer—1. A group of electric circuit elements that can readily be connected to form models of electric networks. From corresponding measurements on the model, it is then possible to infer the electrical quantities at various points on the prototype system. 2. An analog device designed primarily for simulating electrical networks. Synonymous with network calculator.

network buffer—In a computer communications network, a buffer is a storage device used to compensate for a difference in the rate flow of data received and transmitted along the numerous communication lines converging on the data processing center. The communications buffer orders information from many operators and controls the information so that it can be processed by the computer without confusion. The buffer has memory and control circuitry of its own for storing incoming messages that the computer is not ready to process and for storing outgoing messages which have to be delayed because of busy lines.

network calculator—Combination of resistors, inductors, capacitors, and generators used to simulate the electrical characteristics of a power-generation system, so that the effects of varying different operating conditions can be studied in computers.

network, communications—Refers to a set of stations connected together by various communication links. Messages may be sent from any station to any other station, and may pass through several stations along the way.

network communications circuits—In a computer network, there are those circuits that interconnect the nodes of the network, circuits that connect terminals with the network, and those circuits, logical or physical, which provide the end-to-end path between communicating processes. As regards to the circuits that physically connect the nodes in a network, the transmission media can be voice-grade or wideband lines and they can be owned, leased from a common carrier, or dial-up. Voice-grade circuits can be modulated to operate in the range of 110 baud to 9600 baud. Wideband lines operate from 19,000 to 250,000 baud, and some economies of scale exist if there is in fact a need for that kind of bandwidth.

network constant—Any one of the resistance, inductance, mutual-inductance, or capacitance values in a circuit or network. When these values are constant, the network is said to be linear.

network control—This action provides the functions required for intranetwork operation, such as addressing and routing. Facilities may be viewed as those directing the control of switching points rather than providing for the transfer of data between the points.

network, distributed-processing — A distributed-processing network can be any end-user network in which application processing and/or data base accessing (including updates) take place on two or more host computers in the same network. (Note that certain distributed-function terminal systems can be classified as host computers.) A further requirement for a distributed data base network is that host computers have permanent storage-device disks attached for on-line data files. Generally, distributed-processing networks can simultaneously support several large computers as well as a number of micro- or minicomputers. The size of the host computers and their associated bulk memory will depend only on the processing and data base requirements at each individual node location in the network.

network, electrical—1. Any arrangement of electric components, active or passive, with the former implying an internal source of emf or current. 2. Circuit element described by the following letters, e.g., L, having one shunt and one series element; C, one shunt followed by one series element in each leg; T, two series and one shunt element from junction; H, four series and one shunt element; =, one shunt, one series, and one shunt element; O, one shunt, one series in each leg, and one shunt element; lattice (bridge), element between each input terminal to both output terminals; bridged T, T-network with series arms bypassed by fourth element; twin-T, two T-networks overlaying each other. All networks have 4 terminals (quadripole) in a 2-wire line, are balanced or unbalanced to earth potential, and the elements or branches may be complex.

networking — Networking involves the interconnecting of processors within the same enclosure or the same room, across town, or across country. The interconnections are established through common or private carrier communications channels, using data-link control to establish paths, manage the message transactions, and free lines for other users. Techniques, such as synchronous data-link control, implement most of the network functions automatically in hardware and only a few data-link control commands must be added to the application program. As a result, segmenting of the data base and par-

allel processing is often completely invisible to the user.

network intelligence, microcomputer—Distributed-intelligence systems can be more efficiently built with the new generation of microcomputers. The computational and control capabilities allow each micro in the network to perform a dedicated task. The over-all network can provide hardware and software redundancy at an attractive price—compared with a single large processor. Common-memory software and hardware techniques provide one of the newest ways to handle the necessary intercommunication between subsystems. Microcomputer sets that include CPU, memory, and I/O adapters can be purchased inexpensively. In a distributed-intelligence system, each of these units or processors has a dedicated function, typically I/O oriented. Since the system is oriented towards maximum I/O throughput, processor cross-communication is held to a minimum.

network relay—A type of relay (e.g., voltage, power, etc.) used in the protection and control of alternating-current low-voltage networks.

network stabilization—Relates to operational amplifiers and servomechanisms; a network used to shape the transfer characteristics to eliminate or minimize oscillations when feedback is provided.

Neumann principle — Physical properties of a crystal are never of lower symmetry than the symmetry of the external form of the crystal. Consequently, tensor properties of a cubic crystal, such as elasticity or conductivity, must have cubic symmetry, and the behavior of the crystal will be isotropic.

neutral—1. Exhibiting no resultant charge or voltage. 2. Return conductor of a balanced power supply, nearly at earth potential, if without a local ground connection. 3. The normal state of atoms and the universe.

neutral conductor—The one nearest in potential to a neutral point (q.v.) in a polyphase power system.

neutralization—1. The nullifying of voltage feedback from the output to the input of an amplifier through the interelectrode impedance of the tube. Its principal use is in oscillation in an amplifier. This is done by introducing, into the input, a voltage equal in magnitude but opposite in phase to the feedback through the interelectrode capacitance. 2. Counteracting a tendency to oscillation through feedback via anode-grid capacitance. Reversed feedback is provided by a balancing capacitance to which is applied voltage equal and in anti-phase to that on the anode. Also balancing.

neutralizing capacitor — A capacitor, usually variable, employed in a radio receiving or transmitting circuit to feed a portion of the signal voltage from the plate circuit back to the grid circuit.

neutral state—Said of a ferromagnetic material when completely demagnetized. Also virgin state.

neutral temperature—That for a thermocouple at which the emf produced has a turning value, e.g., 270 °C for Cu-Fe.

neutron—Uncharged subatomic particle whose mass is approximately equal to that of a proton, which enters into the structure of atomic nuclei. Interacts with matter primarily by collisions.

new input queue—A group or a queue of new messages that are in the system and are waiting for processing. The main scheduling routine will scan them along with other queues and order them into processing.

newton—The unit of force in the MKS system, being the force required to impact, to a mass of one kilogram, an acceleration of one meter per second per second.

nibble—A term used by microcomputer users and technicians to designate a group of 4 bits, and it is rather quaint to consider that it takes two nibbles to make a byte (8 bits). Nibble (or 4-bit) control can be found on many 8-bit machines and 4-bit operations are usually associated with hexadecimal and binary-coded decimal operations. Applications that have a man/machine interface, such as a control keyboard or a numeric display, are good candidates for nibble control.

nichrome—Trade name for a nickel-chromium alloy largely used for heating resistance elements because of its high specific resistance, and its ability to withstand high temperatures.

nickel—(Ni). Silver-white metallic element, at. no. 28, at. wt. 58.71, m.p.

1450°, b.p. 3000°C, electrical resistivity at 20°C, 10.9 microhm/cm. It is magnetostrictive, showing a decrease in length in an applied magnetic field and, in the form of wire, is much used in computers for small stores, the data circulating and being extracted when required.

nickel-cadmium battery—One type is a secondary battery of 1.2 volt, having a cathode of cadmium and a positive electrode of nickel hydroxide. The battery requires practically no maintenance as water is not lost by electrolysis or evaporation. It is now used as a power supply for transistorized tv receivers and for other purposes.

nickel delay line—A delay line utilizing the magnetic and/or magnetostrictive properties of nickel.

nickel-iron (NiFe) secondary cell—An alkali accumulator using a potassium-hydroxide electrolyte. It is lighter and more durable than lead cells and has an emf of 1.2 volts. Also known as an Edison cell.

n-level logic—Pertains to a collection of gates connected in such a way that no more than n gates appear in series.

NMOS—A silicon-gate n-channel MOS process that uses currents made up of negative charges. It makes components smaller, faster, cooler, and more amenable to working with standard power-supply voltages.

no-address instruction—An instruction specifying an operation which the computer can perform without having to refer to its storage or memory unit.

node — 1. In telecommunications, the node is that point in a transmission system where lines or trunks from many sources meet; i.e., a point of concentration. Also, commonly used to refer to that location of a data network where switching is done; e.g., in a packet switched network such as Datapac, the node is where the equipment that does the packet switching function is located. 2. A terminal of any branch of a network, or a terminal common to two or more branches. Also called junction point, branch point, vertex, or nodal point.

noise — 1. Any unwanted disturbance within a dynamic electrical or mechanical system. 2. Any unwanted electrical disturbance or spurious signal which modifies the transmitting, indicating, or recording of desired data. 3. In a computer, extra bits or words which have no meaning and which must be ignored or removed from the data at the time it is used. 4. Random variations of one or more characteristics of any entity such as voltage, current, or data. 5. A random signal of known statistical properties of amplitude, distribution, and spectral density.

noise, ambient—Refers to an acoustic noise existing in a room or other location.

noise, background—1. Refers to extra bits or words that must be ignored or removed from the data at the time the data is used. 2. Errors introduced into data in a system, especially one or more characteristics of any entity such as voltage, current, or data. 3. Loosely, any disturbance tending to interfere with the normal operation of a device or system.

noise, carrier—Refers to residual modulation. Carrier noise is the noise produced by undesired variations of a radio-frequency signal in the absence of any intended modulation.

noise, common-mode—Common-mode noise is picked up by power lines passing through electrically noisy environments, and can distort the input waveform significantly. Most common-mode noise can be eliminated with a multishielded isolation transformer.

noise, delta—Refers to the difference between the 1-state and the 0-state half-selected noise.

noise, diode—1. A standard electrical noise source consisting of a diode operated at saturation. The noise is due to random emission of electrons. 2. One operating as a noise generator, under temperature-limited conditions.

noise, electrical type—Generally, there are two main forms of electrical noise. They are known as steady-state and impulse noise. Steady-state noise is known also as Gaussian noise, thermal noise, white noise, electron hiss, grass (a radar term), and random noise. This is the background noise that is present on all electronic circuits. The data signal must be kept at a higher level than this noise after attenuation. White noise is the type of noise that causes the most problems in voice transmission but is more controllable in data transmission than is the other form of noise—impulse noise. The latter is characterized by peaks of large amplitude and pulses of short duration; that is, pulse widths measured in milliseconds. Pulses of this duration have little or no effect on the human ear and will be heard merely as a click or crack without destroying voice intelligence. Impulse noise can block out data signals, however, and is a significant source of errors in data. This is especially true with high-speed data transmission, where more bits are affected in a given time period.

noise, Gaussian—Refers to noise which designates that the particular voltage distribution is specified in terms of probabilities.

noise immunity—Relates to a measure of the insensitivity of a logic circuit to triggering or its reaction to spurious or undesirable electrical signals or noise, largely determined by the signal swing of the logic. Noise can be in either of two directions, positive or negative.

noise, impulse—Refers to a form of noise characterized by high amplitude and short duration, sometimes occuring as a group of impulses, or burst. Heard on the line as sharp clicks, impulse noise is a common source of error, originating from switching equipment, electrical storms, etc.

noise level—The strength of extraneous signals in a circuit.

noise, modulation—1. Refers to those extra bits or words that must be ignored or removed from the data at the time the data is used. 2. Errors introduced into data in a system, especially in communication channels. 3. Random variations of one or more characteristics of any entity such as voltage, current, or data. 4. Loosely, any disturbance tending to interfere with the normal operation of a device or system.

noise, natural—Refers to noise caused by natural phenomena such as thermal emission, static, etc.

noise ratio—A measure of noise power in a terminated filter or circuit divided by the signal power; expressed in decibels.

noise, reference—Refers to the magnitude of circuit noise that will produce a circuit noise-meter reading equal to that produced by 10 watts of electric power at 1000 cycles per second.

noise, systematic—Refers to noise that may also be classified as random, periodic, or systematic. Systematic noise, a special case of construct noise, is a form of noise inherent in imperfect equipment. For example, if the signal for the character "e" were always replaced by the signal for character "z" in a message because of equipment failure, this would be a systematic error. Interestingly enough, such systematic errors, once determined, do not interfere totally with a message.

noise, thermal—This is the result of heat-induced vibration, and atom and molecule collisions, e.g., energy generated at all frequencies and combined in a random manner at any instant. Also known as Johnson noise and white noise and considered a basic noise source.

noisy digit—Relates to a digit, usually zero, produced during the normalizing of a floating-point number, and inserted during a left-shift operation into the fixed point part.

noisy mode—In a computer, a floating-point arithmetic procedure associated with normalization. In this procedure, digits other than zero are introduced in the low-order positions during the left shift.

nonarithmetic shift—Refers to a shift in which the digits dropped off at one end of a word are returned at the other in a circular fashion; i.e., if a register holds the eight digits 23456-789, the result of a cyclic shift two columns to the left would be to change the contents of the register to 45678923. Synonymous with logical shift and cyclic shift.

nondestructive reading—Same as nonvolatile. If after reading data to or from a storage unit, the record is unchanged, the term nondestructive or nonvolatile reading is used.

nondestructive readout—1. The copying of information from a computer storage device without altering the physical representation of the information in the device. 2. A particular storage area that cannot be erased and reused, e.g., punched cards or perforated paper tape. 3. A reading

process that does not destroy the data in the source.

nondissipative network—One designed as if the inductances and capacitances are free from dissipation, and as if constructed with components of minimum loss.

nonequivalence element — A specific logic element which has two binary input signals and only one output signal. The variance or variable represented by the output signal is the nonequivalence of the variable represented by the input signals, i.e., a two-input element whose output signal represents 1 when its input signals are different from each other.

nonequivalence operation — A logical operation applied to two operands producing a result depending on the bit patterns of the operands and according to rules for each bit position, e.g., if P = 110110, and Q = 011010, then, R = 101100.

nonoperable instruction — Refers to a type whose only effect is to advance the instruction index counter. Often written as "continue."

nonreturn-to-reference recording—Refers to specific techniques designed to effect a nonreturn-to-zero recording.

nonreturn-to-zero (NRZ)—1. A method of writing information on a magnetic surface in which the current through the write-head winding does not return to zero after the write pulse. 2. A mode of recording in which each state of the medium corresponds to one binary state. In the mode, the state of the recording medium changes when the information changes from 1 to 0 or from 0 to 1. Note: NRZ modified is also often called NRZI.

nonswitched line—Refers to a service or connection between a remote terminal and a computer that does not have to be established by dialing.

nonsynchronous—Not related in speed, frequency, or phase to other quantities in a device or circuit.

nonvolatile memory — A memory type which holds data even if power has been disconnected. A magnetic memory is nonvolatile, an ultrasonic one is volatile (it does not comply with the above criterion).

nonvolatile storage — Storage media that retains information in the absence of power and which will make the information available when power is restored.

No Op—Abbreviation for no operation. 1. A specific computer instruction that causes the computer to perform no operation. 2. Refers to an instruction commanding the computer to do nothing, except to proceed to the next instruction in sequence. It is a jump operation in a very limited sense. Its only effect is to increment the Program Counter by one. It is also used for equalizing the execution time through alternate paths in a control program.

NOR circuit—A gate circuit having multiple inputs and one output that is energized only if all inputs are zero.

normalization routine—Refers to floating-point arithmetic operations related to normalization of numerals in which digits other than zero are developed in the low order; i.e., less significant positions during the left shift.

normalization signal — Refers to the generation, or a restoration, of signals which comply with specified requirements for amplitude, shape, and timing, i.e., such signals are often generated from another signal, and such requirements are most often conventions or rules of specific computers, with little consistency among a great many systems.

normalized form—Concerns a special form taken by a floating-point number which has been adjusted in such a way that its mantissa lies in a specified range.

normal magnetization — Locus of the tips of the magnetic hysteresis loops obtained by varying the limits of the range of alternating magnetization.

notation—1. A manner of representing numbers. Some of the more important notation scales are:

Base	Name
2	binary
3	ternary
4	quaternary, tetral
5	quinary
10	decimal
12	duodecimal
16	hexadecimal, sexadecimal
32	duotricenary
2, 5	biquinary

2. The act, process, or method of representing facts or quantities by a system or set of marks, signs, figures, or characters.

NOT circuit — A computer circuit in which the output signal has a phase or polarity opposite from that of the input signal.

NOT gate—An inhibitory circuit equivalent to the logical operation of negation (mathematical complement). The output of the circuit is energized only when its single input is not energized and there will be no output if the input is energized.

NOT operation — A basic Boolean operation is the NOT function, which specifies that the output will always be the inverse of the input, NOT $1=0$, NOT $0=1$. The gate that produces the NOT function is called an inverter. In general, the inverted value of A is written $\bar{A}$. An inverter changes an input of 1 to an output of 0, and vice versa.

n-plus-one address instruction—A multiple-address computer instruction in which one address serves to specify the location of the next instruction of the normal sequence to be executed.

NRZI—Nonreturn to zero one.

N-type—1. Concerns various semiconductor crystals doped to provide excess electrons. 2. A symbol in flowcharting depicting several options.

nuclear energy—In principle, the binding energy of a system of particles forming an atomic nucleus. More usually, the energy released during nuclear reactions involving regrouping of such particles (e.g., fission or fusion processes). The term atomic energy is deprecated as it implies rearrangement of atoms rather than of nuclear particles.

null—1. A balanced condition which results in a zero output from a device or system. 2. To oppose an output which differs from zero so that it is returned to zero.

null character — Refers to a special control character that serves to accomplish media fill or time fill; for example, in ASCII, the all zeros character (not numeric zero). Null characters may be inserted into, or removed from, a sequence of characters without affecting the meaning of the sequence, but control of equipment or the format may be affected. Abbreviated NUL.

null cycle—The time necessary to cycle through a program without introducing data. This establishes the lower boundary for program processing time.

null set—Refers to a logic or set theory term, i.e., a set which contains no members; an empty set.

null suppression—Refers to the bypassing of all null characters in order to reduce the amount of data to be transmitted. Synonymous with data compaction.

number, check—Refers to a designated number composed of one or more digits and used to detect equipment malfunctions in data transfer operations. If a check number consists of only one digit, it is synonymous with check digit.

number, self-checking—A number, with a suffix digit related to the figure(s) of the number, that is used to check the number for accuracy after it has been transferred or transmitted from one medium or device to another. The suffix or self-check digit is developed using a uniform mathematical procedure designed to detect both erroneous figures and transposed digits. *See* modulo-N check.

numeral, double-length — Refers to a specific numeral that contains twice as many digits as ordinary numerals (in computers) and a number that usually requires two registers or storage locations. Such numerals are most often used for double-precision computing.

numerical analysis—The use of numerical methods to solve mathematical equations, of a form that usually involves more complex processes or relationships, e.g., integration, by means of trial and error.

numerical aperture—This is a measure of the amount of light that can be injected into an optical cable as a function of the distance between the end of the cable and the light source. It is the sine of a half-angle of the cone within which light rays will propagate through a cable.

numerical control—1. A manufacturing technique controlled automatically by orders (called commands). These are introduced in the form of numbers—which may be entered by a decade switch, or by a dial switch like the one on a telephone. 2. Refers to the control of machine tools, drafting machines, and the like, by punched-paper or magnetic tapes suitably encoded with directive information. As most numerically controlled devices have very limited logical or arithmetic capability (to keep costs low), they relay on their input tapes for detailed and explicit guidance. This may mean 8 bits for very 0.001 inch of motion, or a great amount of data on the tape. It is common for a computer to prepare the control tapes, using information presented in a more manageable and concise form.

numerical control, direct—Abbreviated DNC. A system connecting a set of numerically controlled machines to a common memory for part-program or machine-program storage, with provision for on-demand distribution of data for the machines. Direct numerical-control systems typically have additional provisions for collection, display, or editing of part programs, operator instructions, or data related to the numerical-control process.

numerical control, hand-wired—A numerical-control system wherein the response to data input, data handling sequence, and control functions is determined by the fixed and committed circuit interconnections of discrete decision elements and storage devices. Changes in the response, sequence, or functions can be made by changing the interconnections.

numerical-control system — A system controlled by the direct insertion of numerical data at some point. The system must automatically interpret at least some portion of the data.

numerical-control tapes — Refers to a punched-paper tape, or plastic tape with magnetic spots, that is used to feed digital instructions to a numerical-control machine, e.g., an automated cutting or forming machine thus guided. Tolerances as fine as 1/10,000 of an inch can be achieved on unattended units. Tapes are developed with digital computer programs.

numerical data—Data in which information is expressed by a set of numbers or symbols that can only assume discrete values or configurations.

numerically controlled machine — Refers to computer controlled machinery used in manufacturing or processing.

numeric coding—A system of abbreviation used in the preparation of information for machine acceptance in which all information is reduced to numerical quantities, in contrast to alphabetic coding.

numeric constant—In some systems, a numeric constant is a self-defining term that is treated as an octal or decimal depending upon the conversion mode in effect at the time the term is encountered. Initially, numeric terms beginning with a zero are treated as octal numbers. Those not beginning with a zero are treated as decimal numbers.

numeric pads—These are numeral key groupings like those used on adding machines. The pads speed up the entry of numeric data by limiting the hand movement required of the operator.

numeric word — A special word composed exclusively of characters from a numeric code.

O

object code — The basic program; the output from a compiler or assembler which is itself executable machine code, or is suitable for processing to produce executable machine code.

object deck—A stack of punched cards forming a computer program in machine language. Usually prepared from an equivalent source deck by the compiler for the machine.

object language—Refers to the language which is the output of an automatic coding routine. Usually object language and machine language are the same. However, a series of steps in an automatic coding system may involve the object language of one step serving as a source language for the next step and so forth.

object program—1. A source program that has been automatically translated into machine language. 2. The final or "target" program is referred to as the object program. The source program is developed first, and this is translated into the machine program for internal computer operation. 3. A set of machine language instructions for the solution of a problem, obtained as the end result of a compilation process. It is generated from the source program. 4. The absolute coding output by a processor program. *See* source program.

OCR—Abbreviation for optical character recognition. Refers to recognition by machines of printed or written characters based on inputs from photoelectric transducers.

octal — A numbering system basic to computer operation. A positional notation system using 8 as a base, instead of 2, as in binary, or 10, as in decimal.

odd-even check — Refers to an automatic computer check in which an extra digit is carried along with each word, to determine whether the total number of 1s in the word is odd or even, thus providing a check for proper operation.

odd-even interleaving — Refers to the splitting of memory into several sections and independent paths with the odd-even addresses in alternate sections. This allows even further segmenting than the normal memory interleaving of the read-write memory cycle.

odd-parity check—Refers to a popular check by summation in which the binary digits in a character or word are added, and the sum checked against a single previously computed parity digit; i.e., a check tests whether the number of ones in a word is odd or even. (Synonymous with odd-even check and related to redundancy check.)

off emergency — Refers to a particular control switch on most control panels or consoles which, when pushed, will disconnect all power from the computer system.

off-line — Refers to equipment or devices not under direct control of the central processing unit. Also concerns a description of terminal equipment not connected to a transmission line.

off-line operation—1. Refers to a computer operation which is independent of the time base of the actual inputs. 2. In a computer system, this refers to the operation of peripheral equipment independent from the central processor, e.g., the transcribing of card information to magnetic tape to printed form.

one-address instruction—Refers to an instruction consisting of an operation and exactly one address. The instruction code of a single-address computer may include both zero and multiaddress instructions as special cases.

one element (gate)—Refers to an electrical gate or mechanical device which implements the logical OR operator. An input signal occurs whenever there are one or more inputs on a multichannel input. An OR gate performs the function of the logical "inclusive-OR operator."

one-for-one—Relates to a phrase often associated with an assembly routine where one source language instruction is converted to one machine language instruction.

one-for-one translation—This generally refers to assembly language because an assembler program operates on a one-for-one basis in that each phrase of the language translates directly into a specific machine-language word, as contrasted with high-level languages which translate into "many-for-one" bases.

one-shot logic—*See* pulsed logic.

one-step operation—Refers to a method of operating a computer manually, in which a single instruction or part of an instruction is performed in response to a single operation of a manual control. This method is generally used for detecting mistakes and other debugging procedures.

one-to-zero ratio—1. Refers to the ratio of either the maximum amplitude, or the instantaneous amplitude at some specified time, of a "one" output signal to a "zero" output signal. 2. The ratio of a 1 output to the 0 output.

on-line—Relates to equipment, devices, or systems in direct interactive communication with the central processing unit. May also be used to de-

scribe terminal equipment connected to a transmission line.

on-line data base—Typically, a vast and continuously updated file of information, abstracts, or references on a particular subject or subjects. On-line data bases are designed so that by using subject headings, key words, key phrases, or authors, users can quickly search for, locate, analyze, and print out data.

on-line data processing — Data processing procedures in which all changes to relevant records and accounts are made at the time that each transaction or event occurs. The process usually requires random-access storage. *See* on-line processing.

on-line debugging—Relates to the act of debugging a program while time-sharing its execution with an on-line process program. On-line debugging is accomplished in such a way that any attempt by the "slave" program, undergoing debugging, to interfere with the operation of the process, the program will be detected and inhibited.

on-line diagnostics—Relates to the running of diagnostics on a system while it is on line but at off peak times; necessary in order to save time and to take corrective action without closing down the system.

on-line equipment—Refers to a system of peripheral equipment or devices in which the operation of such equipment is under the control of the central processing unit.

on-line processing — The operation of terminals, disks, and other auxiliary equipment under direct and absolute control of the central processor to eliminate the need for human intervention at any stage between initial input and computer output.

on-line storage—Refers to storage devices, and especially the storage media which they contain, under the direct control of a computing system, and not the shelf or off-line storage of these media.

on-line system—1. A system where the input data enters the computer directly from the point of origin and/or in which output data are transmitted directly to where they are used. 2. A system which eliminates the need for human intervention between source recording and the ultimate processing by a microcomputer.

on-line test facilities—Refers to test facilities (including line-loop tests), error-recovery procedures (including check-point restart), and the collection of traffic and error statistics. The equipment is directly connected to the CPU.

opacity—The characteristic of an object that prevents light from passing through.

op code—1. The operation to be performed. In the example of "3 + 4 = 7," the "+" quantity is the op code or operation to be performed. 2. A command, usually given in machine language. 3. That part of a computer instruction word that designates the function performed by a given instruction. For example, the op codes for arithmetic instructions include ADD (add), SUB (subtract), DIV (divide), and MUL (multiply).

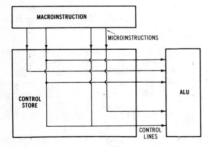

Op code, microcoding.

op code, microcoding—For necessary expansions to the instruction set, many engineers use microcoding as an alternative. Instructions are decoded in a ROM (the control store) and, then, the whole instruction set can be replaced simply by reprogramming the control store. This technique has become standard on minicomputers and mainframes, but because it requires more chip space, different microprocessors use different degrees of microcoding.

Each bit in microcode represents one specific choice (AND/OR, add/subtract, register/memory) and, thus, is called a microinstruction. A com-

plete set of microinstructions is called a macroinstruction, or more simply, an op code.

The expression "macro" is also used in another application. "Macro" capability in an assembler, for instance, means that the user can write the assembly-language "subroutines," (more accurately, functions) that are executed whenever the macroinstruction shows up in the code. The "macro feature" is unrelated to architecture.

open loop—1. Refers to a control system in which there is no self-correcting action for misses of the desired operational condition, as there is in a closed-loop system. 2. A family of automatic control units, one of which may be a computer, linked together manually by operator action.

open-loop control—1. One in which degenerate feedback is not employed. 2. Refers to various control systems designed so that the output variable is directly controlled by the system input, i.e., without feedback.

open routine—Concerns that type routine which can be inserted directly into a larger routine without a linkage or calling sequence.

open running—Refers to, or describes, a teletypewriter connected to an open line or a line without battery. A teletypewriter receiver under such a condition appears to be running, as the type hammer continually strikes the type box but it does not move across the page.

open subroutine — Relates to various subroutines inserted directly into the linear operational sequence; it is not entered by a jump. Such a subroutine must be recopied at each point that it is needed in a routine.

operand—The fundamental quantity on which a mathematical operation is performed. Usually a statement consists of an operator and an operand. The operator may indicate an "add" instruction; the operand thus will indicate what is to be added.

operating code—*See* op code.

operating console, microcomputer—A typical operating console contains all the controls and indicators necessary for the operation of the processor. Typically, it features a switch register (which may be read under program control), LED display indicators, and toggle switches for entering data and operating the processor.

operating system—1. A basic group of programs with operation under control of a data-processing monitor program. 2. An integrated collection of service routines for supervising the sequencing and processing of programs by a computer. Operating systems may perform debugging, input-output, machine accounting, compilation, and storage-assignment tasks.

operating system (software)—A system is composed of both hardware and software in those systems where the modularity and design of the software still is considered an art rather than a science. The hardware must be capable of generating the appropriate stimuli (interrupt) to support concurrent events. The software must be able to logically respond to these events in a reasonable time frame. To effectively coordinate multiple events, some semblance of a controlling piece of software should be present in these systems. This "master" set of software, often called an operating system, allows an application to be subdivided into distinct modules called tasks. With the use of read-only memory chips (ROM or PROM), these operating systems and applications software can reside without any need for "bootable" media such as tape or disk.

operating system (spooling)—If a user program includes several lengthy print requests within a fairly small program segment, there might be a long wait for it to complete its run. Ordinarily, requests would be processed sequentially, but because no one wants to sit waiting, in front of a slow 30-cps printer, a spooling technique has been cleverly devised that lets the operating system do some of the work. Users can structure the DOS to let the disk intercept print requests and store the data for the printer until some later time. Then, print requests can be satisfied at write-to-disk speeds rather than at conventional rates. This approach lets the program, and possibly even several programs, complete execution while the printer grinds away at its normal slow pace.

operating system, supervisory—Refers to an operating system that consists of a supervisory control program, system programs, and system subroutines. A symbolic assembler and macroprocessor, a compiler, and various debugging aids are typically included. A library of general utility programs is also often provided.

operation—1. Generally refers to the action specified by a single computer instruction or a pseudo-instruction. 2. An arithmetical, logical, or transferal unit of a problem, usually executed under the direction of a subroutine. *See also* logical operations, transfer operations, and/or red-tape operations.

operational amplifier—An amplifier that combines functions of amplification and performance of operations. Operational amplifiers are often used as summing amplifiers, analog adders, or sign-reversing amplifiers. Basically, an operational amplifier, or op amp, is a high-gain amplifier capable of amplifying signals from dc to many megahertz. The term "operation" is derived from its most common application, which is to perform a mathematical operation on a signal or set of signals. For example, when the appropriate feedback network is used in conjunction with the op amp, it can change the sign or scale, and differentiate or integrate its input signal. These operations make the applications for operational amplifiers relate to the field of electronic instrumentation and analog signal processing. They represent the greatest use for linear integrated circuits.

operational amplifier, balancing—Refers to the act of adjusting the output level of an operational amplifier to coincide with its input reference level, usually ground or zero voltage.

operational character—Refers to specific characters that, when used as code elements, can initiate, modify, or stop a control operation. Characters may be .used, for example, to control the carriage return, etc.

operation code—*See* op code.

operation cycle—Relates specifically to that portion of a machine cycle during which the actual execution of the instruction takes place. Some operations (i.e., divide, multiply) may need a large number of these operation cycles to complete the operation, and the normal instruction/operation alternation will be held up during this time. *Also called* execution cycle.

operation, dyadic Boolean—A specific Boolean operator that is applied to pairs of operands, in particular, the operators: AND, equivalence, exclusive-OR, inclusion, NAND, NOR, and OR.

operations manual—The manual which contains instructions and specifications for a given application. Typically, it includes components of the operator's manual, the programmer's reference manual, and, sometimes, it also includes a log section.

operator — A symbol which represents an operation to be performed on one or more operands.

operator console—Refers to that particular device or part of the mainframe extension which enables the operator to communicate with the computer, i.e., it is used to enter data or information, to request and display stored data, to actuate various preprogrammed command routines, etc.

operator-indicator lights — The independent operator indicator lights may be used to call the operator's attention to any conditions that the programmer desires. They can be set, cleared, and tested under program control to fulfill the varying requirements of different programs.

operator indicators — 1. Refers to the display lights showing indicator conditions (on the console of the computer). (*See* indicator.) 2. The independent operator-indicator (console) lights that may be used to call the operator's attention to any conditions that the programmer desires. They can be set, cleared, and tested under program control to fulfill the varying requirements of different programs.

operators—Refers to the characters that designate mathematical or logical operations, such as +, −, etc.

operator's console, diagnostic—Refers to a module that allows the operator to verify the proper functioning of the console lights and switches.

op register — A computer register designed to hold the operation code of computer instructions.

optical cable—Optical cable is a generic term that refers to any flexible continuous fiber or group of fibers capable of conducting light from one

end of the filter to the other with relatively low loss. An individual fiber is usually referred to as an optical fiber or optical waveguide, while a group of fibers packaged together to form a cable is called a bundle. A conductor that passes an image without distortion is usually either a coherent-fiber optic or an image conduit. A coherent-fiber optic cable requires that the exact relative location of every fiber must be maintained at both ends of the bundle.

The transmission of information over optical cables offers many advantages, some that are not available with any other technology. These include: immunity to electromagnetic interference, no externally radiated signal, electrical isolation between terminals, broad bandwidth over long distances, and lightweight, flexible, small-diameter cables.

optical character recognition—Abbreviated OCR. Refers to a process of using photosensitive devices to identify graphic characters, often of a special type-font origin.

optical data links — Optical data links, circumvent microwave problems. No FCC licensing is required for some optical links, nor is right-of-way required. Installation is simple, the system is maintenance-free, and information is more secure than it would be if routed over public-access channels. With optical links, any two points within sight of each other can be connected by beams of light—usually from a laser, though other noncoherent light sources are effective up to a couple of miles. Data, voice, printed messages, and video can be transmitted between rooftops or even through facing windows. Video-signal bandwidths are available up to 10 MHz, and data rates range from 4 million bits per second for short-range systems to 9600 bps for long-range laser links.

optical detector — A component that converts light signals from optical fibers to electrical signals which can be further amplified and/or decoded to allow reproduction of the original signal.

optical fiber — The glass, plastic, or plastic-clad silica medium by which light is conducted or transmitted. It can be multimode (capable of propagating more than one mode of a given wavelength) or single mode (one that supports propagation of only one mode of a given wavelength). In general, optical fibers consist of a core of dielectric glass surrounded by a cladding of another material of (generally) a lower refractive index. The material composition, core size, cladding thickness, and so on, are design parameters that influence the attenuation and dispersion characteristics of the system. Silica fibers currently show lower losses, but various forms of glass fibers and plastic-cladded fibers have some advantages during manufacture.

optical fiber bundle—A group of parallel fibers contained within a common jacket. A bundle may contain just a few or several hundred fibers.

optical fiber cladding — The covering material that encases the core of an optical fiber. The cladding material usually has a lower index of refraction than the core material and may be either glass or plastic.

optical numerical aperture—A number that indicates a fiber's ability to accept light. It shows how much light can be off-axis and still be accepted by the fiber.

optical scanner—Refers to a special optical device that scans patterns of incident light and generates analog/digital signals which are functions of the incident light synchronized with the scan—the primary purpose being to generate or "read" digital representations of printed or written data.

optical scanner, bar-code—An optical scanning unit that can read documents encoded in a special bar code, at a hundred character-per-second or higher speeds, is often an element in a data station. The scanner opens up various systems concepts for such tasks as billing, couponing, retail-item control, and other forms of returnable media. The scanner can read either lithographed or computer-printed bar codes. As it scans, it transfers the encoded data to a buffer for direct transmission or to a microcomputer system printer for pretransmission editing (some systems).

optical switch — An optical-semiconductor chip, that can manipulate light beams the way electronic devices manipulate electrons, has been developed by Bell Labs for use as an optical switch. Consisting of a crystalline layer of gallium-arsenide sandwiched between two crystalline layers of gallium-aluminum-arsenide, the experimental device can be switched on in less than 1 nanosecond with as little as 25 pJ of light energy. Turn-off time, which is limited by carrier lifetimes, is currently 40 nanoseconds. However, subnanosecond turn-off times can be achieved by modifying the material.

optical waveguide coupler — One way to combine optical signals without incurring the losses of optical-to-digital conversions is to use optical-waveguide directional-coupler switches. Such a device has been developed from electro-optic lithium niobate ($LiNbO_3$) and fabricated with planar processes similar to those used for electronic ICs. This directional-coupler optical switch is formed by two closely spaced parallel waveguides that have electrodes sitting on top. A voltage applied to the electrodes changes the waveguide's relative phase velocity by means of the electro-optic effect, which in turn controls the amount of light transferred between waveguides on the chip. Switches made this way not only have crosstalk isolation better than 1000 but also can be switched at subnanosecond speeds by only 3 volts.

opto-isolator—A device that modulates data on light beams to electrically isolate systems.

OR—A logic operator having the property that if P and Q are logic quantities, then the quantity "P OR Q" assumes values as defined by the following table:

P	Q	P OR Q
0	0	0
0	1	1
1	0	1
1	1	1

The OR operator is represented in both electrical and FORTRAN terminology by a "+," i.e., P + Q.

OR circuit — An electrical gate or mechanical device which implements the logical OR operator. An output signal occurs whenever there are one or more inputs on a multichannel input. An OR gate performs the function of the logical "inclusive-OR operation."

orderly closedown—Refers to the stopping of a system in such a way that ensures an orderly restart and no destruction of messages. When a system is forced to stop, an orderly closedown provides that all records are updated that should be updated and that no records are erroneously updated again when the restart is made. Furthermore, all incoming and outgoing transmissions are completed, with a message sent to the terminals which notifies the operators of the closedown.

ordinary symbol—Refers to assembler programming. A symbol that represents an assembly-time value when used in the name or an operand field of an instruction when used in the assembler language. Ordinary symbols are also used to represent operation codes for assembler-language instructions.

OR gate.

OR gate—1. An electric circuit that implements the OR operator. 2. That specific gate which implements the OR operator. 3. A circuit element whose output is logical if any of the inputs are logical. The truth table for a 2-input OR gate is shown below.

Inputs		Output
A	B	Q
0	0	0
1	0	1
0	1	1
1	1	1

origin—Refers to basic coding, the absolute memory address of the first location of a program or program segment.

OR operator—A logical operator that has the property that P or Q is true, if P or Q, or both, are true.

oscillator—A source of alternating current of any frequency, which is sustained in a circuit by a vacuum tube or transistor, using the positive feedback principle. There are two types: (1) stable-type, in which the frequency is determined by a line or a tuned LC circuit, with the waveform being substantially sinusoidal, and (2) relaxation-type, in which the frequency is determined by resistors and capacitors, with the waveform having a considerable content of harmonics. Also applies to mechanical systems, with velocities being equivalent to currents.

oscillator, Armstrong—Refers to a specific oscillator in which feedback is achieved through coupled plate and grid circuit coils.

oscillator, Colpitts—Relates to a specific oscillator in which two resonant-circuit capacitors are used, with a tap between the two capacitors.

oscillator crystal—A piezoelectric crystal used in an oscillator to control the frequency of oscillation.

oscillator, Hartley—Refers to a specific oscillator circuit in which the coil of the resonant circuit is tapped.

output enable—The signal that controls the output. The fundamental purpose of the output enable signal is to provide a completely separate means of controlling the output buffer of the memory device, thereby eliminating bus contention.

output formatter — Refers to special programs used to produce disk or tape versions of assembled microprocessor programs in formats that are compatible with any of the following microprogram storage media: (1) mask programmable ROMs, (2) laser encodable ROMs, (3) PROMs, (4) assemblers, (5) ROM programmers, and (6) ROM emulators.

output mode — During this mode of transmission, data is transferred out of the central computer.

output module—Refers to the part of a machine which translates the electrical impulses representing data that is processed by the machine into permanent results, such as printed forms, punched cards, or magnetic writing on tape.

output module valve—Refers to some systems which have a device designed to translate the output data of computers into analog signals which are suitable to position and control valves of other devices.

output record—1. Refers to a specific record written to an output device. 2. The current record stored in the output area prior to being output.

output register—The basic register that holds data until it can be output to an external device.

output stream — Refers to diagnostic

messages and other output data issued by an operating system or a
processing program on output devices especially activated for this purpose by the operator.

output table—1. Refers to a peripheral
output device that plots the curves of
variables as functions of other variables. 2. A hard-copy output device
that presents the results of a plotter
system, which is designed to develop
curves, graphs, charts, and other
graphic output.

outside loop—Generally, outside loops
are considered as nested loops when
loops within them are entirely contained. The outside loop executes the
control parameters that are being held
constant while the current loop is
being carried through its possible
values.

overflow—1. An overflow condition results, in many cases, when an arithmetic operation generates a quantity
beyond the capacity of the register.
This is also referred to as an arithmetical overflow. An overflow status
bit in the condition-code register can
be checked to determine if the previous operation caused an overflow. 2.
The digit arising from this condition, if
a mechanical or programmed indicator, is ·included, otherwise the digit
may be lost. 3. Overcapacity.

overflow, arithmetic—1. In an arithmetic operation, the generation of a
quantity beyond the capacity of the
register or location which is to receive
the result; overcapacity. The information contained in an item of information which is in excess of a given
amount. 2. The portion of data that
exceeds the capacity of the allocated
unit of storage. 3. Overflow develops
when attempts are made to write
longer fields into a field location of a
specific length; a 12-digit product will
overflow a 10-digit accumulator.

overflow check indicator—Refers to a
device which is turned on by incorrect, or unplanned for, operations in
the execution of an arithmetic instruction, particularly when an arithmetic
operation produces a number too
large for the system to handle.

overflow indicator—Relates to a bistable trigger which changes states
when overflow occurs in the register
with which it is associated. It may be
interrogated and/or restored to the
original state.

overflow operation—Relates to that part
of the result of an operation which
exceeds the capacity of the intended
unit of storage, and actions which relate to cause the generation of overflow.

overflow position—Relates to an extra
position in the register in which the
overflow digit is developed.

overhead (operating system)—Pertains
to the distribution of operating time
for the checking, monitoring, scheduling, etc., portions of the executive
system over all jobs or tasks related
to the total cost of the complete system. It is usually developed by percentages and ratios.

overlapping data channel—Refers to a
data channel that allows asynchronous operation of its input/output devices and programs processing by
the central processing unit.

overlay — 1. A popular technique for
bringing routines into high-speed
memory from some other form of storage during processing, so that several
routines will occupy the same storage
locations at different times. It is used
when the total memory requirements
for instructions exceed the available
high-speed memory. *See also* segment. 2. Several sets of information
which time-share a block of storage
to conserve space. New information
that is required is laid over information that is no longer needed. Generally, the sets of information are not related, except that they are needed in
the same program at different times.
The same data for successive cases
is not an overlay. The overlay concept thus permits the breaking of a
large program into segments which
can be used as required to implement
problem solution.

overlay, executive—The "Call Overlay"
command can cause an executive to
input a task or subroutine from the
disk into the area of memory specified by the calling task, and on the
caller's priority level. When the overlay task or subroutine has completed
its execution, control is passed back
to the caller (if it has not been completely overlaid), to another overlay,
or to the normal exit path from the
task level. This feature allows large
programs or groups of programs,

which work together to perform one function, to run in smaller segments of main memory than would normally be possible.

overlay (load) module — Concerns a load module that has been divided into overlay segments, and has been provided by a linkage editor with information that enables the overlay supervisor to implement the desired loading of segments when requested.

overlay manager—Some systems provide for a run-time management of disk overlays, automatically loading program sections from disk as needed.

overlay path—Refers to the segments in an overlay tree between a particular segment and the root segment, inclusive.

overlay program—Concerns a program in which certain control sections can use the same storage locations at different times during execution.

overlay region—Relates to a continuous area of main storage in which segments can be loaded independently of paths in other regions. Only one path within a region can be in main storage at any one time.

overlay segments—Refers to overlaying (replacing) one program segment with another.

overlays, memory—In many types of systems, the monitor remains resident in lower memory at all times. Object programs are loaded into memory, starting at the end of the monitor. The program loader resides in upper memory. Object programs cannot be loaded into the loader area. This area can be overlayed by common storage. Part of the loader can also be overlayed by library subroutines. In addition, programmers can specify that sections of their own program may overlay each other when needed.

overlay tree — Refers to a specific graphic representation showing the relationships of segments of an overlay program and how the segments are arranged to use the same main storage area at different times.

overlay vs. virtual memory—The use of overlay allows a programmer to instruct the CPU to move data from a peripheral device to an area of memory presently containing part of a program. That part of the memory that is being overlaid (replaced) is stored in a peripheral. This differs from virtual memory in that overlays are specified and controlled by the user, while in virtual memory systems, the machine pretends to have a larger memory in a fashion not seen by the programmer.

overload — An analog computer overload relates to a condition existing within or at the output of a computing element that causes a substantial computing error because of the saturation of one or more of the parts of the computing element.

overload module testing—Relates to the destructive read-off or use caused by overloading or underloading the computer components. This causes failure of substandard units. The test is designed to minimize nonscheduled down time.

overrun — Overrun can usually occur when data are transferred to or from a nonbuffered control unit operating with a synchronous medium, and the total activity initiated by the program exceeds the capability of the channel.

overshoot—1. Extent to which a servo system carries the controlled variables past its final equilibrium position. 2. For a step change in signal amplitude, undershoot and overshoot are the maximum transient signal excursions outside the range from initial to final mean amplitude levels.

overwrite—Refers to the activity of placing information in a location and destroying the information previously contained there.

oxide-isoplanar technology — Oxide-isolated isoplanar technology has been applied to an injection-logic configuration. One example is a 4096-bit I^2L random-access memory. The part has a nominal access time of 100 nanoseconds, making it more than twice as fast as older NMOS 4-kilobit dynamic RAMs.

oxygen (O) — Odorless gaseous element, at. no. 8, at. wt. 15.9994, m.p. −218.8°C, b.p. −182.970°C. It is chemically very active and forms one-fifth of the atmosphere.

P

P—The symbol for power, primary winding, permeance, or the plate of an electron tube.

pack—In computer programming, pack refers to the act of combining several fields of information into one machine word.

package—A housing for a semiconductor in which the die is mounted. The contacts of the semiconductor are wired to the leads of the package so that the device can be used by mounting the package in a circuit.

package, ceramic—Refers to an industry standard high-performance high-reliability package made of three layers of Al_2O_3 ceramic and nickel-plated refactory metal. In some types, the die cavity is sealed with a glazed ceramic lid, using a controlled devitrified low-temperature glass sealant. Package leads are of Kovar, nickel-plated and solder-dipped for socket insertion or soldering.

package, cer-DIP—Cer-DIP dual-in-line packages generally have the same high performance characteristics as the standard three-layer ceramic package, yet approach plastic in cost. It is a military-approved type package, with excellent reliability characteristics. The Cer-DIP concept has been around for a number of years and some manufacturers lead the technology with this package, having eliminated the device instability and corrosion problems of earlier Cer-DIP processes. One brand package consists of a 96% Alumina (Al_2O_3) base and the same material lid, hermetically fused onto the base with Corning 7583 solder glass (at approximately 475 °C). Inert gases are sealed inside the die cavity. Generally available in: 16-, 18-, 22-, 24-, and 28-pin configurations.

packaged software — Also called "canned," it usually consists of generalized programs that are prewritten and debugged, and are designed to perform one or more general business functions, such as accounts receivable, accounts payable, general ledger, payroll, or inventory control. The advantages of software packages are their lower cost and their prewritten, debugged, and operational status. The disadvantage is that as a generalized approach to a general problem they may not directly meet a user's specific needs.

package, plastic — A typical plastic dual-in-line package (DIP) is the equivalent of the widely accepted industry standard, refined by manufacturers for MOS/LSI applications. Many packages consist of a silicon body that is transfer-molded directly onto the assembled lead frame and die. The lead frame is often Kovar or Alloy 42, with the external pins tin plated. Internally, some use 50 micro-inch gold spot on each die attach pad and on bonding fingertips. Gold bonding wire is attached with thermocompression gold ball bonding technique. Materials of the lead frame, the package body, and the die attach are all closely matched in thermal expansion coefficients, to provide optimum response to various thermal conditions. During manufacture, every step of the process is rigorously monitored to assure maximum quality of the plastic package. Generally, they are available in 14-, 16-, 18-, 22-, 24-, and 40-pin configurations.

pack, disk—Refers to various removable direct-access storage devices containing magnetic disks on which data are stored. Disk packs are mounted on a disk storage drive.

package, TO — Refers to an industry standard metal-can package for small lead-count dies. The package generally consists of a Kovar body, a pure nickel lid, and Kovar leads, brazed in with a glass seal. The lid is sealed onto the body by cold welding, which assures hermeticity of the package.

packaging—1. The physical process of locating, connecting, and protecting devices, components, etc. 2. The type of packages and the methods in which it is possible to mount the finished semiconductor chip (depending on factors such as heat dissipation, size, etc.). Packages can be plastic, ceramic, Cer-DIP, or other types.

packaging density — 1. The number of devices or equivalent devices in a unit volume of a working system. 2. In a computer system, the number of units of information per dimensional unit.

packaging, microprocessors — In general, package sizes with a small number of pins are easier to physically install into a system, while microprocessors in packages with a large number of pins are easier for interfacing. Thus, package size is important to many system designers during product design.

packed format—A binary-coded decimal format in which two decimal digits are represented within a single byte of storage. This is accomplished by eliminating the zone bits.

packet, electronic mail—In an electronic mail system, individual information "packets" are formed by the work terminal. In addition to the message, each packet contains procedural information in a form determined by protocol: address, routing, security, and error-recovery information, etc. Once a message packet is assembled, the sending terminal gives it to an "intelligent" communications network that automatically routes the message and delivers it to the addressee.

packet format—Refers to a group of bits, including data and control elements, that is switched and transmitted as a composite whole. The data and control elements and, possibly, error-control information are arranged in a specified format.

packets (charge-coupled device) — A device in which operation depends on the movement of discrete packets of charge along or beneath the semiconductor surface. The charge packets are stored in potential wells and are transferred serially with little charge loss by translating the potential wells. A charge-coupled device operates like a shift register.

packet switching—Packet switching, in which data are separated into bursts, or packets, of fixed length, so they can share a channel with other such bursts, is a new form of digital communications service that is economically attractive, particularly in transaction applications. The segmentation and reassembly of messages and the separate routing of packets are completely invisible to the host computers and terminals. Even under complicated routing conditions, the entire process of sending a complete error-free 8-packet message from source to destination takes only a fraction of a second.

A packet-switched network employs dynamic allocation that moves messages from sender to receiver by way of intermediate nodes. Each node on a packet net needs software to identify which messages to keep and which to move on. This is in addition to the node software required for packetizing and assembling message strings at each node. The advantage of the packet-switched allocation method is that if a line fails, the user still receives the message through a new path automatically determined by the network. In packet switching systems, the failure of a single link does not interrupt any transmission because all nodes are connected by at least two paths and packets are automatically routed around any link that might be defective. In some systems, the line scheme is fixed. That makes it economical for high-volume users. Packet switching is suited to intermittent computing where no primary traffic route exists. The dedicated-line approach allows a carrier more reliability through a more static environment.

In most public data networks based on packet switching, the price is distance-insensitive, with the user being charged for actual utilization, rather than for a facility, as in a leased or dial-up network. Packet switching, instead of structuring charges on the duration of the transmission or on the geographic distance between source and destination, enables charges to be based upon the quantity of data sent. As a result, users may process data with little concern for the geographic locations of computers and terminals.

packet transmission—Refers to the use of short standardized packets. A packet-switching network is able to store and forward messages very rapidly, typically, within a fraction of a second. This is made possible by the use of very high-speed switching computers in which messages (packets) are stored in fast-access core memory exclusively, rather than on the slow-access storage devices (electromechanical disk drives) employed in conventional message-switching systems. Flow-control techniques are designed to ensure that main storage does not become overloaded, while still maintaining line loadings as close to maximum as possible. Thus, packets are stored only momentarily at each node and pass very rapidly from node to node through the network. Any delay is but a fraction of a second. Packets are almost continuously checked for errors during transmission and are retransmitted, if necessary, until they have been correctly received. In addition, all messages are acknowledged from destination to source to ensure against their loss. The error-checking code used is so powerful that, typically, undetected and uncorrected errors occur only once in about a trillion (10^{12}) bits transmitted.

pack field strength—Refers to limit of magnetizing forces associated with a field.

packing density — 1. In a digital computer, packing density refers to the number of units of desired information contained within a storage or recording medium. 2. The number of units of useful information contained within a given linear dimension, usually expressed in units **per inch**, i.e., **the** number of binary digital magnetic pulses or the number of characters stored on a tape or disk, per linear inch, on a single track, by a single head.

packing factor — 1. The number of pulses or bits of information that can be written on a given length of magnetic surface. 2. Refers to the number of units (words, bits, characters, etc.) that can fit in something of a defined size (per inch, per record, etc.).

pack (to) — Refers to the process of compressing data in a storage medium by taking advantage of known characteristics of the data, in such a way that the original data can be recovered.

pad—1. Small preset adjustable capacitor used to regulate the exact frequency of oscillation of an oscillator, or a tuned circuit in an amplifier or filter; padder, trimmer. 2. Fixed atten-

uator inserted in a waveguide to obviate reflections. 3. Device which introduces transmission loss into a circuit. It may be inserted to introduce loss or to match impedances. 4. Relatively large metalized areas on the surface of a device or chip to which leads may be bonded or test probes applied. Also called bonding pads, lands.

pad character—Refers to character inserted to fill a blank time slot in synchronous transmission, or inserted to fulfill a character-count requirement in transmissions of fixed block lengths.

padding—Refers to a procedure used to fill out a block of information with dummy records, words, or characters.

page—1. Typically, a page is a set of 4096 consecutive bytes. Applied to main storage, a set of 4096 consecutive bytes, the first byte of which is located at a storage address that is a multiple of 4096 (an address whose 12 low-order bits are 0). 2. A subdivision of a program that can be moved into main memory by an operating system or by hardware whenever the instructions of that subdivision need to be performed. A program will be divided into pages in order to minimize the total amount of main memory storage allocated to the program at any one time. The pages will normally be stored on a fast direct-access store.

page addressing—Refers to a specific procedure of memory addressing utilized with some specific microcomputers. The addressing capability is limited to less than the total memory capability available. But, using page addressing, memory is divided into segments (pages), each of which can be addressed by the available addressing capability.

page protection—The memory protection and control of dynamic mapping is an asset even in systems with smaller memories. The programmer has control of read and/or write protection for each of the 1024 pages in memory. For example, because the system and the user have independent memory maps, the programmer may specify a page of memory be unprotected for the operating system, but write protected for the user. The result is a page of memory that can be altered by the operating system, but only read by the user.

pages, multiple-base—In multiuser systems, each user can have a complete base page while the system also maintains a base page. This large space for base-page links or for direct addressing for both user and system allows users to write large programs without linking or common area limitations (in some systems).

paging — Refers to a procedure for transmitting pages of information between main storage and auxiliary storage, especially when done for the purpose of assisting the allocation of a limited amount of main storage among a number of concurrently executing programs.

paging algorithms, virtual memory — Refers to a task to bring into main memory the appropriate pages before attempts are made to use the information in them. If a page is not transferred from auxiliary storage until it is actually needed, then paging is said to be done by demand. Look-ahead schemes have been implemented on other systems with some success. However, demand paging appears to be as good as the best look-ahead policies. As much or more time could be spent in looking ahead as in waiting for a page to be brought in when using demand paging. For this reason, and its ease of implementation, demand paging is often chosen over any look-ahead scheme.

pair, binary—An electronic circuit having two stable states, two input lines, and two corresponding output lines that are such that a signal exists on either one of the output lines, if and only if, the last pulse received by the flip-flop is on the corresponding input line. A flip-flop or binary pair can store one binary digit (bit) of information, i.e., it is a bistable device.

paired cable — Refers to cables that have individually insulated conductors and which are twisted together two at a time for easy selection and use.

PAL—1. Abbreviation for Programmable Array Logic. Refers to a family of devices designed to replace standard TTL logic. A single PAL unit can replace from four to ten SSI/MSI packages and PAL devices are fully field-programmable to provide the utmost in design flexibility and efficiency. The basic logic implementation of a PAL is the familiar AND-OR array, where the AND array is programmable and the OR array is fixed. The standard AND-OR logic and the flexible I/O programming of a PAL device provides a wide-ranging design and production efficiency. Thus, many logic modifications can be made more quickly and easily with a PAL device than with discrete random logic. PALs are manufactured using TTL Schottky bipolar techniques, the same as those used to make fusible-link PROMs, and they are packaged in 20-pin DIP packages. An npn emitter-follower array forms the programmable AND array. Pnp inputs provide high-impedance inputs to the array; outputs are standard TTL drivers. Like PROMs, the PAL unit has an array of fusible links. Unlike the PROM, a PAL is a programmable AND array driving a fixed OR array. In contrast, a PROM is a fixed AND array driving a programmable OR array. Typical PAL propagation delay time is 25 nanoseconds. 2. Abbreviation for Phase Alternation Line system, one of three color-television systems proposed for an European color standard. The systems are similar in that they separate the luminance and chrominance information and transmit the chrominance information in the form of two color difference signals. The systems are different in the processing of the chrominance information. In the PAL system, the phase of the subcarrier is changed from line to line requiring the transmission of both a line-switching signal and a color burst signal.

panel, control—A device or component of some data processing machines, which permits the expression of instructions, in a semi-fixed computer program, by the insertion of pins, plugs, or wires into sockets or hubs in the device, in a pattern to represent instructions and, thus, making electrical interconnections that may be sensed by the data-processing machine. Synonymous with plugboard and related to pinboard.

panel, graphic—Refers to various master control panels which, pictorially and usually colorfully, trace the relationship of control equipment and the process operation. They permit an operator at a glance, to check on the operation of a far-flung control system by noting dials, valves, scales, and lights.

panel, maintenance control—Refers to a specific panel of indicator lights and switches on which are displayed a particular sequence of routines, and from which repair men can determine changes to execute.

panel, operator control—Generally, the various operator control panels contain all the switches and indicators needed for the operation of the central processor. Bit-by-bit register display and manual entry into the registers are provided by convenient indicator push buttons. The control panel is used primarily for initial setup prior to a program run or for debugging purposes, rather than to exercise control over a running operation.

paper tape—Refers to strips of paper capable of storing or recording information. Storage may be in the form of punched holes, partially punched holes, carbonization or chemical change of impregnated material, or by imprinting. Some paper tapes, such as punched-paper tapes, are capable of being read by the input device of a computer or a transmitting device, by sensing the pattern of holes which represent the coded information.

paper-tape automatic development system—Typically, this is a stand-alone system for the paper-tape-oriented small memory user. It consists of the most commonly used loaders and utilities supplied on a single paper tape with a small executive program that causes the utilities to be loaded at the highest possible memory address (regardless of memory size) in order to leave maximum room for the user's program. Such a system includes programs such as Debug, Binary Load, Binary Dump, Binary Verify, and Object Loader.

paper-tape reader — A device that senses the holes in a perforated tape and translates them into electrical signals.

parabolic interpolation — Refers to a procedure used, usually connected with numerical control of a machine tool, to control the center line of a cutter path. Also, smoothly blended surfaces can be constructed from parabolic segments (spans), each defined by three programmed points (also of which each span shares with its neighbor). Spans may vary in length and still blend.

parallel — 1. In microcomputers, the simultaneous transmission of, storage of, or logical operation on a character or other subdivision of a word, using separate facilities for the various parts. 2. The simultaneous transmission or processing of the individual parts of a whole, such as the bits of a character or the characters of a word. When characters are dealt with simultaneously (not one after another), the transmission is serial by character, parallel by bit.

parallel addition—Refers to a technique developed so that all the corresponding pairs of digits, or the two numbers, being added are processed simultaneously during one cycle of execution with one or more cycles being used to propagate and adjust for any carries which may have been generated.

parallel by character — Refers to the handling of all the characters of a machine word simultaneously in separate lines, channels, or storage cells.

parallel input/output card — A typical full parallel input/output card has the necessary handshake flags for conventional parallel interface and contains all the required addressing circuitry to allow each card to be addressed anywhere from location to location. In some systems, both input and output data have their own 8-bit latch for buffering, including necessary logic to allow an adjacent channel to be a control channel. Thus, adjacent channels can be used to set up flags and, also, clear flags and interrupts.

parallel operation—1. Relates to processing all of the digits of a word or byte simultaneously by transmitting each digit on a separate channel or bus line, as contrasted with consecutive or serial operation. 2. The performance of several actions, usually of a similar nature, simultaneously, through provision of individual similar or identical devices for each such action; particularly the flow or processing of information. Parallel operation is performed to save time over serial operation. Parallel operation usually requires more equipment.

parallel partitioning—*See* pipeline partitioning.

parallel-plate package — Refers to a technique for packaging circuits, i.e., the construction of wiring and other connecting techniques to increase high packing density and to provide for easier automatic production, assembly, and maintenance.

parallel priority, multibus — This technique uses a priority encoder-decoder arrangement. The arrangement is fairly simple. A separate bus request line from each arbiter feeds into the encoder, which generates a binary address for the highest priority line. The address is then decoded to select a predesignated highest priority requesting arbiter via its bus priority in line. When the system bus becomes idle, the selected arbiter allows its master to access the bus. While this technique requires external logic, the logic is simple to implement and can be used effectively where many arbiters are present on the system bus.

parallel processing—1. In a microcomputer, the processing of more than one program at a time through the use of more than one active processor. 2. Processing more than one program at a time on a **parallel basis**, where more than one processor is active at one time (distinguished from multiprocessing where only one processor is active on one program at a time).

parallel processing, loosely coupled— There are two very similar approaches to building a loosely coupled parallel-processing system. They have similar software ramifications but differ in potential speed. One configuration uses one very high-speed bus (or two, for redundancy) to interconnect a number of central processors. Each CPU has its own memory and a copy of the operating system. Peripheral devices are usually attached separately to each processor, but they may be multiported to allow for both shared-data access and an alternative path in the event a CPU fails.

parallel processing types — There are four general kinds of parallel processing: single instruction, single data stream (SISD); multiple instruction, single data stream (MISD); single instruction, multiple data stream (SIMD); and multiple instruction, multiple data stream (MIMD). Most single computers in use today are SISD-type machines. This type of processor serially executes instructions that operate on a single stream of input data. Yet, within a single central processor, there are various functions that can be completed in parallel to enhance system performance. Such a scheme is called pipelining.

parallel run test—Refers to the running of the old system and the new system side-by-side while using the same data as input. Doing this ensures that both systems agree, that the user can run the new system, and that it operates with success in the real world.

parallel-search memory — A memory where the storage locations are identified by their contents rather than their addresses. This enables faster interrogation to retrieve a particular data element. Synonymous with associative storage.

parallel storage—1. Computer storage where all bits, words, or characters are equally available. 2. Refers to storage in which all bits, characters, or (especially) words are essentially equally available in space, without time being one of the coordinates. Parallel storage contrasts with serial storage. When words are in parallel, the storage is said to be parallel by words. When characters within words (or binary digits within words or characters) are dealt with simultaneously, not one after the other, the storage is parallel by characters, or parallel by bit, respectively.

parallel transfer—Refers to a procedure of data transfer in which the characters of an element of information are transferred simultaneously over a set of paths.

parallel transmission—In a microcomputer, the system of information transmission in which the characters of a word are transmitted (usually simultaneously) over separate lines, as contrasted with serial transmission.

paramagnetic material — Material having a permeability slightly greater than that of a vacuum; broadly considered nonmagnetic.

parameter — 1. Variable which, for a particular purpose, combines with other variables in microcomputers. 2.

An arbitrary constant, which has a particular value under specified circumstances (in physics). 3. A variable that can take the place of one or more other variables (in mathematics). 4. In a subroutine, a quantity that may be given different values when the subroutine is used in different main routines or in different parts of one main routine, but which usually remains unchanged throughout. any one such use; in general, a quantity used to specify input/output devices, to designate subroutines to be included, or used otherwise to describe the desired routine to be generated.

parameter, macro — Refers to specific symbolic or literal elements in the operand part of a macro statement, which will be substituted into specific instructions in the incomplete routine to develop a complete open subroutine.

parameter testing—Tests of individual sections or subroutines of a program to assure that specified inputs produce the desired outputs.

parameter word—A word in a subroutine which contains one or more parameters that specify the action of the subroutine, or words which contain the address of such parameters.

parametric subroutine — A subroutine which involves parameters, such as a decimal-point-coded subroutine. The computer itself is expected to adjust or generate the subroutine according to the parametric values chosen.

parametron—Refers to a unique device composed of two stable states of oscillation; the one is twice the frequency of the other and, thus, has a capability of storing one binary digit.

parity bit—1. A redundant bit added to a group of bits so that an inaccurate retrieval of that group of bits is detected. 2. A binary digit appended to an array of bits to make the sum of all the bits always odd or always even.

parity check—1. A computer-checking method in which the total number of binary 1s (or 0s) is always even or always odd. 2. A summation check in which the binary digits, in a character or word, are added, and the sum checked against a single previously computed parity digit; i.e., a check tests whether the number of 1s in a word is odd or even.

parity check, even — Concerns a technique of detecting when bits are dropped by adding one bit to all odd numbers of bit patterns used to signify a character; thus, all characters would be represented by an even number of bits. A failure to have such representation would be called a parity error.

parity flag — A specific indicator that signals whether or not the number of digits in the logic one condition is an odd or even value. The indicator is often used for error checking purposes during I/O operations.

parity interrupt—Refers to an interrupt that occurs because of a parity check (parity error).

partial RAMs—A partial RAM is an "almost good" part in which some bits are inoperative. The development of the semiconductor industry has been marked by a decrease in yields as densities increased. The 64K-bit dynamic MOS RAM is no exception to this failing. On some of these chips as much as one-half or more of the bit locations are unusable because of less than ideal yields. Nevertheless, such RAMs are viewed by many semiconductor manufacturers and by some users as perfectly good parts, only smaller in size. Thus, one can conceivably buy two 64K-bit dynamic MOS RAM chips in order to get 64K bits of effective memory storage.

partitioning — Subdividing one large block into smaller subunits that can be handled more conveniently, e.g., partitioning a matrix.

parts programming system, automatic —Abbreviated APPS. APPS is a computer system that automatically generates parts programs for numerically controlled machine tools. It consists of a computer, a digitizer, a video terminal, a tape-punch interface, and associated software. APPS is applicable to XY, single-pass operations—such as flame and laser cutting, welding, and the milling of gaskets or template-type parts. The system is particularly useful for freeform part shapes, but it works well with both straight lines and arcs. Much less time is required to prepare programs, and a specialized skill is not required.

To use the APPS system, the operator traces a 2-dimensional path with the digitizer stylus, using a foot switch to control the segmenting of the trace.

The stylus path is stored in the computer and a summary of the statistics of the trace is presented on the system's terminal. If the trace characteristics are satisfactory, the computer analyzes the coordinate data and, within the resolution of the digitizer, determines a set of straight line and arc commands that will smoothly approximate the desired path.

party-line—Party-line is used in its telephone sense to indicate a large number of devices connected to a single line originating in the CPU.

party-line driver—A line driver used to fan out to multiple receivers via a transmission line. Also called bus driver.

Pascal—A language designed to enable teaching of programming as a systematic discipline and to do systems programming. Pascal is a block-structured programming language in the style of ALGOL. Programs consist of two parts: a heading names the program and specifies the variables it will use, and the body of the program, called a block, follows. A block is further subdivided into six sections. The first four sections declare the labels, constants, data types, and variables. The fifth names and precedes an actual procedure or function. The last section, called the statement section, contains the executable code for the named function or procedure.

Labels identify statements so they can be referenced. Constants equate numbers with names for use throughout a program, like pi = 3.14. Data types are numerous; furthermore, structured types can be defined to include arrays, records, sets, and files. Each named variable must be followed by its type. Procedures can be put within procedures, and the statements for each must be preceded with the keyword "begin" and terminated with the word "end." Operators are defined for multiply, divide, add, subtract, logical, and relational, and numerous control statements are allowed.

Pascal compiler/interpreter—The most common translation method for the Pascal language is one that compiles code for a processor called the P-machine, which the actual processor simulates. (The exception is the Western Digital Pascal MICROENGINE, which is a microprogrammed P-ma-

chine.) This combination is usually called a compiler-interpreter, because simulating a P-machine is the same as interpreting P-code. (There are several Pascal compilers that will produce machine code directly.) This method of compiling an intermediate code, which is then interpreted, is sometimes used for COBOL and ALGOL, also.

Pascal computer systems — Some microprocessor hardware is designed exclusively for direct high-level language execution, and the processor is incorporated into a single-board computer system. This type of system will directly execute the Pascal intermediate code (called P-code) that is generated by a Pascal compiler. Since the P-code output from the Pascal compiler represents an ideal architecture for a computer executing Pascal programs and since these systems directly execute P-code (no interpreter), these programs will execute up to five or more times faster than will equivalent systems.

Pascal P-code — Some manufacturers have designed a microcomputer around a language instead of the other way around. The language is Pascal. One way to compile this high-level programming language is to do it in two steps. First, Pascal source code is compiled into its intermediate code, P-code. Then, the P-code is executed interpretively on the host machine. This interpreter is actually an idealized stack machine and can be implemented in software. That is, with the proper routines, a processor can be turned into a pseudo-machine whose native language is the P-code.

passivation—The formation of an insulating layer directly over the semiconductor surface to protect the surface from contaminants, moisture, or particles. Usually an oxide of the semiconductor is used; however, deposition of other materials is also used. Typically, a coating of an electrically inert material, such as glass or silicon dioxide, is used to protect semiconductors or resistors from environmental contamination. Unpassivated nickel-chromium resistors, for example, will open in the presence of water and a large applied dc potential.

passive element—1. A fundamental element of an electric circuit that is not the source of energy, such as a resistor, inductor, or capacitor. 2. Elements incapable of power gain, such as resistors, inductors, capacitors, transformers, or diodes.

pass, sorting—The processing of each file record once, for the purpose of reducing the number of strings of sequenced records and increasing the number of sequenced records per string.

password—1. Refers to a word or string of characters that is recognizable by automatic means and that permits a user access to protected storage, files, and input or output devices. 2. The unique set of digits or characters assigned to a user as part of his identification number in communicating with the computer.

patch—1. A section of coding inserted into a routine (usually by explicitly transferring control from the routine to the patch and back again) to correct a mistake or alter the routine. 2. A special routine linked to the program by unconditional transfers of control; used for checking or correcting programs. 3. To correct or change the coding at a particular location by inserting transfer instructions at that location, and by adding the new instructions and the replaced instructions elsewhere.

patchboard—A removable board containing hundreds of terminals into which patch cords (short wires) are connected (these determine the different programs for the machine). To change the program, the wiring pattern on the patchboard or the patchboard, itself, must be changed.

patch cord—A handy flexible connector/conductor with receptacles or connectors at each end that is used to interconnect sockets of plugboards.

patch panel—An arrangement for terminating channels and terminal circuits in which plug-ended cords are inserted into jacks corresponding to the channels or terminals to be interconnected. *See also* control panel.

patchplug—A specialized plug of metal or plastic which functions as a patch cord. The patchplug is cordless in contrast to a standard plug which has a wire for jumping or connecting two terminals. A patchplug usually has an insulating handle.

pattern generator, computer-controlled—A major advance in mask making took place in the early 1970s with the introduction of computer-controlled pattern generation equipment. This pattern generator produced a 10x emulsion reticle from a magnetic tape input. This equipment generated more complex reticles with a high degree of accuracy, and it eliminated the problems previously encountered during the artwork cutting operation and the use of the first reduction camera.

pattern recognition—1. The identification, by automatic means, of shapes, forms, or configurations. 2. The recognition of shapes or other patterns by a machine system. The patterns may be either a physical shape or a speech pattern.

PC, pc—Abbreviation for programmable controller, printed circuit, and program counter.

pc board, dual-side mounting—This technique involves attaching chip-type components (resistors, capacitors, transistors) to the bottom, or solder side, of a pc board with an epoxy adhesive. Axial-leaded components are then inserted through the top side in the normal fashion. Therefore, both sides of the pc board can be used, shrinking circuit area. Besides its most obvious advantage of allowing greater circuit density, this technique offers advantages in reduced labor cost, improved high-frequency performance, and increased reliability.

pc board fabricating processes—There are two important methods for fabricating pc boards, the additive method and the subtractive method. The subtractive method calls for the printing of a chemically resistive ink or paint in a kind of stenciling operation on an insulating board with previously applied copper foil. Acid is used to selectively etch away unwanted metal to leave the desired pattern on the board. The additive method, increasing in popularity among pc board makers, also typically employs a printing process, but the pattern covers only those areas where metal is not desired. Thus, selective plating can be performed on the unclad insulating board which has been treated to accept the plating metal, usually electrolysis copper.

pc board technology—Pc board technology follows many of the photolithographic procedures used to make hybrid circuits, passive resistor networks, and even integrated circuitry. The track-like metallic wiring paths are laid down on thin insulating boards, typically epoxy-impregnated fiberglass. A number of different methods employing a variety of chemical and mechanical processing steps are involved. Regardless of procedures, three basic steps are common to all printed-circuit technology: design, photography, and manufacturing.

pc board testing—In pc board testing, a known data stream is fed into the circuit's input and a shift-register measurement is made at each node of a known-good board. A signature is yielded for each point on the board in much the same way as feeding an analog signal into an analog pc board, under fixed conditions, yields a repeatable waveform at each node on the board. By tracing faulty signatures back through a board, as in tracing erroneous waveforms through a troubleshooting tree, a technician can locate the faulty node precisely.

pc board test language—Languages for the tester processors have been specifically designed for the unique requirements of testing. As a result, a plug-in personality board and a specific test language can be as powerful as most large minicomputer-based testers. Some tester languages are capable of loading registers, transferring data to latches or other internal registers, generating repetitive routines with DO loops and nested DO loops, performing unconditional and conditional jumps, as well as checking input lines and generating timing delays and pulses.

p-channel charge-coupled device — A charge-coupled device that is fabricated so that the charges stored in the potential wells are holes.

p-channel metal-gate process — Of all the basic MOS processes, the p-channel metal-gate process is the oldest and the most completely developed. It has served as the foundation for the MOS/LSI industry and still finds use today in some devices. Several versions of this process have evolved since its earliest days. Typically, a thin slice (8 to 10 mils) of lightly doped n-type silicon wafer serves as the supporting substrate or body of the MOS transistor. Two closely spaced, heavily doped p-type regions (the source and the drain) are formed within the substrate by selective diffusion of an impurity that provides holes as the majority electrical carriers. A thin deposited layer of aluminum metal (the gate) covers the area between the source and the drain regions, but it is electrically insulated from the substrate by a thin layer (1000-1500 A) of silicon dioxide. The p-channel transistor is turned on by a negative gate voltage and conducts current between the source and the drain by means of holes as the majority carriers.

The basic p-channel metal-gate process can be subdivided in two general categories: high threshold and low threshold. Various manufacturers use different techniques (particularly so with the low-threshold process) to achieve similar results, but the difference between them always rests in the threshold voltage (V_t) required to turn a transistor on. The high-threshold (V_t) voltage is typically —3 to —5 volts, and the low-threshold (V_t) voltage is typically —1.5 to —2.5 volts.

peak transfer rate—Refers to a particular rate at which data are transmitted through their channel, but measured during the time data are actually being transmitted, i.e., tape transfer rates are measured in terms of characters per second, discounting gaps between blocks, words, etc.

Peltier coefficient—Energy absorbed or given out per second, due to the Peltier effect, when unit current is passed through a junction of two dissimilar metals.

Peltier effect — Phenomenon whereby heat is liberated or absorbed at a junction when current passes from one metal to another.

pen, light — An optional device, used in conjunction with the incremental display, that can greatly extend its usefulness. It is a high-speed photosensitive device that can cause the computer to change or modify the display on the cathode-ray tube. As the pertinent display information is selected by the operator, the pen signals the computer by generating a pulse. Acting upon this signal, the computer can then instruct other points to be plotted across the tube face in accordance with the pen movements, or it can exercise specific options previously programmed without the need for separate input devices.

pen recorder, dual — Accepts inputs from two separate sources and charts each versus time. Input spans are separately selectable so two signals may be simultaneously recorded although of different amplitudes. Pens cross freely to produce continuous traces on many systems.

period—The time required for one complete cycle of a regular, repeating, series of events.

periodic—Repeating itself regularly in time and form.

periodic damping—Damping in which the pointer of an instrument oscillates about the final position before coming to rest. The point of change between periodic and aperiodic damping is called critical damping.

periodic pulse train — A pulse train made up of identical groups of pulses repeated at regular intervals.

peripheral bus—A data direction register or DDR is used to establish each individual peripheral bus line as either an input or an output. Each of the DDR's 8-bit positions corresponds to a peripheral data line and a 0 or a 1 written into a bit position causes that line to function as an input or output, respectively (some systems).

peripheral compatibility — Although small computer peripherals appear to be similar, there are many differences at the detail signal-control level that can lead to incompatibility between a particular peripheral and a particular processing system. Interfacing, signal timing, signal-control lines, data formats, and other facilities must be considered and matched between a specific peripheral and the processing unit. The supplying source often will support a particular peripheral for one machine processor but not for another machine processor.

peripheral control — Peripheral control lines may be programmed to act as an interrupt input or peripheral control output. As an input, these lines have high input impedance and are generally compatible with standard TTL. As an output, they are compatible with standard TTL, and they may also be used as a source of up to 1 milliampere at 1.5 volts to directly drive the base of a transistor switch. The functions of these signal lines are often programmed with the control register.

peripheral controllers — The physical peripheral device that actually handles data input or output is normally looked at as being the principal processing connection to the outside world. However, there is a second level of this connection—the peripheral controller. Peripheral controllers are essentially electronic hand-shake type units that take signals from peripherals and condition them to the point where they can be received and recognized by the driver software in the processor hardware. Peripheral controllers often contain temporary storage buffers, error-control hard-

Peripheral controllers (Courtesy Datum Inc.).

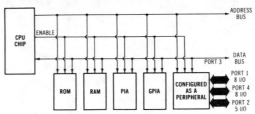

Peripheral control transfers.

ware, timing control hardware, and other sophisticated processing units. In many small computer systems, the electronics and actual processing architecture of the peripheral controller is often larger, more sophisticated, and more significant than what is actually contained inside the data-processing unit itself. In fact, many peripheral controllers are more expensive than the actual central processing hardware of the system.

peripheral control transfers — Peripheral controls regulate the transfer of data between the central processor and peripheral devices. Specifically, they reconcile the mechanical speeds of the peripheral devices with the electronic speed of the central processor, and minimize the interruption of central processor activity due to peripheral data transfers.

peripheral disk file—File management systems are generally available for use with the floppy disk peripherals. These file management systems can be accessed by various macro-language programs. They have complete sets of utility programs for update, copy, purge, or addition of files.

peripheral driver—A circuit designed to interface a digital device with an external nondigital device such as a lamp, a light-emitting diode, or a data bus.

peripheral equipment — 1. Units which work in conjunction with a microcomputer but are not a part of it (e.g., a tape reader, analog-to-digital converter, typewriter, etc.). 2. In a data-processing system, any equipment, distinct from the central processing unit, that may provide the system with outside communication or additional facilities. 3. The auxiliary machines which may be placed under the control of the central computer. Examples of this are card readers, card

punches, magnetic-tape units, and high-speed printers. Peripheral equipment may be used on-line or off-line depending upon computer design, job requirements, and economics.

peripheral interface adapter—Abbreviated PIA. Some microprocessors have incorporated LSI devices that are exclusively dedicated to enhance their I/O capabilities and, thus, simplifying the interfacing task of the design engineer. The typical peripheral interface adapter provides a universal means of interfacing peripheral equipment to the microprocessing unit (MPU). The device is capable of interfacing the MPU to peripherals through various bidirectional peripheral data buses and control lines. Often no external logic is required for interfacing to most peripheral devices. The functional configuration of the PIA is programmed by the MPU during system initialization. Each of the peripheral data lines can be programmed to act as an input or as an output, and each of the control/interrupt lines may be programmed for one of several control modes. The unit also provides handshake control logic signals for synchronizing I/O devices to the microprocessor. This allows a high degree of flexibility in the overall operation of the interface.

peripheral power supplies—Peripherals tend to be heavy consumers of electric energy within a computer system. Most of them contain mechanical or rotational drive components, such as drive motors, solenoids, relays, and other electromechanical parts, that require considerably more power than the low-voltage electronic signal units of the processors. Peripherals usually require separate power supplies to support their functioning. In large computers, which are normally completely integrated with their peripherals and where the processor is organized and closely connected, a single power supply is usually provided to service all units. However, in small computers, where it is never known exactly which components will be installed on a particular system, each device usually has its own independent power-supply source.

peripheral processors—The processing capability of some typical computer systems is distributed between the central processor subsystem and up to seven peripheral processors, which operate asynchronously with CPU and with each other. CPU subsystems often consist of a memory subsystem and the CPU. Each class of peripheral devices is controlled directly by its own peripheral processor. Functionally, the

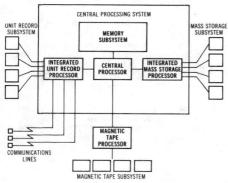

Peripheral processors.

use of separate peripheral processors, each having its own memory, firmware, microcode, and logic units, frees the CPU for other internal processing functions concurrent with the execution of peripheral and communications activities. The communications capabilities of some systems are implemented by up to three communications controllers, with each capable of supporting as many as 15 synchronous and/or asynchronous lines.

It is in minicomputers that peripheral processing is perhaps the most prevalent and practical approach. Peripheral processors are commonly found in minicomputer systems—as device controllers, array processors, communications and I/O front ends, and even as system consoles. A major reason for their popularity is that few,

if any, design changes in the CPU or bus structure are required for implementation. Also, many modern I/O controllers are peripheral processors. They contain microprocessors and control I/O devices in smart ways that take a burden from the host CPU. Some of these controllers use 8-bit MOS microprocessors; others which handle faster data-rate devices, use bit-slice, microcoded logic.

Peripheral processors generally operate as slaves to a host processor but have their own memory, input/output bus, and peripherals. Using direct-memory-accessing techniques, they can also access the memory or peripherals of the host's system. *See also* processor, peripheral.

peripheral programs—After the peripheral has been selected and evaluated for each interface and system problem, the software designer can generate the programs necessary to support these devices. Each MOS LSI peripheral will need initialization, maintenance, and diagnostic/recovery routines. By approaching each interface task as a separate but related activity, the programmer can more easily generate routines for that function and also speed his debug cycle by breaking a large job into smaller, more manageable tasks. This technique also offers inherent modularity to the total system software project.

permalloy—Group name for class of high permeability nickel-iron alloys. Also another group of molybdenum permalloy materials, e.g., Mo 4%, Ni 79%, Fe 17%.

permanent dynamic storage—Refers to a distinct type or form of dynamic storage. Examples are a magnetic disk or tape cassette, in which the maintenance of the data stored does not depend on a flow of energy.

permanent error—An error which is not eliminated by reprocessing the information a limited number of times.

permanent fault—Faults are failures in performance in the manner required or specified. Sporadic faults are intermittent while permanent faults are repetitious, but these may escape attention when they do not result in a failure to perform some particular tasks, or are known and easily correctable.

Personal computers.

permatron — A hot-cathode gas-discharge diode, gated by an applied magnetic field.

permuted cyclic code — Refers to a specific code in which characters are represented by words of a fixed number of bits but which are arranged in a sequence so that the signal distance between consecutive words is 1 or unity.

permuted index — A form of document indexing that is developed by producing an entry in the index for each word of specific interest and by including the context in which it occurs; most often restricted to title words.

personal computers — Personal computers are often defined as those that are low cost (relative to mini and standard systems), based on tiny microcomputer chips and, thus, portable, personally controllable, and easily used. There are several classifications — home, hobbyist, professional, business, very small business, appliance, and more.

personality cards—Inside some PROM programmers, a microcomputer tailors the program to the PROM the development team has decided to use. A programmer often directs the data to be stored through "personality cards" that provide the appropriate timing patterns, voltage levels, and other requirements. The programmer is partitioned so that new personality cards can be inserted as new PROMs are developed.

personality modules — A personality module is the hardware interface between a control unit and a particular PROM. There are more than 200 PROM types and they vary in number of bits, pinouts, package size, power requirements, and programming techniques. Various firms make three kinds of personality modules: dedicated, generic, and gang. Dedicated modules are for specific PROMs with unique characteristics. Generic modules (with appropriate pinout adapters and configurators) permit programming of families of PROMs. Gang modules enable the programming of multiple PROMs simultaneously. Personality modules function with many types of control units. A typical personality module contains the specialized interfacing, power supplies, and programming instructions that are unique to the particular PROM or family of PROMs being programmed (pulse width, number of pulses, duty cycles, and threshold level). In many cases, a single module enables the user to program several types of PROMs.

PERT network — Abbreviation for Program Evaluation and Review Technique. It is a critical path analysis using computer techniques. The use of PERT requires an extensive analysis of an overall project in order to list all the individual activities or jobs which must be performed in order to meet the total objective. These activities are then arranged in a network that displays the sequential relationship among them. This analysis must be extremely thorough and detailed if it is to be realistic. PERT provides a means of reporting and analysis for project administrators. Information required can be developed and the areas which impose the greatest time restrictions on the completion of a product can be highlighted. Areas with an excess of time for completion, called stack areas, are also highlighted. *See* critical path.

phase dictionary—Refers to an abbreviated table of contents that contains the phase name and load addresses of the phases to be loaded for a given application.

phase encoding, redundant — An encoded system in which zeroes and ones are represented by different width pulses. Each pulse can be given once or repeated for a certain amount of time. It is called redundant (repeated) phase encoding; e.g., the hobbyist cassette Kansas City Standard is redundant because all of the information is contained in the first portion of the pattern. Redundant phase encoding is actually frequency-shift keying (fsk).

phase jitter—1. Refers to a type of unwanted random distortion which results in the intermittent shortening or lengthening of the signals. 2. Peak-to-peak phase deviation of a transmitted carrier signal. An excessive phase jitter causes errors in high-speed phase-modulated modems. Phase jitter generally originates in frequency-division multiplexers in carrier systems.

phase library—Refers to a specific directoried data set that contains program phases that are processed and entered by the linkage editor, the source from which program phases are loaded for execution.

phase-locked loop (PPL) motor control —Microprocessors can offer important advantages in phase-locked loops for dc motor control. Though unusual, this all-digital technique proves straightforward and effective for these reasons:
- The fixed cycle time of the processor is derived from a crystal-controlled clock. Use of this consistent timing provides the system accuracy.
- A digital PPL that uses pulse-width modulation performs a count-and-compare function. The processor's arithmetic and branching capabilities are suited to perform these tasks.

phase-locked oscillator — Concerns a specific parametric oscillator which can be made to oscillate in one of two phases relative to the pump frequency and, thus, can act as a storage cell.

phase logic—Phase logic is what transfers the machine from one operational phase to another, such as fetch, indirect, execute, and interrupt. In some systems, flip-flops and combinatorial next-state logic are used to establish the current phase and the next phase. To minimize costs, phases are often merely microcoded subroutines.

phase modulation recording—Refers to a specific procedure or method for the magnetic recording of bits, in which each storage cell is split into two parts and each is magnetized in opposite senses, with the sequence of these senses indicating whether the bit represented is a zero or a one.

phase, object—*Same as* phase, run.

phase, run—An occasion on which the target program (after compiling) is run and often called the run phase, the target phase, or the object phase.

phase shift—1. A time difference between the input and output signals of a system. 2. A change in the phase of a periodic quantity. 3. A change in time relationship of one part of a signal waveform with another, with no change in the basic form of the signal. The degree of change varies with frequency as a signal passes through a channel.

phase shifter—A device in which the output voltage (or current) may be adjusted to have some desired phase relationship with the input voltage (or current).

phase, sorting—An arbitrary segmentation of a sort program. Many sorts are segmented into three phases: initialization phase, internal phase, merge phase.

phase splitter—Refers to a technique of producing two or more waves which differ in phase from a single input wave.

phase, target—*Same as* phase, run.

phase velocity—The velocity at which a point of constant phase is propagated in a progressive sinusoidal wave.

phasing — 1. Causing two systems or circuits to operate in phase or at some desired difference from the in-phase condition. 2. Adjusting a facsimile-picture position along the scanning line.

phasing capacitor—A capacitor used in a crystal filter circuit for neutralizing the capacity of the crystal holder.

phoneme—A primitive unit of auditory speech in a given language.

phonemes, voice synthesizer—One type synthesizer relies on phonemes, the most basic of speech sounds, stored as 6-bit words in a separate memory chip. The speech IC contains the circuits for selecting the phonemes and connecting them to generate words and sounds. An important adjunct to the chip is a stand-alone development system with which a user develops the words to be generated. The system contains the general rules of speech used to formulate the phoneme sequence. It converts the sequence into the digital code to be stored in the memory chip. Normally, a user types a sentence or phrase into the development system, which breaks each word into phonemes and, then, into the code. In some applications, the synthesizer chip itself can independently access the phonemes stored in memory. A microprocessor may be needed if the reproduced phrases reach a certain complexity—for example, if the words to be spoken go beyond a relatively simple phrase or sentence, or if choices among different possibilities must be made.

phosphor characteristics, white/green—The use of P4 (white) phosphor in data displays arose naturally from its use as a standard monochrome television phosphor, but a trend in the direction of green phosphor has appeared since IBM began using a green phosphor in the Series 3270 terminals. Green corresponds to the peak of the human eye's spectral response, and many of the phosphors that minimize flicker resulting from interlaced scan and 50-Hz refresh are green. A terminal designer can control the choice of phosphor as a part of the crt display-module specifications.

phosphor dots—Refers to the elements in the screen of the crt which glow in the three primary colors.

phosphorescence—Concerns the property of emitting light for a period of time after the source of excitation is taken away, i.e., electrostatic storage tubes and cathode-ray tubes (crt's) use this capability or phenomenon to cause a trace on the screen to remain after the transient signal causing the signal is removed; it is, thus, a form of temporary storage.

phosphor, P4—Low in cost and readily available, P4 (white) phosphor is a standard monochrome tv-receiver material that permits good focus and small spot size. It's a medium- to medium-short-persistence phosphor (depending on the manufacturer); i.e., the glow activated by the electron beam fades away fairly rapidly, leaving no cursor trail or temporary ghost characters. As is characteristic of medium- and medium-short-persistence phosphors, P4 resists phosphor burn—the formation on the unlit crt face of a permanent dark pattern caused by often-repeated portions of the character format. (Susceptibility to burn is somewhat proportional to persistence; longer persistence phosphors are more likely to burn.) Because of its relatively short persistence, though, P4 phosphor is not suitable for interlaced operation. Its European equivalent is W.

phosphor, P31 — A green phosphor of medium-short persistence, P31 is more luminescent than P4, has good focus and small-dot-size capabilities, and is highly resistant to phosphor burn. It presents a slight cost premium, however, and, like P4, it is not suitable for interlaced operation. The European equivalent of P31 phosphor is GH.

phosphor, P39 — A yellow-green long-persistence phosphor, P39 operates down to 25 Hz without flicker and, because of its longer persistence, is used almost exclusively in interlaced displays. It exhibits fairly good luminescence and, when used in a high-quality display, provides small dot size and good focus capabilities. Because of the long persistence of P39, however, characters on the screen fade slowly, so a moving cursor leaves a momentary trail. Moreover, because it burns easily, it is not suitable for data displays in which the format remains fixed for long periods of time. The European equivalent of P39 is GR.

photocell — 1. A specific vacuum tube which converts light into electrical energy. 2. A resistive, bulk-effect type of photosensor; used when it is desirable to wire several photoreceivers in series or in parallel. 3. Fundamentally, this is a solid-state photosensitive electron device whose current-voltage characteristic is a function of incident radiation.

photocell light checks — Checks performed on data read from cards passing through a card reader.

photocell matrix—An optical character recognition term for a device capable of projecting an input onto a fixed two-dimensional array of photocells to develop a simultaneous display of the horizontal and vertical components of the character. The time necessary to scan the character is related to the response time of the photocells.

photoconductivity—Property possessed by certain materials of varying their electrical conductivity under the influence of light.

photodiode—1. Combination of photoconducting cell and junction diode into a two-electrode semiconducting device. Widely used as an optical-sensing device for data processing. 2. A special type of diode that allows a current flow proportional to the amount of light striking it. This may be thought of as a transistor with light providing the base current. Almost all transistors will, when removed from their protective cases, function as photodiodes. 3. A diode whose junction changes resistance (photoconductive diode) or generates a voltage (photovoltaic diode) when illuminated by infrared, visible, or ultraviolet light.

photoelectricity—Emission of electrons from the surface of certain materials by quanta exceeding certain energy (Einstein).

photoemissive—Refers to the effect in which electrons are emitted from the surfaces of certain specific materials at particular threshold levels of frequency of incident electromagnetic radiation, i.e., as visible light, infrared, or ultraviolet, as used in phototubes.

photogrammetry — Photogrammetry is the process of making precise dimensional measurements through photography, generally using twin pictures to produce a stereoscopic effect for three-dimensional measurements. The most common application is aerial photogrammetry for making maps. There are terrestrial applications in such fields as architecture, medicine, animal husbandry, and engineering. Photogrammetry is described as an art form as well as a scientific record.

photographic storage—1. Generally refers to high-density storage of data in binary form on photographic disks for quick reference purposes. 2. Photographic copies of data shown on direct-display cathode-ray tubes. 3. Facsimile copies of readable documents or of the direct output of the processor. 4. Any storage schemes utilizing photographic processes. This includes various microimage systems, computer-output mcrofilm, and binary data storage on photographic media.

photo-isolator — A solid-state device that allows complete electrical isolation between the field wiring and the controller.

photolithographic diffusion windows—Photolithographic techniques are used to etch selective openings on a passivating oxide layer. Such openings serve as diffusion windows from which controlled amounts of impurity doping can be introduced into the single-crystal silicon substrate or the epitaxial layer. Using photographic techniques, the diffusion windows can be greatly reduced in size without sacrificing the accuracy of their alignment or lateral dimensions.

photolithography—Refers to a process used to print the masks on a silicon wafer. It involves the use of photosensitive emulsion and selective etching analogous to commercial lithography.

photolithography mask layers — Generally, an initial layout of an integrated circuit is normally done at a scale several hundred times larger than the final dimensions of the finished monolithic chip. This initial layout is then decomposed into individual mask layers, each corresponding to a masking step used during the fabrication process. The individual mask layers are then reduced photographically to the final dimensions of the integrated unit. The reduced form of each of these patterns is then contact-printed on a transparent glass slide to form a photographic "mask" of the patterns that are to be etched on the SiO_2 surface. To facilitate batch-processing, a large number of such masks are contact-printed on the same glass slide, forming a "masking plate." The plate is sufficiently large enough so as to cover the entire surface of the silicon wafer to be masked. Thus, in a single masking operation, an array of a large number of identical masks can be applied simultaneously over the wafer surface. During the masking operation, the mask is transferred from the masking plate to the wafer surface by photolithographic techniques.

photo-optic memory—A specific memory or storage unit that uses an optical medium. For example, a laser might be used to record data on photographic film.

photo optics—The combination of an input light source and a photoreceiver that produces an output signal. They are assembled either separately or in a single package.

photoreceiver—A unit consisting of a photosensor, focusing lens, and a protective enclosure.

photoresist—Masking material used in the etching of semiconductor devices or integrated circuits.

photoresist coatings — The coated resist should be free of heterogeneous fillers, crystallites, or particulate matter. Large particles scatter or diffract radiation or cause edge roughness. The coating should be free of voids that act as easy channels for unwanted attack of the etch solution on the substrate. Sometimes protrusions from the substrate or from a mask brought into near contact with the resist create defects in the coating. The coated resist must also show good adhesion to metals and oxides, such as silicon, silica, aluminum, aluminum oxide, tungsten, copper, gold, and magnetic alloys. The exposure that creates a desired relief image in the resist should be short enough to be compatible with a high throughput of substrates.

photoresist process—Process used to selectively remove the oxidized surface of a silicon semiconductor slice. The photoresist material is an organic substance which polymerizes under an exposure to ultraviolet light and, in that form, resists attack by acids and solvents.

When a resist film becomes more soluble as a result of exposure, it acts in a positive tone or as a positive resist; when it becomes less soluble, it acts as a negative resist. Negative working photoresists crosslink and gel in the exposed area and become insoluble, while positive resists generally increase their acidity in the exposed area and become more soluble in a dilute, aqueous base.

After the solvent develops a relief image, it is dried and hardened. Etching then transfers the image to the substrate. The resist "resists" the action of the etching solution and, hence, its name. Alternatively, the relief image can act as a physical closure around an area in which a plating or some other deposition process occurs on the substrate. Finally, stripping the resist away leaves a positive or negative image of the relief pattern on the substrate.

photoresists, negative—Negative photo resists are formulated from three essential ingredients: a chemically reactive polymer, a photosensitive agent that starts the chemical reaction, and a solvent.

photoresists, positive—Positive photoresists, like negative resists, are formulated from three ingredients: an acidic polymer that dissolves or disperses in an aqueous base, a photosensitive inhibitor in solution, and a solvent. The exposure destroys the photosensitive solution inhibitor. This compound, usually a quinone diazide, absorbs light and undergoes a series of reactions that convert it from a neutral hydrophobic material to an acidic hydrophilic material. The solution inhibition is destroyed because the inhibitor has lost its resistance to an aqueous base. In exposed areas, the photoresist is now readily attacked by the aqueous basic developer. The acidic polymers chosen for use in positive resists are either weakly acidic, such as phenol containing polymers, or strongly acidic, such as acrylic acid containing polymers.

photovoltaic cell — *See* photovoltaic sensor.

photovoltaic sensor — A photovoltaic sensor or photovoltaic cell is one which absorbs light and produces an output voltage. A pn junction forms a barrier in the semiconductor to separate electron pairs as in a conventional diode or transistor, and the voltage across the junction is a function of the photons impinging on it. When connected to a suitable load, a considerable current can be maintained. The most common materials used for cell construction are silicon and selenium; others include germanium and gallium arsenide.

Silicon photovoltaic cells do not exhibit serious light history effects and have a good speed of response times ranging from 1–100 microseconds. They can be biased for even faster response. Photovoltaic devices are self-generating and do not require external power supplies. This makes them useful in applications such as camera light meters and in tape and card readers. They can also be used for direct energy conversion, i.e., the solar cell.

PIA—*See* peripheral interface adapter.

PIA bus interface—The PIA in many systems is used to provide 8- or 16-bits of external interface and four control lines at addressable locations in standard system memory. The I/O bits can be accessed in two words of 8-bits each, but each I/O bit is individually programmable to act as either an input or an output. All operating characteristics of the interface can be established by writing from the processor to the Data Direction and Control Registers of the PIA. This is required at the time of system Reset and permitted at any other time, in most systems. All devices connected to the processor have the same interface as a memory—a fundamental characteristic of most microbus systems. The register-select lines serve the same purpose in the PIA as the address lines do in a memory. For this reason, they are normally connected directly to the low-order address lines of the system. Chip selects are again provided for partial address decoding.

PIA Read/Write — On some systems, this signal is generated by the MPU to control the direction of data transfers on the data bus. A low state on the PIA Read/Write line enables the input buffers and the data are transferred from the MPU to the PIA on the "E" signal if the device has been selected. A high on the Read/Write line sets up the PIA for a transfer of data to the bus. The PIA output buffers are enabled when the proper address and the enable pulse "E" are present.

piezoelectric—1. The property of certain crystals, which: (1) Produce a voltage when subjected to mechanical stress, and (2) Undergo mechanical stress when subjected to a voltage. 2. A term applied to the phenomenon whereby certain crystalline materials develop useful electrical pressures (voltages) when the material is subjected to variable mechanical pressures, strains, or stresses; conversely, the materials develop mechanical strains or stresses when electrical voltages are applied.

piezoelectric crystal — 1. A piece of natural quartz or other crystalline material capable of demonstrating the piezoelectric effect. A quartz crystal, when ground to certain dimensions, will vibrate at a desired radio frequency when placed in an appropriate electric circuit. 2. A crystal that converts mechanical pressure into an electrical signal or converts a signal into a pressure.

pilot system—Concerns a specific collection of file records and supplementary data that is obtained from the actual operations of a business over an extended period of time, and which is used to effect a realistic system for testing by closely simulating the real-world environment.

pinboard—Refers to a type of control panel which uses pins rather than wires to control the operation of a computer. On certain small computers that use pinboards, a program is changed by the operator removing one pinboard and inserting another. Related to panel, control.

p-i-n diode — A semiconductor pn diode with a layer of an intrinsic semiconductor incorporated between the p and n junctions.

pip—Significant deflection or intensification of the spot on a crt giving a display for identification or calibration. Particularly applied to the peaked pattern of a cursor signal or device.

pipeline—Computers that execute serial programs only, whether standard, mini, or micro, are referred to as pipeline computers.

pipeline partitioning—In many applications, significant improvements in performance may be achieved by using more than one processor in the system. Two ways of allocating or partitioning system functions among multiple processors is by pipeline and parallel partitioning. In pipeline partitioning, system functions (tasks) are divided among several processors, so that data flow through the system is primarily serial. Each processor performs its portion of system functions, and then calls upon another processor to perform another set. An example of pipeline partitioning is when one processor performs data acquisition and buffering, while a second uses the data to perform digital signal processing. However, parallel partitioning allocates system functions among several processors at a time, in such a way that each processor performs a separate system task in parallel. An example is a system where one processor performs an industrial process-control loop, while another monitors and controls a varying parameter, such as temperature.

pipeline processing—Pipelining is employed to obtain faster microprocessor configurations. With the addition of an n-bit register at the output of microprogram memory, the microprocessor can be operated in what is called the pipeline mode. Based on the status of the various addresses, instruction, and control buses, the master clock is halted at an arbitrary location in the program for both serial and pipeline configurations. It is seen that the advantage of pipelining is increased speed; for example, fetching of instruction n ± 1 is performed while the instruction (n) is being executed. The one disadvantage of pipelined processing is that conditional instructions can only test the results of previous instructions. In other words, instruction n can only test for overflow generated by the previous instruction n-1 or n-2, etc. In some cases, this will result in the pipelined machine requiring more storage than a serial machine because the serial machine can, for example, execute an "Add and branch if zero" instruction in a single microinstruction while the pipeline machine will require two microinstructions to perform the same function. *See also* parallel processing types.

pipeline transparency—One of the greatest benefits of instruction pipelining is its transparency to the user. When implemented properly, the performance of instructions can be increased significantly without affecting the code already written. The actual execution of an instruction can be divided into four distinct parts. First, the instruction must be fetched from memory. Then, it must be interpreted, or decoded. Next, the operand or operands must be fetched from memory. Finally, the instruction must be executed. If all these operations are performed serially for successive instructions, as on an assembly line, the next instruction can be fetched while the first one is decoded, and so on. If the "pipe" can be kept full, the incremental time to complete an instruction can be reduced to just the execution time. Instruction pipelines can become a hindrance, however, when the program branches to an instruction other than the next one in line. To circumvent this, parallel pipelines are used—one for the current instructions and others for the most likely branch instructions.

pipelining—Refers to the overlapping of fetch and execute cycles within a processor. After the fetch unit has passed a decoded instruction on to the execution unit, it places the next one in the instruction queue.

pipelining, hardware—Hardware pipelining is a widely used technique that is used for speeding up a computer by performing operations concurrently. For example, a floating-point multiplication has three stages, each of which takes a machine cycle to complete. The product of the mantissas of the two operands starts in the first stage and is completed in the second stage, while the exponents of the two operands are added, and any normalization and rounding of the product is performed during the third stage. By pipelining (or staggering and overlapping) the sequential operations of many multiplications, the speed of the multiplier hardware is improved. Although there is a delay of three machine cycles before the completion of the first multiplication, once the pipelining begins, a new result emerges each cycle.

pixel—Short for picture element. A pixel is a small rectangular division of the video screen. The smaller the rectangle, the sharper the picture will appear to be, and the more rectangles there will be. Thus, the higher the resolution, the greater is the amount of computer space that is needed to store the pixels.

pixel/bit levels—Bits are related to image brightness. The brightness or gray level of a pixel, when digitized, is given a value from a specified set of allowed values—a quantized level. The number of quantized levels can be expressed as 2^n levels or as B bits. The number of levels corresponding to a byte (i.e., 8 bits) is equal to 2^8 or 256 levels and is frequently encountered.

pixel vs. resolution—A pixel, or picture element, is a spatial resolution element and is the smallest distinguishable and resolvable area in an image, for example, the display on a crt monitor. It can also describe the smallest distinguishable variation over time in a signal sequence. The term pixel is not, strictly speaking, applicable to an analog image, but it is tempting to equate pixel to limiting resolution. In general, however, actual pixel resolution is less than limiting resolution. Limiting factors include: spatial resolution capability, noise, shading, geometric distortion, black signal-level instability, nonproportional response to illumination, and overall instabilities.

PLA—*See* programmable logic array.

PLA advantages—PLAs are particularly suited to decoding where AND–OR logic is most often used. The inclusion of logic in the array provides a distinct space advantage over ROMs for performing this function. As such, they are likely to be used in code converters, computer-instruction decoding, and I/O device command decoding. Other PLA advantages include a significant reduction in the logistics problems during manufacturing due to fewer device types, a slight increase in systems reliability due to decreased part count and interconnections, system-power reductions, and decreased board-space requirements.

PLA disadvantages—PLAs suffer from several disadvantages. First, until recently, the only two ways to program PLAs were to either mask program them or have interconnections burned in by a laser. This required designers to be very sure that the design was correct prior to committing to masks (which cost between $500 and $1000

each). The second disadvantage is that PLAs are slow compared to random-logic equivalents. A third disadvantage has been a lack of user application knowledge of PLA design techniques. A fourth PLA disadvantage is price—while a single PLA costs about $25 (in volume quantities), one can easily, and as cheaply, purchase 40 or more SSI–MSI TTL gates to perform the same function (with higher performance).

planar—A type of semiconductor device and the process technology that is used to fabricate it, in which all of the pn junctions terminate at approximately the same geometric plane on the surface of the semiconductor. However, devices using similar technologies, but having one or more diffused areas lying in a slightly different but parallel plane are also considered planar (e.g., buried collector, etc.).

planar integrated circuit — One produced on a thin silicon wafer; the same technique as is used for planar transistors.

planar network—A network in which no branches cross when drawn on the same plane.

planar process — A basic part of the technology used for silicon transistors, it is a combination of oxidation, selective oxide removal, and, then, heating to introduce doping materials by diffusion. Silicon, rather than germanium, is the predominant semiconductor material. As applied to semiconductor devices, the term is used to mean that the monolithic components fabricated by this process extend below the surface of the silicon substrate. However, the plane surface of the semiconductor remains relatively flat and unaltered through the sequence of the different fabrication steps. Planar process technology is comprised of five independent processes: epitaxy, surface passivation, photolithography, diffusion, and thin-film deposition.

planar process advantages—As compared with earlier solid-state device fabrication techniques, the planar process offers two unique advantages that make it ideally suited for integrated circuits: (1) The semiconductor junctions are protected on the surface by an oxide layer and are not exposed to air. This results in low leakage currents and high reliability. (2) Photographic reduction, masking, and etching techniques are used to determine device geometries, thus making possible very small dimensions and the simultaneous fabrication of a large number of devices and circuits on the same silicon surface.

planar transistor—A form of transistor constructed by etching a thin slice of semiconductor and characterized essentially by a parallel-plane electrode configuration protected by an oxidized surface.

plasma—1. A wholly or partially ionized gas in which the positive ions and negative electrons are roughly equal in number. Hence, the space charge is essentially zero. 2. The region in which gaseous conduction takes place between the cathode and anode of an electric arc. 3. Ionized gaseous discharge in which there is no resultant charge, the number of positive and negative ions being equal, in addition to un-ionized molecules or atoms. The term is also used as a synonym for the positive column in a gas discharge. 4. A plasma is a volume of ionized gas atoms capable of supporting a current. The plasma contains a substantial group of free radicals—electrically neutral atoms that can form chemical bonds. The free radicals react with photoresists and substrate coatings to etch them.

plasma torch — One in which solids, liquids, or gases are forced through an arc within a water-cooled tube, with consequent ionization; de-ionization on impact results in very high temperatures. Used for cutting and depositing carbides.

plasmatron—Discharge tube in which anode current can be regulated by control of plasma, either by a grid or through the electron stream originating the plasma.

platinum—A heavy, almost white metal that resists practically all acids and is capable of withstanding high temperatures.

platinum contacts — Used where currents must be broken frequently (e.g., in induction coils and electric bells). Sparking does not damage platinum as much as it does other metals. Hence, a cleaner contact is assured, with minimum attention.

PL/M—PL/M is a powerful structured high-level algorithmic language in which program statements can naturally express the program algorithm. This frees the programmer to concentrate on the system implementation without concern for the burdensome details of assembly-language programming (such as register allocation, meanings of assembler mnemonics, etc.). Since PL/M programs are implementation-problem oriented and are more compact, use of PL/M results in a high degree of engineering productivity during project development. This translates into significant reductions in initial software development and follow-on maintenance costs for the user. PL/M is an assembly language replacement that can fully command the 8080 CPU and future processors to produce efficient run-time object code. PL/M was designed to provide additional developmental software support for the MCS-80 and other microcomputer systems, permitting the programmer to concentrate more on his problem and less on the actual task of programming than is possible with assembly language. PL/M is derived from PL/1 with emphasis on those features that accurately reflect the nature of systems programming requirements.

PLMX—PLMX is a universal high-level language for microprocessors. It can be used with all 8- or 16-bit microprocessors and was designed primarily for use in microcomputer product development systems and in real-time process-control applications. PLMX syntax is identical to PL/M, so the entire library of existing PL/M programs can be compiled under PLMX. PL/M programs may be used on microprocessors other than the 8080 through the PLMX compiler. PLMX is a true compiler, allowing fast compiling times—useful for real-time applications. It has been developed as a user-oriented language. There are no arbitrary formatting rules or line numbers. Comments may occur anywhere in the source text, except within reserved words, identifier names, and numbers.

PL/1 programming language—A computer programming language which has some features of FORTRAN and some features of COBOL, plus others.

PL/1-80—PL/1-80 is ANSI's general-purpose subset of full PL/1, tailored

Plotter (Courtesy Hewlett-Packard Co.).

into a language for 8080, 8085, and Z80 users who expect the software revolution that they've seen in hardware—better results at lower cost. PL/1-80 works harder than any other general-purpose language for business, science, research, and education according to many users. A typical PL/1-80 software package includes a native code compiler, a comprehensive subroutine library, a linkage editor, and a relocating macroassembler.

plotter—Refers to a visual display or board in which a dependent variable is graphed by an automatically controlled pen or pencil as a function of one or more variables. The typical new generation of recorders are designed to meet more sophisticated recording needs. RS-232 compatible, under microprocessor control, they often record from either an analog or digital source, functioning as either a strip chart recorder or as a digital plotter.

plotting board—Refers to an output unit which plots the curves of one or more variables as a function of one or more other variables.

plugboard—1. In a computer, a removable board having many electric terminals into which connecting cords may be plugged in patterns varying

for different programs. To change the program, one wired plugboard is replaced by another. 2. For punched-card machines, such as sorters, it is a removable panel consisting of an array of terminals which may be interconnected by short electrical leads according to a prescribed pattern and, hence, can designate a specific program. An entire prewired panel may be inserted for different programs. 3. A control panel or wiring panel.

plugboard unit—A chassis which can be removed or inserted into the rest of the equipment by merely plugging or putting in a connecting socket.

plugging chart—Refers to a diagrammatic chart displaying where plugs or wires are to be inserted into a plugboard. Other information displayed relates to placement and setting of switches, digit emitters, and other specific uses of the plugboard.

plug-in unit — 1. Refers to an assembly of electronic components of a standard type, wired together, which can be plugged in or pulled out of a unit of equipment easily. 2. A self-contained circuit assembly.

plug, program-patching—Refers to a relatively small auxiliary plugboard patched with a specific variation of a portion of a program and designed to be plugged into a relatively larger plugboard patched with the main program.

plus zone—Refers to bit positions in a computer code which represent the algebraic plus sign.

point contact — 1. A pressure contact between a semiconductor body and a metallic point. 2. Condition where current flow to a semiconductor is through a point of metal, e.g., the use of the end of a metal wire as in a "cat's whisker."

point-contact diode — A diode which obtains its rectifying characteristic from a point contact.

point-contact rectifier—One comprising a metal point pressing on to a crystal of semiconductor and delivering holes when made positive.

point-contact transistor — A transistor having a base electrode and two or more point-contact electrodes.

point effect—The phenomenon whereby a discharge will occur more readily at sharp points than elsewhere on an object electrode.

pointer—A word giving the address of another main memory storage location. Pointers automatically step through memory locations. Automatically stepping forward through consecutive locations is known as autoincrement addressing; automatically stepping backwards is known as autodecrement addressing. These modes are particularly useful for processing tabular or array data.

pointing—A method of allowing a nontypist operator to enter data items. A "menu" of items is displayed on the screen; the operator chooses one by pointing at it with a system device, such as a light pen, stylus, or terminal cursor, or, on a "touch" screen, with a finger.

point-junction transistor — A transistor having a base electrode and both point-contact and junction electrodes.

point-of-sale—Point-of-sale (POS) systems are systems for automating various aspects of retail operations. Such systems are electronic and many directly involve EFTS (electronic funds transfer system). The general types of functions performed by POS systems are:

  1. Inventory control and other functions internal to the retail establishment. Data entered on an electronic cash register becomes input to a store-wide or chain-wide file of such data.

  2. Credit authorization. A purchaser's credit card is read by a terminal and a central computer verifies that the card is valid and that the purchaser's credit is sufficient to cover a sale. Such systems provide the means for establishing a zero floor limit for all credit transactions.

  3. Credit verification. A merchant obtains verification from a bank's central computer that a purchaser's demand account balance is sufficient to cover a sale.

  4. Electronic funds transfer. Some EFTS projects include POS terminals that are card-activated and which debit a customer's account and credit a merchant's account in order to effect payment for a sale. All POS functions could be integrated in a single EFT system. In such an integrated system, communications between banks and retail terminals would be handled by special switching and processing centers. Compatibility and standardization of POS/EFTS are important. Some standardization of cards and terminals may be necessary, since merchants may be unwilling to handle several different types. On the other hand, sharing of terminals may pose antitrust problems.

point-of-sale central controller—Refers to a specific central controller. Some types poll up to 120 of the data entry stations and record the data on 9-track magnetic tape. The central controller can also operate directly on-line with the computer as well as recording on magnetic tape.

point-of-sale terminals—Most of these are designed primarily for off-line operation in multiterminal installations. A central unit is used to record data from multiple point-of-sale units connected by direct wiring to a 9-track magnetic-tape device. The central unit includes:

  1. A magnetic-tape unit.
  2. A control unit.
  3. A communications interface.

Point-of-sale terminals
(*Courtesy NCR Corp.*).

4. A scanner or multiplex unit.
5. A buffer.

Arithmetic operations are performed in the terminal, which is programmable to a limited extent. Originally point-of-sale terminals were used in department stores and other large retail outlets. Now supermarkets are their biggest users. One point-of-sale recorder or "electronic cash register" on the market today includes:

1. A tag reader for reading merchandise tags.
2. A keyboard with numeric and function keys for the operator entry of data.
3. A printer which prints sales slips and an internal audit tape.
4. A 13-digit numeric display for displaying data entered through the keyboard.
5. A cash drawer.
6. A buffer memory.
7. A logic and control unit.
8. An optional magnetic-tape unit and communications modem.

point-to-point connection—This is a method of connecting single terminals, either hard-wired or via a full duplex modem, to the more commonly available computer interfaces. When data transmission is in character mode, it enables terminals to be connected as direct replacements to teletypewriter-like devices.

polar—1. Pertaining to, measured from, or having a pole (e.g., the poles of the earth or of a magnet). 2. A situation in which a binary 1 is represented by current flow in one direction and binary 0 by current flow in the opposite direction.

polar coordinates—A system of coordinates in which a point is located by its distance and direction (angle)

from a fixed point on a reference line (called the polar axis).

polar crystals—Crystals having a lattice composed of alternate positive and negative ions.

polar diagram—A diagram in which the magnitude of a quantity is shown by polar coordinates.

polarity—1. General term for the difference between two points in a system which differ in one respect; e.g., potentials of the terminals of a cell or an electrolytic capacitor, the windings of a transformer, a video signal, the legs of a balanced circuit, the phase of an alternating current. 2. Having two opposite charges, one positive and the other negative. 3. Having two opposite magnetic poles, one north and the other south. 4. Distinction between positive and negative electric charges (Franklin). 5. Distinction between positive (north) and negative (south) magnetic poles of an electro or permanent magnet; these poles do not exist, but describe locations where the magnetic flux leaves or enters a magnetic material.

polarization—1. The magnetic orientation of molecules in a piece of iron or other magnetizable material placed in a magnetic field, whereby the tiny internal magnets tend to line up with the magnetic lines of force. 2. The direction of the electric vector in a linearly polarized wave radiated from an antenna.

polarizing slots — Also called indexing slots. One or more slots placed in the edge of a printed-circuit board to accommodate and align certain types of connectors.

polish notation—1. A specific form of prefix notation. 2. A method of algebraic statement representation that has the advantages of conciseness and unique logical interpretation.

poll — Refers to a systematic method, centrally controlled, for permitting stations on a multipoint circuit to transmit without contending for the line.

polling—1. Refers to an important multiprocessing method used to identify the source of interrupt requests. When several interrupts occur simultaneously, the control program makes the decision as to the one that will be serviced first. 2. Refers to a technique by which each of the terminals sharing a communications line is periodically interrogated to determine whether it requires servicing. The multiplexer or control station sends a poll which, in effect, asks the terminal selected, "Do you have anything to transmit?" 3. A flexible, systematic, centrally controlled method of permitting terminals on a multiterminal line to transmit without contending for the line. The computer contacts terminals according to the order specified by the user, and each terminal contacted is invited to send messages. 4. Refers to a centrally controlled method of calling a number of transmission points to permit them to transmit information.

polling characters—Refers to a set of characters designed to be peculiar to a terminal and the polling operation. Response to these characters indicates to the computer whether or not the terminal has a message to send.

polling interval—Refers to a time interval set between polling operations if no data is being transmitted from the polled station.

polling, line-shared—Throughout polling sequences, the sharing device routes the signals to and from the polled terminal and handles the supporting tasks, such as making sure the carrying signal is on the line when the terminal is polled, and inhibiting transmission from all terminals that are not connected to the computer. There are two types of devices used in this technique — modem-sharing units and line-sharing units. They function in much the same way to perform similar tasks—the only significant difference being that a line-sharing unit has an internal timing source, while a modem-sharing unit gets its timing signals from the modem it is servicing.

polling list—Concerns a specified list containing control information and names of entries in the terminal table. The order in which the names are specified determines the order in which the terminals are polled.

polling programs—Generally refers to a series of packages that transfers files from one processor to another and selects from among programs on the basis of various call routines. Some perform asynchronously (often at 1200-baud full-duplex) or synchro-nously (often 2000, 2400, or 4800 baud). Such programs may be called auto-dial, auto-answer, and any other type name used for unattended operation.

polling schemes—There are two basic polling schemes. In ring polling, the I/O devices are weighted equally and are polled sequentially and serviced at the same rate. In priority polling, all I/O devices are unequally weighted, so that certain of them are polled more often than others and are given a higher rate of service. Priorities established in a polling scheme are relative. That is to say, a higher-priority device, while getting more frequent CPU attention, cannot override an "in-service" lower-priority element.

polling, time-sharing—Polling is a technique for controlling the use of lines, by an agreed protocol, for those devices that are trying to share a common transmission path. The devices are rigidly controlled (so that only one of them sends information along a line at any instant) by an exchange of control signals or messages between them. Sometimes polling is governed by the central computer which sends a control message to each terminal, in turn, inviting it to transmit an information message. The terminal replies either with such a message or with a control message indicating it has nothing to report.

polycrystalline structure—The granular structure of crystals which have uniform shapes and arrangements.

polyesters — A class of thermosetting synthetic resins having great strength and good resistance to moisture and chemicals.

polymorphic — Capable of existing in more than one crystal form.

polystyrene—A clear thermoplastic material having excellent dielectric properties, especially at ultrahigh frequencies.

polystyrene capacitor—A low-loss precision capacitor with a polystyrene dielectric.

polythene or polyethylene — A tough waxy thermoplastic material that is flexible and chemically resistant. A good insulator. Mechanical properties are changed by irradiation. Symbol Tn (Alkathene).

polyvalence—The property of being interrelated in several ways.

polyvalent notation—Refers to a method for describing salient characteristics, in condensed form, using two or more characters, where each character or group of characters represents one of the characteristics.

porcelain-on-steel technology—A recent significant development has been the use of cheap but strong porcelainized steel substrates with modified thick-film materials used for the circuitry. Early in the 1970s, several major firms placed screened thick-film conductors onto small porcelain-on-steel boards for use in flash-bulb arrays for low-cost cameras. By the late 1970s, manufacturers like the Erie Ceramic Arts Co. in Erie, PA, Alpha Metals Inc. in Jersey City, NJ, and General Electric's Lamp Department in Cleveland, OH, all produced electronic-grade (low-ion-content) porcelain-on-steel devices. The porcelainized-steel substrates allow thick-film techniques for applications to boards as large as any epoxy-glass printed-circuit board. Punching and forming steel prior to porcelainizing can eliminate hardware. The steel core distributes heat to eliminate hot spots and improve power dissipation.

Replacing conventional printed-circuit-board laminates and alumina substrates with porcelainized-steel substrates (PSS) is gaining momentum. The method for producing porcelainized steel is not new and is fairly straightforward. Low-carbon steel, typically 18–22 gauge, is coated with a layer of 0.005- to 0.1-inch-thick porcelain enamel material. The steel plate can be punched and formed into various shapes, with many holes for discrete component attachment. Thick-film conductive and resistive inks can then be fired onto the porcelain to form hybrid substrates or porcelainized-steel printed-circuit boards.

port—1. A place of access to a system or circuit. Through it, energy can be selectively supplied or withdrawn. Also, various measurements can be made. 2. An opening or connecting opportunity. Device terminals that provide electrical access to a system or circuit are examples. The point at which Input or Output is in contact with the CPU can be considered a port. 3 An entrance to or an exit from a network. 4. In data communications, that part of a data processor which is dedicated to a single data channel for the purpose of receiving data from or transmitting data to one or more external remote devices. 5. The term "port," by itself, refers to all of its associated hardware. When the port is used as a "data port" or an "I/O port," it is controlled by its Data Direction Register. 6. A port is a collection of individual I/O lines. The number of lines is equal to the length of the basic microprocessor word. *See also* I/O lines/ports.

portable compiler—This device is used to enter, edit, and compile control programs written in a higher-level process-control language. It generates machine-language programs from the higher-level language. These machine-language programs are then loaded into the process controller. The compiler must be a portable device and capable of being carried to the job site. It must have the following additional facilities.

1. Keyboard with which to enter program and control information.
2. Printer or display to permit the display of several lines of program simultaneously.

portable computer systems—Users are beginning to want systems that provide checks and balances at the point of entry, and are not just electronic notepads. For this type of system, a portable capacity is required and this has resulted in the appearance of

Portable computer systems (Courtesy Computer Devices, Inc.).

versatile portable microcomputers with a range of features that are both flexible and convenient.

The efforts of one manufacturer have produced such devices as (1) a portable microcomputer with a bar code reader option that allows users to enter alphanumeric bar code data via a hand-held wand, (2) a portable microcomputer that is able to support up to four double-density minidiskettes that are each about the size of a dictionary, and (3) a portable microcomputer that has a keyboard, minicassette storage, and a 50-cps thermal printer. The efforts of other manufacturers are producing portable microcomputers that have such features as 12K bytes of program and 64K bytes of data memory, an alphanumeric keyboard and display, communication couplers, and a multicode optical scanner.

port pins—The term "port," by itself, refers to all of its associated hardware. When the port is used as a "data port" or as an "I/O port," it is controlled by its Data Direction Register and the programmer has direct access to its pins using the port's Data Register. Typically, the port pins are labeled as P_{ij} where i identifies one of the ports and j indicates the particular bit that is referenced (some systems).

port selector — The major features of the telephone dial network that are sometimes taken for granted are the contention and port selection provided by the telephone rotary. The number of terminals usually exceeds the number of computer ports and the telephone rotary allocates ports on a first-come, first-served basis, providing a busy signal when all computer ports are occupied. Where several different computers are available in one computer center or where different services are available on different ports of the same computer, different telephone numbers may be used to permit access to each class of service. However, an alternative approach to dial-up phone access is to use a port selector to control and coordinate terminal access to a computer facility. Such a device can integrate dedicated terminal connection with dial-up access, if required, providing the advantages of both without the disadvantages of either.

The port selector is installed between the computer (or computers) and the terminals. Like the telephone rotary, it provides first-come first-served contention between terminals for the available computer ports. But unlike the telephone rotary, this facility is available to all terminals, whether their connections are dial-up or dedicated. The contention facility provided by a typical port selector reduces the number of computer ports needed to support a given number of terminals without requiring dial-up access. A port selector can also provide multiple-computer access for dedicated dumb terminals, or can restrict access to certain computer ports from certain terminals. It can also operate independently of the computer to transmit special messages to terminal users to advise of system problems and scheduled restoral of service after downtime.

In the simplest applications, all terminals are in contention for all ports, but the ports may also be partitioned into "classes" to provide contention for each of several computer systems. When multiple port classes are defined to the port selector, the user enters the desired class (i.e., computer system) from his terminal keyboard, rather than dialing a different telephone number for each system.

port selector, intelligent—An intelligent port selector normally is installed as a replacement for telephone dial-up access. However, the ability to dial different telephone extensions to obtain access to different computer systems or to different application programs running on the same computer system must be reproduced in the intelligent port selector. The intelligent port selector can be used to retain the contention and port selection facilities previously provided by the telephone rotary when Single Message-Unit Rate Timing forces a change from dial-up terminal connections to private wires or leased lines. With a port selector, terminal connections can be made as cost-effectively as possible for each individual terminal, by direct-interface cable, limited-distance line driver or local data set, or by modem over dial-up or dedicated lines, without restricting the freedom of any terminal to access any computer port. In addition, the selector can maintain usage statistics, enabling the computer manager to monitor usage of each group of computer ports. The port selector thereby enables proper access management and significantly improves the manager's ability to ensure optimum service to all terminal users, while keeping port costs minimal.

In addition to the more basic applications, the intelligent port selector monitors the status of each port attached to it and maintains a table defining whether it is enabled, disabled, or busy. Disabled ports are automatically removed from the port selection process. Thus, it is an inherent capability of the intelligent port selector to provide fall-back switching by selectively enabling or disabling groups of ports. Ideally, however, port selection should be accomplished from the terminal keyboard so as to avoid the cost and space requirements of a separate port selector unit at the terminal site.

port selector (time-division switch) — The heart of some port selectors is a time-division switch — a solid-state electronic version of the electro-mechanical crossbar switch used in most conventional telephone exchanges. The time-division switch operates under the direction of a microcomputer, which controls all connections and disconnections. Once a connection is established, operation is completely transparent. The time-division switch transfers data directly from terminal to port at very high speed; the microcomputer controller is activated again only when the connection is to be broken. To the computer port, the selector may appear either as a dedicated terminal or as a modem emulating the full answering sequence of a Bell 103 modem. Each port interface on the selector has a class defined in the selector's control memory. However, this class definition can be modified at any time.

Terminals can be connected to the port selector by direct cabling or by the use of line drivers, local data sets, or modems on dial-up or leased lines. With some selectors, the terminal operator requests connection by depressing any key on his keyboard.

port sharing—Usually refers to a "port concentrator" that allows several asynchronous terminals to share one computer port with a minimum of user programming. Using a port concentrator, one computer port can communicate with up to 16 channels on a remote system by means of a simple asynchronous or synchronous protocol. Computer software to support the protocol usually must be written by the customer.

In certain applications, e.g., point-to-point systems that feed a single computer port, port sharing offers the advantage of decreased response time. In these systems, port sharing enables high-speed modems to operate, in the "carrier on" mode, which eliminates modem set-up time. Eliminating the modem set-up time greatly improves the response time for the entire system.

ports, input-output — Each processor can have a number of I/O ports. Some are associated with external system activity; others are used for information exchange with other system processors. Low-cost microcomputers are particularly adaptable to communications via their I/O ports. In practice, ports are part of the I/O section of a processor.

POS—*See* point-of-sale.

positional operand—Refers to assembler programming and an operand in a macroinstruction that assigns a value to the corresponding positional parameter declared in the prototype statement of the called macrodefinition.

positive ion—An atom which has lost one or more electrons and, thus, has an excess of protons, giving it a positive charge.

positive logic — In positive logic, the positive voltage level at the inputs is defined as a "one" and the negative voltage level is defined as a "zero." In contrast, in negative logic, the negative voltage level at the inputs is defined as a "one" while the positive voltage level is defined as a "zero."

postbyte—Some opcodes are followed by a byte that defines a register or set of registers to be used by the instruction. This is called a postbyte.

post mortem routine — 1. A diagnostic routine for locating a malfunction in a computer or an error in a coding problem. 2. A routine which, either automatically or on demand, prints information concerning the contents of the registers and storage locations at the time that a routine is stopped, in order to assist in the location of any mistake in coding. 3. Concerns a service routine useful in analyzing the cause of a failure, such as a routine that dumps out the content of a store after a failure.

post processor — Refers to a set of computer instructions that transform tool-centerline data into machine-motion commands, using the proper tape code and format required by a specific machine-control system. Instructions such as feed-rate calculations, spindle-speed calculations, and auxiliary-function commands may be included in the instructions.

power fail, automatic restart — 1. The power-fail facility provides a processor interrrupt when a power low signal is received from the primary power source. Sufficient time is then available to preserve the contents of the working registers in the memory. The auto-restart feature enables processing to resume, at the point of interruption, when power is restored. 2. Refers to a specific power-fail interrupt which provides an interrupt when a loss of primary power is detected. Typically, a minimum of one millisecond of computer operation is assured after the interrupt. Power-restart interrupt occurs when the power is applied and is up to normal operating levels, and the processor is placed in the run mode.

power-fail logic — Refers to specific logic circuits that protect a system in the event of primary power failure. Circuits automatically store current operating parameters. When power is restored, the circuits make use of this information to continue proper operation.

power fail/restart—Refers to a provision that monitors power-supply voltage to make an orderly shutdown upon power failure and an automatic restart when power is restored.

power-failure interrupt — A signal that occurs on many machines for the purpose of informing the machine that the external power is failing. Usually a power-failure interrupt will not destroy the operating status of the machine because most machines store enough power internally to go through a predetermined number of instructions.

power frequency deviations — Frequency deviations are a shifting of the basic power-line frequency of 60 hertz. Frequency deviations are generally not a problem in the United States. Apparent frequency shifts are sometimes recorded but these usually turn out to be power-phase shifts, not true frequency changes. Frequency shifts can cause random disk errors if the pack rotation speed is affected.

power-on reset—In some systems during power turn-on, it is necessary to initialize the CPU to a known state such that the proper sequence of events can occur. This initialization is accomplished by input of a "power-on" signal which is generated external to the power system. The CPU receives this signal, initializes the internal logic states, and, at the same time, generates a synchronized power-on output signal which can be used to initialize other circuits.

power problems (sags/surges)—There are five basic categories of power-line problems—short-term sags and surges, long-term fluctuations, transient impulses, complete voltage interruptions, and frequency variations. Sags and surges are changes in the amplitude of the ac sine wave. Sags or surges generally last from several cycles to several hundred cycles. These types of voltage fluctuations are usually caused by large electrical loads being turned on and off. High-voltage surges cause equipment damage. Voltage sags can cause pseudo power failures or operating system crashes, and can also cause what *appear* to be intermittent software failures.

power semiconductor devices—Power semiconductor devices distinguish themselves from small-signal semiconductor devices by their ability to handle heavier currents, higher voltages, and the dissipation of higher power levels. They have taken over the rectification, switching, and amplifying tasks formerly performed by vacuum tubes and thyratrons. Solid-state devices capable of handling one watt of power or more, at room temperature, are considered to be power devices. Included are rectifiers, transistors, and thyristors, a category that involves silicon-controlled rectifiers (SCRs) and triacs. These are discrete devices whose operation differs

Power supplies, switching (Courtesy Boschert, Inc.).

little from their small-signal counterparts. Plastic packaging is widely used for devices in the lower power-handling ratings, while metal cans are more prevalent in the higher power ratings.

power supplies, switching — A power supply (usually with a dc output) that achieves its output regulation by means of one or more active power-handling devices which are alternately placed in the "on" and "off" states. They are distinguished from linear power supplies which use power-handling devices to achieve regulation. The conduction of these devices is varied continuously over a wide range but seldom (if ever) do they reach the full "off" or full "on" condition. Switching power supplies make extensive use of semiconductors and, thus, are smaller and lighter than the other types. Switching power supplies also benefit from the many new developments in advanced semiconductor components. Long-term trends toward smaller, lighter, and more functional systems favor switchers. The trend toward rising prices for copper and steel also favors the use of switching supplies (which are based on semiconductors) rather than ferroresonant and linear supplies (which require large copper-wound steel-core transformers). Switching supplies minimize power dissipation to avoid excessive heating and power reliability. The energy efficiency rating for switchers ranges from 55% to 90% while linear supply efficiencies run from 50% down to 15% or less.

power-supply basics — All active electronic projects and equipment require a power supply. A battery supply is convenient for low-power and portable applications. For the majority of applications, however, the ac, or line-operated, power supply is more practical for equipment that requires moderate to high power and where portability is unimportant. A building-block approach starts off with the power transformer/rectifier/filter system that is basic to all line-operated supplies. This is followed by voltage and current regulation and with the error amplifier used in the power supplies found in the most sophisticated electronic equipment. Many users design their power supply to suit their needs. A basic power supply has a power transformer that steps down (or up) the input voltage from the ac line to roughly the voltage needed for the project. The low voltage at the transformer's secondary then goes through a rectifier system, where it is converted to a pulsating dc. The filter system then smooths out the pulsations to make the dc voltage at the supply's output more like the steady-state dc characteristic of batteries.

power-supply circuit — 1. A unit that supplies electrical power to another unit. It changes ac to dc and maintains a constant voltage output — within limits. 2. An electronic circuit that converts an input ac voltage into an output dc voltage.

power-supply efficiency — The ratio of output power to input power expressed as a percentage. This is generally measured under full load at nominal line voltage.

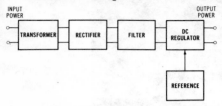

Power-supply operation
(*block diagram*).

power-supply operation — The modern regulated power supply is manufactured using many solid-state components and consists of the following basic sections: a transformer, a rectifier, a filter, a dc regulator, and a voltage-reference source. The transformer takes the ac-line voltage, normally 115/230 V ac, and transforms it into the desired voltage level for the supply output. This secondary voltage is then full-wave rectified to give a dc voltage. The rectified voltage has a very high ripple and must, therefore, be filtered to give a smooth dc output. The filter may take various forms from a single capacitor to the more elaborate inductor-capacitor combinations. Most modern power supplies, however, use a single-capacitor filter

since the dc regulator that follows the filter effectively rejects the ripple at the output.

power-supply types—Some individuals believe that the primary considerations that determine power-supply performance in commercial data-processing applications involve available technologies, not manufacturing technique. The four basic types of supplies—linear, switcher, ferroresonant, and hybrid—can be distinguished by nearly a dozen key features: cost, reliability, noise-protection (radiated and conducted), holdup time, input strappability (115 or 230 V ac), heat dissipation, size, weight, output overvoltage protection, output regulation (line and load), and auxiliary outputs (when the main-supply output is 5 V). In terms of units in use, linear supplies are far more popular than the other types. The basis of a linear power supply is a 60-Hz (50-Hz) transformer, followed by a rectifier and a series-pass regulating circuit. In a ferroresonant supply, a transformer with a resonant secondary circuit is followed by a rectifier and low-level filter.

power-switching modules—These modules typically provide isolated output voltages for driving solenoids, motor starters, and other high-power devices, and they accept inputs of from 12 to 120 volts while providing high-

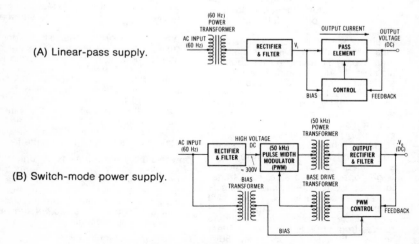

(A) Linear-pass supply.

(B) Switch-mode power supply.

Power-supply types.

voltage isolation. Both ac and dc modules are available.

power system problems — Power system problems can significantly affect computer reliability and data base integrity. Computer power and wiring problems usually appear as repeated hardware failures on one device or throughout the entire system. They can also manifest themselves as intermittent, nonrepeatable software problems (hangs, loops, unexplained halts, data base corruption, destroyed file labels, etc.).

power transformer — 1. A transformer used to raise or lower the supply voltage to the various values required by heater, bias, and other circuits. 2. In electronics, a transformer used to introduce the energizing supply into an instrument or system (distinct from a signal transformer).

power transistor—1. A transistor, usually of an alloy-function type, capable of handling high current and power. 2. One capable of being used at high power ratings; i.e., of the order of 100 watts, and generally requiring some means of cooling. 3. Power transistors are used either as amplifiers or switches. It has been estimated that one-third of all power transistors are used to switch power, in some form, in power supplies, inverters and converters, and automotive ignition systems. Amplifier applications include their use as radio-frequency sources and their application in oscillators.

power transistors, MOS — Most MOS power transistors are n-channel devices. Although p-channel devices can be built just as easily as n-channel ones by the simple interchanging of n- and p-channel regions, there is a difference in their performance when compared with n-channel MOS-FETS.

In n-channel MOSFETs, the majority carriers are electrons, while in p-channel devices, the majority carriers are holes. Since holes have about one half the mobility of electrons, p-channel "on-resistance" for a given device is about twice as high as that of an n-channel structure, unless about twice the n-channel's area is used in a p-channel structure. A larger p-channel structure means more capacitance and a higher cost

than does an equivalent "on-resistance" n-channel one.

preallocation — The technique of not beginning execution of a process until all of the resources it requires have been allocated to it.

pre-analysis—Refers to an initial review of the task that is to be accomplished by the microcomputer in order to increase the efficiency of that task.

pre-assembly time—Refers to the specific time at which an assembler processes macrodefinitions and performs conditional assembly operations.

precision—1. The quality of being sharply or exactly defined, i.e., the number of distinguishable alternatives from which a representation was selected. This is sometimes indicated by the number of significant digits the representation contains. 2. The degree of discrimination with which a quantity is stated, e.g., a three-digit numeral discriminates among 1000 possibilities. Precision is contrasted with accuracy, i.e., a quantity expressed with 10 decimal digits of precision may only have one digit of accuracy.

precision, double-length—Pertaining to twice the normal length of a unit of data or a storage device in a given computing system; e.g., a double-length register would have the capacity to store twice as much data as a single-length or normal register; a double-length word would have twice the number of characters or digits as a normal or single-length word.

precondition—A preliminary condition as defined by a type of logic instruction. Generally, one or more preconditions are programmed prior to an output instruction.

predictive control—A type of computer control which allows a digital computer to include a dynamic control loop for repetitive comparison of pertinent factors.

pre-edit programs—A checking of the application or operational program before the test run. A pre-edit run can remove such things as disobedience to established supervisory, main-memory program-segmentation rules, etc.

pre-fix—Refers to a special system with

a complex priority structure. The stopping of the scheduling routine from transferring control among programs by the use of suppression bits. A method by which the application program registers its status in a priority table by means of prefixes and suffixes for the use of the scheduling routine.

prefix notation—Refers to a technique of forming one-dimensional expressions without the need for brackets by preceding, with a string or vector of operators, an operand string or vector which may itself contain operators upon operands.

preliminary review—Refers to an examination or evaluation of matters related to processing procedures of an organization in an attempt to offer guidance in the preparation of plans, proposals, or goal-designs previous to installation of computer system equipment.

preparatory function—Refers to a command changing the mode of operation of a control, such as from positioning to contouring, or calling for a fixed cycle of the machine.

preprocessor—Refers to emulation, a program that converts data from the format of an emulated system to the format accepted by an emulator.

preset—1. Refers to an activity to set the contents of a storage location to an initial value. 2. To establish the initial control value for a loop.

presettable I/O conditions—1. Presettable I/O conditions allow the programmer to verify microinstructions that perform I/O data transfers before actual peripherals are connected to the system. 2. A single set of switches can be used to preset the I/O bus input. It might also be helpful to provide a register that can be used to trap and display data transferred out during an I/O microinstruction.

prewired external circuitry—Refers to connectors that are prewired to extend some I/O systems. Because some units use the wire-wrap technique, it is not difficult for the user to arrange the connectors in any way that is convenient.

PRF—Abbreviation for pulse repetition rate. Refers to the measure of the number of electric pulses per unit of time experienced by a point in a com-

puter; usually the maximum, normal, or standard pulse rate.

primary electrons — 1. Those incident on a surface whereby secondary electrons are released (see also primary ionization). 2. Those released from atoms by internal forces and not by external radiation as with secondary electrons.

primary emission — Electron emission arising from the irradiation (including thermal heating) or by the application of a strong electric field to a surface.

primary ionization—1. In collision theory, the ionization produced by the primary particles; in contrast to total ionization, which includes the secondary ionization produced by delta rays. 2. In counter tubes, the total ionization produced by incident radiation without gas amplification.

primary store—1. The main store built into a computer, but not necessarily the fast-access store. 2. Relatively small immediate or very rapid access store incorporated in some computers for which the main memory is a slower secondary store.

primitive — 1. A basic or fundamental unit, often referring to the lowest level of a machine instruction or lowest unit of language translation. 2. Operation provided by a kernel for use in synchronization.

printed circuit—1. A circuit in which the interconnecting wires have been replaced by conductive strips that are printed, etched, etc., onto an insulating board. It may also include similarly formed components on the baseboard. 2. Refers to resistors, capacitors, diodes, transistors, and other circuit elements which are mounted on cards and interconnected by conductor deposits. 3. Special boards (cards) that are treated with a light-sensitive emulsion and exposed. The light thus fixes the areas to be retained. The "card" is placed in an acid bath and the acid bath eats away those portions which are designed to be destroyed. The base is usually a copper-clad card (board).

printed-circuit assembly — A printed-circuit board to which separable components have been attached. 2. An assembly of one or more printed-circuit boards, which may include several components.

printed-circuit board — Also called a

card, chassis, or plate. An insulating board onto which a circuit has been printed. The printed-circuit or pc board should more accurately be termed a printed-wiring or pw board to reflect its true function. Basically, it is an insulating board complete with metallic wiring paths for point-to-point connections, but it may also include metalized connecting surfaces and heat sinks or heat radiators. The boards may be single-sided, double-sided, or multilayer—actually sandwiches of boards where high-density interconnections are required. Printed-circuit boards, either single-sided, double-sided, or multilayer, may be manufactured with plated-through holes, with a metal trace pad surrounding the hole on both sides of the printed-circuit board. The plated-through hole is desirable to provide a sufficient surface for the solder to wet and, thereby, be pulled up by capillary attraction along the lead through the hole to the top of the printed-circuit board. This provides the best possible solder connection between the printed-circuit board and the leads of the device.

printed-circuit card—A card, usually of laminate or resinous material of the insulating type, used for the mounting of an electrical circuit. Together, the base and circuit make up the card.

printed circuit, ceramic — Refers to a material usually used only for very small printed-wiring applications since large ceramic pieces tend to be brittle and are not as flexible as phenolic or glass epoxy. Ceramic material is chosen when extreme dimensional stability, at very high temperatures, is required.

printed-circuit connector — Describes two different situations:
1. Edge (or card) connectors: The connector serves as the socket for the edge of the pc board.
2. Two-piece connectors: The terminals of one of the connectors are inserted into the pc board and wave soldered (or the connector body is bolted to the board), and its contacts interconnect with the other connector, which is usually terminated to a cable.

printed-circuit defects — Defects in printed-wiring boards of all types consist either of open circuits, shorts, or potential arc-over points. Open circuits are generally caused by a break in the conductor, while short circuits are usually caused by the bridging of solder between conductors. Arc-over occurs when the gap between adjacent conductors is so small that an arc can occur at higher voltages.

printed-circuit design — The object of the design stage is to determine the extent and scope of circuitry to be assigned to one board and to work out an effective procedure for interconnecting all the active and passive circuit elements with the metallic conductors lying in one, two, or more routing patterns on or in the same board. After a precise conductor routing is established, an artwork master several times larger than the final size of the pc board is prepared. Some are prepared manually by applying black tapes to transparent stable plastic sheets or, alternatively, by cutting and stripping away an opaque coating on a stable base material such as glass. The circuit-pattern photographic masters are used to make the screen and masks for the photoresistive or printing steps which follow. The masters may also be used to prepare drill templates for drilling stacks of boards simultaneously. For more complex boards, there may be an economic advantage to the use of numerical control for drilling board holes; the control tapes may be prepared with the aid of a computer. Certain economies may be achieved by making dies and punching out the necessary holes.

printed circuit, double-sided — Refers to a printed-wiring method — where greater complexity is required; both sides of the insulating material contain the printed-wiring pattern. Again, components are mounted solely on one side. Connections between the conductors of two opposite sides can be made by insertion of a metal conductor, such as eyelets, rivets, or a simple wire. For many applications, plated-through holes are used. In this process, conductive material is deposited inside the holes connecting the two printed-wiring patterns and, subsequently, plating is applied to provide a firm connection between the material in the hole and the land pattern on each side.

printed-circuit epoxy-type coatings — These coatings are excellent mechanical and thermal protection, as well as electrical insulators, but do not lend themselves for easy repair. Removal of the epoxy coating to gain access to a solder connection is usually complicated.

printed circuit, glass epoxy laminate— Refers to the most widely used pc material. It is available in green and blue colors, is considerably more translucent than phenolic material, and has an excellent temperature stability and considerably greater strength than phenolic materials.

printed-circuit gold plating—Gold is a metal that provides excellent solderability, withstands corrosion for long periods of time, and provides low-resistance surfaces. Gold plating is particularly important when using plug-in boards.

printed circuit, multilayer — Refers to printed wiring with a technique that uses several layers of printed-wiring patterns, each mounted on a thin insulating material, and carefully aligned and molded together. This technique invariably uses plated-through holes to provide the connection of conductors that are in the internal conducting layers to those that are on the outside conducting layers of the printed-wiring pattern.

printed-circuit nickel plating — Nickel may be used as a substitute for gold or rhodium, but most often is used directly over the copper, and below the gold or rhodium plating to provide a hard base for thin layers of gold or rhodium.

printed circuit, phenolic — Refers to a usually brownish board material used in commercial applications where temperature, great stability, and reliability are not too essential.

printed circuit, polyvinyl fluoride—Refers to materials that provide excellent insulating capability and withstand extreme environmental conditions as well, but are more difficult to repair. The polyvinyl fluoride material must be scraped away before soldering.

printed-circuit rhodium plating—A material that is used because of its hardness and surface stability for extreme environmental and wear conditions. Fingers on printed-circuit boards that

mate with connectors and switch surfaces are usually rhodium-plated for long wear.

printed circuit, single-sided—Refers to a conductor pattern that is contained on one side of the board with the components mounted on the opposite side. Component leads and connections pass through suitably placed holes and are soldered onto the conductor.

printed-circuit solder plating — Refers to the mixture of tin and lead to improve solderability and prevent corrosion.

printed-circuit special lacquers—These provide good insulation but can be melted with a soldering iron to permit repair of selected portions of an assembly.

printed-circuit switch—A special rotary switch that can be connected directly to a mating printed-circuit board — without wires.

printed component — A type of printed circuit device intended primarily for electrical and/or magnetic functions other than point-to-point connections or shielding (e.g., printed inductor, resistor, capacitor, transmission line, etc.).

printed contact — The portion of a printed circuit that connects the circuit to a plug-in receptacle and performs the function of a plug pin.

printed element—An element, such as a resistor, capacitor, or transmission line, that is formed on a circuit board by deposition, etching, etc.

printed wiring — A conductive pattern formed on the surface of an insulating baseboard by plating or etching.

printed wiring, substrate—A conductive pattern printed on a substrate.

printer, electrostatic — Electrostatic printers use specially coated paper. The image is formed by the transfer of an electrostatic charge onto the dot area of the paper. The dots comprise the desired characters and the final image is formed by "developing" the electrostatic image with a toner.

printer, nonimpact — Differing significantly from drum and train printers, various nonimpact printers create a high-charged image on the paper. Then a toner is passed over the paper and all high-charged areas attract the toner. After that, a heat process affixes the toner to the paper (on many types of units).

printer port — Refers to the outlet that permits a printer connection to the terminal; for hard-copy records of data transmission.

printer, thermal — Thermal printers (which are also called electrosensitive printers) form an image on a specially treated piece of paper by heating the elements of the matrix at the time when desired points are at the proper positions on the paper. Thermal printers frequently have a five-element comb that progresses across the paper forming the vertical dimension of the character, and the horizontal dimension is formed by moving the comb across the paper. The image is formed by the physical burning of the chemicals in the paper.

priority indicators—Code signals which form a queue of data awaiting processing so that data are handled in order of importance.

priority interrupt table—Refers to a table that lists the priority sequence of handling and testing interrupts used when a computer doesn't have fully automatic interrupt handling capability.

priority modes—Refers to the organization of the flow of work through a computer. The mode depends upon the sophistication of the system and the machine, and will vary from a normal noninterrupt mode to a system in which there are several depths of interrupt.

priority ordered interrupts—Some time-sharing computers are capable of having over 200 priority ordered interrupts for external lines. This extensive interrupt capability permits a terminal to be attached to more than one interrupt line. If the attached interrupts cover a range of priorities, by selectively arming and disarming the external interrupt lines, the executive program can change the relative priority of a terminal's attention requests allowing different classes of service or response to be given to the terminal.

priority sequence — The sequence in which various entries and tasks are processed or peripheral devices are serviced. Priorities are based on analyses of codes associated with an entry or task, or the positional assign-ment of a peripheral device within a group of devices.

private automatic branch exchange (PABX) — A private automatic exchange that provides for the transmission of calls to and from the public telephone network.

private line or **private wire**—Refers to a channel or circuit furnished a subscriber for his exclusive use. Also called a leased line.

privileged instructions — 1. Often various measures for protecting against the subprogram of one problem misusing the I/O devices of another problem's subprogram are provided by restricting all I/O commands to the supervisor state. A subprogram requests I/O action by issuing a supervisor call instruction. The supervisory subprogram can then analyze this request and take the appropriate action. 2. Several instructions are privileged; that is, for those machines with the program-protect option, a privileged instruction will not be executed when the computer is in nonprivileged mode. Instead, a designator flag is set and a processor interrupt occurs.

privilege states, processor — The processor operates in one of two states of privilege: the "user" state or the "supervisor" state. The privilege state determines which operations are legal, is used by the external memory-management device to control and translate accesses, and is used to choose between the supervisor stack pointer and the user stack pointer in instruction references. The privilege state is a mechanism for providing security in a computer system. Programs should access only their own code and data areas, and ought to be restricted from accessing information which they do not need and must not modify.

probable error — The amount of error which, according to the laws of probability, is most likely to occur during a measurement.

probe—1. A resonant conductor which can be placed into a waveguide or cavity resonator to insert or withdraw electromagnetic energy. 2. A test lead which contains an active or passive network and is used with certain types of test equipment. 3. A rod placed into the slotted section of a transmission line to measure the standing-wave ratio, or to inject or extract a signal. 4. The mechanical interface to a system under test. A basic probe consists of a ribbon cable terminating in a pod with flying leads. The pod contains input buffers and, sometimes, other circuitry, which can, for example, set the logic threshold.

problem board—1. Refers to a removable panel containing an array of terminals that may be interconnected by short electrical leads according to a prescribed pattern and, hence, a specific program. The entire prewired panel may be inserted into the system for different programs. 2. A control panel or wiring panel. (*See* control panel.)

problem definition—Refers to the act of compiling logic in the form of general flowcharts and logic diagrams so as to clearly explain and present the problem to the programmer. This is done in such a way that all requirements involved in the run are presented.

problem diagnosis—Refers to the analysis that results in identifying the precise cause of a hardware, software, or system failure.

problem language — The language a computer programmer uses in stating the definition of a problem.

problem-oriented language — 1. In a computer, a source language suited to describing procedural steps in machine computing. 2. A language designed for convenience of program specification in a general problem area rather than for easy conversion to machine-instruction code. The components of such a language may bear little resemblance to machine instructions. 3. A machine-independent language where one needs only to state the problem, not the how of solution.

procedural and exception tests — Refers to the various procedure and exception tests designed to check machine control and operation before processing. They consist of test data covering all or most of the conditions that can arise during the run, as well as a control panel and/or program which will reprocess the test data and check out machine components. The control panel is inserted, or the program loaded, or both. The test data is

then read into the machine and processed. The results are compared against predetermined answers. If they are satisfactory, actual processing can begin. In some installations, these tests are made only at the beginning of each working day; in others, they are made before specific runs.

procedure-oriented language — 1. Refers to various machine-independent languages which describe how the process of solving the problem is to be carried out. Usually oriented toward a specific class of procedures, i.e., .FORTRAN is oriented toward algebraic procedures; COBOL is oriented toward commercial procedures. 2. A problem-oriented language that facilitates the expression of a procedure as an explicit algorithm; for example: FORTRAN, ALGOL, COBOL, or PL/1, etc. 3. A programming language designed for the convenient expression of procedures used in the solution of a wide class of problems.

process control—1. Automatic control of industrial processes in which continuous material or energy is produced. 2. Pertaining to systems whose purpose is to provide automation of continuous operations. This is contrasted with numerical control, which provides automation of discrete operations.

process-control analog modules—Provides conversion of both analog-to-digital and digital-to-analog signals, with amplifiers, multiplexers, sample-and-hold, and signal-conditioning modules available.

process-control block—A data structure that uniquely defines a given process.

process-control computer — A digital computer designed for a process-control system, and generally limited in instruction capacity, word length, and accuracy. Generally, only simple software is required.

process control, industrial—Industrial processing applications are as wide and varied as the degrees of control that individual processes may require. Some general process-control application areas are: precious metals production, cement production, environmental control, pilot plants, chemical processes, petroleum refining, and many others. The data acquisition and control system provides maximum flexibility in the types of process data that it can accept, and in the variety of output signals and data format that a computer may exercise.

process controller — This computer controls the process to which it is attached and executes the machine language programs to accomplish this control.

process-control loop—Control devices linked to control a phase of a process.

process-control system—1. Descriptive of systems in which computers are used for the automatic regulation of operations or processes. Typical are operations in the production of chemicals wherein the operation control is applied continuously and adjustments necessary to regulate the operation are directed by the computer in order to keep constant the value of a controlled variable. Contrasted with numerical control. 2. In a typical process-control system, the control program is stored in ROM and is executed by the CPU to sample switch closures, variable-voltage levels, or digital information from other systems or central panels. Information is stored in RAM and is manipulated by appropriate algorithms. It is then output to switch controllers in order to turn on lights or solenoid drivers, or to d/a converters and buffers to drive such things as linear positioners or variable oven heaters. When appropriate, information is output to furnish status information back to the central system through adaptive signal-conditioning interface circuits.

processing section—The portion of a computer that does the actual changing of input into output. This includes the arithmetic and logic sections.

processing, serial — Pertaining to the sequential or consecutive execution of two or more processes in a single device such as a channel or processing unit. Contrast with parallel processing.

processor—1. In hardware, a data processor. 2. In software, a computer program that performs functions, such as compiling, assembling, and translating for a specific programming language. 3. Processor modules execute basic instructions that can be functionally grouped into five categories: register operations, accumulator operations, program-counter and stack-control operations, Input/Output operations, and machine operations. 4. A unit in the programmable controller which scans all the inputs and outputs in a predetermined order. The processor monitors the status of the inputs and outputs in response to the user-programmed instructions stored in memory, and it energizes or de-energizes outputs as a result of the logical comparisons made through these instructions. 5. A processor is a digital device (usually) capable of performing arithmetic and Boolean operations on a digital representation of data. It is capable of storing and retrieving data and instructions, and is capable of conditioning the execution of its instructions based on input data and other computations. A multiplexer would not be considered a processor, but a processor could perform multiplexing.

processor, arithmetic—These are specialized number-crunching machines that are able to perform rapid high-precision arithmetic over a large dynamic range. They are very popular for speeding up the throughput of computer systems used in scientific applications. Often called array processors because of their optimization for performing repetitive calculations on an array of data, these peripheral arithmetic processors are not to be confused with machines having an internal array architecture, such as vector processors. Applications include flight simulation, radar signal analysis, X-ray tomography, image analysis, speech synthesis, and nuclear reactor monitoring.

processor, array—*See* processor, arithmetic.

processor, associative — The associative processor is an unusual type of reconfigurable array system. In a sense, its basic operating principle is the reverse of that for a serial processor. The associative processor is based on a "search memory." Unlike a RAM—which accepts the address of a memory location as input and outputs the contents of the location—the search memory accepts the contents of the memory as input and outputs flag settings to indicate the location.

processor, attached—A typical attached

processor is one that is added to the main central-processing unit, sharing its channels and memory. Often, both processors are controlled by one multiple virtual storage (MVS) operating system which automatically balances the workload for highest productivity under user-selected priorities. Large multitasked jobs may be completed rapidly if both tightly coupled processors can be applied to them. There is no need to divide data files because both processors use the same main memory and system-control program (some systems).

processor, auxiliary—An auxiliary processor is, effectively, a device controller, acting as a subsidiary to a master microcomputer on the same bus. Because of its programmability, it is more powerful and flexible than a conventional (nonprogrammable) controller would be.

processor, back-end — Back-end processors, also sometimes called database computers, consist of specialized integrated circuits that combine the disk controller and the data-base management functions. On-line archives will provide a thousand or more megabytes of storage at a price commensurate with microcomputer-based systems, thus allowing users to keep all their data permanently online. Thus, back-end processors and on-line archives are expected to cause an impact on the small disk market.

processor, bit-slice—This approach to microprocessors allows microcomputer organizations of variable word sizes, with processor units separated into 2-, 4-, or 8-bit slices on a single chip. These devices can be paralleled to yield an 8-, 12-, 16-, 24-, or 32-bit microcomputer when assembled with the other necessary "overhead" components of the system. Thus, 16-bit microprocessors constructed from these components can be assembled into microcomputers that perform in the minicomputer class.

processor-dependent interrupt — One specific example of a processor-dependent interrupt condition is the "presence bit condition." It is caused by a program being executed on a processor, that is executing an operand call, which addresses a descriptor with a presence bit of zero.

processor, distributed — According to the architecture of some distributed processors, each microprocessor can access one 450-nanosecond semiconductor cache memory holding between 16,000 and 128,000 words. (Each processor also has its own control memory.) The work is doled out with a "mailbox" concept—when one microprocessor is ready for more work, it accesses a mailbox to get its next task. The distributed nature of the architecture allows extra communications interfaces or disk control units (or additions to the data-base management system) to be made simply by plugging in another microprocessor card. All cards can be identical. For example, if one customer wants to run the system with several host computers talking to a few disks, extra communications cards are added; if another customer wants to expand the data-base management function, extra data-cards are added there also.

processor evaluation module—Understanding and using the evaluation modules is often the first step in understanding different types of microsystems. There are many different evaluation modules of which the processor module is the basic or key module. The processor module is a printed-circuit card that contains all the necessary components of a microprocessor set including: a crystal-controlled clock-generator circuit, a power-on initialization circuit, one CPU, two RAMs, and, in some systems, two I/Os. That is, it contains everything except the ROM. The contents of the ROM is the system microprogram and it is developed by the customer, and is, therefore, often unique to each product and application.

processor, floating-point — A typical floating-point processor will contain four 64-bit program-accessible accumulators, a 32-bit status register, and 56 single- and double-word instructions. It will be able to execute arithmetic instructions between floating-point accumulators and, also, between memory and any of the floating-point accumulators. When floating-point computation must be interrupted, a single instruction saves the contents of all accumulators and status registers in a hardware stack. Another instruction reverses the process. Distributed parallel logic mounted on the floating-point and the fixed-point processor boards allows a program to execute floating-point arithmetic while the CPU does other processing.

processor, front-end — A typical technique being used to handle many asynchronous lines is the small computer that serves as a line controller for the large processor. The small computer not only can serve as a line scanner and a controller, but it can handle a number of "supervisory" tasks that would normally be done by the large processor, such as error detection, character echoing (on a full-duplex line), user validity checking, etc. There are two basic design approaches to the communication front-end of a small processor: single-bit buffers and line scanning.

processor, I²L slice—A typical I²L 4-bit processor slice has 1500 gates operating at delays of 25 nanoseconds. It is designed to work with existing families of TTL LSI processor parts. A 4-bit Schottky TTL slice increases speeds into the 1- to 10-ns range.

processor input-output channel — Abbreviated PIO channel. (1) A processor input-output channel is used to communicate with low-speed character-oriented devices that are asynchronous in nature. Each item of data is transferred to or from an addressed device, via the accumulator, by executing an input-output instruction for each transfer. Input-output instructions, in addition to transferring data, are also used to test the status of a device, and to initiate input or output operations. The PIO channel is capable of transfer rates of up to 50,000 or more words-per-second. (2) A processor input-output channel enables data transfer between the accumulator and a selected input-output controller and device, as directed by the execution of a series of input-output transfer (IOT) instructions.

processor interrupt facility—The interrupt facility provides a processor interrupt when an input-output device is ready to send or receive data, or a power failure is detected. If the interrupt facility is enabled when an interrupt occurs, the processor can, for example, disable the interrupt facility, store the contents of the program

counter in location 0, and execute location 1.

processor interrupts—Processor chips can be equipped with an interrupt line which allows the enabling or disabling of interrupts. Input to the interrupt recognition logic can be generated by an external-event detection module which implements the detection of, and response to, application-defined events or power-failure conditions. Enabling and disabling interrupts can be performed under program control. Serial communication between the processor and external equipment is often furnished by an integral universal asynchronous receiver/transmitter. Through this interface, programs can be loaded from an external peripheral device such as a paper-tape loader or other system communicating directly with external data bases.

processor interrupts, internal—Internal processor interrupts are generated whenever an unimplemented instruction, memory parity error, memory write protect violation, privileged instruction violation, or power failure is detected.

processor, I/O — The I/O processor executes its own programs to initialize, maintain, and perform diagnostics on all peripherals. It completely handles all "bookkeeping" and timing functions required by the peripherals, and communicates with the main CPU only when it has valid data to be examined or processed in conjunction with the execution of the main CPU program. The I/O processor will usually have its own RAM for buffer storage functions and, in order to enhance the I/O structure's real-time throughput, a simple access to DMA control functions is maintained.

processor, microprogrammed — A microprogrammed processor is really a computer within a computer. The microprocessor can often emulate the instruction set of earlier computers, control the front panel in the halt mode, operate the automatic bootstrap, and implement the enhanced instruction set. Compatibility at the base instruction-set level is far more important than at the microprogram level. Microprograms are typically small compared to applications programs, and experience has shown that it is relatively easy to convert these small programs from one type of microcode to another type of microcode.

processor module — A typical processor module (PM) contains a single-chip MOS/LSI microprocessor along with the integrated logic and control circuitry necessary to operate as a parallel 8-bit central processing unit. Single-chip microprocessors contain various general-purpose registers, condition flip-flops, instruction control and decoding logic, and a memory stack. The microprocessor support logic consists of a clock, an input multiplexer, I/O control logic, interrupt recognition logic, and a universal asynchronous receiver/transmitter plus data, memory, and address bus gating.

Communication between internal registers and logic and other MPS modules and peripheral devices is generally conducted through an 8-bit bidirectional data port integral to the processor chip. The _internal stack often contains the program counter and other registers for nesting several levels of subroutines. This addressing capability permits accessing up to 16K or more memory locations that can be mixtures of RAM or ROM.

processor, peripheral—Peripheral processors are usually microprogrammed and include Read-only storage, Read/Write memory, and an arithmetic and logic unit. Microprogrammed functions can be executed at the peripheral subsystem level considerably reducing CPU busy time for I/O operations. *See also* perpiheral processors.

processor status word — Generally the processor status word (PSW) contains information on the current processor status. This information includes the current processor priority, the condition codes describing the arithmetic or logical results of the last instruction, and an indicator for detecting the execution of an instruction to be trapped during program debugging. The PS word format determines this. Certain instructions allow programmed manipulation of condition code bits and loading or storing (moving the PSW).

Certain memory locations have been reserved by convention for interrupt and trap handling and for peripheral device registers. Other addresses are usually reserved for trap and device-interrupt vector locations. Several of these are reserved in particular for system (processor initiated) traps.

processor vs. controller—Although interrelated, the functions of processor and controller differ greatly. Suitability of a microprocessor to perform a given control function, either separate from or in addition to the computational function, is dependent on factors such as the number of inputs and outputs involved, the time allowable to respond to inputs, the resolution required at the outputs, and the complexity of the algorithm. When there are many inputs and outputs, and the computation required is a long complex algorithm involving various pressures, temperatures, and positions, a separate controller can provide information and maintain, or change, outputs according to the previous execution of the algorithm by the processor. Even when the computational function is separated from the control functions, a high-performance controller may require a more specialized architecture than is available in any off-the-shelf microprocessor.

process scheduler — The operating-system module that determines which processes will execute and in which order.

product development system—Usually this is a complete system including a general-purpose computer system, a mass storage device, an intelligent crt console, a printer interface, and a complete system-software package. This total-system concept means that all the elements of this integrated package work together as a system. It also eliminates the risks involved in procuring assorted devices, which may work today but may not work with tomorrow's software. Enhancements to software can be easily implemented when the various system components are known, and the power of the system is better utilized when all components are defined.

productive sampling tests—Those tests normally made by either the vendor or the purchaser on a portion of a production lot for the purpose of determining the general performance level.

program — 1. A set of instructions arranged in a proper sequence for directing a digital computer in performing a desired operation or operations (e.g., the solution of a mathematical problem or the collation of a set of data). 2. To prepare a program (as contrasted with "to code"). 3. A sequence of audio signals transmitted for entertainment or information. 4. The basic computer preparation procedure. The computer is practically useless without accurate worthwhile programming. Programs are designed and written to solve problems, control processes and procedures, and are generally referred to as software. 5. A plan for the solution of a problem. A complete program includes plans for the transcription of data, coding for the computer, and plans for the absorption of the results into the system. (The list of coded instructions is called a routine.) To plan a computation or process from the asking of a question to the delivery of the results, including the integration of the operation into an existing system. Thus, programming consists of planning and coding, including numerical analysis, systems analysis, specification of printing formats, and any other functions necessary to the integration of a computer in a system.

program, assembly — Also called a translator. A process that translates a symbolic program into a machine-language program before the working program is executed. It can also integrate several sections or different programs.

program, automatic-controller — The controller enables the user to program his automatic-control sequences, usually with simple inexpensive equipment, working directly from a ladder diagram or Boolean algebra, and without any special computer language or training. It also allows him to change programs or expand his operation, right on the plant floor.

program, check—1. A system of determining the correct program and machine functioning, either by running a sample problem with similar programming and a known answer, or by using mathematical or logic checks such as comparing A times B with B times A. 2. A check system built into the program or computers that do not have automatic checking. This check system is normally concerned with programs run on computers that are not self-checking internally. *Related to* check, automatic.

program, compiling—Refers to a particular program (often called a translator) which translates from macro language into another language; i.e., from one programming language into another programming language. *See* compiler.

program, control—1. A control system which automatically holds or changes its target value on the basis of time, to follow a prescribed program for the process. 2. A sequence of instructions which prescribes the series of steps to be taken by a system, a computer, or any other device.

program-controlled I/O—In some systems, two basic instructions (one for input and one for output) are used for transferring information to and from controllers on the byte I/O bus under programmed control. These instructions permit transfers between the device controller and the A register, B register, or memory. Up to eight or more types of input and eight or more types of output instructions can be defined for a particular controller. Generally, these include function output, data output, status input, and data input, and are determined by a device order in the control byte of the I/O instruction.

program-control transfer—Refers to the transfer of operational control among two or more independent programs being operated concurrently. This function makes possible the operation of compute-limited programs concurrently with input/output-limited programs. Operational control is transferred to a compute-limited program whenever the I/O-limited programs must wait, pending completion of requested I/O functions. This function of the executive program allows an installation to make maximum use of its total computer facility.

program control unit—Refers to a specific unit in a central processor that controls the execution of the computer instructions and their sequence of operations.

program conversion—Refers to installations that have been in operation for several years and have gone through several conversion processes. Conversion is the so-called "controlled transition" from an old system to a new one. It involves careful planning for the various steps that have to be taken, and equally careful supervision of their execution.

program, correction—Most users can be assured that the first time they assemble or compile a program, it will contain errors in logic and instruction syntax. If a user's program is written in a compiler language, the source and object programs will be too unlike for them to follow and understand the object program execution steps. Nearly all the program corrections must be made by generating results, and then checking through logic to determine why the results are wrong.

program counter — Abbreviated PC. 1. A program counter contains the address of the next instruction byte to be fetched from memory and is automatically incremented after each fetch cycle. 2. Refers to one of the registers in the CPU that holds addresses necessary to step the machine through the various programs. During interrupts, the program counter saves the address of the instruction. Branching also requires loading of the return address in the program counter.

program counter operation—A program counter (PC) controls the program sequence. It contains the address of the memory location from which the next instruction is fetched. During the instruction fetch, contents of the program counter are transferred to the memory address register. The program counter is normally incremented by one after an instruction fetch; however, the contents of the program counter may be modified by branch instruction. The memory-address register (MAR) contains the address of the memory location that is currently selected for reading or writing. The instruction register (IR) contains the instruction that is currently being executed by the CPU. A temporary register (TEMP) latches the result of the arithmetic-logic unit before it is sent to the destination register to avoid race conditions. A link is used as a carry flip-flop for two's complement arithmetic; a carry out of the accumulator complements the link. The link may be rotated as part of the accumulator and can be cleared, set, complemented, and tested under the program control. The multiplier-quotient register (MQ) is a program-accessible register for temporary data storage. MAR, IR, and TEMP are also used as internal registers for microprogram control. (Some systems.)

program, cross-assembler—Microcomputers generally do not have enough memory or are not equipped with the necessary peripheral devices to support many utility programs. In such a situation, another computer is used to perform the assembly or compilation, and the programs used are called cross-assemblers or cross-compilers. For example, a microcomputer program might be cross-assembled on a time-sharing system. Punched-tape or disk output from the time-sharing terminal would then be loaded into the microcomputer for testing.

program design, microprocessor—Program design, the single most important part of the software development, bridges the gap between the hardware and software (or firmware, when the program is put into ROMs). Involved here are the over-all system operation, the hardware design, and the kind of programs to be written. The program design should define every step of the system operation from the point-of-view of the microprocessor. It should also establish the necessary "handshaking" between the peripherals and the microprocessor, and between the peripherals and the external circuitry.

program development system—For program development, some suppliers provide a microprogramming development package, whereby users can make, simulate, and debug programs on a system that has a crt display, keyboard, dual or single floppy-disk drives and, optionally, a hard-copy printer.

program, diagnostic trace — Refers to a particular type of diagnostic program used for the performance of checks on other programs or for demonstrating such operations. The output of a trace program may include instructions of the program that is being checked and the intermediate results of those instructions arranged in the order in which the instructions are executed.

program editor—These are often string editing programs that instruct the CPU to search out and alter certain blocks of data (strings) in the program being developed. The editor is very useful when users desire to change an instruction that has been repeated throughout a program.

program error—A mistake made in the program code by the programmer, operator, or a machine-language compiler or assembler.

program, executive—Refers to various programs that control loading and relocation of routines and which, in some cases, make use of instructions that are unknown to the general programmer. Effectively, an executive routine is part of the machine itself (synonymous with supervising system and supervisory program). 2. A set of coded instructions designed to process and control other sets of coded instructions. 3. A set of coded instructions used in recognizing automatic coding. 4. A master set of coded instructions.

program generation system (PGS)—Allows the user to output selected areas of memory in object-program format and, also, load programs into memory. It will load object programs produced by itself and those produced by the memory load builder or assembler.

program generator—Generally, a large detailed program which permits a computer to write other programs automatically. Generators are usually of two types.
1. The character-controlled generator, which operates like a compiler in that it takes entries from a library tape, but is unlike a simple compiler in that it examines control characters associated with each entry, and alters instructions found in the library according to the directions contained in the control characters.
2. The pure generator is a program that writes another program. When associated with an assembler, a pure generator is usually a section of program that is called into storage by the assembler from a library and which, then, writes one or more entries in another program. Most assemblers are also compilers and generators. In this case, the entire system is usually referred to as an assembly system. (Related to problem-oriented language.)

program instruction — Refers to designed sets of characters, together with one or more addresses (or no address), that define an operation and which, as a unit, causes the computer to operate accordingly on the indicated quantities; a machine instruction to specific functions. Types: actual, arithmetic, blank, branch, control, direct, effective, execution, executive, extract, halt, hold, jump, machine, macro, programmed, and pseudo.

program, interactive — An interactive system-generation program, once loaded from the appropriate media (e.g., magnetic disk or tape), immediately initiates a dialogue with the operator to determine the configuration parameters. The required system modules and support processors are selected from the system-generation media, based upon these configuration parameters.

program, internally stored—Refers to a set or sequence of instructions stored in memory, i.e., a program or routine that is stored within the computer (internal memory) as contrasted to those programs which might be stored externally on paper or magnetic tapes, or on disks, etc.

program interrupt transfers — A program interrupt system may be used to initiate programmed data transfers in such a way that the time spent waiting for device status is greatly reduced or eliminated altogether. It also provides a means of performing concurrent programmed data transfers between the CPU and the peripheral devices. This is accomplished by isolating the I/O handling routines from the main-line program and using the interrupt system to ensure that these routines are entered only when an I/O device status is set, indicating that the device is actually ready to perform the next data transfer, or that it requires some sort of intervention from the running program.

program library—1. Refers to a collection of available computer programs and routines. 2. Same as a partitioned data set (in some systems).

program library, microcomputer — A typical library includes: text editor, assembler, and loader, a subroutine for driving, a RAM test program, a program to control the tape motion of tape drives, logic subroutines AND,

XOR, IOR, LOGIC, a decimal addition routine, exerciser programs, teletypewriter keyboard input routines, PROM programming software packages, an a/d converter using DAC, a PROM duplication and verification program, a BCD-to-binary conversion routine, and others.

programmable array logic — Abbreviated PAL. PALs borrow the proven fusible-link technology from bipolar PROMs so that users can "write-in-silicon" the small digital functions used for applications like computer-control stores, character generators, and data-storage tables. PALs, which are the equivalent for four or five IC packages, fit in complexity between small- and medium-scale logic parts and the very complex gate arrays. They help solve three problems: decreasing board space (because of more and more concern about board density), the reduction of inventory (because less logic parts will need to be stocked) and the ability to make "quickie" design changes (by limiting design changes to fuse changes in the PALs, thus avoiding board changes). Programmable-array logic chips, more than any other component, affect the 32-bit design, performance, and personality of many 16-bit processors. A PAL is a programmable AND array providing inputs to a fixed OR array, and is often packaged in 20-pin DIPs.

programmable calculators — Programmable calculators are available at prices ranging from $79 to $1000 and with simple instruction execution times that range from about 10 μsec to 300 μsec. A high-level man-machine interface is one of the most attractive features of these popular forms of programmable logic. In its simplest form, programmable calculator programming is accomplished by keystrokes stored to form a sequence of operations. This sequence can then be repeated on demand by the user. Higher-level programmable calculators include simple storage devices to allow easy program change and storage. As one approaches the very high end of the programmable calculator spectrum, the calculators begin to look like microcomputers. Programmable calculators in this class are elements in data-communications nets, perform remote job-entry (RJE),

functions as instrumentation system controllers, and have disk, cartridge and line-printer peripherals. BASIC is run interpretively on several calculators in this class with the programming facilitated by special keys and alphanumeric keyboards. However, even these high-level calculators maintain their dual nature so that simple problems can be quickly solved by several keystrokes while more difficult problems demand a greater programming effort. Many scientific- and engineering-oriented programmable calculators use algebraic langauge and observe the hierarchy of mathematics. These instruments feature programmable ROM memories, expandable program memory, an external magnetic-storage capacity, and are available with printer, plotter, and display. Problems are entered just as users would write their equations. Numbers can be entered from the keyboard in scientific notation, floating point, or in mixed format, and will be displayed in the same form.

programmable clock—A programmable clock offers several methods for accurately measuring and counting time intervals or events. It can be used to synchronize the central processor to external events, count external events, measure intervals of time between events, or provide interrupts at programmable intervals. It can be used to start the a/d converter at predetermined intervals or from an external logic input. In some systems, the clock operates in one of two program modes: single interval or repeated interval.

programmable communications interface—Abbreviated PCI. The PCI accepts programmed instructions from the microprocessor and supports many serial data-communication disciplines, both synchronous and asynchronous, and in the full or half-duplex mode. The PCI serializes parallel data characters received from the microprocessor for transmission. Simultaneously, it can receive serial data and convert it into parallel data characters for input to the microcomputer. A typical programmable communications interface is a universal synchronous/asynchronous data-communications controller chip designed for microcomputer systems. It interfaces directly to the microprocessor and may be used in a polled or interrupt-driven environment.

programmable communications interface (USART)—The typical universal synchronous/asynchronous receiver/transmitter (USART) chip is designed for data communications. It is used as a peripheral device and is programmed by the central processing unit to operate with virtually any serial data-transmission technique. One type USART accepts data characters from the CPU in a parallel format and converts them into a continuous serial data stream for transmission. It can simultaneously receive serial data streams and convert them into parallel data characters for the CPU. A signal is transmitted to the CPU when the unit can accept a new character for transmission or when it has received a character for the CPU. Also, the CPU can read the complete status of the unit at any time, including data-transmission errors and control signals. Most USARTs have TTL-compatible inputs and outputs, operate from a single 5-volt power supply, and have a single TTL clock.

programmable concentrators—A concentrator is a device used in data communications to multiplex numerous low-speed communications lines onto a single high-speed communications line. Since many concentrators have become programmable, they can perform automatic speed recognition to accommodate different-speed devices automatically, whereas, multiplexers are limited to a single speed or a predetermined set of speeds. Concentration may be a function of a general-purpose minicomputer that is also acting as one of the switching computers in a network.

programmable controller—1. Abbreviated PC. A solid-state control system that has a user programmable memory for storage of instructions to implement specific functions such as: I/O control logic, timing, counting, arithmetic, and data manipulation. A PC consists of a central processor, an input/output interface, memory, and a programming device which typically uses relay-equivalent symbols. A programmable counter is purposely designed as an industrial control system that can perform functions equivalent to a relay panel or a wired solid-state logic-control system. 2. Quite often,

programmable controllers replace solid-state logic modules. They are used in industrial control as direct replacements for electromechanical control relays. PCs are designed to provide the user with the benefit of solid-state reliability while avoiding its pitfalls. Programmable controllers are provided with shielding or noise-immune logic, i.e., designed-in isolation from high-voltage inputs and outputs. In addition, the control logic, rather than being point-to-point wired as with solid-state modules, is programmable. PCs can be programmed in a familiar manner, often directly from a ladder diagram. Therefore, minimal training is required to implement a PC and, thus, more effort can be spent on designing the control logic rather than designing a control panel.

programmable controller capability — Solid-state controllers are designed to replace relay-logic control and to automate systems. Low-cost and compact, many provide a programmable automatic control system that exceeds the performance of any conventional hard-wired relay control panel in controlling, monitoring, and protecting industrial machines, processes, and production lines. The controller permits revision and reprogramming of the system without disturbing equipment or control devices or cables, without rewiring the control panel, and without losing the program security inherent in hard-wired systems. The simple modular construction of many controllers permits the system designer to choose both the size and characteristics needed for his control system. By using standard modules, he can tailor the controller to handle as few as 16 inputs and 8 outputs, and as many as 512 inputs and 256 outputs—with or without timing and counting. He can also perform arithmetic and shift-register functions.

For almost any working environment, programmable controllers now offer the same advanced technology as general-purpose computers: semiconductor memory, microprocessor-based CPUs, and special interfaces for master/slave distributed-control applications. PCs should be considered as a new breed of computer-based hardware that is designed specifically for the hot, damp, dirty, and otherwise unsavory working conditions often found in industry. The emphasis is on replacing electromechanical control relays with something smaller, cheaper, and more reliable without introducing any new complications.

programmable controller characteristics — Programmable controllers are systems that use a primitive language (generally a scheme of ladder-diagram symbols or English-like logic statements), that can be translated to an intermediate code by a portable programming device. The controller itself contains a small control program that reads and interprets this intermediate code. Generally, programmable controllers sacrifice virtually all of their analog, communications, and data-handling capabilities in exchange for their programming simplicity. Some of these systems also allow machine-language subroutines. Two substantial advantages of these controllers are their ease of programming and the portability of the programming equipment.

programmable controller input — The standard programmable controller will accept inputs from limit switches, push buttons, pressure switches, proximity switches, and thermostats. It can deliver outputs to solenoid valves, motor starters, clutches, brakes, and indicator lights. Typically, the PC interfaces with the outside world at 110 V ac, 60 Hz, while operating internally at a 5- or 15-V logic level.

programmable interval timer—This allows the user to accomplish accurate timing functions without employing timed program loops. Typical applications of the device are real-time clock interrupt generation, event counting, delay generation, and delay measurement. A number of recent microprocessors have interval timers built in.

programmable logic — Programmable logic can be used to solve problems ranging from extremely simple combinations of elementary logic to controlling the financial system and production flow of an entire corporation. The tools to support development of these systems range from simple Karnaugh maps to extremely complex operating systems and high-level languages. In surveying this spectrum of devices and tools, one encounters a myriad of tradeoffs which confuse the path to the best price performance solution for the problem at hand. This is further compounded by the speed with which new devices and tools are developed and the dynamic nature of the roles and characteristics of existing devices.

programmable logic array — Abbreviated PLA. 1. PLAs provide the sum of partial-product outputs for a given set of inputs. This is accomplished by mask programming the interconnections in the input array of AND gates and the connection of the outputs of these AND gates to the inputs of an output array of OR gates. 2. A general-purpose logic circuit (an integrated circuit) that contains an array of logic gates that can be connected (programmed) to perform various functions. 3. A PLA is an orderly arrangement of logical AND and logical OR functions. In application, they behave very much like a glorified ROM, but a PLA is primarily a combination logic device. A programmable logic array is an alternative to a ROM which uses a standard logic network programmed to perform a specific function. PLAs are implemented in either MOS or bipolar circuits.

programmable logic devices—*See* programmable logic spectrum.

programmable logic spectrum — The programmable logic spectrum breaks down into two distinct categories—programmable logic devices and programmable logic systems. Each of these categories can be further broken down and ordered by the flexibility and capability of its individual elements. Programmable logic devices can be defined as relatively simple entities which, of themselves, do not comprise an entire computing system. Included in this category are random logic, FPLAs, PLAs, ROMs, EAROMs, RAMs, CAMs, and microprocessors. Programmable logic systems, on the other hand, are self-contained ASMs (Algorithmic State Machines) that include all of the elements of computer-control, arithmetic and logic functions, memory, I/O, and the required software to make them implement the desired functions. Included in this category are microcomputers, programmable calculators, minicomputers, and large-scale computers. Obviously this spectrum is wide, overlapping, and replete with jargon that blurs distinctions between devices, systems, and categories.

programmable logic systems—See programmable logic spectrum.

programmable logic types—Logic has two significant forms—combinatorial logic and sequential logic. Combinatorial logic circuits produce outputs dependent only on input states and delays encountered in the logic path. Sequential logic, on the other hand, produces an output that is dependent on input states, delays, the presence of a discrete timing interval, and the previous state of the logic array.

programmable memory — Refers to a type of memory whose locations are addressable by the computer's program counter, i.e., a program within this memory may directly control the operation of the arithmetic and control unit.

programmable point-of-sale terminal—Refers to various terminals that contain both a read-only microprogram memory and a semiconductor memory. The terminals can operate either on-line over a communication link with a central computer or can store transaction data on a magnetic tape which can then be polled automatically by the computer.

programmed check — 1. A means of checking for the correctness of a computer program and machine functioning, either by running a similarly programmed sample problem with a known answer (including mathematical or logical checks) or by building a checking system into the actual program being run. 2. A check of machine functions performed by the machine in response to an instruction included in a program.

programmed input-output—For greater flexibility, programmed I/O provides transfers between the external interface and some specific registers. It is especially effective in applications where data must be examined immediately upon input (such as message handling, keyboard response, etc.) or where data is the result of a computation which must be output immediately.

programmed input/output channel device—Refers to the program control of information transfer between the central processor and an external device which provides the fastest method of operating on data received from peripheral equipment. The programmed input/output channel allows an input directly to the accumulator where the data can be acted on immediately, thus eliminating the need for a memory reference by either the channel or the program. Likewise, output data may be sent directly from the accumulator to an external device.

programmed input/output instructions—Programmed I/O instructions can be combined with sense-and-skip instructions to produce a single instruction that performs a test and transfers only if the test result is satisfactory. For example, in some systems, the two functions "sense for ready" and "input" can be combined in one "read" instruction. And, these instructions are interruptible.

programmed learning—Refers to an instructional methodology based upon alternating expository material with questions coupled to branching logic for remedial purposes. May be implemented in book form (programmed text) or in computers (tutorial computer-assisted instruction, CAI).

programmed logic—Refers to the internal logic design that is alterable in accordance with a precompleted program that controls the various electronic interconnections of the gating elements, i.e., the instruction repertoire can be electronically changed, or the machine capability can be matched to the problem requirement.

programmed logic array — See programmable logic array.

programmer check — A check procedure designed by the programmer and implemented specifically as a part of his program, as contrasted with an automatic or built-in check that is built into the computer hardware.

programmer control panel — A programmer's control panel is generally supplied along with the microcomputer to provide access to the CPU registers and the memory. It generally includes an array of data switches, data and address indicators, and function switches. Using the programmer's panel, the operator may address, load, and examine memory and CPU registers, and control the operation of the microcomputer.

programmer-defined macros — Refers to specific segments of coding, which are used frequently throughout a program, that can be defined at the beginning and used and referenced by a mnemonic code with parameters. This increases coding efficiency and readability of the program.

programmer, EEROM—A unit that provides a means of programming a single electrically erasable ROM (EEROM), or an EEROM module, from paper tape or from an integral hex keyboard and display. EEROMs are electrically erasable and, therefore, need not be removed from the module or socket to be erased and reprogrammed. Included is a RAM buffer which permits editing of any EEROM. The equipment may also be used as a ROM emulator.

programmer's console diagnostic—Refers to a routine that tests most of the console logic in an automatic loopback test. It tests lights and switches with operator intervention.

programmer tools (microprocessor) — Generally, a programmer's tools, software and hardware, are designed for generating the system's programs. This programmer support includes assemblers, simulators, editors, and debug programs. Some of these programs are available on commercial time-sharing devices, while others run on the microprocessor system under design. For a very small system with minimal software requirements, a time-share assembler and simulator can be useful. If the software grows much larger than 200 lines of code (or greater than 1K bytes), however, the processing and connect time for time-sharing grows very expensive. However, these software systems, on time-share, can be valuable in the early stages of any project for programmers who must learn the specifics of the microprocessor and prepare for stand-alone software aids.

program, micro—1. Refers to a program of analytic instructions which the programmer intends to construct from the basic subcommands of a digital computer. 2. A sequence of pseudo-commands which will be translated by hardware into machine subcom-

mands. 3. A means of building various analytic instructions as needed from the subcommand structure of a microcomputer. 4. A plan for obtaining maximum utilization of the abilities of a digital computer by efficient use of the subcommands of the machine.

programming—1. Definition of a computer problem resulting in a flowchart diagram. 2. Preparing a list of instructions for a microcomputer to use in the solution of a problem. 3. Selecting various circuit patterns by interconnecting or "jumping" the appropriate contacts on one side of a connector plug.

programming, background—Refers to a type of programming of no specific urgency, as regards to time, but which may be preempted by a program of greater urgency and priority. Contrast with foreground programming.

programming control panel—Refers to a type of panel, made up of indicator lights and switches, by which a programmer can enter or change routines in the computer.

programming languages — A universal programming language that satisfies everyone's needs is still not available. COBOL is used for large business systems, RPG for small business systems, FORTRAN, Ada, and C for scientific users, BASIC for instructional time-sharing, PL/1 for the programmer who has everything (including a large computer memory), and there are a host of other languages. Also, once users have written a source program in a higher-level language, a special program called a Compiler is necessary to convert the program to a sequence of machine instructions which become the binary object program. The compiler breaks out statements using format identifiers and delimiters, and builds up executable binary-code sequences from standard modules. Thus, a compiler gives the programmer an option in his choice of a programming language. The compiler takes care of much of the programmer's decision-making task, such as: choosing register assignments, assigning memory areas to programs and subroutines, and linking labels in one program with addresses in another program. If users were to program in a compiler language, the compiler will, for all practical purposes, become the computer; users could program for years and never know or care how many registers the computer has, or what the instruction set is; they need not be aware that the compiler has a host computer. But, if users want to make full use of all of the ranges, flexibilities, and capabilities of a computer, they will program in assembly language.

programming languages (types of) — The major kinds of programming languages are: (1) Assembly, or symbolic, machine languages — a one-to-one equivalence with computer instructions, but with symbols and mnemonics as an aid to programming. (2) Macroassembly languages, which are the same as assembly, or symbolic, machine languages, but which permit macroinstructions to be used for coding convenience. (3) Problem-oriented languages for expressing problems. (4) Procedure-oriented languages for expressing methods in the same way as that expressed by algorithmic languages. Procedure-oriented languages may be further divided into: (A) Algebraic languages (numerical computation), (B) String-manipulating languages (text manipulation), (C) Simulation languages, and (D) Multipurpose languages (such as PL/1).

programming module—Refers to the input to, or output from, a single execution of an assembler, compiler, or linkage editor; a source or program module. Hence, a program unit that is discrete and identifiable with respect to compiling, combining with other units, and loading.

programming of peripherals—In some systems, two distinct functions are relegated to the software: setting the data direction and control register patterns at the time of system initialization and the handling of interrupts. Setting the data direction and control register patterns establishes the operating characteristics of the I/O device. Handling the interrupts in a system is often a problem of software polling. A polling and corresponding program are required.

Such a polling approach is usually the lowest cost alternative for identifying interrupts, but may in some instances be too slow. For such applications, hardware may be added to the system to achieve priority encoding of the various interrupt requests. The encoded value of the interrupt request can then be used as a system address to transfer control to the appropriate response routine. This is referred to as "interrupt vectoring."

programming, structured — See structured programming.

programming word length — Word length is a determining requirement for analog resolution, computational accuracy, character length, and width of parallel digital inputs or outputs. Microprocessors are generally structured for fixed word lengths or for modular expansion by a parallel combination of building block chips. Some manufacturers offer 2-bit and 4-bit "slices" of a central processing unit (CPU). In some microprocessors, the word lengths for addresses exceed those for instructions. A large address word eliminates the need to manipulate smaller—4- and 8-bit—data registers to obtain 12- to 16-bit addresses. Higher-speed parallel, rather than time-multiplexed serial, addressing is a resulting benefit. In general, longer word lengths for either addresses or instructions provide higher system throughput and more powerful memory addressing, while shorter word lengths require somewhat less hardware and smaller memories.

program module — A set of programming instructions that is treated as a unit by an assembler, compiler, loader, or translator.

program parameter—1. In a subroutine of a computing system, an adjustable parameter that can be given different values on the several occasions when the subroutine is used. 2. Refers to a parameter incorporated into a subroutine during computation. A program parameter frequently comprises a word stored relative to either the subroutine or the entry point and dealt with by the subroutine during each reference. It may be altered by the routine and/or it may vary from one point of entry to another. Related to parameter.

program, partial — A specific program that is incomplete by itself and, generally, a specification of a process to be performed on data. It may be used at more than one point in any particular program, or it might be made available for inclusion in other programs, i.e., a subroutine. It is often called a subprogram, an incomplete program, etc.

program reference table (PRT)—Refers to an area in memory for the storage of operands, references to arrays, references to segments of a program, and references to files. Permits programs to be independent of the actual memory locations occupied by data and parts of the program.

program register—Also called program counter, or control register. The computer control-unit register into which is stored the program instruction being executed, hence controlling the computer operation during the cycles required to execute that instruction.

program requestor—On some systems, the program requestor, which controls execution of all background programs, is one of the major interfaces between the system and the process engineer. It automatically sets up sequences for tests, execution, and language processing that is required for developing and running supervisory programs. It manages the time-sharing of all background activity on the basis of priorities and job statements.

program run—Refers to the actual processing of or by a computer program.

program scheduler—A facility that allocates use of the central processing unit among programs in storage, based on priority.

program segmentation — Various control programs consist of one or more program segments. Program segments are the logically discrete units, such as the main program and the subprograms, which comprise a user's complete program. Program segments consist of sequences of program statements. Any number of program segments are allowed in a user program. The first program segment must be the main program. The main program names the overall program and is where execution begins. All other segments are subprograms; each subprogram must be named. Control and data can be passed in both directions between segments. No segment may call itself, or one of its callers, or the main program. Program segments take the following forms:

1. Main program form: Program Statement, Declaration Statement(s), Executable Statement(s), END Statement.
2. The subprogram form includes: Procedure Statement, Declaration Statements, Executable Statement(s), END Statement.

The Declaration Statements define variables and constants. They must precede the Executable Statements in a program. The Executable Statements are those which result in the generation of one or more executable machine instructions.

program, segmented — Refers to one written in separate segments or parts. Only one, or some, of the segments may fit into memory at any one time, and the main portion of the program, remaining in memory, will call for other segments from backing storage when needed, with each new segment being utilized to overlay the preceding segments.

program, sensitive-error — In a computer, this refers to an error arising from the unforeseen behavior of some circuits, discovered when a comparatively unusual combination of program steps occurs.

program, sensitive-fault — Refers to a fault that appears in response to some particular sequence of program steps.

program, service—Refers to the various classes of standard routines that assist in the use of a computing system and in the successful execution of problem programs, without contributing directly to control of the system or production of results.

programs, micro/macro — A very detailed level of control is provided at the microinstruction level. These microinstructions may be used to obtain a macro-, or machine-language, instruction set, which is then used to write control programs for the microprocessor. New machine-language instructions may be defined by coding new microroutines. In this way, an instruction set can be tailored to an application. Control programs can often be written in microcode. This provides increased execution speed and more detailed control at the expense of more difficult programming. Microprocessors that are not microprogrammable contain fixed general-purpose instruction sets, which are often adequate for most applications.

program, stand-alone—Refers to various programs that operate independently of system control. Generally, it is either self-loading or loaded by another stand-alone program.

program statements (assembler)—The statement is the basic unit used to construct assembly-language programs. Each statement begins in character position 1 of a source line and is terminated by a carriage return, or a semicolon (;). On some systems, use of the semicolon enables multiple statements to be coded on the same physical source line. If a statement extends past character position 72, for example, the assembler ignores all succeeding characters until a carriage return is encountered. The text of a statement may be preceded by one or more blank positions. The first non-blank position may then contain any one of the special characters.

program status word (PSW)—A computer word containing information used in interrupt processing and, also, for other purposes. *See* PSW.

program step—Refers to a phase of one instruction of command in a sequence of instructions. Thus, a single operation.

program stop instruction — A stop instruction built into the program that will automatically stop the machine under certain conditions, or upon reaching the end of the processing, or upon completing the solution of a problem.

program storage—Refers to a portion of the internal storage reserved for the storage of programs, routines, and subroutines. In many systems, protection devices are used to prevent inadvertent alteration of the contents of the program storage.

program storage unit chip circuits (PSU) — PSU chips serve principally for storage of programmed instructions and nonvolatile data constants used during program execution. The PSU can interface directly with the CPU without use of buffer circuits. PSU chips may also contain a program counter, stack register, local interrupt control, and a timer. Medium complexity systems can be designed

by adding additional PSU chips directly to the basic CPU chips and the PSU set.

program storage, word determination —A microcomputer program may be defined as a sequence of individual instructions which, when executed by the microcomputer, cause, or effect, a desired solution to a set of operations. Instruction and data words can be mixed and stored in any way. However, on examining the contents of a word in memory, there is no way of telling whether the word's pattern represents data or an instruction. The logic of a computer program has the sole responsibility for determining whether the contents of a memory word are data or an instruction.

programs, user—A group of specific programs, subprograms, or subroutines that have been written by the user, as contrasted to manufacturer-supplied programs.

program tape—Refers to a specific tape which contains the sequence of instructions required for solving a problem and which is read into a computer prior to running a program.

program test — Refers to a checking system used before running any problem, in which a sample problem of the same type, with a known answer, is run.

program testing time—1. Refers to the machine time expended for program testing, debugging, and volume and compatibility testing. 2. Refers to the time that is used for the testing of the machine or system, to ensure that no faults exist or no malfunctions are present, by using special diagnostic routines either for circuit testing or to discern status of conditions or components. Such time could be included in fault time after the repair of the fault and is usually included in scheduled maintenance time.

program, TRACE — This type program instructs the CPU to display the contents of any combination of registers or memory throughout the execution of the program being developed. Unlike many debug routines which instruct the computer to halt at certain selected breakpoints, TRACE programs allow users to command the computer to print the contents of any selection of registers in memory and, then, resume program execution—all automatically.

projection aligner—Also called reduction projection, wafer stepper, and direct-step-on-wafer machine. These items refer to the alignment of a semiconductor chip with a mask pattern and the reduction of the size of that mask pattern. In use, an ultraviolet (UV) source is shone through the blown-up portion of an IC wafer pattern, commonly known as a reticle. The reticle's pattern is projected down through a reduction lens onto the surface of a resist-covered wafer. After exposure, the projection table is mechanically stepped to a new area for another exposure.

PROM — 1. A programmable read-only memory is generally any type that is not recorded during its fabrication but which requires a physical operation to program it. Some PROMs can be erased and reprogrammed through special physical processes. Information stored in the PROM can be altered electrically or through a combination of ultraviolet light erasing and electrical writing, but not at normal operational speeds and voltages. 2. A semiconductor diode array that is programmed by fusing or burning out diode junctions.

PROM copying — "Clean," or unprogrammed, PROMS may be programmed from previously written (programmed) PROMS by using a special programmer. Using the special programmer, the "written" PROM is placed in a MASTER socket and the "clean" PROM in a COPY socket. The RESET button is depressed; then, the START button. The special programmer automatically copies data, advances address, and repeats the operation until the maximum address is reached. A START light on the programmer goes out when the programmer stops.

PROM programmer control unit — A typical control unit is a low cost, portable, and highly versatile solution to programming requirements for MOS and bipolar PROMs. Conversational interaction with the operator makes it simple to use in engineering, quality assurance, or in the field. Some contain a microprocessor system that gives the capability to handle a wide variety of options which interface with tty paper-tape readers and punchers, minicomputers, and a host of other equipment. These interfaces are available as standard options to the systems. Various personality modules may be plugged into the control unit to program most PROMs now being manufactured. In many cases, a single module enables the user to program several different types of PROMs. Some units are portable and are packaged in a high-impact carrying case, but they can also be bench mounted.

PROM programmer personality cards —These generally refer to universal programmers. When some users buy a programmer, they often want to program several or all of the more than 200 PROMs currently available. Luckily, plug-in personality card sets are available for each PROM type. This eliminates the need to buy additional programmers to accommodate different PROMs and it gives users maximum design flexibility in terms of device costs and capability.

PROM programmer system—Generally a PROM programmer system consists of a PROM programmer containing a microprocessor, a high-speed paper-tape reader and interface, and a visual display terminal. The binary data are read in through the high-speed paper-tape reader and stored in one of four or more RAM banks, after which the PROM contents are compared with the data in the appropriate bank to verify that the data were correctly loaded. Data transferred to the PROM are simultaneously displayed in octal format on the display screen. A letter code is also displayed beside each data byte which indicates the number of attempts necessary to successfully load that data byte. In the event of a failure to load the data, the bad location is flagged and the erroneous data are displayed. In defining a program, it is frequently necessary to make single-location changes to a PROM. The programmer system allows the operator to copy the PROM contents into one of the RAM banks and to edit the data in the RAM bank as necessary. The edit is initiated by entering the edit function request, followed by the bank number and the starting address, in octal code. The system responds with the contents of the addressed location and positions the cursor under the first digit. After the operator alters the data at one location, the system responds with the data at the next sequential location, which may be altered in turn. If any changes involve changing bits from low to high, the PROM may be immediately reprogrammed. Otherwise, the PROM must first be erased and then totally reprogrammed with the edited data in the bank.

PROM programmer, universal — This refers to programming instruments that are capable of programming all available PROM types.

PROM programming—To store microprograms, the PROM has to be programmed. For this, machine-language programming is the basic method of programming. The machine-language user is expected to have a sound understanding of the microcomputer organization and know the significance of the instruction set. Machine language is the most efficient method to use on the PROM chip. It is also the easiest method to write programs that have stringent timing requirements. There are two general ways of programming a PROM; one is to satisfy the control requirements for a particular address, apply some sort of pulsed voltage to the appropriate connection, and then proceed to the next location. The other is to put the information on a mark/sense card or paper tape.

To program a device, keyboard data are entered into a copy PROM. A hexadecimal character defines each four bits at each address location in the PROM. Both address and data are displayed for verification prior to actual programming. The unit automatically reads the PROM to verify correct programming. To duplicate a device, data in a master PROM are automatically programmed into the copy PROM. Prior to programming, the operator can enter data corrections for up to 16 words. To verify, data in the master PROM are automatically compared to data in the copy PROM. The programmer halts on a mismatch and displays the address and data in the master PROM (in hexadecimal) and the data in the copy PROM (in binary). The operator can continue comparing beyond the mismatch. Vertification of two matching PROMs takes about two seconds.

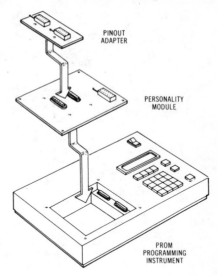

PROM programming machines.

PROM programming machines — Putting information into a PROM involves altering the internal physical structure of the device and requires equipment designed specifically for this purpose. The physical changes involve one of three dominant technologies:

1. Avalanche-induced migration of metal ions.
2. High-temperature fusing of metal or silicon links.
3. Avalanche-injected electrons on an isolated gate.

PROM chips can be programmed with many types of specific machines. Some PROM programming machines are "Manual Switches" that have 8 data switches and 8 address switches with associated LEDs indicating the "on/off" condition of each switch. The address to be programmed is set by the address switches, data are set in by the data switches, the Write mode is enabled, and the data are entered into the PROM. This sequence is repeated for each address requiring data. Other machines have keyboards that allow input, via keyboard, of the address and the data in a hexadecimal value. The input is displayed on an n-digit alphanumeric display that is part of the programming device. The left-most two digits generally display the address, the middle digits display data, and the last two digits display the contents of the address shown in the left-most display.

MOS EPROMs are programmed one word at a time and bipolar PROMs are programmed one bit at a time. All of these programming differences suggest the need for a wide variety of programming equipment. To accommodate the many programming techniques, equipment manufacturers have developed programming instruments with pluggable "personality modules." This allows one control unit to handle all the differing devices by interchanging low-cost modules, or "personality cards." Also, in recent years, PROM manufacturers have been standardizing the family or "generic" programming techniques within their own product lines. This has allowed the equipment manufacturers to further lower programming equipment costs by making available interchangeable pinout adapters for their personality modules.

proof listing—Refers to a designed report prepared by a processor which shows the coding as originally written, any comments that may have been written, and the machine-language instructions produced.

propagated error — An error occurring in one operation and affecting the data required for many subsequent operations, so that the error is spread through most of the material processed.

proprietary program—When the development of a program is controlled by an owner through the legal right of possession and title, it is a proprietary program. Commonly, the title remains with the owner, and its use is allowed with the stipulation that no disclosure of the program can be made to any other party without prior agreement between the owner and user.

protectable memory—A type of memory that does not lose information upon loss of power.

protected key, terminal—When this key is depressed, the character marked by a cursor on the screen can be protected from strikeover. The character is protected; it cannot be removed from the screen if another key

in its position is struck. Protected fields are very useful when forms are set up on the screen and labeled. The forms and the labels are usually protected, so that when the form is filled in, the form is not accidentally erased. Once a protected field is set up, it is often desirable to give it special prominence on the screen for ease of identification. Or, it may be desirable to highlight information other than protected fields.

protected locations—1. Refers to locations reserved for special purposes, and in which data cannot be stored without undergoing a screening procedure to establish suitability for storage therein. 2. Block locations reserved for special purposes, such as in main storage or on disk files. Data may be read from, but nothing may be written into, these locations.

protection key—Refers to a specific indicator associated with a task that appears in the program status word whenever the task is in control, and which must match the storage keys of all storage blocks that it is to use.

protocol—A protocol is essentially a set of conventions, or rules, between communicating processes on the format and content of messages to be exchanged. To make implementation and usage more convenient, in sophisticated networks, higher-level protocols may use lower-level protocols in a layered fashion.

protocol, bit-oriented — As with any form of communication, rules, whether implicit or explicit, are necessary if messages are to be received and interpreted properly. In the case of data communications, the increasing capability and complexity of equipment and rapidly rising software costs have called forth the development of more efficient sets of rules, or protocols. Recent protocols for data-link control have switched from a character- to a bit-oriented approach. This approach uses position instead of control characters to define the various parts of a message, thereby boosting throughput and greatly simplifying implementation. In addition, the newer protocols provide advanced error-checking techniques, data transparency, and full-duplex capability.

protocol chip—Traditional hardware approach have been strongly impacted by the emergence of the multiprotocol chip. This device performs the basic task of assembling received serial data characters, and serializing transmitted characters. It also performs the data transparency function of bit-stuffing or byte-stuffing, as well as CRC (cyclic redundancy check) polynomial generation and checking. Many of the devices incorporate modem control functions, the interchange signals between the data circuit and the data terminal equipment. Most devices are bus-oriented and contain multiple registers, designed to interface with an 8- or 16-bit data bus of a microprocessor. The advantage of a multiprotocol chip is that it reduces the number of support circuits and permits adaptability to various line protocols on the same hardware interface. Nonetheless, these protocols have been designed to operate over synchronous serial-transmission interfaces. However, a word-count protocol such as digital data communications message protocol (DDCMP) can operate over synchronous and asynchronous serial or parallel interfaces.

protocol, data-base — Under the data-base-access protocol imposed by most information storage and retrieval applications, only host commands and specified data fields will pass between the host and the controller according to standard procedures.

protocol functions—In most communications systems, protocols are required for bit synchronization, in order that the receiver will know when a bit starts and ends so that it can be sampled. This is necessary for character synchronization, so that the receiver can determine which bits belong to a character, and for message synchronization, so that the receiver can recognize the special character sequences that delineate messages. Typical protocols include the blocking of transmission into messages employing start-of-text and end-of-text (STX/ETX) or other similar markers, and a positive/negative acknowledgment procedure (ACK/NAK). Additional error detection and correction is provided by longitudinal redundancy checks (LRC).

protocol levels — A complex hierarchy exists in protocol usage. At the lowest level is the synchronous communications protocol governing the exchange of information between switching computers. Next, the so-called first-level protocols control the exchange of information between a host computer and its interface. Using these two protocols in its implementation is the level-two protocol controlling the exchange of information between host computers. Level-three protocols control the information exchange between actual processes where a process may be a computer program or a user terminal. At this level are the protocols that are very relevant to the user in relation to the utility of the network.

protocols, user level—Refers to specified sets of user-oriented protocols that have been developed and are continuing to be extended. Such protocols include: the initial connection protocol, which can be used by all processes to initiate a communication link with remote processes; the file transfer protocol, for the transmittal of large files from one computer to another; and the remote job-entry protocol, for communicating batch variety.

proton—An elementary particle, of positive charge and unit atomic mass; an atom of lightest isotope of hydrogen without its electron. Appears to be joined with neutrons in building up a nucleus of atoms, there being Z protons in the nucleus—where Z is the atomic number. (Each chemical element can have a variable number of neutrons to form isotopes.) It is the lightest baryon (rest mass 1.00758 amu), and believed to be the only one completely stable in isolation.

prototype boards — An alternative to wire-wrap boards are prototyping cards, which are essentially perforated boards that have been constructed on a printed-circuit card and designed to conform to the physical conventions of a particular mini- or microcomputer. Since these printed-circuit cards are often double-sided, all of the standard card-edge fingers for connection to standard bus signals appear. Interconnection between components may be through wire-wrap sockets or soldered connections, in many instances.

prototype boards, evaluation systems —A typical development cycle using a second-generation microcomputer development system is one without in-circuit emulation capability. At the conclusion of the hardware and software design phase, the development effort splits into two segregated efforts. Hardware development continues with the construction of key hardware (e.g., memory and memory-decode circuitry, critical I/O circuitry) on prototype boards which plug into the development system backplane. The engineer uses these prototype boards to evaluate new system concepts using development system diagnostics. Hence, prototyping at this level is restricted to the bus architecture of the development system for support.

Software development continues from the design stage through code preparation, translation, and verification phases in the development system. Once the software is debugged in the development system, and the stand-alone prototype has passed preliminary tests, the time-consuming systems integration phase begins. Here, for the first time in the development cycle, final systems software is run on the production prototype and the necessary hardware and software modifications are made to correct system bugs. Finally, a production test takes place using a specially constructed piece of test equipment.

prototype debugging, microcontroller — A prototype debug program can verify that the written program operates as intended. A simulator, in some systems, has a modifiable program storage in place of a read-only memory so that changes can be quickly made directly from the front panel. The front panel provides a program display and a control to single step through the program and verify that each instruction operates as intended. All I/O points can be displayed, with the I/O points set to specific values, and the registers and working storage can be examined to verify program operations.

prototype printed-circuit board—Refers to a double-sided, plated-through board used for designing custom interfaces to some systems.

prototyping—Prototyping represents the initial design development stage wherein, at first, it is certain that errors will be discovered which will require design changes. It is in this period that design aids, emulation techniques, and supportive design techniques are essential to quick design.

prototyping cards — See prototype boards.

PRT — Abbreviation of program reference table. Consists of the locations reserved for program variables, data descriptions that give information about data arrays, and other program information. When a program references a word in its PRT, the relative address of the word is used, never the absolute address. The relative address of any particular location is based on its position relative to the beginning of the PRT.

pseudocode—1. Refers to an instruction that is not meant to be followed directly by a computer. Instead, it initiates the linking of a subroutine into the main program. 2. Refers to various codes that express programs in source language; i.e., by referring to storage locations and machine operations by symbolic names and addresses that are independent of their hardware-determined names and addresses. (Contrasted with machine-language code.) 3. An arbitrary code, independent of the hardware of a computer and designed for convenience in programming, which must be translated into computer code if it is to direct the computer.

pseudodynamic memory—See pseudostatic, semistatic, pseudodynamic, quasi-dynamic memory.

pseudo-instruction—1. A symbolic representation in a compiler or interpreter. 2. A group of characters having the same general form as a computer instruction, but never executed by the computer as an actual instruction. (Synonymous with quasi-instruction.) 3. An instruction written in an assembly language designating a predetermined and limited group of computer instructions for performing a particular task.

pseudorandom codes—Refers to some digital codes having the appearance of a random sequence but of finite length. Therefore, they repeat and are not truly random. They are useful for synchronization and controlling sequences.

pseudorandom number sequence — A sequence of numbers, determined by some defined arithmetic process, that is satisfactorily random for a given purpose, such as satisfying one or more of the standard statistical tests for randomness. Such a sequence may approximate any one of several statistical distributions; i.e., uniform distribution or a normal (Gaussian) distribution.

pseudostatic RAM — Much of the dynamic memory technology has been carried over to a class of memory called pseudostatics. These memories contain dynamic storage areas, along with all the necessary support circuitry on the chip to perform the refresh, thus making the entire memory appear static to the external world. (One example of these memories is the Mostek 4816.) These memories are available in 8-bit-wide data paths so that interfaces to the microprocessor require but a single package. The byte-wide configuration also permits the RAMs to be directly substituted for UV EPROMs, PROMs, and even ROMs, thus permitting programs to be developed in RAM and a "permanent" memory substituted.

pseudostatic, semistatic, pseudodynamic, quasi-dynamic memory — The official term is still not determined but any one of the preceding names describes a memory with dynamic storage cells and apparent static operation (refresh that is transparent to the user). Since this is basically a dynamic memory, precautions with respect to supply noise must be taken. However, a power supply with a margin for high current transients and with adequate decoupling should have no trouble handling a board full of quasi-static memories. Quasi-static RAMs hope to approach the cost/bit and power/bit potential of dynamic designs. The user-transparent refresh should offer the ease-of-use of static RAMs.

PSW — Abbreviation of program status word. Refers to a word in main storage that is used to control the order in which instructions are executed. Also, used to hold and indicate the status of the computing system in relation to a particular program.

pull-down resistor — A resistor connected across the output of a device or circuit to hold the output equal to or less than the 0 input level. Also used to lower the output impedance of digital or analog devices. It is usu-

ally connected to a negative voltage or ground.

pull operation—Refers to an operation in which an operand (or operands) is taken from the top of a pushdown stack in memory and placed in a general register (or registers). The operand remains in the stack unaltered; only a pointer value indicating the current top-of-stack is changed.

pull-up resistor — A resistor connected across the output of a device or circuit to hold the output voltage equal to or greater than the input transition level of a digital device. It is usually connected to a positive voltage or to the plus supply.

pulse amplifier—Refers to an amplifier with a very wide frequency response that can amplify pulses without distortion of the very short rise time of the leading edge.

pulse amplitude—1. A general term for the magnitude of a pulse. For a more specific designation, adjectives such as average, instantaneous, peak, rms (effective), etc., should also be used. 2. Maximum instantaneous value of a pulse.

pulse amplitude modulation—1. Refers to the form of modulation in which the amplitude of the pulse carrier is varied in accordance with successive samples of the modulating signal. 2. The coding of a continuous or analog signal onto a uniformly spaced sequence of constant-width pulses by amplitude-modulating the intensity of each pulse, i.e., similar to am radio broadcasts except that the carrier is a pulse and not a sine wave.

pulse analyzer—Equipment for analyzing pulses to determine their time, amplitude, duration, shape, etc.

pulse carrier—1. A carrier consisting of a series of pulses. Usually employed as subcarriers. 2. A carrier wave comprising a series of equally spaced pulses.

pulse, channel—Refers to the channel pulse representing intelligence on a channel by virtue of its time or modulation characteristic.

pulse code — 1. The modulation imposed on a pulse train to convey information. Loosely, a code consisting of pulses, e.g., Morse, Baudit, binary. 2. A code in which sets of pulses have been assigned particular meanings. 3. The binary representations of characters.

pulse-code modulation—1. Abbreviated PCM. Pulsed modulation in which the signal is sampled periodically, and each sample is quantized and transmitted as a digital binary code. 2. The sampling and quantization of signals in the transmission of analog data. The value of the quantized sample is transmitted as a distinct pattern of pulses, i.e., the value can be expressed as a binary number and transmitted as a sequence of pulses representing 1s and spaces representing 0s. 3. The form of modulation in which the modulating signal is sampled and the sample quantized and coded so that each element of the information consists of different kinds and/or numbers of pulses and spaces.

pulse counter—A device that gives an indication or actually records the total number of pulses that it has received during a given time interval.

pulse digit—1. A code element comprising the immediately associated train of pulses. 2. A particular drive pulse corresponding to a one-digit position in some or all of the words in a storage unit. In some techniques, it may always be an inhibit pulse or always an enable pulse. These are more acceptable names for the general term.

pulse, drive—1. A pulsed magnetomotive force applied to a magnetic core. 2. A particular pulse of current in a winding inductively coupled to one or more magnetic cells which produces a pulse of magnetomotive force.

pulsed logic — Signal modification that produces output independently of input signal duration. Pulse duration (swell) is usually adjustable. Also referred to as one-shot logic.

pulse equalizer — A circuit that produces output pulses of uniform size and shape when driven by input pulses that vary in size and shape.

pulse, gate—Refers to a pulse which enables a gate circuit to pass a signal. Usually the gate pulse is of longer duration than the signal to make sure that coincidence in time occurs.

pulse, gating — A pulse which permits the operation of a circuit.

pulse generator—1. A device for gen-

erating a controlled series of electrical impulses. 2. The circuit in a crt transmitter that generates the basic timing pulses for blanking and synchronization.

pulse interleaving—A process in which pulses from two or more time-division multiplexers are systematically combined in time division for transmission over a common path.

pulse jitter—A relatively slight variation of the pulse spacing in a pulse train. It may be random or systematic depending on its origin, and is generally not coherent with any imposed pulse modulation.

pulse string — A particular group of pulses that happen in time sequence at a point in a circuit, i.e., an amplitude vs. time plot of the pulses appears as though the pulse group occurs in space sequence or along a line, thus, the terms pulse string or pulse train.

pulse, strobe—Refers to a pulse used to gate the output of a core-memory sense amplifier into triggering a register. Also called sample pulse.

pulse, synchronization — Refers to pulses introduced to keep all components operating in order or step, i.e., into transmitters and receivers to keep order, or timing pulses into a master clock to keep all logic gates operating in order in synchronous computers.

pulse train—1. Also called pulse group of impulse train. A group or sequence of pulses of similar characteristics. 2. *Same as* pulse string.

pulse train generator—Refers to a circuitry system or device that, with a signal stimulus, produces a fixed number of equally spaced pulses.

pulse-width recording—A procedure or method for the magnetic recording of bits in which each storage cell comprises two regions that are magnetized in opposite senses with unmagnetized regions on each side, i.e., the "zero" bit is represented by a cell containing a negative region followed by a positive region.

pulse, write—Refers to a drive pulse (or the sum of several simultaneous drive pulses) that, under suitable conditions, can write into a magnetic cell or set a cell, i.e., usually to a "one" condition.

punched card—Also called IBM card. A piece of cardboard on which information has been coded in the form of holes (to be read by a machine). The holes can be of many shapes, and may be punched either by machine or by hand.

punched paper tape—Refers to paper tape on which information has been (or may be) stored or recorded in the form of partially punched (chadless) holes. Each character of information is punched in binary representation in a column across the width of the tape. There are usually five to eight punch positions (channels or levels) per column. The channels, or levels, run in rows parallel to the length of the tape. The punch positions are normally spaced ten to the inch.

pure generator — Refers to a unique generator that is a routine capable of writing another routine. When this is tied to an assembler, the pure generator is usually a section of a program found on a library tape and it is called into storage by the assembler, which then writes one or more entries in the routine.

push-down list—A list of items in which the last item entered becomes the first item of the list and the relative position of each of the other items is pushed back one.

push-down nesting — As data is transferred into storage, each word in turn enters the top register and is then "pushed down" the column from register to register to make room for the subsequent words as they are assigned. When a word is transferred out of the storage (again, only from the top register), other data in the storage moves back up the column from register to register to fill the space left empty. This is accomplished either through programs or the equipment itself.

push-down queue — A last-in/first-out (LIFO) method of queuing in which the last item attached to the queue is the first to be withdrawn.

push-down stack—A register developed to receive information from the Program Counter and store address locations of the instructions which have been pushed down during an interrupt. This stack can be used for subroutining. Its size determines the level of subroutine nesting in a 16-word register. When instructions are returned, they are popped back on a last-in/first-out (LIFO) basis.

push operation—Refers to an operation in which an operand (or operands) from a general register (or registers) is stored into the new top location of a push-down stack (in memory).

push-up list — A list of items in which each item is entered at the end of the list and the previous items maintain their same relative position in the list.

push-up storage—A technique in which the next item of data to be retrieved is the oldest, i.e., has been in the queue the longest.

Q

Q—1. Symbol of merit for an energy-storing device, resonant system, or tuned circuit. Also called magnification factor, quality factor, Q-factor, or storage factor. 2. A register used as an accumulator extension, which is necessary for efficient multiply-divide programming.

Q address—A source location in internal storage, in some types of equipment, from which data are transferred.

QAM—Abbreviation for quadrature amplitude modulation. A high-speed modem modulation technique employing both differential phase modulation and amplitude modulation.

quad bus transceiver — A component that consists of four separate receiver-transmitter combinations, designed for use with a bidirectional bus system, such as a data bus.

qualifier—A name used to qualify another name with an action similar to an adjective in English grammar, i.e., to give additional information about a name or to distinguish the named thing from other things having the same name. In COBOL, the technique of making a name unique by adding IN or OF, and another name, according to defined rules and procedures.

quality control—That process whereby systematic and regular review of the timeliness, accuracy, completeness, etc., of data entry is accomplished.

quantification—An act of quantifying or giving numerical value to the measurement of an item, i.e., to attempt to give discrete values to human characteristics using statistical terms, numerical indicators, or weights.

quantity—1. A constant, variable, function name, or expression. 2. A positive or negative real number in the mathematical sense. The term quantity is preferred to the term number in referring to numerical data. The term number is used in the sense of natural number and is reserved for "the number of digits," "the number of operations," etc.

quantization—1. The process whereby the range of values of a wave is divided into a finite number of subranges, each represented by an assigned (quantized) value. 2. The subdivision of a continuous range of values into a finite number of distinct elements, and a process similar to analog-to-digital conversion; the approximation of a real (or infinite-precision) value by a number of prespecified resolution. For example, the conversion of a 1- to 100-volt signal to a 12-bit number.

quantization distortion — In communications, quantization is a process in which the range of values of a wave is divided into a finite number of smaller subranges, each of which is represented by an assigned (or quantized) value within the subrange. Note: "Quantized" may be used as an adjective modifying various forms of modulation, for example, quantized pulse-amplitude modulation.

quantization uncertainty — Refers to a specific gauge or measure of the uncertainty, particularly that of the irretrievable information loss, which occurs as a result of the quantization of a function in an interval where it is continuous.

quantize — To subdivide the range of values of a variable into a finite number of nonoverlapping subranges or intervals, each of which is represented by an assigned value within

the subrange; e.g., to represent a person's age as a number of whole years.

quantizer—A device that converts an analog measurement into digital form.

quantizing error—The inherent uncertainty in digitizing an analog value due to the finite resolution of the conversion process.

quantum—1. Refers to a unit of processing time in a time-sharing system that may be allocated for operating a program during its turn in the computer. More quanta may be allocated to higher-priority programs than to lower-priority programs. 2. One of the ranges or discrete values resulting from quantization.

quantum electronics — Refers to a branch of science concerned with amplification or generation of microwave power in solid crystals, governed by quantum mechanical laws.

quantum number—One of a set, describing possible states of a magnitude when quantized, e.g., nuclear spin.

quantum statistics—Those dealing with the distribution of the particles of a given type among the various possible energy values.

quantum theory—The theory developed from Planck's Law. There is a quantum theory for most branches of classical physics.

quartz crystal—1. Also called a crystal. A thin slab cut from a piece of quartz and ground to a thickness at which it will vibrate, at a desired frequency, when supplied with energy. It is used to accurately control the frequency of an oscillator. 2. A piezoelectric crystal that regulates an oscillator frequency.

quartz delay line — 1. A delay line in which fused quartz is the medium for delaying sound transmission or a train of wave. 2. A sonic delay line using a length of quartz crystal as an acoustical medium and with sound waves representing digital data being propagated over a fixed distance.

quartz oscillator—One whose oscillation frequency is controlled by a piezoelectric quartz crystal.

quartz thermometer — One with digital readout obtained by beating a temperature-dependent quartz oscillator against a temperature invariant one.

quasi-dynamic memory—*See* pseudo-static, semistatic, pseudodynamic, quasi-dynamic memory.

quasi-instruction—*See* pseudo-instruction.

query—A specific request for data, instructions, characteristics of states of switches, position in a queue, etc., while the equipment is computing or processing.

Query language—1. A class of English-like languages that allows nonprogrammers to inquire about the contents of a data base and receive fast responses. Although the ability to specify the contents of the output is usually powerful and flexible, formatting and arithmetic abilities are usually limited. More sophisticated reports are better developed with a report writer. 2. An English-like language, incorporated in some data base management systems, that acts as an impromptu report generator.

query station—Refers to a specific unit of equipment that introduces requests or queries for data, states of processing, information, etc., while the equipment is computing, or processing, or communicating.

queue—1. Refers to waiting lines resulting from temporary delays in providing service. 2. A line or group of items waiting for the attention of the processor—usually in main memory and chained together by address words.

queue, automatic—Relates to a specific series of interconnected registers that are designed to implement either a LIFO (last-in/first-out) queue or a FIFO (first-in/first-out) queue without program manipulation. For a FIFO queue, new entries to the queue are placed in the last position and automatically jump forward to the last unoccupied position, while removal of the front entry results in all entries automatically moving forward one position. Also called push-down storage and push-up storage.

queue control block—Refers to a special control block that is designed to be used in the regulation of the sequential use of some programmer-defined facility by a set of competing tasks.

queued access method — Any access method that automatically synchronizes the transfer of data between the program using the access method and the input/output devices, thereby eliminating delays for input/output operations. (The primary macro-instructions used are GET and PUT.)

queued content-addressed memory — Refers to an as-yet experimental automatic memory structure that contains a series of parallel automatic queues (q.v.). The front member of each queue is content-addressable in the usual fashion.

queue discipline—Refers to the methods selected to determine order of service in a queue, i.e., LIFO (last-in/first-out) or FIFO (first-in/first-out), etc.

queued sequential-access method — Refers to a version of the basic sequential-access method (BSAM). When this method is used, a queue is formed of input data blocks that are awaiting processing or of output data blocks that have been processed and are awaiting transfer to auxiliary storage or to an output device. Abbreviated QSAM.

queued telecommunications access method — A method that is used to transfer data between main storage and the remote terminals. Application programs use GET and PUT macro-instructions to request the transfer of data, which is performed by a message control program. The message control program synchronizes the transfer, thus eliminating delays for input/output operations. Abbreviated QTAM.

queues, direct-access — A group of queues or, more specifically, message-segment chains of queues residing on a direct-access storage device. The group can include destination and process queues.

queuing — Pertains to a study of the patterns involved and the time required for discrete units to move through channels, e.g., the elapsed time for auto traffic at a toll booth or employees in a cafeteria line (in queuing theory).

queuing list—Refers to a list frequently used for scheduling actions in real time on a time-priority basis. Appends are made following the ending item. The beginning item is always the removed item.

queuing, message—Controls the order

in which messages are stored, processed, and transmitted.

queuing theory—Refers to a form of probability theory useful in studying delays or line-ups at servicing points.

quick-break — A characteristic of a switch or circuit breaker, whereby it has a fast contact-opening speed that is independent of the operator.

quick disconnect—Refers to a type of connector shell which allows for very quick locking and unlocking of two connector parts.

quiescent—1. At rest; specifically, the condition of a circuit when no input signal is being applied to it. 2. General term for a system waiting to be operated; e.g., a vacuum tube ready to amplify or a gas-discharge tube ready to fire.

quiescent current—Current in a vacuum tube or transistor, in the absence of a driving or modulating signal. Also, standing current.

quiescent operating point — The state or condition that exists under any specified external condition when the signal is zero.

quiescing—Refers to the stopping of a multiprogrammed system by means of the rejection of new jobs.

Quincke's method—A method for determining the magnetic susceptibility of a substance, in solution, by measuring the force acting on it in terms of the change of height of the free surface of the solution, when placed in a suitable magnetic field.

QUIP — A 64-lead integrated-circuit package developed jointly by Intel Corporation and the 3M Company. It has two rows of pins instead of one along each longitudinal edge, so that the 64 pins are contained in 1⅝ inches of length. This size enhances strength and rigidity, and the consequent shortening of the internal metalized conductors results in low pin-to-pin capacitance, lead resistance, and inductance. A QUIP can be dismantled with a small screwdriver, and a special set of probe contacts along the top of the unit allows access for measurements while the QUIP is operating in its socket.

quoted string — Refers to assembler programming, where a character string, enclosed by apostrophes, is used in a macro-instruction operand to represent a value that can include blanks. The enclosed apostrophes are part of the value represented.

qwerty—Refers to the typical typewriter keyboard which starts with these six letters, left-to-right, in the top row below the numerals.

R

rack mounting—Refers generally to the metal or other type of frame or chassis on which panels of electrical, electronic, or other equipment may be mounted, such as power-supply units, amplifiers, etc.

radiation—1. The propagation of energy through space or through a material. It may be in the form of electromagnetic waves or corpuscular emissions. The former is usually classified according to frequency, e.g., Hertzian, infrared, (visible) light, ultraviolet, X-rays, gamma rays, etc. Corpuscular emissions are classified as alpha, beta, or cosmic.

radix—Also called the base. The total number of distinct marks or symbols used in a numbering system. For example, since the decimal numbering system uses ten symbols (0, 1, 2, 3, 4, 5, 6, 7, 8, 9), the radix is 10. In the binary numbering system, the radix is 2, because there are only two marks or symbols (0, 1).

radix notation, fixed—A positional representation in which the significances of successive digit positions are successive integral powers of a single radix. When the radix is positive, permissible values of each digit range from zero to one less than the radix, and negative integral powers of the radix are used to represent fractions.

radix point—1. Also called base point, and binary point, decimal point, etc., depending on the numbering system. The index that separates the integral and fractional digits of the numbering system in which the quantity is represented. 2. The dot that delineates the integer digits from the fractional digits of a number. Specifically, the dot that delineates the digital position involving the zero exponent of the radix from the digital position involving the minus-one exponent of the radix. The radix point is often identified by the name of the system, e.g., binary point, octal point, or decimal point. In the writing of any number in any system, if no dot is included, the radix point is assumed to follow the rightmost digit.

RAM—Abbreviation for random-access memory. This type memory is random because it provides immediate access to any storage location point in the memory by means of vertical and horizontal coordinates. Information may be "written in" or "read out" in the same very fast procedure.

RAM and ROM, mixing — A unique memory cross-addressing capability allows the mix of RAM and ROM memory in order to benefit from both in a mixed memory system. All program instructions, which do not change, are permanently stored in ROM. All data, which does change, are allocated space in RAM. RAM can be used as scratchpad memory using an indirect addressing scheme associated with ROM. Combined configurations of ROM/RAM offer the advantages of both memory types. The main program can be stored in nondestructive ROM while the RAM can

be used as scratchpad for Write instructions and data storage.

RAM array organization—In addition to the wide variety of memory types, there are many variations within each family that define the array organization, the output type, and the basic device structure. For example, there are actually three basic types of RAM structures—dynamic, static, and pseudostatic, as well as three basic array organizations—$\times 1$, $\times 4$, and $\times 8$. In general, dynamic memories, because of their extensive use in computer main-memory systems, are exclusively organized in the $\times 1$ format. This way, the multiplexed address bus and the data I/O structure are most efficient for large systems, and error detection and correction circuitry is easily added.

Static memories, on the other hand, are available in $\times 1$, $\times 4$, and $\times 8$ organizations, since each type is best suited for a different application. For example, the $\times 1$ units are effective for large-capacity (4K words and up) cache memories, the $\times 4$ units suit writable control stores that typically have under a few K words, while the $\times 8$ RAMs are very handy for microprocessor systems needing only a few K bytes of RAM.

RAM data words—The RAM portion of the memory is used to store data words. These data words are often changed and must be easily accessed. Each word is stored in RAM at a known location called an address (words in ROM also have addresses). If the microprocessor is instructed to

RAM—48K board (Courtesy Vector Graphic Inc.).

fetch a word from the RAM, it places the address of the word on the address bus. The RAM will send that word to the microprocessor through the data bus.

RAM design-error corrections—As systems become more and more complex, an increasing number of design errors are discovered after the system is installed. Prior to the introduction of RAM, error-correction changes were made by physically making wiring changes in the field or by replacing portions of the hardware. With RAM, many of these repairs can be made by distributing a new control program and writing it into the control store. Since machines using RAM have hardware control-store loaders, this is very simple to do. For example, in many machines, the control store can be loaded through the card reader by enabling a special loading mode with a switch.

RAM, latched output—This is an output in which the output data remains valid after the memory cycle. This feature can work against users if they do not need the latch but tie the outputs of several devices together. A more desirable feature is a control function that latches the output. This approach is common with newer memories (e.g., the $\overline{CAS}$-controlled output on 16K and 64K dynamic RAMs).

RAM loader—A program used to read a program from an input device, and, usually, into some type of random-access memory.

RAM memory-save option—In a power outage, the RAM memories that contain the program and the last data scan lose their stored information. However, in systems equipped with a custom initialization ROM, restoration of power automatically restores the full program to the RAMs, starts the clock, and initiates data scanning in the AUTO mode. But for some applications, a preprogrammed ROM is not desired for each different setup. To avoid program data loss and timing loss, the memory-save option powers the RAMs for ten or more minutes from an internal bank of batteries. These cells are kept fully charged during normal operation, and are automatically cut in if a transient or outage occurs. If more than 5 minutes of protection is desired, external bat-

teries can be provided. The memory-save option returns the system to scanning in the AUTO mode when line power is restored.

RAM memory system characteristics—In some system designs, a block diagram of a RAM memory system can be split into three main sections as follows. The first section is comprised of the address buffers, Read/Write, and Chip-select decoding logic. The second section consists of the data-bus buffering and the memory array itself. The memory array can consist of sixteen memory devices (4K words x 1-bit) organized into two rows of 4096 bytes each. The third section of the block diagram comprises the refresh and control logic for the memory system. This logic handles the timing of the refresh handshaking with the data bus that requests a refresh cycle, the generation of the refresh addresses, synchronization of the power-fail signal, the multiplexing of the external memory clock with the internal clock (used during standby), and the generation of the −5-V supply on the board (by a charge pump method).

RAM, partial—To improve the yield of their production lines, semiconductor manufacturers have taken to packaging devices that have less than the total designed storage—devices usually referred to as *partials*. Partial 16K dynamic RAMs are already available from some manufacturers, and the first volume appearance of the 64K devices will probably be in the form of ''partials.'' Far from being inferior parts whose operation is questionable, these parts are tested to the same functional standards as whole devices. Such RAMs enable memory-board builders to bring dependable products to market in the earlier stages of a memory family's development or when full-storage parts are scarce. There are many reliable memory-board designs in which partials can be used.

RAM refresh operation—A refresh operation consists of a specified number of Write cycles (some memories require a Read cycle) on the least-significant address bits of the memory within a given period of time. All dynamic MOS random-access memories require a periodic refresh operation to ensure that stored data is retained. The number of Write or Read cycles will vary depending on the memory circuit. The dynamic MOS RAMs presently available require either 16, 32, or 64 Write or Read cycles within a 2 ms period. Unfortunately, the periodic refresh requirement of dynamic MOS RAMs increases the cost and reduces the overall performance of the memory system. For example, additional logic is required to ensure that the memory system is properly refreshed.

RAM refresh rate—Also called the refresh frequency. The number of refresh operations (cycles) that must be performed in the maximum refresh time interval. For example, the 16K dynamic RAM requires 128 refresh cycles at least every 2 milliseconds to maintain data.

RAM refresh time interval—Also called the refresh period. The time between the successive refresh operations that are required to restore the charge in a dynamic memory cell.

RAM register simulators — Refers to programs that functionally simulate execution of microcomputer programs. Simulators are interpretive and provide bit-for-bit duplication of microprocessor instruction executing timing, register contents, etc. Direct user control over execution conditions (RAM/register contents, interrupts, I/O data, etc.) are provided.

RAM/ROM memory — There are basically two kinds of memory devices used in microcomputer systems: data memory and program memory. The data memory has information being continually entered and removed. It must be capable of both read and write functions and it must store the variables from the system (numbers, alphanumeric characters, etc.). This calls for an alterable memory such as a random–access memory (RAM). Program memory, normally in the form of a ROM or PROM, stores fixed instructions which constitute programs to be executed by the system. Since this information does not change regularly, the ROMs should be nonvolatile or nonalterable.

RAM, self-refresh—In a dynamic RAM, a method of asynchronously refreshing during a battery backup mode of operation with only one control pin held active.

RAM storage functions—RAM consists of a number of random-access memory devices that are used to store the macrocode (user program) under execution. Its size also varies with user requirements as limited by the addressing capability of the microprocessor.

RAM subroutine calls — Random-access memories have modifiable contents. For subroutine calls and interrupts, the 16-level or larger stacks are used to hold the return addresses and the contents of the state register. On some systems, when the microprocessor is in the noninterrupt state, one block of registers and condition code is accessible and interrupt requests may be honored. When the microprocessor is honoring a request, an interrupt is set equal to 1. During this time, another block of register and condition code is addressed by the processor. Further interrupt requests are kept pending until the current interrupt is serviced. Since the two or more blocks of registers and condition codes are transparent to the microinstructions, common subroutines can be used by the interrupt service routines and the background program.

random access—1. Access to a computer storage under conditions whereby there is no rule for predetermining the position from where the next item of information is to be obtained. 2. Describes the process of obtaining information from or placing information into a storage system where the time required for such access is independent of the location of the information most recently obtained or placed in storage. 3. Describing a device in which random access can be achieved without effective penalty in time.

random-access device—A unit that is designed so that access time is independent of data location and system history.

random-access memory — 1. Abbreviated RAM. A memory system for which the access time is independent of the location being addressed. 2. A memory whose information media are organized into discrete locations, sectors, etc., each uniquely identified by an address. Data may be obtained from such a memory by specifying the data address(es) to the memory, i.e., bubbles, drum, disks, cards, etc.

random-access storage—1. A storage medium in which the time required to obtain information is statistically independent of the location of the information most recently obtained. 2. A type of storage in which access can be made directly to any storage regardless of its position, either absolute or relative to the previously referenced information.

random logic design — Refers to systems designed using discrete logic circuits. Numerous gates are required to implement the logic equations until the problem is solved. Even then, the design is not completed until all redundant gates are weeded out. Random logic design is not a realistic guarantee of optimum gate count.

random logic testing—A test pattern for random logic testing on a tester typically consists of three parts: (1) the logical inputs and expected outputs, (2) the microprogrammable multiprocessor control-memory image, and (3) directive messages for operator action. The programmer has the choice of using binary, hexadecimal, or octal formats depending on convenience. Inputs and outputs are defined by the system logic interface panel and can be hand-wired or under software control. The choice typically depends on the types of cards to be tested. The control memory determines the sequence that the stimuli stored in the data buffer memory is applied to the module under test. The sequence of data patterns and the expected results are easily modified under microinstruction control. Based upon failed output data, directive messages can tell the operator to replace a device, probe a certain group of devices, or look in a general area for faults. Particular provision is made for on-line module debug with real-time operation simulation.

randomness — A condition of equal chance for the occurrence of any of the possible outcomes.

random noise—Also called fluctuation noise. A large number of random overlapping transient disturbances.

random-noise correction—Most all random noise is characterized as a lack of organization. Because it is random,

its periodicity and amplitude are difficult to predict. If the noise remains below a determined threshold level, it usually will not interface with a signal; if the noise does not, system parameters must be adjusted to minimize its effects.

random number—1. A set of digits constructed of such a sequence that each successive digit is equally likely to be any of N digits to the base n of the number. 2. A number formed by a set of digits selected from a random table or sequence of digits.

random-number generator—A type of machine routine, or hardware unit, designed to produce a random number or a series of random numbers according to specified limitations.

random processing — Information and data records are processed in the particular order specified by the control system and not in the order in which they are stored.

random sequence—A sequence that is not arranged by ascending or descending keys, as in alphanumeric or numeric sequences, but is instead arranged in an organized fashion in bulk storage, by locations determined by calculations performed on keys to develop addresses. The calculations are repeated in order to acquire the address and locate the item desired.

random variable—1. Also called variate. The result of a random experiment. 2. A discrete or continuous variable which may assume any one of a number of values, each having the same probability of occurrence.

rapid access — Rapid access is often synonymous with random access and is contrasted with sequential access, i.e., dependency upon access of preceding data.

rapid-access loop—Refers to a section of storage, particularly in drum, tape, or disk storage units, that has a much faster access than the remainder of the storage.

rapid-access memory — In computers having memories with different access times, the section that has much faster access than the remainder of the memory.

rapid-access storage—*Same as* storage, high speed.

rate, action—A type of control action in which the rate of correction is made proportional to how fast the condition is going awry. This is also called derivative action.

rate-grown transistor — Also called graded-junction transistor. A variation of the double-doped transistor, in which n- and p-type impurities are added to the melt.

rate, residual-error — The ratio of the number of bits, unit elements, characters and blocks incorrectly received but undetected or uncorrected by the error-control equipment, to the total number of bits, unit elements, characters, and blocks that are sent.

rate, scan—A frequency at which data are compared or read to various predetermined sets of criteria, for the purpose of seeking certain data.

rate test—Refers to various problems chosen to determine whether the computer or a program is operating correctly.

rate, undetected-error—*Same as* rate, residual-error.

ratio, read-around — *Same as* read-around number.

RCTL (resistor-capacitor-transistor logic)—Same as RTL except that capacitors are used to enhance switching speed.

raw data—Data that has not been processed; they may or may not be in machine-sensible form.

reactance modulator—Refers to a circuit capable of acting as a variable capacitor. A second variety of reactance modulator acts as a variable inductance or coil.

reactive—Pertaining to either inductive or capacitive reactance. A reactive circuit has a higher reactance than resistance.

reactive mode—Refers to a condition of communication between one or more remote terminals and a computer, in which each entry (usually batch) causes certain actions to be performed by the computer, but does not necessarily include an immediate reply. Contrasts with mode, conversation.

read — 1. The process of introducing data into a component or part of an automatic data-processing machine. 2. To copy, usually from one form of storage to another, particularly from external or secondary storage to internal storage. 3. To sense the mean-ing by arrangements of hardware. 4. To accept or copy information or data from input devices or a memory register, i.e., to read out; to position or deposit information into a storage or output medium, or a register, i.e., to read in. 5. To transcribe information from an input device to internal or auxiliary storage. 6. To sense the presence of information in some type of storage, which includes RAM memory, magnetic tape, punched tape, etc.

read-after-write verify — Refers to a function for determining that information currently being written is correct as compared to the information source.

read-around number — The number of times a specific spot, digit, or location in electrostatic storage may be consulted before spillover of electrons will cause a loss of information stored in surrounding spots.

read-back check—Concerns a specific check of accuracy of transmission in which the information that was transmitted to an output device is returned to the information source and is compared with the original information, to ensure accuracy of output.

read cycle, microprocessor—During a Read cycle, the microprocessor receives data from memory or a peripheral device. The processor (of one major system) reads bytes of data in all cases. If the instruction specifies a word (or double word) operation, the processor reads both bytes. When the instruction specifies byte operation, the microprocessor uses an internal address (A0) bit to determine which byte to read and then issues the data strobe required for that byte.

read cycle time—The time interval between the start and end of a read cycle.

read, destructive—The sensing of data using a process which inherently destroys (erases) the record of the data that has been read. In some storage, reading is destructive, but such data are usually regenerated after each readout. In tapes, bubbles, disks, etc., reading is usually accomplished without destruction.

reader—1. Refers to a device capable of sensing information stored in an off-line memory media (cards, paper tape, magnetic tape) and which generates equivalent information in an on-line memory device (register, memory locations). 2. Any device, which has the capability of sensing, detecting, or converting data, i.e., transferring to another form or medium.

reader, character — A specialized device that can convert data (represented in one of the type fonts or scripts readable by human beings) directly into machine language. Such a reader may operate optically or, if the characters are printed in magnetic ink, the device may operate magnetically or optically.

reader, document — An input device which can read documents as a human would, so that data can be directly and easily put into a computer for processing. Although document readers cannot read human script as yet, they can read a large variety of hand-printed and typed documents; for example, bank checks with the account numbers printed in magnetic ink, and specially formed numbers made by the raised letters on credit cards.

reader, film—A unit of peripheral equipment which projects film to permit reading by clients or customers of the data stored on the film, such as microfilm or microfiche. Also, a device that converts patterns of opaque and transparent spots on a photofilm to electrical pulses that correspond to the patterns.

reader/interpreter—Refers to a specific service routine that reads an input stream, stores programs and data on random-access storage for later processing, identifies the control information contained in the input stream, and stores this control information separately in the appropriate control list. A reader/interpreter may be considered very nearly the opposite of an output writer.

read in—1. Refers to the act of placing data in storage at a specified address. 2. To sense information contained in some source and transmit this information to an internal storage.

read-in, microcomputer — 1. To copy, usually from one form of storage to another. 2. To sense the meaning of an arrangement of hardware representing information. 3. To extract information.

reading rate—In a microcomputer, the number of characters, symbols, etc., that can be sensed by an input unit in a given time.

reader, optical—1. A device based on the principle that the special shape of each character printed on the input media is capable of being identified by a reading device. For example, the audit-journal from a cash register, if printed in a distinctive optical font, could be used as the input media to a computer. As the optical reader reads each character from the input media, it translates the data into electrical impulses that, in turn, are transmitted to the computer for processing. 2. A device to read printed and typewritten material directly, without converting it into other intermediate formats. It recognizes all letters of the alphabet, standard punctuation, numerals zero through nine, and special symbols used in programmed functions. It handles documents, and continuous fan-fold sheets.

reader, photoelectric—A unit of peripheral equipment that has the capability of converting data, in the form of patterns of holes in such storage media as tapes or cards, into electrical pulse patterns by means of photosensitive diodes and transistors, i.e., a reader used for rapid input to a computer and one which usually can also drive a printer, plotter, etc.

reading, destructive — A reading process that destroys the source data.

reading, nondestructive — A reading process that does not destroy the data in the source.

read-only memory (ROM)—A memory in which the contents are not intended to be altered during normal operation. The term "read-only memory" implies that the content is determined by its structure and is unalterable (e.g., mask programmable ROM). Most ROMs are n $\times$ 8 (words $\times$ bits/word) to work with popular microprocessors. There are also special-purpose ROMs, such as character generators, with a 7-bit-wide output word and an addressing structure to output one hundred and twenty-eight 9 $\times$ 7 characters.

readout — 1. The manner in which a computer displays the processed information, e.g., digital visual display, punched tape, punched cards, automatic typewriter, etc. 2. To sense information contained in some internal storage and transmit this information to a storage external to the computer. 3. To copy data from specified addresses in storage into an external storage device. 4. The act of removing and recording information from a computer or an auxiliary storage. 5. The information that is removed from computer storage and recorded in a form that the operator can interpret directly. 6. To sense information contained in the internal storage of a computer and transmit this information to an external storage unit.

readout device—Refers to a device, consisting usually of physical equipment, that records the computer output either as a curve or as a set of printed numbers or letters.

read pulse—A pulse applied to one or more binary cells to determine whether a bit of information is stored there.

read wire—A particular drive pulse (the drive wire or drive winding) inductively coupled to one or more magnetic cells and, thus, the pulse of magnetomotive force which is then produced.

read/write counter — Data are transferred between the main memory and peripheral devices via read/write channels. Associated with each channel are read/write counters. These counters store the starting and current addresses of the data being transferred by the read/write channel.

read/write cycle—The sequence of operations required to read and write, e.g., restore memory data.

read/write cycle time—The time interval between the start of a cycle in which the memory is read and new data are entered, and the end of that cycle.

read/write head—1. The device that reads and writes information on tape, or disk storage devices. 2. A small electromagnet used for reading, recording, or erasing polarized spots, which represent information on magnetic tape, disk, or other media.

read/write memory — A memory in which each cell may be selected by applying appropriate electrical input signals, and the stored data may be either (A) sensed at appropriate output terminals, or (B) changed in response to other similar electrical input signals.

ready—Refers to the status or condition of being ready to run. A program, task, or hardware device that is in a ready condition needs only a start signal in order to begin operation.

ready status word—Concerns a particular status word indicating that the remote computing system is waiting for entry from the terminal.

real time—1. In solving a problem, a speed sufficient to give an answer within the actual time the problem must be solved. 2. Pertaining to the actual time during which a physical process transpires. 3. Pertaining to the performance of a computation during the actual time that the related physical process transpires in order that results of the computation can be used in guiding the physical process.

real-time bit mapping — Abbreviated RTBM. Real-time bit mapping is often used as a production technique; it is also used to find mask defects and to overcome process problems. But, memory users as well as manufacturers can profitably employ it. For example, part purchasers may use it to look at the possible pattern sensitivities of incoming devices so that they can gear their test procedures to hunt for them. They can also use it to determine a device's sensitivity to parameter variations—changes in supply level, for instance—so that they can set practical design rules for their products. Having once done so, they need have less worry about board-design changes adversely affecting product performance and lead time.

The "real-time" in the technique's name refers to the gathering of data. When this is done, the "catch" RAM is addressed in parallel with the device under test using unscrambled addresses—addresses that are based on the topological location of cells inside a device rather than the scheme adopted by the manufacturer for his pinouts. Thus, the stored data can provide a picture of the physical area in the device in which problems occur.

real-time batch processing — The requirements for real-time action are known frequently to occur in peaks and valleys. In many businesses, these requirements tend to increase from early morning through the middle of the day and to taper off from then on. In other businesses, the occurrence of these demands may be sporadic. The real-time system is so designed that it will automatically, as its facilities are freed from the dynamic demands of real-time processing, load them up with the ordinary day-to-day backlog of less urgent work of the familiar batch-processing type—typically, the sequential processing of sequentially ordered files, such as accounts receivable, accounts payable, or payrolls.

real-time clock — Refers to a device that provides interrupts at twice the ac line frequency. For example, it allows maintenance of an accurate time-of-day clock and the measurement of elapsed time.

real-time clock diagnostic—Refers to a routine that tests proper functioning of the real-time clock operation.

real-time clock-interrupt operation—A real-time clock interrupt occurs when a preset clock count in a unique memory location is incremented to zero. The clock-count location is automatically advanced at each clock time. The real-time clock interrupt is enabled and disabled under program control. Some clock units can provide 13 or more programmable time bases—from one microsecond to one hour. A 1-MHz crystal-controlled oscillator typically generates the clock module's frequency standard. When enabled, the module informs the computer at the completion of each time interval.

real-time clock, microcomputer — In many microcomputer applications, a precision time display, such as a real-time clock or an accurate time delay, must be generated to sequence program flow or to supervise assigned programming tasks. A typical application is a data-acquisition system. Numerous measuring stations producing different physical quantities must be polled for data at predetermined rates to obtain a sufficient number of samples per unit time for each quantity; thus, this system would require a multicycle timer. Also, each sampled value must be associated with its real-time position.

real-time debug program—Functionally equivalent to a stand-alone "debug" utility program, a real-time debug program allows the user to test, examine, and modify a program task while the real-time application program is running.

real-time executive—Real-time executives usually are multitasking executive systems that handle all aspects of priority scheduling, timing, interrupt servicing, input-output control, intertask communications, and all necessary queuing functions. Real-time executives are very compact modular systems that greatly simplify the programming required in real-time applications. Many are completely open-ended. Any number of user-defined software tasks can be supported with the hundreds of software priority levels available. A typical configured executive system consists of the resident nucleus of memory together with the base page locations. A variable amount of storage, lying below the resident nucleus, is required for system tables. The remainder of memory is available to the user for the storage of task programs and data. The executive may be configured with standard I/O routines for various microcomputer interface controllers—teletypewriter or data terminals, analog-to-digital converters, digital-to-analog converters, character printers, etc. A single copy of each standard I/O routine is sufficient to service multiple devices of the same physical type. The executive is modular in design permitting the user to include special-purpose I/O routines at the time of system generation. Standard entry and exit conventions simplify the task of preparing such routines for incorporation into a specific executive configuration. Executives are designed for operation with specific microcomputer systems. The executive program package often consists of a reference document and some types of disks.

real-time input — Refers to instantaneous input to a real-time system, i.e., input that goes into the computer as the activity occurs.

real-time mode—Refers to a mode of operation in which data that are necessary to the control and/or execution of a transaction are affected by the results of the processing. Real-time processing is most usually identified with great speed, but speed is relative. The essence of real-time operation is concurrency—simultaneity. Real time is refinement in the integration of data processing with communications. Real time eliminates slow information-gathering procedures, dated reporting techniques, and lax communications; it ensures that facts within the system are as timely as a prevailing situation, as current as the decisions which they must support. Real time provides answers when answers are needed, and delivers data instantly whenever the need for that data arises. Incoming information is edited, updated, and made available on demand at every level of responsibility. Imminent departures from established standards are automatically detected, and management is notified in time for action.

real-time operation—1. Refers to those data processing techniques designed to allow the machine to utilize information as it becomes available, as opposed to batch processing, which processes information at a time unrelated to the time the information was generated. 2. Operations performed on a computer in time with a physical process so that the answers obtained are useful in controlling that process. 3. The use of the computer as an element of a processing system, in which the times of occurrence of data transmission are controlled by other portions of the system or by physical events outside the system, and cannot be modified for convenience in computer programming. Such an operation either proceeds at the same speed as the events being simulated or at a sufficient speed to analyze or control external events happening concurrently.

real-time remote inquiry — On-line inquiry stations permit users to interrogate the computer files and receive immediate answers to their inquiries. In industry, the stations can be located at dozens of remote locations, such as office, factory, or warehouse. Such a system permits all levels of industrial management to obtain immediate answers to questions about inventories, work in progress, sales, etc.

real-time software, microprocessor — It's the software that distinguishes various real-time microprocessor systems. Software ties together the processor and the peripheral capabilities of the systems. Specifically, the software is organized around two major operating systems: one for program development and one for on-line real-time operation. These two systems must be totally compatible, with the programs developed capable of being directly loaded for execution. In larger configurations, they operate on-line as a background task system.

real-time system—1. A real-time system may be defined as a communications-oriented, data-processing system capable of performing batch-processing functions while concurrently processing inquiries, messages, and data transfer, and generating responses in a time interval directly related to the operational requirements of the system. 2. A system in which information is processed in time to influence the process being monitored or controlled.

reasonableness checks—Refers to various program tests made on information reaching a computer system, or being transmitted from it, to ensure that the data falls within a given range. It is one form of error control.

receiver — 1. Any device equipped for reception of incoming electrically transmitted signals. 2. A device that transforms a varying electrical signal into sound waves or another usable form.

receiver card—An internal plug-in unit containing the printed-circuit wiring and components for a receiver. A typical receiver card accepts ASCII data and translates it into parallel digital data. A receiver card consists of a receiver module, a clock module, and all necessary pull-up resistors. As in a transmitter card, some receiver cards are supplied already programmed for teletypewriter operation at 110 baud, but by using programming jumpers, all the original receiver flexibility is available.

receiver gating—The application of operating voltages to one or more stages of a receiver, only during the part of a cycle when reception is desired.

receiver isolation—Refers to the attenuation between any two receivers connected to the system.

receiver register—One type is an 8-bit

shift register that inputs the received data at a clock rate determined by the control register. The incoming data is assembled to the selected character length and is then transferred to the receiver holding register with logic zeroes filling out any unused high-order bit positions.

record—Refers to a collection of fields; the information relating to one area of activity in a data-processing activity, i.e., all information on one inventory item. Sometimes called item.

record blocking—Concerns the practice of grouping records into data blocks that can be read and/or written to magnetic tape in one operation. This enables the tape to be read more efficiently and reduces time required to read or write the file.

record format—Refers to the design of the contents and organization of a record; ordinarily, a portion of a program specification.

record interface, audio cassette—Refers to a popular storage device that allows virtually unlimited memory storage for data or software. Operates by modulating audio frequencies in the record mode. Demodulates recorded data in playback mode. Connects to any better-quality cassette tape recorder.

recording density—Refers to the number of bits per a unit of length of a single linear track in a recording medium.

recording head—A magnetic head that transforms electrical variations into magnetic variations for storage on magnetic media.

records, grouping of — Refers to the combining of two or more records into one block of information on tape to decrease the time wasted due to tape acceleration and deceleration, and to conserve tape space. This is also called blocking of records.

records, overflow—Refers to those records that cannot be accommodated in the assigned areas of a direct-access file and which must be stored in another area. They can be retrieved by means of a reference that is stored in place of the records in their original assigned area.

recoverable error—Refers to an error condition that allows the continued execution of a program.

recoverable synchronization — Concerns a specific ability to recover or re-establish synchronization automatically when synchronization is lost. It is an important operational feature because disturbances on a communications channel will often upset synchronization.

recovery from fallback—Refers to the restoration of a system to full operation from a fallback mode of operation after the cause of the fallback has been removed.

recovery procedures error—Refers to procedures designed to help isolate and, where possible, to recover from errors in equipment. The procedures are often used in conjunction with programs that record the statistics of machine malfunctions.

recovery program, automatic — Refers to a specific computer program which enables a computer system to keep functioning when a piece of equipment has failed.

rectifier crystal—Refers to diodes that are manufactured with a junction of a base metal and some type of crystalline element, for example, silicon or germanium. Such diodes contrast with vacuum tube diodes and are used in computing equipment to perform logic, buffering, and current conversions necessary for switching and storage transfers.

rectifier diode—A device for converting alternating current into direct current. Two types are silicon and selenium diodes. Those of silicon are often applied for low forward-voltage drops, and signal and power rectification, while those using germanium provide a high rectification ratio, a high inverse-breakdown point, and high signal and power rectification.

recursion—1. The continued repeating of the same operation or group of operations. 2. Any procedure (A) which, while being executed, either calls itself or calls another procedure (B), which in turn calls procedure A.

recycling programs—Refers to an organized arrangement for recycling programs through a computer, when alterations have been made in one program that may change or have an effect on other programs.

red-tape operation—Refers to operations which do not directly contribute to the results, i.e., those internal operations that are necessary to process data, but do not, in themselves, contribute to any final answer.

redundancy — 1. The employment of several devices, each performing the same function, in order to improve the reliability of a particular function. 2. In the transmission of information, that fraction of the gross information content of a message that can be eliminated without loss of essential information.

redundancy check—Refers to an automatic or programmed check based on the systematic insertion, in a message, of bits or characters that are used for error-checking purposes; they are redundant, as they can be eliminated without the loss of essential information. Parity checking is a form of redundancy checking.

redundancy check, longitudinal — An error-control device or system based on the arrangement of data in blocks according to some preset rule, with the correctness of each character within the block being determined on the basis of the specific rule or set.

redundancy check, vertical—Refers to an odd parity check performed on each character of a transmitted block of ASCII-coded data as the block is received.

redundant character—Refers to a character specifically added to a group of characters, to ensure conformity with certain rules, which can be used to detect computer malfunction.

redundant codes — Refers to a self-checking code which is a binary-coded decimal value with an added check bit. Three redundant code examples are the biquinary code, the two-out-of-five code, and the quibinary code.

reed switch — Refers to a special switching device that consists of magnetic contactors which are sealed into a glass tube. The contactors are actuated by the magnetic field of an external solenoid, an electromagnet, or a permanent magnet.

reentrant—That property of a program that enables it to be interrupted at any point by another user, and then resumed from the point of interruption. Reentrant programs are often found in multiprogramming and time-sharing systems, where there is a re-

quirement for a common store of so-called public routines that can be called by any user at any time. The process is controlled by a monitor that preserves the routine's environment (registers, working storage, control indicators, etc.) when it is interrupted and restores that environment when the routine is resumed for its initial use.

reentrant code—A specific set of instructions that form a single copy of a program or routine which is shared by two or more programs, as contrasted to the conventional method of embedding a copy of a subroutine within each program. Typically, reentrant routines are composed completely of instructions and constants that are not subject to modification during execution.

reentrant program—A program (or portion) that can be used simultaneously by different routines. Programs can call themselves repeatedly, or may call a routine that, in turn, calls a reentrant-coded program again.

reentry point—The point at which an instruction or a program is reentered from a subroutine or main program is called the reentry point.

reference address — 1. Addresses that are used in converting related addresses to machine-language addresses. 2. An address used as a reference for a group of related addresses.

reference instruction — An instruction designed to allow reference to systematically arranged or stored data.

reference listing — Refers to a list printed by a compiler to indicate instructions as they appear in the final routine, including details of storage allocation.

reference program table — Refers to that section of storage used as an index for operations, subroutines, and variables.

reference time — In a microcomputer, an instant chosen near the beginning of a switching routine as an origin for time measurements. It is taken as the first instant at which either the instantaneous value of the drive pulse, the voltage response of the magnetic cell, or the integrated voltage response reaches a specified fraction of its peak pulse amplitude.

reference voltage—Refers to an analog computer; a voltage used as a standard of reference, usually the nominal full scale of the computer. Also, a constant unit of computation used in normalizing and scaling for machine solution.

reflected code—Any binary code that changes by only one bit when going from one number to the number immediately following.

reformatting — Refers to the act of changing the representation of data from one format to another, usually with the data being input from a machine-readable source. Reformatting may include the translation or conversion of data values from one character set to another, such as from ASCII to EBCDIC.

refreshing—A process of constantly reactivating or restoring information that decays or fades away when left idle. For instance, the phosphor on a crt screen needs to be constantly reactivated by an electron beam in order to remain illuminated. Cells in dynamic memory elements must be repeatedly accessed in order to avoid a fading away of their contents.

regenerate—The restoring of information that is electrostatically stored in a cell, or on the screen of a cathode-ray tube, in order to counteract fading and other disturbances that are prevalent with this type of information.

regeneration—1. The process of returning a part of the output signal of an amplifier to its input circuit in such a manner that it reinforces the excitation and, thereby, increases the total amplification. 2. Periodic restoration of stored information. 3. The inclusion of logic in a system design to permit the generation of data (when required) from basic formulae as opposed to storage of large volumes of static data.

regeneration, pulse—Refers to the process of restoring a series of pulses to original timing, form, and magnitude.

regenerative memory—A memory device whose contents gradually vanish if not periodically refreshed.

regenerative reading—Refers to a specific read operation which involves the automatic writing of data back into the positions from which it is extracted.

regenerative storage—Refers to storage such as in a crt (cathode-ray tube) that needs to be regenerated to maintain the image.

region—1. In relative coding, a group of location addresses that are all relative to the same specific reference address. 2. A group of machine addresses that refer to a base address.

regional breakpoints—Regional breakpoints give the user a powerful tool in debugging multiprocessor systems. A bug in any one processor can destroy data in the common memory, producing a system failure. Previously, emulators did not offer a direct method for tracking down these memory accesses. With regional breakpoints, however, any memory access into a group of preset user-selected locations (1000 to 2000, for example) sets a breakpoint.

register—1. A digital computer device capable of retaining information, often that contained in a small subset (e.g., one word) of the aggregate information. 2. A temporary storage device used for one or more words to facilitate arithmetical, logical, or transferral operation. Examples are the accumulator, index, instruction, and other registers. The accessibility to the CPU is basic to registers. The number of registers in a microprocessor is one of the prime criteria for judging its worth. 3. A memory device capable of containing one or more computer bits or words. A register has zero-memory latency time and negligible memory access time. 4. A term to designate a specific computer unit for storing a group of bits or characters.

register, accumulator — Refers to that part of the arithmetic unit in which the results of an operation remain, and into which numbers are brought to and from storage.

register, address—A register in a microcomputer where an address is stored.

register address field—The part of a microcomputer instruction that contains a register address.

register addressing—Refers to an addressing mode using a register as the effective address of one of the operands, mainly to shorten instruction size.

register, arithmetic—Refers to the particular register in a microcomputer that holds operands required for certain operations, e.g., it may hold the multiplier for multiplication, or the addend for addition.

register arrangement—The number of registers in a microprocessor is considered by many to be the most important feature of its architecture. Registers in a microcomputer have many varied and different uses. The ways that they may be used are embodied in the instruction set and the most important resource to many programmers is the set of CPU registers. The more registers there are, the less likelihood there is of main storage references. To be considered in conjunction with the addressing modes is the register arrangement. Some systems have: general-purpose registers, a hardware stack pointer, and a program counter. Registers not dedicated to any specific function can be used as determined by the instruction that is decoded; they can be used for operand storage. For example, contents of two registers can be added and stored in another register, they can contain the address of an operand or serve as pointers to the address of an operand, they can be used for the autoincrement or autodecrement features, or they can be used as index registers for convenient data and program access.

register, base — Refers to a register whose contents are used to modify a microcomputer instruction prior to its execution.

register, buffer memory—1. A register in which a word is stored as it comes from memory (reading) or just prior to its entering memory (writing). *See* register. 2. The memory buffer serves as a buffer register for all information passing between the processor and the main memory, and serves as a buffer directly between main memory and peripheral equipment during data-break information transfers. The memory buffer is also used as a distributor shift register for the analog-to-digital converter.

register, cache — Refers to a small, high-speed memory buffer between the processor and main memory where often-used data are duplicated. Most often uses content-addressable registers.

register, circulating — 1. Refers to a

shift register in which the stored information is moved right or left, and the information from one end is reinserted at the other end. In the case of a one-character right shift, the right-most character reappears as the new left-most character and every other character is shifted one position to the right. 2. A register in which the process, as in the preceding statement, is continuously occurring. This can be used as a delaying mechanism.

register, console display — Refers to sets of indicator lights on a computer console that display the bit-pattern contents of registers.

register, control—1. A register which holds the identification of the instruction word to be executed next in time sequence, following the current operation. The register is often a counter that is incremented to the address of the next sequential-storage location, unless a transfer or other special instruction is specified by the program. (Synonymous with program counter, and contrasted with program register.) 2. The accumulator, register, or storage unit that stores the current instruction governing a computer operation; an instruction register.

register, data (microcomputers) –– The data registers, when addressed, store the data present on the MPU data bus during an MPU Write operation. This data will also appear on those peripheral lines that have been programmed as PIA outputs. If a peripheral line is serving as an input, the corresponding bit position of the data register can still be written into by the MPU; however, the information on the data bus will not appear on that peripheral data line. During an MPU Read operation, the data present on peripheral lines programmed as inputs are transferred directly to the MPU data bus. The PIA control registers allow the MPU to establish and control the operating modes of the peripheral control lines. By means of these lines, control information is passed back and forth between the MPU and peripheral devices.

register, delay-line—A unique register incorporating a delay line plus a means for a signal regeneration and a feedback channel. Thus, the storage of data in serial representation is achieved through continual circulation.

register, designation — A register into which data are being placed.

register, double-word — Refers to microcomputer registers that are used together to hold a double word (a 16- or 32-bit word).

register, external — These registers, which can be referenced by the program, are located in control storage as specific addresses. These are the locations (registers) that the programmer references when he desires that some sort of computational function be carried out.

register, file — A bank of multiple-bit registers that can be used as temporary storage locations for data or instructions and is often referred to as a stack.

register, index—A specific register that contains a quantity which may be used to modify memory addresses.

register, indirect-addressing—A procedure or addressing mode that utilizes the contents of memory-pointer registers to indicate a memory address.

register, input-buffer — That device which accepts data from input units, or media, such as magnetic tape or disks and then transfers this data to internal storage.

register, input/output—Refers to registers that temporarily hold input and output data.

register, instruction—A temporary storage device that retains the instruction code of the instruction currently being executed.

register length—The number of digits, characters, or bits that a register can store.

register, memory-address — Abbreviated MAR. A special location in memory that is selected for data storage or retrieval and which is determined by the MAR. This register can directly address all words of the standard main memory or those in any preselected field of extended main memory.

register, multiplier-quotient—The register used to contain a multiplier in multiplication and the quotient in division.

register, program — 1. Register in the control unit that stores the current instruction of the program and controls computer operation during the execution of the program. 2. A temporary storage device or area which retains the instruction code of the instruction being executed.

register, PSW — Abbreviation for program status word register. A register that contains the processor-status information resulting from the previous operation (carry, borrow, overflow, zero flags, interrupt status).

register, shift—A microcomputer register that is capable of shifting data as directed.

register, sequence — Controls the sequence of the instructions.

register, sequence control — A hardware register that is used by the computer to remember the location of the next instruction to be processed in the normal sequence, but which is subject to branching, execute instructions, and interrupts.

register, shift—A register in which the characters may be shifted one or more positions to the right or left. In a right shift, the rightmost character is lost. In a left shift, the leftmost character is lost.

register, stack-oriented — Many microprocessors offer stack-oriented registers that can be accessed only in a last-in/first-out basis—the so-called LIFO, or pushdown, stack. These are used for subroutine nesting, interrupts, and for temporary storage of data. They can be either on the chip (a hardware stack) or external to the processor in memory (a software, or pointer, stack). The hardware stack permits higher-speed operation, but it has limited size. The size of the software stack may be as large as available memory space permits, but the stack must be maintained by the program.

register, standby—A register in which accepted or verified information can be stored so as to be available for a rerun in case the processing of the information is spoiled by a mistake in the program, or a malfunction in the computer.

relation—Refers to assembler programming; the comparison of two expressions to see if the value of one is equal to, less than, or greater than the value of the other.

relational breakpoints — Relational breakpoints occur after either a memory Read or a memory Write that is followed by a second memory Read or Write. Some systems have this capability, which was formerly reserved for more expensive development systems. Other low-cost emulators rely on tandem breakpoints. They can specify two memory Read or Write operations, one following the other, but not a Read followed by a Write or vice versa. Some systems also permit a breakpoint to be specified after an I/O Read or Write followed by a second I/O Read or Write.

relational operator—Refers to assembler programming; an operator that can be used in an arithmetic or character relation to indicate the comparison to be performed between the terms in the relation.

relative address—Refers to an address that will be altered to an absolute address at the time the program is being run on the microcomputer.

relative address label—Refers to a label used to identify the location of data in a program by reference to their position with respect to some other location in that program.

relative addressing—Permits addresses to be specified relative to the address of the current instruction (program counter), e.g., to provide position independence.

relative addressing, microprocessor— Relative addressing shortens the address part of the instruction by permitting references within some narrow range relative to a CPU register. In many systems, that register is the program location counter. The address field of the instruction is added to the program location counter's value (in some cases, with sign extension) to arrive at a datum address. In larger computers, the base-displacement form of addressing is used; this relative form uses a special (base) register plus the displacement carried as an abbreviated address in the instruction to compute a storage address.

relative addressing mode—Refers to a basic mode that specifies a memory location in the CPU's program location-counter register (on some systems). This addressing mode is used for branch instructions, in which case an op code is added to the relative address to complete the branching instruction.

relative coding—Refers to a code in which all addresses are specified or written with respect to an arbitrarily selected position, or in which all addresses are represented symbolically (in a computable form).

relative time clock—Abbreviated RTC. Using a relative time clock, the executive keeps track of time. At every relative time-clock (RTC) interrupt, the interrupt service routine returns control to the executive, which checks to see if a higher-priority device is seeking execution or if a program wants to be turned "on."

relay—An electromechanical device in which contacts are opened and/or closed by variations in the conditions of one electric circuit and, thereby, affect the operation of other devices in the same or in other electric circuits.

relay contacts — Contacts that are closed or opened by the movement of a relay armature.

relay, electromagnetic — Refers to an electromagnetic switching device having multiple electrical contacts that are operated by an electrical current through a coil. It is used to complete electrical circuits with an applied control current and, also, as a mechanical binary counter.

relay, reed—A special switching device which consists of magnetic contactors that are sealed into a glass tube. The contactors are actuated by the magnetic field of an external solenoid, electromagnet, or a permanent magnet.

relocatable assembler — A relocatable assembler generates an object program with memory addresses entered as displacements from a relative program origin, or as external references.

relocatable expression—Refers to assembler programming: an assembly-time expression whose value is affected by program relocation. A relocatable expression can represent a relocatable address.

relocatable macroassembler — A program that permits instruction groups to be combined for execution, using symbolic addresses. The typical relocating macroassembler provides a quick way to create a microcomputer code in a modular fashion. The design supports absolute or relocatable object-code formats, global definitions, external references, macros and conditional assembly. Optionally, a cross-reference and/or symbol table may be generated, and the size of the symbol table is only limited by available storage on the disk. All diagnostic messages are routed to the system console with the pertinent line number, the error and the statement itself, so it is not necessary to wait for a listing to locate erroneous statements (some systems).

relocatable program—Refers to a program that is written so it may be located and executed from many areas in memory.

relocatable program loader—Refers to a program that assigns absolute origins to relocatable subroutines, object programs, and data, assigns absolute locations to each of the instructions or data, and modifies the reference to these instructions or data.

relocatable term—Refers to assembler programming; a term whose value is affected by program relocation.

relocatability — Concerns a capability whereby programs or data may be located in a place in memory at different times without requiring modification to the program. In some units, segments of the program and all data are independently relocatable with no loss in efficiency.

relocating object loader—Refers to a device that is used to load and link object programs produced by assemblers. Binary programs produced by the binary dump and link editor programs can also be loaded. This program satisfies external references between separate program segments, generates linkages to externals as required, and maintains a common literal pool for usage by the completed program complex. When loading library subroutine packages, this program selectively loads only those segments required to satisfy external references.

relocation dictionary—Refers to a part of a program that contains information necessary to change addresses when it is relocated.

relocation, dynamic — The act of as-

signing absolute addresses when a program is loaded into memory.

relocation, static—The act of assigning absolute addresses at linking time.

remote-access storage and retrieval—Refers to various remote-access storage-and-retrieval systems that involve applications such as reservation systems, insurance companies, credit checking, and similar real-time operations.

remote batch — A method of entering jobs into the computer from a remote terminal, at a convenient time.

remote-batch processing — Refers to computer programs or data being entered into a remote terminal for transmission to the central processor. Jobs can be "batched" before transmission. Results of the processing may be transmitted back to the originating point. Also called remote job entry; abbreviated RJE.

remote console—Refers to various terminal units in a remote computing system. Some of the distant consoles are equipped with facilities to transmit and receive data to and from the central processor. Connection to the processor is normally made through a remote computing system exchange.

remote control monitoring systems — Various remote control equipment systems relate to the status monitoring control and supervision field. Due to their unique scanning and encoding techniques, as well as modular construction, they can monitor a single remote site or they may be used for complete control and supervision of a large system. Configurations are easily arranged for multipoint operation, continuous reporting or polled scanning, dedicated or shared displays, and transmission of analog functions. Automatic reporting and control may be accomplished because of computer-compatible codes that allow direct computer or tty interfacing.

remote-control signals — Some microcomputers have signal lines for the Run, Halt, and Reset functions, as well as Load and Power On. These signals permit the processor to be operated from a remote-control panel located up to 50 feet or more from the processor. The function of each remote-control signal is indicated. Examples are: Remote Halt Indicator, Remote Run Indicator, Remote Power On, etc.

remote data concentration—Refers to communications processors that are used for the multiplexing of data from many low-speed lines or terminals (or low-activity lines or terminals) onto one or more higher speed lines.

remote debugging—Refers to using remote terminals in a mode suitable for testing of programs, most frequently found in systems designed for scientific or engineering computation.

remote inquiry—Refers to inquiry stations which, when operated on-line, permit humans to interrogate the computer files and receive immediate answers to inquiries. In industry, they can be located at dozens of remote areas.

remote job entry (RJE) — 1. One type RJE allows various systems to share the resources of a batch-oriented computer at speeds of up to 4800 baud. This enables such tasks as data transmission, report generation, file updating, and the compilation and running of computer programs in COBOL, FORTRAN, or RPG. The processor gives the user access to centrally located data files and access to the power necessary to process those files. Emulators are compatible with various terminals that are available. 2. Refers to processing of stacked jobs over communication lines via terminals typically equipped with line printers. Small computers also can operate as RJE stations if equipped with communications adapters. 3. *See also* remote-batch processing.

repeat counter—The repeat counter is used to control repeated operations, such as block transfer and repeated search commands. To execute a repeated instruction "k" times, the repeat counter must be loaded with "k" prior to the execution of the instruction. A repeated sequence may be suspended to process an interrupt, with circuitry providing for the completion of the repeated sequence after the interrupt has been processed.

repeatability—The closeness of agreement among a number of consecutive measurements of a constant signal, approached from the same direction. Repeatability is expressed as maximum nonrepeatability in percent of span or counts of error.

repeatability, timer — The maximum timing variation between repetitive operations, generally expressed as a percentage of the set time. In most cases, the repeatability band falls well within the specified accuracy band. Sometimes called *repeat accuracy,* the characteristic is commonly referred to in the timer industry as *accuracy.*

repeater—Refers to a system component which reconstitutes signals into standard voltages, currents, and timing.

repertoire, instruction—1. Refers to the set of instructions that a computing or data processing system is capable of performing. 2. The set of instructions that an automatic coding system assembles.

report generation—Refers to the production of complete output reports, from only a specification of the desired content and arrangement and from specifications regarding the input file.

report generation parameters — Refers to the automatic creation of reports according to user specifications. To use the report generator, the programmer merely prepares a set of parameters defining control fields and report lines. These parameters are used as input to the report generator that produces a symbolic program. The assembled version of this program accepts raw data as input, edits it, and generates the desired reports.

report generator—1. A special computer routine designed to prepare an object routine that, when later run on the computer, produces the desired report. 2. A problem-oriented language capable of automatically generating the machine instructions required to transform an input file into a desired report. *See* generator. 3. A techique for producing complete data-processing reports by giving only a description of the desired content and format of the output reports, and certain information concerning the input file.

report program generator—Refers to a type of processing program that can be used to generate object programs which will produce reports from existing sets of data. Abbreviated RPG.

report program generator language — Abbreviated RPG. A popular problem-oriented language for commercial programming, especially in smaller installations. Like COBOL, RPG has a powerful and relatively simple input/output file manipulation (including table look-up), but is relatively limited in algorithmic capabilities.

report program generator II—Abbreviated RPG II. RPG II is a software processor adhering to accepted industry standards that provides a convenient means of preparing reports from information available in computer-readable form. RPG II can also establish and update information files in conjunction with report generation. RPG II features array processing, ISAM and direct-file processing, and extended calculation operations. A report program generator provides a programming method for producing a wide variety of reports. These may range from a listing of a disk file or a tape reel to a precisely arranged, calculated, and edited tabulation of data from several input sources.

RPG II is a powerful business-oriented programming language that can be a primary language for small-business computer users. RPG II is a result-oriented language. RPG II is oriented toward the business-user's problems, describing reporting requirements rather than being aimed primarily towards computer procedures. With RPG II, routine report and file updating jobs can be programmed and debugged very quickly. While RPG II is a sophisticated report generator, it was designed for conciseness and ease of use. Only a few commands are needed to create and maintain files and to generate reports. However, for more complex applications, RPG II has a complete range of advanced commands that makes it as versatile and as powerful a language as COBOL.

request for repetition, automatic (ARQ) —Refers to a system employing an error-detecting code and so arranged that a signal detected as being in error automatically initiates a request for retransmission.

request to send—One of the basic data set interchange leads defined in EIA Standard RS-232-B.

rerun point — In a computer program, one of a set of preselected points located in a computer program such that, if an error is detected between two such points, the problem may be rerun by returning to the last such point instead of returning to the start of the program.

rerun routine — 1. A computer routine designed to be used, in the event of a malfunction or mistake, to reconstitute a routine from the previous rerun point. 2. The rerun of a program usually starting from the last previous rerun point, after an interruption caused by an error or other fault.

rescue dump — A rescue dump (R dump) is the recording on disk or tape of the entire memory, which includes the status of the system at the time the dump is made. R dumps are made so that in the event of power failure, etc., a run can be resumed from the last rescue point (R point) rather than rerunning the entire program.

reset—1. To restore a storage device to a prescribed state. 2. To place a binary cell in the initial, or zero, state. (Also see Clear.) 3. To return a register or storage location to zero or to a specified initial condition.

reset key, error—Refers to a push button that, when pushed, acknowledges an error and resets the error detection mechanism indicated by the check light. This is required to restart a program after an error has been discovered in batch mode.

reset pulse — 1. A drive pulse which tends to reset a magnetic cell. 2. A pulse used to set a flip-flop or magnetic core to its original state.

reset switch — The reset switch, when toggled, generates a master reset condition. The processor is halted, all internal registers are set to zero, the interrupt facility is disabled, the input/output interface is initialized, and the program counter is set to a specific range. The reset switch also functions as an indicator test in that all indicators are illuminated when the reset switch is toggled. (Some systems.)

resident compiler—Although many microprocessors require a cross-compiler—one that runs only on a larger machine—resident compilers that use the microcomputer itself to produce their programs are technically feasible with the advanced state of micro-computer development and inexpensive peripherals. Such a compiler requires several passes to reduce a source program to machine language, using the developmental system itself, and eliminating the need for large-system support.

resident macroassembler — A resident macroassembler translates symbolic assembly-language instructions into the appropriate machine-operation codes. In addition to eliminating the errors of hand-translation, the ability to refer to program addresses with symbolic names makes it easy for the user to modify programs by adding or deleting instructions. Full macro capability eliminates the need to re-write similar sections of code repeatedly and greatly simplifies the problem of program documentation.

resident program—Refers to a program that is permanently located in storage. For example, the nucleus in main storage or a system library on direct-access storage.

resident software — Various resident software packages operate stand-alone terminals and systems without dependence on outside hardware. Some packages consist of advanced macroassemblers, text editors, disk operating systems, file maintenance systems, and real-time debugging procedures. These resident software packages are often stored on diskettes when they are not in use and can be loaded into the terminal CPU in less than one minute.

residue check—Refers to a check in which each operand is accompanied by the remainder obtained by dividing this number by N, the remainder then being used as a check digit or digits. Synonymous with modulo-N check.

resist—In the preparation of a printed-circuit board, a material, such as ink, paint, metallic plating, etc., that is used to protect the desired portions of the conductive material from the action of the etchant, solder, or plating.

resist-etchant—Any material deposited onto a copper-clad base material to prevent the conductive area underneath from being etched away.

resistor-transistor-logic, RTL — Logic performed by resistors. Transistors are used to produce an inverted output.

resolution—1. The smallest incremental step in separating a measurement into its constituent parts. In a digital system, resolution is one count in its least significant digit. 2. The ratio of maximum to minimum readings of a measuring system. 3. The process of separating the parts which compose a mixed body. 4. A measure of the smallest possible increment of change in the variable output of a device.

resolver—1. A means for resolving a vector into two mutually perpendicular components. 2. A transformer, with a coupling between primary and secondary that can be varied. 3. A device that separates or breaks up a quantity, particularly a vector, into constituent parts or elements, e.g., the mutually perpendicular components of a plane vector.

resolver differential—A device used for zero shift or offset in numerical control systems that utilize resolver or flat-type feedback. It is electrically connected between the reference and the feedback. When the shaft of the resolver is turned, it shifts the phase of the reference signal to the position-feedback unit and creates the signal that tells the slide to move.

resonant-gate transistor — A type of field-effect transistor with a mechanically tuned input, obtained by a vibrating cantilever assembly.

response time—1. The time (usually expressed in cycles of the power frequency) required for the output voltage of a magnetic amplifier to reach 63% of its final average value in response to a step-function change of signal voltage. 2. The time required for the pointer of an instrument to come to apparent rest in its new position after the measured quantity abruptly changes to a new, constant value. 3. The amount of time elapsed between generation of an inquiry at a data communications terminal and receipt of a response at that same terminal. Response time, thus defined, includes: transmission time to the computer, processing time at the computer, including access time to obtain any file records needed to answer the inquiry, and transmission time back to the terminal.

restart procedures, checkpoint — Refers to various checkpoint and restart procedures, which are techniques associated with computers. They make it possible, in the event of an error or interruption, to continue processing from the last checkpoint rather than from the beginning of the run. These techniques are included in applications that require many hours of processing time, since heavy machine scheduling and deadlines generally do not permit a complete rerun. To establish checkpoints, processing intervals are determined, each being based upon a certain number of items, transactions, or records processed. At each interval or checkpoint, the stored program identifies input and output records and, then, records them along with the contents of important storage areas such as counters and registers. At the same time, accuracy of processing up to that point is established. Restart procedures are the means by which processing is continued after an error or interruption.

restore—1. Refers to the return of a cycle index, a variable address, or other computer word to its initial value. *See also* reset. 2. Periodic regeneration of charge, especially in volatile condenser-action storage systems.

restorer pulse generator—Refers to a specifically designed generator that generates pulses for special timing or gating in a digital computer; i.e., pulses that are used as inputs to the gate of a device to aid in pulse-shaping and timing.

retentivity—The degree or ability of a material to retain magnetic flux.

return address—1. Relates to that part of a subprogram that connects it with the main program. 2. A process to gather or unite two or more separately written, assembled, or compiled programs or routines into various single operational entities; i.e., to complete linkage. Some computer systems have special programs called linkage editors to correct address components into symbols or to perform relocation to avoid overlapping. 3. A communications line between two or more stations or terminals.

return from zero time — The elapsed time between the end of a pulse at full strength and the start of the absent electrical flow or some lower level on electrical flow. Contrasts with rise time.

return to bias (RB)—Refers to a mode of recording in which the state of the recording medium changes from a bias state to another state and returns to record binary 1.

return to zero (RZ)—A pulse that ends any time during a reference cycle.

reverse scan—Refers to a particular editing operation designed to suppress zeroes, i.e., to replace them with blanks and eliminate the zero suppression word mark.

reverse video—This allows black characters on a white field in any area of the screen, and is useful for displaying several types of information at one time on the crt.

rewrite—Also called regeneration. In a storage device where the information is destroyed by being "read," the restoring of information into the storage area.

ribbon cable—The term "ribbon cable" can refer to etched flexible circuit flat cable, round conductor laminated cable, round conductor extruded cable, or bonded round conductor cable. The word cable is usually omitted.

ribbon cable connectors—Devices that are designed to terminate ribbon cable with round connectors.

ribbon contact connectors—A rectangular connector with a self-wiping contact. *Not to be confused with* ribbon cable connector.

right shift—Refers to an operation in which digits of a word are displaced to the right. This has the effect of division in arithmetical shift.

ring counter—A loop of interconnected bistable elements such that one and only one is in a specified state at any given time and such that, as input signals are counted, the position of the element in the specified state moves in an ordered sequence around the loop.

ripple — 1. The ac component arising from sources within a dc power supply. Unless otherwise specified, ripple is the ratio, expressed in percent, of the root-mean-square value of the ripple voltage to the absolute value of the total voltage. 2. The excursions above and below the average peak amplitude. 3. The percent of ripple is the ratio of the effective time. Often used to describe a form of bandsplitter that periodically rearranges the frequency displacement of sub-bands.

ripple counter — Refers to a binary counting system in which flip-flops are connected in series. When the first flip-flop changes, it affects the second, which affects the third, and so on. If there are ten flip-flops in a row, the signal must go sequentially from the first flip-flop to the tenth.

ripple filter—A low-pass filter that is designed to reduce the ripple current but at the same time permit the free passage of the dc current, e.g., from a rectifier.

rise time — The time required for the leading edge of a pulse to rise from 10% to 90% of its final value. It is proportionate to the time constant and is a measure of the steepness of the wavefront.

robot — Refers to a specific device equipped with sensing instruments for detecting input signals or environmental conditions, but with a reacting or guidance mechanism that can perform sensing, calculations, etc., and with stored programs for resultant actions, i.e., a machine running itself.

robot capability—Properly programmed, a robot can solve problems in the two general areas of visual inspection and identity and attitude analysis. Available routines have the capability to extract the 2-dimensional outline of the image of an object, locate corners, find holes, and separate multiple objects, identify an object on the basis of its distinguishing features, and specify the grip points, acquisition, and orientation of a workpiece. In one set of laboratory experiments, the developmental system has identified each of four different foundry castings and determined their position and orientation so that the system's manipulator can pick them up off a conveyor belt.

robotic artificial intelligence — Robots with "artificial intelligence" have recently moved into factories from research labs. These machines can "see" with television eyes and "feel" with artificial skin and pressure transducers. They can move their fingers, arms, and legs using feedback control circuits. And, in a functional sense, they can "think" in order to make their own decisions without continuous human control, by using computer programs that operate on sensory inputs.

robotics—Refers to a specific area of the field of artificial intelligence. Robots have been designed by industrial firms as well as research institutes to perform relatively simple tasks such as arranging blocks, assembling simple pumps, and mounting wheels on automobiles. The use of industrial robots is an important trend since robots can increase productivity and relieve workers from dehumanizing tasks. The technology of systems and cybernetics is undergoing a rapid growth and will have a profound effect on society.

roll-in/roll-out — Generally refers to a return (roll-in) to a main or internal storage unit of data and programs, that has been previously transferred (roll-out) from main or internal memory units to various external or auxiliary units.

roll-out—To record the contents of main storage in auxiliary storage.

ROM—Abbreviation for read-only memory. 1. A blank ROM can be considered to be a mosaic of undifferentiated cells. Many types of ROMs exist. A basic type of ROM is one programmed by a mask pattern as part of the final manufacturing stage. PROMs are "programmable" ROMs. PROMs are relatively permanent although they can be erased with the aid of an ultraviolet irradiation instrument. Others can be electrically erased and are called EPROMs. 2. A device where information is stored permanently or semi-permanently and can be read out, but not altered in operation.

ROM basics—The need for a fast non-volatile memory was answered first by the read-only memory (ROM). Practically all ROMs are random access. Information is stored in mask-programmable ROMs at the time of manufacture. Ones and zeros are programmed into the device to indicate the presence or absence of a control-gate voltage, which determines whether the addressed transistor is "on" or "off." The permanence of this technique is obvious, and the speeds range from 200 nanoseconds

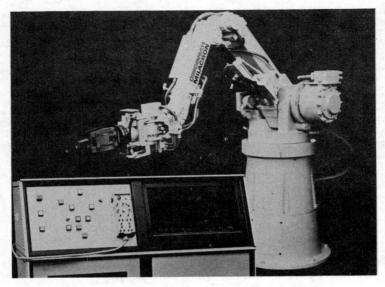

Robotics (Courtesy Cincinnati Milacron, Inc.).

(ns) to 800 ns access time for MOS ROMs.

ROM bootstrap—Nearly every computer uses at least one ROM program, the most common one being a ROM bootstrap loader. The bootstrap loader is a minimum program which, if everything in memory has been wiped out, will allow the programmer to recreate his main memory load.

ROM errors — Single errors occur at random as a result of flaws in the chip, or occasionally when a bit in a programmable ROM reverts to its unprogrammed state—unlikely in recent versions of programmable ROMs. Any single error changes the parity of its column from odd to even. Multiple errors in a single word change the parity of every column involved. They occur only rarely. If a data output line is stuck at 1 or 0, there may be a short-circuit to ground or to a power line from wiring connected to that output, or the output driver circuit may be dead. Since most ROMs have a total capacity equal to a power of 2, the number of words is even, and the stuck output line looks like an even number of 1s or an even number of 0s—thus creating an even parity. (This is one reason why even parity

in the check word won't work.) If an address input line is stuck at 1 or 0, it may similarly indicate a short circuit somewhere in or near the ROM, or a dead bit position in the address input buffer. This fault renders exactly half of the words inaccessible; an attempt to read all the words in the memory will read the other half twice, necessarily generating even parity. (Even if a user perversely loads a whole ROM with two identical groups of words, the contents of the one location reserved for a check word must necessarily be different from its image in the other half of the memory.) Likewise, if two address lines are stuck, a sweep of the ROM reads one quarter of the words four times, again giving even parity.

ROM, field-alterable—Generally, these work with many popular microcomputers and minicomputers. They are often packaged on a single pc board. Some field-alterable ROMs can be programmed at the single-bit level. With capacitive-type units, the alteration is almost as simple as a pencil erasure. Any discrete bit in storage can be reprogrammed repeatedly, even while the system is operating.

ROM functions—ROM is used to store

the microprogram or a fixed program depending upon the microprogrammability of the CPU. The microprogram provides the translation from higher-level user commands, such as ADD, MPY, etc., down to a series of detailed codes recognizable by the microprocessor for execution. The size of the ROM varies according to user requirements within the maximum allowed capacity that is dictated by the addressing capability of the microprocessor.

ROM loader—Refers to a typical binary loader program that is implemented in read-only memory. It eliminates the manual bootstrap loading procedure. Typically, a ROM loader consists of a 3 inch × 2.5 inch (7.5 cm × 6.25 cm) printed-circuit card that plugs into sockets located inside the processor enclosure and comes complete with doumentation.

ROM, mask-programmed control — Some microcomputers can be tailored to design requirements through use of a mask-programmed control ROM. In effect, the designer can choose, within limits, the basic machine-language instruction set as he writes the microprogram. In some systems, this flexibility simplifies use of a microcomputer as an emulator of another computer. The instruction set of the other computer is microprogrammed into the microcomputer control ROM. Execution of a program instruction corresponds to selection of the equivalent microroutine. Microprogramming can also be used for critical short routines in applications where speed is of the essence. The routines can be executed faster when written in the basic control language of the microcomputer. A single machine-language instruction triggers the routine. The microprogram instructions are more elemental than the usual machine-language instructions. Each instruction controls limited simple operations in the microcomputer. A sequence of instructions is required for most machine-language instructions.

ROM, mask vs. bipolar — The primary difference in read-only memories is in the forming of the open or closed contact; that is, in the design of the cell. In mask-programmable read-only memories, the contact is made by selectively including or excluding a small conducting jumper during the final phase of semiconductor manufacture. In bipolar-programmable read-only memories, the contact is made with a fusible material of such that the contact can later be opened, allowing the data pattern to be configured by the user after the device has been manufactured.

ROM microprogramming — By microprogramming a ROM on the microprocessor chip, a logic designer can implement in one package, together with some ancillary memory, a function that often took 50 or more TTL packages. Designs can be changed by a simple software program, and reprogrammable ROMs can be used to change systems in the field. In effect, design engineers must become programmers in order to discard many tedious, but formerly essential, logic optimization techniques. The disadvantages of ROM programming apply to microprogramming. It is relatively slow and expensive, and users must be absolutely sure their logic is correct before encoding a microprogram, since debugging costs are high. Another disadvantage of microprogramming is that all computer programs that use microprogrammed instructions are executable only on computers that hold the required microprogram. Those individuals who microprogram their own microcomputer will find that it may soon become the only machine in the world on which their computer programs will run. The most serious disadvantage of microcomputers that are constructed using microprogrammed CPUs, though, is their slow speed. A normal CPU can be designed to execute a number of operations in one cycle. This is possible because a fixed number of unique logic sequences will enable the entire instruction set. It is most unlikely that the signal sequences will be in any modular form; i.e., if the execution sequence were altered from c-d-e-f to c-e-f-d, the entire signal sequence, from the start to the end of the instruction, may have to be altered. But a microprogrammable computer specifically allows users to string program execution steps together and thus create their own instruction set. That means signal sequences must be modular; and to be modular, most instruction steps will be triggered by the cycle clock pulse and will require an entire cycle. Users have to be sure that their program is right before they enable it into a ROM. On most microcomputers, once enabled, the program gives no flexibilities that are not an inherent outcome of the encoded instruction sequence. This can be inconvenient. However, if users plan to load data from a peripheral device, process it in some way, and then store it, there is no reason why they should not include in the ROM program some instructions to read data from the selected peripheral device.

ROM-oriented architecture — A ROM-oriented architecture is one in which the microprocessor instruction set can be executed completely from ROM without the need for external RAM. This requires an internal stack for subroutines and internal registers for indirect addressing operations. The instruction set needs logical instructions for bit manipulation, in addition to good byte manipulation. Decimal arithmetic capability is also desirable. For many purposes, memory size need not be large. A small memory size implies efficiency in addressing, indicated by short memory- and decision-branching instructions.

ROM/RAM simulator—Refers to a program that enables designers to develop and test machine-code software in microprocessors, bit-slice, and minicomputer systems. Most have an expandable word length beyond 128 bits (including word lengths in excess of 40 bits). Users can run the system at full speed without wasting PROMs, and diagnostic tests can be conducted on assembly-line systems with minimum down time on many systems.

ROM reprogrammability — The fuse PROM, of course, is a one-time programmable circuit, and although the UV EPROM can be wiped clean with a UV lamp, many applications won't have a lamp available. In both cases, special programming circuits are required to generate the high voltage or current pulses that perform the actual bit programming. A partial solution is available with the electrically alterable ROMs (read-mostly memories) and the newer electrically erasable PROMs—EAROMs and EE-PROMs, respectively—which can be

wiped blank by electrical signals, either one word at a time or all at once, and which can then be electrically reprogrammed with new data.

ROM simulator—A ROM simulator is a general-purpose instrument that is used to replace ROMs or PROMs in a system during program debug. Because it offers real-time in-circuit simulation, it can be used in the engineering prototype, preproduction version, or production model to find and correct program errors or to add new features. The ROM simulator provides the software documentation required during debug and, often, a user-configured assembler makes program development a relatively simple task. A ROM simulator is an important tool for designers of ROM-based systems. Because it is a general-purpose instrument, it can be used from project to project with different processors. The use of a ROM simulator provides a simplified and inexpensive means of altering microprograms by enabling the loading, displaying, or modifying of the contents of any microprogram address.

ROM testing—Circuits that use ROMs to replace hard-wired logic tend to have many feedback loops. In many cases, technicians troubleshoot the ROMs along with the rest of the circuit—a practice that can lead to confusion. Therefore, it is best to install sockets for the ROMs so that the memories can be checked prior to installation on the board. This not only simplifies the test but also provides a breakpoint in the loops. The sockets can also be used to connect to the test equipment during checkout. Thus, the test system can be directed to generate ROM patterns while the system monitors the results coming back as inputs to the ROM. (Inputs to the ROM for address lines are usually a function of the previous ROM address pattern.) Circuits with ROMs also tend to have many jumps and subroutines so that it is often difficult to verify whether the instruction sequence follows the right course. Single-step capability is easy to implement at points where an external break is advisable.

rotate—Refers to a process of moving in a circular manner each bit in a register, either to the right or left.

Thus, each bit that leaves one end of the register enters the other end.

routine—1. A set of computer instructions arranged in a correct sequence and used to direct a microcomputer in performing one or more desired operations. 2. A series of microcomputer instructions which perform a specific limited task.

routine, closed — Refers to a routine which is not inserted as a block of instructions within a main routine but is entered by basic linkage from the main routine.

routine, correction—Concerns a particular routine that is designed to be used in or after a microcomputer failure, malfunction, or program or operator error, and which, thereby, can reconstitute the routine being executed before another error or malfunction, and from the most recent or closest rerun point.

routine, direct-insert—1. A separately coded sequence of instructions that is inserted in another instruction sequence directly in low order of the line. 2. A directly inserted subroutine to the main-line program specifically where it is required. 3. A subroutine that must be located and inserted into the main routine at each place it is used.

routine, floating-point—A set of subroutines that can cause a microcomputer to execute floating-point arithmetic. These routines may be used to simulate floating-point operations on a microcomputer with no built-in floating-point hardware.

routine, independent—Refers to a routine that is executed independently of manual operations, but only if certain conditions occur within a program or record, or during some other process.

routine, input — A routine, sometimes stored permanently in a microcomputer, to allow reading of programs and data into the machine (bootstrap).

routine, interrupt control—Refers to a microcomputer routine that is entered when an interrupt occurs (for analysis of the interrupt cause).

routine, minimum-latency — Refers to programming in such a way that minimum waiting time is required to obtain information out of storage.

(Contrasted with random-access programming.)

RPG II—*See* report program generator II.

RPG II compiler—An RPG II compiler supports sequential, indexed-sequential, and direct-access disk files. One type of compiler also contains powerful table and array-handling facilities. Typically, RPG II reads and compiles statements at a fast rate of one hundred per minute. It also has the capability of calling assembly language subroutines. One specific RPG II compiler has been designed to execute in 64K bytes. However, the compiler also has the ability to create a temporary work file on disk, if necessary, to handle the compilation of very large programs. The compiler generates relocatable code that is linked with the run-time library to produce a load module.

R-S flip-flop — A flip-flop consisting of two cross-coupled NAND gates having two inputs designated "R" and "S." A "1" on the "S" input and a "0" on the "R" input will reset (clear) the flip-flop to the "0" state, and "1" on the "R" input and a "0" on the "S" input will set it to the "1" state. It is assumed that "0s" will never appear simultaneously at both inputs. If both inputs have "1s," the flip-flop will stay as it was. A "1" is considered nonactivating. A similar circuit can be formed with NOR gates.

R-S-T flip-flop—A flip-flop having three inputs, "R," "S," and "T." This unit works the same as the "R," "S" flip-flop except that the "T" input is used to cause the flip-flop to change states.

RS-232-C compatible controller — This module is a serial-to-parallel/parallel-to-serial converter with control lines designed to interface the microcomputer system to most asynchronous modems (especially those which are Bell 103 or 202 equivalent). Six different baud rates are often available: 110, 300, 1200, 2400, 4800, and 9600. Data word length can be selectable from 5- to 8-bits, inclusive. One or two stop-bit capability is also often selectable. If parity is selected, it may be further selected to be either odd or even.

RS-232 interface—1. Refers to the interface between a modem and the associated data-terminal equipment;

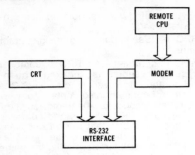

RS-232 interface.

it is standardized by EIA Standard RS-232. 2. An industry standard for asynchronous data communications, the EIA Standard RS-232 defines a 25-pin connector interface and the signals required to interface a terminal with a modem. It does not provide timing specifications, however, and almost half of the pins in the connector are not standardized. As a result, pin connections vary among crt terminal manufacturers. 3. For voiceband modems, the interface leads are single leads with a common ground return. Polar-type signals are specified with a minimum amplitude of +3 V at the terminating end. The maximum allowable voltage is +25 V. A ground-potential difference between equipment of up to 2 V is allowed for by specifying that the driver source must provide a +5-V signal. The terminating impedance is required to be in the 3000–7000 ohm range. The drivers typically provide voltages in the range of +6–10 V, with a source impedance of a few hundred ohms. A negative polarity indicates the binary state "1," marking, or an OFF control state. The positive polarity indicates the binary state "0," spacing, or an ON control state.

RS-232-C standard—The Electronic Industries Association (EIA) in conjunction with the Bell System, independent modem manufacturers, and the computer manufacturers, developed a standard for the interface between the Data Communications Equipment (DCE) provided by the carrier, and the Data Terminal Equipment (DTE) provided by the data-processing hardware manufacturers. This standard, which uses binary serial interchange, is called RC-232-C, for which the C

reflects the latest revision. Some newer standards, such as RS-422, RS-423, and RS-449 have been developed for both high-speed and/or digital interfaces, but RS-232-C is still the standard to which modem/computer equipment interfaces are designed. In many instances, the modem is referred to as the DCE, and the data-processing hardware is referred to as the DTE.

RTBM—*See* real-time bit mapping.

RTE—Abbreviation for real-time executive. This software system provides a multiprogramming, foreground-background system with priority scheduling, interrupt handling, and program load-and-go capabilities.

RTL—Abbreviation for resistor-transistor logic. Logic is performed by resistors. Transistors are used to produce an inverted output.

RTV—A room-temperature vulcanizing elastomer. A protective covering applied over an entire chip to protect it from its surroundings. The RTV is usually a silicone rubber compound.

ruby laser — Refers to an optically pumped ruby crystal producing a very intense and narrow beam of coherent red light. It is used in light-beam communication and for localized heating.

run—1. One routine or several routines automatically linked so that they form an operating unit, during which manual interruptions are not normally required to be made by the computer operator. 2. One performance of a routine on a microcomputer involving loading, reading, processing, and writing. 3. The execution of one or more programs that are linked to form one operating program.

runaway—Refers to a condition which arises when one of the parameters of a physical system undergoes a large, sudden, undesirable, and often destructive increase.

run book—Refers to material needed to "code document" a microcomputer application, including problem statement, flowcharts, coding, and operating instructions.

run indicator—The run indicator is illuminated whenever the processor is in the RUN mode.

run switch—The run switch, when toggled, causes the processor to commence instruction execution beginning at the address contained in the program counter.

run-time routines—Refers to sequences of instructions capable of performing specific operations which are used by programs that have been compiled by a high-level language compiler. Run-time routines are used when it is time to execute ("run") the machine-language programs that have been produced.

run-time support packages—Designers of high-level languages have to deal with problems of software interfacing and program size. Their languages often include special packages of high-speed assembly-language routines that are linked and loaded with the user's final compiled program. These routines, collectively called run-time or object-time support packages, perform operations such as computing transcendental functions, floating-point multiplication, checking array bounds on array references, and handling run-time program errors. Size and interfacing problems are minimized by structuring each package as a library that is completely transparent to the user. Thus, the linker auto-

matically searches the code library, extracts only the routines called by the high-level language program, inserts them, and links them to the final compiled code.

R/W RAM refresh — Dynamic R/W RAMs add the additional problem of refresh. Refresh creates problems in I/O-to-memory and CPU-to-memory interaction. Balancing of CPU, asynchronous memory refresh, and real-time semi-asynchronous I/O memory bandwidth demands is a difficult but solvable system design problem.

R/W RAM volatility — Despite all the positive aspects of semiconductor memory, it, like all other technologies, does have negative influences on system design. The first such influence one encounters is the volatility of the data in R/W semiconductor RAMs. While the problem can be overcome with a battery-backup power subsystem, the cost, complexity, and inconvenience of such a subsystem may prohibit its application to the problem. Making this battery-backup system reliable and cost effective presents a sizable design challenge to the system designer.

S

sample/hold amplifier—A typical integrated-circuit sample-and-hold amplifier consists of a high-performance operational amplifier, a low-leakage analog switch, and a JFET integrating amplifier—all fabricated on a single monolithic chip. An external holding capacitor, connected to the device, completes the sample-and-hold function. With the analog switch closed, the unit functions like a standard op amp; any feedback network may be connected around the device to control gain and frequency response. With the switch open, the capacitor holds the output at its last level, regardless of input voltage. Typical applications for the devices include sampled data systems, d/a deglitchers, analog demultiplexers, auto null systems, strobed measurement systems, and a/d speed enhancement. Most are packaged in a standard DIP

package and are pin-for-pin compatible with the various major systems.

sampling gate—A device which must be activated by a selector pulse before it will extract information from the input waveform.

sampling oscilloscope — A type of oscilloscope in which the input waveform is sampled at successive points along the waveform instead of being continuously monitored.

sampling period—Refers to a specific measured time interval between observations in a periodic sampling control system.

sapphire—A gemstone used on the tip of quality phonograph needles. Also used for bearings in precision instruments and as a substrate for integrated-circuit chips (SOS or Silicon-on-Sapphire).

sapphire substrates (SOS)—The boost given to MOS memory performance by sapphire substrates is the basis for a fully static 4096-bit RAM on a chip which includes word and bit decoders, sense circuits, and cell matrix. By reducing parasitics, SOS substrates let geometries be tighter. The complementary transistors and load resistors can be directly connected to the flip-flop to save cross-over space between interconnections.

Conventional sapphire manufacturing is a three-step format. First, a disc of crystalline sapphire is rotated and drawn upward so that the resulting crystal is a cylindrical boule slightly larger in diameter than the final substrate. The boule is ground down to its final diameter, then, sliced by a diamond-edged saw and polished. A layer of silicon is deposited on the substrate, which is then ready for the first IC-making steps. A newer process of growing sapphire substrates for integrated circuits, in ribbons instead of in cylindrical boules, has cut the cost of raw materials for silicon-on-sapphire CMOS by almost 80%. As a result, CMOS/SOS, already competitive in price with CMOS circuits built on bulk silicon wafers, are now challenging NMOS devices.

Prototype quantities of sapphire ribbons are being produced that are 3 inches wide, 1/32 inch thick, and about a yard long. The ribbons have to be pulled vertically from a melt of aluminum oxide. However, ribbons can be pulled continuously. Pulling sapphire ribbons is basically simple: aluminum oxide pellets are fed from a hopper into a high-temperature chamber. Touch the top of the melted oxide with a small sapphire crystal. Then, slowly draw the crystal up from the melt so that a single large crystal of sapphire grows as the aluminum oxide cools.

satellite computer—1. One used to relieve a central processing device of relatively simple but time-consuming operations, such as compiling, editing, and controlling input and output devices. 2. A processor connected locally or remotely to a larger central processor, and performing certain processing tasks — sometimes independent of the central processor, sometimes subordinate to the central processor.

saturated molecule — One in which each bond of every atom in the backbone of the molecule holds another atom.

saturation — 1. The state of magnetism beyond which a metal or alloy is incapable of further magnetization — i.e., the point beyond which the B-H curve is a straight line. 2. A circuit condition whereby an increase in the driving or input signal no longer produces a change in the output.

saturation noise—1. Refers to extra bits or words that must be ignored or removed from the data at the time the data is used. 2. Errors introduced into data in a system, especially in communication channels. 3. Random variations of one or more characteristics of any entity such as voltage, current, or data. 4. Loosely, any disturbance tending to interfere with the normal operation of a device or system.

save-and-store function—See definition for streaming.

scalar—1. A quantity that has magnitude but no direction (e.g., real numbers). 2. A circuit with two stable states which can be triggered to the opposite state by appropriate means (a bistable circuit).

scalar product—That product of two vector quantities which is a scalar function when the result is a scalar quantity, e.g., work=force $\times$ displacement. Known as the inner product and denoted algebraically by a dot between the vectors (or by a round bracket enclosing them). The scalar product's magnitude is given by the product of the vector amplitudes, and the cosine of the angle between them, i.e., $A \cdot B = AB \cos \theta$.

scalar quantity — Any quantity which has magnitude only—e.g., time, temperature, quantity of electricity.

scale — 1. The theoretical basis of a numerical system. 2. A series of markings used for measurement or computation. 3. A defined set of values, in terms of which different quantities of the same nature can be measured. 4. In a computer, to change the units of a variable so that the problem is within its capacity. 5. To alter the units in which all variables are expressed; to bring all magnitudes within bounds dictated by need, register size, or other arbitrary limits.

6. A range of values frequently dictated by the computer word-length or routine at hand.

scale factor—1. In analog computing, a proportionality factor that relates the magnitude of a variable to its representation within a computer. 2. In digital computing, the arbitrary factor which may be associated with numbers in a computer to adjust the position of the radix point so that the significant digits occupy specified columns. 3. The factor by which the number of scale divisions indicated or recorded by an instrument must be multiplied in order to compute the value of the measurand. 4. A value used to convert a quantity from one notation to another.

scaling — 1. An electronic method of counting electrical pulses occurring too fast to be handled by mechanical recorders. 2. The changing of a quantity from one notation to another.

scaling factor—Also called the scaling ratio. The number of input pulses per output pulse required by a scaler.

scaled process technology — Scaled process technology will be the process that permits the manufacture of the next generation of semiconductor components. "Scaled" refers to circuits in which all physical dimensions, horizontal and vertical, have been reduced by a scaling factor, as has the operating voltage. This differs from "squeezing" in that three dimensions rather than two are impacted. In scaling theory, all parameters are scaled by a factor K. For a 5-volt part scaled from 12 volts to 5 volts, the scaling factor K is 5/12ths. This approach yields a "brute force" process that will not necessarily be manufacturable. Therefore, to be used, a slight modification to the straightforward scaling technique must be made.

scan—To examine every reference or every entry in a file routine as a part of a retrieval scheme. Occasionally, to collate.

scanner—Refers to an instrument that automatically samples or interrogates the state of various processes, files, conditions, or physical states, and initiates action in accordance with the information obtained.

scanner, analog input—Refers to a device which will, upon command, connect a specified sensor to measuring equipment and cause the generation of a digit count value that can be read by the computer.

scanner, bar-code—An optical scanning unit that can read documents encoded in a special bar code, at thousands of characters per second speed. The scanner opens up various systems concepts for such tasks as billing, couponing, retail item control, and other forms of returnable media. The scanner can read either lithographed or computer-printed bar codes. As it scans, it transfers the encoded data to a buffer for direct transmission, or to its internal computer, or to printers for pretransmission editing (some systems).

scanning rate—Refers to the speed at which a computer can select, convert, and compare an analog input variable to its high and/or low limits.

scan, sensor—Refers to a type of sequential interrogation of lists of information or devices under process control. This develops a collection of data from process sensors by a computer for use in calculations, usually working through a multiplexer.

scatter loading—A procedure or process of loading a program into main memory in such a way that each section or segment of the program occupies a single connected memory area (in some systems, a "page") but the several sections of the program need not be adjacent to each other. Usually implemented by a virtual memory structure. In some systems, physical memory can be assigned in noncontiguous nonsequential pages to multiple users. Pages can be loaded or stored with a single "scatter load." The programmer is thus given greater control of memory by allowing nonsequential segments of main memory to be stored sequentially.

scatter read—The ability of a computer to distribute data into several memory areas as it is being entered into the system from magnetic tape or disk.

scheduler system, time-sharing — A time-sharing scheduler system performs multiprogramming. This allows several programs to reside in memory simultaneously and to execute concurrently. Time-sharing tasks, in one type of system, run in a system-controlled time-sharing partition. The scheduling algorithm of an executive program controls the switching, execution, and disposition of the programs. The time-sharing scheduler maintains several prioritized queues. The service required by a particular task determines which queue it is placed in. Highly interactive tasks are placed in the highest-level queue, given very short time slices, and receive frequent service. Tasks that are primarily CPU-bound are placed in the lowest-level queue, given relatively long time slices, and receive less frequent service.

Schmitt limiter—A bistable pulse generator that gives a constant amplitude output pulse provided the input voltage is greater than a predetermined value.

Schmitt trigger circuit — The Schmitt trigger circuit is a pulse amplifier used to convert sine waves and other wave forms into pulses. Its operation is similar to the one-shot multivibrator, except that the input signal and not a coupling capacitor determines its output voltage. Like a dc coupled amplifier, it has one RC connection between transistors; however, a degree of positive feedback is provided through a common-emitter resistor. This speeds up the rise time and defines the input voltage level at which the output is switched from high to low, and vice versa. The difference between the voltages at which the circuit will snap high and low is called the hysteresis or backlash voltage. By careful design, this can be controlled to desired levels. Also, some special Schmitt circuits are designed to trigger at specific voltage levels and act as voltage-level detectors.

Schottky barrier charge-coupled device—A buried-channel charge-coupled device that uses a Schottky barrier junction to isolate the transfer gate.

Schottky barrier diode—1. A high frequency junction diode used for ultrahigh-speed switching. 2. A junction diode with the junction formed between the semiconductor and a metal contact rather than between semiconductor materials, as in the case of an ordinary pn diode.

Schottky barrier height—The Schottky barrier height is always less than the energy gap of the semiconductor. Thus, for a given voltage, the current flowing in a Schottky barrier diode is orders-of-magnitude larger than in a pn diode of the same area; but, the forward current follows the same exponential law, doubling for every increase of 18 mV in forward voltage, i.e., increasing tenfold for every voltage increase of 60 mV.

Schottky bipolar parallel, bidirectional bus driver—Refers to a unit that has three-state outputs that enable it to isolate and drive external bus structures associated with bipolar systems. The driver and receiver gates have three-state outputs with pnp inputs. When the drivers or receivers are tristated, the inputs are disabled, presenting a low current load, typically less than 40 μA, to the system bus structure.

Schottky circuits—The Schottky barrier diode has many desirable characteristics. By 1970, a great deal of progress had been made in the understanding and manufacturing of these diodes. Metal-silicide and refractory-metal contacts assured high temperature stability and the surface effects of silicon were better understood and controlled. All the major TTL manufacturers introduced a line of Schottky TTL circuits where all the transistors that normally would be saturated are equipped with anti-saturation Schottky barrier-clamp diodes. These Schottky TTL circuits are very fast but, since the emphasis is on speed, they consume more power than normal TTL and their short rise and fall times cause interconnection problems.

Schottky clamp—The Schottky clamp in an I²L gate reduces logic swings which, in turn, reduces gate delays. The clamps can be built with just one additional mask step directly into the p-diffusion wells, so that as a result very little space is wasted. When equipped with Schottky clamps, I²L gates operate at the 5-nanosecond gate propagation-delay time needed for high-performance applications. This speed is to be contrasted with the 9-nanosecond operation of non-Schottky gates.

Schottky diode—A Schottky diode, also called a "hot carrier diode," offers two big advantages over the conventional pn-junction diode—very high speed due to extremely short recovery time and a substantially lower forward-voltage drop for a given current, or an order-of-magnitude higher current for the same voltage. The more familiar pn-junction diode that exists at the boundary of two differently doped sections inside a semiconductor crystal relies on minority carriers for current transport. In contrast, a Schottky diode is formed by the metal-to-semiconductor contact at the surface of the semiconductor crystal and relies on majority carriers for current transport (electrons in the case of n-type semiconductor). Charge storage is negligible and forward-to-reverse recovery is extremely fast.

Schottky diodes, saturation delay — With the use of Schottky diodes, the saturation delay normally encountered in saturated logic (TTL, DTL, and RTL) can be avoided. These logic families operate by turning their transistors either fully on or fully off. However, the amount of base current required to turn on a transistor is critical. Too little current will not turn the transistor on sufficiently. Too much current will turn the transistor on quickly; however, when the base current is interrupted, the transistor will continue to conduct until the excess charge in the base disappears (usually through thermal recombination).

Schottky TTL cell, inverted — This cell has much in common with the I²L approach. It consists of a pair of inverted transistors in a cross-coupled flip-flop configuration, with emitter-base resistors as loads. The inverted transistor flip-flop requires no isolation in the horizontal direction since its collector, which serves as an emitter, is shared with the cells in the same row. In the vertical direction, however, the flip-flop does require isolation from the emitter-follower transistors. The compact 10-mil² cell that results, even with conventional processing tolerances, packs a 1024-bit RAM onto a chip only 130 by 180 mils in area.

Schottky TTL, low-power—Low-power Schottky TTL devices consume one quarter the current and power of conventional TTL devices and use both Schottky diode clamping and advanced processing to regain the speed that is lost because of the lower internal charging currents. Schottky families offer performance superior to conventional TTL devices while saving 75% of the power dissipation.

Schottky, Walter — Walter Schottky, a German physicist, who invented the screen-grid tube in 1915, was born in June, 1886, in Zurich, Switzerland. He received doctorates in engineering and natural sciences from the University of Berlin and spent several years as a professor at the universities of Wurzburg and Rostock. He also worked in the research department of Siemens, the German telecommunications giant. Most of his early research dealt with electrons and ions in vacuum tubes. He invented the screen-grid tube in 1915 and later discovered an irregularity in the emission of thermions, known as the "Schottky effect"—the reduction in the minimum energy required for electron emission under the influence of an electrical field. During the 1930s, Walter Schottky worked mainly on the theory of semiconductor physics which, at that time, had the bad reputation of being the "physics of dirt effects" or the study of "order-of-magnitude effects." Semiconductors such as selenium and copper-oxide rectifiers, overvoltage protectors, and photovoltaic cells were used commercially but there was no clear understanding of their theory of operation. Walter Schottky established the boundary-layer theory for crystal rectifiers that explained how special concentration and potential conditions exist in the boundary layer of the semiconductor and how these conditions depend on the current through the rectifying junction. Walter Schottky remained active in semiconductor research for several decades until his death in 1956.

scratchpad — A "nickname" for CPU memory. It pertains to information that the CPU stores or holds temporarily. It is a memory containing subtotals for various unknowns that are needed for final results.

screen enhancement, character—Typically, characters can be enhanced on the screen, in a variety of ways, to suit the video requirements of various applications. These enhancements, or attributes as they are commonly called, can include half-intensity, blink, blank, reverse video, half brightness, underscore, double-width characters, and meaningful combinations thereof. However, all vendors are not alike, meaning user accessibility can be limited, or the video attribute codes may take up valuable space on the screen.

screening—A process of selection.

screening, character—There is a great deal of flexibility offered by the manufacturers of intelligent terminals with regard to character definition. Characters are formed within a dot matrix, typically within a 10-by-10 dot matrix on the screen. The data that forms each of the character dots are stored in some type of memory device, either a ROM or RAM. A ROM memory pattern cannot be changed. However, data can be rewritten in a RAM any number of times or whenever the user wishes to change the character font pattern. Thus, the RAM character set requires that the RAM be loaded upon power-up with data from another source, either from a floppy disk or from a CPU. Effectively, the data has to be stored in the terminal every time the system is powered-up. The beauty of this arrangement is that whenever you want to change your character set —say from an English character definition to Hebrew, French, Finnish, or even mathematical symbols—by simply loading this one individual RAM area, you can instantly redefine the character set. Also, some manufacturers can build in a right-to-left character-progression capability that will handle Middle Eastern languages.

screen shift, half-dot — The phrase "one-half-dot shift" is a terminology that refers to movement on a 10-by-10 character-cell grid. This capability allows for finer character definition for a highly curved symbol, such as a G or the hump on an M. When a terminal requires the use of italics or a set of specialized symbols, it might be beneficial to consider a terminal that has the half-dot shift capability. Additionally, if a specific terminal will always use a specific set of characters, then a ROM character generator should be specified. However, for a terminal that is going to constantly have several character sets, it is best to use a RAM character generator. In either case, most intelligent terminals should be able to address up to two different character generators.

scrolling—This feature permits manipulating, sending, or receiving messages that are larger than the screen capacity. Terminals with scrolling features need additional local memory for storing extra lines or pages of nondisplayed data. By depressing appropriate keys, the terminal operator can view the additional lines or pages on the display screen. With direct-memory access, scrolling is often automatic. When the processor is told that the bottom of the screen has been reached, the characters on the screen are made to move up by one row. The top row swings around to the bottom. This new bottom row can then be erased. The same locations in memory are used both before and after the scroll. Since each segment is stored in the memory buffer, data may be scrolled forward or backward (up or down) a line or a segment at a time.

sealed circuits—Refers to circuits that are sealed in place. They are very tiny but are far more rugged than their larger, more cumbersome counterparts. Sealed circuits permit the development of electronic systems that take only a fraction of the space required by ordinary wire circuits.

secondary memory—A particular storage that is usually of large capacity, but also with longer access time, and which most often permits the transferring of blocks of data between it and the main storage.

second-level addressing—Refers to the addressing of a computer instruction which indicates a location where the address of the referenced operand is to be found. In some computers, the machine address indicated can itself be indirect. Such multiple levels of addressing are terminated either by prior control or by a termination symbol.

second source—Refers to manufacturers of devices other than the original one that designed or began the manufacture of the device.

section debugging, microprogram — One of the best ways to check out a microprogram is to debug it in sections. This can be done by first setting up system conditions that will force a section of code to be executed. Secondly, insert Halt instructions at critical test points in the microcode. Suppose the designer sets up system conditions that should force the system to JUMP TO EXIT 4. For some reason, the system never gets there but wanders off to some other point in the program. Inserting Halt instructions (Jump to Self if no Halt instruction exists) for JUMPs to Exits 1, 2, and 3 will cause the system to halt at one of these points and the designer can determine where the program bug is. The designer will probably find a simple coding error has caused the problem. This condition is usually hard to find by simply reading over the code. Probably the most important rule for the microprogrammer during debug is to break his program up into a number of small segments and debug each of these. After the programmer is satisfied that each segment works, he can begin to check out the remainder of the microcode which ties the pieces together. At this point in time, additional bugs will probably be discovered in the previously checked-out sections of the code.

sector formatting, disk—In addition to formatting a disk into tracks and sectors, information must be written in every sector. Furthermore, the beginning of every sector must be clearly defined. Two techniques are used for this purpose—soft sectoring and hard sectoring. A hard-sectored disk begins every one of its sectors with an actual hole punched in the disk. The disk drive is equipped with a photoelectric sensor and whenever a hole is detected in the disk, the beginning of a new sector is identified. Soft sectoring, on the other hand, uses a single hole to mark the beginning of sector zero and all subsequent sectors are identified through a timing track that is read from the disk.

security monitor microprocessors—Single-chip 16-bit microprocessors have often replaced minicomputers or multiple dedicated microprocessors in some complex control and data-processing applications. Some are used in plant-security monitoring systems that monitor and, in some instances, control an entire plant operation. One CPU chip can act as a data-acquisition/alarm scanner, while another CPU can form a central control/acknowledgement terminal. Some functions monitored are: plant power (peak demand, total consumption, and output) and environmental qual-

ity (air contaminants, temperature, and air flow). Various transducers, thermocouples, and sensing devices measure the required analog variables and provide inputs to an analog multiplexer. The CPU scans these input points at preselected time intervals by supplying an address to the analog-multiplexer and starting the a/d conversions.

security terminal (plant)—A computerized security system offers many organizations the best possible solution toward preventing vandalism, theft, and unauthorized admission. A typical system might consist of a centrally located computer and, at each plant entrance, a data terminal and an additional employee/visitor identifying device. Employee data can be entered into a computer by the personnel department. Updated information can be transmitted via the primary terminal by inputting the badge number of an employee and stating whether he is authorized admission or not.

seek—Computer process for locating specific data in a random-access store. Each memory location inspected is a "seek" and the number of seeks governs the total search time.

seek time—Refers to the time that is needed to position the access mechanism of a direct-access storage device at a specified position.

segment—1. In a routine, the part short enough to be sorted entirely in the internal storage of a computer, yet containing all the coding necessary to call in and jump automatically to other segments. 2. To divide a program into an integral number of parts, each of which performs a part of the total program and is short enough to be completely stored in internal memory. 3. A set of data that can be placed anywhere in a memory and can be addressed relative to a common origin. The origin and number of locations of a segment are called its base address and its length.

segmentation overlays—A segment of a program is defined as that portion of memory that is committed by a single reference to the loader. Usually, a segment overlays some other segment and may have within itself other portions which, in turn, overlay one another, i.e., subsegments. That part of a segment that is actually brought into memory when the loader is referenced is called the fixed part of a segment. Segments are built up from separate relocatable elements, common blocks, or other segments.

seizing signal — Refers to a specific signal that is often translated at the start of a message to initiate a circuit operation at the receiving end of a circuit.

selective dump—Usually a library subroutine that is called to be used when other computer programs are running and a dump is desired.

selector—An automatic switching operation in a computer process that enables a logical choice to be made, based on results of the processing already carried out.

selenium (Se)—At. no. 34, at. wt. 78.96, sp. gr. 4.81, m.p. 217°C, b.p. 685°C. A nonmetallic element that is an important semiconductor and exists in a number of allotropic forms. The "grey form" becomes electrically conducting when irradiated with light.

selenium rectifier—One depending on a barrier layer of crystalline selenium on an iron base. Widely used in power supplies for small electronic apparatus.

self-adapting—This refers to a capability of a computer system to change its performance characteristics In response to its environment.

self-contained control—A photoelectric or proximity control in which all three phases of control—scanning, signal conditioning, and output—occur in a single device.

self-defining term—Refers to assembler programming of an absolute term whose value is implicit in the specification of the term itself.

self-diagnostic — The hardware and firmware within a controller that allows it to continuously monitor its own status and indicate any fault which might occur within it.

self-instructed carry—A system of executing the carry process in a microcomputer by allowing information to propagate to succeeding places as soon as it is generated, without receipt of a specific signal.

self-relocating program — Refers to a specific program that can be loaded into any area of main storage, and

which contains an initialization routine to adjust its address constants so that it can be executed at that location.

self-resetting loop—Refers to a type of circuit which contains instructions restoring all locations affecting the operation of the loop to their initial condition as an entry of the loop.

self-scanned photodiode arrays — In self-scanned photodiode arrays, each pixel consists of a photodiode and a MOSFET (field-effect transistor). The n-type region of the photodiode acts as the source of the FET, the gate is connected to a row line, and the drain is connected to a column line. The charge integrated by the photodiode is transferred to the column line when the FET is gated by the vertical digital-scan register.

semantic error—1. One which results in ambiguous or erroneous meaning of a microcomputer program. Most programs have to be debugged to eliminate these errors before use. 2. Refers to errors in the meaning or intent of the programmer and which are definitely his responsibility. Consequently, he is provided with an extensive set of debugging aids for manipulating and referencing a program when in search of errors in the logic and analysis sections.

semantics—Refers to the relationships between symbols and their intended meanings independent of their interpretation devices.

semaphore/flag, I/O — Conditional input/output techniques generally employ a single flip-flop, either a flag or a semaphore, to synchronize the data transfer between a microcomputer and a peripheral device. The output from the flag goes only to the microcomputer, whereas, the output from the semaphore goes both to the microcomputer and the input/output device. In view of the trend toward distributed and parallel processing in microcomputer systems, it is worthwhile to investigate in some detail the use of semaphores and flags. Various firms offer a simplified flowchart to depict the data transfer between a source of data and an acceptor of data (in the presence of a semaphore). Generally there are two semaphore states. A high (logic 1) condition indicates that data are available to the acceptor from the buffer; a low (logic 0) condition indicates that data have been received by the acceptor from the buffer, and that the buffer is now empty and can accept new data from the source. The source and acceptor influence each other's sequence of events. For example, as long as the semaphore is sensed low by the source, no new data can be provided to the buffer; while the semaphore is sensed high by the acceptor, this acceptor cannot acquire new data from the buffer.

semicompiled — Refers to a specific program which has been converted from source language into object code by a compiler, but which has not yet had those subroutines, explicitly or implicitly called by the source program, included.

semiconducting material — A solid or liquid having a resistivity midway between that of an insulator and a metal.

semiconductive—Refers to an electric device which is composed of high conductive metals and low conductive insulators designed to change the nature or strength of electric flows in various circuits.

semiconductor — 1. A material with an electrical conductivity between that of a metal and an insulator. Its electrical conductivity, which is generally very sensitive to the presence of impurities and some structural faults, will increase as the temperature does. This is in contrast with a metal, in which conductivity decreases as its temperature rises. 2. A material whose resistivity is between that of conductors and insulators, and whose resistivity can sometimes be changed by light, an electric field, or a magnetic field. 3. An electronic device whose main functioning parts are made from semiconductor materials, such as germanium, lead sulfide, silicon, and silicon carbide, and whose conducting characteristics are between metals and insulators.

semiconductor, discrete — A discrete semiconductor device is one in which a *single function* is performed by a *single semiconductor* structure. Discrete devices usually involve one to three junctions. This definition is only important in that it differentiates between discrete devices and "integrated-circuit" (IC) semiconductor

devices. ICs involve more than one structure; usually many are combined in a single device by a single manufacturing operation.

semiconductor doping—Doping is the carefully controlled adding of impurities, such as arsenic or antimony, to the basic germanium or silicon semiconductor material to produce an n-type material. The addition of dopants such as aluminum, indium, or gallium will produce a p-type material. These impurities are called "donors" and "receptors," respectively.

semiconductor, germanium crystal — Germanium is a gray-white metal that, as used in electronics, takes a crystalline form. As a metal, germanium should be an excellent conductor, but it actually is not. The reason for this odd behavior is that the four extra electrons in the outer shell of the germanium atom form a strong bond with the four extra electrons in the outer shell of a neighboring atom in the crystal, and consequently are not free to move easily. To get an appreciable current through the material, a heavy voltage would have to be connected across the crystal—a process which might destroy the crystal's regular structure. Pure germanium is, therefore, a difficult material in electronics. However, if it is tinged with small quantities of an impurity, it can be tremendously useful. This action of doping is an important process in the manufacture of semiconductors. If the germanium crystal is doped with tiny amounts of arsenic, a metal whose atom has five extra electrons, the crystal will accept an arsenic atom into its structure. But, only four of the arsenic atom's extra electrons can form a bond with a germanium atom in the crystal, thus leaving one electron free to roam. The arsenic atom now becomes a positive ion since it has lost an electron; it is called a donor because it has given an electron to the germanium. Crystals doped to obtain free electrons are said to be n-type, with the "n" indicating that unbound negative charges are present. By a similar but reverse process, pure germanium can be converted to a "P," or positive, type of crystal in which there is not only a lack of free electrons, but actually a deficiency of electrons.

semiconductor, high-frequency — A

transistor, diode, or integrated circuit designed to operate at frequencies above 3 MHz.

semiconductor, high-power—A transistor, diode, or integrated circuit that can dissipate more than one watt of power.

semiconductor, intrinsic — A crystal of germanium, or silicon, substance that conducts electric currents of an electric field due to the presence of mobile "holes" and "electrons," but which is not as efficient a conductor as copper, silver, gold, or aluminum where the carrier density is greater; since the property is that of a crystal, it is called intrinsic. See also: donor, acceptor, and semiconductor.

semiconductor, intrinsic and extrinsic —Semiconductors in which the electrical properties are not modified by the presence of impurities or imperfections, in the crystal lattice, are called intrinsic semiconductors. Extrinsic semiconductors, however — those dependent upon impurities for their particular electrical characteristics—form the bulk of the types used in solid-state devices. Extrinsic semiconductors, in which the current carrier is the electron, are called n-type materials, because the electron is a negative carrier of charge. Conversely, materials in which the conduction is due, in the majority, to the apparent movement of "holes" is called p-material, because the hole acts as a positive carrier.

semiconductor junction—Refers to the junction between the donor and acceptor impurity semiconducting regions in a continuous crystal; a region produced by one of several techniques, e.g., alloying, diffusing, doping, drifting, fusion, growing, etc.

semiconductor, low-frequency — Typically, a transistor, diode, or integrated circuit designed to operate at frequencies below 3 MHz.

semiconductor, low-power — Typically, a transistor, diode, or integrated circuit that dissipates less than one watt of power.

semiconductor materials — A material whose resistivity is between that of conductors and insulators, and whose resistivity can sometimes be changed by light, an electric field, or a magnetic field. Typical semiconductor materials are crystalline metals, compounds, and alloys, most notably germanium and silicon. Selenium sulphide, copper oxide, and the gallium-arsenide, gallium-phosphide families are also used. All of these materials have, in common, the fact that, when prepared as metallurgically pure crystalline forms, they are poor conductors . . . but, when "doped" by the addition of very tiny amounts of some other substance (for example, phosphorus or boron for silicon), they can be made to conduct electrical current.

semiconductor memory — A memory whose storage medium is a semiconductor circuit. Generally, semiconductor memory components are constructed using one of three basic technologies: (1) bipolar, (2) n-channel MOS, or (3) p-channel MOS. Early designs favored p-channel MOS since that technology had already been developed for other componentry by the time it was realized that semiconductors could offer an economically feasible alternative to cores. There are many significant variations within each of the three technologies. To most experts, it now appears that over the long term, n-channel technology will be the dominant process that will be used in the construction of semiconductor memory and processing components—at least for a time. However, complementary MOS (CMOS) is fast gaining popularity as a semiconductor process.

semiconductor memory design—Semiconductor memories are basically either static or dynamic. CCDs and bubble memories, however, use various serial-transfer techniques. A memory design can be considered in two parts: array and periphery. Each block on a design marked "16K," represents one-fourth of the memory array of a 64K RAM. Everything else on the die is periphery. The periphery feeds data, addresses, and control signals to the array, which stores the data. Each storage cell or storage location is capable of storing 1 bit of data. When specifying the bit storage capacity of a memory, the letter K means $2^{10} = 1024$ bits. Thus, 64K = 65,536 bits.

semiconductor, n-type — Relates to a semiconductor crystal material that has been doped with minute amounts of an impurity which will produce donor-type centers of electrons in the crystal lattice structure. Because electrons are negative particles, the material is called n-type, and conduction is primarily by using electrons as the majority carrier of electric current.

semiconductor, p-type — A semiconductor crystal material that has been doped with very tiny amounts of an impurity that will produce acceptor-type centers in the crystal lattice structure. Since it has a deficiency of electrons or negative particles, the material is called a p-type semiconductor. P-type semiconductors have "holes" as the majority carriers.

semiconductor trap — Refers to lattice defects in a semiconductor crystal that produce potential wells in which electrons or holes can be captured.

semimetals — Materials such as bismuth, antimony, and arsenic having characteristics that class them between semiconductors and metals.

semistatic memory—*See* pseudostatic, semistatic, pseudodynamic, quasidynamic memory.

sense amplifier, memory — A circuit used to sense the output level of the storage elements of a memory and used to convert that measurement to a form compatible with the logic output elements.

sense recovery time—The time interval needed to switch a memory from a Write mode to a Read mode and to obtain valid data signals at the output.

sensing element—That specific portion of a device that is directly responsive to the value of the measured quantity.

sensor—Refers to a transducer or other device whose input is a quantitative measure of some external physical phenomenon and whose output can be read by a computer.

sensor based — Refers to the use of sensing devices, such as transducers or sensors, to monitor a physical process.

sensor-based computer — A type of computer designed and programmed to receive real-time data (analog or digital) from transducers, sensors, and other data sources that monitor a physical process. The computer may also generate signals to elements that control the process. For example, the computer might receive data from a gauge or flowmeter, compare the data with a predetermined standard, and

then produce a signal that operates a relay, valve, or other control mechanism.

sensor-based system — Refers to an organization of components, including a computer whose primary source of input is data from sensors and whose output can be used to control a related physical process.

sensor card—One typical card was developed to handle logic levels and loads that are not TTL-compatible. Depending on instructions from the microcomputer, the board will operate in several modes: high-level input sense, medium-current switch to ground, or a combination of the first two modes where the sense circuitry is enabled to test the loads for open-circuit burnout. There are 32 multipurpose channels provided, all uniquely addressable. In the load-testing mode, any of the outputs can be checked by disabling the drivers and testing for open-circuit load voltage.

sensor control system — One type of system is able to sense many inputs and can drive medium-power outputs. It is a plug-compatible turnkey control system with all the software and hardware furnished for home systems. Input devices can be TTL gates or any form of switch contacts, including thermostats, reed switches, microswitches, joysticks, key switches, and numeric keypads. The system can be used to sense for either an open or closed condition. A software timing and control program (STAC) lets the user specify and execute complex timing, sensing, and control sequences without having to program. It also lets him write programs that can call STAC as a subroutine.

sensor devices — Temperature, flow, pressure, and level units form the four types of sensors that are most frequently interfaced to data-acquisition subsystems. Other types of analog sensors account for only a small percentage of all inputs. Some of the largest data-acquisition systems have 1000 or more analog inputs, while a small system will have 32 inputs or less.

sensor input/output unit — A typical basic unit consists of a power supply, a terminator card, and slots for eight sensor I/O feature cards mounted in a one-half-width unit. Any of the following types of cards can be used: digital input/process interrupt, nonisolated; digital input/process interrupt, isolated; digital output, nonisolated; analog input control (with analog-to-digital converter); programmable multirange amplifier; reed relay multiplexer; solid-state multiplexer; and analog output.

sensor, reflective—This type of device is not only suited for the typical reflective-surface applications, such as end-of-tape/beginning of tape (EOT/BOT) and mark sensing; but it is also particularly useful in those nontransmissive applications that must detect the absence or presence of a mechanical object, such as a card or a paper. A typical standard reflective sensor incorporates a GaAs infrared LED that is spectrally matched with a high-speed silicon phototransistor.

sentinel—A symbol used to mark the beginning or end of some piece of information in digital-computer programming.

separator—Refers to a specific character developed to be used for the demarcation of the logical boundary between those items of data that are referred to as separate and distinct units.

sequence—1. An arbitrarily defined order of a set of symbols, i.e., an orderly progression of items of information or of operations in accordance with some rule. 2. To put a set of symbols into an arbitrarily defined order, i.e., to select A if A is greater than or equal to B, or select B if A is less than B.

sequence checking—Refers to a routine that checks every instruction executed and prints out certain data, e.g., to print out the coded instructions with addresses and the contents of each of several registers. Or, it may be designed to print out only selected data, such as transfer instructions and the quantity actually transferred.

sequence counter—A hardware register that is used by the microcomputer to remember the location of the next instruction to be processed in the normal sequence, which is subject to branching, execute instructions, and interrupts.

sequence processor—An enhancement to local memory that enables users to loop a portion of the memory for a predefined time, or allow them to define subroutines and branching within local memory. This function is totally software controlled.

sequencer register—A computer register that controls the sequence of instructions.

sequence timer—A succession of time-delay circuits arranged so that completion of the delay in one circuit initiates the delay in the following circuit.

sequential-access storage — A form of digital computer storage in which the items of stored information become available only in a one-after-another sequence regardless of whether all or only part of the information is desired.

sequential computer, logic-controlled —Refers to a specific sequential computer with the capability of executing instructions in a sequence designed by particular built-in logic, i.e., a fixed-sequence, but one which can be overridden or changed by an instruction. A highly unique and almost single-purpose computer that has little or no concurrent action.

sequential control — Digital computer operation in which the instructions are set up in sequence and fed to the computer consecutively during the solution of a problem.

sequential control, PLA — A programmable logic array (PLA) can be used effectively in sequencing applications to implement flowcharts of state diagrams, condition-driven look-up tables, or arbitrary state sequencers. The input set could come from external control points ("qualifying inputs") or from the PLA outputs that are coupled through feedback latches ("current state inputs").

sequential logic—Refers to a circuit arrangement in which the output state is determined by the previous state of the input.

sequential operation—The performance of actions, one after the other in time. This refers to actions that are of a large scale, as opposed to the smaller-scale operations that are referred to by the term "serial operation." For an example of sequential operation, consider: $A*(B*C)$. The two multiplications indicated follow each other sequentially. However, the processing of the individual digits in each multiplication may be either parallel or serial.

sequential sampling — A sampling inspection in which the decision to accept, reject, or inspect another unit is made following the inspection of each unit.

serial—1. Pertains to the time-sequential transmission of, storage of, or logical operations on, the parts of a word in a computer—the same facilities being used for successive parts. 2. The handling of one item after the other in a single facility, such as a transfer or "store" in a digit-by-digit time sequence, or the processing of a sequence of instructions one at a time, i.e., sequentially.

serial adder—Refers to a logical unit that adds two binary words, one binary bit-pair at a time. The least significant addition is performed first, and then, progressively more significant additions, including carries, are performed until the sum of the two numbers is formed. Saves hardware at the expense of operating time.

serial bit—Refers to a method of sequentially moving or transferring a contiguous set of bits, one at a time, over a single wire, according to a fixed sequence.

serial chip memories—Serial memories include both the conventional shift memories and the more exciting products such as the charge-coupled device (CCD) and the magnetic-bubble memory device (MBD). Both CCDs and MBDs are high-density, potentially low-cost devices that are especially attractive for use in replacing rotating memories in computer systems, as well as for other slow mass-memory applications in terminals.

serial communications — Serial communication minimizes the number of channels required which reduces costs and also eliminates data synchronization problems that are associated with receiving parallel data. Thus, a means is provided (typically) to convert parallel computer or terminal data to a serial bit stream at one end of the communications channel and then assemble the received serial bit stream into parallel data characters at the other end.

serial input/output card, RS-232 — A full RS-232 interface card has a signal compatibility to a conventional RS-232 interface. Typically, the card uses a UART and has divider logic to allow for presettable baud rates from 110 to 19,200. It uses an adjacent channel for control if desired.

serial input/output controller—Abbreviated SIO. The typical serial input/output controller is a dual-channel multifunction peripheral component designed to satisfy a wide variety of serial data-communications requirements in microcomputer systems. Its basic function is as a serial-to-parallel, parallel-to-serial converter/controller, but — within that role — it is configurable by systems software so that its "personality" can be optimized for a given serial data-communications application. An SIO is capable of handling asynchronous formats, synchronous byte-oriented protocols (such as IBM Bisync), and synchronous bit-oriented protocols (such as HDLC and SDLC). This versatile device can also be used to support virtually any other serial protocol for applications other than data communications (cassette or floppy-disk interfaces, for example). The SIO can generate and check CRC codes in any synchronous mode and can be programmed to check data integrity in various modes. The device also has facilities for modem controls in both channels. In applications where these controls are not needed, the modem controls can be used for general-purpose I/O.

serially reusable—1. A reusable program that is not necessarily re-enterable. 2. The attribute of a routine that, when in main storage, the same copy of the routine can be used by another task after the current use has been concluded.

serial operation — 1. Computer operation in which numbers are processed one character at a time—as opposed to parallel operation, where several numbers are processed simultaneously. 2. The flow of information through a computer in time sequence, usually bit-by-bit but sometimes by characters. 3. A type of information transfer within a programmable controller, whereby the bits are handled sequentially rather than simultaneously, as they are in parallel operation. Serial operation is slower than parallel operation for equivalent clock rate. However, only one channel is required for serial operation.

serial-parallel—1. Having the property of being partially serial and partially parallel. 2. A combination of serial and parallel, i.e., serial by character, parallel by bits comprising the character. 3. Descriptive of a device which converts a serial input into a parallel output.

serial/parallel converter module — A typical 8-bit transmitter/receiver serial/parallel module makes possible asynchronous full-duplex operation between a computer and a remote application. The modules are used in pairs, one located with the computer and the other placed in the remote location. They transfer data up to 10,000 feet on twisted-pair cable at rates from 1.25K to 80K baud.

serial priority, multibus — This technique, used for medium-sized systems, eliminates the need for external encoder-decoder logic. Instead, priority is established by daisy-chaining the bus arbiters together; the bus-priority output of the highest-priority arbiter is connected to the bus request of the next highest priority, and so on. The number of arbiters that can be chained together is a function of the bus-system clock and the propagation delay from arbiter to arbiter. Normally, at a 10-MHz bus-clock frequency, only three arbiters can be daisy-chained.

serial programming — 1. Programming of a digital computer in such a manner that only one arithmetical or logical operation can be executed at one time. 2. The programming of a computer so that no arithmetical or logical operation can be executed concurrently, e.g., a sequential operation.

serial storage — Refers to the common types of storage in which time is one of the coordinates used to locate any given bit, character, or word (especially word). Storage in which words (within given groups of several words) appear one after the other in time sequence, and in which access time therefore includes a variable latency or waiting time of zero to many word-times, is said to be serial-by-word storage. Storage in which the individual bits comprising a word appear in time sequence is serial-by-bit storage. Storage for coded decimal or other nonbinary numbers, in which the characters appear in time sequence, is serial-by-character storage, i.e., magnetic drums are usually serial-by-word but may be either serial-by-bit or parallel-by-bit, or serial-by-character and parallel-by-bit, etc.

serial transfer—Data transfer in which the characters of an element of information are transferred in sequence over a single path.

serial vs. parallel communication—Serial transmission is slower than parallel transmission; however, it requires only one channel or line. This saves the cost of leased or direct-dial parallel lines. Also serial transmission lines are easier to operate when using them with cassette units and slow electromechanical teleprinters for communications over ordinary telephone lines. The two types of serial transmission modes are synchronous and asynchronous.

service routine—Refers both to a routine designed to assist in the actual operation of a computer and to a broad class of routines that are standardized at a particular installation for the purpose of assisting in the maintenance and operation of the computer, as well as the preparation of programs, as opposed to routines, for the actual solution of production problems. This class includes monitoring or supervisory routines, assemblers, compilers, diagnostics for computer malfunctions, simulation of peripheral equipment, general diagnostics, and input data. The distinguishing quality of service routines is that they are generally standardized so as to meet the servicing needs at a particular installation, and are independent of any specific production-type routine requiring such services.

servo — General term for a system in which the response is determined by a drive that is actuated by the difference (error) between a set target and the actual response. A servo system aids or replaces human action, by force, time of operation, or location. Error quantity (value) usually requires a vacuum tube or transistor amplification.

servo control systems—The choice of a servo is highly application dependent, but basically two types are used: dc servos and stepping motors.

415 servo function generator ● setpoint control

Stepping motors are purported to be more compatible with computers, being quasi-digital in nature. However, little simplification is actually achieved using stepping motors, and their peculiarities can be rather troublesome. A typical dc servo control system has two feedback control loops: a velocity control loop and a position control loop. The former uses a tachometer for velocity feedback to the amplifier—no software function is necessary, while a digital shaft encoder, mechanically connected to the servomotor (either directly or through gearing), provides position feedback.

servo function generator—Refers to a function generator consisting of a position servo driving a function potentiometer.

servo link — Refers to a mechanical power amplifier that permits low-strength signals to operate control mechanisms that require fairly large powers.

servomechanism — 1. A closed-cycle system in which a small input power controls a much larger output power in a strictly proportionate manner, e.g., movement to a gun turret may be accurately controlled by the movement of a small knob or wheel. 2. Any closed-loop feedback type of control system. A servomechanism consists of the following elements (which may be distinct or combined-function elements of hardware): (A) An input signal or command line, to indicate the desired state. (B) An output sensor, capable of monitoring the actual output state. (C) A comparator which determines the deviation from the desired state, based on the above two signals. (D) An effector, which has the power to modify the output state or condition. The important feature of a servomechanism is its four-part closed-loop organization as outlined above. Its actual physical implementation or field of application is immaterial.

servomechanism, positional—1. An automatic feedback control system in which one or more of its signals represent mechanical motion. 2. A servomechanism in which a mechanical shaft is positioned, usually in the angle of rotation, in accordance with one or more input signals. Frequently, the shaft is positioned (excluding

transient motion) in a manner linearly related to the value of the input signal.

servomechanism rate—A servomechanism in which a mechanical shaft is translated or rotated at a rate proportional to an input signal amplitude.

servomotor—A motor used in a servo system. Its rotation or speed (or both) are controlled by a corrective electric signal that has been amplified and fed into the motor circuit.

servo multiplier—An analog computer term relating to a multiplying unit which has a position control capability. The unit also has a capability of multiplying each of several different variables, represented by analog voltages, by a single variable.

servo system — An automatic control system for maintaining a condition at or near a predetermined value by activation of an element such as a control rod. It compares the required condition (desired value) with the actual condition and adjusts the control element in accordance with the difference (and, sometimes, the rate of change of the difference).

set—1. To place a storage device in a prescribed state. 2. To place a binary cell in the 1 state. 3. A permanent change, attributable to any cause, in a given parameter. 4. A collection of elements having some feature in common or which bear a certain relation to one another, e.g., all even numbers, geometrical figures, terms in a series, or a group of irrational numbers.

set breakpoint—In some systems, the set breakpoint command is issued with respect to a program under test and causes a breakpoint to be set into a specified memory location. When the program attempts to execute the instruction at the breakpoint location, control is transferred back to Debug. Debug clears the breakpoint, preserves the contents of the accumulator, link, and program counter for the executing program, and, then, types out the breakpoint number, the breakpoint location, and the contents of the accumulator and link (some systems).

setpoint—In a feedback control loop, the point which determines the desired value of the quantity being controlled.

setpoint control—A process may be intelligently controlled at the site, thus eliminating hard-wired logic and extensive master-remote communications. In setpoint control, an analog signal is checked against specified limits, and commands are sent to a relay driver or electronic circuit to actuate control points. Gas or water flow is a typical example. If the meter signal exceeds its upper (lower) limits, a close (open) command is sent to the valve that controls the flow rate.

set symbol—Refers to assembler programming; a variable symbol used to communicate values during conditional assembly processing.

set theory—Refers to a study, in the mathematical sense of the rules, for characterizing groups, sets, and elements, i.e., the theory of delimiting or combining groups.

sexadecimal digit—A digit that is a member of a set of sixteen digits: 0 through 9, and A, B, C, D, E, or F, used in a numerical notation system using a radix of 16. *Same* as hexadecimal.

sexadecimal (hexadecimal) notation—Notation using the base 16.

Shannon equation — Equation in information theory which gives a theoretical limit to the rate of transmission of binary digits, with a given bandwidth and signal/noise ratio.

shared-bus system — The shared-bus approach offers the advantage of free access to both memory and peripheral devices by each of the processors in a configuration. A disadvantage is seen in an environment where the combined activity of high-speed I/O and memory access exceeds the speed of the bus. In most minicomputers, where system buses operate at rates ranging from 1.5 to 5 megabytes per second, the aggregate activity can easily overburden the bus. In addition, not all bus designs can handle the arbitration required for multiple CPU masters on a common bus. This capability must therefore be designed in initially.

shared-executive system — A key feature of tightly coupled systems is the sharing of a single memory among various CPUs. Most tightly coupled systems also use a single shared operating-system executive to control the execution of tasks. Thus, provisions for synchronization, interlock-

ing, and interprocessor communication must be made in the hardware to accommodate a true multiprocessor operating system. The major difference between configurations is the method of accessing the memory.

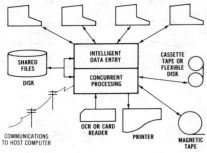

Shared-memory systems.

shared-memory systems—In many systems, tightly coupled user networks all share a common memory which can be accessed either through (A) a shared bus, (B) a multiported memory system, or (C) a crossbar switching network. Such systems also generally share an operating system executive.

shared storage—The ability to share main storage between two CPUs. This means that either machine can insert information into storage and either machine can access the data and use it.

sharing — 1. Refers to the interleaved time use of one device; hence, a method of operation in which a computer facility is shared by several users concurrently. 2. The apportionment of intervals of time availability for various items of equipment so as to complete the performance of several tasks by interlacing (contrasted with multiprogramming). 3. The use of a device for two or more purposes during the same overall time interval, accomplished by interspersing the computer actions in time.

sheath—1. Excess of positive or negative ions in a plasma, giving a shielding or space-charge effect. 2. The covering on a cable. 3. The can protecting a nuclear fuel element.

shell — 1. Shell-like magnet in which magnetization is always normal to the surface and inversely proportional to the thickness. The strength of the shell is the product of magnetization and thickness of shell. 2. Theoretical concept of a double layer of poles, i.e., multitudinous magnetic dipoles, which is, in general, not a plane. 3. Pattern of orbital electrons surrounding the nucleus of an atom, characterized by principal quantum numbers.

shielded line—1. Line or circuit that is specially shielded from external electric or magnetic induction by shields of highly conducting or magnetic material. 2. Transmission line enclosed within a conducting sheath, so that the transmitted energy is enclosed within the sheath and not radiated.

shielded pair — Refers to a balanced pair of transmission lines within a screen, to mitigate interference from outside.

shielded transmission line — A transmission line, the elements of which confine the propagated electrical energy inside a conducting sheath.

shield, electrostatic—Refers to a metal mesh used to screen one device from the electric field of another.

shift — 1. Displacement of an ordered set of computer characters one or more places to the left or right. If the characters are the digits of a numerical expression, a shift is equivalent to multiplying by a power of the base. 2. To move information serially right or left in a register(s) of a computer. Information shifted out of a register may be lost, or it may be re-entered at the other end of the register. 3. Refers to the removal of the digits of a number (or characters of a word) from one end of a number or word and their insertion, in the same sequence, at the other end.

shift, end-around carry — A carry sent directly from the high-order position to the least-significant place, i.e., using nine's complement addition to subtract numbers.

shifting register—Refers to a particular register that is designed to be adapted to perform shifts, i.e., a delay-line register whose circulation time may be increased or decreased so as to shift the content.

shift instruction, accumulator—A computer instruction that causes the contents of an accumulator register to shift to the left or right.

shift-out character—1. Refers to a code extension character that substitutes an alternative set of graphic characters (upon which agreement has been reached or which have been designated using code extension procedures) for the graphic characters of the standard character set. 2. A code extension character that can be used by itself in order to substitute another character set for the standard character set, usually to access additional graphic characters.

shift pulse—A drive pulse that initiates the shifting of characters in a register.

shift register—1. A register that provides short- or long-term storage for either serial or parallel operation. 2. A register in which the stored data can be moved to the right or left. 3. A memory in which data words are entered serially and shifted to successive storage locations. The data word can be read when it has been sequentially shifted to the output. 4. A program, entered by the user into the memory of a programmable controller, in which the information data (usually single bits) are shifted one or more positions on a continual basis. There are two types of shift registers: asynchronous and synchronous.

shift register, bubble memory — A device that stores data as the absence or presence of tiny right-cylindrical domains of magnetization in a magnetic medium. Bubble memories operate as shift registers with complex control signals for the various magnetic fields required. (Bubble memories are not made using standard semiconductor technology.)

shift register, flip-flop — Shift registers are made up of a number of flip-flops joined together in tandem or chain fashion. Each flip-flop is triggered at the same time by the same clock pulse, and this shifts the "0" and "1" states from one flip-flop to the next. In addition to shifting, individual flip-flops can be set and their outputs are also individually available. This means that data can be entered serially (shifted) or parallel, and they can be taken from the shift register in either serial or parallel form.

shift unit, data handler—In some systems, a data handler consists of the arithmetic/logic control, the shift control, and the bit control. The arithmetic/logic unit performs data manipulations such as: addition, subtraction, negation, increment, decrement, logical AND, logical OR, logical exclusive-OR, and their logical complements. In one specific system, the shift unit is capable of shifting the contents of any register from 1 through 7 shifts, left or right, within one cycle. The bit control unit can clear, set, complement, or test any bit or any register of the local memory or of the I/O buffer/control.

short-haul modems—These are devices for sending data over short distances. Actually, the distances may be up to many miles. The devices generally assume that they will be connected to another device of the same type over a circuit that employs only wires (which is not true of all circuits in today's world). The main advantage of these devices is that they usually are less expensive than equivalent-speed general-purpose modems.

short instruction format—A "standard" length (i.e., one-word) instruction as opposed to a "long" instruction. Most instructions are of this type.

shrinkable tubing—A nonmetallic tubing that is fabricated to allow a non-reversible decrease in its diameter upon the application of heat. It is used to provide insulation or mechanical protection to conductors, cables, splices, and terminations.

SI—Abbreviation for superimpose.

side-shielded—A sensor that "senses" only to the front of its face and ignores metals to its side. However, the presence of such side metal may cause a slight shift of operating characteristics.

sign — 1. A symbol that distinguishes negative from positive quantities. 2. A symbol that indicates whether a quantity is greater or less than zero. 3. A binary indicator of the position of the magnitude of a number relative to zero.

signal — 1. A visable, audible, or other conveyor of information. 2. The intelligence, message, or effect to be conveyed over a communication system. 3. A signal wave. 4. The physical embodiment of a message. 5. A detectable impulse (voltage, current, magnetic field, or light impulse) by which information is communicated through

an electronic or optical means, or over wire, cable, microwave, or laser beams.

signal charge—A quantity of electrical charge in a potential well (or a discrete region of a bucket-brigade device) that, in conjunction with the bias charge (if used), defines the signal level.

signal conditioner, industrial—In harsh industrial environments, some signal conditioners feature high noise rejection, filtering, input protection, and excellent temperature stability in order to assure measurement integrity. Economical and easy to use, they provide a prepackaged, cost-effective analog signal-handling and interface capability for a wide variety of transducers or process signals.

signal conditioning — To process the form or mode of a signal so as to make it intelligible to, or compatible with, a given device, including such manipulation as pulse shaping, pulse clipping, digitizing, and linearizing.

signal converter — A particular transducer designed to convert one standardized transmission signal to another. Signals on this type circuit originate in the data-terminal equipment to select whether the signal converter is to be conditioned to transmit or to receive.

signal conversion — The process of changing a signal from one form to another as in mixing or modulating.

signal element — 1. Also called a unit interval. That part of a signal which occupies the shortest interval of the signaling code. It is considered to be of unit duration in building up signal combinations. 2. A pulse or signal. An absence or presence of voltage or current in a communication medium.

signal frequency noise — Refers to noise that lasts for a significant time period and is highly localized in frequency.

signal generator — An oscillator, designed to provide known voltages (usually from 1 volt to less than 1 volt) over a wide range of frequencies; used for testing or ascertaining performance of radio-receiving equipment. It may be amplitude, frequency, or pulse-modulated.

signal, interrupt—A signal that causes a processor to suspend the current execution and transfer control to special interrupt-handling software. Vectored interrupts use a set of memory locations that have the addresses of interrupt-service routines to which control is transferred.

signal level—The level at any point in a transmission system, as measured by a voltmeter (VU meter) across the circuit when properly terminated; a level expressed in dB or VU in relation to a reference level, now 1 mW in 600 ohms.

signal processors, digital—Macro arithmetic processors (MAP) allow minicomputers and large scientific computer systems to perform complex mathematical operations in real time, while still acquiring data. The programmable MAP can provide the host computer with the capability of a fast-Fourier-transform processor, array processor, display processor, image processor, voice processor, or data-acquisition system. The main advantage of MAP is its speed and its fast powerful signal-processor memory and its input/output capacity. It is available with multiported memory having cycle times of 125 or 500 nanoseconds and can optimally be addressed in 8-, 16-, or 32-bit words. A multiprocessor, MAP consists of up to 4 arithmetic processors, a control processor, up to 4 multiported memories, up to 64 input/output devices, and the host computer. The control processor is a stripped-down version of a minicomputer. It has some arithmetic capacity but no memory of its own, since it is used to set up I/O operations and calculate addresses and address patterns (some systems).

signal shaping and filtering—Refers to procedures that are used in modems to confine the signal to a specific frequency band, to minimize influence of noise, and to control intersymbol interference. The long-haul portion of a typical voice-channel facility has a well-defined frequency band determined by the channel-bank filters.

signal-to-noise ratio—Also called signal-noise ratio. 1. Ratio of the magnitude of the signal to that of the noise (often expressed in decibels). 2. In television transmission, the ratio in decibels of the maximum peak-to-peak voltage of the video television signal (including the synchronizing pulse) to the rms voltage of the noise

at any point. 3. The ratio of the amount of signals conveying information to the amount of signals not conveying information.

signal tracing—The tracing of a signal through each stage in order to locate a fault.

signal transducer—Refers to a particular transducer designed to convert one standardized transmission signal to another.

signal transmission — 1. Conveying electrical energy over a distance by wires, either to operate controls or make indications (telemetering), process acoustic information (telephony, broadcasting), or pass pictorial information (facsimile, television). Also used to denote radio, optical, or acoustic wave propagation. 2. Conveying electrical energy from point to point along a path. 3. The sending of data to one or more locations or recipients. 4. The sending of data from one place for reception elsewhere. 5. In ASCII coding and communications, a series of characters including headings and texts.

signals, supervisory control—Refers to characters or signals used to indicate the various operating states of circuit combinations. These characters or signals may automatically actuate equipment or indicators at a remote station.

signature analysis—1. A technique for data compression, in which the entire data record is compacted into one or more hexadecimal words through an algorithm that weights each bit equally. For all practical purposes, this signature is unique to the data and may be compared to a known-good signature. 2. This refers to the conversion of bit patterns into easily identifiable alphanumeric equivalents. One system compresses a long data stream into a unique readily recognizable "signature" of four hexadecimal characters. This signature enables users to isolate system faults right down to a single node or component level. Signature analysis will not fill all testing needs; it can tell only whether or not a particular node is operating correctly. It cannot tell what the problem is or why it occurred, only what component must be replaced to fix the system. On the other hand, signature analysis can detect problems caused by out-of-tolerance components.

signature image system—On some systems, 2K to 4K bits of information can be stored on a disk subsystem for later retrieval. The storage subsystem contains both the disk and a processor that accepts requests for signatures, retrieves the stored data, and then transmits the compressed signature data to the correct crt terminal, where it is displayed by the display subsystem. Often a signature request can be made via dial-up lines just by entering such information as an account number or a credit card number into the keyboard of a terminal. Then, when the stored signature is displayed on the crt screen, the operator can determine its validity by comparing the displayed signature with the signed document prepared by the customer. (*See also* signature recognition.)

signature recognition — An electronic writing tablet does not need to scan a document. Instead, it senses the motion of the stylus. By means of sophisticated sampling techniques, various tablets can accurately store and transmit an entire handwritten signature using only about a hundred point-samples, even when telephone transmission is of a low quality. This reduces transmission costs. In recognizing handwritten numerals, the electronic writing tablet senses the dynamic characteristics of a digit as it is being written.

sign, check indicator—Refers to an error-checking device, indicating no sign or improper signing of a field used for arithmetic processes. The machine can, upon interrogation, be made to stop or enter into a correction routine.

sign control, flip-flop — Refers to the control of a specific flip-flop which is used to store the algebraic sign of numbers.

sign digit—A character ($+$ or $-$) used to designate the algebraic sign of a number.

significant digit — A digit that contributes to the precision of a number. The number of significant digits is counted beginning with the digit contributing the most value, called the most-significant digit, and ending with the one contributing the least value, called the least-significant digit.

silica gel—A moisture-absorbent chemical used for dehydrating wave guides, coaxial lines, pressurized components, shipping containers, etc.

silicon—1. A nonmetallic element that is mixed with iron or steel during smelting to provide desirable magnetic properties for transformer-core materials. In its pure state, it is used as a semiconductor. 2. A nonmetallic element having semiconducting properties, and occurring in two allotropic forms — dark, gray crystals and a brown amorphous powder. Used for transistors and certain crystal diodes. Characteristics are at. no. 14, at. wt. 28.086, sp. gr. 2.42, m.p. 1420°C, energy gap 1.12 electron-volts, dielectric constant 12.

silicon anodization—The discovery that silicon can be anodized opened an unexpected path to cheaper, denser, faster integrated circuits. The low-temperature process produces, in one step, the dielectric needed to isolate the active elements on a chip, thus adding the advantages of dielectric isolation to any semiconductor technology, whether bipolar or metal-oxide-semiconductor. Normally, device isolation requires two or three extended oxidizing and diffusion steps at temperatures in excess of 1000°C. But, the anodizing process eliminates one and often two mask applications, depending on the circuit design. It should, therefore, ultimately reduce the energy consumed in processing as well as cut the front-end wafer cost by 25%. Circuit complexity is also increased: bipolar large-scale ICs can double in density. Silicon anodization improves performance by lowering the capacitance between elements and increasing transistor gain and speed. The improvement is especially evident in such new bipolar circuit forms as integrated-injection logic and low-power Schottky transistor-transistor logic. In improved I²L circuits, for example, current gains have increased tenfold, and cutoff frequencies have been multiplied by five. However, the use of an anodizing process in the fabrication of integrated circuits is not new; in many circuits, buried conductors are built by anodizing aluminum. But, silicon, itself, had never before been anodized and transformed into a dielectric deep enough for IC isolation.

silicon avalanche photodiodes — The silicon avalanche photodiode is the solid-state counterpart of the photomultiplier tube. It has an internal gain mechanism due to impact ionization, very high responsivity, high gain-bandwidth product, and fast time-response characteristics.

silicon crystal processing, Cz method —In the conventional Czochralski, or Cz, method, polycrystal silicon is heated in a silica crucible to a temperature of about 1420 °C. A crystal seed is immersed in the silicon melt, and then pulled, while rotating, to obtain single-crystal silicon. The application of extreme heat, however, causes thermal convection currents in the melt, and the roughly activated melt surface causes a fluctuation of melt temperature, preventing a smooth crystal growth. In addition, large quantities of oxygen, that are produced by the chemical reaction between the silica crucible and the silicon melt, dissolve into the melt and find their way into the crystal, causing defects in the crystals, and distortions and warpage in the wafer-production process.

silicon crystal processing, MCz method —By simulating a zero-gravity environment through the use of a high magnetic field, Sony Corporation has developed a new crystal-growing process for producing single-crystal silicon. Called the magnetic field Cz (or MCz) method, the approach is similar to the method of growing other high-quality crystals in a zero-gravity environment. The MCz method is a modified form of the Czochralski (or Cz) method that is currently employed to produce single-crystal silicon. By using the MCz method, crystal defects, wafer distortion and warpage, and resistivity fluctuation can all be minimized considerably. The decrease in crystal defects reduces noise and improves the electrical characteristics of microcircuit devices, while the decrease in wafer distortion and warpage allows the etching of densely integrated circuit patterns.

The Sony method uses the same crystal-pulling system as the Czochralski technology, but the application of a high magnetic field of about 2000 gauss suppresses the thermal convection of the silicon melt. The suppression of convection current smooths the melt surface and reduces temperature fluctuation to a constant level. This ensures a smooth and uniform crystal growth with virtually negligible growth striations caused by localized impurities such as oxygen. The optimum level of oxygen concentration in the crystal can be controlled by adjusting the magnetic field and the rotating speed of the crystal. Thus, the oxygen content in the crystal can be reduced to one-tenth of that which is present when using the Cz method. Researchers at Sony Corporation say that the improved quality of the silicon will improve the production yield of semiconductor devices—with 4200-gate devices improving from a 40% production yield to about a 70% yield.

silicon diode — Also called a silicon detector. A crystal detector used for rectifying or detecting uhf and vhf signals. It consists of a metal contact held against a piece of silicon in a particular crystalline state.

silicon doping — Doping of silicon with impurity atoms alters the electronic structure of the substance in such a way that carriers of electric charge are easily freed from the atomic lattice. A silicon atom has four electrons in its valence, or outermost, shell, and in a pure crystal, these electrons form pairs that are shared by adjacent atoms. As a result, each atom is surrounded by eight electrons, an inherently stable configuration. An n-type semiconductor can be made by replacing a few atoms of silicon with those of an element, such as phosphorus, which has five electrons in its valence shell. The extra electron has no part to play in the bonds between the atoms of the crystal, and so, it readily becomes a mobile charge carrier. In a p-type semiconductor, the impurity introduced is an element, such as boron, with three electrons in its valence shell. Each impurity atom gives rise to a deficiency of one electron, called a hole. A hole has a net positive charge, and under an applied voltage, it can move from atom to atom through the crystal structure.

silicone—1. A member of the family of polymeric materials that are characterized by a recurring chemical group which contains silicon and oxygen atoms as links in the main chain. These compounds are presently derived from silica (sand) and methyl chloride. One of their important properties is resistance to heat. 2. A family of synthetic materials consisting of a backbone of alternating atoms of silicon and oxygen, usually with associated carbon atoms. They generally have a low vapor pressure and can withstand extremely high temperatures.

silicon gate — Generally refers to an MOS technology process that uses silicon as the material for the gate of the transistor.

silicon-gate complementary MOS — Some microprocessors are designed by using state-of-the-art "silicon-gate complementary MOS" technology which offers a high packing density with a good speed performance, noise immunity, and extremely low power dissipation. The internal logic structure is fully static in nature and allows the clock to be stopped between instructions, cycles, or minor cycles. In addition, it requires a single +5-volt supply. All the signals are fully TTL compatible. The design has been optimized to minimize external packages, thus reducing the overall system cost, in comparison with other microprocessors that require multiple supply voltages and support chips. The ability of complementary MOS technology to withstand a larger variation of supply voltages and temperature ranges automatically qualifies these microprocessors for military applications, an area ignored, so far, by most microprocessor developers.

silicon growing, directional-solidification method — In the directional-solidification method of growing silicon, a seed crystal placed at the bottom of a silicon melt grows to conform to the shape of the crucible. The directional-solidification method differs from the conventional Czochralski method in that the crystal is not pulled from a silicon melt contained in a crucible, but is instead grown from a seed at the bottom of the melt. The silicon crystal grows upward and outward from the seed as the 1400 °C temperature of the melt is lowered. Fully grown, the crystal assumes the shape of the crucible, pressing up

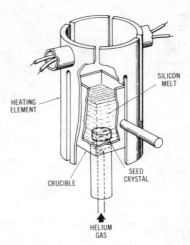

Silicon growing, directional-solidification method.

against it, and this is the point where the production problem lies.

The process uses a graded-silica crucible with a high density at the interior that grades to a lower density at the outside. A tenacious bond is formed between the silicon and the silica in the crucible wall. Then, at the cooling stage, the silicon, in tension with the wall, contracts 10 times faster than the container and, thus, can crack. However, the crucible breaks before the ingot fractures, as wanted.

silicon-nitride passivation — Silicon-nitride passivation is acknowledged as a process which enhances IC reliability. Various circuits utilize a primary passivating layer of silicon nitride to protect the devices from ionic contamination. This layer is deposited below the final layer of metallization, which is itself protected by a layer of phosphorous silicon dioxide. This double protection prevents mechanical and ionic damage to the circuit and greatly enhances its operational lifetime.

silicon-on-sapphire (SOS) — SOS technology resolves the problem of parasitic capacitance by removing surplus substrate conducting material after all gates have been generated. Parasitic capacitance, the problem resolved by SOS, is the principal disadvantage of n- or p-channel MOS; this is a prob-

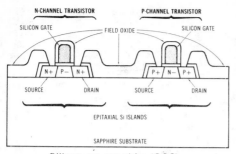

Silicon-on-sapphire (SOS).

lem that is not resolved in any way by CMOS or bipolar technology. Note that SOS is not a substitute for CMOS or bipolar technologies. In theory, it could be used with any of the technologies. SOS technology is a process in which a thin layer is grown on a sapphire substrate, and then selectively removed leaving small silicon "islands" that are made into MOS transistors. The essence of SOS technology is that instead of using an n- or p-type substrate, the doped substrate material is grown on an inert base. Artificial sapphire is chosen as the inert base because its coefficient of thermal expansion is almost exactly equal to that of silicon. This is important, since LSI circuits heat up when operating, with the result that even a small difference in the coefficient of expansion would cause the silicon to separate from the base on a hot chip. All standard techniques can be used with SOS. Because the sapphire substrate is a true insulator, not a semiconductor, this technique drastically reduces all parasitic capacitance and leakage current. It also should be possible to place transistors much closer together, with very high packing density. SOS technology is moving relatively slowly and sapphire substrates are still very costly; however, SOS is a potent technology that should play an important role in high-performance memories.

silicon, polycrystalline—Polycrystalline silicon is a material made up of many single crystals that have a random orientation and it is of great importance in solid-state electronics. Devices like floating-gate memory systems, charge-coupled devices, and static and dynamic RAMs depend on

the electrical characteristics of polysilicon and on oxides grown over polysilicon. However, a major problem with these ICs, which rely on alternating layers of silicon and oxide, is that asperities on the surface of polysilicon lead to electric-field enhancement and consequent breakdown problems. One solution to the problem is to expose the polysilicon film to an intense laser beam prior to oxidation so as to melt down and smooth the surface asperities without creating unwanted heating in underlying material.

silicon rectifier—1. One or more silicon rectifying cells or cell assemblies. 2. By simple definition, a silicon rectifier is a pn junction, with p-type material forming the anode and n-type material forming the cathode. It rectifies by permitting current to flow more easily in the forward direction than it does in the reverse. Hence, when alternating current is applied across the two terminals, current flows freely during only half the cycle.

silicon rectifying cell — An elementary two-terminal silicon device which consists of a positive and a negative electrode and conducts current effectively in only one direction.

silicon resistor—A resistor of a special silicon material that has a fairly constant positive temperature coefficient, making it suitable as a temperature-sensing element.

silicon solar cell — A photovoltaic cell designed to convert light energy into power for electronic and communication equipment. It consists essentially of a thin wafer of specially processed silicon.

silicon steel — Steel containing 3% to 5% silicon. Its magnetic qualities make it desirable for use in the iron cores of transformers and in other ac devices.

silicon transistor—One formed from a silicon crystal, sometimes specified in preference to germanium because of its higher temperature stability.

silicon transistor logic circuits—Logic circuits using silicon transistors instead of germanium components.

Silicon Valley — Refers to the general area below San Francisco centering around Sunnyvale, California, where a large concentration of semiconductor manufacturers have located their headquarters and many of their manufacturing facilities. (Also called Silicon Gulch.)

silicon wafer manufacture — Roughly speaking, wafers are basically made of sand (silicon dioxide), and in the first manufacturing step, the sand is reacted with carbon to form 99% pure silicon and CO_2. The silicon is then reacted with hydrogen chloride to form trichlorosilane. $SiHCl_3$ is an industrial chemical with many other uses. (The trichlor can be distilled as required to increase purity.) At this point, the poly supplier takes over. The trichlorosilane is decomposed in a hydrogen atmosphere with electric current to form pure free silicon which grows in ingots (rods). The rods are not single-crystalline, but rather are polycrystalline: hence the name "poly." Poly is the basic material that is melted in a crucible to feed the growth of crystals in the Czochralski method.

silver (Ag)—Noble metal, at. no. 47, at. wt. 107.870, sp. gr. 10.5, m.p. 960.5 °C, b.p. 2180 °C. The best electrical conductor and the main constituent of photographic emulsions.

silver mica capacitor—A high-stability, low-power-factor, fixed capacitor prepared by vacuum deposition of silver on thin mica sheets.

simulate—1. Refers to the activity of representing certain features of the behavior of a physical or abstract system by the behavior of another system, e.g., to represent a physical phenomenon by means of operations performed by a microcomputer or to represent the operations of a microcomputer by those of another microcomputer. 2. To represent the functioning of a device, system, or microcomputer program by another, i.e., to represent the functioning of one microcomputer by another, to represent the behavior of a physical system by the execution of a microcomputer program, or to represent a biological system by a mathematical model. 3. To imitate one system with another, primarily by software, so that the imitating system accepts the same data and executes the same microcomputer operations.

simulation — 1. A type of problem in which a physical model, and the conditions to which the model may be subjected, are all represented by mathematical formulas. 2. The representation of physical systems and phenomena by microcomputers, models, or other equipment, e.g., an imitative type of data processing in which an automatic computer is used as a model of some entity, i.e., a chemical process. Information enters the microcomputer to represent the factors in the real process, and the microcomputer produces information that represents the results of the process, and the process itself. 3. In microcomputer programming, the technique of setting up a routine for one microcomputer to make it operate as nearly as possible like some other microcomputer. 4. As related to analog or digital computers, a development representation of physical systems, in which information provided to the computer is represented by the process variables; an example would be a chemical process. The processing completed by the computer is a representation of the process itself and the output of the computer represents the results of the processes simulated.

simulator — Refers to highly specific programs that emulate, imitate, or substitute the logical operation of various microprocessors. These programs are often designed to execute object programs generated by a cross-assembler on a machine other than the one being worked on. Simulators are very useful for checking and debugging programs prior to committing them to ROM firmware.

simulator, cross—Cross simulators are often used on larger host computers to programmatically simulate actions of a microcomputer. The primary problem, however, is that extensive program testing and simulation of real-time external events, such as signals input from a device controller, is tedious and expensive. Thus, cross simulators are principally used to step-through subroutines and program modules independent of the electronic environment. A simulator is extremely useful, however, when exact execution time must be determined for time-critical program segments.

simulator, diagnostic routine—When a system goes to production, many of the checkout routines can be used by manufacturing in the final system test. Users have found that putting diagnostic routines in a simulator is the most effective way of reducing the time required to check out a system and to locate system hardware failures. Therefore, the simulator can be used as an effective piece of manufacturing test equipment.

simulator/debug utility — This allows any microcomputer programs that are generated to be simulated and debugged on the larger computers or prototype systems.

simulator, hardware—A hardware simulator is a program written for a microcomputer. This program will provide interactive control over the debugging of other microcomputer programs by plugging a number of PROMs into the board. The minimum configuration required is a prototype card with 3 RAMs and a teletypewriter for a typical system. When fully stuffed with 16 RAMs, test programs up to 512 bytes (locations) in length may be accommodated. In one system, the hardware simulation program itself occupies 9 full ROMs. Generally, the hardware simulation program has two basic functions: (1) to simulate the execution of a test program, tracing its progress, and apprehending gross errors, and (2) allow the user to dynamically interact with and/or modify his test program, in order to facilitate the debugging process. These two functions are implemented by means of a set of directives or commands that the user types in at the teletypewriter keyboard. Some of the directives call for type-outs by the simulator program, some of the directives signal the input of data or program modifications, and some of the directives involve both type-outs and input response or data. (Some systems.)

simulator programs—These are special programs to emulate execution of microprocessor programs. Simulators are interpretive and provide bit-for-bit duplication of microprocessor-instruction execution timing, register contents, etc. Direct user control over execution conditions (RAM/register contents, interrupts, I/O data, etc.) usually is provided.

simulator program, UART—A Universal Asynchronous Receiver/Transmitter (UART) is a large-scale integration circuit with a complexity that is comparable to that of a typical 4-bit microcomputer. Its functions may be easily transformed to a program for execution by an 8-bit microcomputer. A system program would then pass parallel characters to the UART simulation program just as if it were a hardware UART. The UART simulator also processes the serial data stream between the microcomputer and the cassette interface.

simulator, ROM — The ability to set, lock, and monitor the ROM address register provides a convenient means for identifying the location of errors and documenting individual program changes. The simulator enables the user to insert the hundreds of little changes he will make during the debugging of his program. Some of these changes will be made to correct actual errors in the microcode. However, the majority will be inserted in an effort to locate and diagnose mistakes. Once the designer has the proper instrumentation at his disposal, system checkout can proceed quickly.

simulator, software — Many potential sources of error exist in a microcomputer program of even modest complexity. For some systems, software simulators provide one of the most useful tools for testing programs. Input data to the simulator consist of an assembled program, or object file, written for the microcomputer. In addition, various commands are available to control the simulated execution of the program. The simulator output contains representations of various registers, flags, and memory locations. These are shown as they would appear inside the microcomputer. The simulator commands allow designers to obtain selected outputs at simulated instants.

simultaneity—Refers to the facility of a microcomputer to allow input/output on its peripherals to continue in parallel with operations in the central processor.

simultaneous computer — Refers to a computer that contains a separate unit to perform each portion of the entire computation concurrently, the units being interconnected in a way determined by the computation. At different times in a run, a given interconnection carries signals representing different values of the same variable, for example, a difference analyzer.

simultaneous I/O bus interface — I/O bus interfaces generally consist of drivers and receivers of the I/O bus. In many systems, the I/O command register can simultaneously contain the 8 I/O commands needed to control devices and buffer memories. Up to 256 I/O devices or up to 65,536 words of 8-bits in buffer memories may be addressed through these data bus lines.

simultaneous operations—In some systems, the input and output channels for the microcomputer are designed for maximum performance and flexibility. Any channel may control any input or output device within its speed range. This universal ability to attach any device is a major achievement of combined computer and I/O design. All I/O operations may be simultaneously performed with program processing by the microcomputer data channels. An especially powerful feature of these channels is the ability of the system to execute a complete sequence of I/O instructions—a small program independent of the main program. This capability, together with special features in the I/O control units, permits the channel to perform such outstanding operations as the searching of a disk file independently from the main microcomputer program. The processing program is not interrupted until the complete I/O sequence is finished or unless an error condition occurs.

single- and multiple-pass programs—A single-pass program generates the desired end result in one computer run. A multiple-pass program generates intermediate outputs which require additional processing to obtain the end result.

single-board computer controller—With the advent of the single-chip microprocessor with its internal general-purpose registers, flip-flops, logic, and memory, there has arisen a device called the single-board computer. With the addition of external ROM, RAM, logic, etc., it is possible to use the single-chip processor and build a microcomputer onto a single pc board. Typically, many single-board microcomputers are ideally suited for use in controller applica-

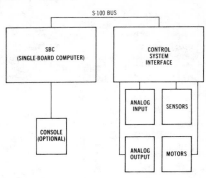

Single-board computer controller.

tions by connecting to a system interface that is constructed on just one additional board. Both the single-board computer and the single-board system interface are connected to the system bus, and the interface board can contain analog to digital converters, digital to analog converters, triacs, relays, opto-isolators, or any other circuitry that is required to interface the microcomputer to the controlled processes. Optional direct-control circuits can be coupled directly to parallel or serial I/O ports in the form of a console terminal. For data processing, the single-board microcomputer can be coupled with the boards of other systems to provide the essential components for a complete system. By having a disk controller, a RAM, and a video terminal controller operating from the bus, a complete data-processing system will be ready to provide an interface with the devices required by the user's application.

single contiguous allocation—A memory-allocation scheme that assigns all available memory as one block.

single step—A method of operation of a microcomputer in which each step is performed with manual control.

single-step debugging — An important first step in system debug is to check out in a single-step mode the simplest instructions that enable information to be entered into registers and which permit system states to be set up. Once this has been done, short routines that set up system states can be written. Then, the response of the microprocessor to these states can be checked. For example, one might want to determine if the microprocessor is capable of testing for a negative result on an arithmetic operation. To do this, a program to generate a negative result is written and entered into the simulator. Then, a test is made to determine if the microprocessor can detect this condition. If the test fails, a loop can be written so this sequence is repeated over and over again until the reason for a failure can be determined.

single-step mode — The single-step mode is derived from correctly timed transitions on the halt-signal input. It forces the processor to execute a single bus cycle, by entering the "run" mode until the processor starts a bus cycle, and then changing to the "halt" mode. Thus, the single-step mode allows the user to proceed through (and, therefore, debug) processor operations one bus cycle at a time.

single-step operation — Refers to a method of operating an automatic computer manually, in which a single instruction or part of an instruction is performed in response to a single operation of a manual control. This method is generally used for detecting mistakes.

SIO—Abbreviation for serial imput/output controller.

skeleton table macro—A macro assembly-program internal table that contains the prototypes of all the macro-definitions in a program.

skip bus — Refers to a specific central processor bus that is shared by I/O interfaces and is utilized in order to test devices associated with each interface and the conditional branching of the program as a result of the testing.

skip code—A functional code that instructs the machine to skip certain predetermined fields in memory.

skip flag (SF)—The skip flag is typically a 1-bit register that represents a true/false skip condition with respect to the instruction being executed by the processor.

skip instruction—Refers to an instruction to proceed to the next instruction; a blank instruction. Same as instruction, no-op.

skip test — Refers to a specific type of microinstruction that is designed and utilized for conditional operations based on the state of readiness of various devices or the conditions of a register.

slave—Refers to a unit of electronic gear under the control of signals from some type of master equipment.

slave/master relationship — Refers to communication between two devices on the bus in the form of a master-slave relationship. At any point in time, there is one device that has control of the bus. This controlling device is termed the "bus master." The master device controls the bus when communicating with another device on the bus, termed the "slave." A typical example of this relationship is a processor, as the master, fetching an instruction from memory (which is always a slave). Another example is a DMA device interface, as the master, transferring data to memory (the slave). Bus master control is dynamic. The bus arbitrator on the processor module, for example, may pass bus control to a DMA device. The DMA device, as the master, could then communicate with a slave memory bank. On some systems, the bus is used by the processor and all I/O devices. There is a priority structure to determine which device gets control on the bus. Every device on the bus that is capable of becoming a bus master is assigned a priority according to its position along the bus. When two devices that are capable of becoming a bus master request use of the bus simultaneously, the device with the higher-priority position will receive control.

slave microcomputer architecture — There is a significant difference between slave computing and multiprocessing. A slave microcomputer comes with its own memory and I/O, and it operates in parallel with, and on the same bus with, the host processor. It has minimal software problems. Typically, a slave microcomputer has an on-chip ROM and RAM, one or more general-purpose I/Os, an extended instruction set, and a full access to the memory and peripherals of a higher-capability microprocessor system. Thus, without affecting the host microcomputer, the slave microcomputer is able to perform peripheral functions.

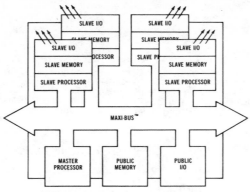

Slave microcomputer architecture.

slave microcomputers — Microcomputers have evolved in a number of directions with the standard type (the most common) being the general-purpose microcomputer. Typically they have on-chip ROM and RAM, general-purpose I/O, and a memory that is generally in the 1K and 4K range. One such general-purpose device is the "slave microcomputer."

Slave microcomputers have specialized I/O ports that allow them to be appended to microprocessor systems of higher capability. The microcomputer in this mode of operation is programmed to perform a peripheral function for the microprocessor system, such as controlling a keyboard, printer, or other device. One manufacturer (Computer Automation, Inc.) has implemented the slave microcomputer concept to design their LSI 4/10S (the "S" stands for slave) to work with their NM4 and LSI-2 master microcomputers. The 4/10S slave is a well-equipped CPU with a 32K-byte RAM memory, four private I/O ports, a real-time clock, and an extended "NAKED MINI 4" instruction set. It has full access to the master microcomputer's memory and peripherals. By inserting an LSI 4/10S slave microcomputer board into the chassis, Computer Automation, Inc., is able to add to the processing power of their NAKED MINI microcomputer. Working in parallel with a master microcomputer, up to four 4/10S slave microcomputers can process all kinds of off-loaded tasks, such as communications protocol jobs, process control work, and complex calculations. This is accomplished without slowing down the host microcomputer's own processing chores.

slave mode — Refers to the mode of computer operation in which most of the basic controls affecting the state of the computer are protected from the program.

slave peripheral-processor control — Control of a slave peripheral processor is generally the same as for any

Slave microcomputers (Courtesy Computer Automation, Inc.).

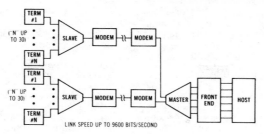

Slave support processors.

I/O device with direct-memory access (DMA). A simple device driver is often sufficient to control its functions. In addition, if a problem can be partitioned and is for a special purpose, a peripheral processor may notably improve execution of the task.

slave station—A type of station to which a master station intends to (or does) send a message. Also referred to as a "receiving station" or a "data sink."

slave support processors — Several kinds of support circuits can pick up where the processor leaves off. For example, "slave" circuits, one of the earliest concepts, are dedicated functional blocks that operate like a peripheral device. Downloaded by the processor, the slave, such as the various math circuits that have been developed by several manufacturers, often operates 10 to 100 times faster than the CPU, interrupting the CPU when the operation is complete so that the CPU can transfer the result back into its accumulator or into a memory location. In a multilink configuration, with links in simultaneous operation, each link can transmit at up to 9600 bits/second with dynamic load sharing (typically). Alternatively, either link can operate at 19.2K bits/second while the other is on standby.

slice—1. Refers to a special type of chip architecture that permits the cascading or stacking of devices to increase word bit size. 2. Those parts of a waveform lying inside two given amplitude limits on the same side of the zero axis.

slice architecture—In "slice" architecture, a section of the register file and ALU in a microcomputer is placed in one package. In some systems, the registers are all 4 bits wide; others accommodate 2 bits. Each end of

each register is accessible through the ALU at the chip's edge; two or more of these "slices" can be cascaded together to form larger word sizes. Whether instruction lengths are identical to data-word size or not depends upon how the control portion of the processor is organized. In some systems, another chip in the set provides 8 microprogrammed control sections.

slice, bipolar — Bipolar/LSI microprocessor slices offer several advantages over standard MOS. The bipolar speeds of "bit slice" processors, or microcontrollers, assure a precise emulation of conventional systems, which employ standard bipolar circuits. By using microprogramming techniques, designers can replace scores of SSI and MSI packages and at reduced power. And, in applications such as minicomputers, processor slices provide the hardware flexibility to reduce equipment size without changes in existing software. One major 4-bit bipolar slice system can process both binary and BCD data and provide parity for error checking. The 4-bit slice contains an ALU, a data latch/mask and shift network units, an accumulator, and I/O bus control sections. The data input and output ports are organized to allow use of the slice in a wide variety of system bus structures.

slice/memory interface circuit — Any processor circuits must have access to main-memory storage. In one specific family, this chore is handled by a Slice/Memory Interface circuit. This circuit contains the necessary memory data and address storage. In addition, there is logic for more complex addressing techniques (paging, associative memories, etc.).

slice systems, bipolar—No matter how different a manufacturer's new family of bipolar LSI circuits may appear, certain circuit blocks are common to all bit-slice systems. In addition to the processor slice itself, the functions of control register, timing, slice-memory interface, and carry look-ahead are all needed to expand the system. In every configuration, the control register contains the logic necessary to accomplish microprogrammable control. It includes a 4-bit-wide data path, which can be expanded to larger words, plus enough storage and logic to address and control the memory circuits. It can also handle status, branching, and interrupt functions. In the arithmetic-and-logic-unit block, the computational logic sits side-by-side with data-routing paths and the input/output ports that handle the control-register inputs and memory outputs. The timing function ties the other functions together by providing the various clock phases needed to drive all parts of the system. Where the systems generally differ is in what they offer in system capability and speed. Some systems, by virtue of their 2-bit format, are probably the most flexible. But this versatility is achieved at the expense of the number of chips needed for a complete CPU system—usually twice as many as the others need for a system of given complexity.

slices, time—Refers to an allotment of computer time for a particular task to be accomplished (a concept used in multiprogramming or time sharing).

slicing techniques, fixed abrasive—For any ingot technology to meet its cost goals, silicon ingots must be sliced efficiently and with minimum cost. One system uses the Fixed Abrasive Slicing Technique (FAST) which combines the low-cost equipment and labor features of multiblade slurry slicing with low-cost expendable materials costs. The FAST approach fixes abrasives on the cutting edge only, thus reducing kerf width and abrasive cost. With the FAST approach, diamonds (the best abrasive available) are metal-bonded to the bottom of high-strength wires. These wires are assembled into a multiwire blade pack, stretched to high tension, and reciprocated back and forth to saw through the silicon ingots. FAST is a new slicing technology and, therefore, involves both machine and blade development. The combined savings in abrasives, kerf width, and labor result in an economic breakthrough in wafer slicing. Smooth surfaces with damage of less than 5 microns and no edge chipping are produced, minimizing surface preparation for device fabrication. The FAST program is in the development stage with a prototype machine expected to be available in 1981/1982 which will slice ingots that are up to 15 centimeters in diameter and 30 centimeters long.

slow-scan television—A technique used by ham operators. Many have developed a slow-scan television system using a microprocessor and a few inexpensive analog interface cards. They find it a vast improvement over both the earlier analog system (the image quality of which was low) and the digital systems (which were very complex and expensive). A typical slow-scan television system using a microprocessor permits amateur radio operators to transmit video signals in about 1/1000 of the bandwidth used by commercial television.

small-scale integration — Abbreviated SSI. Any integrated circuit which has fewer than 12 equivalent gates. (*See* LSI.)

"smart" interactive terminals—Refers to the new "smart terminals" term used to identify an interactive terminal in which part of the processing is accomplished by a microcomputer or microprocessor contained in the terminal itself. This type of terminal is sometimes referred to in literature as an "intelligent terminal." To be considered a smart terminal, the computing capability of the microcomputer in the terminal must be available to the user in a way that permits him to program it to perform part of his unique application.

"smart" terminals — In its most rudimentary form, a smart terminal contains a crt, a keyboard, a serial-communication I/O device, and a microcomputer. The microcomputer controls text editing, formatting, and the protocol of communication with the host computer system. Such terminals can incorporate peripheral memory devices like tape cassettes, can be programmed independently of their roles in the larger computer system, and can, therefore, serve several useful functions, both on- or off-line. For example, the microcomputer can serve as a communications controller and handle tasks like line switching. Microprocessor-controlled interactive smart terminals often have the following characteristics:

1. Self-contained storage.
2. User interaction — with the terminal or the central computer.
3. A stored program.
4. Part of the processing is accomplished in the terminal.
5. On-line operation via a communications line with a large central computer and data base.
6. Human-oriented input — keyboard, light pen, etc.
7. Human-oriented output — serial printer, crt, etc.

SME—Abbreviation for Society of Manufacturing Engineers.

smooth contact—Refers to a socket or pin contact that has a significantly smooth profile, i.e., a flush surface and not one which has a locking spring projecting from its side; one that is locked to the connector body by other methods.

snapshot debugging—Refers to a type of diagnostics and debugging technique in which the programmer specifies the start and end of program segments where he wishes to examine the contents of various registers and accumulators. The snapshot tracing may indicate the contents not only of the various accumulators and registers but also of specified memory locations.

snapshot jump — Refers to a dynamic partial printout during computing at breakpoints and checkpoints, or of selected items in storage.

SNOBOL—This refers to a problem-oriented language that facilitates string manipulation and pattern-matching operations.

socket strips—The main alternatives to soldering are socket strips and wire wrapping. Socket strips are plastic boards with small sockets on a 1/10-inch grid. The sockets are bused together to allow the rapid connection of DIP and other standard components. Jumpers are made from solid stripped hook-up wire, usually No. 22 AWG. The wire is pushed into a socket to make the connections.

Socket strips are made in sizes that range from one which holds a single 14-pin DIP package to large assemblies capable of holding several hundreds of components and furnishing regulated power, signal generation, switches, indicators, etc. They are generally used for circuit development as they are not easily adapted to building multiple copies or connectors to other equipment. They are initially expensive but allow repeated use of components and do not damage the components; users can even save and re-use the wire jumpers. This makes socket strips ideal for educational use where many circuits are to be studied.

soft error—An occasional random loss of data. The reason for the error is normally not identifiable, nor is it repeatable on a device tester.

soft error, alpha radiation — Dynamic RAMs rely on a charge stored in cells; the level of charge determines the cell's bit state (logical 1 or 0). The charge used to determine the bit state could be upset and altered by alpha radiation coming from trace elements in a ceramic package. The resulting soft errors—in which a bit is switched from a 1 to a 0, or vice versa—cause no circuit damage and leave no telltale signs to indicate that they ever occurred. (Soft errors can, however, be detected and reversed using error-correction circuitry.)

soft limited integrator—Refers to integrators in which the inputs cease to be integrated when the output tends to exceed specified limits. In a soft limited integrator, which is used for lower cost or convenience and where precision is of less importance, the output may exceed the limits.

soft limiting—Refers to a circuit of nonlinear elements that restrict the electrical excursion of a variable in accordance with some specified criteria. "Hard limiting" is a limiting action with negligible variation in the output in the range where the output is limited. "Soft limiting" is a limiting action with appreciable variation in the output in the range where the output is limited.

software—1. The term software was invented to contrast with the "iron" or hardware of a computer system. Software items are programs, languages, and procedures of a computer system. Software libraries for microprocessors are being built and assembled with heavy competition among suppliers, both manufacturers and distributors. 2. Refers to the internal programs or routines prepared professionally to simplify programming and computer operations. Uses permit the programmer to use his own language (English) or mathematics (algebra) in communicating with the computer. 3. The various programming aids that are frequently supplied by the manufacturers to facilitate the purchaser's efficient operation of the equipment. Such software items include various assemblers, generators, subroutine libraries, compilers, operating systems, and industry-application programs.

software "bus" — This is a standard software interface (analogous to the hardware interface between microcomputer modules) that allows for communication between software modules, both standard and custom. The software designer can incrementally add modular software capability to his application, just as the hardware designer incrementally adds hardware capability.

software, canned — Also called packages. Generalized programs that are prewritten and debugged and are designed to perform one or more general functions. Business functions include accounts receivable, accounts payable, general ledger, payroll, or inventory control.

software, co-routine — The co-routine approach to software organization provides an alternative to conventional hierarchical structures. It is a useful tool in applications that require two interactive programs to alternately behave as main control programs. Examples include test drivers and other program development and testing aids, as well as certain categories of language processors. Although implementations of co-routine structures vary as a function of application and processor architecture, they are straightforward and require only minimal resources and operational overhead.

software, cross—Cross-software packages let users take advantage of the tools of a larger computer system in order to develop software for their own target system.

software, cross-assembler — Cross-assemblers translate a symbolic representation of the instructions and data into a form that can be loaded and executed by a microcomputer. A cross-assembler is defined as an assembler executing on a machine other than the one used to generate the code for the desired unit. Initial development time can be significantly reduced by taking advantage of a large-scale computer's processing, editing, and high-speed peripheral capability. Programs are written in the assembly language using mnemonic symbols both for instruction and for special assembler operation. Symbolic addresses can be used in the source program; however, the assembled program will use absolute address. Many assemblers, designed to operate interactively from a terminal, are written in standard FORTRAN IV and can be modified to run on most large-scale machines.

software cross-products (microprocessor)—These devices include assemblers, simulators, and various compilers. They develop versions of programs which are used for assembly, simulation, or compilation of programs. A cross-assembler, for example, is functionally identical to other resident assemblers. Compilers are machine-oriented systems-programming languages designed specifically to generate various internal codes. Assemblers often have full macro capability and allow for conditional assembly (meaning that at the time of assembly, one of several sections of code may be chosen).

software, custom—These are programs designed specifically to meet one user's particular requirements. Advantages are that any specific need can be directly addressed (within the capability of the hardware), and the software will conform to the business instead of the business conforming to the software. One disadvantage is that custom software is more likely to have "residual bugs" after its installation. Another disadvantage is the cost. Since development costs can only be distributed to one user, the price of a custom software system is somewhat higher than a comparable packaged system.

software design approach—A software design begins with functional specifications, but it is translated into a sequence of instructions, rather than into an array of gates. The paper design usually involves a flowchart, which shows events graphically in the proper order, together with conditions that can cause the order of events to change. The first step can be a high-level flowchart, which closely resembles a block diagram. This is broken down into a form in which each block in the flowchart represents a single instruction in the program. Standardized shapes of blocks in the flowchart diagram have evolved so that one person can more easily follow the logic of another person's work.

software development process — The steps of a basic software development cycle are as follows:

1. Problem statement.
2. Design of abstract algorithms and the data structures.
3. Construction of flowchart and data layouts.
4. Coding of the program in the chosen language.
5. Source-code preparation in machine-readable form, often using a source-code editor.
6. Translation to object code or machine code (using assemblers, compilers, and linkage editors).
7. Transmission of machine code to the target environment (using loaders).
8. Run-time checkout of the executing code (using debuggers).
9. Documentation.

This series of identifiable steps serves only to illustrate roughly the various activities that are traversed from the problem statement to the tested, properly running, well-documented program.

The problem statement can take a number of forms, each of which expresses the software development task to be performed; this problem statement serves as a goal for the creative energies of the software designer. Initial decisions are made. Abstract data structures are envisioned. Abstract algorithms are invented, discovered, deduced, or induced. What once was a problem statement becomes a deterministic algorithm. This solution can be represented in a flowchart or other representation of the algorithm, and the program can be coded in whatever language is chosen. This code is "desk checked" and prepared in machine-readable form so that it is acceptable to the language translator. The assembler or compiler translates this source code into object code or machine code. From there, the machine code is loaded into the target environment and will be subsequently tested, debugged, and documented.

software documents—Refers to all the documents and notations associated with a microcomputer; i.e., manuals, circuit diagrams, etc. Also, refers to all the programs and routines associated with the microcomputer; i.e., compilers, special languages, library routines, etc.

software house—Refers to a company which offers software support service to users. This support can range from simply supplying manuals and other information to a complete counseling and computer programming service.

software interrupts — A software interrupt is an instruction that will cause an interrupt and its associated vector fetch. Various software interrupts are useful in handling operating-system calls, software debugging, trace operations, memory mapping, and software development systems.

software kernels — On some systems, small software kernels that reside on each component computer cooperate and exchange data via the communication system in order to implement a single virtual machine. Programs are written, compiled, and tested independent of the hardware configuration. A separate system-generation facility allocates parts of the compiled program among the processors in the system. This allows programs to be loaded onto expanded or reduced hardware configurations without change. *See also* kernel.

software library — Most manufacturers support their users with extensive software libraries. All of the software tools required for the development of user application programs are generally available. These are operating and executive systems, high-level languages, assemblers, loaders, editors and utilities, etc. In addition to their use as development tools, the executive systems, arithmetic libraries, and input/output drivers are available for use as building blocks in user-application programs. Once the application program is written, additional software tools, such as "debug" and "real-time debug," are available to help users find and correct errors and make improvements. A complete library of diagnostics is usually also available to both verify proper hardware operation and troubleshoot many problems.

software, microcomputer — Standard software for many microcomputers includes an assembler, a loader, a debugging utility, a source-edit utility, and diagnostic programs. The assembler translates symbolic assembly-language programs into executable machine programs. The loader loads object tapes produced by the assembler or debugging utility. The debugging utility aids program checkout and features multiple breakpoints, instruction trace, and several other standard functions. The source-edit utility is used to generate assembly-language source tapes or modify existing source tapes. The diagnostics are used to verify processor operation. The cross-assembler enables programs written for the microcomputer to be assembled on various mini- or large computers.

software, microprocessor — In microprocessor applications, the designer-programmer tries to implement a design (previously done by logic designers on paper) through on-line programming of the microprocessor. Instead of using gate logic such as AND, OR, NAND, and NOR, the designer-programmer uses the mask, compare, and jump instructions. Most microprocessor applications involve a mixture of control operations and application computations that are interleaved in the program mainstream. Assembly language is predominant. Because of modularity and the obvious repetitious nature of so many operations, subroutines are used extensively, and subroutine nesting is facilitated by the stack register organizations in many of these units.

software monitor, small system — The typical small system monitor is a program that provides the user with certain maintenance and debugging functions which would normally be provided in a limited way on systems that include a control panel. The "monitor" is included on diskette with many small computers. The monitor is intended to be used in conjunction with the various Disk Operating Systems (DOS). Commands to the monitor are entered into the system via the terminal, using a format consistent with the DOS commands. Command editing facilities that are compatible with the user's BASIC editing features are often included in the monitor.

software, multilevel—Many applications involve the use of a multilevel software approach. In many systems, the microcomputer program that implements the visible functions of the microcomputer system (sometimes called the application program) is actually being controlled by another program, called an operating system. The operating system keeps track of system resources, such as input/output devices and memory, and coordinates the sharing of these resources between multiple applications programs. Complexity in the growth of microcomputer applications continues as does software applications. The word processor of today will grow into an all-electronic office. Home computers or small-business computers will become network elements as they are interconnected to share messages or data. Factories will employ up to 10 microcomputers per employee in sophisticated control applications. The software task of coordinating these multiprocessor systems is becoming a real crisis for system designers.

software package — Refers to various computer programs or sets of programs used in a particular application, such as a payroll/personnel package, scientific-subroutines package, etc.

software package, utility—Refers to a comprehensive library of utility software available for most series of microcomputers. The library generally includes:

1. Loading and debugging program.
2. Text editor.
3. Resident assembler.
4. Floating-point package.
5. Cross-assembler.
6. PROM programming software.
7. Tape conversion program.
8. Multiply/divide package.

software prototyping systems — One software development approach uses a combination of hardware and software called a prototyping system. Prototyping systems provide program assembly, on-line execution, and debugging. A general-purpose prototyping system allows the designer-programmer to be more creative and productive in the design of a particular microcomputer application. As a result, companies in this business either design a prototyping system as their first product or buy it. Using an on-line teleprinter, the designer-programmer assembles, edits, and stores the program in the RAM associated with a computer in the prototype system. Switching to the "operate" mode, the microprocessor in the application system accesses the program in the prototyping system as if it were in its own ROM, and the check-out procedure begins.

software simulator—An item of development software is the simulator. Simulators operate on computers other than the microcomputer and they simulate the operation of the microprocessor itself. This allows the programmer to test his microcomputer independently of the state of the development of the actual microcomputer hardware and allows him to perform his testing in larger, more capable, more convenient computers. The fundamentals of programming a microcomputer are the same as the fundamentals of programming any other computer. However, the microcomputer may require the application of additional cleverness and perseverance, because the typical microcomputer has a small word size (8 or 16 bits and, sometimes, 32 bits or, worse still, only 4 bits) and it runs slowly (5 to 20 milliseconds for a typical instruction). If the microcomputer is to be used in a real-time application with tight constraints, the programmer will have to produce a pretty "tight" code. If the application requires calculations, it may be necessary to use multiple-precision arithmetic—this means more coding and longer execution times.

software stack—Some microprocessor units use software stacks—an area in read-write memory that is set aside under program control. An on-chip

hardware stack often provides increased performance. For hardware stacks to be generally useful, there should also be on-chip indicators for "stack full" and "stack empty," which increases chip area. However, the on-chip hardware required for a software stack consists primarily of a stack-pointer register and an appropriate increment/decrement control. An indication of overflow and underflow is not so critical as for an on-chip hardware stack, since the software stack can be easily expanded in system memory.

software trace — Execution of one instruction at a time while the register status is displayed.

solderless connector — A device for clamping two wires firmly together to provide a good connection without using solder. A common form is a cap with tapered internal threads, which are twisted over the exposed ends of the wires.

solderless wrap — Also called wire-wrap. A method of connection in which a solid wire is tightly wrapped around a rectangular, square, or V-shaped terminal by means of a special tool.

solid—A state of matter in which the motion of the molecules is restricted. They tend to remain in one position, giving rise to a crystal structure. Unlike a liquid or gas, a solid has a definite shape and volume.

solid circuit—1. A semiconductor network fabricated in one piece of material by alloying, diffusing, doping, etching, cutting, and the use of necessary jumper wires. 2. Modification of properties of a material, i.e., silicon, so that components can be realized in one mass (i.e., resistors, capacitors, transistors, diodes). 3. Subminiature realization of a circuit in three dimensions, e.g., the buildup as parts of a semiconductor crystal, or by etching or deposition on a substrate.

solid error—Refers to an error that always occurs when a particular piece of equipment is used.

solid state — 1. Refers to various electronic components of solid materials as opposed to vacuum and gas tubes. 2. Pertains to various types of electronic components that convey or control electrons within solid materials. Transistors, germanium diodes, and magnetic cores are solid-state components; vacuum and gas tubes and electromechanical relays are not.

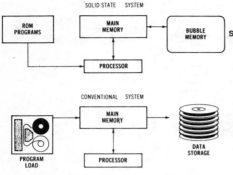

Solid-state computer systems.

solid-state computer systems — Combining ROM program storage with bubble memory creates an interesting solid-state high-performance computer system. The bubble memory provides secondary read-write storage with better access time than available with mechanical disks. The ROM supplies a program storage that eliminates the loading time required by mechanical peripherals. Without the burden of mechanical drives, a solid-state system is well adapted to small applications. Consequently, microprocessor-based terminals and other small applications are likely to be the first products to exploit this technology combination. Later, as bubble memory becomes cost-effective at the multimegabyte level, solid-state systems will be able to satisfy larger system applications.

solid-state device—1. Any element that can control current without moving parts, heated filaments, or vacuum gaps. All semiconductors are solid-state devices, although not all solid-state devices (e.g., transformers) are semiconductors. 2. Relates to the electronic components used to convey or control electrons within solid materials, e.g., transistors, germanium diodes, and magnetic cores. Thus, vacuum and gas tubes are not included.

solid-state element — Refers to electronic components whose operation does not require current to pass through a space or a vacuum. As a direct result, power needed to push current through the element is greatly reduced, and there is often no need for special cooling because there is very little heat built up.

solid-state imagers—A solid-state imager may soon replace the standard vidicon camera tube. Solid-state imagers have a number of very attractive advantages. They are small, rugged, and lightweight, operate at low voltage, and use little power. These features make them ideal for compact color cameras, particularly for general-consumer use with video cassette recorders. While most development effort has been directed toward imagers using charge-coupled device (CCD) shift registers, major strides are also being made with self-scanning imagers.

solid-state integrated circuit — The class of integrated components in which only solid-state materials are used.

solid-state physics—Branch of physics which covers all properties of solid materials, including electrical conduction in crystals of semiconductors and metals, superconductivity, and photoconductivity.

sonic delay line—A delay line using a medium providing an acoustic delay, such as mercury or quartz delay lines.

SOS—Abbreviation for silicon-on-sapphire. 1. Refers to an increasingly popular semiconductor manufacturing technology in which metal-oxide semiconductor devices are constructed in a thin single-crystal silicon film grown on an electrically insulating synthetic sapphire substrate. 2. Refers to the layers of material, and indirectly to the process of fabrication of the devices which achieve bipolar speeds through MOS technology by insulating the circuit components from each other.

SOS applications — SOS technology should suit microprocessor applications since all the advantages of CMOS circuitry could be retained at the high packing densities required to keep cost down. System clock rates at up to 15 MHz at 10 volts should be possible with basic machine-cycle times (typically eight clock pulses) of about 0.5 microsecond. In counter applications, circuit outputs normally clock at some submultiple of the input frequency. This application is ideal for SOS circuits since all high-frequency operation is on-chip. Besides time-keeping applications, SOS counters should also be useful in communication equipment where high-speed divide-by-N counters could be used in frequency synthesizers. Portable operation will also be possible because of low power drain. In bulk-silicon circuits, it is often difficult to use more than one supply voltage on the same chip since, for many transistors, the wafer itself forms a common substrate. Source voltage is then restricted because voltages above or below the substrate potential will either forward-bias the source-substrate junction or increase transistor threshold voltages. In SOS circuits, on the other hand, it is possible to use any number of supply voltages on the same chip without a substrate effect or diode interaction. SOS circuitry, then, should be particularly useful in level-shifting applications or in single-chip integrations of circuits which operate at different supply voltages. Another opening for SOS circuits is in multiplexing where a high degree of isolation between switches is needed. Thus, the areas where CMOS-on-sapphire technology can best be applied are in timekeeping, memories, microprocessors, high-speed counters, level shifters, and multiplexing. All these applications require a high degree of circuit complexity, plus fast low-power operation.

SOS fabrication — Irrespective of whether SOS technology is used with n- or p-channel MOS, CMOS, or bipolar technology, just two extra fabrication steps are required to implement the SOS portion of the process. Instead of starting with an n-type substrate, start with a sapphire wafer and deposit a layer of silicon on the substrate; then, dope the silicon to n-type material. After etching away oxide for metal contacts, etch away all the surplus base material.

SOS technology — A technology that has developed significant importance recently is silicon-on-sapphire (SOS). Based on the use of a nearly perfect insulating sapphire substrate, and combining (to a degree) the high density, low power, and low cost of MOS technology with the high speed of bipolar technology, SOS offers the further advantage of TTL compatibility. N-channel SOS devices were used recently in their first major commercial computer application: a computer processor on a single semiconductor chip.

SOS transistor characteristics—Unlike bulk CMOS processes, in which all p- and n-type transistors share a substrate, each SOS transistor has its own substrate which is insulated electrically from the others by the sapphire — no direct connection is made to any substrate. But substrate potentials remain fixed (at least in the dc case) for standard enhancement-type transistors at one diode-drop below or above the source potential. Since source and substrate voltages move together, the dependence of the threshold voltage on source potential, which is often a problem in bulk-silicon processes, is eliminated.

source—1. The device which supplies signal power to a transducer. 2. In a field-effect transistor, the electrode that corresponds to the cathode of a vacuum tube. 3. A region from which majority carriers flow into the channel.

source-code instructions—In many microprogrammed processors, source-code instructions are interpreted in the instruction register as pointers to the microprocessor programs that emulate the particular instruction set being executed. In the conventional approach, on the other hand, each instruction is decoded and executed with specific control logic wired into the machine. The conventional method sometimes has an advantage in speed over microprogrammed control, but it requires that the hardware and the instruction set be fixed at an early stage in the design of the system. Thus, it is inflexible and adding new capabilities is often difficult and expensive.

source deck—Stack of program cards that are ready to be inserted into the compilers of some computers which are operated by punched cards.

source editors—Source editors are programs that facilitate the entry and modification of the source code into a computer system for later translation, on-line storage, off-line storage, or listing on a printer for later reference. Without a source editor, the programmer would have to go through a tedious process of building his program on a unit-record physical medium like cards, or through a virtually impossible process using a sequential medium like paper tape. Source editors are best designed when they take into consideration the characteristics of the language being entered and the type of communications terminal used.

source file editor — Refers to a line-oriented editor that operates in an operating system environment. Editing of programs can be done sequentially by their assembler-produced source-statement line numbers. A source file editor produces a resultant updated file while preserving the original master file.

source-language debugging—Refers to correcting or debugging information that is requested by the user and displayed by the system in a form consistent with the source programming language.

source-language translation — The translation of a program to a target program; for example, of FORTRAN, COBOL, etc., to machine language, with the instructions being equivalent in the source program. The translation of a program to an automatic or problem-oriented language, such as FORTRAN, with the translating process being completed by the machine under the control of a translator program or compiler.

source library program — A collection of computer programs in compiler language and/or assembler language.

source macrodefinition—Refers to assembler programming; a macrodefinition that is included in a source module. A source macrodefinition can be entered into a program library; it then becomes a library macrodefinition.

source module—Refers to a particular organized set of statements in any source language that is recorded in machine-readable form and suitable for input to an assembler or compiler.

source program—1. A program that can be translated automatically into machine language. It thereby becomes an object program. 2. A computer program written in a language designed for ease of expression of a class of problems or procedures by humans, e.g., symbolic or algebraic. A generator, assembler, translator, or compiler routine is used to perform the mechanics of translating the source program into an object program in machine language.

source statement — 1. Refers to program statements written in other than machine language, usually mnemonics or three-character symbols. There are many types of source-language instructions — executive statements, assembly statements, etc. 2. Statements written by a programmer in symbolic terms that are related to a language translator such as an assembler or a report program generator.

source-tape cross-assembler — The cross-assembler often performs the same functions as the assembler, but it is written to operate on another type computer. The cross-assembler generally requires a minimum of 4K words of memory and is often supplied on a specific format binary tape or disk.

source-tape preparation—Refers to a program to provide a means of preparing and/or editing symbolic source tapes. In edit mode, commands are typed on the teletypewriter keyboard to perform the corrections and produce a new source tape. When preparing programs, the backspace, insert, and delete functions allow the operator to correct typing errors.

space—1. Generally refers to a site intended for the storage of data, e.g., a site on a printed page or a location in a storage medium. 2. A basic unit of area, usually the size of a single character. 3. One or more space characters. 4. To advance the reading or display position according to a prescribed format, e.g., to advance the printing or display position horizontally to the right or vertically down.

space charge—1. The electrical charge caused in space by the presence of electrons or ions. 2. The electron cloud around the hot cathode of a vacuum tube.

space lattice — A three-dimensional regular arrangement of atoms that is characteristic of a particular crystal structure. There are 14 such simple symmetrical arrangements that are known as Bravais lattices.

spark chamber — Radiation detector in which tracks of ionizing particles can be studied by photographing a spark following the ionization. It consists of a stack of parallel metal plates with an electric field between them that is raised nearly to the breakdown point.

spark spectra—The most important way of exciting spectra is by means of an electric spark. The high temperature reached will generate the spectrum lines of multiple-ionized atoms as well as of uncharged and single-ionized ones, as distinct from the arc spectrum (q.v.). Evaporation of metal from the electrodes leads to additional lines not associated with the gas through which the discharge takes place.

speaker-dependent/-independent systems—There are many ways of dividing voice systems. One way is deciding if they must be "trained" by individual users. All speech systems are either speaker dependent or speaker independent. A speaker-dependent system recognizes only those voices it has been trained to recognize; it works best in applications with only a few users. To train a system, each speaker must repeat every active vocabulary word or phrase several times to store a recognizable digitalized voice pattern in memory. When that individual subsequently uses the system, each spoken word is compared against the stored patterns. These systems are unaffected by voice inflections, regional accents, and other speech changes, are easy to learn, and can be used over telephone lines because they are designed to accommodate both noise on the line and background noise. Speaker-independent systems make larger vocabularies available to fewer users, typically, ten or less. They are sensitive to minor voice changes, must be trained by each successive user, and can be affected by noisy telephone lines or by background noise.

speaker-dependent recognition systems—Such systems require "training" in which each human subject repeatedly verbalizes each word in the system vocabulary to provide the templates, or voice-reference patterns, to which comparisons are later

made for word recognition. Early data seems to indicate that recognition accuracy under high noise or vibration conditions improves if the training is done under similar conditions, but that accuracy then declines when conditions become less harsh.

speaking board—Refers to one of several speech-synthesis modules that typically has a 24-word vocabulary in English, German, or Arabic. It contains a voltage converter, an audio filter, an amplifier, a volume control, and a 2-inch speaker.

special-purpose logic—Proprietary features of a programmable controller that allow it to perform logic not normally found in relay ladder logic.

specific magnetic moment — Refers to the value of the saturation moment per unit weight of a magnetic material, expressed in emu/gm. The specific magnetic moment is the most convenient quantity in which to express the saturation magnetization of fine-particle materials. The specific magnetic moment of pure gamma ferric oxide is approximately 75 emu/gm at room temperature.

specific routine—A routine to solve a particular mathematical, logical, or data-handling problem in which each address refers to explicitly stated registers and locations.

spectrum—1. Arrangement of components of a complex color or sound in order of frequency or energy, thereby showing distribution of energy or stimulus among the components. A mass spectrum is one showing the distribution in mass, or in mass-to-charge ratio of ionized atoms or molecules. The mass spectrum of an element will show the relative abundances of the isotopes of the element. 2. The range of electromagnetic radiations, from the longest known electrical wave to the shortest cosmic ray. Light, the visible portion of the spectrum, lies about midway between the two extremes. 3. A graphical representation of the distribution of the amplitude (and sometimes phase) of the components of a wave as a function of frequency. A spectrum may be continuous or, on the contrary, contain only points corresponding to certain discrete values.

speech analyzer—A speech analyzer is a low-cost speech-recognition labo-

Speech analyzer (Courtesy Heuristics, Inc.).

ratory system that allows ordinary voice input to computers. One example model, the "Speechlab™," by Heuristics, Inc., (California), includes one S-100–compatible pc board and components, a microphone, a "SpeechBasic" BASIC programming language, an experiment manual, speech-recognition software, a tutorial on human speech, and construction and test manuals. The hardware consists of a high-fidelity microphone, three bandpass filters, a zero-crossing detector, an analog-to-digital converter, time averagers, and decoding logic. "Speechlab™" is a laboratory speech-recognition system capable of running many different algorithms for speech recognition. Under the "SpeechBasic" software control that is provided, samples of speech waveforms are collected, analyzed, and classified. "Speechlab™" features graded experiments to introduce new concepts and techniques so the user can acquire enough knowledge to use "SpeechBasic" to develop new algorithms and tailor the system to his own needs.

speech analyzer language—"Speech-Basic" is a modified version of 4K Palo Alto Tiny Basic, which with a new command, SPEECH, added, completely controls the "Speechlab™" hardware. The recommended minimum computer memory for use is 4K of RAM. However, with more memory, more elaborate experiments and a larger vocabulary are possible. The 4K-byte demonstration program provided with "Speechlab™" works well with a 16-word vocabulary. Cooperative users can expect over 95% correct recognition. The "Speechlab™" system uses graded experiments to introduce new concepts and techniques so that a user can acquire enough knowledge to use the "SpeechBasic" programming language to develop new algorithms and tailor the "Speechlab™" system to his or her own needs.

speech chip, CVSD—CVSD is the abbreviation for continuous variable-slope delta-modulation detector. This type of detector chip takes a ROM code and creates a facsimile of a sound waveform under the direction of an 8-bit processor. The chip was originally aimed at telecommunications speech and signal processing applications. It uses self-aligned silicon-gate complementary-MOS circuitry (for its low-power, high-speed advantages), along with dielectric isolation and on-chip resistors. Ordinarily, no microprocessor control or external components are required for the recovery of digitized speech; the chip does all its own data conversion and processing.

speech chip, FIFO buffer—One type of speech chip has the capability of accepting data from either a compatible

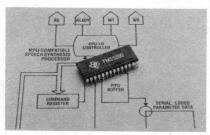

Speech chip, FIFO buffer (Courtesy Texas Instruments Incorporated).

128K-bit ROM or an onboard 128-bit first-in/first-out (FIFO) buffer. The FIFO buffer allows the storage of speech data in programmable read-only memories (PROMs), eraseable PROMs, random-access memory (RAM), or other random-access storage media such as disk or bubble memories. Organized as a 16-byte parallel-in serial-out device, the FIFO buffer frees the central processing unit (CPU) to tend to other tasks during the 50 milliseconds that it takes for the speech chip to exhaust the data that is in the FIFO. The speech chip allows verbal communication from microprocessor-based systems. It is a speech-synthesis processor that is specially designed for easy interface to a standard microprocessor having an 8-bit data bus.

speech recognition systems — Computer recognition of speech refers to the capability of a computer to identify a message spoken by a human and then produce an appropriate response to that message. Some basic functions involved in speech recognition are:

1. Speech transmission — human speech coded for fast inexpensive transmission over long distances, and then decoded at the receiving end.
2. Speech recognition — The replacement of the human at one end of a voice-grade line with a computer that not only records a message but also understands the message and produces an appropriate response.
3. Speech output—the mechanical duplication of human speech (either by voice response or speech synthesis).
4. Verification and identification—

verification of the accuracy of the information and the identification of the speaker.

speech synthesis — Refers to various programs that translate English text into synthetic speech. Some programs apply a limited set of letter-to-sound rules to individual words, and "sounds" them out the way a child does. Thus, it does not require a separate dedicated computer system, separate storage for a large data base, or a large amount of computer time to break up and attempt to understand sentences. In an average sample of English text, a system will pronounce about 95% of the words correctly, and most of the errors will be obvious enough to be detected by the human operator.

speech systems, discrete — Most early systems recognized isolated words (or discrete speech); that is, words spoken one at a time with a distinct pause between each word. These are the systems used most often when a large number of people must have access. A connected speech system, or connected-digit sequence system, will allow the speaker to string together a few words or numbers without pausing. There are some continuous-speech recognition systems currently available and working in laboratories and in robotic experiments.

speech systems, dual computer—Some types of speech systems consist of two computers—one handles input/output interface functions and the other does the actual word recognition. The *I/O computer* detects a ringing phone or a human voice, answers the call or prepares to receive information, verifies access codes, converts analog phone inputs or voice patterns into a digital signal, and sends the digital signal to the other computer. The I/O computer also initiates the proper response, either with recorded messages or voice synthesis. As each word is spoken into a telephone or microphone, the sound is converted into an analog signal and, then, into a digital code.

The second computer, or *word recognizer,* matches each spoken word with word patterns stored in memory —either the patterns of an operator who has "trained" the system, or a master pattern consisting of many different pronunciations of the same vocabulary word. The word is recognized when an "in range" match is made between the incoming signal and a stored word pattern. The accuracy of each recognized word is verified via a crt display or a voice feedback, in which a voice response unit repeats the words or digits recognized.

spin block—A loop created when a process keeps checking the state of a flag or status bit while waiting for an event to occur. The process executes the test for an indefinite period of time unless the situation is corrected.

spooling — Refers to a procedure of temporarily storing data on disk or tape files until another aspect of processing is ready for the data (such as printing it).

spooling devices—Some devices, such as cassette tape, can be shared through the use of virtual-device techniques—combinations of the two major management schemes. A common strategy, termed spooling (an acronym for Simultaneous Peripheral Operations On Line), allows reading and copying to a disk of the files stored on tape. When a program tries to read from the tape, the spooling routine intercepts the request and converts it to a read-from disk. Because the disk can be shared, the technique for all intents and purposes converts the tape unit to a shared device. Also, an input/output processor (IOP) can be used to store data from low-speed devices, such as terminals and paper-tape readers, either in memory or on disk, until the transmission is complete. The IOP can then transfer the data at high speed when it is needed by an application program. Conversely, output data ultimately destined for a low-speed device, such as a printer, can be temporarily spooled to disk and then printed later. This permits batches of data to be gathered or distributed by low-priority programs that run in the background, essentially using up "spare" CPU and IOP cycles. Applications programs that use or produce the data can execute faster because they are not bound by the low-speed devices. Thus, spooling is extremely useful in preventing slow-speed printers and other devices from slowing down system throughput.

spooling, I/O—Operating systems can increase I/O efficiency by a technique called *spooling*. If data are being typed out on a low-speed terminal, like a teletypewriter, and its buffer is filled, the task must be suspended until the buffer is emptied. By spooling—temporarily storing the data on a disk, and transferring it to the device buffer when space is available—the amount of main memory necessary for buffering can be reduced.

sporadic fault — Faults are failures in performance in the manner required over specified conditions, and sporadic faults are intermittent faults.

spring-finger action—Refers to operations of electrical contacts to permit a stress-free spring action to develop contact pressure, i.e., used in sockets of printed-circuits and in many other types of connectors.

sputtering—In a gas discharge, the removal of atoms from a cathode by positive ion bombardment, like a cold evaporation. These unchanged atoms can be deposited on any surface and are used to coat dielectrics with thin films of various metals.

stable—1. Said of systems not exhibiting sudden changes, particularly atoms which are not radioactive. 2. Used to indicate the incapability of following a stated mode of spontaneous change, e.g., beta-stable means incapable of ordinary beta disintegration but could be capable of isomeric transition or alpha disintegration, etc. 3. State of an amplification system when it satisfies the Nyquist criterion, either conditionally or unconditionally.

stable oscillation—One for which amplitude and/or frequency will remain constant indefinitely. N.B. — A statically stable system may be dynamically unstable and follow a divergent oscillation when subjected to a disturbance. In this sense, the term dynamically stable means that an induced oscillation will be convergent, i.e., of decreasing amplitude.

stable state—Refers to the phase with which oscillations begin; that phase will continue each time the oscillations are restarted, until the circuit is switched to the opposite state or phase by another input signal.

stable trigger circuit—Refers to a circuit which is binary, i.e., has two states, each requiring an appropriate trigger for excitation and transition from one state to another. Also called binary pair, trigger pair, and flip-flop.

stability—The ability of a component or device to maintain its nominal operating characteristics after being subjected to changes in temperature, environment, current, and time. It is usually expressed in either percent or parts-per-million for a given period of time.

stack—1. The stack is a reserved area of memory where the CPU automatically saves the program counter and the contents of working registers when a program interrupt occurs. The stack normally forces users to return from interrupts in the same order that interrupts occurred. 2. The stack is generally a block of successive memory locations that are accessible from one end of a last-in/first-out (LIFO) basis. The stack is coordinated with a stack pointer that keeps track of storage and retrieval of each byte or word of information in the stack. A stack may be any block of successive information locations in a read/write memory.

stack architecture — Many microcomputers have a stack architecture wherein any portion of the external memory can be used as a last-in/first-out stack to store/retrieve the contents of the accumulator, the flags, or any of the data registers. Many units contain a 16-bit stack pointer to control the addressing of this external stack. One of the major advantages of a stack is that multiple-level interrupts can easily be handled since complete system status can easily be saved when an interrupt occurs and can, then, be restored after the interrupt. Another major advantage is that an almost unlimited subroutine nesting is possible.

stacked-job processing — A procedure of automatic job-to-job transitions, with little or no operator intervention.

stack, main memory — Some systems permit an unlimited number of stacks to reside in main memory with two of them operational at any moment. The operating system has access to all stacks simply by placing new stack addresses in the current stack pointers. Each operational stack has its own stack pointer, its individual upper and lower limit detectors, as well

as its stack fault vector which points to the user's diagnostic and recovery program.

stack-oriented registers—Many microprocessors offer stack-oriented registers that can be accessed only in a last-in/first-out basis—the so-called LIFO, or push-down, stack. These are used for subroutine nesting, interrupts, and for temporary storage of data. They can be either on the chip (a hardware stack) or external to the processor in memory (a software, or pointer, stack). The hardware stack permits higher speed operation, but it has limited size. The size of the software stack may be as large as available memory space permits, but the stack must be maintained by the program.

stack pointer—Stack pointers are coordinated with the storing and retrieval of information in the stack. The stack pointer is decremented by one immediately following the storage in the stack of each byte of information. Conversely, the stack pointer is incremented by one immediately before retrieving each byte of information from the stack. The stack pointer may be manipulated for transferring its contents to the index register or vice versa. The address of a location is at the top of the stack. Abbreviated SP.

stack pointer register—A stack pointer is a register that comes into use when the microprocessor must service an interrupt. (An interrupt is a high-priority call from an external device to the central processing unit that it must suspend temporarily its current operations and divert its attention to the interrupting task.) However, a CPU must store the contents of its registers before it can move on to the interrupt operation. It does this in a stack, so named because information is added to its top, with the information that is already there being pushed further down. The stack, thus, is a last-in/first-out type of memory. The stack pointer register contains the address of the next unused location in the stack.

stack, push-down—A push-down stack is essentially a last-in/first-out (LIFO) buffer. As data are added, the stack moves down, with the last item added taking the top position. Stack height varies with the number of stored items, increasing or decreasing with the entering or retrieving of data. The words "push" (move down) and "pop" (retrieve the most recently stored item are used to describe its operation. In actual practice, a hardware-implemented pushdown stack is a collection of registers with a counter which serves as a "pointer" to indicate the most recently loaded register. Registers are unloaded in the reverse of the sequence in which they were loaded. The principal benefit of the pushdown stack is as an aid to compiling. By reducing the use of registers necessary for temporary storage, stack architecture can greatly decrease the number of steps required in a program, thereby reducing costs.

stack, virtual memory—A major benefit in the use of virtual memory is when it is necessary to swap pages between primary and secondary storage. The object of page swapping is to move that material which is most likely to be needed in the immediate future to primary memory, and to remove that which is least likely to be needed. An algorithm that has found acceptance is to remove the least-recently used pages from primary memory as that space is required for newer pages. The pushdown stack is an ideal hardware implementation of this algorithm. Page references are added to the stack in the order in which the pages are retrieved from secondary storage; stack levels correspond to available page storage capacity of primary memory, with the bottom of the stack always identifying the least-recently used page.

stand-alone network systems — These are dedicated networks that can include both local and remote data sources. A typical network is a system that interconnects branch offices with a headquarters computer, or provides communication between various departments within an office complex, or permits the inquiry/response processing of a dynamic data base.

standard interface—Refers to that specific form of (matching) interface, previously designed or agreed upon, so that two or several units, systems, programs, etc., may be easily joined or associated.

standard subroutine—Refers to a subroutine that is applicable to a class of problems. *See also* library subroutine.

standby register—A register in which accepted or verified information can be stored in order to be available for a rerun in the event of a mistake in the program or a malfunction in the computer.

start-of-message character—A character or group of characters transmitted by a polled terminal to indicate addresses of stations to receive the message.

start-of-text character — Refers to a specific control character in a communications text that is designed to terminate and separate a heading and mark the beginning of the actual text.

state switcher — For an inexpensive power-loss backup system, a manual break-before-make device (if a break in power is permissible) can handle the switchover from line power to inverter output. But, usually, a solid-state power-loss sensing circuit, called a state switcher, is employed to accomplish the transfer automatically, and as quickly as possible. Solid-state switchover circuits—generally referred to as static-transfer, or bypass, switches—can be designed to take up high in-rush (or even fault) currents.

static cell memory—Basically a cross-coupled flip-flop. Some power is consumed at all times through the two load resistors. However, some newer designs reduce the power required to maintain the state of the flip-flop by using high resistance poly-silicon load resistors.

static check — An equipment setup check performed by comparing measurements taken in the reset mode or the hold mode for a single value of the independent variable, and including the initial rates of change, with the results received from some alternative method of computation. This type of check reveals the static errors and often reveals the instantaneous values of dynamic errors.

static dump—A dump that is performed at a particular point in time with respect to a machine run, frequently at the end of a run.

staticizer—1. A storage device for converting time sequential information into static parallel information. 2. A type of buffer.

static magnetic cell—That specific binary storage cell in which two values of one binary digit are represented by different patterns of magnetization, and in which the means of setting and sensing the contents are stationary with respect to the magnetic material.

static magnetic storage — Refers to storage of information that is fixed in space and available at any time, e.g., flip-flop, electrostatic, or coincident-current magnetic-core storage.

static memory — Refers to a memory device that contains no mechanical moving parts. Also, a memory device that contains fixed information.

static MOS circuits — MOS memories are produced with either static or dynamic circuits. Static memory cells are cross-coupled bistable circuits wherein information is stored by one of the two stable states. Most static MOS memory cells use six transistors for each cell or bit location.

static RAM — Data is stored in a conventional bistable flip-flop and need not be refreshed.

static RAM chip — Refers to an integrated circuit used for storing information and which uses electronic "latch" circuits internally. Unlike leaky dynamic chips, no refreshing is required for static chips.

static read/write memory—A typical n-channel MOS memory that is designed and organized to be compatible with the various MPUs. Its data, address, and control-line organization and functions match those of the MPU, all signal levels are TTL-compatible, and clocks or refreshing are often not needed.

static subroutine — A digital computer subroutine involving no parameters other than the addresses of the operands.

station, earth — Refers to special communications. Ground terminals that use antennas and associated electronic equipment to transmit, receive, and process communications via satellite. Future cable systems may be able to interconnect by domestic communications satellites, creating regional and national cable networks.

statistical data recorder — Under disc operating system (DOS) operation, a feature that records the cumulative error status of an I/O device on the system recorder file. Abbreviated SDR.

statistical multiplexing—Statistical multiplexing, sometimes referred to as intelligent time-division multiplexing (ITDM) or data concentration, is a relatively new technique. Like time-division multiplexing, it is a digital system, but instead of sampling each channel at a fixed rate, it dynamically allocates time on the line to the various channels according to their relative activity. When a channel is inactive, the statistical multiplexer ignores it entirely, making idle bits or characters unnecessary. And, when many channels are highly active at the same time, the multiplexer stores data in memory until it can be transmitted without overloading the line.

Statistical multiplexing is an advanced technology for dynamically sharing telephone lines between multiple data streams, with each representing terminal-computer, terminal-terminal, or computer-computer traffic. Not only does statistical multiplexing save communications costs, it also significantly enhances line quality. A variety of low-end statistical multiplexers/data concentrators have become available during the past few years. They are simple to use and also correct data errors resulting from noisy telephone lines. All statistical multiplexers are not created equal, however. In fact, most are restrictive limited-use products that do not meet professional data-communications standards.

This technique optimizes data throughput by allocating time slots on a statistical basis—so that the busiest equipment gets the largest allocation of time; and the least busy, the smallest.

Some statistical multiplexers can also offer multidrop capability—employing data protocols to tag data packets for the drop points. Also, some types of statistical multiplexers combine the advantages of frequency division and time division. They can provide other advanced features, also, such as error protection and data compression. Statistical multiplexing also enables a much faster terminal operation without requiring the use of very high-speed modems or without susceptibility to line errors.

statmux port concentrators—In a statistically multiplexed system, some problems can be overcome with the use of port concentrators, which reduce the host software requirement by more than half. A port concentrator functions as a single-channel master statmux (statistical multiplexer), enabling a computer port to communicate with multiple channels attached to a remote statmux that is using a simple asynchronous or synchronous protocol. Transmissions to and from the computer consist of simple lines of text, preceded by a terminal address.

status bits—Parameterization is a technique of recording parameters, which characterize a system, in storage elements such as status bits. Status bits are frequently used in information-processing systems to store information about the conditions of the device. Frequently, program words can be saved if it is possible to set certain bits based on a condition of the network and, then, test these bits at subsequent instruction times. Microprograms can frequently be shortened by the use of status bits. Branches in the microprogram frequently can be made a number of instruction cycles after the status bits are set. This eliminates premature branching and the unnecessary duplication of microinstructions.

status register—On some systems, the status register provides storage for the arithmetic, control, and software status flags.

status word — 1. Refers to words that provide information necessary to resume processing following the servicing of an interrupt. 2. Computer words containing various information used to control processing.

status word, device (DSW)—Refers to a computer word containing bits whose condition indicates the status of devices.

status word, program (PSW)—On many systems, the PSW is stored at a fixed location, the address of which depends on the type of interruption. The system then automatically fetches a new PSW from a different fixed location, the address of which is also dependent on the type of interruption. Each class of interruption has two fixed locations in main storage—one to receive the old PSW when the interruption occurs and the other to

supply the new PSW that governs the servicing of that class of interruption. After the interruption has been serviced, a single instruction uses the stored PSW to reset the processing unit to the status it had before the interruption (some computers).

status word register—Refers to a group of binary numbers that inform the user of the present condition of the microprocessor.

STD process—The STD process (semiconductor on thermoplastic on dielectric) permits freedom of choice of IC devices and the choice of appropriate substrate. STD is useful in the broadest possible frequency range, and permits use of controlled-batch processing, computer-aided design techniques, and precise photolithographic technology. In the STD process, all interconnections, including the films, metallizations, chips, and layers of fluorinated ethylene proplyene copolymer, are deposited on the substrate at one time, using a proprietary vacuum technique.

steady state — 1. A condition in which circuit values remain essentially constant, occurring after all initial transients or fluctuating conditions have settled down. 2. Said of any oscillation system which continues unchanged indefinitely.

steady-state characteristics—Refers to those particular characteristics relating to a condition, such as a value, rate, periodicity, or amplitude, which exhibit only negligible change over an arbitrarily long period of time. They may describe conditions in which some characteristics are static, while others are dynamic.

steady-state deviation—The difference between the final value assumed by a specified variable after the expiration of transients and its ideal value.

steady-state oscillation — Also called steady-state vibration. Oscillation in which the motion at each point is a periodic quantity.

step-and-repeat systems (direct-on-wafer) — The introduction of more VLSI devices with tighter design rules requires new methods of wafer exposure. Recently introduced equipment performs the step-and-repeat process directly on the wafer. These direct-step systems, a modification of existing mask-making step-and-repeat equipment, expose the wafer through a 5× or 10× reticle, and can improve defect density and registration. Automatic focusing, which compensates for wafer distortion resulting from high-temperature wafer processes, will improve critical dimension control, and will produce 1.5-micron line widths.

step-and-repeat systems (mask making) — Step-and-repeat systems, as used in mask making, can also be used directly to expose small sections of a wafer in steps. A small-lens system for a small field of view—say, the size of a microscope objective — is easier to make distortion-free than a large one. And, an effective alignment system necessary to mesh the circuit sections is not a major problem. Also, the step-and-repeat method can use masks five to ten times larger than the finished circuit, which makes mask making easy. However, production throughput is low with such an approach. On the other hand, scanning-projection systems can increase the low throughput while retaining the effectiveness of step-and-repeat methods with small optical fields.

step-by-step switch—Refers to a switch that moves in synchronism with a pulse device, such as a rotary telephone dial. Each digit that is dialed causes the movement of successive selector switches to carry the connection forward until the desired line is reached.

step counter—Refers to a counter used in the arithmetical unit to count the steps in multiplication, division, and shift operation.

step-down transformer—The reverse of the step-up transformer, i.e., in an electrical transformer, the transfer of energy from a high to a low voltage.

step function—A function which is zero for all time preceding a certain instant, and has a constant finite value thereafter.

step index fiber optic cable — Cable that is constructed with optical fibers. *See* step index fibers.

step index fibers — Fibers that have a sharp boundary between core and cladding are called *step index* fibers. The reflection at the boundary is not a "zero-distance" phenomenon. The ray, in being reflected, is actually entering a minute distance into the cladding, and there is some loss. This loss can be seen as a faint glow along a length of unjacketed lossy fibers carrying visible flux. To reduce such reflection loss, it is possible to make the rays turn less sharply by reducing the index of refraction gradually, from core to cladding, rather than sharply. A fiber of such a form is called a *graded index* fiber.

stepper motor—Also called a stepping motor, it is used frequently in electromechanical devices like printers. It rotates by a fixed amount every time it receives an electrical pulse. Stepper motors are generally the best solution when designers want precise economical movements with minimum wear.

stepper-motor controller—This system avoids the one-pulse, one-step operation that requires a host computer to tie itself down to a stepper motor. A function-oriented stored-program stepper-motor controller allows the user, or host computer, to program it and forget it. One typical device executes 22 high-level instructions, either in command mode or as a sequence of internally-stored commands, using single-byte code such as "P" for position, "R" for rate, and "S" for slope. Parameter values can be expressed either in ASCII-decimal for keyboard programming or binary code from the host computer. Parallel or serial communication can be used. The stored program capability allows the use of "DO-WHILE" program looping and "WAIT-UNTIL" operation. Ten different operational modes allow absolute

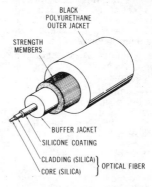

Step index fiber optic cable.

or relative positioning, full- or half-step operation, hardware or software control of direction, start/stop, etc. Numerous input and output control lines allow synchronizing the device with external events or devices and also allow each step to be triggered.

stepping motor—Refers to one device in which rotation occurs in a series of discrete steps that are controlled electromagnetically by individual (digital) input signals. *See also* stepper motor.

stepping switch — Refers to a special switching device or relay having "n" discrete conditions and which advances from one condition to the next each time it receives an input pulse.

step response—Refers to a time response of an instrument when it is subjected to an instantaneous change in input from one steady-state value to another.

step response time—Refers to an element or system in which the time required for an output to make the change from some initial value to a large specified percentage of a steady-state value, either before or in the absense of overshoot, is a result of a step change to the input. This is usually stated for a 90%, 95%, or 99% change.

stochastic—Refers to any system operation in which an element of chance cannot be excluded.

stochastic noise — Refers to that which maintains a statistically random distribution.

stop bit—Refers to the last element of a character designed for asynchronous serial operation that defines the character space immediately to the left of the most significant character in accumulator storage.

stop, dynamic—A specific stop in a loop that consists of a single jump instruction which effects a jump to itself.

stop element (bit) — Refers to the last element of a character in a start-stop (asynchronous) serial transmission; used to ensure recognition of the next start element. When the Baudot 5-level transmission code is used, it is 1.42 mark bits.

stop, optional—A miscellaneous function command that is similar to program stop except that the control ignores the command unless the operator has previously actuated a manual selector to validate the command.

storage—1. The act of storing information (*see also* store). 2. Sometimes called a memory. Any device in which information can be stored. 3. A computer section used primarily for storing information in electrostatic, ferroelectric, magnetic, acoustic, optical, chemical, electronic, electrical, mechanical, etc., form. Such a section is sometimes called a memory, or a store (in British terminology). 4. Pertaining to a device into which data can be entered, in which they can be held, and from which they can be retrieved at a later time.

storage allocation—Executive program control of internal (main memory) and external (e.g., disk or tape cassette) storage devices may range from helping the programmer map the contents of memory to complicated dynamic-storage allocation in a multiprocessing system.

storage capacity—Also called memory capacity. The amount of information that can be retained in a storage (memory) device. It is often expressed as the number of words (given the number of digits and the base of the standard word).

storage, cartridge — An alternative to the Philips cassette designed for digital applications. Data rate and capacity are typically five times the figure available for cassettes, with a much greater reliability.

storage, cassette — Cassettes provide the least expensive means of storage with several million bits capacity per cassette, typically with a 10-kilobit/data rate. The most popular units are the upgraded versions of the Philips cassette. Quality is highly variable, however, depending on the manufacturer. *See also* cassette.

storage, cathode-ray tube — Refers to the (usually) electrostatic storage characteristics of cathode-ray tubes in which the electron beam is used to sense the data.

storage cell—Refers to an elementary unit of storage, for example, a binary cell, a decimal cell.

storage, common block — Refers to a block of storage locations in a digital computer that is associated with information or data required both in the main program and in a specific sub-program.

storage cycle—1. Refers to a periodic sequence of events occurring when information is transferred to or from the storage device of a microcomputer. 2. Storing, sensing, and regeneration form parts of the storage sequence.

storage cycle time—Refers to the time required in milliseconds, microseconds, nanoseconds, etc., for a storage cycle.

storage, dedicated—The allocated, reserved or obligated, set aside, earmarked, or assigned areas of storage that are committed to some specific purpose, user, or problem, i.e., an exclusively reserved space on a disk storage unit for an accounting procedure, problem, or data set.

storage device, mass — Mass storage devices are the means of collecting, organizing, and retrieving large volumes of data. Many manufacturers offer small mass storage devices that are tailored to a customer's needs. One typical dual-cassette magnetic-tape drive permits a total of 180,000 characters of on-line storage, at low cost. Where higher capacity and speed are required, a dual floppy-disk drive might be an appropriate device. It uses diskettes for low-cost random-access mass memory. Some disks are capable of storing up to 128K 12-bit words, or 256K 8-bit bytes. For economical mass storage, some disk cartridge systems can provide 1.6 million words of high-density memory per disk drive. Generally, a controller can support four disk drives. A fully expanded system can offer over 6 million words of storage.

storage, dynamic—1. Refers to stored computer data that remain in motion on a sensing device. For example, an acoustic delay line or a magnetic drum, as opposed to static storage. 2. The storage of data on a device, or in a manner, that permits the data to move or vary with time and, thus, the data is not always available.

storage, electrostatic—1. The storage of data on a dielectric surface such as the screen of a cathode-ray tube, in the form of the presence or absence of spots bearing electrostatic charges. These spots can persist for a short time after the electrostatic

charging force is removed. 2. A storage device so used.

storage element—One unit in a memory, which is capable of retaining one bit of information. Also, the smallest area of the surface of a charge-storage tube which retains information different from that of neighboring areas.

storage, fragmentation—Refers to the inability to assign real storage locations to virtual addresses because the available spaces are smaller than the page size.

storage, high-speed — A specific storage device that has relatively short access time, as compared to the main memory of the CPU, i.e., at least significantly shorter in time than other devices in the same computer system, such as disk-tape storage.

storage key—Refers to a special set of bits designed to be associated with every word or character in some block of storage, which allows tasks having a matching set of protection key bits to use that block of storage.

storage location, temporary—Refers to a specific area of memory which has been set aside for data that is in process of intermediate states of computation, i.e., such storage is often called "scratch-pad" memory in the CPU.

storage, macroinstruction — Macroinstructions, defined by sequences of microinstructions, are often implemented in read-only storage (ROMs or PROMs). In-circuit ROM simulation reduces the number of changes that will be required in the transition from development prototype to production units, and thus reduces the likelihood of errors. Because of the longer programs associated with macroinstruction-level programming, trial-and-error debugging techniques play a larger role in minimizing the amount of time required to generate error-free code. Easily alterable program storage simplifies trial-and-error techniques and allows the user to write simple test loops to exercise small portions of code.

storage, magnetic core — Often refers to main storage, or a storage device, in which binary data are represented by the direction of magnetization in each unit of an array of magnetic material, usually in the shape of toroidal rings, but also in other forms.

storage, microprocessor—Storage and memory are terms that are used interchangeably. The most important types of storage for microprocessors are: ROM, RAM, PROM, paper tapes and magnetic-tape cassettes, disks, etc.

storage, minidisk — These are smaller lower-capacity versions of the disk storage units that are used with larger computers. The simplest forms have a single disk and fixed magnetic heads. Popular configurations combine one fixed with one removable disk. Storage capacity is several million bits and up. However, the larger units may be too expensive for microcomputer applications and may offer more capacity than is needed.

storage, mixed—Refers to a type of storage whose elements are arranged in a matrix so that access to any location requires the use of two or more coordinates, i.e., cathode-ray tube storage, core storage, etc., which use coincident-current selection.

storage, primary—Refers, most often, to the fastest storage device of a microcomputer and the one from which instructions are executed. (Contrasted with auxiliary storage.)

storage protection — 1. Stored programs, library subroutines, and other data which may have to be retained in a memory indefinitely are all allocated to a protected storage block. With multiprocessing, more complex storage protection is required to ensure that a program being processed does not attempt to utilize storage associated with a different program. 2. Refers to a feature that includes a programmed protection key which prevents the read-in of data into a protected area of main memory and, thus, prevents one program from destroying another.

storage, random-access — Refers to storage in which the time required to obtain information is independent of the location of the information. This strict definition must be qualified by the observation that we usually mean relatively random. Thus, magnetic drums are relatively nonrandom access when compared to magnetic cores for main storage, but are relatively random access when compared to magnetic tapes for file storage.

Synonymous with random-access memory.

storage, secondary—Refers to the storage facilities that are not an integral part of the microcomputer but are directly connected to and controlled by the microcomputer, i.e., magnetic tape cassettes.

storage, serial — Refers to a storage technique in which time is one of the factors used to locate any given bit, character, word, or groups of words that appears one after the other in a time sequence, and in which access time includes a variable latency or waiting time of from zero to many milliseconds. A storage is said to be serial-by-word when the individual bits comprising a word appear serially in time, and a storage is serial-by-character when the characters representing coded decimal or other nonbinary numbers appear serially in time.

storage, slow—A storage module or device whose access time is longer when viewed in relation to the speeds of arithmetic operations of the central processing unit (CPU) of the microcomputer and which are more lengthy when compared to other faster-access peripheral units.

storage, static—Storage or information that is fixed, e.g., flip-flop, electrostatic, etc.

storage switch — Refers to a manually operated switch or group of switches, most often on computer consoles, that permit operators to read register contents.

storage time—1. The time during which the output current or voltage of a pulse is falling from maximum to zero after the input current or voltage has been removed. 2. In a transistor, the time required to sweep current carriers from the collector region when the switch is turned off.

storage tube — A tube which stores charges such as those deposited on a plate or screen in a crt, with a subsequent scanning by the electron beam, thus detecting, reinforcing, or abolishing the charge. Due to the phosphors used in a storage tube, some images that are produced must be viewed in a darkened room.

storage, virtual—Refers to a conceptual form of main storage which does not really exist, but is made to appear as if it exists through the use of hardware and programming.

storage, volatile — A storage media of such that if the applied power is cut off, the stored information is lost, i.e., acoustic delay lines, electrostatic tubes.

store—1. To introduce or retain information in a device from which the information can later be withdrawn. 2. A British synonym for storage. 3. To transfer an element of information to a device from which the unaltered information can be obtained at a later time. 4. *See also* storage.

store and forward—Refers to communication systems in which messages are received at intermediate routing points and recorded (stored). They are then retransmitted to the ultimate recipient or to a further routing point.

stored program—A set of instructions in a microcomputer memory specifying the operations to be performed and the location of the data on which these operations are to be performed.

straight-line code—Refers to repetition of a sequence of instructions, with or without address modification, by explicitly writing the instructions for each repetition. Generally, straight-line coding will require less execution time and more space than equivalent loop coding. If the number of repetitions is large, this type of coding is tedious unless a generator is used. The feasibility of straight-line coding is limited by the space required as well as by the difficulty of coding a variable number of repetitions.

straight-line coding — Any computer program that can be completed by carrying out sequentially each program instruction, i.e., one without any branch points or loop instructions.

strain — Relates to the dimensional change in a medium when subject to a mechanical, or other form of, stress. It is specifically defined as the ratio of the dimensional change (in length, area, or volume) to the original (or unstrained) dimension.

strain gauge — A specific sensor that produces a voltage or resistance change when a force is applied.

strain gauge element — This refers to nickel wire or printed-circuit resistance mat cemented to a surface under stress and used either (A) to measure the static strain in terms of the change in resistance of the element, or (B) to measure the dynamic strain resulting from vibration, in terms of the consequent modulation of a steady current passed through the element.

stranding effect — The propensity of a stranded conductor to exhibit a higher dc resistance than does a solid conductor of the same material and cross-sectional area. It is due to the relatively longer distance that current must travel when following a stranded conductor's helically configured wires.

stray radiation — Direct and secondary radiation from irradiated objects that does not serve a useful purpose.

streaming—Fixed disk drives require removable media backup systems that provide a save-and-restore function. Recording data in a "streaming mode" provides a solution to the problem. Thus, "streaming" ¼-inch Cartridge Magnetic-Tape Drives are ideal backup choices for systems designers. A streaming drive allows essentially all of the available tape in the cartridge to be used for data storage by eliminating the traditional starting and stopping between data blocks and the associated interblock gaps. By eliminating the gaps, the data are recorded in what appears to be a continuous stream on the tape using a serpentine track arrangement (i.e., no rewind between tracks, and full read-while-write data verification). Also, because starting and stopping becomes very infrequent, tape speed can be increased with a resultant increase in transfer rate. Streaming also eliminates the necessity for rapid start/stop servo electronics and mechanics, which results in a real cost savings, as well as a reduction in power requirements and associated heat dissipation.

streaming digital cartridge tape drives — Custom-tailored to provide media backup for Winchester disks, a new pair of streaming digital cartridge tape drives can furnish up to 20M bytes of storage on one industry-standard ¼-inch ANSI/ECMA data cartridge. The two units—one storing 10M bytes on two tracks; the other, 20M bytes on four tracks—can each transfer 5M bytes of data in 1 minute. Interfacing the drives is a process similar to that for a semiconductor first-in/first-out (FIFO) memory.

Streaming digital cartridge tape drives (Courtesy Data Electronics, Inc.).

Operating in the streaming mode, these drives do not require interrecord gaps. Additionally, because they record in a serpentine fashion, they also do not require rewinding to get to the next track. Optional error-detection and -correction circuits keep Read errors below 1 in 10^{10} bits.

streaming drive data verification — A streaming digital cartridge tape drive verifies data "on the fly" with a read-while-write check. That is, reading what is written in real-time checks the data. Further, this read-while-write checking does not accept signals that are lower than a very conservative threshold level. A normal Read operation can detect significantly lower levels. In addition, a check character is appended to each data blockette for verification of the data during Read passes. Further, decade, format, and address checks are made during read-while-write operations, as well as during Read-only operations. All of these taken together reduce, to a very small probability, the chance of an undetected error occurring during streaming. Prudent design would probably add an error-detection scheme to the data transmitted within the system. This arrangement would provide transmission failure detection, which the streamer cannot detect. Adding a check character to each block would provide for this eventuality.

streaming formatter/controller — A streaming formatter/controller separates incoming data into blockettes,

and inserts between each blockette an internal address, resync, and error-checking characters. During the Write mode, the data are verified within the drive and marginal data are rewritten without stopping the tape. In the Read mode, the extra characters are stripped, and only data are returned to the host. When examined, a streaming controller interface looks like a semiconductor memory element. The "streamer" may be thought of as a nonvolatile first-in/first-out (FIFO) memory, and can be integrated easily into a system. Complex timing and data-handling requirements are eliminated.

streaming/incremental-recording tape systems — Drives for ¼-inch-cartridge magnetic tape are available in two operative modes. One is known as streaming, and the other is the more traditional incremental-recording technique. Streaming is a method that allows essentially all of the available tape in the cartridge to be used for data storage by eliminating starting and stopping between data blocks. The associated interblock gaps used in incremental recording are also eliminated. By eliminating the gaps and by recording in a serpentine-track arrangement, data are recorded in what appears to be an essentially continuous stream on the tape. Incremental recording writes data in blocks with each data block bounded by interblock gaps. This provides for such techniques as file management, selective erase, track select, and the capability to change

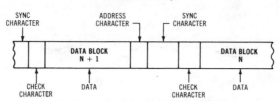

(A) Data format for streaming mode.

(B) Data format for incremental-recording mode.
Streaming/incremental-recording tape systems.

or add to existing records. However, the use of interblock gaps means that some potential recording capacity must be sacrificed.

STRESS—Acronym for Structural Engineering Systems Solver. A language useful for structural-analysis problems in civil engineering. For design applications, larger problems, and more sophisticated modeling and analysis, this language has been replaced with STRUDL. Implemented on several computers, primarily small types.

string—1. In a list of items, a group of items that is already in sequence according to a rule. 2. A set of records that is in ascending or descending sequence according to a key contained in the records. 3. A string is a data structure that groups a number of characters into a sequence.

string, alphabetic—A sequence of letters from the same alphabet, i.e., a character string.

string, character—1. A group of characters in a one-dimensional array, in an order due to the reference of relations between adjacent numbers. 2. A sequence or group of connected characters, that are connected by codes, key words, or other programming or associative techniques.

string language — The MUMPS language is a high-level English-like language. It consists of a relatively few, but powerful, commands and functions, and contains extensive call and overlay facilities. The language is heavily string-oriented with operators and functions for such string operations as pattern verification, collating, extracting, searching, and concatenating. In addition, it contains a complete set of arithmetic and Boolean operators.

string length — The number of records in a string.

string manipulation — Refers to a procedure designed for manipulating groups of contiguous characters.

string processing — ASCII-character string expressions may include literal strings, string variables, and subscripted string variables, which select substrings. Statements permit strings to be entered, concatenated, compared, printed, and stored in data files. Strings can be of any length limited only by available main memory.

string variable ROM—A string variable ROM provides a computer with the ability to accept and manipulate alphabetic as well as numerical information. It expands the language of the computer to include string variables without sacrificing any of the special function keys or read/write memory. The new commands provided by the string ROM are of three main types: input, manipulation, and output.

strip-chart recorder — A recorder that automatically makes a plot of a variable versus time on graph paper. The paper is moved at a constant speed under a pen or other writing device as the variable is recorded.

stripe card reader—A device that decodes information contained in a stripe of magnetic tape imbedded in a plastic card.

Stripe card reader/encoder
(*Courtesy American Magnetics Corp.*).

stripe card reader/encoder—One typical unit is said to be a field-proven, economical means for reading and encoding magnetic stripe cards, badges, and passbooks. The unit possesses patented dual heads that are independently suspended and gimbal-mounted for less head and card wear, and for increased reliability with warped and contaminated cards.

stripe card standards—The published ANSI standard calls for a three-track format, with recording done serially-by-bit on each track. Looking ahead a bit, some observers see the credit card of the future as having an imbedded microprocessor chip, and using a high-density magnetic stripe as its memory. Powered by the reading unit or an internal battery, it could acquire a variety of data from remote sources, identify itself upon request, and encrypt its own data for transmission.

stripe recording, magnetic—Refers to a magnetic recording, such as the magnetic material that is deposited in stripe form on a document or card; the term magnetic stripe recording is most often used.

strip, magnetic-file—A file storage device that uses strips of material with surfaces that can be magnetized for the purpose of storing data.

strobe—1. General term for the detailed examination of a designated phase or epoch of a recurring waveform or phenomenon. 2. The enlargement or intensification of a part of a waveform as exhibited on a crt. Also called linearity control. 3. Process of viewing vibrations with a stroboscope; colloquially, the stroboscope itself. 4. The selection of a desired point or position in a recurring event or phenomenon, as in a wave, or in a device used to make the selection or identification of the selected point. 5. A selection signal that is active when data are correct on a bus.

strobe pulse — Also called sample pulse. A pulse used to gate the output of a core-memory sense amplifier into a trigger in a register.

strobe release time—The time required for a circuit output to reach the logic threshold voltage after the strobe signal changes from the inhibiting level to the enabling level.

strobe signal—A signal used to enable or disable a circuit function.

stroked characters — Stroked characters are similar in concept to dot-matrix characters because the characters are formed through the use of a series of short strokes. The advantage over dot-matrix characters is the variety of different fonts that can be formed.

structured interrupt — Most peripheral integrated-circuit device controllers employ open-drain outputs to facilitate "wired-OR" single-wire interrupt systems. Peripherals also employ versatile command and status words to inhibit the interrupt output easily and to provide for uniform polling among all peripherals.

structured programming — The phrase was originally applied to coding and is now used as a shorthand for a collection of techniques designed to be used to make the programming art more rigorous. The techniques include restricting the size of the code being produced to one coding sheet, restricting the numbers and kinds of program structures, allowing only one entrance and one exit, and avoiding the GOTO. However, the phrase is now used by many to encompass a whole range of techniques that apply to every stage of producing and managing software systems. In the structured programming procedure, documentation is designed in and becomes a byproduct of every stage, rather than being carried out after the system has been built. In structured programming, testing is done in stages as is documentation. Instead of waiting until all of the program modules have been completed and linked together for the first time, each module is debugged and tested as a unit. As the modules are hooked together (first two, then three, and so on), a series of integration tests, using sample code and dummy data where necessary, is performed. As a result, the final system test, using real data, is made less difficult.

structured programming, microcomputer — Most of the languages for microcomputers include some means of practicing structured programming, at least, in the narrow sense of using properly nested IF and iteration statements without GOTOs. This and other structuring facilities are essential elements of Pascal, which was designed for teaching programming methodology. In various ways, ALGOL, PL/1, FORTH, LISP, FORTRAN 77, and C also achieve this level of structure. A language that doesn't can still be used for structured programming if the user writes his code in a structured version of the language and, then, translates it either by hand, or by means of a preprocessor, to the standard version of the language. Several FORTRAN and COBOL preprocessors are available, and one version of COBOL, MicroCOBOL from CAP-CPP, Inc., has structured programming forms built in. Availability of particular structuring facilities — procedures, recursion, concurrency, separate compilation, and so forth— varies. Each is available in some programming languages but not all, and each may take different forms in different languages, or even in different dialects of the same language.

STRUDL — Abbreviation for structural design language. An outgrowth or extension of STRESS designed to provide a language for analysis and design of structures.

stunt box — 1. A device for controlling the nonprinting functions of a teletypewriter terminal. 2. The unit which controls the response of stations to selective calling signals.

subaddress—Refers to a portion of an input/output device that is accessible through an order code. For disk storage units, the module number is the subaddress.

subcommand—Refers to a request for an operation that is within the scope of work requested by a previously issued command.

submicron—A particle whose diameter is less than a micron.

submicron applications impact — Submicron technology principally affects magnetic bubble technology and semiconductor memories. Although the first submicron structures will probably range to about 64 kilobits for RAM, "million-bit chips" are possible. These structures mean that submicron devices will have better economics than rotating disk or drum on head-per-track memory systems. This super-LSI technology is expected to appear in new products where increased complexity can still be utilized. The one-chip medium-size computer quickly becomes a reality in conjunction with its one-chip memory or, alternately, a minicomputer will tend to have everything on one chip.

subminiaturization — The technique of packaging miniaturized parts in which unusual assembly techniques are used to give increased volumetric efficiency.

submodulator — Refers to a low-frequency amplifier which immediately precedes the modulator in a radiotelephone transmitter.

subprograms — Subprograms are program segments that perform a specific function. A major reason for using subprograms is that they reduce programming and debugging labor when a specific function is required to be executed at more than one point in a program. By creating the required function as a subprogram, the statements associated with that function may be coded once and executed at many different points in a program.

subroutine—1. In computer technology, the portion of a routine that causes a computer to carry out a well-defined mathematical or logical operation. 2. Usually called a closed subroutine. One to which control may be transferred from a master routine, and which returns control to the master routine at the conclusion of the subroutine. 3. Refers to either part of a master program or routine that may be "jumped" or "branched" to or to an independent program in itself but usually of smaller size or importance. 4. A subroutine is a series of computer instructions used to perform a specific task for many other routines. It is distinguishable from a main routine in that it requires, as one of its parameters, a location specifying where to return to the main program after its function has been accomplished.

subroutine instructions — In most systems, subroutines, called programmed instructions, may be used as if they were single commands by employing one of the programmed instructions of the repertoire. This capability allows the programmer to define his own special command, through the use of subroutines, which may be changed by the operating routine if desired.

subroutine library—Refers to a set of standard and proven subroutines that is kept on file for use at any time.

subroutine, static—Refers to a subroutine that involves no parameters other than the addresses of the operands.

subroutine status table—Refers to the program or routine used to maintain a list of subroutines in memory and to get subroutines from a file as needed.

subsequent counter—Refers to a specific type of instruction counter designed to step through or count micro-operations; i.e., parts of larger operations.

substrate — In microelectronics, the physical material on which a circuit is fabricated. Its primary function is to provide mechanical support, but it may also serve a useful thermal or electrical function.

substrate (bulk) — The base material

upon which or in which a field-effect transistor is fabricated.

substrate (of a microcircuit)—Refers to the supporting material upon which or within which an integrated circuit is fabricated, or to which an integrated circuit is attached.

substrates, multilayer—Multilayer substrates are a facet of hybrid technology that has come of age. A few years ago, manufacturers could go in only two directions—X and Y—when trying to add more interconnects to a hybrid. But, since a hybrid substrate is quite small, there wasn't too far to go. Currently, multilayer techniques allow three or four layers of interconnects with up to six or seven layers of circuitry, without making the substrate larger. Instead, the substrate is made deeper. Layers of conductors are separated by layers of glass; the conductors are fed through from level to level.

subsystem—Refers to a self-contained portion of a system that performs one of the major system functions, usually with only minimal interaction with other portions of the system.

subsystem support chips — These include serial and parallel I/O ports, timers and event counters, arithmetic chips, interrupt controllers, DMA controllers, and memory controllers. These components are defined according to bus compatibility, supplier, model number, technology and packaging, and price and availability.

subtracter — Refers to a device that is capable of forming the representation of the difference between two numbers which are represented by signals applied to the inputs of the device. Types: full subtracters, parallel and serial.

subtracter-adder—A logic element designed to act as either an adder or a subtracter in accordance to the control signal applied to it.

suite of programs—A suite of programs is generally a collection of separate but interrelated programs run one after another to do a single major job.

sum check—Refers to a specific check developed when groups of digits are summed, usually without regard for overflow. That sum is checked against a previously computed sum to verify that no digits have been changed since the last summation.

summing junction — In computing amplifiers or operational amplifiers, various input impedances are each connected from a separate input terminal of a unit to a common point. This point is called a summing junction and it is connected to the feedback impedance.

supercomputer, theoretical — A theoretical supercomputer using Josephson circuit technology may soon be within reach. Such a supercomputer has been defined by researchers at the Thomas J. Watson Research Labs, according to IBM researchers of exploratory cryonic technology. But they were quick to point out that the final realization is not around the corner when they described the specifications for the machine at an advanced computing techniques seminar. The machine would include a processor containing 300,000 circuits, with a cycle time of 1 nanosecond. Also included would be a cache memory of 256K bytes featuring a 2-nanosecond access, and a 64-Mbyte main memory with a 7-nanosecond access. The whole system could be packed into an 8 × 8 × 10-cm box and would dissipate 10 watts.

superconducting amplifier—One using superconductivity to give noise-free amplification.

superconductivity—1. The decrease in resistance of a certain material (lead, tin, thallium, etc.) as its temperature is reduced to nearly absolute zero. When the critical (transition) temperature is reached, the resistance will be almost zero. 2. The physical characteristic displayed by certain materials whose resistance to the flow of electric current becomes zero below a specified temperature. (A magnetic field can change its threshold value of temperature at which super conductivity occurs and such phenomenon is used in cryogenic devices.) 3. Superconductivity was first observed in 1911 by students of the Dutch scientist Kammerleigh Onnes, who found that the electrical resistance of a rod of frozen mercury fell to zero when the rod was cooled to four degrees Kelvin (—269 degrees Celsius). Subsequently, other scientists discovered that a variety of materials could be made to superconduct when sufficiently cooled. In such a state, a current, once induced in a material, will circulate indefinitely without any need for additional energy. Thus, superconductors can potentially carry extremely high currents without loss. Over the past 20 years, new materials —such as niobium-tin, niobium-titanium, and niobium-germanium—were developed which could withstand magnetic fields up to 200,000 gauss. Materials were also developed with higher transition temperatures. Niobium-germanium, for example, becomes superconducting at 23 K, allowing cooling with liquid hydrogen rather than with the rarer liquid helium needed for temperatures below the boiling point of hydrogen. In the past few years, new techniques have been developed which greatly ease fabrication of normally brittle superconductors.

superimpose — Refers to the process that moves data from one location to another, superimposing bits or characters on the contents of specified locations.

superimposed circuit—Refers to an additional channel that is obtained in such a manner from one or more circuits (which are normally provided for use by other channels) so that all channels can be used simultaneously, without mutual interference.

supervising system—1. Refers to a program that controls loading and relocation of routines and, in some cases, makes use of instructions which are unknown to the general programmer. Effectively, an executive routine is part of the machine itself (synonymous with supervisory program and program, executive). 2. A set of coded instructions designed to process and control other sets of coded instructions. 3. A set of coded instructions used in realizing automatic coding. 4. A master set of coded instructions.

supervisor—A monitor or executive routine that controls the proper sequencing and positioning of segments of computer programs in limited storage during their execution.

supervisor mode—Refers to a mode of operation under which certain operations, such as memory-protection modification instructions and input/output operations, are permitted.

supervisor overlay — A control routine that initiates and controls fetching of overlay segments on the basis of information recorded in the overlay module by the linkage editor.

supervisory communications — These are supervisory routines that control the access and direct the transfer of data between the user's programs and a remote terminal or another computer. Communications routines support switched (dial-up), or non-switched, point-to-point connections using binary synchronous or start-stop line control.

supervisory console — Generally, the supervisory console includes that operator's control panel, a keyboard and typeprinter, and a control unit for the keyboard and typeprinter.

supervisory program—A program used to control the execution of the various user programs, manage the allocation of memory and peripheral device resources, and safeguard the integrity of the system as a whole by careful control of each user program. In a multiprogramming system, the supervisory program provides the means for assigning memory pages to a user program and preventing that user from making any unauthorized access to the pages outside his assigned area. Thus, a user can effectively be prevented from accidentally or willfully destroying any other user program or the system executive program.

support circuits, bubble memory — Aside from the simple circuits, such as the field-coil drivers and the sense amplifier, bubble-system support typically consists of a circuit that keeps track of the bubble position and controls the flow of data to or from the host system bus. Also part of that interface is a circuit typically used to generate all the timing for the various bubble control and generation pulses. Some suppliers added a third circuit that not only formats and buffers the data but also provides error correction using a proprietary algorithm. Each manufacturer's circuits are dedicated to the company's own family of bubble-memory chips and cannot easily be interchanged, even if the bubble devices have the same number of bits and are organized similarly. All these circuits, though, will permit system expansion to well beyond a single bubble-memory cell. One firm's concept, using its family of support components, will permit

systems with capacities of up to 256 Mbits to be assembled.

support software, microprocessor — The implementation of microprocessors into product design is aided by support tools that include hardware reference manuals, cross-assemblers and simulators with manuals, and prototyping boards that allow I/O personalization for unique interfaces. The reference manuals include a detailed description of the internal organization and operation of the MPU, its instruction set description, its system implementations, and the peripheral chip descriptions and applications. Software support for many units consists of a cross-assembler and simulator written in ANSI FORTRAN IV. Some salient features of typical assemblers are a relocatable loader and macroinstructions.

support system—1. Refers to programming systems used to support the normal translating functions of machine-oriented, procedural-oriented, and problem-oriented language processors. 2. A collection of computer programs used to aid the production and checkout of a system. 3. The combination of the skills, techniques, and equipment needed to operate and maintain a system.

suppressor, line-surge—A device used to protect microcomputers and other electronic equipment from ac line surges. A typical surge suppressor absorbs transients that exceed the protection level, and a ferrite filter suppresses spikes and transients that fall below the level of the surge protector. The typical unit will fit in the palm of the hand and will plug into a standard ac outlet; the equipment to be protected plugs into the unit.

surface barrier — Potential barrier across the surface of a semiconductor junction due to diffusion of charge carriers.

surface-barrier transistor — One in which very thin barriers (by means of etching techniques) are used, thus permitting the frequency range to be extended to 100 MHz.

surface channel — A transfer channel created at the semiconductor-insulator interface.

surface-channel charge-coupled device (SCCD)—A charge-coupled device in which the potential wells are created at the semiconductor-insulator interface and the charge is transferred along that interface.

surface leakage — That leakage along the surface of a nonconducting material or device. May vary widely with contamination, humidity, etc.

surface lifetime—The lifetime of current carriers in the surface layer of a semiconductor where recombination takes place most readily.

surface recombination velocity—Electron-hole recombination on the surface of a semiconductor occurs more readily than in the interior, hence, the carriers in the interior drift towards the surface with a mean speed termed the surface recombination velocity (SRV). Defined as the ratio of the normal component of the impurity current to the volume charge density near the surface.

surface-state charge density—Refers to the net charge density on the surface of a semiconductor. Both the charge density and the energy levels may be influenced by such factors as the insulation layer, surface discontinuities, chemicals, light, and any electrical or magnetic field that is present.

swap — Refers to systems using time sharing; means to write the main-storage image of a job to auxiliary storage and the reading of the image of another job into main storage.

swapping—Refers to a design of memory multiplexing in which jobs are kept on a backing storage and are periodically transferred entirely to an internal memory to be executed for a fixed time slice.

switchboard loop jack—A patch panel with rows of jacks for physical access to local loops (maximum capacity of 90 channels). Each column of four jacks accesses one local loop and consists of looping jacks, a set jack, and a miscellaneous jack (some systems).

switched message network — A communications service in which customers may communicate with each other, such as TELEX and TWX.

switching applications—Refers to message-switching applications where the computer is used to accept messages from terminals, route the messages over trunk lines (at perhaps higher speeds) to remote message-switching computers, and to provide certain reliability functions, such as an audit trail and error control. Message switching is a somewhat different application of computer communications in that there is no user processing involved. The sole purpose of the system is to communicate messages from one point to another point.

switching circuit — A circuit that performs a switching function. In computers, this is performed automatically by the presence of a certain signal (usually a pulse signal). When combined, switching circuits can perform a logical operation.

switching diode, crystal — Relates to various diodes that are manufactured with a junction of a base metal and some type of crystalline element, for example, silicon or germanium. Such diodes contrast with vacuum diodes and are used in computing equipment to perform logic and buffering current conversions necessary for switching and storage transfers.

switching equipment — Refers to devices which allow users to select specific communication circuits on demand. Such switching equipment may operate either manually or in automatic mode and is designed to provide alternate facilities in case of line malfunctions, circuit overloads, or other operational conditions.

switching systems — These add a new dimension of flexibility to communication networks. Using a minimum number of interconnecting lines, either leased or switched common carrier, a number of data sources and destinations can be interlinked with each other and with a common data base.

switching techniques, hybrid—A typical hybrid switching technique satisfies a variety of data communication user types. In circuit switching, a physical link is held through the network for the duration of the call, and this switching method provides the user with minimum network transit delay and full transparency. With packet switching, user information is inserted into data blocks called packets, and the actual switching is done on packets. Each packet is transmitted through the network via a virtual or logical connection, which results in an effective sharing of facilities and lower communication costs to a user.

switch register — The switch register consists of up to 12 (or more) data-entry switches that are used to manually alter the contents of the accumulator, program counter, or memory data register. The switch register can also be read under program control.

switch stepping — Refers to a special switching device or relay having "n" discrete conditions and which advances from one condition to the next each time it receives an input pulse.

symbol—1. A simplified design representing a part in a schematic circuit diagram. 2. A letter representing a particular quantity in formulas. 3. In some systems, a symbol consists of up to eight letters and digits beginning with a letter. Symbols are defined by their appearance as statement labels or equality symbols. The value of a symbol, defined as a label, is the value of the location counter at the time the label was encountered. The value of a symbol, defined by equality, is the value of the expression appearing on the right of the equal sign. 4. A conventional representation of a concept, or a representation of a concept upon which agreement has been reached.

symbolic—Programming languages are sometimes described as symbolic. The programs refer to storage locations and machine operations by symbolic names and addresses which are independent of their literal hardware-determined locations. A symbolic name is a label used in programs to reference data peripherals, instructions, and the like. In practice, symbolic means representing something by the use of everyday alphanumeric symbols.

symbolic addresses—1. The programmer can refer to memory locations by symbolic name, rather than actual numeric address and the assembler will translate these, as well as the instructions. The assembler usually runs on a larger computer, although some assemblers run directly on their microcomputer-based development systems. The assembler requires significantly less development and check-out time than manual translation, and there are fewer coding errors. 2. Also called a floating address. In digital computer programming, a label chosen in a routine to identify a particular word, function, or other information that is independent of the location of the information within the routine.

symbolic assemblers—Nearly all manufacturers of microprocessors (and mini- and maxicomputers as well) provide symbolic assemblers. These are programs that ease the programming task by eliminating the need to translate instructions manually into machine-readable form. The designer can express his program in terms of mnemonics, which are abbreviations that suggest individual instructions. Then, the assembler translates each mnemonic instruction into its binary representation.

symbolic assembly system—Refers to the symbolic language itself and to the symbolic assembler that can translate it. A symbolic assembly program can minimize the time required for assembling a program. It permits the programmer to recover errors on-line without having to restart the assembly process. The programmer can insert corrections from the keyboard during assembly. The assembler also provides the programmer with a means of entering linkage and of mapping common data. Instructions, data, memory addresses, and address modifiers can be coded and entered in symbolic rotation.

symbolic code — Refers to a specific code designed to express programs in source language; i.e., by referring to storage locations and machine operations by symbolic names and addresses that are independent of their hardware-determined names and addresses.

symbolic coding—1. In digital computer programming, any coding system using symbolic rather than actual computer addresses. 2. Broadly, any coding system in which symbols other than actual machine operations and addresses are used.

symbolic concordance program — Refers to a program that is used to produce a cross-referenced list of all the symbolic names in a program. This is of use in debugging or modifying programs, especially large ones.

symbolic debugging—Symbolic debugging means the user need not refer to both linker maps and assembly listings in order to locate particular sections of a program code. The user need only specify a label name in order to reposition the debugger display to the required location. The debugger can also evaluate arithmetic expressions to make the location of particular program steps even easier. A single-stepping facility allows the user to trace the flow of the program and simultaneously watch the registers change. Tracing allows the user to see back in time as the program approaches a breakpoint.

symbolic language—1. Refers to that portion of a microcomputer program prepared in any coding other than the specific machine language, and so required to be assembled or compiled before it can be carried out. 2. A programming language that expresses addresses and operation codes of instructions in symbols convenient to humans rather than in machine language.

symbolic logic—1. Refers to the study of formal logic and mathematics by means of a special written language which seeks to avoid the ambiguity and inadequacy of ordinary language. 2. The mathematical concepts, techniques, and languages as used in reference 1, whatever their particular application or context. Synonymous with mathematical logic and related to logic.

symbolic macroassembler—A symbolic macroassembler allows the programmer to code programs using mnemonic operation codes and symbols to define machine instructions. A comprehensive set of directives facilitates subroutine linkage, conditional assembly-nested macrodefinitions, and manual or automatic control of extended memory.

symbolic math system — The typical symbolic mathematics system enables users to solve such problems as polynomial multiplication, symbolic differentiation and integration, simplification of trigonometric expressions, and exact solutions of nonlinear equations. These programs perform actual symbolic operations taught in algebra, trigonometry, and calculus courses, as well as arithmetic, using exact rational operations with precision as high as 600 digits. Various systems run on 8080-, 8085-, and Z80-based and other microcomputer systems using TRSDOS, standard CP/M, Cromemco CDOS, or other specific operating systems.

symbolic name—Refers to a label used in programs, that are written in a source language, to reference data elements, peripheral units, instructions, etc.

symbolic parameter—Refers to assembler programming; a variable symbol declared in the prototype statement of a macrodefinition. A symbolic parameter is usually assigned a value from the corresponding operand in the macroinstruction that calls the macrodefinition.

symbolic programming—1. A program using symbols instead of numbers for the operations and locations in a computer. Although the writing of a program is easier and faster, an assembly program must be used to decode the symbol into machine language and assign instruction locations. 2. The use of arbitrary symbols to represent addresses in order to facilitate programming.

symbolic unit — 1. Refers to a mnemonic in the symbolic units table which refers to an input/output device. A symbolic unit may be assigned to an entire input/output device or to a portion of a device. 2. In coding a program, the designation used to refer to external storage, with the actual storage to be used during a particular execution of the program to be determined later.

symbol library — Some systems allow the storage of symbols that are standard to the user's application. No restrictions with regard to size or number are placed on the symbol function. Any construction is acceptable to the symbol library. Typically, symbols can be used to create other symbols and no restrictions as to number of levels are imposed. Symbols when used can be accessed graphically with a light pen. Also, a symbol can be assigned an access name if, because of size, graphic access would be inconvenient.

symbol manipulation — Refers to the formal use of symbol manipulation that results in a specific list-processing language, because data are usually not numerical. The first real list-processing language, IPL (or Information Processing Language), was developed by Newell, Shaw, and Simon in 1957.

symbol variable—Refers to assembler programming; a symbol used in macro- and conditional-assembly processing that can assume any of a given set of values.

synchronization, frame—Some form of frame synchronization is required between transmitting and receiving parties in synchronous data transmission. Most common of the methods is to precede the block with a unique bit-pattern sequence. The receiver searches for this unique pattern so that it can obtain proper frame synchronization. The number of bytes and the synchronization code employed differ among the various protocols.

synchronizer—1. A unit used to maintain synchronism when transmitting information between two devices. It may merely control the speed of one device (e.g., by clutch) or, if the speeds are very different, may include buffer storage. 2. A storage device used to compensate for a difference in a rate of flow of information or time of occurrence of events, when transmitting information from one device to another.

synchronizing clocks—Every microprocessor system needs some kind of synchronizing clock mechanism, and most of the MOS processors require two-phase clocks. In the simplest case, the user need only supply a crystal or a series RC network to establish the time constant of the on-chip clock. Some firms offer a special clock-generating chip. At the other extreme, some systems require a four-phase nonoverlapping clock signal system. Although all manufacturers publish a sample clock circuit, most of these are not easy to use in production; they have four interacting variable controls which must be adjusted for optimum pulse repetition, rate, and width. Many microprocessor systems make use of DIP-packaged crystal clocks.

synchronometer—A device which counts the number of cycles in a given time. If the time interval is unity, the device becomes a digital frequency meter.

synchronous—1. Refers to the same frequency and phase. 2. Having a constant time interval between successive bits, characters, or events.

synchronous clock—1. An electric clock driven by a synchronous motor, for operation on an ac power system in which the frequency is accurately controlled. 2. Refers to a microcomputer in which each event, or the performance of each operation, is initially based on the results of a signal generated by a clock. 3. Even in the case of static circuitry, a clock frequency is generally used to keep the various events in the microcomputer in step and running at the proper rate. This action results in synchronous operation, as contrasted with asynchronous operation. In a synchronous system, the clock must be sufficiently slow to allow the slowest circuit sufficient time to switch. In an asynchronous system, the length of time for an operation is determined only by the operating speed of the circuits. Dynamic circuitry is inherently synchronous in operation.

synchronous communications satellite—Refers to one with an orbital period equal to the time of rotation of the earth on its axis and launched so that it remains directly above the same geographical point on the earth's surface. This facilitates the control of the aerial assembly of ground stations operating in conjunction with the satellite.

synchronous computer—A digital computer in which all ordinary operations are controlled by equally spaced signals from a master clock.

synchronous data transmission—Refers to a system in which timing is derived through synchronizing characters at the beginning of each message.

synchronous gate—Time gate controlled by clock pulses and used to synchronize various operations in computer or data-processing systems.

synchronous inputs—1. Refers to those terminals on a flip-flop which allow data to be entered but only upon command of the clock. These inputs do not have direct control of the output such as those of a gate but only when the clock permits and commands. Called J-K inputs or ac set-and-reset inputs. 2. Those terminals in a flip-flop which can affect the output state of the flip-flop independent of the clock. Called set, preset, reset, or dc set-and-reset, or clear.

synchronous machine — A machine which has an average speed exactly proportionate to the frequency of the system to which it is connected.

synchronous operation — Refers to a type of operation in which each event or the performance of each operation starts as a result of a signal generated by a clock.

synchronous serial-data adapter — In some synchronous systems, the synchronous serial-data adapter converts the microprocessor's parallel data to serial data and, vice versa, with error-detection and -correction during transmission and reception. Some two-chip high-speed modems are available that provide high data transfer-rate capability, and a clocking source.

synchronous shift register—A shift register that uses a clock for the timing of a system operation and where only one state change per clock pulse occurs.

synchronous transmission — Refers to a mode of transmission using a precisely timed bit stream and character stream.

syndetic—1. Refers to connections or interconnections. 2. Pertains to a document or catalog with cross references.

synergetic—Refers to a combination of every unit of a system, which when combined develop a total larger than their arithmetic sum (also called synergistic).

syntactic error — Syntactic errors are considered the responsibility of the system and are further categorized as follows: Composition—typographical errors, violations of specified form of statements, and misuse of variable names (e.g., incorrect punctuation, mixed-mode expressions, undeclared arrays, etc.). Consistency — statements that are correctly composed but conflict with other statements (e.g., conflicting declaratives, failure to follow each transfer statement with a numbered statement, etc.). Completeness—programs that are incomplete (e.g., transfers to nonexistent statement numbers, etc.).

syntax — 1. Refers to the relationship among characters or groups of characters, independent of their meanings or the manner of their interpretation and use. 2. The structure of expressions in a language. 3. The rules governing the structure of a language. 4. The relationships among symbols.

syntax checker—Refers to a program that tests source statements in a programming language for violations of the syntax of that language.

synthetic language—Refers to a pseudocode or symbolic language. A fabricated language.

system — 1. Refers to a collection of parts united by some form of regulated interaction; an organized whole. 2. A collection of service routines that sequences programs through a microcomputer, provides conversion, I/O, and debugging subroutines, and which makes helpful remarks to the operator, is known as an operating system. 3. As used in some computing installations, the system includes, and defines the interrelationship of, hardware, service routines, processing procedures, and accounting methods.

system and level registers—Within the processor architecture of some systems, two categories of registers exist: system registers and level registers. System registers contain system-wide information used by the operating systems and appear singularly within the processor. Level registers are used by a task in process at a particular priority level and are replicated for each interrupt level. This structure provides general-purpose registers for ease of programming while replicating these registers on priority levels for fast interrupt response. System registers can be accessed by a program only when the CPU is operating in privileged state (in other words, by the operating system).

system check — Refers to a computer performance using external program checks, not check circuits built into the hardware.

system check module—Relates to a device which monitors system operability if power fails or if deviations from desired computer operations develop. It initiates appropriate emergency actions by the computer.

system control panel — Many system

control panels are divided into three major sections: the operator control section, which contains only those controls required by the operator when the processor is operating under full supervisory control; the operator intervention section, which contains additional controls required for the operator to intervene in normal programming operation; and the customer engineering section, which contains controls intended only for customer engineering use in diagnostics and maintenance. Manual control operations are held to a minimum by the system design and operating system. The result is fewer operating errors.

system definition, microprocessor — System definition involves the major tasks to be performed by the microprocessor—which is assumed to be the central control device of the system. Data formats should be established to maximize processor control. The over-all system timing is included in this design phase to ensure that all functions can be handled within the timing constraints. Based on the system definition, the basic program structure can then be defined. Each input channel to the microprocessor represents a major program, assuming the use of more than one input device. In addition, an executive program should be written to control the over-all operation of the system. Various routines—based on the different functions or command codes supplied — further subdivide the main program.

system design—1. The specification of the working relations between all the parts of a system in terms of their characteristic actions. 2. System design consists of selecting the basic architecture used to implement the functional specifications. System partitioning assigns portions of the system to hardware and software, and subdivides hardware functions among LSI packages. In the case of logic design for digital circuits and circuit design for analog circuits, designers using the specifications developed for each LSI device at the partitioning step create designs for the LSI devices themselves.

system design aids, microcomputer— In addition to complete circuit and applications documentation, most suppliers provide all the software and hardware aids needed to design various kinds of equipment. The user manuals provide a detailed description of these design aids: 1. Support hardware (evaluation modules); 2. Support systems (special development and test equipment); 3. System design aids (documentation); and 4. Support software. In addition, personal design assistance usually is immediately available by phone, through computer links, or from special service companies. Software and hardware support is available for most phases of the development of a microcomputer and its associated computer program(s). For example: evaluation and development modules containing various test devices are usually available. These modules provide an economical and fast means of actually building and testing a proposed microcomputer system before committing to firmware.

system diagnostics — Refers to programs resembling the operational program rather than a systematic logical-pattern program which will detect overall system malfunctions rather than isolate or locate faulty components.

system engineering—A method of engineering approach whereby all the elements in the control system are considered, even the smallest value and the process itself.

system firmware — Many systems include system firmware building blocks. They can be used in various systems and often assure that only application software peculiar to the application need be written by the user. The following are firmware/software system building blocks: the multiprogramming executive, a macroassembly language interpreter, an input/output control system, a disk file management system, and others.

system generation (SYSGEN) — On some systems, when a user installs a system, he or she performs a "system generation" (or SYSGEN) to create a supervisor and data-management support for a particular configuration, and to include the program products that have been ordered. During system generation, the source library, the object library, and the system history area are established on these systems. The characteristics of the required spooling support are also defined.

system hardware, industrial-control—A typical industrial microcomputer system can be divided into five basic parts. They are the microprocessor and its associated memory, the interface modules that connect the microcomputer system to external devices (such as limit switches, push buttons, and motor starters), the equipment needed to program the microcomputer, a program analyzer that is used to analyze and diagnose the operation of the microcomputer-based system, and a system tester that allows the user to check the microprocessor memory and interface modules to see if they are functioning properly.

system interface (microprocessor) — Refers to devices that interconnect all the other support hardware.

system language — In a system language, program statements generally correspond directly with machine-level instructions, and conversely, every machine operation is reflected in a high-level language statement. Because of this correspondence, system-language programs usually translate efficiently to the machine-language level, and the programmer finds all the machine's facilities directly available to him. Nevertheless, some hardware designers, particularly those newly introduced to software systems, may prefer to work at a comfortable level, which may mean programming in absolute machine code initially and then moving to assembly language as more capability is required. Similarly, they can easily make the transition to a high-level language when programming in assembly-language becomes tedious.

system loader — Refers to one of the supervisor routines. It is used to retrieve program phases from the main image library and load them into main storage.

system log — Refers to a data set in which job-related information, operational data, descriptions of unusual occurrences, commands, and messages to or from the operator may be stored. Abbreviated SYSLOG.

system monitor—A typical system monitor, which often resides in the first 1K

to 4K of memory, enables the user to load and execute programs that are stored on tape, disk, or other external devices. The user can also write device drivers coded to suit his own particular I/O needs. Programs loaded and executed under monitor supervision can be passed parameters to control their operation.

system multiplex (MUX)—To interleave sequentially and transmit two or more messages on a single data channel. In some systems, the MUX cards feed each channel, in turn, into the measuring circuit and microprocessor under control of the program.

system noise—1. Refers to extra bits or words that must be ignored or removed from the data at the time the data is used. 2. Errors introduced into data in a system, especially in communication channels. 3. Random variations of one or more characteristics of any entity such as voltage, current, and data. 4. Loosely, any disturbance tending to interfere with the normal operation of a device or system. Refers to the random energy generated by thermal and shot effects in the system.

system organization, industrial—An industrial microcomputer system consists of a central processor unit (CPU) module (which provides system control and performs the various arithmetic and logical functions), one or more programmable read-only memories (which store the system instructions or program), one or more random-access memories (which are used for data storage), one or more input/output modules (which accept inputs from the system being controlled and which transmit control signals to that system), a power supply and regulators, a communications bus flat cable (which provides the signal path to tie the various modules together), the necessary mounting hardware, and possibly, an interrupt control module (which is used to handle interrupt signals from devices being controlled).

systems analyst—A systems analyst is a person who defines the applications problem, determines system specifications, recommends equipment changes, and designs data-processing procedures. He devises data-verification methods and prepares block diagrams and record layouts from which the programmer prepares flow-charts. He may assist in or supervise the preparation of flowcharts.

systems and support software—Refers to the wide variety of software that includes assemblers, compilers, sub-routine libraries, operating systems, application programs, etc.

systems handbook—Refers to a concise distillation of the major characteristics of the instruction set including operation codes, addressing modes, and microprocessor status for each instruction. Also includes reference to the primary aspects of system implementation including chip interfaces and timing. This document is aimed at the experienced user who understands the basics of the family and requires a concise reference book.

system software—System software generally includes a debugging program and a basic operating system, a text editor, an assembler, a linking loader, and an I/O operating system. The debugging program and basic operating system provides the user with the capabilities of address modifications, memory dumps, absolute loading, and diagnostic running of programs with breakpoint processing. The text editor offers the user editing capability for creating and maintaining source files. Text can be added, modified through a number of useful functions, and prepared for disk or tape. The assembler will have the full ranges of instructions, often with the options of either relocatable or absolute code, plus macro capacity. A linking loader is often available to load relocatable codes. An I/O operating system facilitates the details of I/O programming. Most companies provide system software free or at low cost. System software provides the following savings: it shortens the time needed to write and debug applica-

tions programs, and it provides much of the routine software commonly used by most applications. By making effective use of hardware, system software can reduce the size of the total system necessary for various applications.

systems support, microcomputer — In supplementing the microprocessor system itself, support should be provided by the manufacturer to simplify the application of the processor and the development and prototyping of the end product. This category includes documented manuals, application literature, area field specialists, and prototyping systems. Also generally useful are program-development software and the ability to fashion the microprocessor into different configurations.

system support programs — Refers to those processing programs that contribute directly to the use and control of the system and the production of results: the job control processor, the linkage editor, and the utility programs.

systems test—1. Refers to the running of the whole system against test data. 2. A complete simulation of the actual running system for purposes of testing out the adequacy of the system. 3. A test of an entire interconnected set of components for the purpose of determining proper functioning and interconnection. 4. The running of the whole system of runs making up a data-processing application against test data.

system timer—A hardware system timer is a standard feature of many present-day computers. In the data mode, it provides time stamps for monitored events (time-of-day clock). In the control mode, it generates interrupts that can be used to drive sampling monitors (interval timer).

T

table—Refers to a collection or ordering of data (such as square root values) laid out in rows and columns for reference, or stored in a computer memory as an array. In computing,

elements of such a table would be obtained by direct calculation where possible (table, look-at) to save storage. If this were not possible, the whole array would be stored and the element required would be determined by a comparison search (table, look-up).

table, decision — Refers to a specific table of all contingencies that are to be considered in the description of a problem, together with the actions to be taken. Decision tables are sometimes used in place of flowcharts for problem description and documentation.

table, graphics—*See* tablet menu.

table, look-up—Refers to various processes or procedures for searching identifying labels in a table so as to find the location of a desired associated item. By extension, a digital computer instruction which directs that the above operation be performed. The techniques are used primarily to: (1) obtain a derived value for one variable when given another where the relationship cannot be easily stated in a formula or algorithm, (2) to convert a discontinuous variable from one form to another (e.g., convert from one code to another), or (3) to provide conditional (logical) control functions (e.g., converting from symbolic to actual addresses or determining which of several discrete processes should be applied for a given state).

table look-up instruction—Refers to a specific instruction designed to speed reference to stored data which are specifically arranged, i.e., in a table or in tabular form. This instruction will direct a microcomputer to automatically search for a named argument in a table in order to locate and retrieve a desired result, i.e., an operation performed instead of a calculation, in most cases. However, tables and instructions vary considerably among different computers and programs.

table, reference program — Refers to that section of storage used as an index for operations, subroutines, and variables.

table, symbol—*See* tablet menu.

tablet menu — On some systems, the commands and instructions for board design are positioned on system tablet menus which include frequently used component symbols. Stored in the graphic system's data base, the symbols are easily retrieved to create a schematic by activating the tablet with an electronic pen. The menus include two standard component libraries, one consisting of schematic/logic symbols and the other pcb components.

tactile keyboard—Designed for calculators, digital tv and fm receivers, terminals and other applications, this type of keyboard has three component layers. Just below the keys (not provided with some units) is a sheet of Mylar that is, first, screened on its bottom side with a conductive pattern and, then, "bubbled" by heat and pressure deformation. These bubbles invert when they are depressed by the keys into spaces in the second layer (a Mylar sheet with a circular opening at each key position). As a bubble inverts, the conductive area on its underside contacts the third layer (a screened circuit board) to complete the switch closure.

talking terminal—This type of terminal is a computer-independent, asynchronous, ASCII, dial-up device that can be connected to any computer allowing this type of communication. The hardware for the terminal consists of a speech synthesis device, a microprocessor, a keyboard, and an acoustic coupler. Software to provide the control of the speech synthesizer resides in the terminal's microprocessor system, permitting computer independence. A talking terminal was used extensively with the University of Illinois' PDP-10 computer and proved to be a very satisfactory means of communication between a computer system and a blind computer scientist.

tape back-up, ½-inch—The availability of ½-inch tape offers a reliable means of having a back-up storage that has the additional advantage of having an IBM-compatible format. Transfer of data can be accomplished at a very high rate and the storage capacity can be quite large. However, ½-inch tape drives are relatively expensive, bulky, troublesome to transport, and power consumptive, thereby limiting their application to large systems. Also, with this media, trained personnel are required to thread the tape onto the reel-to-reel recorders.

tape cable—Refers to a type of cable containing flat metallic ribbon conductors, all lying side by side in the same plane and imbedded in a material that both insulates and binds them together. *See also* ribbon cable.

tape cartridge, ¼-inch — The ¼-inch tape cartridge is an ANSI standard, commonly available, environmentally protected media that can be easily used without any special training. The "protection" increases the read reliability and the resultant recovery of data. Many cartridges may be stored within a small area such as a desk drawer. The media is low cost, lightweight, suitable for interchange of data via the mail, reliable, and available from multiple sources. The corresponding ¼-inch cartridge drives used are low cost, small, power efficient, and can offer an optimum solution for the fixed-disk back-up application.

tape certification — Certification is a process by which storage blocks (or sections for marking of tape length) are put on tape and aligned for use (on specific systems). *See also* tape characteristics.

tape characteristics—Tape characteristics are variable. One type of Mylar tape has a specially formulated plastic sheath overcoating which serves as a protector for the heads. The result is long-lasting Read/Write heads and consistent tape reliability. Some tape is offered certified (formatted) and uncertified (unformatted). Certification is a process by which storage blocks (or sections for marking off tape length) are put on the tape and aligned for use on specific systems. Uncertified tape comes blank, with no blocks. Some firms guarantee that uncertified tape is certifiable.

tape data validation — A typical unit tests the parity of each incoming character. A substitute flag character is recorded and a resettable counter is incremented if a 200-character block contains one or more flag characters. An option at each terminal will cause the retransmittal of blocks which fail parity tests. A Read-after-Write test is performed on the computer tape. Blocks failing this test are erased, defective tape is bypassed, and the block is rewritten. The buffers and speed of the tape drive allow six Write attempts without disturbing the flow of data.

tape drive—A mechanism for controlling the movement of magnetic tape, which is commonly used to move magnetic tape past a reading or writing head, or used to allow automatic rewinding.

Tape drives, streaming
(*Courtesy Data Electronics, Inc.*).

tape drives, streaming—Streaming tape drives that are directed toward fixed Winchester-technology disk back-up application have a large data capacity, fast access speed, and a reasonably sized package. However, there are software complications. They do not provide the Read-after-Write facility that many memory systems are programmed for. Instead of creating interrecord gaps on the tape by decelerating and stopping the tape with its Erase head energized, a streaming tape drive creates the gaps electronically as the tape streams by the Read, Write, and Erase heads from one end to the other without stopping. Despite this potential software problem, streaming tape systems — so called because of the absence of the stop-and-go motion of other tape drives— do offer several advantages. They offer a choice of speeds and a choice of data transfer rates. One new unit (Data Electronics, Inc.) is microprocessor controlled with either a serial or parallel interface provided. It has an I/O buffer included as well as an interface that simulates a semiconductor FIFO memory.

tape head—Refers to the part of a tape deck or cassette unit that reads to and/or writes information from the tapes. These days, many tape units have two separate heads, one for reading and one for writing. The typical device allows a logical Read-after-Write check on some decks, thus ensuring meaningful information has, in fact, been put on to the tape.

tape loadpoint — The position of magnetic tape where reading or writing can begin.

tape, magnetic—Refers to a storage device consisting of metal or plastic tape that is coated with a magnetic material. Binary data are stored as small magnetized spots arranged in column form across the width of the tape. A Read/Write head is usually associated with each row of magnetized spots so that one column can be read or written at a time as the tape is moved relative to the head.

tape package, floating-point — A floating-point package is a collection of subroutines for arithmetic and conversion operations on floating-point numbers. Since these are normally assembled with the user's program, the floating-point package is supplied only in the form of a source program tape with an assembly listing and the user's manual for a specific microcomputer.

tape transport—Refers to the mechanism which moves magnetic or paper tape past sensing and recording heads and is usually associated with data-processing equipment. Synonymous with tape drive.

target language — The language into which some other language is to be properly translated.

target phase — An occasion on which the target program is run is often called the run phase, or the target phase, or the object phase; i.e., most often this terminology is used when compiling has taken place.

task management — Refers to a set of functions of the control program or routine which controls the use of system resources, other than the input/output devices, by tasks.

task management software functions — The task management functions provide a set of basic functions to the user for controlling the program execution environment. The services often provided are: task dispatcher, basic overlay support, timer support, supervisor call.

task queue—Refers to a queue which contains all the task control blocks that are in the system at any one time.

telecommunications—1. Any communication of information in verbal, written, coded, or pictorial form by electric means, whether by wire or by radio. 2. Refers to processes for conveying from one location to another, by electrical means, information that originates or is recorded in alphabetic, numeric, or pictorial form, or as a signal that represents a measurement. This includes telemetering, telegraphy, and facsimile as well as voice and television. (Also known as data transmission.)

telecommunications access method (TCAM) — The Telecommunications Access Method (TCAM) is a communication subsystem designed to exchange messages between a communication network and a set of message queues, according to information contained in control blocks and message headers. The program

Tape transport—magnetic tape (Courtesy Datum Inc.).

that controls these operations, called the Message Control Program (MCP), is coded for each particular installation using a set of system macros, which invoke various parts of the TCAM software.

teleconference—A conference between persons who are remote from one another but linked together by a telecommunications system.

telematics—Telematics is the term used to encompass the accelerating technological revolution in the related fields of telecommunications, computers, microchips, and data banks. It is the vogue word in the European countries.

telemeter — 1. To transmit analog or digital reports of measurements and observations over a distance (e.g., by radio transmission from a guided missile to a control or recording station on the ground). 2. A complete measuring, transmitting, and receiving apparatus for indicating, recording, or integrating the value of a quantity at a distance by electric translating means.

telemetering—Also called telemetry or remote metering. Measurement which, through intermediate means, can be interpreted at a distance from the primary detector. A receiving instrument converts the transmitted electrical signals into units of data, which can then be translated by data reduction into appropriate units.

telemetry—1. Transmission to a distance of measured magnitudes by radio or telephony, with suitably coded modulation (e.g., amplitude, frequency, phase, pulse). 2. Remote sensing of operating systems by an instrument that converts transmitted electric signals into units of data.

telephone Borsht functions — Subscriber-line interface circuits (SLICs) are supposed to satisfy, in theory, what is known as the Borsht functions. These are B for battery feed, O for overvoltage protection, R for ringing, S for signaling, H for the two-to-four-wire hybrid functions, and T for test features. Just how these functions are defined and which are important depends on whether the chip is used in the U.S. or Europe, whether it is in a PBX or a central office, and how many auxiliary chips are acceptable.

telephone data-carrier system (DCS)— The typical data-carrier system (DCS) provides simultaneous voice and data communications. This makes terminal hookups easier and less expensive

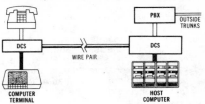

Telephone data-carrier system (DCS).

than various other methods. The DCS can be plugged into a standard telephone line without interfering with normal telephone service. This ability cuts terminal installation and relocation time. The system is designed to cost-justify operation on small, low-cost networks. An FCC-registered unit can operate (typically) full-duplex, asynchronous, and up to 9600 bps.

telephone dialer circuit—An MOS telephone dialer circuit is a system that converts push-button closures to rotary-dial pulses which are directly compatible with all existing standard telephone systems. Pulse rate, mark-to-space ratio, and interdigital pause can be easily adjusted. Typically, the last number dialed is stored for automatic redial when desired. Access-pause capability simplifies operation in a PABX or WATS system.

telephone link, microcomputer — The typical telephone communication system operates at a data rate of either 110 or 300 bits per second (bps), allowing the use of simple Bell 103-compatible modems. In order to set the data rate for a transmission, each user must transmit a carriage return character so that the computer can set up the correct data rate. Once the data rate is established, the microcomputer sends out a sign-on message and asks the user to "log in" with an identification code. This identification code can be a membership number, an amateur radio call sign, or some arbitrary name. It is often limited to a length of from 8 to 16 characters. The microcomputer will then indicate the presence or absence of any personal messages addressed to the user who has just logged in.

telephony—The branch of telecommunications that has to do with the transmission and reproduction of speech, and in some cases, other sounds; additional information may also be transferred.

telephotography—Refers to the transmission of pictures over long distances by electrical means. Different from facsimile in the techniques used to scan and reproduce the picture.

teleprinter—The typewriter-like device at one end of a telegraph line. The term is generally used to refer to any printer-plus-keyboard device on any telecommunications link — which is more accurately referred to as a teletypewriter.

teleprocessing — This is a word that IBM invented to describe systems in which remote locations are connected to a central computer by data-transmission circuits — usually telephone lines. Some teleprocessing applications are data collection, teleconferencing, interactive time-sharing, and remote batch processing.

teletext—Teletext refers to the over-the-air broadcast systems, in which the viewer is actively involved in data selection, and Viewdata or Cabletext pertains specifically to the telephone and cable systems. The term "Prestel" belongs to the British Post Office, who chose that name after abandoning its first choice, the too-common "Viewdata." The name of BBC's system is "Ceefax" (see facts). Its twin, ORACLE, is an acronym for Optional Reception of Announcements by Coded Line Electronics. ORACLE is Britain's Independent Broadcasting Authority's service. Japan has used the name of CAPTAIN (Character and Pattern Telephone Access Information Network), while Canada's version is called Telidon, a combination of two Greek words meaning "I see at a distance." The French use 3 names —Titan, Didon, and Antiope—to refer to the various parts of their teletext/viewdata type of systems. Antiope, which also refers to the system as a whole, when translated, stands for "numerical analysis of text and information organized in written pages."

Teletype — Trademark of the Teletype Corporation. Usually refers to a series of different types of teleprinter equipment, such as transmitters, tape punches, reperforators, and page printers, that are utilized for communication systems.

teletypewriter controller — A teletypewriter controller is often incorporated on the same circuit board as the control-panel logic module; thus, it is usually available at no additional expense. This "minimum cost" interface is then operated under program control by the CPU to allow full-duplex communication with a single teletypewriter.

Telex—International network of teleprinter subscriber service; also, a domestic Western Union network.

temporary register (TEMP)—A typical 12-bit TEMP register latches the result of an ALU operation before it is sent to the destination register to avoid race conditions. The TEMP is also used as an internal register for microprogram control (some systems).

temporary storage area — A specific area of memory that has been set aside for data which is in a process of an intermediate state of computation, i.e., in the CPU (Central Processing Unit), such a storage area is often called "scratch-pad" memory.

terminal—1. A point of connection for two or more conductors in an electrical circuit. 2. A device attached to a conductor to facilitate connection with another conductor.

terminal area—In a printed circuit, the portion of the conductive pattern to which electrical connections are made.

terminal boards, customized — Many computer firms and other terminal manufacturers provide many different microprocessor and memory boards, for various businesses and industries, that are used to customize terminals. By using specific ROMs and RAMs and the different programs they contain, terminal functions can be changed or adjusted without redesigning the entire unit.

terminal character sets—The character sets that are available for use with a microcomputer terminal are both varied and many. Characters include alphabetic letters, symbols, and numerals. Letters may be all capitals

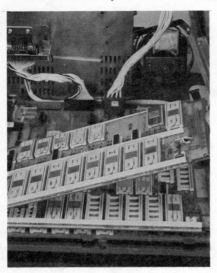

Terminal boards, customized (Courtesy NCR Corp.).

(upper case) or may include lower-case letters as well. Alternate character sets in different languages, such as Cyrillic (Slavic), Farsi (Arabic), or Katakana (Japanese), may also be available, as may be double-width and double-height characters.

terminal chromaticity coordinates — This refers to the ratio of each of the three tri-stimulus values of the color to their sum; thus defining a color quality by its coordinates.

terminal chromaticity diagram — This refers to a diagram in which any one of the three chromaticity coordinates is plotted against any other. Chromaticity of a color is thus plotted as a point.

terminal colorimetry — Refers to the measurement of colors in a manner that simulates the response of the human eye and which is based on a set of conventions.

terminal controller — 1. A typical data terminal controller incorporates the serial-to-parallel and parallel-to-serial conversion circuitry necessary to interface a local teletypewriter or RS-232C-compatible data terminal to a microcomputer. It contains a receiver and a transmitter which operate as independent input and output de-

vices. The receiver converts serial incoming data into parallel input data with parity, framing, and over-run error detection. The transmitter converts parallel output data into serial outgoing data complete with one start bit and either one or two stop bits. Parity generation and checking is a switch-selectable option; the controller is capable (typically) of generating and checking both even and odd parity. 2. The controller is a logic device; it directs all the tasks that the terminal must perform to convert an operation (a keystroke, perhaps) into a sequence of bits for transmission on the communications link. Depending on the particular terminal, the controller may be hard-wired and, thus, was fixed in its functions when the terminal was designed, or, it may be programmable so that its functions and tasks can be suited to a particular application. However, whether hard-wired or programmable, the terminal's controller must perform several basic operations. One of its simpler tasks is to handle the few signals that govern the input or output device. Here, the controller sends or receives signals to start up or shut down such devices as keyboards, card readers, crt screens, character and line printers, magnetic tape drives, magnetic cassettes, and punched-paper tape drives. A control signal also initiates the translation of data from human-readable form to machine-readable form, and vice versa.

terminal, data-operations — The data-line terminal transmits and receives data on a block-by-block basis, using synchronous transmission. A data block consists of data characters preceded by a start-of-block (SOB) character and followed by an end-of-block (EOB) and block parity (B/P) character. Transmission characters are 8-bits in length; 6 data bits, 1 control bit, and an odd-parity bit. Each block transmission is completely protected by both character and block parity. The block-parity character uses an even-parity check for each longitudinal bit level in the data block (some systems).

terminal, desktop microcomputer—This refers to the new type of compact, quick-access, low-cost, minidiskette-based microcomputers that are powerful enough to meet the specialized

*Terminal, desktop microcomputer
(Courtesy Wang Laboratories, Inc.).*

needs of engineers, laboratory technicians, and scientists, but which are flexible enough to meet the data-processing needs of students, accountants, business people, and administrators. One such device, the PCS-11 by Wang Laboratories, Inc., permits both first-time and experienced computer programmers to have a stand-alone computing capability located where the data generation takes place. Various data entry, retrieval, editing, and processing tasks can be performed by the Wang PCS-11. In addition, the available software supports a variety of scientific, technical, and business applications.

terminal diagnostic graphics—On some systems, the terminal contains a diagnostic self-test capability that can test all of the display-generation functions of the system. On one typical system, four sets of display-generation instructions are contained in ROM. Each set of instructions can be accessed either manually or by a microcomputer with just a single control instruction. The accessed set of diagnostic instructions is then executed by the display system to generate test displays.

terminal equipment types — There are three basic systems at present, the standard "dumb" and "smart" pre-programmed single-application configurations and the "intelligent" user-programmable visual-display terminal system. Most systems are based on a common microprocessor and a local memory of from 16K bytes to 96K bytes, which allows the prompting and validation of data as they are input, as well as off-line and on-line operation to a host computer. One typical line of terminals can use or be directly linked to a wide range of modules, which include 12 types of a keyboard, 4 microdisk subsystems, 12 types of a printer, 14 types of a display unit, and various other equipment, such as magnetic card readers. (All these modules are furnished in an attractive common style of packaging.) Typically, the linkage of peripherals is facilitated by an integral I/O interface with its own microprocessor and controller contained on a single chip. The "intelligent" terminals have RAM memory and, with the addition of a microdisk subsystem, become small computers with significant stand-alone capabilities. Some types offer Forms Definition Languages that apparently allow a relatively unskilled user to design and implement a program for his own requirements.

terminal, glass—Refers to a visual-display terminal with an electrostatic deflection-type display. The term sometimes refers to all video "glass" terminals. The displays of these terminals use either screen storage or memory-refreshed raster-scanning techniques to generate visuals.

terminal, intelligent—The heart of any intelligent terminal, its microprocessor, allows the terminal two basic operations that were previously impossible at the terminal level: the ability to make decisions based upon specific guidelines and the ability to perform calculations. The microprocessor allows the intelligent terminal to achieve a combination of rapid response and simplicity in design that was heretofore impossible. The unit's modularity allows it to meet a variety of user requirements, including control of other terminals and a buffering capability for communications interface with the host computer. In other words, more and more of the communications functions can be performed inside the terminal rather than by the CPU. Microprocessors are now being used in all functional areas of intelligent terminal design, including print mechanisms, carriage control, interface control, and maintenance testing. The more intelligence placed in the terminal, the less is required of the host computer. *See also* terminal programmability.

terminal interfaces—The Electronic Industries Association (EIA) has standardized connections, fixing the voltage levels, impedances, connector type, and pin assignments for the standard terminal interface. A similar standard has been prepared by the Consultive Committee on International Telegraphy and Telephony. Manufacturers often list under interfaces, on the terminal specification sheet, such comments as: "RS-232-C," "current loop," "20-mA current loop," "60-mA current loop," or any of a variety of computer/communications names. The RS-232-C interface, for example, specifies a 25-pin connector, of which only 13 pins are assigned definite functions. The 12 others are used, in whole or in part, by different terminal manufacturers for different (or nonstandard) functions. Also, RS-232-C doesn't provide for timing specifications.

terminal keyboards—This refers generally to two basic types—alphanumeric and numeric. Alphanumeric keyboards are typically used for word processing, text processing, data processing, and teleprocessing. Numeric-only keyboards are generally used on touch-tone telephones, accounting machines, and calculators. The touch-tone telephone keyboard has come into significant use as a calculator- and data-input and as a voice-output activated device.

terminal, microprocessor-controlled—The operating characteristics of "smart" terminals are controlled through firmware. The terminal's microprocessor manages memory allocation, data communications, keyboard scanning, and display control. This microprocessor implementation and the use of a single-bus architecture yields a terminal that utilizes electronics and mechanics for a wide range of capabilities and with a potential for future enhancements.

terminal/modem interface operations—Refers to the interfaces between the terminal and the modem. They contain not only digital data signals, but signals for controlling the modem and the data link. For example, when the line is turned around in half-duplex communication, the sending modem must be switched to the receiving condition, and the receiving modem often must be switched to the sending condition. A modem is switched from receive to send through an EIA interface by raising to a predetermined voltage level the control lead designated as "Request to Send." When the modem's "Clear to Send" status lead turns on, it is a signal to the computer or terminal that the modem is ready to transmit data over the data link.

terminal, multidrop—Multidrop refers to when it is possible to have a number of modems, with associated terminals, share or drop off one telephone line. This is distinct from multipoint, where each modem has its own data link with the central computer.

terminal programmability — Programmability is the key to the depth of a terminal's intelligence. Thus, in an intelligent terminal, the microcomputer controls a variety of functions to assist in text-editing and word-processing applications. For example, the keyboard is constructed such that, whenever a key is depressed, a ROM will output an 8-bit key code to the microcomputer as well as outputting an interrupt signal and, possibly, a character repeat signal. To change the key code or repeatability of a key, one simply reprograms the keyboard ROM. Once the key code has been received into the terminal, either a function will be performed or a symbol will be displayed. Any key can be programmed for any function and any key can display any symbol. This is all under user program control. *See also* terminal, intelligent.

terminals, addressable-pollable—A terminal is addressable when it has its own unique identifier. All data sent to the terminal must be preceded by their addresses. Pollable means that the terminal responds to status inquiries from the computer. Each terminal in the system is queried by the computer in succession. The ability of the terminal to respond to the poll and to identify itself is what makes it pollable.

terminals, daisy-chaining — Daisy-chaining is generally the same as multidropping, except that no modems are used; however, the terminals share the same data link. The data link comes from the computer, goes to the first terminal, comes out of the first terminal, and on to the second terminal, etc. All terminals share the same data link and the same computer port.

terminals, graphic — Graphic terminals are display systems with keyboard and/or graphics input devices (light pen, stylus) for the display and manipulation of graphic as well as alphanumeric images. Among the hardware features on some graphic terminals are image transformations in two or three dimensions; zooming and windowing on selected parts of the screen; function, vector, and character generators (circles, ellipses, rectangles, etc.); depth cueing (change in line intensity with depth); and perspective (nonparallel planes define the viewing space). Graphic terminals are often sold with the option of a color crt.

terminals, interactive—Refers to terminals that are generally equipped with a display, a keyboard, and an incremental printer. Optionally, they also include a tape subsystem. Such terminals support interactive, conversational, demand, inquiry, and transaction oriented applications.

terminal, speech-recognition—One of the many ways to implement speech recognition is to incorporate a speech-recognition board into a crt terminal. Many types of speech-recognition boards are specifically designed for crt terminals; they are microprocessor-based pc boards that transform the "dumb" terminal into a voice-identification, voice-actuated, video-display terminal. A noise-canceling microphone usually rounds out the system.

terminal storage, CCD—Some charge-coupled devices (CCDs) are organized as nonvolatile storage devices. A Read function from a CCD does not destroy data. This nondestructive read of the CCD tends to simplify its required I/O electronics. CCDs, however, are not random-access devices; they are serial-storage devices similar in function to the traditional delay line. Effectively operating as an extensive shift register, the CCD must cycle data through a Read point (or points) in order to access the desired stored information. While storage cost is attractively low, the associated

control electronics could easily become significant if any extensive attempt is made to compensate for the serial read characteristics.

terminated line—Refers to a transmission line with a resistance attached across its far end equal to the characteristic impedance of the line, so that there is no reflection and no standing waves when a signal is placed on it at the near end.

terminating—The closing of the circuit at either end of a line or transducer by connection of some device. Terminating does not imply any special condition, such as the elimination of reflection.

terminating symbol — A symbol on a tape that indicates the end of a block of information.

termination—1. The load connected to the output end of a transmission line. 2. The provisions for ending a transmission line and connecting to a bus bar or other terminating device. 3. A distributed network that provides a means of absorbing power incident upon it without any appreciable reflection, or provides a means of terminating a transmission line in its specific impedance.

test card, diagnostic—Refers to a special input/output test card that is used to completely test all I/O functions and the strappable operation configurations. The test card simulates both normal and direct-memory access (DMA) I/O controllers along with special-purpose test logic that allows a complete test of every I/O bus signal. In addition, the test card can provide connections to the power supply to test the Power Fail/Restart function, to the teletype controller to completely simulate a Teletype® machine, to the automatic loader switch to completely test the automatic loader, and to the other jumper option points to allow testing of every possible configuration.

test clips — Test clips offer power- and ground-seeking circuitry that eliminates the need to make separate connections from a power source to the clip. Some have buffered over-voltage protected inputs to prevent circuit loading or LED burnout. Some particular units, while larger in overall size, are connected to the unit under test via a 2-foot cable, allowing the readout section to be positioned without reference to the product under test. Some are also provided with 100 IC reference-schematic cards that can be inserted into the readout unit to aid in interpreting the display.

test data—Refers to a set of data developed specifically to test the adequacy of a computer run or system. The data may be actual data that have been taken from previous operations, or artificial data created for this purpose.

test equipment, microcomputer—Some of the equipment used for microcomputer testing includes the simulator, the in-circuit emulator, and the microsystem analyzer (also called logic analyzer or logic-state analyzer). The simulator is used in the development stage and is a special software program that simulates the logic operation of the microcomputer under development. It is useful for testing and debugging programs prior to committing them to ROM firmware.

tester, modem simulator—One type is able to inject random errors into both transmitted and/or received data. The modem simulator tests the error-recovery performance of any synchronous data-communications system. The unit interfaces with all EIA-compatible synchronous modems and data terminals. It simulates modems by providing clock timing to the data terminals. Error rate and noise density are switch selectable. The noise source is pseudo-random in nature for a precise, uniform, and controlled error rate.

testing, algorithmic pattern-generation—A test method that keeps CPU testing costs down, and can be used to test memories as well, is algorithmic pattern generation. A CPU usually contains an instruction set that specifies an operation in conjunction with an operand. Each instruction is well-defined, in the sense that an exact result can be expected after execution of an instruction over its existing operand. However, it is not always feasible to monitor the executed output of a single instruction. Instead, it may be necessary to execute a series of instructions before a user can monitor the output. Since users are especially interested in their own set of instructions, user-oriented testing of any

CPU can be reduced to verification of all instructions.

testing, comparison—A method for testing microprocessors is to check the difference between a good reference CPU and an unknown CPU; one technique uses two sets of drivers and detectors and two device sockets. The good reference device works with a RAM, ROM, etc. All input data to the reference microprocessor also goes to the unknown device as well. Outputs of the unknown device are compared with the good outputs of the reference device. If the unknown CPU output data matches the reference data, they are passed. One shortcoming of this technique is that the reference microprocessor must be of the highest quality. The test procedure cannot be executed at data rates any faster than that to which the reference microprocessor will respond to correctly. A similar design or masking flaw in both the reference and the unknown device will be undetected since both devices are alike. Real-time cycle-response testing is possible. Implementation is not difficult, chiefly because output data need not be stored in a memory for comparison.

testing, digital components—Signal sources having but one or two output channels often fall short of providing realistic test signals for complicated circuits. Providing stimuli for testing digital components and assemblies is primarily a multichannel affair. A mixture of binary data and pulse-type signals—address, data, clock, flag, enable, strobe, to name a few—usually is required. Because these signals are not always identical in form, digital device testing has generally required an array of interconnected pulse generators and digital pattern generators, or a dedicated automatic system.

testing digital logic circuits—The testability of many digital logic circuits is often a function of the complexity of the input stimulus to the unit under test. In the past, many combinatorial and sequential logics have been adequately exercised with pseudo-random-pattern generators or other repetitive input forms. As the state of the art in logic design progressed, so did the required complexity of the input stimulus. Today's logics are of an extremely complex nature. LSI and the trend toward microdesign have produced high-density logics in very small packages with all but a plurality of input nodes. Common port and bused systems, serialized logics, asynchronous clocks, programmed logic arrays, and ROM-based systems are good examples of difficult-to-test logics. A pseudo-random-pattern generator would have little effect on these systems, even if an input format could be established. Something more powerful is needed. By adding the control abilities of a specialized processor, tester manufacturers have accepted the challenges of the state-of-the-art testing.

testing, RAM—To test large RAM systems requires specialized test equipment. However, small memories embedded in a large circuit board may be easily tested by provision of some access for external controls, such as Read or Write. In the usual circuit implementation, a memory Read cycle forms a subcycle of a CPU instruction. Therefore, it may not be possible to exercise a Read cycle without going through all the motions. If it can be done without unbearable cost and long delay in the development cycle, providing pins for external Read and Write commands (data input and output) can be monitored by means of an IC clip. For dynamic MOS RAMs, refresh requirements present some degree of difficulty. The strategy here is to first thoroughly check out the refresh logic, then test the memory.

testing, saturation — This refers to the testing of a program by pushing through a great many messages in an attempt to find errors that happen infrequently.

testing, self-diagnostic—In the self-diagnostic method, some engineers use a ROM to load into CPU memory (RAM) a worst-case sequence of instructions. The CPU chip is placed within its intended operating environment, including interrupts from peripherals. The instruction set terminates at some identifiable error location. Error indication, usually identified by an instruction routine, shows if the unit fails or passes. Most small users of CPU chips use the self-diagnosis test method because it can be implemented easily with laboratory equipment, or with hardware and as-

sistance from the chip manufacturer. Some shortcomings are: multiple errors may negate each other and be undetected, or the actual cause of a failure may not be diagnosed. Also, without special hardware, external environment conditions, such as interrupts, cannot be tested under worst-case conditions.

testing, stored-response — Stored-response testing encompasses two test development methods and two pattern-generation techniques. Each method stores and executes user-written diagnostics quite differently. With stored-response, users keep an emulation or a simulation program in bulk memory (usually a disk) and, then, apply the program to the CPU under test to generate output data response. Users can simulate the sequence of operation of a CPU in conjunction with all peripheral devices, such as RAMs and ROMs. To do this requires a large RAM or PROM to store a predefined sequence of instructions associated with the appropriate data set. Simulated outputs can be sampled and their logic states identified at a defined sampling period.

test points, edge-connector—Provision for extra test points is very important. However, the points must be easily accessible if they are to be of value. Use of extra edge-connector pins to bring out the test points can minimize test time and simplify the test-fixture design. However, more thought should be given as to what constitutes a good test point. Each test point should be connected to an internal circuit node that can give the system an important clue to the nature of possible failures.

test programs and subroutines — Frequently used test-program segments can be coded once, either as macros or subroutines, and can then be permanently stored on a user-selected device. When generating a device test, these routines can be recalled by the user's test program, thus reducing test-generation time. Test program size is virtually unlimited as subroutines may call subroutines, in up to four levels of nesting, in some systems.

test programs, development system—Some test programs are just a set of self-test programs and diagnostics that verify that the hardware associated with the system is operating correctly. The programs are also helpful in isolating malfunctioning components. Typically, the program for testing the basic hardware is resident in EPROM and is activated by the keyboard TEST key (on some systems).

test programs, simulator and prototype—Design aids and test programs—such as simulators—are often necessary to track down the various subtle errors that appear. Similarly, hardware prototype units are essential to the development of final products. Prototype units generally involve expanded memory capability, teletypewriter or card-reader interface, power supply, chassis, and control panel—in addition to a microcomputer. Besides boosting initial development costs for the designer, the various wide ranges of hardware/software support have required a major investment by some semiconductor manufacturers. One indication of a vendor's seriousness in marketing a particular microprocessor is the availability of hardware/software support for the product.

test program system—A checking system used before running any problem, in which a sample problem of the same type, with a known answer, is run.

test set, in-circuit emulator—The in-circuit emulator is a diagnostic hardware/software test set used in a development system to test the operation of a developed microcomputer system, checking breakpoints and tracing the logical sequence of the completed system's operation. It is an advanced technique of debugging the microcomputer system. Included in some in-circuit emulators are additional options such as multiple in-circuit emulators to control and coordinate two microcomputer systems simultaneously, RS-232 interface capability for on-line testing, and front-panel PROM sockets that allow diagnostic programs to be plugged into the system.

tests, microprocessor — Currently, the primary major test categories available to the engineer are: the self-diagnostic method, the comparison method, algorithmic pattern generation, and stored-response testing.

test strobe—A clock that is independent of data patterns, that is provided to enable logic either in the device under test or in the system.

test transit time — The time required for the stimulus to get from the source to the device under test, for the response to get from the device under test to the detector, and for the detected information to get to the processor. Transit time determines how soon the tester knows whether the device under test passes or fails.

tetrad—A group of four, especially a group of four pulses used to express a digit in the scale of 10 or 16.

text editing—Refers to specific flexible editing facilities that have been designed into a computer program to permit the original keyboarding of textual copy without regard for the eventual format or medium for publication. Once the copy has been placed in computer storage, it can be edited and justified easily and quickly into any required column width and for any specified type font, merely by specifying the format required. Thus, copy for a report or journal can be keyboarded and edited, then justified and outputted directly onto a photocomposition device for publication of the document. If later, there is a request for a reprint in either the original or in an edited form, the computer can quickly produce output suitable for printing by any of several techniques.

text editor—A text editor provides the system user with a convenient and flexible source text-generation system. Source statements are entered via any source input device/file. The entered source text may be output, and statements added, deleted, or modified. The text editor permits the order of statements or groups of statements to be altered at any time. The final text is output to a source device/file for use as an input to an assembler.

text editor, microprocessor—A typical text editor provides facilities for editing a source program (usually assembly language) read in from an external device. The program is stored in an area of memory during the editing process and is written back out to an external device when editing is complete. The user can insert, delete, or replace lines in the text buffer. With a powerful editor, users can accomplish both line and character-oriented text preparation and editing. An advanced development aid removes the tedium from program preparation and alteration. Whether users choose to develop their software on large computers or on small microcomputers, software support can save time and money.

T flip-flop—Refers to a flip-flop having only one input. A pulse appearing on the input will cause the flip-flop to change states. Used in ripple counters.

thermal agitation—1. The movement of the free electrons in a material. In a conductor, they produce minute pulses of current. When these pulses occur at the input of a high-gain amplifier, in the conductors of a resonant circuit, the fluctuations are amplified together with the signal currents and are heard as noise. 2. Also called thermal effect. Minute voltages arising from random-electron motion.

thermal converter—The combination of a thermoelectric device (e.g., a thermocouple) and an electrical heater, thus converting an electrical quantity into heat, and into a voltage. Used in telemetering systems; also thermoelement.

thermal ionization — Ionization due to high temperature (e.g., in the electrically conducting gases of a flame).

thermal light—Refers to a display signal that is visible to a computer operator when the temperature in a piece of equipment is higher than it is supposed to be.

thermal noise — Refers to electromagnetic noise emitted from hot bodies. Sometimes called Johnson Noise.

thermal runaway — The effect arising when the current through a semiconductor creates sufficient heat for its temperature to rise above a critical value. The semiconductor has a negative temperature coefficient of resistance, so the current increases and the temperature increases again, resulting in ultimate destruction of the device. Also thermal catastrophe.

thermal shock — A specified abrupt temperature change applied to a device.

thermal shock test—This test acceler-ates the failure due to mechanical defects that may exist in a semiconductor. Particular emphasis is upon any microscopic fractures on the substrate, poor or weak lead bonds or welds, poor die attachment to the header, and improper seal of the metal cap to the header. This test can be done in several ways under varying conditions, but the test is usually performed by lowering the device into a liquid bath at 125 °C. After stabilization at this elevated temperature, the device is suddenly plunged into another liquid bath at −55 °C. This immersion can be repeated from two to ten times, duplicating in a very short period the stresses a component may experience over more than an ordinary lifetime.

thermionic conduction—Refers to that phenomenon which arises through electrons being liberated from hot bodies.

thermistor—1. A solid-state semiconducting device, the electrical resistance of which varies with the temperature. Its temperature coefficient of resistance is high, nonlinear, and negative. 2. A specific resistor whose temperature coefficient of resistance is unusually high. It is also nonlinear and negative. It is often made by sintering mixtures of oxide powders of various metals and, thus, is a solid-state semiconducting material, in many types of shapes such as disks, flakes, rods, etc., to which contact wires are attached. The resistance of the unit varies with temperature changes and, thus, it is a tester or sensor for temperature change.

thermocouple—1. Also called a thermal junction. A pair of dissimilar conductors joined together so that an electromotive force is developed by the thermoelectric effects when the two junctions at opposite ends are at different temperatures. 2. A specific device that usually has two wires composed of different metals and with the ends of both wires connected to each other to thus form a single loop with the property that if the two junctions are maintained at different temperatures, a difference of electric potential is developed, which is equally divided between the two junctions, and is calibrated with a meter inserted in the loop. Used to measure temperature and current.

thermoelectric effect—The electromotive force produced by the difference in temperature between two junctions of dissimilar metals in the same circuit.

thick film—1. Refers to a method in the manufacturing of integrated circuits, where thin layers of materials are deposited on an insulated substrate (often ceramic) to perform electrical functions; usually only passive elements are made this way. 2. A process employing screen printing of conductive or resistive pastes, and the subsequent firing in a furnace to create conductors, resistors, and capacitors on a ceramic substrate. 3. A technology that uses pastes to form conductor, resistor, and insulator patterns; usually screened onto the substrate and cured by firing at temperatures of 800 °C to 900 °C. While less expensive than thin films, thick-film resistors exhibit somewhat poorer matching and temperature coefficients.

thick film, laser trimming — Trimming plays an essential role in the manufacture of thick-film resistor networks. The process used to define circuit elements on a substrate, based on silk-screening techniques, is fast and inexpensive and has greatly increased the volume of manufactured devices. Trimming each resistor enables them to overcome the inherent limitations of the screening process and increase their yields of accurate and reliable devices. The laser has become an effective tool for trimming resistors because it is fast as well as accurate and it can be controlled in order to produce consistent results.

thick-film resistor chips—Resistor chips are available as thick-film, thin-film, and bulk-metal devices. Designers are probably more familiar with the characteristics and performance of thick- and thin-film resistors than they are with chip capacitors because of the rather extensive use of thick- and thin-film resistor networks in today's electronic equipment. However, this may not be true for bulk-metal chip resistors, generally used only in applications requiring very special performance. Film resistors are formed by depositing a film of conducting material on a nonconducting substrate. By definition, a thick-film resistor is one in which the conducting material is greater than one-millionth of an inch thick.

thick-film resistors, circular—By laser trimming a circular design for thick-film resistors, manufacturers of hybrid circuits can obtain an unusual range of resistor values from any off-the-shelf ink. The circular design provides trim factors—the ratio of as-fired resistance to trimmed resistance —in excess of 1000. In the new design, a round resistor pattern is placed on a ceramic substrate. The pattern interconnects at the center and at the circumference. A dielectric layer separates the center conductor from other parts of the resistor pattern. The appropriate resistor value is selected by laser trimming the thick-film pattern in a spiral outwards from the center.

thick-film technology—1. A technology whereby electronic circuits or elements are formed by applying a liquid, solid, or paste coating, through a screen or mask in a selective pattern, onto a supporting material. This technology also includes films deposited by any other means when the films so formed are 5 micrometers or greater in thickness. 2. Thick-film technology provides a microminiaturization fabrication technique that uses printed conductive paths slightly larger than a human hair. Because thick film lends itself to batch processing, it helps to meet the increasing demand for communication equipment.

thick-film thermal printheads — Solid-state thick-film thermal printheads, that incorporate all circuitry on the substrate, display dramatic improvements in printhead reliability and print quality. Printheads using this technology can be supplied with single-element print widths up to 10 inches (25 cm), can achieve line speeds of 2 ms, and can increase dot density to 8 dots/mm. Both graphics and alphanumerics can be produced with the same head.

Significant improvements in the thick-film and ceramic technologies used in the printheads, coupled with the mounting of all required circuitry directly on the substrate, are responsible for the improvements. The construction technique, as well as the elimination of external drivers, diode matrices, shift registers, and associated cabling, improves reliability and head life.

thick-film/thin-film fabrication — *See* thin-film fabrication.

thick-film/thin-film hybrid fabrication— To form resistors, a resist and etching process is used to remove the gold substrate overlay and the nickel-chromium alloy that is sublimated on the substrate. (*See* thin-film fabrication.) The exposed nickel/chromium alloy then functions as resistors. The entire substrate is heated to 350 °C to stabilize these resistors. The resistors can then be laser- or air-abrasive-trimmed to specific values. Following resistor trimming, selective photoresist masking and copper plating form the ground plane and circuit pads for attaching connector wires. A chassis is used that has the same thermal expansion coefficient as the substrate. This eliminates mechanical stress from differential expansion and contraction. After the patterned substrate is X-rayed to make sure there are no voids in critical electrical areas, the entire module is thoroughly cleaned and vapor-degreased to remove foreign materials. The substrate is now ready for the components — capacitors, inductors, transistors, etc., which are bonded to the substrate with gold epoxy and cured at 125 °C. One important difference between the fabrication of thick-film and thin-film hybrids is the way wires and beam-lead parts are attached to the gold-conductor pattern. For thick-film hybrids, hybrid packagers often use pulse-tip thermocompression.

thick-film/thin-film printing — In hybrid modules, users can make interconnections with the same flexibility as on a card. Most variations that apply to pc cards have their counterparts in hybrid-substrate design and fabrication. Many can use single or multilayer substrates. Users can lay down a circuit's conductor pattern in two ways: with thick- or thin-film "printing." Thick-film paste-printing is simpler and cheaper. Thick-film hybrids allow a wider range of resistor values than do thin-films; they also handle higher currents. Generally, the thick film is made of a conductive, resistive, or insulating material laid down in a pattern that is thicker than 20,000 angstroms (1 Å = 10^{-8} cm). Thick

films are usually associated with hybrid integrated circuits.

Thick films are better for relatively "low-frequency" applications (less than 1 GHz), whereas, the more precise line widths and circuit elements that users can make with thin-film printing are necessary for higher radio-frequency applications. Thick-film hybrid applications are mostly in input/output and interfacing circuits and in power supplies, where the modules perform such functions as amplification, buffering, demodulation, phase detection, and a/d or d/a conversion.

thin film — 1. Having to do with the branch of microelectronics in which thin layers of material are deposited on an insulating base (in a vacuum). 2. Refers to a layer of material that is of (or approximate to) mono-molecular thickness and is laid down by vacuum deposition. Many types of electronic components and complete microcircuits can be produced in this way. 3. A process used to create conductors, resistors, and capacitors on a ceramic or glass substrate. Techniques used are diffusion and evaporation of metals onto the substrate, resulting in very thin deposits (when compared to thick film). 4. A metal film used to fabricate conductors and resistors, usually a few hundred angstroms thick. Some commonly used resistor materials are nickel-chromium, tantalum nitride, and silicon-chromium. These films are usually deposited using sputtering, vacuum evaporation, or electron-beam techniques.

thin-film capacitors — Refers to a type of capacitor constructed by the evaporation of two conducting layers and an intermediary dielectric film (e.g., silicon monoxide) on an insulating substrate.

thin-film fabrication — The difference between thick-film and thin-film technology is basic. Thick film is an additive process with microcircuits built up through several applications of thixotropic paste. But, thin film is subtractive; metal placed on the substrate is etched away until the conductor pattern and other circuit elements are formed.

Thin-film fabrication begins with several tiny holes drilled into the alumina substrate. Eventually, these holes are conductively coated to provide an electrical ground to the module chassis. After drilling, the substrate is washed in high-purity water. Then, thin layers of metal are deposited on the substrate in several successive steps — evaporization, sputtering, and electroplating. First, a nickel-chromium alloy is sublimated (evaporated) onto the circuit side of the substrate (in a vacuum chamber). Rods of nickel-chromium alloy, heated to a temperature just short of melting, cause metal molecules to vaporize and drift up against the substrate. If the substrate is to have resistors, then the resistivity of the alloy deposit is controlled. Nickel and, then, gold are evaporated onto the substrate. The nickel serves as a barrier between the nickel-chromium alloy and the gold. Nickel and gold pellets are melted to liquids within the chamber by electron beams. The liquids then evaporate and condense on the substrate, where they solidify as 2000-Å films. Next, a film of nickel-chromium, followed by a film of gold, is deposited to the back of the substrate, or ground plane. This metal deposition is done by sputtering in a vacuum chamber filled with argon gas, which is excited by a strong rf voltage. Excited argon ions strike a disc of metal and dislodge tiny metallic particles, which then strike the substrate hard enough to stick in place. The particles adhere not only to the flat surface but also to the edges and the insides of the pre-drilled holes in the substrate. The alloy deposit is 400 Å thick, and the gold, 200 Å thick.

Finally, a thin layer of gold about 200 μinch thick is electroplated to both sides of the substrate. The next steps involve etching away the deposition to create the circuitry. But to prepare for etching, a photosensitive resist material, applied to the substrate with an eyedropper, must be spun to remove the excess material. An opaque circuit pattern of the film mask, that is placed over the resist and exposed via a mercury-vapor light, defines the metal to be removed. The light shining through the clear spaces defines the metal to be left. After developing and washing the resist, unwanted gold is easily etched away with chemicals. Selective etchants dissolve the gold, nickel, and nickel-chromium individually. The gold that remains serves as the conductor pattern (some systems).

One important difference between the fabrication of thick-film and thin-film hybrids is the way the wires and beam-lead parts are attached to the gold-conductor pattern. For thick-film hybrids, hybrid packagers often use pulse-tip thermocompression.

thin-film integrated circuitry — Also called two-dimensional circuitry. This refers to microminiature circuitry produced on a passive substrate. Terminals, interconnections, resistors, and capacitors are formed by depositing a thin film of various materials on a substrate. Microsize active components are then inserted separately to complete the circuit. The term "thin film" is used to imply an approximate film thickness of 1μ or less, as compared with the larger geometry and thicker films associated with hybrid integrated circuits.

thin-film magnetic module—A thin-film magnetic module is made by the deposition of magnetic alloys, in a vacuum and under the influence of a high magnetic field, on planes of glass so thin that the direction of their magnetic fields can be switched within several billionths of a second (nanoseconds). This feature allows information to be stored or retrieved at extremely high speeds. The immediate benefits derived from this procedure include savings in processing time, reduced power requirements, and miniaturized storage units.

thin-film memory—Refers to a storage device made of thin discs of magnetic material deposited on a nonmagnetic base. Its operation is similar to a core memory. (*Also see* storage and core memory.)

thin-film microelectronics — Circuits made up of two-dimensional active elements that are mounted or deposited on thin wafers of an insulating substrate material.

thin-film printing—*See* thick-film/thin-film printing.

thin-film processing — The basics of thin- and thick-film processing are quite different. Thin-film processes are critically important to the reliability of integrated circuits, and the IC designer must be aware of the limitations of the materials used (for example, electromigration in aluminum conductors) and the problems that can result in processing (for example, reduction in aluminum thickness at oxide steps). Thick-film technology, however, is only appropriate with hybrid circuits.

thin-film recording heads — Thin-film recording heads and the associated plated media allow dramatic density increases. Thin-film heads allow the resolution of much more closely packed data. This is because the air gap of a recording head can be made much smaller by photolithographic techniques than is possible when the heads are made by hand. Photolithography allows the heads to be made at lower cost, which brings the technology into the reach of many users.

The thin-film techniques used by one firm for its heads are very similar to those used for semiconductor manufacturing. The main difference is that the integrated head is made entirely using a single–bell-jar process. Thus, there is relatively little contamination and a high yield—better than 85%. The heads, 912 per substrate, are made of 100 masked layers of copper, quartz, and an alloy of iron, nickel, and chromium. The copper is used for the inductive coil, the quartz serves as an insulator, and the ferronickel alloy makes up the magnetic circuit, replacing the ferrite body of conventional recording heads. The final thickness of such a head, with 20 turns in the coil, is a mere 10 micrometers. The heads are then coated with glass to strengthen them mechanically.

thin-film resistor chips—A thin-film resistor is, by definition, one with conductive material that is less than one-millionth of an inch thick. Thin-film chip resistors provide significantly better performance than the thick-film types but, obviously, at a higher cost. Their resistance range is very limited compared to that of thick-film chips, typically running from 10Ω to about 300K. Higher values are available usually only on request.

thin-film resistors—A modern high-stability resistor formed by a conducting layer that is a few hundred angstrom thick (on an insulating substrate).

thin-film technology — A technology whereby electronic circuits or elements are formed by vacuum depositing or sputtering films onto a sup-porting material. This technology also includes electrochemical deposition, pyrolytic deposition, vapor decomposition, and similar techniques, when the films so formed are less than 5 micrometers in thickness.

3-D display, retinal image—A 3-D image is actually a "retinal" image containing up to 6 depth cues—even though it is seen on a conventional X-Y monitor or display instrument. A "retinal" image is the same image that the lens of the eye projects onto the retina of the eye. This type 3-D display "system" is a purely analog system using proprietary signal processing to create the "retinal" image. It produces a true 3-D image in real time and is compatible with either analog or digital systems. The 3-D "system" produces higher-quality images for much less cost than any digital systems using either hardware or software to generate 3-D images. Advantages of the "system," when used in a digital system, include relieving the digital computer from doing coordinate transformation, hidden-line-solution perspective generation, etc., much faster image manipulation and no additional digital requirements since the 3-D "system" utilizes the existing recirculating memory and digital-to-analog converters that must exist in any digital display system. The 3-D "system" fits in between the DAC outputs and the deflection inputs of the X-Y display.

three-state logic — A logic family that may be in one of three states rather than the usual two—high, low, or high impedance. In the high impedance state, output voltage is unaltered. Logic in a high impedance state may be easily and permanently connected to a bus.

throughput — 1. Relates to the speed with which problems, programs, or segments are performed. Throughput can vary from application to application, as well as from one piece of equipment to another, even though they are of the same brand or even the same model. 2. The total useful information processed or communicated during a specified time period.

thyristor — Thyristors are electronic switching devices requiring quick pulses of control current to activate them. When the pulse current ceases, the thyristor continues to operate. In effect, thyristors are switches, the two most important of which are silicon-controlled rectifiers (SCRs) and triacs. Formed from alternate layers of P and N materials, thyristors behave like conventional rectifiers, in the presence of current passing in the reverse direction, and as a combination switch and rectifier to current that is passing in the forward direction. Current conduction in the forward direction is controlled by an electrode called the gate.

time constant of integrator — For each input, the ratio of the inputs to the corresponding time rate of change of the output.

time, cycle — Refers to the minimum nonoverlapping time interval between successive accesses to one storage location. Cycle time, typically between 0.5 and 2 μs, is one parameter that allows comparison of speeds. Because other factors, such as instruction set and cycles/instruction, affect computer speed, benchmark programs similar to the required application program should be used to compare speeds.

time-delay circuit—A circuit that delays the transmission of an impulse signal, or the performance of a transducer, for a definite desired length of time.

time discriminator—Refers to a type of signal that is proportional to the time difference between two pulses, its polarity reversing if the pulses are interchanged.

time-division multiplexer (TDM)—A device or process that transmits two or more signals over a common path by using successive time intervals for different signals.

time-division multiplexing, intelligent— *See* statistical multiplexing.

time-pulse distributor—Refers to a device or circuit used for allocating timing pulses or clock pulses to one or more conducting paths or control lines in a specified sequence.

timer, internal — An electronic timer which facilitates monitoring or logging events at predetermined intervals.

time, response — The amount of time that elapses between generation of an inquiry at a terminal and the receipt of a response at the terminal. Response time would be: transmis-

sion time to the computer, processing time at the computer, access time to obtain any file records needed to answer the inquiry, and transmission time back to the terminal.

timer, sequence—A succession of time-delay circuits arranged so that completion of the delay in one circuit initiates a delay in the following circuit.

time-schedule controller — Refers to a specific controller in which the reference input signal (or the set point) adheres automatically to a predetermined time schedule.

time series—Refers to the discrete or continuous sequence of quantitative data assigned to specific moments in time, usually studied with respect to their distribution in time.

time-shared BASIC — Time-shared BASIC is a conversational language designed to provide easy access to computers for the maximum number of people. It is especially useful in management and education where ease of access is important. It is an enhancement of the original BASIC.

time-shared computer utility — Generally, refers to the special computational ability of time-shared computer systems. Programs as well as data may be made available to the user. The user also may have his own programs immediately available to the central processor, may have them on call at the computer utility, or may load them by transmitting them to the computer prior to using them. Certain data and programs are shared by all users of the service; other data and programs, because of proprietary nature, have restricted access. Computer utilities are generally accessed by means of data-communication subsystems.

time-shared system—A system in which available central computer time is shared among several jobs as directed by a scheduling plan or formula.

time-sharing — 1. A computing technique by which more than one terminal device can use the input, processing, and output facilities of a central computer simultaneously. 2. A specific method of operation in which a computer facility is shared by several users for different purposes at (apparently) the same time. Although the computer actually services each user in sequence, the high speed of the computer makes it appear that the users are all handled simultaneously. 3. The use of a device for two or more purposes during the same overall time interval, accomplished by interspersing the computer component actions in time.

time-sharing, conversational — The simultaneous utilization of a computer system by multiple users at remote locations, each being equipped with a remote terminal. The user and the computer usually communicate by way of a higher-level, easy-to-learn computer language.

time slice—Refers to a designed interval of time during which a job can use a resource without being preempted.

time slicing—1. Refers to a feature that can be used to prevent a task from monopolizing the central processing unit and, thereby, delaying the assignment of CPU time to other tasks. 2. In systems with time-sharing, the allocation of time slices to terminal jobs.

timing analyzer—Timing analyzers have an internal clock that allows both synchronous and asynchronous recording. Logic-state analyzers do not have a clock and rely upon external signals to control recording operations. General-purpose analyzer instruments combine the capabilities of both instruments.

timing generator — A time-base reference programmed to operate with the drivers and comparators that define critical timing edges. Delay, width, and rise and fall times are generally the most important timing parameters.

timing master—1. Refers to the primary source of timing signals used to control the timing pulses. 2. The electronic or electric source of standard timing signals, often called "clock pulses" required for sequencing computer operation. This source usually consists of a timing pulse generator, a cycling unit, and sets of special pulses that occur at given intervals of time. In synchronous computers, the basic time frequency employed is usually the frequency of the clock pulses.

timing, microprocessor—Microprocessor timing and clock-generation methods affect the system, because instruction times are based on maximum clock frequencies and cycle times. Users may have to select a lower-frequency clock to optimize some system considerations, such as memory-access time or clock-generator synchronization with external timing.

timing signals — Electrical pulses sent throughout various machines at regular intervals to ensure absolute synchronization.

titanium (Ti)—At. no. 22, at. wt. 47.90, sp. gr. 4.5, m.p. 1850 °C. A metallic element resembling iron, sometimes used for the solid horns of magnetostrictive generators.

toggle—1. Operation of a bistable trigger circuit (a multivibrator with coupling capacitors omitted) which switches between two stable states depending on which vacuum tube (or transistor) is triggered. 2. A flip-flop. 3. Pertaining to a manually operated on-off switch, i.e., a two-position switch. 4. Pertaining to flip-flop, seesaw, or bistable action.

toggle switch—1. A two-position snap switch operated by a projecting lever and used to open or close circuits. 2. A manually operated electric switch, with a small projecting knob or arm that may be placed in either of two positions (on or off) and will remain in that position until changed. 3. An electronically operated circuit that holds either of two states until changed.

tolerance—A permissible deviation from a specified value. A frequency tolerance is expressed in cycles or as a percentage of the nominal frequency; an orientation tolerance, in minutes of arc; a temperature tolerance, in degrees Celsius, and a dimensional tolerance, in decimals or fractions.

tomography, computerized—Refers to the process of obtaining the density distribution within a human body from multiple X-ray projections.

topology, microcircuit — The surface layout design study and characterization of a microcircuit. It has application chiefly in the preparation of the artwork for layout masks that are used in fabrication.

torr—One torr is the equivalent of one millimeter, or 1/760 of atmospheric pressure. *See* vacuum measurement.

touch tablet—An on-screen cursor can be positioned by an easy-to-use "touch tablet." This finger-operated pointing device is used to select and manipulate items on the crt display. As the user moves his finger on the surface of the small rectangular tablet, the cursor moves to track the position of the finger. The mechanism is simple, reliable, and easy to operate. (*See also* definition for trackball, manually operated.)

Townsend avalanche — Multiplication process whereby a single charged particle, accelerated by a strong field, causes, through collision, a considerable increase in ionized particles.

Townsend criterion — The relationship expressing the minimum requirement for breakdown in terms of the ionization coefficients.

Townsend ionization coefficient — The average number of ionizing collisions made by an electron as it drifts a unit distance in the direction of an applied electric force.

trace—1. Refers to an interpretive diagnostic technique which provides an analysis of each executed instruction and writes it on an output device as each instruction is executed. 2. Software that is used for extremely detailed testing of the validity of an applications program or other software.

trace program—Pertains to a trace or diagnostic program used to perform a desired check on another program and which may include instructions as its output, and the intermediate results of those instructions can be arranged in the order in which the instructions are executed. When such a trace program is an interpretive type, it is called an interpretive trace program.

trace, selective — Refers to a tracing routine wherein only instructions satisfying certain specified criteria are subject to tracing. Typical criteria are: (1) instruction type, e.g., arithmetic, jump, or other specific types, (2) instruction location, i.e., a specific region of storage, (3) data location, i.e., a specific region of storage. For criteria case 2, when tracing is performed on transfer or jump instructions, the term logical trace is sometimes used.

trace trap—Trace traps are enabled, on some systems, by a specific bit of the program status word (PSW), and cause processor traps at the end of instruction execution. The instruction that is executed, after the instruction that set the specific trap bit, will proceed to completion and will then trap through the trap vector at another specific address (on various systems). Generally, the trace trap is a system debugging aid and is transparent to the general programmer.

tracing — An interpretive diagnostic technique to record on an output device the execution of each instruction and its results. This technique provides a record of each processed instruction by the recording of all instructions, operands, and results for analysis of the computer run.

tracing, interpretive—Such routines interpret rather than execute directly each instruction in either source language or machine code. The program is simulated in its execution by using accumulators and pseudo index registers which are not identical to the accumulators and registers used by the tracing program; thus, control does not pass from the tracing program to the program which is being traced when a branch instruction is encountered.

tracing routine—Refers to one of many diagnostic routines used to provide a time history of one or more machine registers and controls during the execution of the object routine. A complete tracing routine would reveal the status of all registers and locations affected by each instruction each time the instruction is executed. Since such a trace is prohibitive in machine time, traces which provide information only following the execution of certain types of instructions are more frequently used. Furthermore, a tracing routine may be under control of the processor, or may be called in by means of a trapping feature. Related to trap.

track—1. A sequence of binary cells arranged so that data may be read or written from one cell at a time in serial fashion; for example, a track on a magnetic drum is a path 1-bit wide around the circumference of the drum. 2. In electronic computers, that portion of a moving-type storage medium that is accessible to a given reading station (e.g., film, drum, tapes, disks).

trackball — A ball mounted in a box equipped with position sensors. A trackball does not move the cursor in direct proportion to its position, but instead it transports the cursor in proportion to the speed at which it is rolled and in the direction of its rotation. This method of operation enables a cursor to be precisely positioned because the speed of rotation can easily approach zero. However, by rotating the ball rapidly, the cursor can be moved fast, so as not to cause undue delay.

trackball, manually operated—A manually operated trackball or data tablet provides a means of operator interaction with the displayed images and graphics overlays. This device allows the operator to position the movable target to any location in the display format. The X-Y coordinates of the target location are then available through the standard computer interface. Additional interactive functions that can be performed by a trackball include outlining areas of interest, controlling enhancement algorithms, positioning alphanumeric notations, and defining vectors.

track, primary—On a direct-access device, the original track on which data are stored.

tracks, floppy-disk — The information stored on a diskette surface is organized in concentric tracks. Each track consists of a continuous string of sectors, each of which contains a group of bytes comprising one record of data. Data are recorded in a sector on a bit-serial basis. Bits of information to be stored are first encoded, then recorded in a specific sector. The user's system will, however, determine the particular data-encoding scheme to be used for data storage, depending on the type of recording medium and the bandwidth limitations of the Read channel. The term "information" refers to any sequence of flux transitions written on the diskette consistent with the data-encoding scheme employed by the user.

trailer—1. A record that follows a group of detail records and gives information about a group not present in the detail records. 2. A record that follows a header.

trailer label—The end-of-tape file record that lists summary information concerning that file.

transceiver—1. The combination of radio transmitting and receiving equipment in a common housing, usually for portable or mobile use and employing some common circuit components for both transmitting and receiving. 2. A terminal device that can both transmit and receive signals.

transcribe — To copy, with or without translating, from one external storage medium of a microcomputer to another.

transducer — 1. A device by means of which energy can be made to flow from one or more transmission systems to one or more other transmission systems. The energy may be in any form, such as electrical, mechanical, acoustical, etc. The term "transducer" is often restricted to a device in which the magnitude of an applied stimulus is converted into an electrical signal proportionate to the quantity of the stimulus. Usually, the variations of the phenomenon being measured are referenced to time. 2. An energy converter used to convert one form of energy to another.

transducer devices—Refers to specific elements or devices which have the capability of receiving information in the form of one physical quantity and converting it to information in the form of the same or other physical quantities. This particularly relates to specific cases of devices such as primary elements, signal transducers, and various transmitters.

transducer, expandor—Refers to a specific transducer designed for a given amplitude range of input voltages and which produces a larger range of output voltages. One important type of expandor employs the information from the envelope of speech signals to expand their volume range. Compare with compandor.

transducer, incremental — Refers to a rotary or linear feedback device with discrete on-off pulses. All pulses are the same, and there is always the same number of signals per unit length or per revolution. Direction is determined by special logic circuits.

transfer—1. To transmit, or copy, information from one device to another. 2. To jump. 3. The act of transferring. 4. In electrostatography, the act of moving a developed image, or a portion thereof, from one surface to another without altering its geometrical configuration (e.g., by electrostatic forces or by contact with an adhesive-coated surface).

transfer check—1. Refers to a verification of transmitted data by temporarily storing, retransmitting, and comparing. Also, a check to see if the transfer or jump instruction was properly performed. 2. A check which verifies that information is transferred correctly from one place to another. It is usually done by comparing each character with a copy of the same character transferred at a different time or by a different route.

transfer circuit—A circuit that connects communication centers of two or more separate networks in order to transfer the traffic between the networks.

transfer command—A particular order or instruction that changes control from one part of the program to another part by indicating a remote instruction.

transfer, conditional — 1. Refers to a transfer which occurs only when a certain condition exists at the time the transfer instruction is executed. 2. An instruction which interrupts the normal process of obtaining the instructions in a normal-ordered sequence and specifies a different address if certain programmed conditions occur.

transfer operations—Refers to descriptions of the data path, including terminal, adapter or "modem," and transmission line, and the maximum rate at which they can transfer information. Transmission capability is not the same as the net rate at which information is transferred; there is always an overhead. The maximum information transfer rate is expressed in bits per second (bps). (A bit is a binary digit, the smallest unit of information.) A more meaningful, but less used measure is the transfer rate of information bits (TRIB), which excludes all overhead. Another descriptor commonly used is baud, the number of state changes per second. There are multiple states, thus, each state can represent more than one bit; therefore, the bps is greater than or equal to the baud. For example, a transmission line capable of supporting four states has a bps rate twice its baud rate since each state represents two bits.

transfer table vector—Refers to a specific table that contains a list of transfer instructions of all the programs that are in main memory which enables transfer of control to be made from one program to another program.

transfer time—1. The time required for a transfer to be made in a digital computer. 2. In a relay, the total time (after contact bounce has ceased) between the breaking of one set of contacts and the making of another.

transform—1. To convert a current from one magnitude to another, or from one type to another. 2. In digital computer programming, to change information in structure or composition without significantly altering the meaning or value at the same time. 3. To derive a new body of data from a given one, according to specific procedures, often leaving some feature invariant. Related to translate.

transformation, graphics — The ability to modify a display image by scaling, displacement, and/or rotation.

transformer — 1. An electrical device which, by electromagnetic induction, transforms electric energy from one or more circuits to one or more other circuits at the same frequency, but usually at a different voltage and current value. 2. A component made up of two or more coils wound around the same core.

transient — 1. The instantaneous surge of voltage or current produced by a change from one steady-state condition to another. 2. A phenomenon caused in a system by a sudden change in conditions, and which persists for a relatively short time after the change. 3. A physical disturbance, intermediate to two steady-state conditions. 4. Pertaining to rapid change. 5. A build-up or breakdown in the intensity of a phenomenon until a steady-state condition is reached. The time rate of change in energy is finite and some form of energy storage is usually involved.

transient analyzer — An electronic device for repeatedly producing a succession of equal electric surges of small amplitude and of adjustable waveform in a test circuit and presenting this waveform on the screen of an oscilloscope.

transient area — The space in memory available for user programs and system utilities.

transients, power—Transients are very short duration, high-amplitude pulses. Transients are probably the most common type of "power problem." They exist in all power systems. In some large cities, recent measurements show transients that ranged between 50 and 1000 volts. These impulses are very damaging to integrated circuits. Transients have a tendency to inject both short- and long-term failures into equipment. If users have a system that is "broken" all the time, they could be a victim of undetected transients. Transients may also be generated by improper grounding. A good, solid, computer-grade, single-point ground is a *must* for reliable system operation.

transient voltage suppressor—Besides grounding personnel and equipment, other power devices can be installed on power lines to protect equipment from data loss. One such device is a transient voltage suppressor, a shunt device connected across a power input line to keep the voltage from exceeding a preset level. The transient voltage suppressor can do a better job of suppressing voltage transients than an isolation transformer can because the voltage suppressor dissipates any overvoltage as heat, whereas an isolation transformer usually shunts the overvoltage to chassis ground. This means the energy isn't really dissipated and so it can pop up somewhere else in the system.

transient voltage suppressors, shunt type—Shunt devices, installed across power distribution lines, conduct small leakage current as long as the voltage across it remains below a preset level. When voltage exceeds the clamping level, the device conducts sufficient current to hold the voltage at the clamping level. Developed with silicon pn junction technology, some units are coupled with heavy-duty crowbar circuits to handle extended overvoltage conditions on the ac power system.

transistor—A device made by attaching three or more wires to a small wafer of semiconducting material (a single crystal which has been specially treated so that its properties are different at the point where each wire is attached). The three wires are usually called the emitter, base, and collector. They perform functions somewhat similar to those of the cathode, grid, and plate of a vacuum tube, respectively.

transistor action—The physical mechanism of amplification in a junction transistor.

transistor evolution, APN—Amorphous semiconductor material has found increasing use in the field of semiconductors. Developed first as an electrical switching device, amorphous semiconductor material was then used in thermal-scribed imaging systems, such as solid-state printing. Next, amorphous material found its way into memory storage and, subsequently, into erasable ROM integrated circuits. A most recent amorphous semiconductor advance surfaced when magnetic bubbles were observed by IBM in amorphous thin-film alloys. Since the amorphous emitter transistor offers three output levels, such a component could form the basis of a ternary, or three-level, logic system. This compares to the binary (zero or one) logic system presently used.

transistor flip-flop circuit principles—The most basic of flip-flop circuits consists of two transistors, connected to each other in such a way that when one transistor is cut off, the other conducts. When the flip-flop changes state, the cut-off transistor conducts and the conducting one is cut off. Flip-flops can be made up of two gate circuits connected back-to-back. If the output of the first gate is high (transistor is cut off), it will cause the other gate to turn on (conduct). The "on" gate has a low output, which, connected to the first gate, forces it to maintain its high output; thus, a "locked up" stable condition is obtained. By applying a negative-going signal simultaneously to the second input of each gate, the "on" transistor is turned off, but the "off" transistor is turned on by the fact that it is being fed by a high signal that persists longer because of the RC time constant of the emitter-to-base connection. Thus, the state of the flip-flop has been reversed.

Since the flip-flop is affected only by the negative-going part of the signal, it takes two such signals to change and, then, restore the flip-flop to the original state. In effect, this divides the number of input signals by two. Connecting several flip-flops in series provides a binary-counter chain. In addition to the basic flip-flop described above, there are variations that are triggered by applying a pulse to both emitters, both collectors, or both bases. The trigger pulse may be coupled by means of diodes, capacitors, and/or resistors.

transistorized—Pertaining to equipment or a design in which transistors instead of vacuum tubes are used.

transistor seconds — Also called fallouts. Those transistors that remain after the firsts (units meeting rigid specifications for a specific application) have been removed from the production process.

transistor-transistor logic (TTL)—This is the most common form of IC logic. As a result, the relatively simple process used to produce TTL logic is a natural candidate for memory fabrication, especially since most memories are used with TTL logic. However, the TTL approach—even though the simplest bipolar process—is considerably more complicated and expensive than MOS. Since n-channel MOS devices can now be made as fast in performance as TTL bipolar devices, the importance of the TTL process to the memory market is limited. It will vie with CMOS for those applications represented by small memories of around 256 bits per chip, commonly intermixed with computer logic (distributed memory). The only advantage of both CMOS and TTL in these applications is their 100% compatibility with the logic (i.e., power supplies and signal levels). Of course, n-channel memories can also be made logic compatible at lower-speed (2 to 3 MHz) operations. Slightly larger memories can bear the cost of having less than 100% compatibility, so the lower cost of n-channel will displace TTL CMOS in all but the smallest memories.

transition—The change from one circuit condition to the other—specifically, from mark to space, or space to mark.

transition card — A card which signals the computer that the reading-in of a program has ended and that the carrying out of the program has started.

transition point—A point at which the circuit constants change in such a way that a wave being propagated along the circuit is reflected.

transition region—Also called transition layer, the region, between two homogeneous semiconductor regions, in which the impurity concentration changes.

transition temperature — 1. Refers to that corresponding to a change of phase. 2. That temperature at which a metal becomes superconducting.

translate—To change computer information from one language to another without significantly affecting the meaning.

translation language — The translation from a source language program to a target program; for example, from FORTRAN, ALGOL, etc., to machine language, with the instructions being equivalent in the source program to the automatic or problem-oriented language. The translating process is completed by a machine under the control of a translator program or compiler.

translator — 1. A device which transforms signals from the form in which they were generated into a useful form for the purpose at hand. 2. A device that converts information from one system of representation into equivalent information in another system of representation. For example, one transmission code, such as Baudot, can be translated into another, such as ASCII. In telephone equipment, it is the device that converts dialed digits into call-routing information.

translator package—A computer program which allows a user program (in binary) to be converted into a usable form for computer manipulation.

translators—Translators, a generic term for assemblers and compilers (also interpreters, which have not been used much with microcomputers), are programs that allow the programmer to express his program in a language closer to his native language for later translation into a language acceptable by a machine or subsequent loader. Sometimes translators can only translate from a higher language (closer to English, for example) to a lower language like assembly language (closer to machine language). Translator tools are designed with features to enhance program expression, to provide programmer services, and to remove as much clerical burden as possible.

Translators, language (Courtesy Quasar Co.).

translators, language—Also called information processors. An electronic, talking, language translator has been introduced by at least three different manufacturers — Texas Instruments Incorporated, Quasar Company, and Nixdorf Computer Corporation. With the use of available language modules or capsules, the instrument functions as a language translator that can form thousands of spoken and displayed foreign language words and phrases. Typically, the translator uses speech synthesis, a controller, read-only memories, and language modules (or capsules) to speak and display the language phrases. In addition, the instrument can be used either as a telephone directory, a Las Vegas-type game machine (blackjack, etc.), as a personal date book, or as a data collection system.

transliterate — Refers to the activity to convert the characters of one alphabet to the corresponding characters of another alphabet.

transmission — 1. Conveying electrical energy from point to point along a path. 2. The sending of data to one or more locations or recipients. 3. The sending of data from one place for reception elsewhere. 4. Conveying electrical energy over a distance by wires, either to operate controls or

give indications (telemetering), to give acoustic information (telephony, broadcasting), or to provide pictorial information (facsimile, television). Also used to denote radio, optical, or acoustic wave propagation.

transmission band — Section of a frequency spectrum over which minimum attenuation is desired, depending on the type and speed of transmission of desired signals.

transmission cable—Transmission cables are very critical in the overall system. They can decrease the effect of extraneous noise voltages on system performance by providing shielding. They also greatly affect the signal losses as the transmission length increases. By controlling these losses, cables can permit a single set of system elements to function adequately for both long and short transmission distances. The critical performance parameters of a transmission cable include cost, transmission length, line-series resistance (dc losses), high-frequency losses, type and amount of shielding, and characteristic impedance.

transmission measuring set — A measuring instrument comprising a signal source and a signal receiver having known impedances, and used for measuring the insertion loss or gain of a network or transmission path connected between those impedances.

transmission, parallel — Refers to a method of data transfer in which all bits of a character or byte are transmitted simultaneously either over separate communication lines or on different carrier frequencies on the same communication line.

transmission rate, baud — The rate at which it is possible to transmit a data signal can be expressed in terms of the *baud,* which is a measure of carrier-modulation rate in pulses per second (1 baud = 1 pps). The baud is strictly a statement of signaling speed—that is, it tells how many carrier pulses are available to convey information during each second of transmission, and does not refer to information or its flow. Bits and bits per second (bps), however, are units of information flow, and do not refer to signaling speed. In a true binary system, each pulse contains 1 bit of information; thus, the bit and baud rates are the same. For example, a modem operating at 600 baud transmits information at 600 bps. However, the terms are not interchangeable for there are instants where pulses contain more than 1 bit, such as in most modems that operate at speeds greater than 1200 bps.

transmission schemes, basic — There are three basic transmission schemes available to data-communications systems.

1. *Simplex* — transmission from point A to point B but never from B to A.
2. *Half-duplex*—transmission from point A to point B during one interval, then from point B to point A during another interval. This two-way alternate mode prohibits simultaneous transmissions. With a normal two-wire circuit, the line must be "turned around" before the transmission can reverse. Four-wire circuits eliminate this.
3. *Full-duplex* — simultaneous transmission from point A to point B and from B to A, most often supported by four-wire circuits. However, two-wire circuits can be adapted to full-duplex operation by subdividing the frequency spectrum into receiving and transmitting channels—the technique used in 1200- and 2400-bit/s, full-duplex, two-wire modems.

transmission, serial — Refers to a method of transmission in which each bit of information is sent sequentially on a single channel rather than simultaneously as in parallel transmission.

transmission, synchronous—Refers to a transmission system in which the data characters and bits are transmitted at a fixed rate with the transmitter and receiver synchronized. This eliminates the need for start-stop elements, thus providing greater efficiency. Compare with asynchronous transmission.

transmission system — An assembly of elements capable of functioning together to transmit signal waves.

transmitter card—A typical transmitter card converts parallel digital data into asynchronous serial ASCII format. It consists of a transmitter module, a

Clock module, and all necessary pull-up resistors and shift registers to expand the module's ability to send ASCII control characters. For use in simple ASCII data-transmission applications, only a +5-V power source, a current-loop driver, and a source of data are required.

transmitter-distributor — Refers to the device in a teletypewriter terminal which makes and breaks the line in timed sequence. Modern usage of the term refers to a paper-tape transmitter. Abbreviated TD.

transmitter holding register—In some units, an 8-bit parallel register holds the parallel transmitted data that are transferred from the data access lines (DAL) by a Write operation. These data are transferred to the transmitter register when the transmitter section is enabled and the transmitter register is ready to send new data.

transmitter/receiver chip modes — Transmitter/receiver chips can be operated in synchronous and/or asynchronous modes. Chips with synchronous capability will have one or more SYN-character holding registers and a way of loading these registers with designated SYN-character(s). Synchronous transmitters can be directed to transmit, and synchronous receivers to search for, matching SYN-characters at the beginning of a message. This ensures that data characters are transmitted and received with proper framing. If the processor does not supply a character to the transmitter before the last character has been shifted out onto the line, a condition known as *underrun* occurs. The transmitter will supply a SYN as a fill character to maintain synchronization.

transmitter/receiver circuit—A processor can perform the bit-serialization (transmit) and bit-deserialization (receive) function, and the generation and detection of parity (if any) in software. However, it is more efficient to provide these functions in hardware via a transmitter/receiver circuit (such as the Signetics 2651 PCI). Operated in this manner, the processor is free to perform other work during transmission and reception of characters. For high data rates, a dedicated transmitter/receiver circuit is essential. Basically, the transmit portion of a transmitter/receiver chip consists of parallel data-input lines, a holding register to load data to be transmitted, a shift register to convert the parallel data (to be transmitted) to serial data, and control and timing logic.

transmitter register—In some units, this 8-bit shift register is loaded from the transmitter holding register, the SYN register, or the DLE register. The purpose of this register is to serialize data and present them to the transmitted-data output.

transparency, communications — The successful data-communications network will be totally transparent to its users. It should not be obvious to a person sitting at a terminal whether the computing facility he is addressing is located within the terminal itself, in a controller to which the terminal may be attached, or in some processor remote to the terminal. Nor should the user be aware of how the communication actually occurs. It may also be that the application, with which the user is in communication, is unaware of the physical characteristics of the terminal in use, or of the transmission medium which connects it with the terminal.

transparent multiplexer — "Transparent" means that the multiplexer system does not interrupt the flow of data and interface signals across the cable between the computer port and the attached modem or terminal. Thus, when the multiplexers are installed, the computer, modems, and terminals remain unaware that the multiplexer system is being used. As a result, neither terminal equipment nor computer software has to be changed when a multiplexer system is installed.

transponder—A radio or satellite transmitter-receiver which transmits identifiable signals automatically when the proper interrogation is received.

transportable microcomputer system—With the advent of the Quasar Micro Information System, science fiction has become a fact. The Micro Information System is a microcomputer that can fit into a briefcase. It has a hand-held terminal that operates with micromemory capsules (ROM) with functions such as language

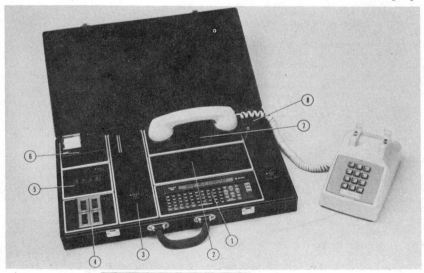

1. Hand-held terminal.	5. Cassette interface.
2. Expandable RAM.	6. Printer.
3. I/O driver.	7. Acoutical coupler.
4. Expandable ROM.	8. AC adapter.

Transportable microcomputer system (Courtesy Quasar Co.).

translation. The terminal also powers optional peripherals. The optional peripherals are an expandable random-access memory (RAM), an input/output driver, an expandable ROM (for up to four additional capsules), a cassette interface, a printer, and an acoustical coupler. The System also has an ac adapter and a video adapter available that can be used with the unit.

trap—1. A selective circuit that attenuates undesired signals but does not affect the desired ones. (Also, see wave trap.) 2. A crystal imperfection which can trap carriers. A crystal lattice defect at which current carriers may be trapped in a semiconductor. These traps can increase recombination and generation or they may reduce the mobility of the charge carriers. 3. An unprogrammed conditional jump to a known location, that is automatically activated by hardware. See trapping. 4. A trap is effectively, an interrupt generated by software.

trap, hardware — Microcomputer systems usually need external equipment for debugging. Certain computer hardware features are often helpful when debugging software and diagnosing software failures. One of these is a hardware "trap"—vectoring the program to a specific address in memory upon the occurrence of a predefined machine state. The attempt to execute an illegal instruction or to address nonexistent memory are examples of "trap-generating" occurrences. These "trap" features are standard on minis but are lacking on micros. The microcomputer programmer cannot, however, really compensate for them in software, so this function in the debug phase of software usually must be replaced by the use of a logic "analyzer" or some other external debug hardware. The microcomputer programmer should become familiar with the use of such devices.

trapped flux—In a material in the superconducting state, magnetic flux linked with a closed superconducting loop.

trapping—1. The holding of electrons or holes by any of several mechanisms in a crystal, thereby preventing them from moving. 2. A feature of some computers whereby an un-

scheduled, i.e., nonprogrammed, jump is made to a predetermined location in response to a machine condition, i.e., a tagged instruction.

trapping mode — Refers to a scheme used mainly in program-diagnostic procedures for certain computers. If the trapping mode flip-flop is set and the program includes any one of certain instructions, the instruction is not performed but the next instruction is taken from location N. Program-counter contents are saved in order to resume the program after executing the diagnostic procedure.

traps — When users debug programs (move blocks of words from one memory location to another), they can insert traps in the object code; at which point, program execution halts and control is returned to the debug program.

traps (interrupts) — Interrupts can be generated within some processors. Called traps, these interrupts are caused by programming errors, hardware errors, special instructions, and maintenance features.

tree structures — Refers to specific switching or data-file addressing structures designed to select an element by reduction cascading or all members of a set by expansion cascades. If used in chained data structures, the addresses associated with each item have multiple pointers to other items, i.e., to the next row member and the next column member.

trigistor—A bistable pnpn semiconductor component with characteristics comparable to those of a flip-flop or bistable multivibrator.

trimming — A method for adjusting the value of a film resistor. Thick films are trimmed using either abrasives or lasers; thin-film resistors are laser trimmed. Automated laser trimming is now possible using computer-controlled systems which are available from several manufacturers.

trinistor—A three-terminal silicon semiconductor device with characteristics similar to those of a thyratron and used for controlling large amounts of power.

triple diffusion process—Basically involves three sequential impurity depositions on a prepared silicon substrate. First, after preparation of the substrate by oxidation, comes the photo-resist mask and etching steps that delineate the collector areas. Some new techniques are applied, such as impurity doping with phosphorous-ion implantation followed by a thermal-distribution diffusion. Second and third, the base and emitter regions are created one after the other in a similar fashion. Next, intraconnections are made by etching electrode contacts through the protective oxide and by depositing the metal system, such as titanium-aluminum (an innovation, which prevents migration and yet allows very narrow line delineations). Finally, the metal itself is etched and the surface is covered with a passivating oxide.

truncate—To terminate a computational process in accordance with some rule, i.e., to end the evaluation of a power series at a specified term.

truncation — 1. Ending of a computational procedure in accordance with some program rule as soon as a specified accuracy has been reached. 2. Rejection of final digits in a number, thus lessening precision (but not necessarily accuracy).

truncation error — The error resulting from the use of an approximation caused by using a finite number of terms of an infinite series.

truth table — 1. A mathematical table showing the Boolean algebra relationships of variables. 2. A representation of a switching function, or truth function, in which every possible configuration of argument-values 0, 1, or true-false is listed, and beside each is given the associated function-value 0, 1, or true-false. The number of configurations is $2^{**}n$, where n is the number of arguments, unless the function is incompletely specified, i.e., "don't care" conditions.

truth table generation testing — This generation technique uses a microprocessor to develop the truth table from a user diagnostic written in the microprocessor's own machine code or assembly language. The generation program can be composed without having to know the internal architecture of the microprocessor. Only knowledge of the functions of the external device pins, as stated in the manufacturer's data sheet specifications, are necessary.

TTL (or T^2L) — Transistor-transistor logic, a kind of bipolar circuit logic that takes its name from the way the basic transistor components are interconnected.

TTL compatible — Usually means that the memory can interface with TTL devices without adding any active components. Some manufacturers mean that an MOS memory does not require high-level inputs but pull-up resistors may be required.

TTL logic—1. Standard TTL logic provides the lowest component cost of conventional logic. It is relatively fast and is unsurpassed for a variety of functions. It's the standard by which all other methods are measured. However, it has at least four disadvantages: high power dissipation, limited noise immunity, inadequate speed for some applications, and limited complexity. 2. TTL logic uses two dc flip-flops with one single-phase clock pulse to control the logic steps in a classic master-slave relationship. TTL is simple to operate, but it requires a lot of components and, consequently, a lot of chip area for LSI fabrication.

TTY — TTY is the common abbreviation for the teletype machine patented by AT&T, but many other teletypewriters now appear like these machines and substitute for them. These units are often equipped with paper-tape readers and punches; the original models were slow and expensive, were very noisy, and required frequent maintenance. 2. Trademark of the Teletype Corporation. 3. Abbreviation for teletypewriter; also, abbreviation for teletypewriter equipment.

tunnel diode—Also called an Esaki diode. A pn diode to which a large amount of impurity material has been added. Its operation is based on the tunnel effect of quantum mechanics. As the voltage across this diode increases, the current first increases, then decreases, and finally increases again. The region where the current falls as the voltage rises is called the negative-resistance region. Charges move through the tunnel diode at the speed of light, as contrasted with the relatively slow motion of electrical charge carriers in transistors.

tunnel effect — The probability that a particle of a given potential energy can penetrate a finite barrier of higher potential.

Turing machine — Refers to a unique and useful mathematical abstraction of a device that operates to read from, write on, and move an infinite tape, thereby providing a model for computer-like procedures. The behavior of a Turing machine is specified by listing an alphabet; i.e., collection of symbols read and written, a set of internal states, and a mapping of an alphabet and the internal states which determine what the symbol written and the tape motion will be, and also what internal state will follow when the machine is in a given internal state and reads a given symbol.

turnkey — 1. A computer console containing a single control, usually a power switch, that can be turned on and off only with a key. 2. Also refers to a design and/or installation in which the user receives a complete running system.

turnkey front panel—Some kit systems can be built with either full programmability or a "turnkey" front panel. The latter eliminates all controls except restarting the processor. There are a number of applications where this is desirable in order to eliminate the possibility of having an operator affect the contents of the memory or the computing cycle. An example might be in a sophisticated intruder-detection system where the only control provided for the operator is essentially "on/off."

turnkey system — Refers to an agreement whereby a supplier will install a computer system so that he has total responsibility for building, installing, and testing the system — including hardware and software.

twin check — Continuous computer check achieved by duplication of hardware and comparison of results.

twin crystal—Refers to imperfect growth of crystals, whereby two lattices have a common face, leading to double resonance and unsuitability for radio oscillator or filter use.

twinning—1. Intergrowth of crystals of near symmetry, such that (in quartz) the piezoelectric effect is not sufficiently determinate. *See* twin crystal. 2. One of two nonphysical defects that occur in quartz crystals. Either defect results from structural misgrowth of otherwise perfect crystals, yet cannot be seen in ordinary light. (A) Optical twinning is the presence of both right- and left-hand quartz in the same crystal. (B) Electrical twinning is the presence of adjacent regions of quartz having electrical axes of opposite poles.

two-address — In a computer, having the property that each complete instruction includes an operation and specifies the location of two registers, usually one containing an operand and the other the result of the operation.

two-level subroutine—Refers to a subroutine which has another subroutine within its own structure.

TWX — Western Union teleprinter exchange service with real-time direct connection between subscribers.

U

UART — 1. Abbreviation for universal asynchronous receiver/transmitter. Refers to a specific device that will interface a word parallel controller or data terminal to a bit-serial communication network. The characteristics of some UARTs are identical to those of an ACIA (asynchronous communications interface adapter). With a UART, control inputs, status outputs, and data buffers are accessible through unidirectional lines. Thus, the I/O bus of the microcomputer requires additional multiplexing for Read or Write operations. The ACIA, however, incorporates the multiplexing circuitry, so that status, control, and data registers are accessible through a single bidirectional bus. 2. A typical universal asynchronous receiver/transmitter (UART) is a single-chip MOS/LSI device that can totally replace the asynchronous parallel-to-serial and serial-to-parallel conversion logic required to interface a word parallel controller or data terminal to a bit-serial communication network. The UART can typically transmit or receive data characters of 5-, 6-, 7-, or 8-bit length. Options allow the generation and checking of odd and even parity, or no parity. The odd- or even-parity bit is automatically added to the character length for transmission. 3. *See* universal asynchronous receiver/transmitter.

UART controller—With a controller, the asynchronous terminal data-input and data-output lines are connected to a universal asynchronous receiver/transmitter (UART) circuit which converts a serial bit-stream into 8 bits of parallel data, and vice versa. The controller checks for a received character by testing the RECEIVE FLAG. An 8-bit character is transferred off the DATA IN lines to a buffer memory area in the controller for further processing. Error conditions are tested to ensure character integrity and, finally, the RECEIVE FLAG is cleared, indicating to the UART modem that the previous character has been transferred (some systems).

UART double buffering — A UART receiver has double buffering so that one character can be read from a buffer as a shift register receives another. The status of each incoming character is checked for parity, framing, and overrun errors. A framing error indicates the absence of a Stop bit, and an overrun error indicates that a character previously received has not been read by the microcomputer.

UART operation modes — A typical UART contains separate transmit, receive, and control paths. In the transmit mode, the microprocessor places an 8-bit byte on the data bus and instructs the UART to transmit the data. The byte is then transferred from the microprocessor to a transmit buffer in the UART. If there is nothing else being transmitted at the time, the contents of the transmit buffer are copied into a parallel-to-serial converter where asynchronous start and stop bits are added. Then, using the transmit clock (T $\times$ C), the bits are shifted out one at a time to the terminal. On the receive side, when a start

bit is detected, the UART assembles a byte of incoming serial data in an 8-bit buffer where it is held until a Read command is received from the microprocessor. The UART then places the byte on the microprocessor's data bus.

UART receiver-transmitter section — The receiver and transmitter section of the UART contains a control and a status register for command and monitoring functions. These registers, as well as the receiver and transmitter buffers, are each assigned an input/output address. The assigned addresses are in addition to those indicated in the input/output section. The communication section has two channels of interrupt: the receiver section and transmitter section. The receiver has priority on simultaneous interrupts. A typical communication section has a 20-mA current-loop electrical interface for tty paper-tape reader control and a control line to energize the paper-tape reader run relay, which is an internal modification to the ASR-33 Teletype® machine. This relay allows computer control of the reader during on-line operation.

UART simulator—The UART is a large-scale integration circuit with a complexity comparable to that of a typical 4-bit microcomputer. Its functions may be easily transformed into a program for execution by an 8-bit microcomputer. A system program would then pass parallel characters to the UART simulation program just as if it were a hardware UART. The UART simulator can also process the serial-data stream between the microcomputer and a cassette interface.

uhf (ultrahigh frequencies)—The range of frequencies extending from 300 to 3000 MHz; also, television channels 14 through 83.

ULA—*See* uncommitted logic arrays.

ultraviolet—Electromagnetic radiation at frequencies higher than those of visible light and with wavelengths of about 200 to 4000 angstrom units.

ultraviolet contrast-control safety goggles—Short-wave ultraviolet light can cause "sunburning" of the eyes and skin. Operators should never look directly into a lighted lamp. Long-sleeved clothing and gloves should be worn. Avoid shining the lamp on reflective surfaces whenever possible. Due to the extremely high intensity of the various lamps, UVC safety goggles are essential in protecting the eyes from short-wave exposure, thus eliminating the "blue haze" effect and avoiding possible eyestrain. Their wraparound styling gives side protection and permits use over regular eyeglasses.

ultraviolet energy—Ultraviolet energy is that portion of the electromagnetic spectrum that is adjacent to, and of a shorter wavelength than, visible light. Scientists define wavelengths in terms of nanometers (1 nm = 10 angstrom units). **Short-wave ultraviolet** light has a wavelength of 200–280 nm. Located in this region is the 254-nm mercury emission line. **Long-wave ultraviolet** light has a wavelength of 320–400 nm. Positioned in this region is the 365-nm mercury emission line. **Multiband** ultraviolet lamps emit 254-nm and 365-nm wavelengths (separately or together) depending on the product model. Extreme care must be taken when using short-wave or multiband lamps. They may cause eyes and unprotected skin to "sunburn." However, complete protection is easily attained. A safe, general, operating rule is:

Always hold the lamp so the light is directed away from you.

Long-wave ultraviolet is usually considered harmless. However, individuals should use adequate protection if they are photosensitive or will be subjected to long exposure times. It is recommended that safety spectacles or safety goggles be worn at all times while operating equipment.

ultraviolet energy definitions — **Luminescence** is the emission of light without heat. **Fluorescence** is light emission by certain substances when excited by ultraviolet energy. Emission ceases when the excitation is removed. **Phosphorescence** is light emission that continues after the exciting source is removed. **Germicidal** is the common name used to describe short-wave ultraviolet light. **Black light** is the common name used to describe long-wave ultraviolet light.

ultraviolet erasable PROMs — ROMs are usually thought of as having permanent binary information programmed into their memories as once information is programmed into an ordinary ROM, it cannot be altered. However, there are various types of ROMs that are both programmable and erasable. These types of ROMs, or PROMs, permit information that is stored semipermanently to be erased and new information to be reprogrammed in. One type of erasable PROM can be erased by a concentrated short-wave ultraviolet light. It is housed in a 16-pin dual-in-line package (DIP) that has a quartz top

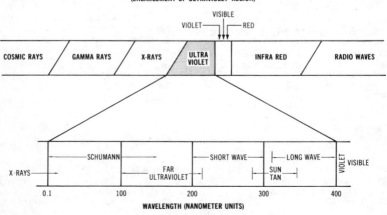

Ultraviolet energy.

which is transparent to short-wave UV light. The unwanted information is erased simply by directing a UV light through the IC's quartz "window" and reprogramming as desired.

ultraviolet lamp—A lamp that provides a high proportion of ultraviolet radiation (e.g., arc lamps, mercury-vapor lamps, or incandescent lamps with bulbs of a special glass that is transparent to ultraviolet rays).

ultraviolet light erasing — EPROMs, or erasable programmable read-only memory chips, may be erased by exposure to a high-intensity short-wave ultraviolet light at a wavelength of 2537 Å. The recommended integrated dose (i.e., UV intensity $\times$ intensity time) is 6W-sec/Cm^2. The devices are made with a transparent quartz lid covering a silicon die. Conventional room light, fluorescent light, or sunlight has no measurable effect on stored data, even after years of exposure. However, after 10 to 20 minutes under a suitable concentrated ultraviolet light source, the device is erased to a state of all zeroes or all ones. It is recommended that no more ultraviolet light exposure be used than is necessary when erasing the EPROM in order to prevent damage to the device. CAUTON: *When using an ultraviolet source of this type, one should be careful to not expose one's eyes or skin to the ultraviolet rays because of the vision damage or burns which might occur. In addition, these short-wave rays may generate considerable amounts of ozone which is also a potential hazard.*

ultraviolet radiation—The electromagnetic radiation in the wavelength range of 4×10^{-5} cm to 5×10^{-7} cm approximately, covering the gap between X-rays and visible light rays.

ultraviolet rays—Radiation in the ultraviolet region.

unallowable digit—Refers to a character or combination of bits which is not accepted as a valid representation by a microcomputer, or the machine design, or by a specific routine, and which suggests malfunctions.

unary operator—Refers to an arithmetic operator having only one term. The unary operators that can be used in absolute, relocatable, and arithmetic expressions are: positive $(+)$ and negative $(-)$.

unbalanced—1. Lacking the conditions for balance. 2. Frequently, a circuit having one side grounded. 3. Relating to an indicated line, electrical transmission, or network in which the impedances measured from corresponding points on opposite sides are unequal.

unbalanced circuit—A circuit, the two sides of which are electrically unlike.

unbalanced line — A transmission line in which the voltages on the two conductors are not equal with respect to ground (e.g., a coaxial line).

unblanked scope — A Z-axis or intensity modulation of the display beam in an oscilloscope or crt. When the screen is unblanked, it will be illuminated because electrons are able to strike the phosphor-coated screen.

unbundling — This generally refers to the pricing of certain types of software and services separately from the hardware.

unbundling, software — Unbundling, which began in earnest in the mid-1970s when certain industry leaders began pricing software and hardware components separately, has made it more difficult for all system vendors to price their products. Software, which was once given away to encourage hardware sales, is now recognized as having value. No vendor today gives away major software elements with a system.

uncommitted logic arrays (ULA)—Uncommitted logic arrays represent a bridge between custom and standard products. They consist of partially processed wafers of standard chip designs, with the customers specifying the interconnections that are needed to make up the functions required. It is possible working with the chips on the wafers to construct a specific customized system. ULAs group the functions of small-scale integration (SSI) and medium-scale integration (MSI) into a single package in order to simplify systems and improve reliability. ULAs represent a kind of "latent logic," allowing a designer to build a fairly efficient system with a smaller parts count without going through either a complex component assembly or a full-scale custom design. For prototype systems, early or small production runs, ULAs are often more cost effective than either standard or full custom products. That cost advantage decreases as production volume increases, because ULA chip sizes cannot be decreased. The chip sizes are constant and the price of a ULA remains the same whether all on-board functions are used or not.

uncommitted storage list—Refers to a list of blocks of storage that are not allocated for any particular use at any specific moment.

unconditional control-transfer instruction — Refers to an instruction which always causes a jump, i.e., an unconditional jump.

unconditional jump—A microcomputer instruction that interrupts the normal process of obtaining the instructions in an ordered sequence and which specifies the address from which the next instruction must be taken.

unconditional transfer of control — 1. In a digital computer that obtains its instructions serially from an ordered sequence of addresses, this refers to an instruction which causes the "following" instruction to be taken from an address that becomes the first of a new sequence. 2. An instruction that switches the sequence of control to some specified location. Synonymous with unconditional jump.

uncorrectable error — If intent of programmer cannot be determined, the CPU prints a diagnostic message, rejects the clause or statement, and continues compilation.

undercut — In a printed-circuit board, the reduction of the cross-section of a metal-foil conductor due to the removal of metal from beneath the edge of the resist by the etchant.

underflow—Refers to the condition that arises when a machine computation yields a non-zero result that is smaller than the smallest non-zero quantity that the intended unit of storage is capable of storing.

unidirectional transducer—Also called a unilateral transducer. A transducer, the output of which cannot be actuated by waves to supply related waves at its input.

unijunction transistor — Also called a silicon double-base diode or silicon unijunction transistor. A three-terminal semiconductor device exhibiting stable open-circuit negative-resis-

tance characteristics. The internal construction consists of a uniformly doped n-type single-crystal semiconductor with ohmic contacts at each end and a wire attached to the emitter between them.

unilateralization—Neutralization of feedback so that a transducer or a circuit has a unilateral response (i.e., there is no response at the input if the signal is applied to the output terminals). While many vacuum tube circuits are inherently unilateral equivalent, transistor circuits require external neutralization.

uninterruptible power supply—Abbreviated UPS. The word uninterruptible covers a multitude of power problems: fast power dropouts lasting just milliseconds and long-term blackouts lasting hours or days; overvoltages, from quick power spikes to long-term high-voltage levels; quick voltage dips and long-term voltage lows. Some power systems can handle no more than 10% of these problems; others can handle all of them. UPS systems are designed to provide continuous computer-quality power under essentially all abnormal utility power conditions, including total loss, for up to 15 minutes typically. This bridges most power outages and permits an orderly shutdown for longer blackouts. If the UPS fails, it automatically switches directly to utility power without disturbing computer operation.

unipolar transistor — A transistor in which the charge carriers are of only one polarity.

unit record equipment—Equipment using punched cards as input data, such as collators, tabulating machines, etc.

universal asynchronous receiver/transmitter — 1. Abbreviated UART. 2. A typical universal asynchronous receiver/transmitter is an MOS/LSI monolithic circuit that performs all the receiving and transmitting functions associated with asynchronous data communications. In a UART, the transmitter converts parallel data bits into serial form for transmission over two-wire lines. The receiver section does the reverse operation. Various systems use a UART with a video display in order to communicate with a microcomputer or another type of display. Coupling it with suitable circuitry, other systems use a UART to record ASCII data from a keyboard or a tape recorder, or it is used with a modem and telephone coupler for transmitting data over telephone lines. UARTs can also be used with centrally monitored burglar and fire alarms, intersection traffic control, and ecological data gathering. The applications in which UARTs can be used are almost limitless. 3. One type of interface is a universal asynchronous receiver/transmitter (UART) that performs two basic operations, receiving and transmitting asynchronous data. When receiving data, the UART converts an asynchronous serial character from the teletypewriter or RS-232 device into the parallel character required for transfer to the CPU bus. This parallel character can then be gated through the bus to the memory, CPU register, or some other device. When transmitting data, a parallel character from the CPU bus is converted to a serial code for transmission to a teletypewriter punch/printer or an RS-232 device. The two data-transfer units are independent, therefore, are capable of simultaneous two-way communication.

universal block channel (UBC) — The universal block channel is a block-mode, direct memory-access channel for high-performance peripheral controllers such as those used with disks and magnetic tapes. The typical UBC has two operating modes—the scan mode and the scan-lock mode. In the scan mode, a UBC supports two concurrent input/output operations. In the scan-lock mode, the UBC operates as a single direct memory-access channel. In addition to direct memory operations, the UBC also functions as a programmed I/O channel and is used for transferring data under CPU/program control between a CPU register and the channel. One type of UBC contains a 48-bit data buffer for each logical channel.

universal devices — At present, there are three such devices: (1) UART, (2) USRT, and (3) USART. A universal asynchronous receiver/transmitter (UART) translates and buffers data between the parallel byte format used by a microprocessor and the asynchronous serial format used by most

low-speed terminals and data communications equipment. Another device, a universal synchronous receiver/transmitter (USRT), translates between parallel and synchronous serial formats. The most recent device in this class is the universal synchronous/asynchronous receiver/transmitter (USART) which handles both synchronous and asynchronous serial formats.

Universal Product Code (UPC) structure.

Universal Product Code (UPC) structure — The Universal Product Code (UPC) is a bar code that has been adopted as the standard by the food industry and is now being printed on some packages. It is a series of parallel lines representing 10 numbers. The first five numbers in code indicate the manufacturer of the item and the second five identify brand, size, and other features. The price is not part of the code. The scanner sends an image of the code to an in-store computer where it is matched with a similar electronic image in memory. The price and product name are sent back to the terminal where they are printed on the customer's bill. All this happens in the time it takes to move the item past the scanning window. Not all packages received at the store have been marked by the manufacturer with the UPC. Store personnel are currently labeling such items with the UPC symbol as they come into the store. Variable-weight meat and produce packages are also labeled with the code, using the electronic scale system, interfaced with a symbol printer that automatically delivers the UPC symbol label ready for manual application.

universal PROM programmer — A universal PROM programmer allows users to program and verify PROMs by initiating PROM programming commands from the system console. The universal PROM programmer peripheral has been created to program programmable read-only memories by plugging personality cards into the appropriate PROM programmer card socket. A typical software-based PROM programmer is a compact lightweight package that has insert/delete data-editing capabilities, and is capable of programming, loading, and verifying several hundreds of different PROM configurations. It can program entire generic PROM families using a single personality module. Hexadecimal keyboard and display plus microprocessor-controlled operations result in a simple operation. Software-based serial and parallel I/O interfaces allow for data communication in key-selectable data-translation formats. Data polarity controls are usually provided, and built-in error-checking routines assure accuracy of all data transfers.

universal synchronous/asynchronous receiver/transmitter (USART)—One type of USART is designed for data communications and is used as a peripheral device. It is programmed by the CPU to operate using virtually any serial data-transmission technique presently in use. The USART accepts data characters from the CPU in parallel format and then converts them into a continuous serial data stream for transmission. Simultaneously, it can receive serial data streams and convert them into parallel data characters for the CPU. The USART will signal the CPU whenever it can accept a new character for transmission or when it has received a character for the CPU. The CPU can read the complete status of the USART at any time. A typical asynchronous communications application uses the USART chip working through an RS-232-C interface circuit to control a cathode-ray-tube terminal. Standard crt control signals are processed by the USART via the RS-232-C interface.

universal synchronous receiver/transmitter—Abbreviated USRT. A typical USRT is a single-chip MOS/LSI device that can totally replace the serial-to-parallel and parallel-to-serial conversion logic required to interface a word parallel controller or data terminal to a bit-serial synchronous communication network. It is a general-purpose communications interface that allows a high-speed synchronous communications device to transmit data to and receive data from a microcomputer system. It connects to the peripheral device via separate serial transmit and receive lines and to the system address bus through a PIA. Often the USRT has separate internal receiver and transmitter sections, which can be blocked by two separate clocks. Many have the capability to handle different word lengths, generate and check parity and other

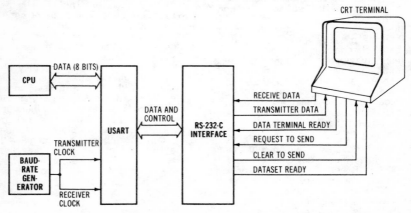

Universal synchronous/asynchronous receiver/transmitter (USART).

conditions, detect sync during receive, and send a fill character during transmit operation. Typically, the USRT is fully double buffered and it internally generates the sync character received and sync character transmitted signals. These programmable features provide the user with the ability to interface with all synchronous peripherals.

unpack—1. In a computer, to separate combined items of information, each into a separate machine word. 2. To decompose packed information into a sequence of separate words or elements.

unwind — To code explicitly, at length and in full, all the operations of a cycle, thus eliminating all red-tape operations in the final problem coding.

UPC code — The Universal Product Code (UPC) symbol adopted by the food industry is a special printed code that consists of a series of vertical bars which reflect light that is emitted by an optical scanner. Human-readable code numbers are printed directly below the UPC bar code. The design of the UPC symbol permits scanning in an omnidirectional manner. *See also* Universal Product Code (UPC) structure.

update—1. To search the file (such as a particular record in a computer tape), selecting one entry, and then performing some operation to bring the entry up-to-date. 2. To put into a master file changes that are required by current information or transactions. 3. To modify an instruction so that the address numbers it contains are increased by a stated amount each time the instruction is performed.

update (verb)—To modify a master file according to current forms of information (often that contained in a transaction field), according to a procedure specified as part of a data-processing activity.

UPS — Abbreviation for uninterruptible power supply.

UPS, float-type configuration—To take full advantage of the isolating and regulating capabilities of a battery-backed uninterruptible power supply (UPS), the float-type configuration must be used. The basic UPS consists of a rectifier/battery charger, a dc-to-ac power inverter, and a battery bank. Under normal conditions, the commercial ac line delivers power to the rectifier/battery charger, and the battery bank is maintained fully charged in a "float" condition. The inverter, also receiving dc power from the rectifier/charger, delivers regulated conditioned ac to critical loads via an automatic, or sometimes manual, transfer switch. If the ac-input fails (blackout) or drops below normal levels (brownout), dc will continue to be supplied to the inverter from the charged battery bank. If the UPS is overloaded or malfunctions, the bypass switch can transfer the load directly to the commercial power mains.

up time—1. The time during which an equipment is either operating or available for operation as opposed to down time when no productive work can be accomplished. 2. The time a computer is operating free of component failure, plus the time the computer is capable of such operation.

upward reference—In an overlay, a reference made from a segment to another segment higher in the same path; that is, closer to the root segment.

USACII—An abbreviation for USA Standard Code for Information Interchange.

USASI—Abbreviation for United States of America Standards Institute; a former name of the American National Standards Institute. Same as ANSI.

user library — A basic library of general-purpose software is furnished by some manufacturers to perform common jobs. To this the user can add his own often-used programs and routines. Programs in the library can be conveniently assembled into an object program by the use of macro-instructions.

user-microprogrammer processors — Current advances in semiconductor technology have led to microprogrammed and user-microprogrammable processors having a variety of microinstruction sequencing capabilities. The primary use of micrograms is as an alternative to hard-wired control sequencers used in the implementation of the control function, in microcomputers with conventional instruction sets; thus, micrograms are used to implement tasks which have a relatively simple logical structure. Microprograms are being used to support special-purpose architectures with instruction sets chosen to simplify programming of certain classes of algorithms; these microprograms are also being used to implement tasks which may have a relatively complex logical structure.

USRT—*See* universal synchronous receiver/transmitter.

utilities—A group of programs that perform duties, such as program checkout, editing, word processing, text preparation, and accounting, that are standard software or installation implemented. Used on all systems.

utilities, cassette—Some types of cassette operating systems offer utility programs that include an interactive editor, linker, on-line debugger, and file interchange utility. These programs are loaded and executed by issuing the monitor's RUN command after the monitor is loaded into memory and the system cassette is mounted.

utilities, data-base operating system— The typical business-oriented database operating system has a complete set of the utilities required for business-processing systems. The normal sort, data-base utilities, memory dump, trace, copies, prints, and restore are the routines generally provided. A number of options are usually also available for backup and recovery.

utility debug—1. A design aid for the programmer in testing and debugging programs and in the performing of utility functions. 2. Abbreviated DBG. On many systems, this is an on-line conversational utility for use in program debugging. DBG offers a wide variety of inspection and control commands, including memory search/inspect/modify and memory print, memory and/or register initialization, memory-to-memory copy of specific regions, a set of selectable relocation registers to provide listing/memory address compatibility, the ability to execute selected program segments using up to two breakpoints, and an automatic escape (TRAP) return to DBG from a "runaway" program.

utility programs—1. Refers to a collection of problem state programs designed for use by a system programmer in performing such functions as changing or extending the indexing structure of the catalog. 2. Off-line routines that are used to load the data base on to disk from other media, and are also used to duplicate the data base as a backup.

utility routines — Utility routines are likely to include: addition, subtraction, and division; trigonometric functions; logorithms, exponentials, and other common mathematical functions; programs to read from and write to all peripheral devices (I/O subsystem with device drivers); and programs to generate text output at a line printer, teletypewriter or crt terminal. The utility routines may constitute a large number of programs, but only those components actually referenced by applications programs will be loaded into memory.

V

VAB (voice answer back) — Concerns various audio response units that can link a computer system to a telephone network to provide voice responses to inquiries made from telephone-type terminals. The audio response is composed from a vocabulary prerecorded in a digital-coded voice or a disk storage device.

vacuum—Ideally stated, a vacuum is an empty space entirely devoid of matter. In actuality, it is a space in which the pressure is far below normal atmospheric pressure, so that the remaining gases do not affect processes carried on in that space. More simply, a vacuum is an enclosure filled with low-pressure gas.

vacuum measurement — The units for expressing the amount of pressure remaining in a vacuum system are based on the force of atmospheric air under standard conditions. This force amounts to 1.03 kg/cm². Gas pressure is stated in terms of the height of a column of mercury supported in a barometer by that pressure. Atmospheric pressure of 1.03 kg/cm² will support a column of mercury 76.0 cm high. In vacuum work, the most common units are the torr and millitorr. One torr is the equivalent of one millimeter or 1/760 of atmospheric pressure. One millitorr is 1/1000 of a torr. The unit derives its name from Torricelli, the inventor of the barometer.

vacuum pumping—The semiconductor industry uses a variety of pumping methods to lower the pressure within chambers. The best-known pumping action is that of the oil-sealed mechanical pump which, by means of an eccentric cam or reciprocating piston, isolates a portion of gas from the vacuum chamber and then compresses it so it can be ejected into the atmosphere. Semiconductor manufacturers use three basic high-vacuum pumping methods: oil diffusion, turbomolecular, and cryogenic.

vacuum seal—One of the major problems in making semiconductor devices is to ensure a perfect vacuum while the aluminum conductors are being deposited on the silicon wafers. Exposure to air can turn the aluminum into an insulating oxide and, thus, ruin the complete wafer. Now there's a better way. The magnetic liquid used as a seal is held in place by magnets. Also, the liquid can even be used to put a vacuum seal around moving parts.

validity check—Refers to one based on limits to the data for a specific problem, e.g., a computed time of day would be rejected if outside the range of 0–24 hours.

validity checking—1. Refers to a procedure for detecting invalid or distinctly unreasonable results, i.e., illogical bit combinations, highly improbable numeric codes, storage addresses, etc. 2. A data screening procedure wherein data input records are checked for range, valid coding, valid representation (i.e., calendar date), etc. Related to input editing.

valid memory address—This output indicates to peripheral devices that there is a valid address on the address bus. In normal operation, this signal should be utilized for enabling peripheral interfaces such as the PIA and ACIA. In many systems, this signal is not three-state. One standard TTL load may be directly driven by this active high signal.

variable — 1. Any factor or condition which can be measured, altered, or controlled (e.g., temperature, pressure, flow, liquid level, humidity, weight, chemical composition, color, etc.). 2. A quantity that can assume any of a given set of values.

variable connector — 1. Refers to a flowchart symbol representing a sequence connection that is not fixed, but which can be varied by the flowcharted procedure itself. 2. The device that inserts instructions in a program corresponding to a selection of paths appearing in a flowchart. 3. The computer instructions that cause a logical chain to take one of several alternative paths.

variable field — A field in which the scalar (or vector) at any point changes during the time under consideration.

variable field length — Refers to data fields that can have a varying number of characters from record to record.

variable function generator — Refers to a particular function generator that operates with reference to a set of values of the function, which are preset within the device, with or without interpolation between these values, i.e., a cam for a mechanical analog representation.

variable-persistence storage monitor— A typical variable-persistence monitor accommodates the display of repetitive phenomena where the persistence is adjusted to let the image fade immediately before the signal is repeated. This is required in applications such as engine analysis, spectrum analysis, and radar/sonar displays.

variable resistance pickup — A transducer whose operation depends upon a variation of resistance, e.g., a thermistor or strain-gauge element.

variable symbol—Refers to assembler programming where a variable symbol does not have to be declared because the assembler assigns it read-only values.

vector—1. The term for a symbol which

denotes a directed quantity; i.e., one that cannot be completely described except in terms of both magnitude and direction, such as wind velocities, voltage and currents of electricity, and forces of all kinds. 2. A quantity having magnitude and direction, as contrasted with a scalar which has quantity only. 3. A 1-dimensional array.

vector algebra—Manipulation of symbols representing vector quantities according to laws of addition, subtraction, multiplication, and division, which these quantities obey.

vector diagram — An arrangement of vectors showing the relationships between alternating quantities having the same frequency.

vectored interrupts — With a vectored interrupt, the interrupt-control logic within the processor recognizes the interrupting I/O device. Each I/O device is assigned a unique device-interrupt address. Once it recognizes an interrupt request, the interrupt-control logic requires the interrupting I/O device to transmit its device-interrupt address to the microcomputer. This address is then used to generate a unique interrupt trap address for the device. The trap addresses, usually located sequentially in the program memory, form the interrupt vector. Each location in the vector contains the start address of a device-service program. The contents of the interrupt vector, defined by the particular interrupt trap address, are loaded into the program counter and program control is automatically transferred to the correct device-service program. Sometimes, the process is simplified by using the interrupt-trap addresses as the interrupt addresses.

vectored interrupts implementation — Interrupts on bus signal lines are implemented in very specific ways. Non-bus-vectored (NBV) and bus-vectored (BV) interrupts permit only one master to respond to a given bus interrupt. The NBV interrupts are handled on the bus master. The vector address is not transferred by the bus, but is generated by the interrupt controller on the master and is then transferred to the processor over the local bus. The slave modules that generate the interrupt can reside on the master module or on other bus modules (some systems).

vector element—The basic element of a vector is a scalar which has a single distinct value. A vector is a set of scalars that share some common attribute; for example, they may be X-axis coordinates in a 3D graphics problem.

vector field — In a given region of space, the total value of some vector quantity which has a definite value at each point of the region (e.g., the distribution of magnetic intensity in a region surrounding a current-carrying conductor).

vector function — A function which has both magnitude and direction (e.g., the magnetic intensity at a point near an electric circuit is a vector function of the current in that circuit).

vectoring, interrupt—Interrupt vectoring is achieved by using a special-purpose single-byte jump instruction that derives the jump address from a part of the instruction code itself. Using the device-interrupt address to specify this bit field, a unique jump address is defined for each I/O device that is used in the system. Vectored-interrupt systems can use nested interrupts so that high-priority interrupts can be rapidly serviced if they occur during a lower priority interrupt.

vector instruction — As an example of how one powerful firmware instruction can facilitate the performance of the operating system, a vector instruction takes an interrupt, stores the machine state, branches to the appropriate device or handle, switches stacks, and allocates a stack frame in just 18 microseconds. This process would take a number of sequential subroutines if it were done by the operating system.

vector, interface—In some systems, the interface vector is the input/output path between the microcontrolled system and the user equipment. Each bit in the interface provides a program-addressable buffered bidirectional path. Both the microcontroller and the user have simultaneous access to each bit for read or write operations. Bits are grouped into 8-bit interface vector bytes to simplify user control of the interface and access by the program. In one system, the processor treats the interface vector as an n-word variable-field random-access storage. Control elements in the interpreter specify the word to be accessed as well as the bit position and the length of the data field to be read or written.

vector interrupt—This term is used to describe a microprocessor system in which each interrupt, both internal and external, has its own uniquely recognizable address. This enables the microprocessor to perform a set of specified operations which are pre-programmed by the user to handle each interrupt in a distinctively different manner.

vector power—A vector quantity equal to the square root of the sum of the squares of the active and reactive powers. The unit is the vector-ampere.

vector processors—These processors are specially designed for performing arithmetic on arrays of data, but they operate on an entire row or column of the array—the so-called vector—at once. Among new computer architectures, there are machines called distributed array processors. They consist of multiple arithmetic and logic units, each of which is associated with its own block of memory and operates on a separate piece of data simultaneously with all the other units.

vector quantity — A quantity with both magnitude and direction.

vector scanning, E-beam—Vector scanning has the potential to write three to four times faster than raster scanning. Vector-scan machines are used for making fine-line masks and, to a lesser extent, for direct writing on wafers and for making 10× reticles. In vector scanning, the beam scans only the areas where circuit features are located, not the total field. The beam creates features by filling in the feature with a raster-type motion, varying spot size and shape, or by finely outlining the periphery of the shape and then filling in the outline in large blocks. After a feature is completed, the beam turns off and goes immediately to the next feature. Regions between features are not addressed, and the addressing structure is very flexible.

vector transfer — Refers to a transfer table used to communicate between two or more programs. The table is fixed in relationship with the program for which it is the transfer vector. The transfer vector provides communication linkage between that program and any remaining subprograms.

Veitch diagram — 1. A graphical technique used for the solution of problems arising in logical circuit design. 2. A table or chart showing information contained in a truth table.

velocity — 1. A vector quantity that includes both magnitude (speed) and direction in relation to a given frame of reference. 2. Rate of motion in a given direction, employed in its higher magnitudes as a means of overcoming the force of gravity. 3. In a wave, the distance travelled by a given phase of a wave divided by the time taken. It is a vector quantity so that it has a magnitude and a direction expressed relative to some frame of reference.

Venn diagrams — Diagrams in which circles or ellipses are used to give a graphic representation of basic logic relations. Logic relations between classes, operations on classes, and the terms of the propositions are illustrated and defined by the inclusion, exclusion, or intersection of circular figures, with shading to indicate empty areas, crosses to indicate areas that are not empty, and blank spaces to indicate areas that may be either. Named for English logician John Venn, who devised them.

verbs, processor — Refers to verbs which specify to the processor the procedures by which a source program is to be translated into an object program. Such verbs do not cause action at object time.

verify—1. To check, usually with an automatic machine, one recording of data against another in order to minimize the number of human errors in the data transcription. 2. To make certain that the information being prepared for a computer is correct. 3. To determine whether a transcription of data or other operation has been accomplished accurately. 4. To check the results of a keypunching operation.

vernier—1. An auxiliary scale comprising subdivisions of the main measuring scale and, thus, permitting more accurate measurements than is possible from the main scale alone. 2. An auxiliary device used for obtaining fine adjustments.

vernier capacitor—A variable capacitor placed in parallel with a larger tuning capacitor and used to provide a finer adjustment after the larger one has been set to the approximate desired position.

vertical parity check — Refers to a check by summation in which the binary digits, in a character or word, are added, and the sum checked against a single previously computed parity digit; i.e., a check tests whether the number of ones in a word is odd or even (synonymous with odd-even check, and related to redundancy check).

vertical polarization—State of an electromagnetic wave when the electric component lies in the vertical plane and the magnetic component lies in the horizontal plane, as in the wave emitted from a vertical antenna.

vertical redundance — In a parity-checking system, refers to an even number of bits in an odd-parity system, or vice versa.

very-large-scale integration — A concept whereby a complete system function is fabricated as a single microcircuit. In this context, a system, whether digital or linear, is considered to be one that contains 1000 or more gates, or circuitry of similar complexity.

v-f band — A voice-frequency band. A transmission facility of approximately 3000-cycle bandwidth, capable of telephone-quality communications.

V format—Refers to a data record format designed so that the logical records are of variable length and each record begins with a record-length indication.

VHS—The ½-inch videocassette format developed by Matsushita Electronics Corporation. VHS stands for Video Home System.

VHSIC programs — A six-year very-high-speed integrated-circuit (VHSIC) project launched by the Pentagon and intended to lead to higher-density components for a new generation of "smart" weapons. The initial target is to make elements measuring 1¼ microns, which later will be brought down to half a micron. Nine teams of contractors are participating in the current study phase, though only three will be funded when component production starts in the mideighties.

video, compressed—The term "compressed video" refers to frequency or bandwidth compression, and the process involves stretching out the picture in time, so that approximately one minute is required to transmit a single image. This is an important consideration, as it means that the camera subject material must be stationary or quite slow in movement in order to reproduce a clear picture. Auxiliary devices for picture "freezing" before transmission may, however, be used for special applications.

video compressor — A typical video compressor converts standard television signals to narrow bandwidths for transmission over voice-grade communications circuits. Still pictures only are transmitted, with a typical frame time being 78 seconds per image for a medium resolution of 256 × 512 picture elements. A companion device, a special video expander, must be used at the receiving location to reconstruct the television image. The system may be used with a normal "dial-up" telephone network, leased lines, radio links, microwave, or satellite channels to provide low-cost visual communications. Typical applications include: conferencing, instruction, medical diagnosis, industrial troubleshooting, remote-site observation, and environmental monitoring. Signals may also be easily recorded on conventional audio tapes or cassettes for later playback.

videodisc pits—Refers to a pickup system that works by reflection. Therefore, the tracks on the disc, which are actually a series of "pits" of information, are coated with a reflective metallic surface. This makes the disc itself, which has a diameter of about

Videodisc pits (Courtesy Magnavox, Inc.).

12 inches and resembles an audio LP record, appear to be made of highly polished metal.

videodiscs, random-access — Videodiscs provide computer-aided audiovisual education that adapts to individual needs. Random-access capability allows the viewer to reach a chosen section among some of the 108,000 frames on a disc in less than 5 seconds. Videodisc players permit either slow- or fast-forward and reverse playback, single-frame forward and backward advance, and optical-scanning speeds. A videodisc user does not have to wade attentively through an entire tape to search out the information he desires.

video display generator — Basically, a video display generator (VDG) addresses the display memory which may be shared with the MPU, and converts the data to analog signals to obtain the proper chroma-bias, R-Y and B-Y signals for the rf modulator. When interfaced to a tv receiver, the VDG chip and the modulator IC chip make various combinations of color information available. Eight colors, all in compliance with NTSC (National Television Systems Committee) standards, can be displayed at five different luminance levels. These combinations provide for three gray shades for both black-and-white tv sets and blank and black conditions.

video display methods—A number of video display methods exist that define how data is stored in RAM and displayed on the screen. Two of the most popular techniques are the fixed-memory and the video-list methods. Simply speaking, in the fixed-memory video technique, every location on the crt screen has a corresponding RAM memory location. Thus, in order to display any characters on the screen, that data must be moved to a specific RAM location.

The video-list technique is quite different; it allows data to reside anywhere in RAM regardless of the screen display position. Simply speaking, the list-driven technique allows the user to have the lines of display data defined by a 4-byte entry in the video list. This 4-byte entry provides useful information concerning the number of characters in a line, double-width/single-width char-

acters, address of characters to be displayed, and so on. Advantages of the video-list technique include smaller memory requirements, faster movement of display data, split-screen displays, and horizontal scrolling, to name just a few.

video-display terminal/light-pen system—A typical video display terminal/light-pen system will consist of a specially configured terminal and a light pen. The system reduces the time and effort required to select information on the display screen. By merely pointing the pen to the desired character position and pressing its tip to the screen, the data are instantly selected for action by the system. One of the features offered by one typical display terminal, for use in the light-pen system, is a paging capability that permits the recovery of top and bottom line rolloffs from internal memory.

video expander—One special type of video expander is a solid-state video memory capable of storing one frame of video information. Data may be fed into the unit at a slow rate and used to build up a continuously refreshed image on a standard television monitor screen. The image buildup process may be continuously observed, and there is no fadeout or image degradation with time in the resulting display. Also, the system can be used as an output display device for data processors or as a slow-scan video communications receiver. The input data can come from the following sources:

1. An fm carrier from a video compressor over standard telephone lines. This signal can also be recorded on a conventional audio tape recorder for subsequent playback.
2. A base-band slow-scan video received from the video compressor over an 8-kHz communications channel.
3. Parallel digital data from a computer or other source of digitized pictorial information.

The video output signal can be displayed on a television monitor or it can be used with other standard television equipment such as a video tape recorder. The output capability of units with the digital I/O option provides easy interfacing with TTL-

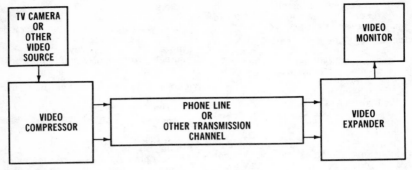

Video expander.

level minicomputers or other digital processing devices.

video frame store—One type is a solid-state video memory, with high-speed a/d and d/a converters, which is capable of digitizing, storing, and displaying a single frame of video information. Individual picture elements can be randomly accessed by computer, processed, then returned to memory. Allows video in, with video or digital out, or digital in, with digital or video out. Easily interfaces with most micro- and minicomputers.

video generator—The scan electronics, which on some systems is commonly called the video generator, incorporates the analog video and synchronization signals required to drive the crt monitor. The configuration of the video generator tailors the display system to a specific application. When necessary, it has multiple generators to meet the demands of both graphics and imaging tasks.

video image generation — Conversion of numeric data into video images can be effected using either vector or raster techniques. Vector generation is limited to the display of lines, but raster scanning (tv) is far more versatile. It can be used to display a greater variety of shapes and gradations of texture. Circular feature-generation algorithms permit circular, globular, and cylindrical objects such as ponds, clouds, and storage tanks to be modeled. Point features can also be defined, positioned, and assigned a color in order to represent airport lighting systems and other point light effects. Various algorithms

are being developed to increase the pictorial realism of simulated scenes with a greater variety of texture, and of shadings of light intensity and color.

video signal—Refers to that part of a tv signal which conveys all the information (intensity, color, and synchronization) required for establishing the visual image in monochrome or color television.

video, single-frame—Single-frame television requires only a small fraction of the bandwidth that is needed by conventional "moving pictures." The results are low transmission costs and relative ease in finding appropriate space within an increasingly crowded radio-frequency spectrum. An enormous amount of information is readily convertible to single-frame format; in fact, virtually anything that is now put on paper or contained in still photographs can be converted. Add audio, as some users have, and a powerful communications system is produced, not quite as flexible as conventional television, but at a fraction of the cost in transmission and program production.

video terminal codes—Between a video terminal and a computer system, information flows in the form of special codes. A good part of that information concerns the characters—letters, numbers, and symbols—that make up the main contents of a company's business files, management reports, etc. Codes for these characters are quite standard; terminal manufacturers use the same character codes as do the computer manufacturers. However, in addition to character codes, another important kind of information also flows between the computer and the terminal in the form of *control codes* that instruct just how the text is to be handled. For example, control codes might instruct the display to "move to the next line" or to "tab to column 35." Each system manufacturer chooses its own control code versions, and imbeds those codes in the programs that operate the computer and perform the business tasks. For a terminal to work properly with a given computer system, the terminals must respond properly to the control codes in the programs used by that system.

video terminal functions — To provide for entry of data into the microcomputer and to display desired information.

videotext — Videotext is an umbrella term used to cover both broadcast teletext and telephone transmission viewdata systems. It is important not for its sophistication, but in its availability and generality. In England, teletext offers an agreed upon set of standards on protocols and display, centralized support via the public switched-telephone network (in the case of viewdata) and redundant television lines (in the case of teletext), and the general availability of terminals in the form of enhanced tv receivers. For the United Kingdom and many other countries, it is the form in which much information will reach homes and businesses. The technology was developed in Great Britain and, then, rapidly gained momentum in France, Japan, and Canada.

Teletext refers to information that is transmitted by broadcasters to business and home screens on an unused portion of the tv signal. The data remains unseen until the viewer, using a hand-held calculator-like keypad, calls it up for display on the screen of his tv set. (The tv set is equipped with a "connector.") With some 800 "pages" of print available from the typical teletext service (as in the United Kingdom in 1980), the "menu" ranges from entertainment to business, and from self-improvement to national affairs. Among the viewing possibilities are news, weather, sports results, daily horoscopes, stock market prices, local super-

market prices, traffic updates, airline schedules, theater and movie listings, local events, home-study courses, and a host of other topics.

Viewdata, a somewhat more versatile technology, offers a greater volume of information. Its flexibility lies in the route taken by the information being transmitted to the television set. Instead of using broadcast signals, a basic telephone connection is utilized. The viewer asks for specific information from the data banks plugged into the system (via his hand-held keypad). The computer obliges by printing the requested materials on the tv screen. This two-way interactivity, allowing the viewer to send and receive information (even a printout), is the technology that leads to the likelihood of electronic banking, schooling, shopping, mail delivery, and other services. *See also* viewdata.

vidicon/computer camera — Refers to one type of vidicon camera that is designed specifically for use with digital and analog computers. The equipment has been designed to shake hands with both types of computer systems, to be used as an "eye" for automated industrial inspection, image analysis, biological research, and for use in college research laboratories.

viewdata—Viewdata is a public name for a type of interactive text service originally developed by the British Post Office. The public name has come to represent the generic name for a two-way tv product, even though there are many competing variations. The basic British viewdata system uses an adapted tv set with a telephone connection and a remote control switch box that looks like a pocket calculator. Viewers press numbers to call for pages of travel information, business information, retail advertising, or constantly updated news. A central computer is signalled through the telephone and responds by finding the appropriate page and flashing it on the viewer's screen. Pages appear in bright colors and block letters; each page includes a list of ten other pages that can be called up for more information. Sometimes, people must search through seven or eight pages to find the one they want. *See also* videotext and teletext.

viewdata (Prestel)—The best-known of the viewdata systems is Prestel, developed by the British Post Office. Prestel contains as much as 170,000 "frames" of information (as compared to 100 frames transmitted via Ceefax).

When the Prestel user calls a local computer for access to the system, a greeting frame and a commencing index appear on the tv screen. The first index is the beginning of a simple tree structure—a prospective theatergoer can press the number corresponding to Entertainment, and then proceed by pressing more buttons to view Theater, London, a certain part of London, a special combination of letters in the beginning of the titles of the plays, and, finally, a number of plays beginning with certain letter combinations. Viewdata systems, such as Prestel, have the capacity of expanding into electronic mail systems. In Prestel, for example, information providers are already writing to one another. (*See* teletext.)

virtual — Conceptual representation as opposed to physical fact; appearing to be rather than actually being.

virtual address—In a computer, an immediate or real-time address. Typically, the virtual address of a word in memory consists of two parts. The first part refers to a page number (a fixed-size block of main memory). The second refers to a location within the block. In operation, secondary memory is connected to these blocks through high-speed I/O devices that permit programs to be swapped directly from disk into any one of the main-memory blocks without interfering with processor operation. This process is known as direct-memory access and allows execution of one user program in one block of memory while programs are being swapped to and from another block.

virtual address space—Refers to virtual storage systems and the virtual storage assigned to a job, a terminal user, or system task.

virtual array — The most visible difference between a real array and a virtual array is the time needed to access a particular array element as a function of where that element is in the array (its referencing order). For very large virtual arrays, the referencing order could noticeably affect program execution time. Knowing the algorithm used by the virtual array processor in order to search the random-access files can help optimize the user's program, but any execution time differences are a small price to pay for the ability to handle the data in the first place.

The shorter access times of random-access files are utilized on some systems to provide a virtual array facility. Instead of moving a data structure into primary memory and then operating on it, the data structure is stored in a random-access file. Whenever the user's program wants to operate on a piece of the data, the system fetches that piece from the file, letting the user pretend that the piece of data is already in primary memory.

The reason for having a virtual array capability is that application programs can use virtual arrays to handle data structures that are too large to fit into primary memory. Large arrays can be stored on a disk, with only a portion of the file in primary memory at any one time. Since virtual arrays (containing string or numerical data) are usually stored as unformatted binary data, I/O conversions can be eliminated during storage and retrieval. This means no loss of precision, nor time wasted doing conversions.

virtual memory — Virtual memory, ideally invisible to the user, involves the transfer of information one page or more at a time between primary and secondary memory, and adds only that time required for page swapping to the normal operating time. This procedure leaves the programmer free to address total storage without concern as to whether primary or secondary storage is actually being addressed and, effectively, includes the large inexpensive capacity of secondary storage in the system. Optimally, a microcomputer should be able to operate either with or without virtual memory without major software modification. While this concept has found wide application in larger computer systems, it has played a lesser role in mini- and microcomputer applications because its simplest implementation is in software alone, which requires a substantial portion of available primary storage capacity. Benefits of virtual memory operation are therefore enhanced when it is implemented by hardware which carries out the data-swapping algorithms. Higher hardware costs are usually more than compensated for by savings in software. Because today's microcomputers are so inexpensive, a virtual memory option would not cost significantly more than an integrated microcomputer plus a secondary disk storage system.

virtual memory concepts—Two important concepts of virtual memory systems are those of address space and memory space. The address space is the set of all locations used by a program, both instruction and data. The memory space is the set of actual hardware locations available on the machine. Programs running under virtual memory will generally have their address space much larger than the memory space. A mapping or some other function from the address space to the memory space is needed. Normally, virtual memory space is needed. In other words, the address used by a program may not correspond to the actual hardware address of the item being referenced. Therefore, something is needed to translate a program or virtual address into a hardware address. Normally, virtual memory systems have special hardware which will intercept all program addresses and send them to be translated. In addition, many systems also have hardware address translation routines which generally involve a hardware table with entries for each page in memory. The entries for a page in such a table would be a virtual address of the first location on the page and its hardware address. If the hardware search of the table fails, the program address is not in memory, and the pager must be entered to bring in the appropriate page.

virtual memory, executive system — A sophisticated storage allocator can allow the programmer to write programs as if main memory were unlimited. This is termed virtual memory. The executive program will keep programs on disk, whenever they are not being used, loading each one into memory whenever it is called for.

virtual memory, FIFO — One possible method to determine the expected time before memory is referenced is the first-in/first-out (FIFO) procedure; the first page into memory will be the first one to leave when replacement is necessary. The advantage to this technique is that it is extremely simple to implement and, therefore, has a low software overhead per reference. On the majority of references to data already in main memory, only the state of presence need be determined, there being no other overhead required. The distance and FIFO methods each have a bad aspect. The FIFO algorithm shows no respect for a program's working set, and ignores the principle of locality. Therefore, this method would probably have more paging activity than other methods.

virtual memory, microcomputer—When accessing virtual memory, the user regards the combination of main and peripheral storage devices as a single large storage space. Consequently, the user can write large programs without worrying about the physical memory limitations of the system. To achieve this, the operating system software places some of the users' programs and data in peripheral storage. When they must be brought into main memory for execution, the system performs an operation called a page swap. Information not currently in use is removed from the main memory and returned to peripheral storage, making room for the new material. For efficiency, when the referenced location has to be brought from the peripheral to main memory, other locations likely to be referenced next are brought also. The essence of virtual memory is that the user, or programmer, does not have to be aware of this process. He or she uses one consistent set of addresses, called virtual addresses. The memory management hardware keeps track of where the information resides at any moment and converts, or translates, the virtual address to its real location in main memory. When the hardware finds the virtual address requested unavailable in main memory, it initiates a swap procedure.

virtual memory pointer — Refers to an aid for storage efficiency. Some computers are designed so that parts of programs and data may be scattered through main memory and auxiliary storage. Various pointers or lists of pointers automatically keep track of the location of these program portions. The user of computers so designed may be unaware of this scattering procedure and most often operates computing procedures as though he were using normal memory.

virtual memory technique — In some systems, to execute a single instruction, all that is required is that the instruction and the data on which it operates be located in the main memory. As far as the execution of the instruction is concerned, the remainder of the program could reside in secondary storage, such as a disk or drum. It is the task of a virtual memory system to ensure that prior to executing an instruction, the instruction and its operand(s) are in main memory. If either is not in memory, then it must be located in the secondary storage (the actual site of virtual memory) and brought into memory. If this retrieval were done on a single instruction basis, the system overhead and execution degradation would be significant.

virtual memory, user-coded — Virtual memory can be provided by a user-determined form of code segmentation. This approach permits a program to be larger than the main memory and avoids the thrashing between disk and memory that often results when segmentation is totally machine determined. Some systems automatically eliminate swap out of segments that are in frequent use. A hardware-implemented variable stack design can sharply reduce the amount of memory required to execute programs. Minor data area can be wasted by unused subroutines. A data stack can also provide variable-size arrays, re-entrant code, recursive programming, and an efficient method of parameter passing to subroutines.

virtual memory vs. mapping — Virtual memory lets addressable program space exceed real memory, while mapping lets real memory exceed addressable program space. Software and hardware for systems with either mapping or virtual memory usually make these benefits transparent to the user by letting him write and run location-independent code. Operating systems may also provide dynamic allocation of memory.

virtual storage—A virtual memory system is organized around a relatively small amount of directly accessible main storage and a large amount of secondary storage in the form of high-speed drums and disks. Programs in these systems can be constructed so as to use a great deal of memory, without worrying about how this memory is going to be allocated in main storage or swapped between main and secondary storage. In typical systems, the virtual memory for all programs is organized in pages of perhaps 4096 bytes, with this organization being transparent to each program. Then, assisted by hardware, the supervisor organizes page transfers between main and secondary storage as required without explicit intervention on the part of the program.

virtual terminal—Refers to a set of conventions characterizing a standard computer terminal, that uses a standard character set and is capable of generating or responding to a standard set of format effect controls. The virtual terminal characteristics are translated into real terminal characteristics by a processor connected to or embedded within a real terminal. Computers offering services through a computer network serve virtual terminals, thus simplifying the programming of terminal support.

visual inquiry station—Refers to an input/output unit which permits the interrogation of an automatic data-processing system by the immediate processing of data from a human or terminal (automatic) source together with the display of the results of the processing—on a cathode-ray tube, in many cases.

VMOS structure (U-groove) — VMOS transistors can be either V-groove or U-groove. VMOS processing with a V-groove uses the silicon area efficiently, but the sharp bottom of the V-groove is a drawback. At the point of the V, a strong field concentration develops between the gate and drain, and the gate oxide layer tends to be quite thin. The result is a limited high-voltage capability, because of gate oxide breakdown, even though the gate does not experience the full drain-to-source voltage.

The V-groove problem can be solved by turning the V into a U. U-groove and V-groove gate geometries are similar, except that, in U-groove,

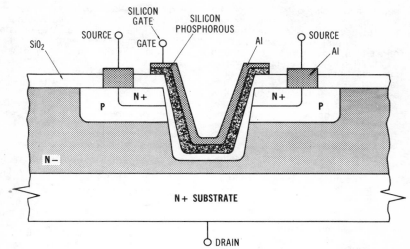

VMOS structure (U-groove).

the etching process that forms the groove stops while the groove is still relatively wide (etched field termination).

The gate area can be covered with a polycrystalline silicon doped with phosphorous (silicon-gate process) to improve manufacturing yields, as well as breakdown voltages. Although polysilicon is an effective ion migration barrier, it is a poor conductor and can slow the device's turn-on.

Therefore, a layer of high-conductivity aluminum is deposited over the polysilicon to improve switching time. Silicon-gate processing has replaced the older metal-gate processing because, among other advantages, the technique results in much lower leakage currents.

VMOS structure (V-groove)—The term VMOS is used to describe a V-grooved device used in integrated-circuit memories in which both

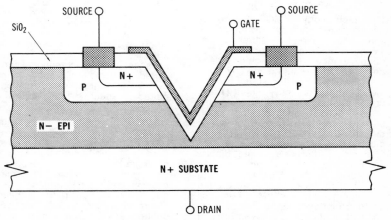

VMOS structure (V-groove).

source and drain contacts are on the top surface. The term, VMOS, refers to the device's construction which causes current flow to be vertical, rather than horizontal, as in standard FETs. This structure overcomes a number of the surface MOSFET limitations. A VMOS structure begins life as an n+ epitaxial substrate into which n and p regions are diffused. A V-shaped groove is then etched anisotropically through the diffusions, and a gate is formed. VMOS devices have several advantages:

1. A low ON resistance, resulting from short channel lengths, can be achieved, and a reduced metallization of the die area, since the source and gate connections are on one side of the die and the drain connections are on the other (vertical current flow).
2. A high gain-bandwidth product due to the low capacitance of VMOS.

VMOS has a very strong selling point. It promises very tight geometries, which in turn promise attractive advantages. A manufacturer can have increased densities and, at the same time, an extremely good speed-power product over and above what would be achieved with NMOS. Also, VMOS is much less susceptible to problems like oxide breakdown—less because, instead of a layer of oxide between the device gates on a chip as is found on other technologies, the air within the V groove provides the isolation.

VMOS technology—VMOS technology has several significant advantages. It allows fabrication of "three-dimensional" transistor structures and requires a much smaller chip surface area than that required for any other planar MOS transistor structure. The VMOS transistors have short (1 micron) channels and large channel width-to-length ratios making possible the design of very-high-speed circuits. The VMOS transistor sinks much larger currents per unit area than planar devices, making bipolar compatibility on the outputs easy. As the source of the VMOS device is a ground plane, a metal bus to ground is not required. The VMOS process has three independent layers of interconnect: diffusion, poly, and metal (not including the ground plane),

which provides about a 40% improvement in area over standard NMOS SiGate devices. Memory devices, such as read-only memories (ROMs), EPROMs, and static RAMs, have about 50% smaller cell sizes relative to NMOS, using VMOS. These cells can be combined with random logic to cover a wide range of applications. The VMOS process has the ability of achieving VLSI (very-large-scale integration) densities and high performance using the current manufacturing photolithographic processes.

voice acceptance terminals — These terminals function conceptually like keyboards and can replace them without special interfacing provisions. In practice, a voice-input terminal accepts spoken signals from the operator and generates digital codes identical to a keyboard's output. In most applications, an unskilled operator can perform the function adequately, usually with better accuracy and with throughput raised 50% or more. The terminal preprocessor uses spectral analysis to resolve the spoken word into 32 speech parameters: unvoiced, energy-burst consonants, vowel and vowel-like consonants, long and short pauses, and other features. The operator stores his speech reference patterns in the microcomputer's RAM, using 1K of memory for each 32 words in the task vocabulary. The operator repeats each word in the vocabulary 10 times in training the terminal to recognize his speech. The microcomputer then compares incoming spoken words with the stored reference patterns and generates the appropriate character string when the incoming word matches a stored word. The terminal's recognition threshold can be varied for commercial applications or the higher degrees of correlation required in security applications.

voice-actuated crt terminal — Consisting of a pc board and a high-quality microphone, one type of speech-recognition system transforms a standard or "dumb" terminal into a voice-controlled video-display console. The board fits easily within the terminal's chassis, and the microphone attaches quickly to a front-panel connector. The microprocessor-based unit voice-controls any program run on the host computer via the crt terminal, recognizing 64 speaker-developed isolated words or phrases at a time. Additionally, several word/phrase groups reside in the computer's memory for use as needed. Standard recognition-rate runs about 99%, increasing to 100% with the use of word/voice-verification loops. System applications can cover virtually every hands- or eyes-busy operation, ranging from medical, laboratory, business, commercial, and industrial uses to utilization by manually handicapped persons.

voice channel — Refers to a circuit of sufficient bandwidth to permit a data-transfer rate of up to 2400 bits per second. Primarily, the term distinguishes this service from a teleprinter grade that utilizes a set or sets of data.

voice-frequency equipment—Refers to equipment which provides the interface between telephone facilities, and between various telephone-switching machines, as well as between telephone-switching machines and subscriber lines, in order to perform the functions of signalling and amplification of voice signals.

voice-grade channel — Refers to a channel that is used for speech transmission that usually has an audio-frequency range of 300 to 3400 Hz. It is also used for the transmission of analog and digital data, as up to 10,000 bps can be transmitted on a voice-grade channel.

voice-grade lines—The common communications line used in normal telephone communications. It is an essential part of most communications systems involving computers and data transmission. A voice-grade line has a bandwidth of 0–3000 hertz.

Voice-grade lines are capable of handling voice transmissions without distortion. These lines are capable of transmitting data at speeds up to 10,000 baud, although they are normally used in systems with transmission-speed requirements of 2400 baud. Lines that are below voice-grade lines (subvoice) are capable of transmitting data for terminals that operate at 15 characters per second. The facility operates at speeds up to 180 baud. Any higher-speed transmission must be handled by voice-grade lines. In contrast, the highest grade facility is the one using

wideband lines. These lines can handle the equivalent of 60 to 120 voice-grade lines.

voice-grade modems—Typical applications for low-speed asynchronous modems (0–2000 bps) include time-sharing operations and as a teletypewriter or crt terminal for computer systems. Medium-speed modems are almost entirely synchronous and operate at speeds ranging from 2000 to 4800 bps over dial-up or leased lines. They are generally used in dial-up two-wire systems that use magnetic-tape units, or in four-wire dedicated multidrop applications with a terminal controller unit. High-speed synchronous modems operate at speeds ranging from 4800 bps to 9600 bps on leased circuits. At these speeds, however, special attention must be given to conditioning and equalization. High-speed modems are typically used for multiplexing applications, higher-speed terminal-to-computer applications, and for airline-reservation systems.

voice-quality synthesizer — The natural-sounding synthetic voice of some units is based on the analysis of real speech. Proprietary computer techniques are utilized for the automatic processing of speech recordings — yours (if of a good quality) or of some other person. The outputs are highly compressed digital codes which operate, in conjunction with a unique voice synthesizer whose circuitry models the human vocal tract to produce a clear, natural, male or female speech, under the control of a communications processor.

voice recognition — Speech systems differ in the manner by which they recognize speech—the way in which they duplicate the human ear-to-brain combination. Speech can be viewed as *waveform patterns;* that is, the vector of numbers that collectively make up a waveform. Speech can be viewed as the product of the human vocal system (analyzed for vocal-chord vibrations, resonances, and other characteristics). Speech can be broken down into various patterns of sound, which is basically the way the brain works. Also, a system can listen only for characteristics, such as timing and vowel pronunciations, that differentiate one speaker from another. Mathematical approaches to speech analysis bring together such disciplines as statistics, theoretic information, signal processing, and pattern classification. Humanistic approaches involve phonetics, linguistics, perceptual studies, and neurology. Most systems use some combination of these approaches and disciplines to perform their recognition function.

voice recognition, connected-speech— With various types of connected-speech recognition systems, users may speak without pausing after each word. (Connected speech is still not quite the same as natural or continuous speech; users still must articulate their words rather distinctly.) One type of terminal has a vocabulary size of 120 words, can handle up to 5 words per spoken sentence (provided the sentence lasts less than 2.5 seconds), and is trained by speaking each word only once (twice for digits). On this system, recognition accuracy is both vocabulary- and user-dependent. But most users seem to quickly learn how to make the subtle adjustments necessary to produce consistent pronunciation. This doesn't mean speaking in a stilted manner. In fact, to the casual listener, it would sound almost like ordinary speech.

voice-recognition dialer — An experimental, voice-controlled, repertory dialing system is being used to permit hands-free telephone dialing. It compares the user's spoken words to stored patterns. To produce the stored patterns, the user initially speaks each name or number twice. The system then can be used to dial any telephone number that corresponds to a name in its memory, or to any number the user speaks. During tests, the system performed well — with no recognition errors, and with only a few requests for repeats (Bell System).

voice-response technology—Voice-response technology is much simpler than speech-recognition technology. One of three procedures is generally used in voice-response operation: (1) playing back prerecorded messages, (2) synthesizing messages by piecing together individually prerecorded words ("synthesis by concatenation"), or (3) synthesizing messages by first forming words from a set of speech elements, or phonemes, and then piecing the words together into sentences ("true synthesis").

Voice entry should not be confused with data-entry devices that, for example, utilize audio or voice responses to verify an order number. The voice-response systems are driven by the same audio tones that are generated by a push-button telephone. The voice-response terminals have customized keypads for specific applications so, in effect, no two user firms have the same keyboard layout.

In a typical parts-order entry application, the voice-response terminal is connected remotely to the host processor via a telephone. Once activated, the operator can key in part numbers and inquire about price, part availability, or order the part. A voice system in the host computer responds to searches of the inventory file that is stored in the computer and sends back synthesized human voice sounds that are heard by the operator through a speaker in the terminal. The voice verifies that the part is ordered, is out of stock, or it utters the price, if a price was requested.

voice-response terminal—One type of Touch-Talk Order Entry System answers incoming calls any time of the day or night, prompts the person calling in a 32-word custom vocabulary in order to obtain required information in a specified sequence, and transfers collected orders to a host computer for processing. Input is via special-purpose Touch-Tone® data-entry terminals over telephone lines. A minicomputer controls the voice-response subsystem and collects order information. Modular software provides a number of options to meet specific application requirements. The basic order-entry processing system includes modems, a crt display station, and a logging printer. Expanded systems can be set up that utilize up to 96 words of voice response and that have modems to support up to 32 phone lines.

voice synthesis — Voice synthesis can be accomplished by stringing together vocal sounds. One method is to break down human speech by phoneme. (The word "cat," for instance, has three phonemes: k, aah, and t.) Word stringing involves storing the sound of each word used. The most natural sounding method is to store whole phrases, but this approach requires a minimum data rate of 1000 bits per second versus a rate of 200 to 300 bits per second for phoneme stringing. Although phrase stringing sounds most like the human voice, it is believed that future products will tend toward phoneme stringing, which will be improved to sound more natural.

tion of clauses and phrases, as well as sentences, are standard. In addition to the manual controls for rate, volume, and pitch, a tone control allows the user to adjust the vocal output for esthetic or ambient-noise considerations.

Voice synthesizer (Courtesy Computalker Consultants).

Voice terminal (Courtesy Interstate Electronics Corp.).

voice synthesizer — A device used to synthesize human speech so that users can vocally communicate with the computer. One low-cost unit is the CT-1 Speech Synthesizer by Computalker Consultants. It is completely self-contained with a chassis, power supply, on-board audio amplifier, software, and interconnecting cable, and it produces a highly intelligible natural-sounding speech. The CT-1 can synthesize human speech in any language or dialect and it can sing and play music, after being programmed by specifying the desired acoustic speech structure. Once the user has the system set down, he or she can get the computer to talk back, vocally debug a program, or tell you what it thinks of someone.

Another type of low-cost single-circuit-board unit is capable of generating an unlimited vocabulary in seven different languages. It generates words by a series of electronic commands that produce the various phonemes from which human speech is constructed. The commands also control the degrees of inflection that contribute to the meaning of each word and phrase. The unit requires eight parallel data bits to create each phoneme—six for phoneme selection and two for inflection. Each 8-bit command selects one of sixty-three phonemes that generates the vocal sound desired. Pauses to allow for separa-

voice terminal—A basic voice terminal is one that consists of a controller, one work station, one asynchronous output interface, and support software. Larger voice terminals are available that have visual feedback and audio response which increases the channel capability. Some voice-logging systems provide cassette reliability and convenience, plus instant recall without recording interruptions. One voice-logging recorder system provides continuous, automatic, audio recording designed to meet the needs of operations that are as diverse as law enforcement, fire and hospital emergency, taxi dispatching, telephone banking, and aircraft control. A biperipheral cassette-tape drive mechanism drives three tape transports which can operate in three modes: continuous, voice activated, or device activated.

voice-waveform digitization—Concerns an approach to digital coding. Voice-waveform digitization methods take samples of the speech waveform and represent the sampled waveform amplitudes by digital binary-coded values. At the receiver, the digital signals are converted back to analog form in an attempt to reconstruct the original speech waveform. Vocoder methods make no attempt to preserve original speech waveform. Instead, the input speech is analyzed in terms of standardized speech features, each of which can be transmitted in digital-coded form. At the receiver, these features are reassembled, and an output speech signal is synthesized. Ideally, the synthesized signal, as it is perceived by the ear, closely resembles the original speech.

volatile—A characteristic of becoming lost or erased when power is removed, i.e., the loss of data.

volatile dynamic storage — Refers to a specific storage unit which depends only on the external supply of power for maintenance of stored information.

voltage comparator — Suitable for use in a variety of applications in logic, control, and instrumentation equipment, voltage comparators are available from most large semiconductor manufacturers as well as a number of the smaller specialty firms. In its basic form, the voltage comparator is essentially a modified differential amplifier with two stable output states, responding when an applied input voltage crosses a pre-established threshold level.

voltage fluctuations — Voltage fluctuations, although occurring for different reasons than noise, affect electronic equipment just as seriously. Voltage fluctuation, as an inclusive term, can be applied to both high-speed voltage transients (spikes and faults) and longer-term brownouts and overvoltages. Transient surges and dips in voltage level occur frequently along ac power distribution lines whenever electrical devices are switched on or off. If voltage is not regulated, such transients produce a variety of damaging effects. Spikes and dips can cause memory loss, affect the performance of timing circuits, and scramble data being transmitted to or from peripherals. In addition, chronic or severe voltage spikes physically degrade and ultimately burn out semiconductor chips.

voltage multiplier—Circuit for obtaining high dc potential from low voltage ac supply, effectively only when load current is small, e.g., for anode supply to crt. A ladder of half-wave rectifiers charges successive capacitors that are connected in series, on alternate half-cycles.

voltage regulation—A measure of the degree to which a power source maintains its output-voltage stability under varying load conditions.

voltage regulation diode—The reverse-biased diode is perhaps the simplest electronic voltage regulator around. Once it reaches its breakdown voltage, the diode will maintain the same voltage over a varying current range until the current reaches the point where the diode ultimately burns up. Except for burning up, this is exactly what the typical zener diode is designed to do. The point at which the zener diode breaks down is known as the "zener voltage" (same as regulator voltage).

voltage regulation load—An occurring change in output voltage of a power source for a specified change in the load. This is often expressed as the percentage ratio of the voltage change.

voltage regulator—A device that maintains or varies the terminal voltage of a generator or other machine at a predetermined value.

voluntary interrupt—Refers to an interrupt to the processor or operating system that is caused by an object program's deliberate use of a function which is known to cause an interrupt and, hence, under program control.

voting processors — On most microcomputer systems, there is only one instruction stream being executed. But, on others, three or more separate microprocessors execute the instructions simultaneously. The name "voting" is derived from a comparison technique where, if any result differs, the erring CPU is "voted" out of the configuration. The remaining units then continue to operate until the faulty CPU is repaired. Often a fourth processor is kept on standby in order to replace an erring processor.

VRAM — Abbreviation for video RAM. Video RAMs generally consist of two primary parts — a digital electronics section that accepts microprocessor commands and formats alphanumeric data which a video-generator section mixes with sync pulses in order to form composite video signals (for input on a video-input stage). A typical VRAM looks like an ordinary 8-bit-wide RAM, and it can be connected directly to the address and data bus of any bus-organized system. Most

VRAMs are particularly suitable for use in microcomputer systems due to their low cost, small size, modular packaging, single +5-volt power supply, and ease of interfacing.

As a low-cost microprocessor/crt interface, VRAMs make many new applications feasible. Microprocessor systems can now display more data at lower cost per character than ever before. Applications now utilizing these devices include word-processing systems, medical-type patient-data monitors, point-of-sale terminals, and PBX telephone systems. Because a designer can program the device for any function, applications are limited only by his or her imagination.

VRC procedure—VRC (vertical redundancy checking) is an odd or even parity check performed on a per-character basis and requires a parity check-bit position in each character. If individual characters are represented by 8 bits, such as when using an 8-level code, 7 bits may be used to represent actual numbers and letters, and the eighth bit may be reserved for checking purposes. The presence or absence of the eighth bit provides the inherent checking feature. For example, in an even parity check, the parity bit is used to make the total number of "1" bits in the character even. If the character contains 4 zeros and 3 ones, then a 1-bit is inserted as the parity bit.

VS—Abbreviation for virtual storage.

VTAM (vortex telecommunications method)—A special data communications software package that organizes and simplifies data-communications programming to serve remote workstations for a host computer.

W

wafer — 1. Refers to the silicon ingot that is cut into thin slices upon which semiconductor devices are fabricated. Also, the slices since the slices as well as the ingots are known as wafers. 2. A thin slice of semiconductor such as silicon or gallium arsenide upon which matrices of individual semiconductor devices can be formed. The wafer is separated, after processing, into the dice or chips which contain the individual devices.

wafer fabrication—This is the sequence of steps that, when applied to a silicon wafer with appropriate masking, produces an array of LSI devices. *See also* maskmaking.

wafer gettering—Gettering of contaminants is done to improve the wafer quality. Lattice damage and strain are produced on the back side of the wafer by fine pitting of the surface with high-intensity laser radiation, providing a means for gettering at any point in the process sequence. There is no risk of damage to the front surface of the wafer in this technique of using lasers. In these applications, the key advantages of laser techniques over thermal techniques are a temporal and spatial control over the heating in the material being processed—extremely short pulses of energy in beam widths that can be adjusted to cover only the areas desired. The cost factor is about the same for laser processing as for thermal processing.

wafer process control system (PCS)— The starting point of the wafer processing flow occurs when the machine operator identifies the lot that is to be processed to the process control system (PCS). The process control system then checks the history file of the lot and the process description in order to determine which operation the lot is scheduled to receive. The automatic "recipe" is transferred from the PCS to the appropriate automatic equipment via a direct computer link. The operator is given wafer-handling instructions for the operation on a computer terminal located at the processing position. The operator then loads the wafers according to the instructions and presses the start button. The operation proceeds to its completion, with alarms logged automatically in the lot history file. Next, the PCS checks the data collected on the processed wafer to ensure conformance to specified limits, and places out-of-spec wafer lots on hold for later examination by the engineering staff. Immediately after a lot successfully completes an operation, it is automatically scheduled for the next operation in its process.

wafer processing—Process control during wafer processing consists of monitoring the electrical and physical properties of all thin-film layers in the device, as well as maintaining close control over the pattern delineation process. The thickness of all thin-film layers is monitored on a lot-by-lot basis. The reflectivity, grain size, resistivity, and adhesion of the metal layers are monitored; in addition, the coercivity, anisotropy, and magneto-resistance of the permalloy are measured on each lot. Control of pattern delineation is achieved with a wafer-by-wafer measurement of the photoresist resolution, alignment, and line width. After etching, the patterned films are inspected and line-width measurements are made on each wafer.

wafer, semiconductor — A relatively large slice (or flat disk) of semiconductor material into which a number of integrated circuits are simultaneously processed and which may be subsequently separated into individual integrated-circuit devices.

waffle pack—Refers to a plastic container, having the appearance of a waffle, that has indentations or slots in it and a cover. It is designed to hold the individual devices in place for transportation purposes.

waiting list—Refers to a procedure for organizing and controlling the data of unprocessed operational programs. These lines are ordinarily maintained by the control program. Synonymous with queue.

waiting state—Refers to the state of an interrupt level that is armed and which has received an interrupt signal, but is not yet allowed to become active.

wait state—A microcycle or an internal state entered by an MPU when a synchronizing signal is not present. It is used to synchronize the microprocessor with a slow memory.

wait time — The time interval during which a processing unit is waiting for information to be retrieved from a serial access file or to be located by a search.

wall energy—Refers to the energy per unit area stored in the domain wall that bounds two oppositely magnetized regions of a ferromagnetic material.

warm-up time—Refers to that particular time that is required, after energizing a device, before its rated output characteristics begin to apply.

WATS wide-area telephone service—A service provided by telephone companies which permits a customer, by use of an access line, to make calls to telephones in a specific zone on a dial-up basis for a flat monthly charge. Monthly charges are based on the size of the area in which the calls are placed, not on the number or length of calls. Under the WATS arrangement, the United States is divided into many zones that can be called, on either a full-time or a measured-time basis.

watt—Abbreviated W. The unit of the electric power required to do work at the rate of 1 joule per second. It is the power expended when 1 ampere of direct current flows through a resistance of 1 ohm.

wattage rating — The maximum power that a device can safely handle.

waveform—1. The shape of an electromagnetic wave. 2. The graphic representation of the wave in (1) above, showing the variations in amplitude with time.

waveform analyzer—An instrument that measures the amplitude and frequency of the components in a complex waveform.

waveform recorders — Waveform recorders are advanced electronic instruments that convert analog signals into digital data and store the information in semiconductor memory. They are the alternative to oscilloscopes and cameras, light-beam oscillographs, and fm tape recorders for recording transient analog signals. Waveform recorders provide excellent time and amplitude resolution, high bandwidth, pretrigger recording, and both analog or digital signal reproduction. The real-time conversion and storage of analog signals (including pretrigger information) makes the waveform recorder valuable in a wide variety of applications, such as acoustics, kinetic chemistry, laser radar (LIDAR), nuclear instrumentation, shock tube physics, video digitizers, and so forth. All of these diverse areas have several things in common: waveform recorders are of most help where the event being studied is either a transient (nonrecurring) event, an event to be computer-processed, or both.

wave function—In a wave equation, a point function that specifies the amplitude of a wave.

waveguide — 1. A system of material boundaries capable of guiding electromagnetic waves. 2. A hollow conducting tube comprising a transmission line within which electromagnetic waves are propagated on a solid dielectric or dielectric-filled conductor. 3. Hollow metal conductor within which very-high-frequency energy can be transmitted efficiently in one of a number of modes of electromagnetic oscillation. Dielectric guides, consisting of rods or slabs of dielectric, operate similarly, but normally have higher losses.

waveguide limits, optical — The waveguiding nature of fibers shows light rays entering the fiber at various angles. The difference in refractive index of the core and the cladding materials establishes a critical angle between the incoming rays and the core-clad interface below which total internal reflection occurs. High-angle rays travel a greater distance than low-angle ones, giving rise to a time delay. Thus, a narrow pulse of light slowly broadens in time as it travels down the fiber, ultimately limiting the information-carrying capacity of the waveguide.

wave shape—Refers to the shape of one cycle of a repeated or periodic phenomenon. A graph representing the successive values of a varying amount (such as voltage, current, pressure, etc.) plotted against another variable (such as time or distance) and usually in rectangular coordinates. The graph represents the characteristics of varying quantity. It is the variation of the characteristic that is the waveform. The graph is its representation.

wave shaping—Modifying the shape of a signal waveform, such as sharpening the rise or fall of a pulse form.

weighted value — The numerical value assigned to any single bit as a function of its position in the code word.

white noise — 1. Random noise (e.g., shot and thermal noise) whose constant energy per unit bandwidth is independent of the central frequency at the band. The name is taken from the analogous definition of white light. 2. The electrical disturbance caused by the random movement of free electrons in a conductor or semiconductor. Since its electrical energy is evenly distributed throughout the entire frequency spectrum, it is useful for testing the frequency response of amplifiers, speakers, etc. 3. Noise which has equal energy at all frequencies. White noise has equal energies within a specified band and zero energy elsewhere if it is band-limited.

Winchester disk drives — Winchester technology permits packing fixed disk capabilities into a unit the size of an 8-inch floppy-disk drive. The advantages of the 8-inch Winchester drive are large capacity, small size, and relatively low prices. Users note that these "hard disk" devices tend to be more reliable than floppy disks, and they also reduce errors and data loss that is caused by media damage. Often, one drive, serving as a shared resource for as many as eight word processors, is used to store address lists and lengthy manuals (among other applications). In addition, the small Winchester drives can be used by stand-alone word processor and personal computer vendors in order to expand functions and to cluster their systems around shared files. A Winchester drive is often tied to a peripheral controller which manages shared memory and output and communications devices for a group of word processors. However, floppy disks are often maintained at the work stations to provide archival storage.

Winchester disk technology — In the mid-1970s, a new disk technology was developed which eliminated most of the undesirable features of hard disks for small computer users—the Winchester hard disk. Winchester drives utilize fast rotating high-den-

Winchester disk drives (Courtesy Pertec Computer Corp.).

sity disks and medium- to high-speed head positioners to achieve performance comparable to the most expensive hard disks. However, to minimize mechanical complexity and the difficulty of use, Winchester drives use fixed or nonremovable media. Because the media is factory installed, the critical head-disk tolerances can be maintained with relatively simple mechanics. The fixed nature of the drive allows the disk chamber to be sealed eliminating the possibility of contamination.

window — 1. A hole formed by etching through an oxide or insulating layer on a semiconductor wafer for the purpose of permitting diffusion into, or deposition onto, a selected area of the semiconductor. 2. A window is a rectangular portion of display memory (not necessarily displayed) which acts, and is treated, as a logical subterminal. Any functional capability that can be applied to the terminal as a whole can be applied to a logical subterminal (window). This translates into an important applications flexibility for the user.

window, enabling—A typical use of an enabling window is to look only at the data section of a message block in a simulated data-communications test. The window would gate out any message headers or control bits in the signal.

Winchester disk technology (Courtesy Kennedy Co., Subsidiary of Magnetics & Electronics, Inc.).

windowing — The division of a crt display into sections (by means of software), allowing the display of data from several different sources.

windowing, crt — Sometimes refers to firmware that allows a three-dimensional portion of the data base to be extracted and presented for viewing within a designated area on the crt screen.

wire-bonding — The method used for connecting chips to substrate conductor patterns, to package pins, or to other chips. Commonly used techniques include thermocompression ball and wedge types, and ultrasonic bond. Wire is usually gold or aluminum, 0.001 or 0.002 inch in diameter.

wired-in — Refers to components connected in circuits, particularly subminiature vacuum tubes and semiconductor devices, which are too small to be safely plugged into a holder.

wired-OR—Externally connecting separate circuits or functions so that the combination of their outputs results in an "AND" function. The point at which the separate circuits are wired together will be a "1" if all circuits feeding into this point are "1."

wired-program computer—A computer in which nearly all instructions are determined by the placement of interconnecting wires held in a removable plugboard. This arrangement allows for changes of operations by simply changing plugboards. If the wires are held in permanently soldered connections, the computer is called a fixed-program type.

wire-wrap — Wire-wrap was developed in the 1950s by Bell Labs as an alternative to soldering. Wire-wrapping consists basically of winding a number of turns of wire around a metal post that has at least two sharp edges. In practice, the metal post has evolved into a standard 0.025-inch square pin. With the correct wire and tension applied during wrapping, a clean metal-to-metal contact results. The corrosion resistance, mechanical stability, and conductivity are good enough for the technique to be used in military equipment. Wire-wrap is widely used in industry for prototype work and, using semiautomatic and automatic machines, for short production runs. Wide usage has brought with it a broad range of hardware such as tools, DIP sockets, edge connectors, and even whole logic boards.

wire-wrap advantages—Wire-wrapping offers the advantage of ease of design, freedom of layout, easy maintainability and parts replacement, ease of design change, good performance, and good density. But, unless users can justify wire-wrapped interconnection for applications on the basis of economics, there is no point in using it. Wire-wrapping would not enjoy its current popularity if it did not offer economic advantages over other techniques. It is far easier to lay out a wire-wrapped system than a printed-circuit board, and there is also an increase in flexibility of component location. Design changes can be implemented by documentation changes. This is considerably easier than modifying printed-circuit artwork and modifying an etched board when a design change is necessary. Replacing a component is also generally easier in a wire-wrapped system because of the plug-in feature inherent in wire-wrapping hardware. Printed-circuit board components can be made pluggable, of course, by the addition of sockets, but sockets on a printed-circuit board represent additional space, assembly labor, and parts cost.

wire-wrap boards—These boards help a designer to extend electronic capabilities without having to resort to a separate packaging scheme. To construct a new peripheral interface — say, between a measuring instrument and an S-100 computer bus— the user inserts components into sockets on the top side of the board; the components are then connected together by wrapping wire around pins that protrude from the opposite side of the board, to obtain the circuit and electronic capabilities required.

wire-wrap tool — A wrapping tool is a pencil-sized shaft with two holes in the end. The larger hole fits over the wrap post and the smaller hole fits over the wire. Wire sizes are 26, 28, and 30 gauge. The tool can be turned by hand, or there are a variety of power drives available. For production work, electric and pneumatic tool drivers are common. In prototype work, battery-powered drivers avoid the inconvenience of a trailing cord.

word—1. A group of characters occupying one storage location in a computer. They are treated by the computer circuits as an entity, by the control unit as an instruction, and by the arithmetic unit as a quantity. 2. A group of bits handled as a unit by a digital computer; generally comprising the largest such group that is handled throughout the central processor as a single unit. Not to be confused with *byte.*

word address format—The order of appearance of character information within a word.

word and byte addressing—Some systems provide both word and byte addressing for most memory reference instructions. This means that users can deal directly with either bytes or full words, as the application requires, without the complications required in microcomputers that are without byte addressing.

word count — Refers to record count. The first word of a record in a backing store file which indicates the length of the record to the housekeeping software and which enables the software to unpack logical records from physical blocks or buckets.

word counter — Block transfer devices that function as bus masters during data transfers and which usually require two registers to hold the parameters of the transfer. One parameter is the transfer word count. In some systems, this register (WC) is loaded by the microcomputer with the two's complement of the number of words to be transferred to or from memory. This number is clocked into the WORDCOUNT register.

word-count register—A separate word-count register keeps track of the progress of I/O transfers. Typically, the register is loaded at the beginning of the operation with the number of data words to be transferred and decremented after each transfer. On reaching zero, the word-count register signals the completion of the transfer operation by generating an interrupt signal.

word generators — Digital signal sources, known as word generators, can produce the simulated digital inputs and outputs of computers, communications equipment, and tape and disk data-storage systems, allowing users to evaluate system components under operating conditions. Word generators produce data either in serial form (useful for testing data-communications gear) or in parallel form (to simulate signals to or from a semiconductor memory stack). The data produced by these generators can be organized into specific binary formats called words or, more commonly, patterns. These can be created, and then reiterated, as required during the test, by presetting the output via switches on the control panel of the word generator, similar to the way one bootstraps a minicomputer. Interfaces are available with some word generators that permit them to be loaded with sequences contained on paper tape or cards.

One of the most common uses of word generators is to debug new circuit designs. The output signal levels and formats from these devices can be changed quickly for use with differing components (e.g., from TTL levels to ECL levels), and can be used in conjunction with other devices, such as programmable digital-width and delay units, to create a complete test facility. Word generators can produce several parallel data streams, or they can be set to produce only one serial data stream, an advantage that increases their flexibility in engineering lab applications.

word length, double—Many arithmetic instructions produce two-word results. With fixed-point multiplication, a double-length product is stored in two A registers of control storage for integer and fractional operations. Integer and fractional division is performed upon a double-length dividend with the remainder and the quotient retained in the A registers.

word-mark — Refers to an indicator to signal the beginning or end of a word, usually in a variable word-length machine.

word, microcomputer — This can be a group, row, or register of binary cells that is typically processed in one simultaneous operation. The word size in a microcomputer is sometimes defined as the number of binary cells contained in the accumulator(s) of the system.

Word modules (Courtesy Texas Instruments Incorporated).

word modules — These are plug-in devices used with the "Speak & Spell" learning aid made by Texas Instruments Incorporated. Speak & Spell comes with a basic vocabulary of the words that are difficult for children to learn to spell. Speak & Spell actually creates speech with microcomputer electronics. Words are spoken in a human voice with inflection and fi-delity. One module features words most commonly used in grades four through six. The module for grades seven and eight follow the same formula. An earlier plug-in module was called Vowel Power. The modules may be inserted in the back of the Speak & Spell machine. Each module contains an integrated circuit in which speech (in a coded digital form) is stored. The plug-in module couples to another circuit in the unit itself, which is an electronic model of the human vocal tract. Just as human speech is created by air impulses passing through the vocal cords and the vocal tract, synthetic speech is generated by processing electrical impulses through a rapidly changing electronic filter. The result is synthetically produced speech that sounds like that which is heard over a telephone.

word-organized storage — Refers to a specific type of storage that is composed of magnetic cells in which each word of the storage has a separate winding common to all the magnetic cells of the word, i.e., carrying the Read pulse and, possibly, the Write pulse also.

word pattern—The smallest meaningful language unit recognized by a machine. It is usually composed of a group of syllables and/or words.

Word processing (Courtesy AM International, Inc.).

word processing—Most word-processing applications operate on various desktop processing terminals. The typical word-processing program uses single-word English-language commands to initiate tasks such as letter writing, filing, editing, and printing. It also can create a mailing list. Editing is performed via function keys, which can center text, search for defined strings of text, and perform tab functions, among others. A typical word processor terminal features a full page video display screen and sophisticated software for maximum recording and editing capabilities.

word-processing center — Word-processing machines are classified as either "stand alone" or "shared logic." A stand-alone machine has one keyboard, one recording unit, and one "computer" for editing. A shared-logic machine has two or more independent keyboards sharing a recording unit and a computer. Shared-logic systems offer more power and economy to businesses that need several keyboards. However, they are inherently more vulnerable to breakdowns, since a single problem can put several keyboards out of commission.

One system designed to permit shared-logic capability while using stand-alone ability is the ForeWord™ word-processing system manufactured by Four-Phase Systems, Inc. The ForeWord™ word-processing system supports up to 16 display stations and 16 printers. It is designed for both general correspondence and long document editing.

word processing, microcomputer—Microcomputer applications have grown to include an office equipment application called word processing, i.e., controlling one or more typewriters that are used to edit text which is stored on cassettes or floppy disks. Before the appearance of microcomputers, this application clearly required a minicomputer. However, to

Word-processing center (Courtesy Four-Phase Systems, Inc.).

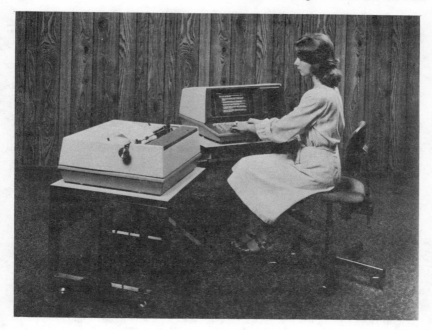

Word processing, microcomputer (Courtesy Lexitron Corp.).

support a small system containing only a few typewriters, the minicomputer was relatively costly to use; the microcomputer has helped bring the cost down to a reasonable level. Needless to say, word processing has received a considerable boost from the development of the floppy disk for a relatively inexpensive text-storage medium. Microcomputers are also appearing in systems designed to handle small business accounting and record-keeping applications. A microcomputer can easily handle these functions in a relatively standardized format if the information traffic is not too heavy.

word-processing terminal—Relates to the preparation and dissemination of letters, memoranda, reports, and articles using office typewriters and word-processing systems.

word recognizer—*See* speech system, dual computer.

word recognizer, discrete — A computer control device that is commanded by human voice, and used for entry of data into a computerized system containing discrete word structure and formatted data fields. Nonintelligent word recognizers are typically limited by a small fixed vocabulary, with all software control being resident in the host computer (typically). Applications programming for these devices is usually expensive.

word time — Refers to: 1. The amount of time required to move one word past a given point. The term is used especially in reference to words stored serially. 2. The time required to transport one word from one storage device to another. Related to time, access.

word, trap—The main storage location used to store the instruction counter and trap identification data.

work area—Refers to a portion of storage in which a data item may be processed or temporarily stored. The term often refers to a place in storage used to retain intermediate results of a calculation, especially those results which will not appear directly as output from the program.

working registers — The major significance of working registers lies in access time and the bit efficiency of instruction words. It takes far fewer bits to specify one of several previously defined working registers than a memory location. Whether these registers are in an external memory or in the CPU is irrelevant, so long as they can be referenced efficiently. But a faster execution time can be obtained with registers that are separate from memory. They can be accessed for Read and Write operations without users incurring excessive memory-cycle delays.

workstation, portable microcomputer — A typical office workstation combines word processing, data processing, and data communications capabilities. Program development software systems are available that make it possible to use the workstation itself to produce specific applications. At least two workstations are needed to support an automated office system — one administrative and one management. Both types of workstations can access all capabilities of the automated system, but each type is tailored to the specific needs of its users. Together, they make a highly productive information management tool.

One easily transportable desktop microcomputer system includes everything needed for a compact word-processing system: a crt with a mini-floppy drive located right under the crt, a full keyboard, a high-speed matrix printer, and, of course, a central processor located inside the unit. The system can be expanded to up to four stations and additional storage capacity can be added. In addition, the whole unit is lightweight.

worst case — Refers to the circumstance or case in which the maximum stress is placed on a system, such as a greater than expected volume.

worst-case design — The worst-case design approach is an extremely conservative one in which the circuit is designed to function normally even though all component values have simultaneously assumed the worst possible condition that can be caused by initial tolerance, aging, and a temperature range of 0 °C to 100 °C.

Workstation, portable microcomputer (Courtesy Durango, Inc.).

WP/DP systems (Courtesy NCR Corp.).

WP/DP systems—Many types of multi-user word-processing systems operate in a time-sharing environment. With these systems, users can easily prepare a wide variety of documents, such as letters, reports, contracts, and technical material. These systems allow the user to interactively create, edit, and print documents. Users may also check a document for spelling errors, as well as selectively merge text information, such as names and addresses with a basic letter. Some systems include features that provide for the integration of word processing and data processing. Users may transfer data-processing information into printed documents and printed documents into the data-processing system. Most users find that WP (word processing) is easy to learn. They can easily control the format of most documents with simple one- and two-keystroke commands. Often, editing keys are labeled and color-coded and, therefore, simple to learn and easy to remember. A typical menu structure allows easy access to various data bases without the need to memorize commands. Transforming raw data into a form that can be transmitted to, and processed by, a larger computer is one of the many roles of an intelligent terminal. A typical system, such as the NCR 7510 by NCR Corporation, includes a communications device (which can link the system with another terminal or computer), a magnetic tape-cassette unit, a keyboard and visual display screen, and a matrix printer.

wpm — The abbreviation for words per minute; a common measure of speed in telegraph systems.

wraparound—Refers to: 1. The continuation of an operation from the maximum addressable location in storage to the first addressable location. 2. The continuation of register addresses from the highest register address to the lowest. 3. On a crt display device, the continuation of an operation, i.e., a Read or cursor movement, from the last character position in the display buffer to the first position in the display buffer.

writable control storage—Writable control storage is the name given to read/write memories used in the control portion of a system. One of the most significant trends in computer-system architecture today is the replacement of ROM in the control store with random-access storage. The trend is significant because it enables the system designer to change the external characteristics of the system. A writable control storage provides more memory for user-written control instructions. The process of using control storage in a host machine in order to give that machine the external characteristics of another device is called "emulation."

writable control-store implementation —There are basically two ways to use a writable control store: as a processor device or as an I/O device. If you set up the writable control store (WCS) as a processor device, special machine instructions will be needed to access it. They will not be required however, if the WCS is treated as an I/O device, which also permits the fast swapping of microprograms in and out of the WCS by direct-memory access. With some systems, the commonly used microprograms and specialized user-written instructions can be put in PROMs. But, for infrequently used microcoded subroutines, the WCS can be loaded and accessed from the programs themselves.

write—In a computer: 1. To copy, usually from internal to external storage. 2. To transfer elements of information to an output medium. 3. To record information in a register, location, or other storage device or medium. 4. To establish a charge pattern corresponding to the input (charge-storage tubes). *See also* Read. 5. To make a permanent or transient recording of data in a storage device or on a data medium. 6. The process of loading information into memory. 7. To record data in a storage device or a data medium. The recording need not be permanent, such as the writing on a cathode-ray-tube display device.

write cycle time—The time interval between the start and end of a write cycle. (The read, read-write, or write cycle time is the actual interval between two impulses and may be insufficient for the completion of operations within the memory. A minimum value is specified that is the shortest time in which the memory will perform its read and/or write function correctly.)

write-read process — To read in one block of data while simultaneously processing the previous block and writing out the results of the preceding processing block.

writing head — Refers to that magnetic head which is designed and used to Write as contrasted with the Read head, with which it is often combined.

writing rate—The maximum speed at which the spot on a cathode-ray tube can move and still produce a satisfactory image.

writing speed—The speed of deflection of a trace on phosphor, or the rate of registering signals on a charge-storage device.

WS—An abbreviation for working storage, that specific area on a disk that is used to hold dynamic or working data. This area is contrasted to both the reserved area which contains permanent information, such as compilers, track and sector information, etc., and the user area designed for semipermanent storage.

X

xerographic printer — Refers to a page printer in which the character pattern is set for a full page before printing, using the principle of xerography.

xerography—1. A nonchemical photographic process in which light discharges a charged dielectric surface. This is dusted with a dielectric powder, which adheres to the charged areas, rendering the image visible. Permanent images can be obtained by transferring particles to a suitable backing surface (e.g., paper or plastic) and fixing, usually by heat. 2. A dry copying process involving the photoelectric discharge of an electrostatically charged plate. The copy is made by tumbling a resinous powder over the plate, causing the remaining electrostatic charge to be discharged, and having the resin transferred to paper or an off-set printing master.

X punch—1. A punch in the X or 11 row of an 80-column card. 2. A punch in position 11 of a column. The X punch is often used to control or select, or to indicate a negative number as if it were a minus sign. Also called an 11-punch.

X-ray lithography — X-ray lithography theoretically can produce greater resolution than UV lithography, having reached better than 0.2 micron in laboratory equipment. However, for production equipment, ultimate resolution capability of X-ray exposure should be between 0.1 and 0.5 micron, according to a 1979 Bell Lab report. Present development work is concentrated on optimizing the combination of X-ray source, membrane mask design, and resist material to minimize energy losses and electron generation in the resist, which degrades resolution.

X-Y plotter—A device used in conjunction with a microcomputer to plot coordinate points in the form of a graph.

X-Y recorder—This refers to a recorder that traces, on a chart, the relationship between two variables, neither of which is time. Sometimes, the chart moves and one of the variables is controlled so that the relationship does increase in proportion to time.

Y

yoke—Refers to a group of heads in magnetic recording which are rigidly fastened and are moved together. They are used for reading and writing on channels which consist of two or more tracks on magnetic tapes, disks, etc.

Y punch — 1. A punch in the Y or 12 row of an 80-column card, i.e., the top row of the card. 2. A punch in position 12 of a column. It is often used for additional control or selection, or to indicate a positive number as if it were a plus sign.

Y signal—A signal that is transmitted in color television broadcasts which contains the brightness and detail information.

Z

Z-axis — The optical axis of a quartz crystal that is perpendicular to both X- and Y-axes.

zener—A semiconductor diode which, under reverse bias, is capable of conducting heavy currents.

zener breakdown — 1. A breakdown caused in a semiconductor device by the field emission of charge carriers in the depletion layer. 2. Temporary and nondestructive increase of current in a diode because of critical field emission of holes and electrons in the depletion layer at definite voltage.

zener diode—One with a characteristic showing a sharp increase of reverse current at a certain negative potential, and suitable for use as a voltage reference. The effect is now believed to be due to Townsend discharge and not to zener current. The device is also known as a breakdown diode or an avalanche diode. A zener diode is a specially treated pn junction with a relatively low reverse breakdown volt-

age. When the inverse voltage applied across the diode is increased beyond the breakdown point, some electrons, injected across the potential barrier, have enough energy to ionize molecules in collisions with them so that more than one electron is knocked loose per colliding electron. This causes a so-called "avalanche" condition resulting in a large increase in current for a small voltage change. As a result, the diode presents the effect of a very low impedance and therefore maintains a fairly constant voltage over a large range of current change.

zero-access store — Fast store from which information is immediately available, e.g., delay line containing one word.

zero adjust — Control for setting the reading of a device to the zero mark in the absence of any signal.

zero compression—A technique of data processing used to eliminate the storing of nonsignificant leading zeros.

zero-cut crystal—Quartz crystal cut at such an angle to the axes as to have a zero frequency/temperature coefficient. Used for accurate frequency standards.

zero fill—Refers to a procedure to fill in characters with the representation of zeros but which does not change meaning or content.

zero frequency — Implication that a complex signal, such as video, has a reference value which must be transmitted without drift.

zero-level address—Refers to an instruction address in which the address part of the instruction is the operand. Same as immediate address.

zero page addressing — In some systems, the zero page instructions allow for shorter code and execution times by only fetching the second byte of the instruction and assuming a zero high-address byte. Careful use of the zero page can result in a significant increase in code efficiency.

zero suppression—The elimination, in computing and data processing, of nonsignificant zeros to the left of the integral part of a quantity, especially before the start of printing.

zone—Refers to: 1. A portion of internal storage allocated for a particular function or purpose. 2. The three top positions of 12, 11, and 0 on certain punch cards. In these positions, a second punch can be inserted so that with punches in the remaining positions of 1 to 9, alphabetic characters may be represented.

zone digit—Refers to the numerical key to a section of a code. Zone digits may be used independently of other punchings for control significance, etc.

z-parameters—The open-circuit impedance parameters of transistors.

zwitterion—A dipolar ion, i.e., an electrically neutral molecule but having a dipole moment. The majority of aliphatic aminoacids form such dipolar ions.

Microprocessors

What is a chip, or a computer chip, or a computer-on-a-chip? To properly answer such questions, it is necessary to know the background and needs of the questioner. Some people do not care what a chip is but want to know what it does, while others are concerned with *how* it does what it does, or how it is *constructed* so that it is able to do what it does. Still others will want to know how many types of chips there are and what are their differences, their capabilities, their costs, and so on.

One type of individual might be satisfied with the following definition:

> A microprocessor chip is a semiconductor device designed as an integrated circuit. It is usually developed from a silicon wafer slice with the use of various doping materials. Then, with the use of microlithography and various large-scale integration (LSI) techniques (usually, the application of electron-beam machinery), many thousands of transistors and other components are connected in patterns that cause them to respond with signals that provide coded intelligence.

Fig. A-1 shows George Sampson, of Bell Labs' Integrated Circuits Laboratory, holding a silicon wafer containing approximately 60 MAC-4 chips and the package in which each will be mounted eventually. Behind him is a blow-up of the layout used to form the tiny microcomputers, each of which contains some 18,000 transistor elements.

A student, office manager, or an executive might be stopped cold by words such as silicon, semiconductor, integration, and the like, and would want to know, "What is an IC, a wafer, a slice?" As we progress, an attempt will be made to put some of the words, the concepts behind them, and their associated processes, manufacturing techniques, and system components into understandable relationships so that the majority of the readers will understand the dictionary definitions better.

The microprocessor is the basic building block for hundreds of new microcomputer control systems. The digital "processor on a chip" performs the same arithmetic, logic, information, and device control that once only the large- and mini-type computers could achieve, but it does it at from one-tenth to one-hundredth of the cost, size, and power re-

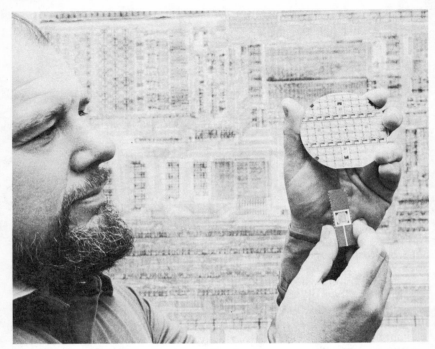

Courtesy Bell Laboratories

Fig. A-1. A silicon wafer that contains approximately 60 Bell Labs MAC-4 chips.

quirements. "Chip sets," a term that has recently evolved into popular usage, have further developed the microprocessor power, expanded the computer memory by using ROM and RAM chips, and with appropriate interface and Input/Output devices completed a total microcomputer system that can be held in one hand. The micropower marvels are also known as microcontrollers and are being designed into "smart" computer terminals, miniature communications switching devices, versatile production machines, and an uncountable number of consumer appliances, and calculating and entertainment devices.

Rapid changes in the microprocessor/microcomputer field continuously spawn several hundreds of new concept, product, and technical definitions. The field of electronics is expanding so rapidly that new terms are constantly being developed and older terms are taking on broader or more specialized meanings. Besides all the major electronic component and computer manufacturers, literally thousands of new companies around the world are rapidly entering the microsystems fields of enterprise. Many engineers, computer and communications professionals, production managers, scientists, teachers, and a wide range of students and other readers now have a deep involvement in the massive microelectronics upheaval. Definitions and concept explanations, both basic and updated, must be offered periodically to help these people and lead them through the new labyrinth of "computerese." Most people attempting to catch up or partially master the many facets of microcomputers will notice their expanding and continuously enigmatic progress. Many will be content to search for and find some common-sense clarifications of the fundamentals concepts and of the computer language. Electronic system designers, although experts themselves, consistently admit that they cannot keep up with all the current developments and advances as the industry churns and almost explodes with discovery and pragmatic utility.

Courtesy Bell Laboratories

Fig. A-2. A digital signal processor chip that is able to make more than a million calculations per second.

Two keys to the success and whirlwind progress of the technology are VLSI (very large-scale integration) and low cost. VLSI is the mastery of intelligently dealing with extremely tiny elements in order to increase the speed of contacts between those elements. The low costs are due basically to the production automation of some of the most complex and difficult designs and processes. The resulting mass sales of these products, due to their powers of programmed machine "intelligence" and the resulting cost-performance characteristics, has caused the price per capability to continue to fall. Another example is the new digital signal processor chip shown in Fig. A-2. New from Bell Labs, it can perform certain complicated real-time data processing tasks that previously were not economically feasible. Able to make more than a million calculations per second, this chip may find use in applications such as speech synthesis, voice recognition, filtering, and tone detection and line balancing in digital communications systems.

Most of the people that will be reading this book will do so because they have noticed microcomputers, microprocessors, and semiconductors creeping into their lives. Housewives see the devices in their microwave ovens, their washers and dryers, and in their children's toys. Office workers see the devices in their typewriters, the copying machines, and in the telephones. And so it goes, from the child to the electronics technician, the microprocessor and microcomputer are gaining more and more prominence in our lives. All of us must learn the "secrets" and "catch words" of the new devices or we will be left behind in the old-fashion mechanical days instead of preparing for the automation of the future.

SEMICONDUCTOR CHIPS

The almost microscopically small semiconductor chips seem to have it all. They contain the microprocessor that has the control and arithmetic abilities, the timing, and the decision-making capabilities. Then, when memory, input/output units, and a few other receptive or inter-

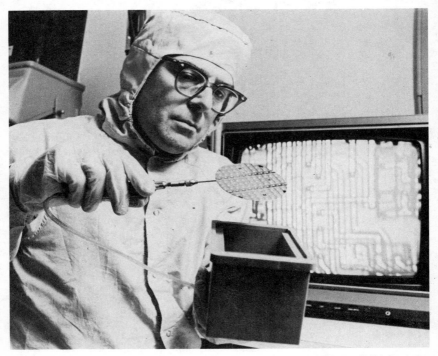

Courtesy Bell Laboratories

Fig. A-3. A wafer containing 64 microcomputer chips.

facing electronics are added to the microprocessor (on the same chip), the "computer-on-a-chip" emerges. Practically all the microprocessors now being manufactured contain these additional devices, so for all practical purposes, the terms microprocessor and microcomputer are very often synonymous. Usually, the terms are now being used interchangeably, even though they do not mean the same. Fig. A-3 shows Process Engineer Mike Grieco of the Integrated Circuits Development Lab (Bell Laboratories, Murray Hill, NJ) holding a wafer containing 64 of their MAC-4 microcomputer chips. The MAC-4 is designed to handle many tasks in telecommunication products and systems. A small portion of one chip appears enlarged 400 times on the video monitor in the background. This is a good example of microminiaturization.

However, it is just not the microprocessor chip that interests us. There are hundreds of chips that range from the memory chips through the signal-processing chips to the peripheral control chips. Now, some newer type chips, the coprocessor and the slave chips, are increasing in popularity. Using a pair of tweezers, engineer Lee Thomas (right in Fig. A-4) holds a MAC-8, the new Bell Labs microprocessor that is as powerful as the processing "brain" of a small computer. Engineer Bob Krambeck (left in Fig. A-4) is holding one of two circuit boards full of electronic components that is equivalent to the new microprocessor. The MAC-8, which is uniquely suited for a wide range of telecommunications applications, is able to execute over 100,000 electronic logic, or "thinking," functions per second while using only 1/10 watt of power.

From the small-scale integration (SSI) and the medium-scale integration (MSI) of the 1960s, we have progressed through large-scale integration (LSI) to very-large-scale integration (VLSI) in the early 1980s. This will certainly evolve by the mid-1980s into ultralarge-scale integration (ULSI), which will include upwards of a million devices on a single chip.

Is it possible to place a billion devices on a single chip? Indeed it is! Dr. Horst Nasko, Director of Research and Development for AEG-Telefunken, the second largest electrical and electronics company in West Germany, noted in June, 1980,[1]

> Superchips are so small and sophisticated, it is expected, ultimately, as many as one billion components may be packed onto one wafer-thin chip no larger than a postage stamp. Even today's mass-produced chips can pack up to as many as a million components into a space no larger than a pea. They are capable of running a factory's automated assembly line, programming computers, and controlling the traffic flows of cities. After that will come the superchips. No larger than the face of an ordinary wristwatch, one superchip will (in theory) be capable of keeping the personnel records for every company in North America or Europe, watch over the world's air traffic, or keep track of every book in every library—anywhere.

---

[1] From *Northern California Electronic News,* European Firms Enter Microchips Race, page 4, July 21, 1980.

Fig. A-4. A microprocessor chip and its equivalent in a circuit board.

How is this possible? The processes and manufacturing devices that are required in order to do this are discussed briefly in the following pages. However, no one denies that the presence and power of the superchips will be coming soon.

16-BIT MICROPROCESSING UNITS

Advances in semiconductor technology have provided the capability to place on a single silicon chip a microprocessor that is at least an order of magnitude higher in performance and circuit complexity than the popular 8-bit systems. The MC68000 is the first of a family of such VLSI microprocessors from Motorola Semiconductor Products Inc. (Fig. A-5). It combines state-of-the-art technology and advanced circuit

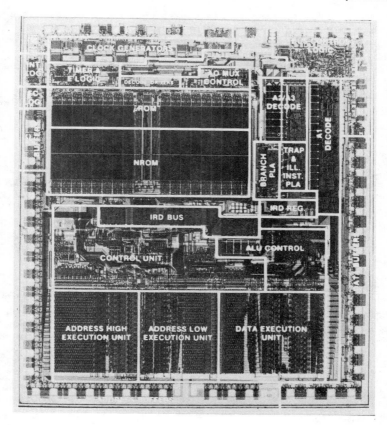

Courtesy Motorola Semiconductor Products, Inc.

Fig. A-5. A VLSI microprocessor sectioned to show its different functions.

design techniques with computer sciences to achieve an architecturally advanced 16-bit microprocessor.

The resources available to the MC68000 user consist of the following:

1. 32-bit data and address registers.
2. Sixteen megabyte direct-addressing range.
3. Fifty-six powerful instruction types.
4. Operations on five main data types.
5. Memory-mapped I/O.
6. Fourteen addressing modes.

The MC68000 offers seventeen 32-bit registers in addition to the 32-bit program counter and a 16-bit status register. The first eight registers are used as data registers for byte (8 bits), word (16 bits), and long-word (32 bits) data operations. The second set of seven registers and the system stack pointer may be used as software stack pointers and base address registers. In addition, these registers may be used for word and long-word address operations. All seventeen registers may be used as index registers.

The family concept has been extremely popular in the microprocessor industry. Motorola pioneered this family concept with the introduction of the M6800 Family in 1974. Led by the MC68000 microprocessing unit in 1979 and followed by a host of peripherals, the M68000 Family offers an engineer a set of building blocks to construct cost-effective solutions to an ever-widening range of complex 16- and 32-bit applications. HMOS technology, performance, and support are but a few of the reasons why the M68000 Family continues to be one of the 16-bit industry leaders. The plan for the M68000 Family is a simple one. Provide the marketplace with a 16-bit family and back it up with support. Some of the support chips are a disk controller (which is a general-purpose, user-programmable interface for Winchester hard-disk drives), a multiprocessor interface unit, and an advanced crt controller (which is a state-of-the-art, user-programmable controller for high-performance, intelligent applications). The disk controller features multiple drive and multiple format capability, M68000 bus compatibility, and single-supply operation, while the crt controller features linked records, multiple cursors, and multiple windows. The multiprocessor interface unit is featured as the key system element for establishing interprocessor communications in moderately coupled distributed processing systems. It also supports point-to-point and multidrop parallel bus interconnection schemes. An I/O processor adds a front-end processing capability to the M68000 Family and off loads the host microprocessor.

32-BIT MICROPROCESSORS

Perhaps a summary statement of the technical press, ". . . a milestone of historic proportions," made after the announcement of FOUR 32-bit microprocessor chip systems clearly stresses the magnitude of this development. It was achieved through the use of very-large-scale integration (VLSI). These developments were first announced and demonstrated in March, 1981, after the 28th International Solid-State Circuits Conference. The details of these systems, their advantages over 8- and 16-bit systems, their potential applications in micromainframes in the immediate future, as well as their impact on industry will be discussed later.

However, a sudden upsurge, at this time, in gate arrays used as custom computer chips was an industry-upsetting development. Also, CMOS technology and the HMOS manufacturing processes suddenly came into near dominance of the microcomputer and memory chips. The reasons and positive aspects of these developments will also be explained and evaluated later.

VLSI

What is the underlying basis of VLSI chip design and how did it get started? This question can perhaps best be answered by one of the technology leaders of a pioneering chip development company. Writing in the company periodical, HUGHESNEWS (March 27, 1981, page 3), Sheldon Welles, director of Independent Research and Development in the Corporate Technical Staff for Hughes Aircraft, stated it as follows:

> With its mind-boggling complexity, large-scale integration (LSI) of electronic circuits has become the vanguard of "the most exciting technical revolution to hit the electronics industry in years." The appeal of today's LSI, and tomorrow's VLSI, lies in its smallness—which makes it the key to many of today's increasingly capable and potent electronic systems in which space and weight are unaffordable luxuries. The intricacies of some VLSI chips on the drawing board are analogous to taking a map of the U.S. that shows every street of every town and village, and reducing that map to the size of a four-inch wafer. Even at this drastically reduced size, however, every intricate detail would remain distinguishable through a powerful microscope. This "road map" on the tiny LSI chip is the means of passing the electronic pulses that accomplish the computing process—it is the circuit. The problem, however, is preparing the "map" so that each "road" leads to its proper destination. The problem has been aggressively attacked by engineers throughout Hughes in a number of LSI development projects in which new ideas in manufacturing and design—including the use of computer-aided design (CAD)—are being explored. The need to disseminate these new ideas led to the first LSI CAD Technology Conference convened "for the benefit of working-level software engineers; those actually developing the computer-aided design software in use by the Groups."

Hughes Aircraft and hundreds of other firms in the "chip" industry have turned almost completely to the use of computer-aided design (CAD) to improve productivity and turn-around time. Few manufacturers have the time to custom design LSIs by hand.

Important developments are continuous without letup in the computer chip business. The areas which show the most dynamic changes are in the areas of function, performance, ease of use, data acquisition cost reduction, increasing reliability and serviceability, and compatibility with other electronic sections of various computer and communications systems. Most industry leaders are convinced that the decade's two most basic challenges and rewards (both based on VLSI) are the 32-bit micromainframe and the wide use of uncommitted gate, or logic, arrays. Writing in the January 8, 1981, issue of *Electronic Design* (pages 142-143), John H. Young, the president and chief executive officer of Hewlett-Packard Company states,

> Very-large-scale integration (VLSI) will be the decade's most important area of technical development—both in computers and in instruments. It totally affects the way we think about designing computers. This technology will encompass custom logic, gate arrays, and large memory arrays (of RAMs, ROMs,

and PROMs) that will influence the architecture, software, packaging, power, and even the user interface with the computer.

Well aware that his company would be one of the four that were about to announce the availability of a micromainframe and, also, that his company was one of the prime leaders in chip-density achievements, he continued:

VLSI makes custom logic an attractive method for creating processors and support systems in CMOS and NMOS technologies. Experimental chips now hold up to 500,000 components. By the end of the 1980s, there will be several million components on a chip. VLSI makes it possible to design computer architectures out of hardware/software modules, which are easy to fit together to form solutions. As an example, it should be possible to place microcomputer systems together, inexpensively, so that their applications can be specified in the natural language of the user, rather than in an unfamiliar microcomputer language.

The Hewlett-Packard CEO concluded his remarks with a comment on another major topic—testability.

. . . is well on its way to being solved. Work done in both industry and the universities has been so fruitful that this area should not be a major problem over the next decade. We have found that, by combining self-testing at the chip subsystem and system levels with high-reliability components, remote diagnostics, and improved test equipment, we can now offer a computer system with a guaranteed up time. In a few more years, we expect down time to be measured in thousandths of a percent.

Other industry leaders also predict that, as magnificent an achievement as was the VLSI 64K-bit RAM, a continuous increase in size would occur so that by the end of the decade, size increases would make available 256-bit, 532-bit, and 1-megabit chips. Most were equally as enthusiastic about CMOS technology, predicting that it would expand in importance—especially for very large systems, due to the need for the reduced power consumption that CMOS provides. Computer-aided design (CAD) and computer-aided manufacturing (CAM), almost all agreed, would allow the development of new products in an acceptable period of time and with a high degree of reliability and quality. The telecommunications leaders saw the use of microcomputers as vital in achieving their four main objectives: lower cost and greater reliability of communications systems, more use of software-driven systems, steady improvements in the human/machine interface, and a greater reliance on digital, light-wave, and satellite transmissions.

DESIGNER PROBLEMS

Designers are primarily concerned with the speed-power relationships of devices regardless of levels of integration. This relationship indicates where an IC family is positioned, with respect to other logic families, in average gate propagation delay (measured in nanoseconds) versus average gate power dissipation (measured in milliwatts). Designer goals are usually for the lowest propagation delay (very fast) with little power dissipation. However, circuit design involves many compromises or trade-offs. In some specific designs, for example, relatively high power consumption (gate power dissipation) will be accepted in order to obtain speeds of a nanosecond or less. ECL is a bipolar logic family respected for its high-speed characteristics, but it has high power dissipation. CMOS, on the other hand, is recognized for its low power dissipation, with an attendent sacrifice in speed, although the speed has been significantly improved recently. Fig. A-6 shows an addition to RCA's expanding line of Microboard products—the CDP18S604 Microboard Computer. This is a complete computer system on a 4.5- by 7.5-inch (11.43 cm by 19.05 cm) card containing a CDP1802 CMOS microprocessor, a 2-MHz crystal-controlled clock, 512-bytes of read-write

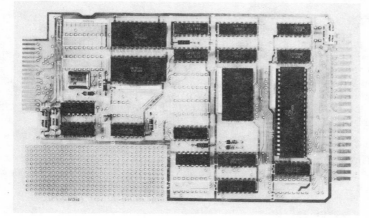

Courtesy RCA

Fig. A-6. The CDP 18S604 Microboard Computer from RCA.

memory, parallel I/O ports, power-on reset, an interface expansion area, and a socket for one or two kilobytes of user-selected read-only memory. The CDP18S604 has all the inherent advantages of low-power static CMOS and the architecture of RCA's COSMAC microprocessor. Powered from a single 5-volt supply, it requires only 4 milliamperes of current when populated with a CMOS ROM. The CDP18S604 is designed to provide the key hardware for a variety of low-cost microcomputer applications enabling the designer to concentrate on software development and the special requirements of his specific application.

Speed-Power Chart

A speed-power chart will show the most significant differences between various logic families, although it is based on measurements made of the simplest devices—gates. In addition to gates, each family has flip-flops, buffers, counters, registers, multivibrators, oscillators, and various interface circuits whose operational efficiencies are not easy to characterize. A convenient reference point on a speed-power chart is the position of the standard TTL family, still the leader in terms of sales. It is positioned at 10 nanoseconds average gate propagation delay and 10 milliwatts average power dissipation.

Low-Power Schottky

Schottky low-power devices offer an 80% improvement in power reduction (10 to 2 mW) with no change in speed. By contrast, CMOS devices offer a speed of 25 to 50 nanoseconds at 1 mW of power. At the far end of the scale, ECL logic offers about an 80% improvement in speed over standard TTL logic (from 10 nsec to 1.5 nsec), but it consumes three times as much power. However, the overall excellent characteristics of the TTL bipolar families have kept them in the front-runner position, so far.

ECL Logic

ECL is a more specialized logic family that also has a noise margin and a fan-out that is inferior to TTL logic. (Fan-out is a measure of the number of other ICs that can be driven by a specific device.) Currently, ECL logic is being used almost exclusively in large computer mainframes where the high speed justifies the high power use. ECL logic is faster than TTL logic because its constituent transistors do not go into full saturation; that is, they do not turn full-on or full-off. The result is higher speed and lower voltages.

CMOS Logic

CMOS is a technology that makes use of both p-channel and n-channel MOS devices on a single substrate; only one of the two complementary devices of the basic gate conducts at any one time. Thus, power dissipation is low—about 1 milliwatt per gate. Still relatively slow, CMOS logic has excellent noise immunity and can be driven from poorly or nonregulated sources. This type of logic is well suited for battery-operated portable tools and instruments.

Integrated Injection Logic

Integrated injection logic, or I^2L, is a form of bipolar logic that is utilized to improve circuit density over what can be obtained with TTL logic. It is based on only one transistor per gate; this results in a power reduction. However, it is most widely used in forming LSI devices; no complete logic families were made using this technique (in the early 1980s).

Gallium Arsenide

Although silicon is expected to be the principal semiconductor material used, for the near future at least, some scientists are working with gallium arsenide and have devised ways of doubling the velocity of electrons through IC chips by using GaAs. The Japanese are believed to be ahead in this area. GaAs semiconductor ICs are more expensive than silicon-based devices, but the advantages of higher transistor density and speed, as well as reduced power consumption, could offset this in time.

SINGLE-CHIP DEVICES

One typical type of single-chip device is the inexpensive Motorola M6805 single-chip microcomputer. It offers HMOS technology to provide both a high level of performance and a combination of features in a cost-effective package. It is made specially for high-volume control applications, such as industrial controllers, appliances, automobiles, and a variety of other consumer products. The M6805 offers three interrupt modes: external, timer, and software. In addition, it has a self-check capability with on-chip testing that is simple and inexpensive. Its I/O lines are organized into three flexible ports with one port able to drive the output devices—the widely used common-cathode LEDs. The 8-bit timer is software programmable with a mask-programmed prescaler.

In 1980 and 1981, the trend was for greater flexibility, larger and easier to use memory capacities, lower power dissipation, and high speed. Also, analog circuitry began appearing more and more on the new single-chip microcomputer products. One of the many was the American Microsystems' 4-bit S2200/2300 device for connecting to the "outside world" of analog devices. Intel Corporation's 8051 Family, with instructions for arithmetic processing, was the successor to Intel's earlier 8048. It contained 4K bytes of ROM and 128 bytes of RAM which could address up to 64K of external program memory and/or up to 64K bytes of data storage. The 8051 could run programs 16 times larger than the older 8048 could and it did it at speeds that were twice as fast. The competitors were National Semiconductor Corporation's 8073 and Zilog's Z-8. Each had instruction sets and architectures that were specially designed for high-level language use.

Some control-oriented processors can better their performance when they gain a counter/timer, more ports, and a larger on-chip ROM and RAM. For example, National Semiconductor Corporation's single-chip 4-bit microcontrollers carry two independent CPUs on one chip. They share a common ROM, RAM, programmed logic array (PLA) instruction decoder, and arithmetic-logic unit (ALU). They have their own program counters, memory-addressed registers, carry bits, and accumulators. The 4-bit CPUs can pull their instructions from different parts of the memory or execute the same instruction on different data—independently. In addition to the dual CPUs, National's 2440 chip has an 8-bit counter-timer that can be software-controlled to establish the desired count and select either the on-chip clock or an external input as a timing source. This is truly exceptional power.

PERIPHERAL INTERFACES

Integrated-circuit peripheral devices belong to two classes: those that control interface functions, such as peripheral and communication controllers, and those that improve system performance, such as hardware floating-point mathematic units. Neither area is rigidly defined;

some devices fit both categories. But all integrated-circuit peripheral devices have one thing in common—improving the cost/performance of processor-based systems.

By acting as a buffer between the CPU and the peripheral device, a peripheral interface can help solve many problems. In its simplest form, the interface might be a register or latch that accepts data at CPU speeds and outputs it at peripheral speeds, or vice versa. However, interfaces range widely in their complexity and programmability.

Fig. A-7 shows a universal wire-wrappable interface IC circuit board from Garry Manufacturing Co. (Division of Brand-Rex Co.) that is designed for use with the Intel SBC 80/10, 80/20 microcomputer system. The board plugs directly into the Intel SBC 604 modular cardcage/ backplane bus system (shown in background) and includes power interface connections for ±5 and ±12 volts dc. The circuit board is a double-sided board with precision screw-machine gold-plated three-level wire-wrappable pins along with card-edge pads for input/output connections and connections for peripheral equipment. The board uses existing software and bus interface while still allowing customizing to meet special applications.

Advanced Micro Computers' Am95/6120 Intelligent Floppy Disk Controller is shown in Fig. A-8. It controls up to four 8- and 5½-inch floppy-disk drives, and it supports any mix of single- and double-density as well as single- and double-sided drives in Multibus®-compatible systems. It has a high-speed data transfer rate of 1.8M bits/second in programmable block, burst, or byte mode. This enhances system throughout.

Fig. A-9 shows industry's first series of interface modules. They are by MDB Systems, Inc., and are for use with Intel's 8- and 16-bit single-board computers. They include a general-purpose bus foundation module and a universal wire-wrap module, and require only one card slot in the Intel computer chassis, which is a significant convenience to the system designer. The MDB general-purpose bus foundation modules provide a flexible and economical interface between the Intel 8- and 16-bit

Courtesy Garry Manufacturing Co.

Fig. A-7. An interface board (foreground) and a cardcage/backplane (background).

Courtesy Advanced Micro Computer

Fig. A-8. A "smart" floppy-disk controller.

computers and the user peripheral devices. The modules consist of basic multibus logic elements plus wire-wrap positions for up to 38 IC devices, utilizing low-profile sockets. (Fourteen 40-pin ICs can also be direct mounted instead.) With the wire-wrap posts on the components side of the board, the modules fit a single slot in the Intel chassis. An extensive selection of designer-wired options permits multiple controller applications, address selection, and interrupt control. The modules have provision for three 50-pin ribbon cable connectors to permit connection to external devices.

Courtesy MDB Systems, Inc.

Fig. A-9. Interface modules.

FROM 8-BIT CHIPS TO MICROMAINFRAMES

In 1976, the "miracle chip" was the 8-bit microcomputer on-a-chip. The whole system was a relatively simple assemblage of a microprocessor, some RAM, and an external teletypewriter. Today, however, microcomputer chips are so complex that the microcomputer can do as much or more than the earlier room-sized machines. Then, in late 1979, much of industry's attention was focused on the high-performance 16-bit microcomputer sets. The new 16-bit "machines" had performance levels that were far greater than the earlier 8-bit "machines." A serious contest developed among the many manufacturers who were working on products to compete in this area. Some, but not all, of the new devices had "look ahead" features in order to assure the buyer that he was not getting "locked-in" to a specific CPU or software. Also, new performance hierarchies began to evolve in the 8-bit microcontroller sector of the market, and many devices were offered at extremely low prices. A few manufacturers had high-performance devices, but they also had their cheaper, faster, or tinier units. Ratings of these were based on their speed, compatibility of software, on-board memory and I/O, and on other performance criteria. The addition of continuing peripheral controller and input/output processor chips and software support encouraged many manufacturers to continue their commitments.

Almost as soon as the first 8-bit microcomputers appeared on the scene, the "big brass" of the semiconductor world declared war on the "big brother" minicomputer systems. Although the minicomputers were 16-bit machines with more accuracy, speed, and a host of other abilities that some felt were beyond the "crude and slow" microcomputer capabilities, the pioneering microcomputer leaders were dreaming of at least catching and meeting the big-selling machines. When the "big three" micro companies (Intel, Zilog, and Motorola) caught them in late 1979, the mini manufacturers were making both superminis and their own micros in order to avoid losing the computer war that seemed about to start. However, the low-cost production methods and mass marketing of the micro manufacturers were in their favor, as was the emergence of the 16-bit microprocessor.

The president of Microsoft, Inc., one of the most successful microcomputer software companies, was reported in many journals (in early 1981) as stating that 16-bit microprocessors will largely replace 8-bit units for general-purpose computing, even for small single-user systems. He felt that 16-bit microprocessors like the Intel 8086, the Zilog Z8000, and the Motorola 68000 would make big in-roads into the 8-bit markets because of their low cost and their ability to handle more than 64K bytes of main memory—a primary advantage. The price differences between the two sizes of chips are small, relatively very small when compared to the increased power and versatility of the 16-bit units. It was noted that Microsoft was quickly changing its 8-bit high-level languages to 16-bit format, and it was felt that most other software houses were bound to follow this lead rapidly.

Basically, 16-bit processing means faster arithmetic and logic devices, a greater data-handling capacity, and greatly improved memory and I/O addressing techniques. Data bus architectures for the 8-bit systems are simply no match for the much more versatile and powerful 16-bit types. Multitasking, alone (and the use of such sophisticated operating systems), puts 16-bit machines far ahead of the 8-bit clique. For example, touch-control keyboards for terminals are now very popular and this requires 16-bit systems. While 4-bit machines work fine for games, calculators, appliances, and the like, and 8-bit systems do very well for simple machine controls, computer peripherals, terminals, and so on, it takes 16-bit machines to realize quality systems in industrial, process, and vehicular control operations. Smart instruments, "really" intelligent terminals, controllers, and communications equipment also require 16-bit machines. Relational Database Systems, Inc., Sunnyvale, CA, offers a UNIX-based system for Z8000 machines.

In early 1981, the trade papers were full of news about 32-bit microprocessors with headlines reading, "3-Chip Micromainframe Shapes Up as a Powerful Performer," "Ada Determines Architecture of 32-bit Microprocessor," "32-bit Microprocessors Inherit Mainframe Features," and "Over a Million Devices Make Up 32-bit CPU and Support Chips." In February, 1981, Intel Corporation revealed its iAPX 432 system. Its three main elements are: a micromainframe executive unit on a 335-mil square chip that accepts, decodes, and executes a continuous stream of microinstructions received from the microinstruction sequencer in the basic computer; a 32-bit computer instruction-decoding unit whose functions are to decode instructions and produce microinstructions and data (this device is 320-mil square and contains over 100,000 transistors); and an I/O interface processor, which is 342-mil square. The iAPX 432 microprocessor 2-chip system (with the third support chip), according to many industry leaders and specialists, is equivalent, in terms of performance, to the IBM 370/158 mainframe computer. The system from Hewlett-Packard Company is enlightening both in itself and the process used to manufacture it. The 32-bit system is made up of six chips that contain up to 600,000 transistors, with more than 450,000 of them on a single chip. The system elements are a 32-bit CPU, an I/O processor, a memory controller, a 128K RAM, and a 528K ROM. The chips were fabricated using a specially developed 2.5-micron pitch process.

When the capabilities of the Intel system were analyzed, it was seen that the 32-bit system is highly useful for heavy number crunching and the handling of lots of floating-point arithmetic, and is ideal for random number generation. It will be especially needed by those who must move great amounts of data, such as in communications, in data base systems, in weaponry, in medicine, in laboratories of various kinds, and so on. The system has an architecture much like several of the older and larger machines as it uses a very large addressing space (up to 4-billion bytes), a virtual memory system, an instruction speed that is equal to or greater than the latest IBM 4331-1 and 4331-2 classes, a content-addressable memory buffer, and a translation look-aside buffer. The separation of the CPU and the I/O processors, and the elimination of all interrupts from the CPU domain, is very similar to the highly successful giant Control Data 6000 system architecture of the early 1960s. The memory management system appears to be modeled after another very large successful mainframe—the Burroughs 5500 of the era that is just a little bit later. Thus, the designers appear to have taken some of the best features of the giant machines that functioned with success in the past and applied them to their system, but at costs that are about 1/1000th of what the large machine prices were back then.

The CMOS 32-bit microprocessor from Bell Labs was implemented using 3.5-micron device features to produce a very large 1.5-cm^2 chip, but the final manufacturing phase was expected to scale this down significantly to almost double the speed, using 2.5-micron lines. The new circuit technique is called Domino CMOS and produces denser circuits that operate at approximately twice the speed of conventional CMOS. The Bell Labs system is a register-based machine with a 17- by 32-bit file that has an architecture that is clearly futuristic. The chip has two independent subunits—one optimized for fetching instructions, the other for executing them. Bell engineers claim that the power of the chip is equal to that of many mainframe systems and will provide three-quarters of the processing power of some of the current medium-sized computers.

Hewlett-Packard Company's 32-bit microprocessor is an NMOS unit with over 450,000 devices incorporated into a high-resistance substrate. It is an 8-mask, silicon-gate device that uses 1.5-micrometer lines and 1-micrometer spaces. The device achieves its density through the use of electron-beam lithography. The microprocessor has a register-based architecture that incorporates a 28- by 32-bit file on a chip. It also includes several other special-purpose units, including an N-bit shifter and a hardware multiplier that yields a 64-bit result from two 32-bit operands in a fast 1.8 microseconds.

A 32-bit microprocessor can address 2^{32} data words while a 16-bit microprocessor can only address 2^{16}. One of the managers of the Intel Special Systems Operations division which developed the Intel 32-bit system stated that they expected the large sophisticated original-equipment manufacturers to begin developing iAPX 432-based products in order to take full advantage of the system "now" (meaning 1981). He predicted that a significant number of iAPX 432s would be used in new markets and applications, as yet undefined, with this remark,

> I believe that the micromainframe's capabilities, size, and price will start lots of creative juices churning, and applications that were previously unrealistic will now be economically attractive.

The 32-bit systems are expected to expand the chip business greatly, not only because they can take over functions that formerly could only be performed by the bigger systems, but because they have the advantages of low cost, small size, and ease of commercial implementation. In its March 2, 1981 issue (pages 116-118), Business Week reported:

> An incredible 150 million of the fingernail-size semiconductor devices were shipped worldwide last year. The market for just the chips alone, virtually nonexistent in 1973, rocketed past $750 million in 1980.

It also quoted unnamed Intel executives as stating that the 32-bit microprocessor is so powerful that it could become the "brains" for such currently unavailable products as office workstations that can understand human speech and industrial robots that could "recognize" the parts on an assembly line. It was also stated that "At least half of the applications that will exist in 5 or 10 years, we can't even imagine today." Business Week also noted,

> The micromainframe and other microprocessors in its class are expected to do more than spawn new applications. Industry watchers say that these integrated circuits are so powerful that new companies and even new industries will spring up to build new end products using these superchips.

However, despite the excitement of the announcements of 32-bit microprocessors from three companies, only the Intel 432 was available as a "sampling kit" in early 1981. The popular 8-bit microprocessor was still being sold in the hundreds of millions in the early 1980s, and the 16-bit machines were making significant inroads in the market place, particularly in communications and office automation devices and systems.

CMOS TECHNOLOGY

The standard explanation of complementary MOS (CMOS) is that it is an inexpensive and popular array technology with a typical cell structure that consists of alternating patterns of 3 n-channel and 3 p-channel transistors, followed by 2 n-channel and 2 p-channel transistors. Each pattern (or cell) carries two gates: a 3-input and a 2-input NAND or NOR gate. The two most prevalent technologies are: (1) silicon-gate CMOS, which offers good density, TTL speeds, and very low power requirements, and (2) metal-gate CMOS, which has been the standard for almost five years but which is more limited in speed and density. It was felt that these deficiencies would restrict its future use but some manufacturers believe that metal-gate CMOS might still remain a viable technology because its speed is being increased by better processing and clever circuit design.

CMOS technology is fundamentally strong and is fully expected to soon dominate the semiconductor field. When compared with n-channel MOS, even the most skeptical admit that there is a need for both processes in the very-large-scale integration (VLSI) area, and that CMOS seems to have the edge. Already, the majority of new MOS chips being designed are using CMOS processes. Harris Semiconductor has been using silicon-gate CMOS for several years and, in 1980-1981, offered a 16K static RAM. Three Japanese companies (Nippon Electric Co. Ltd., Toshiba Corporation, and Oki Electric Industry Co., Ltd.) were the first to announce CMOS microprocessors and were, in early 1981, the only ones producing 16K static CMOS RAMs organized in both 1-bit and bytes (8 bits). They were also the first with superspeed CMOS, as both Toshiba Corporation and the Central Research Lab of Hitachi Ltd. announced and described two 4K CMOS memories that had startlingly fast access times of 18 nanoseconds (typical). As the company that made HMOS scaling a common term and process, Intel Corporation admitted, in early 1981, that "The future is in CMOS." Intel then revealed that they had had a massive CMOS development program underway for the previous two years. They were driven to production faster due to the competition of several CMOS models that popped up early from Japan and elsewhere. Their CMOS process is termed by Intel Corporation as HMOS-CMOS, or simply CHMOS, and it is compatible with their HMOS processing, i.e., it starts with a p-type substrate rather than an n-type substrate as used in most "conventional" CMOS processes.

Although CMOS power dissipation increases with operating frequency, two factors conspire to keep even high-speed CMOS circuits from dissipating more power than do their NMOS counterparts. The first is simply that all elements of the circuits rarely, if ever, toggle at once; quiescent elements of a CMOS circuit draw only minimal leakage currents, compared to the constant drain extracted by NMOS devices. So, while a CMOS circuit can theoretically draw more current, in practice, it never does. It is also noted that the primary method of increasing CMOS speed, i.e., by shrinking the geometries, concurrently decreases the intrinsic power dissipation. This is the key. Low power dissipation becomes increasingly important as chips become denser and denser.

MEMORIES

Memory technology continues to be the most rapidly changing component of a computer system. Memories continue to be built that increase in performance and decrease in price. Both bubble memories and the serial semiconductor technologies (such as charge-coupled devices or CCDs) have the potential to be cheaper than the conventional semiconductor memories. Here again, the Japanese have a strong lead due to their development of these devices for cameras and other imaging systems. Fig. A-10 illustrates a new add-in memory card from Mostek Corporation that is compatible with Data General Corporation's ECLIPSE™* microcomputer models. The new card has three error-correction options and on-board LEDs to allow a failure diagnosis down to the RAM level while running the diagnostics. The basic differences between static RAMs and dynamic RAMs are in the performance characteristics that result from their differently designed storage cell circuits. The developments in memory cells are very often drastic and, generally, very frequent. Pro-Log Corporation has introduced its 7703 STD BUS card which has up to 16,384 bytes of high-speed (350 ns) nonvolatile CMOS RAM memory. An on-board memory-protect circuit monitors the +5-volt dc power and automatically generates a memory-save signal prior to switching to lithium battery backup. Data can be retained without external power for a guaranteed minimum of two years. The 7703 STD card is shown in Fig. A-11. The lithium battery has a shelf life of ten years. A low battery status signal is provided via an LED indicator. No battery charging time is required, allowing instant operation. The 7703 is also provided with Write-protect switches (4K blocks) for preservation of critical data and for nonvolatile program execution from the card.

---

* ECLIPSE is a trademark of Data General Corporation.

Courtesy Mostek Corp.

Fig. A-10. An add-in memory card.

One of the most economical memories in use at the start of the 1980s was the erasable programmable read-only memory available under such names as EPROM (erasable programmable ROM), EEPROM (electrically

Courtesy Pro-Log Corp.

Fig. A-11. A memory card that will retain data two years without external power.

erasable programmable ROM), and EAROM (electrically alterable ROM). The EEPROM is also called E^2PROM. The erasable programmable ROM has the advantage of being able to be reprogrammed electrically in the field, without interrupting in-service equipment operation. Or, it can be reprogrammed remotely via telecom and datacom links. Thus, it saves the labor and system downtime costs usually incurred with changing code in the field. Also, this type of memory is both byte- and chip-erasable. Each byte can be rewritten up to 10,000 times, leading to simple and more flexible systems. Reprogramming is fast; a single-byte program

Courtesy Intel Corp.

Fig. A-12. Industry's fastest and smallest EPROM.

edit takes only 20 milliseconds. Fig. A-12 shows Intel's new 2764 which is the industry's fastest (250 ns) and the smallest (32,400 mils^2). This 64K EPROM in its 28-pin package conforms to the new industry standard universal pinout for high-density ROMs, PROMs, EPROMs, and RAMs. The 2764 is fabricated using HMOS-E, Intel's patented high-performance, metal-oxide-semiconductor process technology, as applied to nonvolatile memories. The HMOS-E process has 3-micrometer channel lengths, which makes for high performance.

The E^2PROM marked the beginning of a abrupt change in memory technology, particularly in a new class of nonvolatile memory usable for many applications, and also usable for a wide range of microcomputer design possibilities. It provides for reconfigurable systems, self-calibrating equipment, self-adjusting machine tools, and self-diagnosing/correcting products.

EPROM ERASERS

The main cause of failure of equipment using MOS EPROMs is in the incomplete erasure of the devices before reprogramming, due to application of the wrong UV intensity or the wrong erasing time for the specific device being erased. The operator can avoid these problems by taking into account a few variables, including: (1) the device to be erased, (2) its previous programming history, (3) the power rating and age of the UV source, and (4) the degree of cleanliness of the EPROM windows and the UV source tubes.

A range of ultraviolet EPROM erasers has been developed to meet the growing need for professional-quality instrumentation in this specialized field by Microsystem Services, High Wycombe, Buckinghamshire, England. Their ME-90/30/10 range of erasers is designed to help the operator take these variables into account automatically, making it simple to recalibrate the instrument when necessary, and thus, prevent under-erasing. The largest instrument in the range, the ME-90, has a capacity to erase up to 90 EPROMs at the same time. It is particularly suited for production applications or larger development laboratories. The ME-90 is shown in Fig. A-13. The large removable radiation drawer incorporated in the ME-90 allows even entire boards to be erased intact. A spare drawer is provided so that the user can be loading one batch while another batch is being erased. Each of the unit's six UV tubes is monitored by a visual failure indicator on the front panel. This is incor-

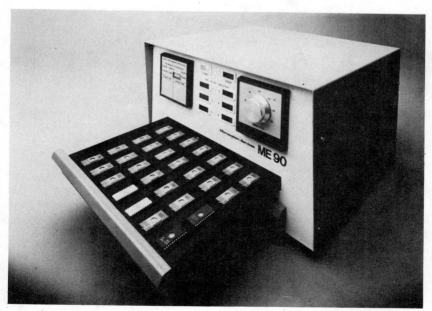

Courtesy Microsystem Services Ltd.

Fig. A-13. An EPROM eraser.

porated to help avoid the possibility of a faulty erasure due to insufficient radiation intensity if one or more tubes are not working properly. The ME-30 is a scaled-down version of the ME-90, with a capacity of 30 EPROMs at one time. It is ideal for medium-sized laboratories. The Type ME-10 is a low-cost unit with a capacity to erase up to 10 EPROMs simultaneously, mainly for service laboratories and smaller program development departments.

BUBBLE MEMORY BOARDS

Bubble memories are being used as peripheral devices rather than as main memory in microprocessor systems. The selection of bubble memory over electromechanical storage devices, such as floppy disks and tape cassettes, centers on such critical factors as reliability in extreme environments (due to their solid-state design and low component count), low incidence of maintenance, and data retention (because of its nonvolatility and speed of operation). High-speed data acquisition, data logging, and critical program storage are typical applications. Data are collected in real-time and stored in the bubble. They are then loaded into the RAM or into a main computer for processing, making

Courtesy Bell Laboratories

Fig. A-14. A message board from Bell System's magnetic bubble announcement machine.

Courtesy Bell Laboratories

Fig. A-15. Test-recording a 24-second message in the announcement machine.

bubbles viable in distributed data processing or stand-alone systems. The total bubble memory market, including the bubble device and its support circuits, is expected to grow in 1982 to a $100-million market and, by 1986, to $500 million. It is believed that these memories will decline in price sufficiently by 1986 to present a serious competition to floppy disks and other mass-storage devices. Fig. A-14 shows Bell Labs supervisor Ron Trupp inspecting a message board from the Bell System's magnetic bubble announcement machine (that operates without any moving parts). This message board is part of a system that can record and announce up to eight different messages. Its predecessor, visible in the background, can handle only one message. The machine uses the magnetic bubble memory technology that Bell Labs invented. In Fig. A-15, Jim Rowley, a Bell Labs engineer, test-records a 24-second message on Bell System's announcement machine, the first of its kind that operates with a magnetic bubble memory. His voice is being recorded via two magnetic bubble packages, each about half the size of a cigarette pack, that are located in the metal containers mounted in the middle of the circuit panel shown at the right of Fig. A-15. The device represents the first application of bubble memory technology.

VOICE SYNTHESIZER CHIP

A new LSI voice synthesizer chip (Fig. A-16) from the Electronic Components Division of Panasonic Company can synthesize up to 63 words

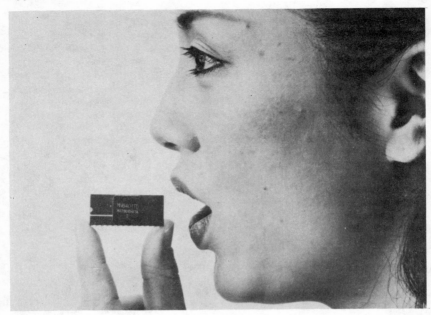

Courtesy Electronic Components Div., Panasonic Co.

Fig. A-16. A voice synthesizer chip.

in about 20 seconds. Designated as the "MN6401," the chip can speak in either a male or a female voice (or a combination of voice and sound). The chip uses the PARCOR (Partial Auto Correlation) system, originally developed by NTT (Nippon Telephone and Telegraph Corporation), that is widely used because of the high quality of its synthesized sound. The MN6401 chip includes a built-in 32K-bit ROM, operates from a single 5-volt dc power supply, has a maximum power consumption of 0.1 watt (20-mA current drain), and is TTL compatible. In those applications where more memory is required, the user can connect an external ROM to the MN6401 chip to enhance the built-in 32K-bit ROM. The chip also includes a speech speed control with six different settings. The chip can be operated by either manual or remote (computer) control.

Panasonic feels that the new voice synthesizer chip will find wide usage in a variety of home electronic products, including home appliances and educational games and equipment, by providing verbal instructions to the user. They expect to be able to start delivery of the chips by the end of 1981.

VIDEODISCS

The technology utilized in the manufacture of videodiscs uses optical lasers, a tellurium media, and holes that are one micron in diameter. Research and experimentation with videodiscs is going on in scores of laboratories around the world. The basic recording and reading techniques are not new. A laser beam is pulse modulated by a data stream originating at a computer. The beam literally burns a hole into the metallic medium every time a logic 1 is transmitted. The surface is left unscathed when a logic 0 is transmitted. Each of the holes is 1 micron (40 microinches) in diameter; the tracks on the disc are between 1 and 2 microns apart. The disc, which rotates at 1800 rpm, has a track density of about 20,000 bpi. The "read" operation is essentially the reverse of the "write" operation in that the "hole" or "no hole" conditions

Courtesy RCA

Fig. A-17. The encyclopedia of the future.

are detected by a scanning laser coupled to some electronics. The electronics transmute the resulting pulses into logic elements for final writing. Prototypes storing more than 2.5 gigabytes of data are expected to be available late in 1981.

The entire contents of a multivolume encyclopedia may someday be stored on the two sides of the 12-inch disc shown in Fig. A-17. It is being held by Dr. Alan E. Bell of RCA Laboratories, Princeton, NJ. He and Dr. Robert A. Bartolini (at left in the photo) received a U.S. patent for the disc which can hold 100 billion bits of information. That is 10 to 100 times the capacity of currently used magnetic storage discs. The key to their patent is a very thin layer of the metal tellurium, which is embedded in the coating structure of the plastic disc. Dr. Bell received a separate patent for the basic coating structure.

To record information on the disc shown in Fig. A-17, an intense beam from a novel semiconductor laser (developed by RCA) burns a series of microscopic-sized pits (holes) in the tellurium. The information is retrieved (read) by a less intense beam from the same laser, which shines through the microscopic pits and is reflected into an electronic light detector by a layer of aluminum below the tellurium. The high-density RCA system has many potential applications including the replacement of conventional X-ray film that requires expensive silver. Other possible uses are in word processing and in the storage of government and business data, as well as in still and moving pictures.

Another device from RCA is their "CED" capacitance electronic disc system which can provide up to two hours of entertainment on a single disc (Fig. A-18). It is designed to combine sound and pictures on a disc that can be played through any brand of NTSC television receiver. As easy to operate as an audio record player, the RCA videodisc player is extremely compact and uses only 35 watts of energy. With its protective sleeve, the disc slides into the front of the player. When the function lever is switched to "play," the disc begins to rotate to reach a speed of 450 rpm. The disc is removed when the sleeve is withdrawn. Each

Courtesy RCA
Fig. A-18. A capacitance electronic disc (CED) system.

"CED" disc can provide up to one hour of visual entertainment on each side of the disc.

The stylus used in the RCA videodisc player is so unique that special computer-controlled processing equipment had to be devised for its manufacture. The stylus tip measures just 1/10,000 of an inch and the tracking force is extremely light—only 65 thousandths of a gram. The high-performance "DuraLife" diamond stylus is designed for years of service under normal use. RCA's goal is to establish the "CED" video-disc system as a worldwide standard for video disc products.

From Quasar Company comes the VHD (video high density) videodisc system shown in Fig. A-19. VHD is claimed to be a major technological breakthrough in video technology, and is said to be able to produce video disc systems capable of playing two hours of programming. The system will offer a full range of special effects and will be capable of high-fidelity sound which will challenge the finest audio discs now being surface. This means that the pickup arm can move freely over the entire produced. The special effects referred to are a stop mode, a search ability, and a slow or fast motion in both forward and reverse, plus random access. The last feature allows the user to not only locate and play a particular portion of a disc but also to play selected portions in any order the user desires. For example, the user could play the fifth song in a concert, followed by the second, etc. These special effects are possible throughout the 2-hour playing time of the VHD disc. The audio quality is said to be outstanding. In addition to the full-range high-fidelity stereo sound tracks, the system is also capable of playing bilingual sound tracks. For example, one audio channel of a program could be in English with the other channel in Spanish. The user would merely choose the desired channel.

The VHD disc can contain up to 54,000 separate images (one hour of programming) per side. The system's electronic tracking system is also an important technological breakthrough. Its highly effective tracking characteristics result from the ability of the VHD stylus to detect the video, audio, and tracking signals simultaneously on the grooveless disc surface of the disc, resulting in special effects capability. The system's

Courtesy Quasar Co.

Fig. A-19. The VHD videodisc system.

compact design results from the fact that the VHD disc is smaller than other videodiscs (10.2 inches vs. 12 inches).

The VHD system and related software are being developed by the three companies jointly owned by THORN EMI Ltd. of Great Britain and Matsushita Electric Industrial Co. Ltd. of Japan—MEI (Quasar's parent company), General Electric Company, and Victor Company of Japan, Ltd. (JVC). These joint ventures consist of a program distribution and artistic production company (VHD Programs Inc.), a videodisc manufacturing company (VHD Disc Manufacturing Co.), and a videodisc player manufacturing company (VHD Electronics Inc.). The initial software library for the VHD system is expected to include over a hundred classic motion pictures from major studios and independent producers.

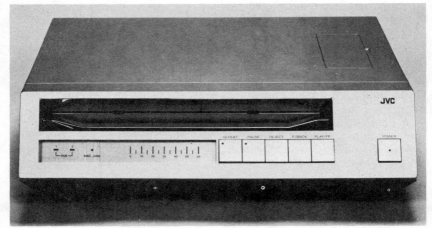

Courtesy US JVC Corp.

Fig. A-20. A capacitive video disc system.

The unit shown in Fig. A-20 is the US JVC Corporation's introduction of their parent company's (Victor Company of Japan, Ltd.) newest most-updated capacitive video disc system. It combines the inexpensive durability of existing capacitive technology with the feature-oriented operation of optical systems. (Computers began using video discs as storage systems in early 1981.)

The videodisc player shown in Fig. A-21 is Pioneer's (U.S. Pioneer Electronics) entry into the video disc field. The player uses a small laser to retrieve the audio/video information stored on the LASERDISC™ record for playback. This laser, while in operation, projects a continuous beam of light on an area measuring no more than one micron (0.001 millimeter) in diameter. As the disc spins at a speed of 1800 rpm, the microfine laser beam is scanned across the surface of the disc. When the laser beam strikes a "pit," it is reflected back into the system. These reflected light pulses comprise the audio/video information etched on the disc in three channels, two for audio and one for video. The two independent audio channels make both stereo and bilingual program-

Courtesy U.S. Pioneer Electronics

Fig. A-21. A videodisc player that uses a small laser beam to retrieve information.

ming possible. Since no direct contact is made with the software by the playback device, the disc is not subject to wear and as a result can be played repeatedly without any loss of fidelity. In addition, the information surface lies beneath a thick transparent acrylic surface so you can handle the disc without fear of damage to the playing surface.

Microcomputers

Cost containment in accounting, sales promotion and development, resource allocation, and labor expense is just one of the reasons for implementing small computer systems. Many banks, hospitals, educational institutions, large businesses, and other institutions are turning to smaller computers instead of large computers to reduce costs. With these much simpler and more effective systems, costs are identified more quickly, response to processed information is more rapid and accurate, and better planning is achieved because more "what-if" calculations can be made quickly and easily. Many low-cost flexible systems provide a quality environment that also demonstrates time savings and efficiencies.

Some of the computers offered to small and very small businesses are, in effect, intelligent assistants offering techniques that lead and prompt users to find the information they need—to complete the job or to follow the procedures required by management. Operators can use specifically designed keys and "HELP" commands; they can call up "menus" of available information, touching the screen or keying in responses as indicated. Many systems can use voice input and output to achieve immediate response in the most often-used applications. Automatic "speller programs" detect and correct inevitable spelling errors. Procedural errors are reported immediately in English, and protected (unerasable) formats are displayed for easy fill-in. Good systems do not interfere with the way people work naturally. "Windowing" on some systems allows segments of several files to simultaneously be displayed on a single screen. Highlights, blinking, underline, movable cursors (position indicators), and easy horizontal or vertical scrolling allow movement of information on to and off of the screen or segments of the screen. All this and more make computer systems convenient and powerful, and quickly useful to inexperienced managers and "knowledge workers." No programming is necessary by the operator. By simply typing a number or letter, or using a light pen or finger (with touch-sensitive screens) pointed appropriately, the menu can be made to provide multiple colors, character sizes, and type fonts; it can bring forth graphs and charts, draw lines, and edit sentences. The menu can also bring forth even more detailed menus for special-subject data base investigation.

Low-cost desktop problem-solving computers put the power to defeat the "business-breaker," administrative overhead, where it is needed most, at the fingertips of knowledgeable users. A typical system is a compact package with the ingredients for interactive computing: a resident LSI ROM-based operating system, a large user memory, disk or cartridge storage, a crt, a user-definable keyboard, multiple and selectable I/O variety, and a low-cost thermal or letter-quality printer, with an optional plotter and crt-screen copier. Many users will add other options, such as voice output synthesizers, voice input recognition systems, light pens, touch-sensitive screens, etc.

Personal computers can be defined as low-cost, small (often portable), personally controllable "turnkey" (plug-and-go) microprocessor-based stored-program ease-of-use systems that accept wide ranges of peripheral memory and input/output equipment. Practically anyone can buy or rent them and use them with a minimum of training. There are endless types of applications. One list has hundreds of distinct applications for computers, and the list increases as more and more people discover even more uses, write more programs, and find more devices and systems to control.

The packaging of more and more capabilities for logic processing, device control, information storage, communications simplicities, and intelligent decision-making onto tiny large-scale integration (LSI) and very-large-scale integration (VLSI) chips, at constantly dropping prices, has amazed everyone both inside and outside the industry. Distributed systems using the computers based on these "cheap chips" have proved more reliable and more economical by far than former standard computers and minicomputers. No computer component has decreased in price more dramatically than microprocessors and programmable memory elements.

CHEAP CHIPS

One of the primary levels of functions in a computer system can be inferred at from the amount of memory that the system contains. Although the typical user might be concerned with the amount of virtual, cache, or external memory (such as disks, etc.) that is available, it is the main memory, composed of ROM and RAM, that is the most significant. Memory contained on single chips has dramatically increased yearly. At the same time, semiconductor chip prices have decreased drastically. This increase in memory capacity at constantly reduced prices has corresponded to the number of increases in functions, power (versatility), and user sophistication.

As an example, low-cost memory permits the construction of very sophisticated video terminals in which one bit of local memory will correspond to each dot position on the screen, permitting simplification of bit-mapped terminals, allow further expansion of gray scale and color capabilities, and improve their cost/benefit ratios. Adding more memory and more versatile microprocessors will make the system operation much easier for the user since so many more functions are either automatically controlled or are made selectable to the user. New microprocessor and memory features improve overall system productivity, providing far more capable displays, more functions usable for video-discs, teletext, and viewdata capabilities, and a greater hard-copy capability (lower cost and greater readability). More powerful micros and more dense and cheaper memory also means that voice input and output can be added inexpensively, image sensors can be far more sophisticated, and remote pickups can be more varied and numerous. Because of these changes and dropping costs, it is predicted that the typewriter, telephone, and file cabinet as we know them will soon disappear in favor of more efficient and cheaper electronic devices.

How do costs continue to decrease as sophistication increases? As chip manufacturing processes become more and more automated, as thousands of chips are made from the same or similar design, costs per chip are cut tremendously. Almost of equal importance is the reduced costs in designing the chip systems (microprocessor, memory, and support chips). One of the most popular ways of accomplishing this is through the use of CAD (computer-aided design). This has had a great success in curtailing both design costs and manufacturing time. CAD is very effective in completing custom designs, just as it was for semi-custom work where the elements are standardized and arranged on a chip. (All the CAD system had to do was design the interconnections.) Another approach is to use off-the-shelf components in an innovative manner, such as adding some custom circuitry to a standard part to make a proprietary product that performs better than the standard part, yet at a cost that is much less than a fully custom device. Another method is to take a standard part (like most LSI components) and use only part of the component for a particular design. This approach is used in many microprocessor designs. The "smart" chip is seldom used to its full potential, yet the wasted capability is so cheap, compared to the cost of a custom design, that it may be safely ignored.

APPLICATIONS

One of the most massive uses of microprocessor and memory chips will be in the "smart" debit card area, such as those pioneered in France. Two such usages are in the counter-top reader (such as used in stores) and in the "fare collection box" reader (such as used with the San Francisco area BART system). Figs. B-1 through B-3 illustrate the devices.

American Magnetics Corporation reports that their Model 44 MAG-STRIPE™ Reader/Encoder (Fig. B-1) is a field-proven economical means for reading and encoding magnetic stripe cards, badges, and passbooks. The unit possesses patented dual heads that are independently suspended and gimbal-mounted for less head and card wear, and for increased reliability with warped and contaminated cards. A similar device was added, in early 1981, by General Telephone and Electronics (GTE), to one of its "system" telephones. The device was called the Micro-Fone (Fig. B-2), and via nationwide multimedia news releases, it was made clear that the unit would handle all types of magstripe cards (VISA, MasterCard, etc.). From the announcement, we find that Micro-Fone is a computer terminal/automatic telephone that can automatically reach up to 14 credit organizations (or manually reach any phone number). It has a magnetic-stripe reader. A quick wipe-through with the credit card starts the procedure. A complete credit verification can take as few as 10 seconds. Micro-Fone can operate through the regular public telephone system, or through packet-switched data communications networks.

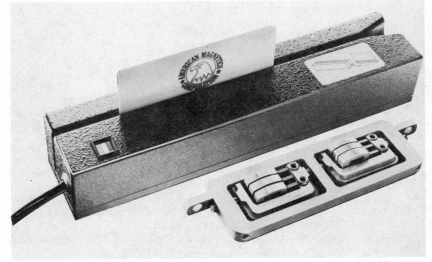

Courtesy American Magnetics Corp.

Fig. B-1. A reader/encoder for use with magnetic stripe cards, employee badges, and bank passbooks.

The automatic fare collection system now operating as part of the San Francisco Bay Area Rapid Transit system (BART) is furnished by IBM. The equipment includes electronic gates, ticket vending machines, and addfare and change machines. Fig. B-3 shows a fare ticket being inserted to upgrade the ticket. The system works as follows:

As customers enter the system, they purchase a ticket, usually for greater than the amount needed to cover the cost of the trip. Later, when the appropriate amount is deposited in an addfare machine, the old ticket is returned magnetically upgraded to the new value, and the patron can use it to open the gate. If the electronic mechanisms encounter problems handling the ticket, the gate flashes a "See Agent" notice, directing the user to obtain help at the station agent's booth. There, a "ticket reader" machine allows the agent to display the information recorded on the ticket's magnetic stripe. With this information, the agent can determine whether the ticket is valid or invalid, coded for exit or entry, or indicates other factors that

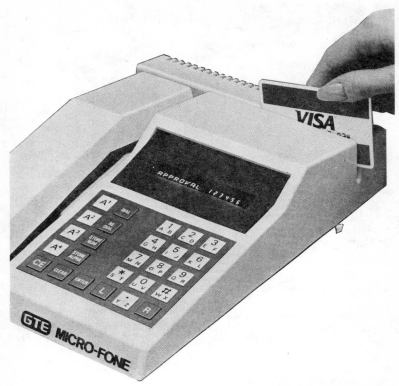

Courtesy General Telephone and Electronics

Fig. B-2. A machine used for automatic credit verification.

could create a problem in automated handling. IBM has provided 607 units of fare collection equipment for BART's 33 stations.

Another use of a microprocessor is in the automobile industry where it is having a giant impact. A tiny digital computer, possessing the same collection and decision-making ability of large computers, was introduced to the automobile industry as part of a Chrysler-developed portable diagnostic tool for lean burn engines. Microprocessors are now involved in all aspects of an automobile—the way it is engineered and built, the way it operates on the road, and the way it is serviced in dealerships. Most 1981 Chrysler-built cars have a microprocessor under the hood, and the 1981 Imperial has more than one microprocessor. The all-electronic instrument cluster receives accurate information on speed, fuel, and time from a microprocessor at the touch of a push button, while another microprocessor controls the Imperial's all-electronic search-tune ten push-button radio. Chrysler Electronics Research

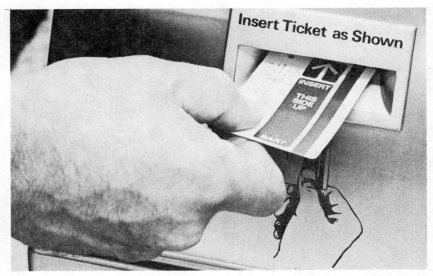

Fig. B-3. A "ticket reader" machine that is used in San Francisco's BART system.

Engineer Judith Pernyeszi is shown in Fig. B-4 holding the microprocessor used to control the automotive electronic items behind her, which includes an electronic engine performance analyzer, a trip computer, and a search-tune radio.

John Call, Engineering Manager of Chrysler's Huntsville Electronics Division, said his company expected to use almost one million microprocessors in its products during 1981. The use of the microprocessor is spreading rapidly in the inspection systems the Huntsville Division develops and builds for assembly plants, and for the diagnostic tools it supplies to dealerships and other service outlets. All of Chrysler's U.S. and Canadian assembly plants use microprocessor-controlled checkout equipment to inspect instrument panel clusters and steering columns, before they are installed in the cars on the assembly lines, to assure excellent quality and lower warranty costs. Mr. Call and his engineering staff feel that microprocessors will continue to take over more functions both inside and outside the car in the next few years so that more diagnostic information will appear on the instrument panel, including messages that will warn the driver of pending maintenance problems before they occur, and, also, control automatic-transmission shifting for smoother engine acceleration without any fuel economy penalty. They feel that someday a tiny computer will be used to sense the wear and tear and other power-train changes that could affect fuel economy and emissions, and will automatically adapt the engine to compensate for the changes. Also, future instrument panels may include a microprocessor-controlled talking instrument that asks the driver and passengers to buckle up.

Courtesy Chrysler Corp.

Fig. B-4. A microprocessor that is used to control various automotive electronic items.

MICROCOMPUTER MARKETS

Perhaps this section should be titled "The semiconductor and small companies move against the giant companies." This action may at first seem incredulous but even more incredulous is that the "big" companies (IBM, Honeywell, Burroughs, etc.) would let the small companies (Radio Shack/Tandy Corp., Apple Computer Inc., Commodore Business Machines, Inc., etc.) take more than one million computer sales away from them. Now, the small companies are threatening to move into the midrange computer area ($30,000 to $60,000 machines) using the super-fast 16-bit microcomputers and the exceptionally strong 32-bit microcomputers.

One of the big market areas has been in the hobbyist area. Figs. B-5 and B-6 show two views of a hobby microcomputer kit system. Built around an RCA COSMAC microprocessor, RCA's COSMAC VIP is a complete computer system that can grow. It has 2K of RAM that is expandable on-board to 4K. It also has a ROM monitor, an audio tone output to a built-in speaker, a power supply, and 8-bit input and output ports to use for the control of relays, sensors, and other peripherals. Fig. B-6 illustrates the COSMAC VIP in use. Its input consists of either a cassette tape recorder or a hexadecimal keypad (not a full keyboard). Extremely inexpensive, it may have a use in the business world, perhaps in an engineer or architect's office, where calculation rather than text storage is important. The VIP has many uses in operations involving relatively small storage needs and comparatively high calculative needs.

Also in the hobbyist or home computer area are the powerful Apple III personal computer (Fig. B-7), and Ohio Scientific's Challenger 1P Series (Fig. B-8). The Apple III personal computer includes a central processing unit with 96K bytes of memory, a built-in floppy-disk drive, an integrated keyboard with a 13-key numeric keypad, and a 12-inch video monitor. Ohio Scientific's new Series 2 C1P offers a sound, music, and voice output capability via a digital-to-analog converter. Its range of screen formats and powerful resident BASIC makes it a very suitable computer for

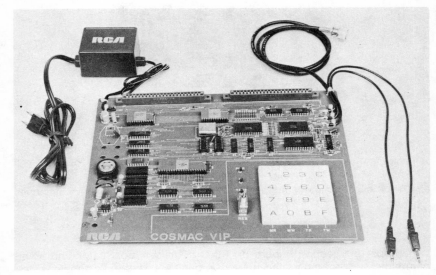

Courtesy RCA

Fig. B-5. A hobbyist microcomputer kit system.

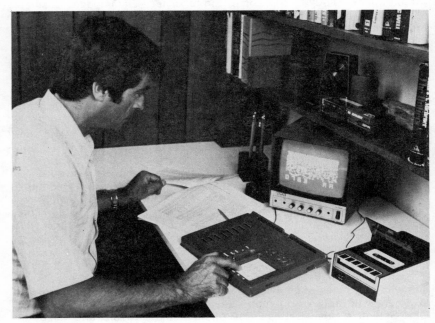

Courtesy RCA

Fig. B-6. The COSMAC VIP in use.

Courtesy Apple Computer, Inc.

Fig. B-7. The Apple III personal computer.

Courtesy Ohio Scientific

Fig. B-8. Ohio Scientific's Superboard II/Challenger C1P microcomputer.

educational applications. With its modem interface, it can be used as an economical remote terminal in conjunction with time-sharing services. It is also useful as a scientific calculator with its advanced floating-point math capability and its "immediate mode" operation. The 8K workspace of the standard machine provides sufficient memory for virtually any cassette-based program.

There still remains a large group of computer professionals who are highly skilled and strongly technically oriented to both large and very large systems, and who do not concern themselves about price. There is also the new computer user who is in the small or medium-sized business class, the professional or educational class, or in the industrial or institutional class. This is the purchaser level at which practically every manufacturer is now aimed. These people and enterprises are seeking "solution systems" with both word and data processing capabilities, graphics capabilities, and communications capabilities. The greatest attention, however, is being paid to the new product developments that have a surprising system capability and versatility at penny-pinching prices (available from manufacturers at the $1000 to $15,000 level). Manufacturers are using these products to "bait" the small business and professional office user with $300 to $1000 "bare bones" systems knowing full well that they or practically no other purchaser can refrain from going out within a week or two to purchase more memory, a better terminal, some voice I/O, better graphics capabilities, or another "complete" system, because the surprising effectiveness of the first "low-cost computer" was a real convincer.

Some examples of the "low-cost computer" are shown in Figs. B-9 through B-13. Fig. B-9 shows the TRS-80 Color Computer, the TRS-80 Pocket Computer, and the TRS-80 Model III—Radio Shack's three newest computers. The Color Computer provides color graphics and

Courtesy Radio Shack

Fig. B-9. Radio Shack's three newest microcomputers.

features instant-load Program Pak™ software that enables the user to instantly program the computer for a variety of educational and recreational purposes. Since it attaches to any color television set, it can easily be used anywhere for home, personal, or educational uses. Weighing only 6 ounces and less than 7 inches long, the Pocket Computer is considered a breakthrough in computer technology. Yet, it is said to be able to do almost any of the smaller jobs that the popular TRS-80 Model I computer can do. Finally, a leader in the TRS-80 family, the Model III desktop computer is designed to meet the needs of many users for more data storage, greater versatility, and higher computing speed. It is highly compatible with the Model I and features the more powerful Model III BASIC language. Radio Shack also has a system to link a home computer with a time-sharing service. Called the Videotex, the system ties in with a time-sharing network such as that offered by CompuServe (Columbus, OH). The unit can be used with the TRS-80 Model II business system to set up internal electronic mail systems, and for order entry and data base searches. Additional functions will be added to include weather, sports, financial news, and up-to-the-minute wire service data.

Hewlett-Packard Company's HP-85 is shown in Fig. B-10. It is a personal computer designed to bring users the capabilities, convenience, reliability, and power that a professional needs. Its biggest users are scientists, engineers, and business professionals. The keyboard, crt display, printer, tape unit, and operating system are all built in one small package. This integration makes the system exceptionally reliable, and gives full computing power in a single convenient and portable unit. The HP-85's BASIC is a conversational programming language that is simple to learn and use, yet more than 150 commands and statements give the power needed to solve many problems.

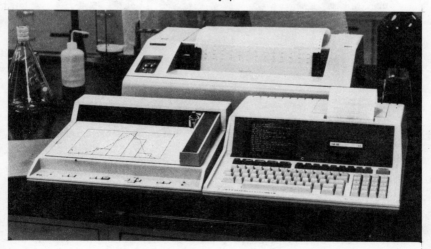

Courtesy Hewlett-Packard Co.

Fig. B-10. The power of Hewlett-Packard's HP-85 is increased with the addition of a plotter and printer.

Fig. B-11 shows Atari's line of personal computer hardware. Clockwise from the lower right is the Atari 830 acoustic modem, the Atari 800 microcomputer, the Atari 822 thermal printer, the Atari 850 RS-232 interface module, the Atari 410 program recorder, the Atari 825 80-column dot-matrix impact printer, the Atari 815 dual disk drive, and the Atari 810 disk drive.

Illustrated in Fig. B-12 is Lear Siegler's video display processor. It is an intelligent terminal that was one of the first implementations of the new concept of packaging a video display device in one compact unit. It contains a 16-bit minicomputer, a crt terminal, and up to 32K words of high-speed RAM memory in the unit. Also available is an integration of a dual floppy disk and a virtual memory operating system packaged in the same unit (designated VDP-1000).

Courtesy Atari, Inc.

Fig. B-11. The "top of the line" in personal computers from Atari.

The Sharp Radicomputer is a fresh design approach to a home computer. It is actually a home entertainment system, personal computer, and calculator all rolled up into one self-contained unit. The Radicomputer can be operated as a conventional combination tv/radio/cassette device. However, when programmed with the computer's special alphanumeric keyboard, the Radicomputer becomes a complete home information center capable of playing games, calculating complex mathematical and scientific equations, computing Biorythms, and balancing household finances. Using Sharp BASIC, the programmer can encode and store data on a standard audio cassette via the 42 graphic signal command keyboard, with the 4.5-inch (diagonal) tv screen serving for the graphic display. The Radicomputer has a 2K-bit memory (expandable to 8K bits). When used alone, the keyboard is a scientific calculator which computes trigonometric functions.

Finally, there is a do-it-yourself unit from Heathkit®. Using concise, easy-to-follow Heathkit® assembly manuals which show you the way from start to finish, you can construct a self-contained, compact unit for up to hundreds of dollars less than comparable systems (Fig. B-14). The Heathkit® H89 All-In-One Computer features two Z80 microprocessors, floppy-disk storage, a smart video terminal, a heavy-duty keyboard, a numeric keypad, and a 16K RAM—all in one compact unit.

Courtesy Lear Siegler, Data Products Div.

Fig. B-12. A video display processor terminal.

It is very necessary that each of the "new breed" of manufacturers study the market carefully, analyzing user requirements, competitive products and prices, and the appropriate support software and hardware for specific or wide-ranging applications. If they do not, they, like the old-line computer companies, will soon fall behind and lose out. Competition is vicious, not only from the price/performance and expanding lower-cost capabilities of everybody's system, but from the "substitutability factor" that has the ability to knock many products out of the market before they are fully introduced. Examples are: (1) Will low-cost Winchester disks knock out floppy-disk systems?, (2) Will bubble memory cassettes do it?, or (3) Will videodisc systems supplant both Winchester disks and bubble memory systems? At the same time, the

Courtesy Sharp Electronics

Fig. B-13. A combination calculator, personal computer, and home entertainment system.

Courtesy Heath Co.

Fig. B-14. The Heathkit® H89.

dropping prices of memory chips must be watched. Also, the prices of the graphics systems and terminals must be watched. Excellent dot-matrix printers and plotters were being sold from slightly below $1000 to between $3000 and $7000. Good quality units began to appear as part of personal portable computer systems, with the total price of computer, acoustic modem, 5-inch crt, and printer less than $800. What is the reason behind this happening? User demands and huge markets continually force innovation and price plunges designed to capture the major part of the market, and to (hopefully) scare competitors out of this apparently low-profit product area, and to (hopefully, again) prohibit other producers from entering such a fiercely competitive market.

Courtesy Sinclair Research Ltd.

Fig. B-15. The Sinclair ZX80.

The major component and microcomputer system suppliers quickly discern the areas of mass-product sales potential. Hundreds of millions of new computer users will quite obviously want cheap, simple, but effective devices with an easy-to-use capability. New products will often "price kill" very efficient products. Figs. B-15 and B-16 demonstrate examples of this. Fig. B-15 shows the Sinclair ZX80 which, at $199.95, is the world's lowest-priced personal computer. Manufactured by Sinclair Research Ltd., of Cambridge, England, and Boston, Massachusetts, the unit, which measures just 6.5 × 8.5 × 1.5 inches (16.5 cm × 21.6 cm × 3.8 cm) and weighs 12 ounces, utilizes a standard home television set for display and a tape cassette recorder for program storage. Fig. B-16 illustrates the prototype of the pocket television invented by Sinclair Research Ltd. It is the first flat-screen television. Measuring just 6 × 4 × 1 inches (15.24 × 10.16 × 2.54 centimeters), the television is being manufactured by the Timex Corporation in Scotland, and is expected

Courtesy Sinclair Research Ltd.

Fig. B-16. Prototype of a flat-screen pocket television set.

to be available in the United States in late 1982. The prototype features a 3-inch (7.62 cm) diagonal black and white flat screen and incorporates an fm radio. The television, which will retail for about $125, will be able to receive transmission almost anywhere in the world.

HAND-HELD COMPUTERS

The hand-held computer is a microcomputer small enough to fit in one's pocket, yet powerful enough to do the jobs that full-size micro-computers do routinely. The first models (by Nixdorf, Seiko, Radio Shack/Sharp, Panasonic/Quasar, and Hewlett-Packard) all fall roughly into the ultrasmall computer category. Hewlett-Packard's HP-41C is a real "computer" because it has all the necessary elements to qualify: memory, processor, I/O, and a full line of peripherals. All the units have some features that many full-size personal computers do not have, such as the ability to run for long periods on battery power alone. Most have user-definable keys, a built-in real-time clock, an uninterruptible storage of user programs, and the ability to produce color images on a color television set (with the addition of optional interface units). Some of the machines are capable of running complex BASIC programs and all are truly portable. A student or other beginner in computer programming can learn a lot with any of these machines, in conjunction with their intro-ductory BASIC books. The hand-held computer is the latest step in the never-ending battle to put more and more capability into less and less space.

The Quasar Portable Computer System (Fig. B-17) can fit into a brief-case. It can be used as a remote terminal to draw information from data

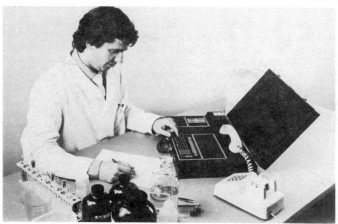

Courtesy Quasar Co.

Fig. B-17. A portable computer system that fits in a briefcase.

stored in a large university or government computer. The battery-operated terminal contains memory capsules (ROM) with functions such as
language translation. Using an ac adapter, the terminal can control optional peripherals, e.g., a programmable memory (RAM), input/output
driver, an expandable capsule memory (up to four additional capsules),
a cassette adapter, a micro-printer, a telephone modem, and a video
adapter. The Quasar Information Processor™, shown in Fig. B-18, can
be used for education, information, communication, or pure entertainment. It accepts up to three memory capsules which can be programmed
for various applications such as language translation, nutrition and calorie guides, and wine selection and bartending guides. Fig. B-19 shows
the hand-held information processor again, this time showing the language capsules. Eight new languages are added to the processor's repertoire—for a total of fourteen—plus five new extra-capacity language

Courtesy Quasar Co.

**Fig. B-18. An information processor that can be used for education,
information, language translation, and pure entertainment.**

capsules, with business terms in four languages, and Las Vegas-type games, such as blackjack. It also has a word game that draws its vocabulary from any language capsule. As shown in Fig. B-20, the battery-operated terminal can be used with a telephone modem to stay in touch while "on the go." The Quasar Hand-Held Computer shown in Fig. B-21 controls accessories in the Quasar Micro Information System (a computer which fits into a briefcase). However, it can be used alone as a world clock with alarm, as a stopwatch, a calculator, a memo recorder, and as an electronic teacher/reference library. It can also be used for translating foreign words and phrases, and for playing hand-held games. A related feature of the hand-held computer is that when the OFF button has been pressed, the computer is still on. It is in a dormant state that only uses enough current to retain the contents of the computer's display image and the CMOS memory and preserve the real-time clock and keyboard functions. A side benefit of this feature is that it is impossible to lose the work you are doing by pressing the OFF key; when you press the ON key, the computer resumes whatever it was doing before it was turned off. To allow use of the computer with minimal prior knowledge of the machine, all functions are selected via a set of nested menus.

From Matsushita Electrical Industrial comes news that they will introduce to the United States, in the spring of 1981, a "hand-held computer" that the company claims will relieve traveling businessmen of the need to carry bulky paper documents. The 9-pound unit, fitted in its own attache case, consists of an 8-bit Rockwell International microprocessor, memory chips, and input/output devices, among them an acoustic coupler (for interfacing a user's central computer) and a video connection that turns an ordinary television screen into a display station.

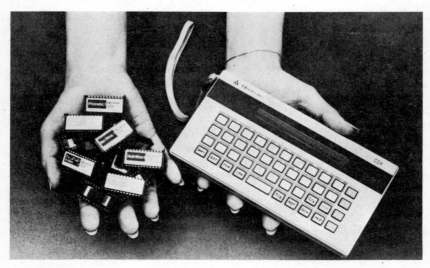

Courtesy Quasar Co.

Fig. B-19. The language capsules used in the information processor.

Courtesy Quasar Co.

Fig. B-20. The battery-operated terminal can be used with a telephone modem to stay in touch while "on the go."

Courtesy Quasar Co.

Fig. B-21. The hand-held computer controls accessories in the Quasar Micro Information System but it can be used alone as a translator, memo recorder, etc.

Fig. B-22. The RL-H1000 hand-held computer system from Panasonic.

Also available in the hand-held category, is the RL-H1000 hand-held computer system (Fig. B-22) introduced in the summer of 1980 by Panasonic. It consists of a full complement of separate peripheral devices, including an input/output interface with the provision for attaching up to six additional peripherals, an acoustic coupler/telephone modem for data bank access, cassette interface, video RAM interface for hookup to a home tv set, a mini printer, and RAM and ROM memory expanders. The variety of uses of the RL-H1000 is limited only by the types of peripheral equipment combined with it and the Program Capsules. Some practical examples are as a time-sharing system and as a personal computer. The RL-H1000, when combined with the acoustic coupler, an optional peripheral, can receive a variety of information by using an ordinary telephone. This information can be displayed on a television set, or if it is desired to retain the information, a printer and/or cassette interface module, also optional, are available. When you put this system to work to serve your needs, you will find that it has a multitude of practical possibilities. You will find that when connected to the optional peripheral equipment, such as a RAM, video RAM, or printer, the Basic Program Capsule provides all of the pleasure of a personal computer system.

COMPUTERS IN EDUCATION

In the United States, in early 1981, a member of the House of Representatives attempted to introduce a bill for a $4-million National Center for Personal Computers in Education, stating that along with other programs in the United Kingdom, the British had recently allocated

$25 million for such a center. He had stated that, "Among the major industrial nations of the world, it is only the United States that is not moving ahead rapidly with a program to assimilate computers into our schools." There are pockets, however, of specific counties and school districts around the United States that are independently moving to purchase personal computers for schools (Fig. B-23). The children are demanding them in order to become better prepared for the massive use of computers in offices, automobiles, factories, etc., and in the fields of science, mathematics, entertainment, etc.

The French have allocated funds to train 10,000 secondary school teachers in computer use.

Courtesy Digital Equipment Corp.

Fig. B-23. Elementary school children enjoy using a computer in the school.

In February, 1981, in a note in a British periodical (the Electronics Weekly), the message read,

> "It was estimated that nearly 50 percent of the secondary schools in England had one or more microcomputers, and eight local educational (boards) provided them for all their secondary schools," MPs were told in a Commons answer last week. The Under Secretary stated that he was urgently considering what steps could be taken to make microcomputers more widely available in secondary schools. The Education Department had 9 million pounds for "microcomputers in education" and the programme was "to promote curriculum development, lay the foundations for improved teacher training, and ensure that good quality educational software was widely available."

Several manufacturers, including Commodore Business Machines, Radio Shack (Tandy Corporation), Hewlett-Packard Company, Texas Instruments Incorporated, and Apple Computer, Inc., have aggressive programs to get their systems into schools at large discounts and, in some cases, as outright gifts to the schools. In one case, a "personal use" innovation in classroom instructional computing is offered by Digital

Courtesy Digital Equipment Corp.

Fig. B-24. A "personal use" innovation in classroom instruction computing is offered by Digital Equipment Corporation.

Equipment Corporation (Fig. B-24). The firm's Educational Products Group said its CLASSIC (for *CLASS*room *I*nteractive *C*omputer) is the industry's first self-installable portable minicomputer system.

COMPUTERS IN BUSINESS

Realizing the dominant successes of the Japanese manufacturers in the radio, tv, calculator, and camera departments, the computer research leaders were undecided about how to handle the growing microcomputer market. Fujitsu, Ltd. and Hitachi Ltd. were the major systems leaders in Japan, followed by Toshiba Corporation, Mitsubishi Electric Corporation, and Nippon Electric Co. Ltd. The other five manufacturers that make up the "Big 10" are Sharp Electronics, Tokyo Sanyo Electric Co., Ltd., OKI Electric Industry Co., Ltd., Matsushita Electronics Industries (Panasonic, Quasar, etc.), and Sony Corporation. All of these firms had personal and small computers on sale in Japan in 1980-1981, and most were either offering products in the United States or were planning to do so. But, there was a second group of firms marketing low-cost systems in the U.S. or about to do so. These were Sord Computer Systems, Casio and Canon (both calculator sales leaders), Ricoh and Minolta (both copier leaders), Nikko Telecommunications, JDL (Japan Digital Labs), and others. More than half of these companies had products in the Japanese markets by 1979 and were now advancing into the world markets. These are all very competitive machines and systems. There is a "free-for-all" battle in the home and small business computer market for the market percentages, and the "weak sisters" will fall by the wayside.

An expandable small business computer featuring a step-by-step programming aid was announced by Sharp Electronics. The complete system, designated the Sharp YX-3200 Business Computer, includes a central processing unit (CPU), high-resolution crt display with green characters, dual-drive floppy disk, and an impact printer. The desktop system, designed with an expandable 32K ROM and a 64K RAM, features an automatic program generator which poses questions to the user that, when answered by a yes or no, in most cases, designs the desired program. The YX-3200 can accommodate up to 72K ROM and 128K RAM.

The TX Series of microcomputers from Canon feature a 6809 microprocessor, with extended BASIC and assembly language, a 20-column alphanumeric video display, and a built-in 26-column triple-copy impact printer. The models have 15K bytes of user memory which can be expanded to 31K bytes. Each model in the series has an RS-232 interface port and a modem port.

Figs. B-25 and B-26 show of the Astra series of small business computers available from NEC Informations Systems, Inc., Lexington, Mass. The four models of the Astra series of small business computers range

Courtesy NEC Information Systems, Inc.

Fig. B-25. The Astra series of computers are adaptable for use in large-scale distributed data processing networks.

in size from a one-crt station with 128KB memory to a 32-station system with a main memory of up to 512KB. Integrated applications software includes sales-order processing, sales analysis, inventory control, accounts receivable, accounts payable, general ledger, and payroll for the first-time computer user. Extensive communications capabilities makes the Astra computer series adaptable for use in large-scale dis-

Courtesy NEC Information Systems, Inc.

Fig. B-26. A small business computer that features three languages, multiple communications, and text processing.

tributed data processing networks (Fig. B-25). The Model 205 Small Business Computer shown in Fig. B-26 features three languages, multiple communications, and text processing for businesses ranging from $500,000 to $5 million while the Astra Business Management Series Model 205 system offers an inventory control specialization consisting of an operator station with a display screen, two diskette drives, a full-function printer, software, instruction manual, and pocket reference card.

Panasonic has simplified the operation of various digital and analog devices with the introduction of a unique one-touch key-mat (Fig. B-27). The man-machine interface is approximately the size of a standard keyboard. The key-mat may be utilized to improve data processing and control applications, such as data entry and automatic equipment control. While standard keyboard operation requires a typist, Panasonic's unique man-machine interface removes this requirement. The interface consists of one switch panel and one removable cartridge mechanism.

591   *Microcomputers*

With 96 customized legends per page and 24 pages per cartridge, the interface has 2304 legends for each cartridge. By employing the maximum 15 interchangeable cartridges, the unit makes 34,560 legends available to any application. Any page is accessible to the operator in less than one second. Easy entry of numeric data is assured by the 10-key numeric pad. System function keys are also provided. The Panasonic key-mat is microprocessor controlled and may be programmed to supply all necessary information to a controller. For example, a single keystroke can generate a character, a word, a line, or a page of information. Fig. B-28 illustrates Panasonic's Model BC-5000 computer with the one-touch key-mat and a printer.

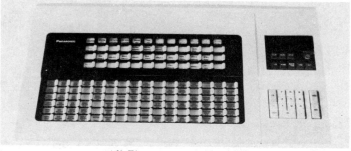

(A) The one-touch key-mat.

(B) The easily insertable cartridge.

Courtesy Panasonic Co.

Fig. B-27. Panasonic's one-touch key-mat man-machine interface.

The low-cost Displaywriter System from IBM (Fig. B-29) is a desktop text-processing system for offices. It has a number of innovative features and is modular, allowing users to tailor and expand the system as their needs change. The software-based system can actually check the spelling of about 50,000 words using an electronic "dictionary." The Displaywriter can also communicate with other office equipment over ordinary telephone lines. The Displaywriter guides operators with messages in clear English text on a tv-like screen and allows them to enter text in a continuous stream. The system can divide the text into lines and pages and can even create "justified" text, with all lines of equal length. Words with misspellings are highlighted on the screen of

Courtesy Panasonic Co.

Fig. B-28. The Model BC-5000 computer with printer and key-mat.

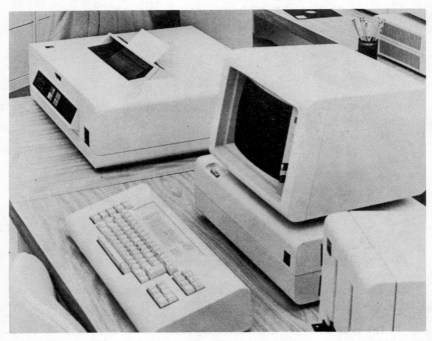

Courtesy IBM

Fig. B-29. A desktop text-processing system.

the electronics "dictionary" to check the spelling of words (Fig. B-30). In seconds, it checks both common English words and special terminology, such as used in science and medicine. The spelling verification aid works when the operator commands the system to compare the typed text to words in the "dictionary." Any unmatched word is highlighted by the system. The operator then simply enters any necessary correc-

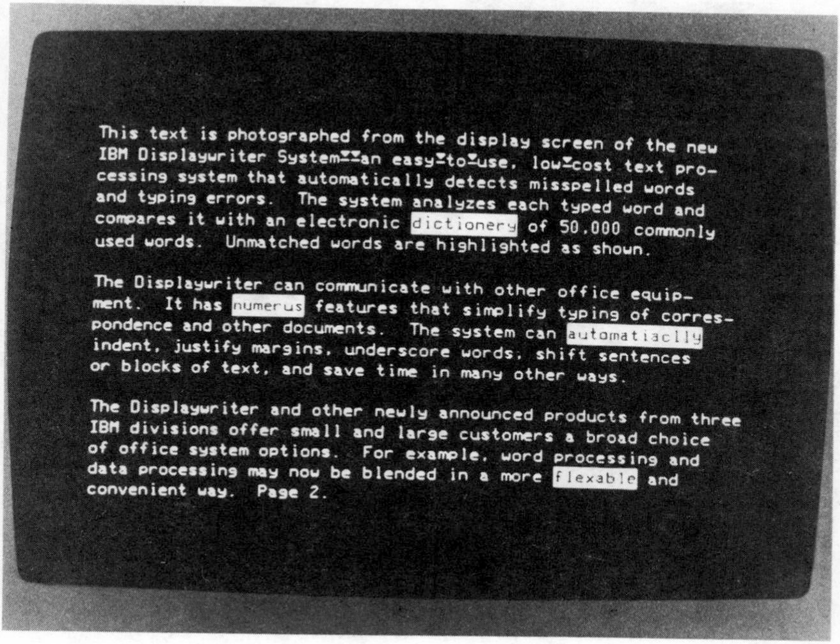

Courtesy IBM

Fig. B-30. Misspelled words are highlighted on the screen of the IBM Displaywriter.

tions. The system has an electronic memory which provides up to 229,376 characters of information. Other options include three printers of different speeds, and a paper handler which automatically moves each sheet into position. The building-block Displaywriter System can be custom-ordered from more than 20 separate components, features, and options.

Sony Corporation has entered the office automation business with an entirely new concept in typing and word processing. The conventional typewriter, as we know it, has been in use throughout the world for the past one hundred years. Sony's "Typecorder," virtually an office in a briefcase, represents a unique fundamental departure from its basic operation. The new unit developed by Sony uses no paper. It is noiseless, portable, and lightweight—only 3 pounds. It is battery driven and compact enough to fit neatly into an attache case (Fig. B-31). Words typed on its standard-sized keyboard are displayed on a LED readout and recorded on a magnetic microcassette tape. The Typecorder can also be used as a recorder for dictation and transcription, or to record meetings and conferences. The Typecorder (a name derived from its function as a typewriter/recorder) uses a microprocessor for totally electronic typing, correcting, and editing as the text is being composed or reviewed.

Courtesy Sony Corp.

Fig. B-31. Sony Corporation's Typecorder, a combination typewriter and recorder, is noiseless, portable, and lightweight.

After the microcassette has been recorded, the text can be dealt with in a number of ways. It can be: (1) printed on paper with Sony's portable Silent Compact printer, (2) processed using Sony's Series 35 Word Processor, (3) processed using existing word processors with communication capability and, then, printed out on most letter-quality printers through Sony's Communication/Printer Interfacing Unit, (4) typed out on conventional electric typewriters by employing Sony's Actuator Unit for electric typewriters, (5) punched out on a Telex tape using Sony's Telex Tape Puncher, and (6) transmitted over telephone lines to a central office, through an acoustic coupler, to be processed with any of the above mentioned equipments. The unit also has "steno" functions for speedy and simplified typing. Its briefcase portability makes it ideally suited for use on airplanes and trains by traveling business people and others on the move. Sony's Tapecorder comes with several accessories. Clockwise from top center in Fig. B-32 is the actuator unit (permitting Typecorder text to be typed out on conventional electric typewriters), the

Courtesy Sony Corp.

Fig. B-32. The accessories of the Typecorder which make it one of the most versatile writing tools ever invented.

Telex tape puncher, the portable printer, the basic Typecorder unit, the acoustic coupler (which transmits data over telephone lines to a central office), and the Communication/Printer Interfacing Unit (which conveys text from the Typecorder to existing word processors to be printed out).

Courtesy ASEA, Inc.

Fig. B-33. Robot system being used to check car body integrity.

ROBOTICS

Industrial workers are pressing nowadays for vastly improved working environments. At the same time, companies have to increase productivity to maintain or improve their position in the market arena. Industrial robot systems have been making a distinct contribution to fulfilling these requirements. The robot can work continuously day in and day out in environments which, for human beings, would be uncomfortable or dangerous. The illustrations in Figs. B-33 and B-34 show how the industrial robots from ASEA, Inc. can contribute to increased productivity and relieve human workers of hazardous, physically exhausting, and boring tasks. Fig. B-33 shows the world's first robotic system being used to check auto body integrity at Volvo's Torslanda, Sweden plant (installed in 1978) while, in Fig. B-34, a robot is spot welding a sheet metal housing.

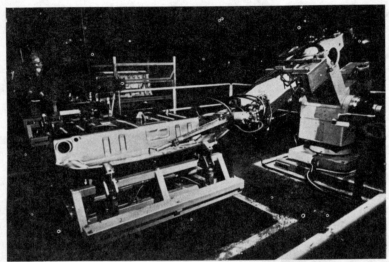

Courtesy ASEA, Inc.

Fig. B-34. Robot spot welding a sheet metal housing.

What is a robot? Robots cover an extremely wide range of sophistication. They have existed for many years, but mainly as parts of various laboratory experiments. (Now, "basement and garage" tinkerers, along with the toy manufacturers, are experimenting and trying to build their own ROBOT.) Simply, and quite restrictively stated, robots are made up from some rather basic components—metal and plastic piping, connectors, electronic components, wires, and various sundry parts. Now, the microprocessor and the microcomputer are being used. The use of single-chip microcomputers can result in the saving of time, parts, and money, because most of the required software can be entered into the chip's on-board memory. Digital devices used in combination with analog devices add considerable versatility to transducers, sensors, etc.

Other components needed are the manipulator, the controller, power supply, and so on. Manipulators usually consist of mechanical linkages and joints that can move in various directions when driven, either directly or indirectly, by the actuators. Feedback data, in either digital or analog form, are transmitted to the controller from the sensing devices, which monitor or cause positioning of the linkages and joints. Older models used a cylindrical, spherical, or jointed-spherical coordinated system that had one basic arm mounted on a vertical column, which was, in turn, mounted on a rotating base. Now, the arms (usually two or more) move in and out, and up and down, on a column, with both the arms and the column rotating as a unit on the base.

Courtesy Unimation, Inc

Fig. B-35. A robot pouring 1200 °C molten glass.

Jointed arms typically have six axes of motion—upper arms, forearms, shoulder joints, elbow joints, wrist joints (providing up to three additional movements), with a roll or rotation in a plane perpendicular to the end of the arm; with pitch or rotation in a vertical plane through the arm; with yaw or rotation in a horizontal plane through the arm; and with various other movements. Controllers initiate and terminate the manipulator motion in chosen sequences and at specified points, store both the arm position and sequence data in memory, and communicate with ancillary devices, such as printers, voice-actuated devices, etc. (for reporting). Energy is provided from the power supply and that energy may be electrical, hydraulic, or pneumatic. Television has permitted experi-

Courtesy Texas Instruments Incorporated

Fig. B-36. A robot sorts calculator parts.

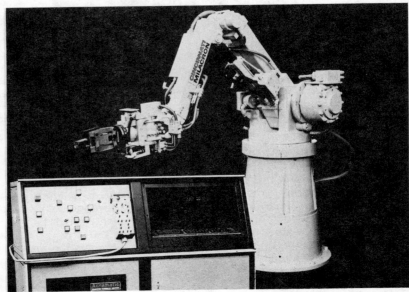

Courtesy Cincinnati Milacron

Fig. B-37. A T³ industrial robot.

menters and others to give the robots sight, allowing the robot to search for and recognize specific parts, devices, etc.

Some of the robot manufacturing companies are: Auto-Place Inc., Unimation, Inc., Prab Conveyors, Inc./Robots Division, ASEA, Inc., Cincinnati Milacron, AMF Electronics Division, Nordson Corporation, and De Vilbiss Company.

Some examples of robots and their uses are shown in Figs. B-35 through B-37. An UNIMATE 2000 Series robot pours molten glass (at 1200 °C) into a mold in the Smethwick glassworks of Chance Brothers (Fig. B-35). Then, in Fig. B-36, an in-house developed robot is sorting calculator parts at Texas Instruments Incorporated. The T[3] industrial robot (in the background in Fig. B-37) utilizes a Cincinnati Milacron Acramatic control for ease of entry, edit, and diagnostic functions. The hand-held unit (shown in the center of the control unit in Fig. B-37) is used to "teach" job functions. The control permits program playback with modifications and additions. The Acramatic control incorporates a minicomputer, cathode-ray tube, and keyboard console.

VIEWDATA AND TELETEXT SERVICES

Many studies have been made and analyzed on just how many consumers are willing to pay for either a viewdata or teletext terminal, what features they want included most, how they normally use their telephones, and just how willing they are to tie their telephones into an information delivery system. And, there are other questions that many participants in the new electronic marketplace have been unable to answer. Uncertainty over such issues has cast some concern about the future of the new information/entertainment operation.

Several surveys on the subject have been conducted by Britain, France, West Germany, and, in the United States, by CBS, AT&T, and many others. Businesses were questioned as to their present methods of collecting information in order to provide data on how those methods may change with the introduction of the new electronic media. These surveys also provided assessments of future markets for individual products and determined for several firms the "go-ahead" viability of their comprehensive information/entertainment packages.

Viewdata

At least half a dozen major companies have taken steps toward entering the viewdata market, the interactive service that turns a tv set into an information terminal (Fig. B-38). One of the first companies was Knight-Ridder Newspapers which began testing its Viewtron interactive service in Coral Gables, FL. It has been stated that Knight-Ridder plans to make a major acquisition of a cable-tv network. (Any 2-way home information service needs either a cable or a telephone connection to work, at least, under present technological constraints.) Another company has also been inching its way to a big viewdata capability, but from the manufacturer—rather than the provider—end. It is the Jerrold Division of General Instrument. Jerrold conducted field and marketing tests for a home-security system that uses a 2-way communication be-

Fig. B-38. Four examples of electronic news.

tween microprocessor-driven terminals and a computer-controlled head-end unit. Cablevision of Long Island was the first Jerrold client to offer the security system. The Jerrold system reportedly allows for easy up-grading to accommodate other 2-way services such as opinion polling and banking at home.

Foreign Viewdata Services

In November, 1980, the public viewdata system of West Germany, Bildschirmtext, operated by the Deutsche Bundespost (DBP), the German postal service, went live with links to third-party data bases that are maintained by private companies. This followed an announcement by the British Telecom that negotiations were under way with the DBP for the purchase of third-party data base software. Nine external computers had been connected to the trial computers (of the Bildschirmtext market) in Berlin and Dusseldorf, West Germany, and viewdata terminal users had direct on-line access to them.

Teletext Standards

Who is ahead of the United States in the viewdata/teletext race? France, England, Austria, Belgium, Sweden, Germany, Switzerland, Australia, Venezuela, Hong Kong, and Holland were all listed in 1980 as being among the countries whose public and private television networks are a year or so ahead. Why is this major ancillary tv service bogged down in committees, proposals, and tests? Some say because of commercial power ploys. For example, the NHK in Japan has developed a teletext system called Captains, and in Canada, the Department of

Communications (DOC) has fielded a teletext operation dubbed Telidon. In England, both Ceefax and Oracle were operational in 1979, while Telediffusion de France offered Antiope as part of their regular operations in 1980.

However, in the United States, teletext, viewdata, etc., were in disarray as far as any progress was concerned. The Federal Communications Commission had three goals: (1) efficient use of the limited and very valuable spectrum space in the vertical interval, (2) the adoption of the best available technology which could lead to a reliable and flexible teletext service for the largest segment of the U.S. viewing public, and (3) a teletext system whose economics would make it reasonably affordable to the widest range of television receiver buyers.

An example of an electronic news display is shown in Fig. B-39. Teletext provides viewer-controlled access to hundreds of pages of information, from news to weather to advertising. KSL Television, in Salt Lake City, was the first U.S. station to broadcast a Teletext signal simultaneous with regular programming.

Courtesy KSL Television, Salt Lake City, Utah

Fig. B-39. Teletext provides viewer-controlled access to hundreds of pages of information.

Electronic Yellow Pages

In late 1980, stories began to appear that information of products and services, of the type currently advertised in the yellow pages of the telephone book, would soon be provided in an electronic format. The pioneers of the service were two newspapers, the *Arizona Republic* and the *Phoenix Gazette,* who formed a joint-venture company, RG Cable, and sell both classified advertising and editorial content on three leased channels to the cable companies. As previously noted, AT&T has reportedly designated electronic yellow page service as one of the first activities of its southwestern subsidiary.

It is hoped that the availability of electronic yellow pages will help stimulate the move towards the installation of more home terminals. The same terminals used for electronic yellow page access can also be used for sending and receiving electronic mail.

In France, the government-controlled Post, (the post office, telephone, and telegraph organization) is moving ahead with a plan to phase out paper telephone directories over the next 15 years, with a complete elimination of telephone books by 1995. Consumers will be provided with a simple tv-like terminal device (with a keyboard), enabling them to request "on-line" directory information. The French expect that the savings on paper, and the printing and distribution of paper directories, coupled with a reduced workload on directory-information operators, will more than pay for the required terminals and computer hardware.

MISCELLANEOUS

There are a lot of devices and functions being produced or, at least, tested which may or may not be feasible and profitable to manufacture. As all marketable items depend on the whims and tastes of the consumer, many devices will not make it into the consumer market because some sales/marketing agent will not have enough faith in the product and its use by the consumer.

PicturePhone Service

AT&T's PicturePhone Meeting Service is complete and automatic (Fig. B-40). The meeting initiator calls up for a room in the city at which the meeting is to take place. From there on, all arrangements are made. The attendees arrive and "meet" with people all over the country and all over the world. Right now, this is economically feasible for large corporations, but it should also be an everyday event for future businesses, both large and small.

Ink-Jet Printer

The Silonics QUIETYPE ink-jet printer shown in Fig. B-41 employs "drop-on-demand" printing to form 7×9 dot-matrix characters. Basically, drop-on-demand ink-jet printing involves the conversion of electrical signals to images on plain paper using a simple one-step process and a special print head that contains seven individual ink ejectors. The images can be numbers as in a document printer or copy machine. At the most sophisticated end of the spectrum, even color photographs could be produced by this method. Since the drop-on-demand technique is so simple, it permits the development of equipment that is low-cost and extremely reliable.

At the heart of the QUIETYPE printer is a revolutionary head (superposed at the top of Fig. B-41). About the size of a matchbook and weighing 50 grams, the print-head ejector consists of a piezoelectric transducer, an ink-delivery channel, and a nozzle. Upon receiving an electrical pulse, the piezoelectric transducer deforms the wall of the associated ink-delivery channel. This slight sudden reduction of channel volume propels an ink drop toward the paper.

Courtesy AT&T

Fig. B-40. A conference using electronic means.

Satellite Communications

During 1979 and 1980, GTE Satellite Corporation placed in operation various remote monitor and control systems for its earth stations in California, Florida, Hawaii, and other states. The stations are a part of a domestic satellite communications system operated jointly by GTE and American Telephone and Telegraph Company for interstate long-distance calling. Provided by GTE Communications Products, these are computer-controlled systems with detailed visual displays believed to represent the first installation of its type. With systems to enable a single operator at a "master" station to monitor and control all operating functions at various earth stations, they permit surveillance of crucial operations and report any change of status. For each of the stations, the network controller can perform such operations as changing the position of antennas or modifying the output power of the radio transmitters. Fig. B-42 is an artist's rendering of the three Comstar satellites and the seven earth stations in the joint AT&T-GTE domestic communications satellite system.

Voice Recognition

In maintaining its position as a leader in the emerging semiconductor technologies, General Instrument Microelectronics has designed a voice synthesis module containing three MOS/LSI devices. The module, designated VSM2032, incorporates a single-chip speech synthesizer with a time-shared two-stage filter section, a microcomputer, and a standard 32K ROM. The three MOS/LSI devices are fabricated with n-channel ion-implant technology, resulting in proven reliability. The VSM2032 (shown in Fig. B-43) features a complete speech system, storage of approximately 30 seconds of speech, custom vocabulary availability, 32

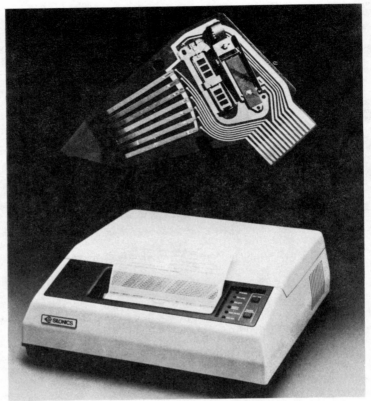

Courtesy Silonics, Inc.

Fig. B-41. An ink-jet printer.

words and syllables that combine to form over one billion phrases, and an audio output of 200 mW.

Speech synthesis products are intended for use in many industrial and consumer applications including control and instrumentation equipment, telecommunications and radar systems, automotive warning systems, and security systems—virtually every product that requires activation. The VSM2032 lends itself to those customer applications where very complex word repertoires or high-quality speech synthesis may be required.

As amazing as the human voice is, it has one drawback—how it is perceived. The ear cannot recognize (or use) much of what is spoken. Your own voice, on a tape recording, is often greeted by, "That's not me talking, is it?" It was to this unique phenomenon that General Instrument's engineers addressed themselves; human-like speech without unrealistically large memory requirements.

A voice-response terminal is illustrated in Fig. B-44. The terminals

Courtesy AT&T

Fig. B-42. Artist's rendering of the AT&T–GTE joint communications satellite system.

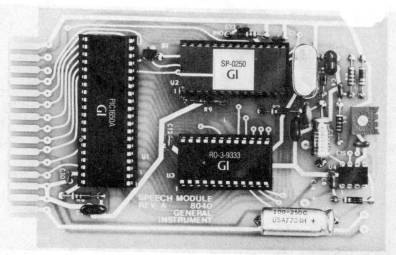

Courtesy Microelectronics Div., General Instrument Corp.

Fig. B-43. A voice synthesis module.

acoustically couple to the telephone headset, and transmit Touch-Tone®
codes. Replies are received from the microcomputer in voice tones. Cost
of the terminals is a small fraction of the costs necessary for a standard
FSK terminal, such as a teletypewriter or keyboard-crt's. Data entry/
inquiry applications, such as credit checking, order entry and status
checking, price quotations, and others can be implemented with a voice-
response system and one of the voice-response terminals.

Fig. B-44. A voice-response terminal.